THE COMMON LAW

CHITTY
ON
CONTRACTS

Third Cumulative Supplement
to the
Twenty-Ninth Edition

Up-to-date to July 31, 2006

LONDON
SWEET & MAXWELL
2006

Published in 2006 by
Sweet & Maxwell Limited of
100 Avenue Road London NW3 3PF
http://www.sweetandmaxwell.co.uk
Typeset by Interactive Sciences Limited, Gloucester
Printed in Great Britain by Athenaeum Press, Gateshead

A CIP catalogue record for this book is available from the British Library

ISBN Main Work (full set)   0 421 842601
ISBN Supplement -10   0 421 930608
ISBN Supplement -13   978 0 421 930605

No natural forests were destroyed to make this product,
only farmed timber was used and re-planted.

[iii]

HOW TO USE THIS SUPPLEMENT

This is the Third Cumulative Supplement to the Twenty-Ninth Edition of *Chitty on Contracts*, and has been compiled according to the structure of the two main work volumes.

At the beginning of each chapter of this Supplement the mini table of contents from the main volume has been included. Where a heading in this table of contents has been marked with a square pointer, this indicates that there is relevant information in the Supplement to which the reader should refer. The symbol □ indicates that the Cumulative Supplement contains new material. The symbol ■ indicates material that is unchanged from the previous Supplement.

Within each chapter, updating information is referenced to the relevant paragraph in the main volume.

TABLE OF CONTENTS

	PAGE
Table of Statutes	ix
Table of Statutory Instruments	xvii
Table of Non-UK Statutory Material	xxiii
Table of Cases	xxvii
Table of European Cases	lxv

VOLUME I

PART ONE—INTRODUCTION

PARA.

1. Introductory — *S. J. Whittaker* — 1–001

PART TWO—FORMATION OF CONTRACT

2. The Agreement — *G. H. Treitel* — 2–001
3. Consideration — *G. H. Treitel* — 3–001
4. Form — *S. J. Whittaker* — 4–001
5. Mistake — *H. G. Beale* — 5–001
6. Misrepresentation — *H. G. Beale* — 6–001
7. Duress and Undue Influence — *H. G. Beale* — 7–001

PART THREE—CAPACITY OF PARTIES

8. Personal Incapacity — *S. J. Whittaker* — 8–001
9. Corporations and Unincorporated Associations — *D. D. Prentice* — 9–001
10. The Crown, Public Authorities and the European Community — *P. Mitchell* — 10–001
11. Political Immunity and Incapacity — *C. G. J. Morse* — 11–001

PART FOUR—THE TERMS OF THE CONTRACT

12. Express Terms — *A. G. Guest* — 12–001
13. Implied Terms — *A. G. Guest* — 13–001
14. Exemption Clauses — *A. G. Guest* — 14–001
15. Unfair Terms in Consumer Contracts — *S. J. Whittaker* — 15–001

PART FIVE—ILLEGALITY AND PUBLIC POLICY

16. Illegality and Public Policy — *D. D. Prentice* — 16–001

PART SIX—JOINT OBLIGATIONS, THIRD PARTIES AND ASSIGNMENT

17. Joint Obligations   *A. S. Burrows*   17–001
18. Third Parties   *G. H. Treitel*   18–001
19. Assignment   *A. S. Burrows*   19–001
20. Death and Bankruptcy   *D. D. Prentice*   20–001

PART SEVEN—PERFORMANCE AND DISCHARGE

21. Performance   *E. G. McKendrick*   21–001
22. Discharge by Agreement   *E. G. McKendrick*   22–001
23. Discharge by Frustration   *E. G. McKendrick*   23–001
24. Discharge by Breach   *E. G. McKendrick*   24–001
25. Other Modes of Discharge   *E. G. McKendrick*   25–001

PART EIGHT—REMEDIES FOR BREACH OF CONTRACT

26. Damages   *D. R. Harris*   26–001
27. Specific Performance and Injunction   *G. H. Treitel*   27–001
28. Limitation of Actions   *A. Burrows*   28–001

PART NINE—RESTITUTION

29. Restitution   *G. Virgo*   29–001

PART TEN—CONFLICT OF LAWS

30. Conflict of Laws   *C. G. J. Morse*   30–001

VOLUME II

31. Agency   *F. M. B. Reynolds*   31–001
32. Arbitration   *A. G. Guest*   32–001
33. Bailment   *E. G. McKendrick*   33–001
34. Bills of Exchange and Banking   *R. J. A. Hooley*   34–001
35. Carriage by Air   *D. McClean*   35–001
36. Carriage by Land   *P. J. S. MacDonald Eggers*   36–001
37. Construction Contracts   *J. Uff and S. Hughes*   37–001
38. Credit and Security   *A. G. Guest*   38–001
39. Employment   *M. R. Freedland*   39–001
40. Gaming and Wagering   *G. H. Treitel*   40–001
41. Insurance   *P. J. S. MacDonald Eggers*   41–001
42. Restrictive Agreements and Competition   *R. Whish*   42–001
43. Sale of Goods   *A. G. Guest, F.M.B. Reynolds and D. R. Harris*   43–001
44. Suretyship   *S. J. Whittaker*   44–001

TABLE OF STATUTES

Where a reference indicates significant discussion of the statute in the text, it is in **bold**. Where a reference is to a footnote, it is *italic*.

1677 Statute of Frauds (29 car. 2
        c.3) 4–063A, 44–049
        s.4 .... *4–027*, 4–078, 44–051
1710 Gaming Act (9 Ann. c.19) 40–A001,
              40–A005, 40–051—40–054,
              40–056, 40–059, 40–088
        s.1 .... *40–A005*
1828 Statute of Frauds Amendment
        Act (Lord Tenterden's
        Act) (9 Geo.4 c.14) *6–041*
1835 Gaming Act (5 & 6 Will. 4
        c.41) 40–A001, 40–A005,
              40–051—40–054, 40–056,
                                      40–059
1845 Gaming Act (8 & 9 Vict.
        c.109) 40–A001, 40–A005,
              40–032A, 40–054, 40–056,
                                      40–059
        s.18 ....*3–167*, 40–001, 40–018,
              40–025, *40–029*, *40–030*, 40–044,
                      40–047, *40–050*, 40–083
1870 Apportionment Act (33 & 34
        Vict. c.35) *29–070*
1882 Bills of Exchange Act
        (45 & 46 Vict. c.61)—
        s.46(2)(c) *34–046*
        s.47(1)(b) *34–046*
1882 Married Women's Property Act
        (45 & 46 Vict. c.75)—
        s.11 .... *18–118*
1892 Gaming Act (55 & 56 Vict.
        c.9) 40–A001, 40–A005,
              40–032A, 40–059, 40–088
        s.1 ....*40–042*, 40–045
1906 Marine Insurance Act (6 Edw. 7
        c.41) 40–A003
        s.4 ....40–A003
        s.4(1) *40–A003*

1906 Marine Insurance Act—*cont.*
        s.4(2) *40–A003*, 40–005
        s.4(2)(a) *40–A003*
        s.4(2)(b) *40–A003*
1909 Marine Insurance (Gambling
        Policies) Act (9 Edw. 7
        c.12) 40–A003, *40–005*
1925 Law of Property Act (15 & 16
        Geo. 5 c.20) 1–082C
        s.73 .... *1–077*
        s.74 .... *1–077A*
        s.74(1) *1–082*, 1–082G
        s.74(1A) *1–082C*
        s.74(1B) *1–082G*
        s.74A(1) *1–082F*
        s.74A(2) *1–082F*
        s.139 1–041
        s.141 1–041
1925 Land Registration Act (15 & 16
        Geo. 5 c.21) 1–039
1925 Land Charges Act (15 & 16
        Geo.5 c.22)—
        s.110(1) 4–056A
1930 Third Parties (Rights against
        Insurers) Act (20 & 21
        Geo.5 c.35) *18–123*
        s.1(3) 18–123
1947 Crown Proceedings Act (10 &
        11 Geo. 6 c.44) 10–011
        S.21(2) 10–011
        s.39(1) *10–002*
        Sch.2 .... *10–002*
1950 Statute Law Revision Act (14
        Geo. 6 c.6) *10–002*
        s.1 .... *10–002*
1954 Landlord and Tenant Act (2 & 3
        Eliz. 2 c.56) 1–039
        Pt II 1–039

1961 Carriage by Air Act (9 & 10
      Eliz.2 c.27)—
      s.2(1) *35–015*
      Sch.1, Art.1(2), (3) *35–021*
      Sch.1, Art.1(3) *35–048*
      Sch.1, Art.5(1) *35–057*
      Sch.1, Art.6(1), (2), (5) *35–057*
      Sch.1, Art.7 .... *35–057*
      Sch.1, Art.10(1) *35–057*
      Sch.1, Art.11(2) *35–057*
      Sch.1, Art.12(1), (2) *35–064*
      Sch.1, Art.12(4) *35–064*
      Sch.1, Art.13(1) *35–064, 35–065*
      Sch.1, Art.13(2) *35–065*
      Sch.1, Art.13(3) *35–068, 35–069*
      Sch.1, Art.19 .... *35–072*
      Sch.1, Art.20 .... *35–072*
      Sch.1, Art.21 .... *35–072*
      Sch.1, Art.22(2) *35–063*
      Sch.1, Art.22(2)(a) *35–055, 35–063*
      Sch.1, Art.22(3) *35–063*
      Sch.1, Art.23 .... *35–068*
      Sch.1, Art.24(1), (2) *35–022,
                                           35–070*
      Sch.1, Art.24(1) *35–069*
      Sch.1, Art.26(2), (4) *35–056,
                                           35–067*
      Sch.1, Art.28(1) *35–024*
      Sch.1, Art.28(2) *35–025*
      Sch.1, Art.29(1) *35–026*
      Sch.1, Art.29(2) *35–026*
      Sch.1, Art.30(1), (2) *35–048*
      Sch.1, Art.33 .... *35–031*
      Sch.1, Art.34 .... *35–030*
      Sch.1, Art.35 .... *35–056, 35–067*
      Sch.1A *35–021, 35–022, 35–024,
          35–025, 35–026, 35–030, 35–031,
          35–048, 35–055, 35–056, 35–063,
          35–064, 35–065, 35–067, 35–068,
               35–069, 35–070, 35–072*
      Sch.1B *35–021, 35–022, 35–025,
          35–026, 35–030, 35–031, 35–048,
          35–055, 35–056, 35–063, 35–064,
          35–065, 35–067, 35–068, 35–069,
               35–070, 35–072*
1964 Trading Stamps Act (c.71) *13–030,
          14–127, 43–013, 43–062*
1966 Commonwealth Secretariat Act
      (c.10) *11–019*
1967 Misrepresentation Act (c.7)—
      s.2 ....6–067, 6–099
      s.2(1) 6–067, *28–010*
      s.2(2) 6–108
1968 International Organisations Act
      (c.48) *11–018*
1968 Gaming Act (c.65) *40–014*, 40–015,
          40–051, 40–054, 40–057,
                                           40–088
      s.16 ....*40–A001*, *40–A005*, 40–077

1971 Unsolicited Goods and Services
      Act (c.30) *2–004*
1973 Supply of Goods (Implied
      Terms) Act (c.13) 43–311
1973 Employment Agencies Act
      (c.35)
      s.31 .... *39–027*
      Sch.7 .... *39–027*
1974 Carriage of Passengers by Road
      Act (c.35) 36–082
1974 Consumer Credit Act (c.39) 1–039,
          30–007, 30–099, 34–222,
          38–012A, 38–014, 38–033,
          38–041B, 38–043, 38–056,
               38–058, *43–249*
      s.8(1) 38–014
      s.8(3) 38–015
      s.16 ....38–015, 38–036, *43–134*
      s.16(6C) ....38–129—38–132, *38–133*,
               38–192—38–206, 38–493
      s.16(7) *38–041*
      s.16(7A) *38–041*
      s.16A 38–014, 38–015, *38–034*,
                           38–041A, *43–134*
      s.16B 38–014, 38–015, 38–019,
          38–034, 38–041B, 38–056, *43–134*
      s.16B(1) ....38–022—38–023
      s.16B(1)(a) *38–042*
      s.16B(4) 38–041B
      s.17(2) *38–042*
      s.18 38–044
      s.26 .... *38–058*
      s.27A *38–011*
      s.40 38–059
      s.43(3) 38–061
      s.55(1) 38–070
      s.58 .... 38–070, 38–494
      s.69(7) 38–098
      s.75 .... *38–454*
      s.77A 38–117A
      s.78(4) 38–119, 38–143C
      s.82(2) ....38–129—38–132
      s.82(3) *38–131*
      s.82(3) *38–133*
      s.83(1) 38–475
      s.86A ... 38–143A—38–143C, *38–148*
      s.86B 38–143A, 38–143B,
                           38–143D, 38–183
      s.86C 38–143A, 38–143C,
                           38–143D, 38–183
      s.86D 38–143D
      s.86E 38–143E
      s.86F 38–143F, 38–253
      s.88(2) *38–148*
      s.88(3) *38–150*
      s.88(4) *38–148*
      s.88(4A) *38–148*
      s.127(3)—(5) 38–083
      s.129(1)(ba) 38–183, 38–183A
      s.129A 38–183A

1974 Consumer Credit Act—*cont.*
    s.130A 38–186A, 38–261
    ss.137—140 ....*7–111*, 38–005,
        38–192—38–206, 38–264, 38–323,
                38–414, *38–432*
    s.140A 38–493
    s.140A(5) *38–041*
    ss.140A—140D *7–111*,
        38–192—38–206, 38–264, 38–323,
                38–414, *38–432*
    s.140B 38–493
    s.145(1)(da) 38–208
    s.145(1)(db) 38–208
    s.145(4) *38–209*
    s.146(5A)—(5D) 38–214
    s.151 38–220
    s.152 38–220
    s.154 38–220
    s.156 38–220
    s.158(1) *38–215*
    s.158(4) *38–215*
    s.176 ....38–055A
    s.176A 38–055A
    s.177(3) *38–499*
    s.185 38–079
    s.185(2)—(2D) *38–119*
    s.185(5) 38–014, 38–056, *38–147*
    s.185(6) *38–072*
    s.187A 38–143E, 38–143F
    s.189(1) 38–014, 38–056,
            38–192—38–206, *43–134*
1975 Sex Discrimination Act (c.65) 2–175,
                      30–109
    s.66 27–076
    s.71 27–021
    s.82(1) 2–175
1976 Fatal Accidents Act (c.30) 36–106
    s.4 36–106
1976 Race Relations Act (c.74) *30–109*
    s.8(1A) *30–109*
    s.62 .... *27–072*
1977 Rent Act (c.42)—
    Sch.I, paras 2, 3 .... *1–041*
1977 Unfair Contract Terms Act
    (c.50) 15–010A
    s.3(1) *15–032A*
1978 Interpretation Act (c.30)—
    s.16 .... *40–A004, 40–A005*
1978 State Immunity Act (c.33)—
    s.2 .... *11–021*
    s.2(2) *11–021*
    s.9 .... *11–020*
    s.14(3) *11–004*
    s.14(4) *11–003, 11–004*
1978 Civil Liability (Contribution)
    Act (c.47) 17–032, 20–015
    s.1(4) 17–032
    s.10 .... *28–051*

1979 Carriage by Air and Road Act
    (c.28)—
    s.4 .... *35–063*
1979 Credit Unions Act (c.34)
    s.11(5) 38–256
1979 Estate Agents Act (c.38) *31–015*
1979 Sale of Goods Act
    (c.54) .... 8–070—8–079, 36–090
    s.3 43–021
    s.3(2) . ...8–070—8–079
    s.14(3) *37–077*
    s.52 27–017
1980 Limitation Act (c.58) 1–039, *28–134*,
                      43–261A
    s.3(2) 43–261A
    s.14A 6–067, *28–010, 28–011*
    s.14A(8) *28–011*
    s.14A(8)(a) *28–011*
    s.14A(9) *28–011*
    s.14A(10) *28–011, 28–033*
    s.14B *28–012*
    s.24(1) *28–015*
    s.27A 43–261A
    s.29 .... *28–100*
    s.29(5) *28–095*
    s.30(2) *28–100*
    s.31(7) *28–103*
    s.32(1)(b) *28–086*
    s.32(1)(c) 29–042, 29–084
    s.36(1) *28–134, 28–135*
1981 Supreme Court Act (c.54)—
    s.37 ....*32–101, 34–236*
    s.138 43–260
    s.138B *43–233*
    s.138B(1) *38–390*
1982 Supply of Goods and Services
    Act (c.29)—
    s.4 1–128
1983 Mental Health Act (c.20) *8–077*
    Pt 7 ....8–070—8–079
1984 Foreign Limitation Periods Act
    (c.16) *30–159*
1985 Companies Act (c.6) 1–077, *1–082*,
                  1–082A, 1–082C
    s.36A *1–077A*
    s.36A(1) *1–082G*
    s.36A(2) *1–077*
    s.36A(3) *1–080*
    s.36A(4) *1–077, 1–080, 1–082G*
    s.36A(4A) *1–082G*
    s.36A(5) *1–077, 1–080, 1–082*,
                      1–082B
    s.36A(6) *1–082F*
    s.36A(7) *1–082C*
    s.36AA(1) *1–082F*
    s.36AA(2) *1–082F*
    s.309A *41–088*
    s.309B *41–088*
    s.309C *41–088*
    s.349(4) 34–046

1985	Companies Act—*cont.*	
	s.459	*32–043*
1985	Enduring Powers of Attorney Act (c.29)	8–070—8–079
1985	Housing Act (c.68)—	
	s.82	6–108
	s.84	6–108
	Sch.2 ground 5	6–108
1986	Insolvency Act (c.45)	*34–313*
	s.345	*20–033*
	Sch.B1 para.69	*43–233*
	Sch.B1 paras 70—72	*43–233*
1986	Company Directors Disqualification Act (c.46)—	
	s.11	16–005
1988	Road Traffic Act (c.52)	41–093
1989	Law of Property (Miscellaneous Provisions) Act (c.34)	4–063A
	s.1	*1–077, 1–077A, 1–082H*
	s.1(2)	1–082A, *1–082B*
	s.1(2)(a)	*1–077,* 1–082A
	s.1(2)(b)	1–082A, *1–082C, 1–082F*
	s.1(2A)	*1–082B*
	s.1(3)	*1–082D*
	s.1(3)(b)	*1–082D*
	s.1(4)(b)	*1–082D*
	s.1(4A)	*1–082C*
	s.1(5)	*1–082E*
	s.1(9)	*1–082H*
	s.1(10)	*1–082H*
	s.2	4–056A, 4–060, 4–063, 4–063A, 4–070, 4–073, 4–078
	s.2(1)	*3–114, 3–139,* 4–073, 4–078
	s.2(5)	*3–114,* 4–073, 4–078
1989	Companies Act (c.40)	1–082F
	s.130(2)	*1–080, 1–082, 1–082G*
1990	Human Fertilisation and Embryology Act (c.37)—	
	Sch.3 para.4(1)	*3–088*
1990	Courts and Legal Services Act (c.41)—	
	s.58(3)	*16–056*
1992	Carriage of Goods by Sea Act (c.50)	*30–064*
1992	Trade Union and Labour Relations (Consolidation) Act (c.52)—	
	s.46	39–219
	ss.145A–145F	39–111—39–112
	ss.146–151	39–111—39–112, 39–219
	s.152	39–219
	s.238A	39–220
	s.238B	39–220
1993	Charities Act (c.10)—	
	s.65(1)(a)	*3–019*
1993	National Lottery Act (c.39)	*40–014*

1995	Merchant Shipping Act (c.21)—	
	s.183	*36–101*
	s.184	*36–101*
	s.184(5)	*36–101*
1995	Disability Discrimination Act (c.50)	*30–109, 39–131, 39–146*
	s.13(1)(c)	*3–038*
	s.21F	*27–072*
	s.21F(2)(b)	*27–022*
	s.68(1), (2)–(4A)	*30–109*
1996	Police Act (c.16)—	
	s.25(1)	*3–063*
1996	Employment Rights Act (c.18)	30–109
	s.43M	39–113
	s.80F	*39–140*
	s.94(1)	*2–175*
	s.98B	39–215
	ss.98ZA—98ZH	39–216A
	s.123	26–077
	s.196(2)	30–109
	s.196(3)	30–109
	s.230(1)	*2–175*
	s.230(2)	*2–175*
1996	Arbitration Act (c.23)	*11–019*
	s.1(c)	32–132
	s.5(1)	*30–183*
	s.18	32–065
	s.44	*32–101*
	s.48(4)	*30–183,* 32–101
	s.48(5)(c)	*32–093*
	s.67	*32–101*
	s.68	*30–183, 32–016, 32–101,* 32–143A, 32–145
	s.69	*32–016,* 32–143A
	s.69(1)	*1–039*
	s.72	*32–046*
	s.72(1)	32–065
	s.76	32–059A
	s.101	*11–004*
1996	Trusts of Land and Appointment of Trustees Act (c.47)—	
	s.14	*34–271*
1996	Housing Act (c.52)—	
	Pt VII	15–014–15–017, *15–021*
1997	Social Security (Recovery of Benefits) Act (c.27)	*39–198*
1998	Competition Act (c.41)	42–082
	Sch.3 para.2	42–104
1998	Human Rights Act (c.42)	*1–039, 39–215*
	ss 3, 4	**1–032**
	s.3	1–041
	s.6	1–042
	s.6(1)	1–042
	s.6(3)	1–042
	s.6(3)(b)	1–042
	Sch.1, Pt II, art.2	*27–023*

1999 Employment Relations Act
       (c.26) 39–027
       s.10 39–258
       ss.10–12 39–258
1999 Contracts (Rights of Third Par-
       ties) Act (c.31) 18–002, 18–087,
                     27–008, 31–083, 31–132,
                                          41–093
       s.1(1)(b) 18–087
       s.1(2) 18–087
       s.1(4) 18–087
1999 Contracts (Privity) Act—
       s.1(6) 31–110
2000 Financial Services and Markets
       Act (c.8) 1–042, 6–027, 6–149,
                         38–001A, 38–012A,
                         38–222A, 40–A002
       Pt VI 6–027
       s.22 ....40–A003
       s.73A(4) 6–027
       s.81 6–017
       ss.84–87R 6–027
       s.86 6–017
       s.86(1) 6–089
       s.87G 6–017
       s.90(11) 6–089
       s.90(12) 6–089
       s.102A 6–027
       s.412 ....40–025, 40–041, 40–059
2000 Postal Services Act (c.26)—
       s.90 35–074
2001 Regulatory Reform Act (c.6) 1–077
       s.1 ....1–077—1–082
2002 Proceeds of Crime Act
       (c.29) 29–137
       Pt 5 Ch.2 ....43–261A
       s.281 ....43–261A
       s.267 43–233
       s.288 ....43–261A
       s.328 34–317
       Sch.7 43–233
2002 Police Reform Act (c.30)—
       Sch.4 para.10 43–233
2002 Enterprise Act (c.40) ... 31–015, 34–313
       Pt 8 30–100
       s.11 14–131
       s.248 43–233
       Sch.16 43–233
2003 Communications Act (c.21)—
       Sch.17, para.47 38–040
2003 Courts Act (c.39)—
       s.109(3) 38–390, 43–233, 43–260
       Sch.7 43–260
       Sch.7, para.10 43–233
       Sch.7, para.11 38–390
       Sch.10 ....38–390, 43–233, 43–260

2004 Gangmasters Licensing Act
       (c.11) 39–032
       ss.12–14 39–032
2004 Statute Law (Repeals) Act
       (c.14)—
       s.1(1) 36–082
       Sch.1, Pt 14 36–082
2004 Employment Relations Act
       (c.24) 39–220
       s.27(3) 39–093
       ss.27–28 39–220
       s.29 ....39–111—39–112
       ss.29–32 ....39–111—39–112
       s.31 ....39–111—39–112
       s.32 39–219
       s.37 39–258
       s.40 .... 39–111—39–112, 39–215
       ss.44–46 39–076
2004 Companies (Audit, Investiga-
       tions and Community En-
       terprise) Act (c.27)
       s.19 41–088
2004 Civil Partnership Act (c.33)—
       s.70 18–118
       s.73 3–073
2005 Mental Capacity Act
       (c.9) .... 8–070—8–079, 31–033
       Pt 2 ....8–070—8–079
       s.1 .... 2–100, 8–070—8–079
       s.2 2–100
       s.2(1) ....8–070—8–079
       s.2(2)–(4) ....8–070—8–079
       s.2(5) ....8–070—8–079
       s.3 ....8–070—8–079
       s.4 ....8–070—8–079
       ss.5–6 ....8–070—8–079
       s.7 .... 8–070—8–079, 43–021
       ss.9–14 ....8–070—8–079
       s.15 ....8–070—8–079
       ss.15–19 ....8–070—8–079
       s.16(1) ....8–070—8–079
       s.16(2)(a) ....8–070—8–079
       s.16(2)(b) ....8–070—8–079
       s.16(3) ....8–070—8–079
       s.17 ....8–070—8–079
       s.18 ....8–070—8–079
       s.18(3) ....8–070—8–079
       s.19(6) ....8–070—8–079
       ss.19–20 ....8–070—8–079
       s.20(6) ....8–070—8–079
       s.45 31–165
       s.66 31–165
       Sch.6 para.24 43–021
2005 Disability Discrimination Act
       (c.13) 39–131
       s.12 ....27–022, 27–072

2005   Gambling Act (c.19) *3–017*,
                    40–A001—40–A005,
                40–001, 40–005, 40–014,
                40–015, *40–018, 40–029,*
                40–032A, *40–042*, 40–044,
                40–045, 40–047, 40–052,
                40–053, 40–077, *40–082*,
                    40–083, 40–088
          Pt 13 40–047
          Pt 14 .... *40–A007*
          Pt 17 ....*40–A001*, 40–A003
          s.1(a) 40–A005
          s.2 .... *40–A002*
          s.3 .... *40–A003*
          s.3(1) *40–A003*
          s.6 ....*40–A003*, 40–014
          s.6(1) 40–014
          s.9 ....*40–A003*, 40–002
          s.10 .... 40–A002, 40–A003
          s.11(1) *40–A003*
          s.11(1)(b) *40–A003*
          s.12(1) *40–A003*
          s.15 .... *40–A002*
          s.18 40–001
          s.20 .... *40–A002*, 40–A007
          s.33(1) *40–A005*
          s.33(1)(b)(v) *40–A005*
          s.33(1)(b)(vi) *40–A005*
          s.33(2) *40–A002*, 40–A005
          s.37(1) *40–A002*, 40–A005
          s.37(2) *40–A005*
          s.37(7) *40–A005*
          s.42 ....*40–A002*, 40–A005
          s.46 .... *40–A002*
          s.48 .... *40–A002*, 40–A005
          s.50 .... *40–A002*
          s.58 .... *40–A005*
          s.81 ....*40–048*, 40–052, 40–059
          s.81(2)(a) *40–A005*
          s.81(2)(b) *40–A005*
          s.83(1)(a) *40–A005*
          s.83(1)(b) *40–A005*
          s.140 .... *40–A007*
          s.143 .... *40–A007*
          s.177 ....*40–048*, 40–052, 40–059
          s.177(2)(a) *40–A005*
          s.183 .... *40–A005*
          s.245 .... *40–A005*
          s.296 .... *40–A002*
          ss.297–302 .... *40–A002*
          s.334 ....*31–154, 31–157*, 40–A001
          s.334(1) *40–A001*
          s.334(1)(c) *3–167*
          s.334(1)(e) *40–025, 40–041*
          s.334(2) *40–A001*

2005   Gambling Act—*cont.*
          s.335 .... *40–A002*,
                    40–A005—40–A007
          s.335(1) *3–016, 3–050*, 40–A001,
                40–A004—40–A006, *40–025,*
                40–030, 40–032, 40–032A,
                40–042, 40–044, *40–048*, 40–052,
                    40–059, 40–083, 40–088
          s.335(2) **40–A005, 40–A006**,
                    40–048, 40–052, 40–059
          s.336 .... **40–A007**, 40–083
          s.336(1) 40–A007, *40–083*
          s.336(2) *40–A007*
          s.336(2)(b) 40–083
          s.336(3) *40–A007*
          s.336(4) 40–A007
          s.336(4)(a) *40–A007*
          s.336(5) *40–A007, 40–083*
          s.337(1) *40–A004*
          s.337(2) *40–A007*
          s.337(3)(a) *40–A007*
          s.337(3)(b) *40–A007*
          s.338 ....40–A007
          s.338(1) *40–A007*
          s.338(2) *40–A007*
          s.338(3) *40–A007*
          s.338(4) *40–A007*
          s.339 40–047
          s.356 .... *40–025, 40–041*
          s.356(3)(d) *3–167*
          s.356(4) *3–167*
          s.358(1) 40–A001
          Sch.17 ....*3–167, 40–025, 40–041*

2005   International Organisations Act
          (c.20) *11–018*
          ss.1–3 .... *11–019*

2005   Finance (No.2) Act (c.22)—
          s.3 .... *29–086*

2006   Equality Act (c.3) *27–072, 30–109*
          Pt 2 27–072
          Pt 3 27–072
          s.1 27–072
          s.23(1)(a)(i) 27–072
          s.24 27–072
          s.24(3)(a) 27–072
          s.33 27–072
          s.33(1)(g) 27–072
          s.33(1)(h) 27–072
          s.34 27–072
          s.40 ....*27–021, 27–072*, 27–076
          s.46 27–072
          s.47 27–072
          s.66 27–072
          s.81(1) 27–072
          s.91 ....*27–021, 27–072*, 27–076
          Sch.3 para.12 ....*27–021, 27–076*
          Sch,3 para.27 27–072
          Sch.4 ....*27–021, 27–072, 27–076*

2006 Consumer Credit Act (c.14) *30–007,*
30–099, 34–222, 38–005,
38–012A, 38–014, *43–015,*
43–016, 43–017, 43–134,
43–329
ss.1—4 .... *34–222*
s.2 .... 38–014, 38–033
s.2(2) *38–033*
s.2(3) 38–061
s.3 ....38–041A
s.4 ....38–041B
s.5(1) 38–015
s.5(2) ....38–022—38–023
s.5(3) *38–042*
s.5(4) *38–209*
s.5(5) *38–215*
s.5(6) *38–215*
s.5(8) 38–014, *38–056, 38–147*
s.5(9) *38–072*
s.6 ....38–117A
s.7(3) *38–079, 38–119*
s.8 ....38–143A
s.9 ....38–143B
s.10 ....38–143C
s.11 ....38–143D
s.12 ....38–143E
s.13 .... 38–143F, 38–253
s.14(1) *38–148, 38–150*
s.14(2) *38–148*
s.14(3) *38–148*
s.15 38–083

2006 Consumer Credit Act—*cont.*
s.16(1) 38–183
s.16(2) 38–183A
s.17 .... 38–186A, 38–261
s.18 ....38–143E
s.19 .... 38–039, 38–493
ss.19—22 ...*7–111,* 38–192—38–206,
38–264
s.22(2) *38–041*
s.23 38–056
ss.23—58 38–058
s.24 38–208
s.24(5) *38–499*
s.25 38–208
s.25(3) *38–220*
s.25(4) *38–220*
s.26 ....*38–058,* 38–059
s.29(2) 38–367
s.33 38–011
ss.59—61 ....38–004A
s.70 ....*7–111, 38–041,*
38–192—38–206, 38–264
s.71 ....38–012A
Sch.2 ....38–004A
Sch.3 ....38–012A
Sch.3 paras 14—17 38–192—38–206
Sch.4 ....*7–111, 38–041,*
38–192—38–206, 38–264
2006 Work and Families Act (c.18)
s.12 .... *39–140*

TABLE OF STATUTORY INSTRUMENTS

Where a reference indicates significant discussion of the statute in the text, it is in **bold**. Where a reference is to a footnote, it is *italic*.

1976 Consumer Transactions (Restrictions on Statements)
Order (SI 1976/1813) *38–354,
38–423, 38–424, 38–435*

1981 Transfer of Undertakings (Protection of Employment)
Regulations (SI
1981/1794) 39–171, 39–216,
39–255, 39–256

1983 Consumer Credit (Guarantees
and Indemnities) Regula-
tions (SI 1983/1556) 38–164

1983 Consumer Credit (Cancellation
Notices and Copies of
Documents) Regulations
(SI 1983/1557) 38–077, 38–079,
*38–118, 38–122, 38–166,
38–462, 38–496*

1983 Consumer Credit (Settlement
Information) Regulations
(SI 1983/1564) *38–032*

1986 Insolvency Rules (SI
1986/1925)—
r.2.85 .... *34–313*
r.4.90 .... *34–313*

1987 Carriage of Passengers and
their Luggage by Sea (Do-
mestic Carriage) Order (SI
1987/670) *36–101*

1988 Consumer Protection (Code of
Practice for Traders on
Price Indications) Ap-
proval Order (SI
1988/2078) 43–154

1989 Consumer Credit (Exempt
Agreements) Order (SI
1989/869) *38–037*

1990 Carriage by Air Acts (Imple-
mentation of Protocol
No.4 of Montreal, 1975)
Order (SI 1990/1312)
Art.1(3) *35–021*, 35–048
Art.12(1), (2) 35–064
Art.12(4) 35–064
Art.13(1) *35–064*, 35–065
Art.13(2) 35–065
Art.13(3) *35–068*, 35–069
Art.19 35–072
Art.20 35–072
Art.21 35–072
Art.22(2)(a) *35–055*, 35–063
Art.24(1), (2) *35–022*, 35–070
Art.24(1) 35–069
Art.26(2) *35–056*, 35–067
Art.26(4) *35–056*, 35–067
Art.28(1) 35–024
Art.28(2) 35–025
Art.29(1) 35–026
Art.29(2) 35–026
Art.33 35–031
Art.34 35–030
Art.35 .... *35–056*, 35–067

1993 Money Laundering Regulations
(SI 1993/1933) 34–224, 34–249,
34–356

1995 Public Offer of Securities Regulations (SI 1995/1537) *6–017,
6–027, 6–089*, 6–149

1995 Landlord and Tenant (Covenants) Act 1995 (Com-
mencement) Order (SI
1995/2963) *44–009*

1998 Air Carrier Liability Order (SI
1998/1751) 35–007–35–010,
35–035

1998 Civil Procedure Rules (SI
1998/3132) *34–120*, 37–254A
   r.11 32–048
   r.12.6 .... *34–120*
   r.17.4.2 .... *28–118*
   Pt 21 8–072
   r.21.1(2)(b) 8–077
   r.21.2 8–077
   r.21.10(1) 8–077
   Pt 24 32–049
   r.72.4 .... *34–324*

1999 Unfair Terms in Consumer
Contracts Regulations (SI
1999/2083) 15–010A, 15–032A,
          15–076, 15–086, *27–025,*
                    31–123
   reg.5 ....15–032A
   reg.5(1) 15–032A, 5–060
   reg.5(1)–(4) *15–032A*
   reg.6(2) 15–036A, 15–036B
   reg.9 15–093

2000 Consumer Credit (Conduct of
Business) (Credit Refer-
ences) (Amendment) Reg-
ulations (SI 2000/291) *38–058*

2000 Air Navigation Order (SI
2000/1562)—
   art.113 35–012
   art.115 35–012

2000 Consumer Protection (Distance
Selling) Regulations (SI
2000/2334) *2–062, 30–100,*
                  38–475, 40–026
   reg.16(3) *30–063, 30–100*

2001 Financial Services and Markets
Act 2000 (Regulated Ac-
tivities) Order (SI
2001/544) *38–039*

2001 Stop Now Orders (EC Directive) Regulations (SI
2001/1422) *30–100*

2001 Financial Services and Markets
Act 2000 (Regulated Ac-
tivities) Order (SI
2001/544) 38–036
   art.61 .... *38–491*
   art.85 ....*40–A003*
   art.90 .... *38–491*
   art.91 .... *38–491*

2001 Money Laundering Regulations
(SI 2001/3641) *34–224, 34–249,*
                    34–356

2001 Financial Services and Markets
Act 2000 (Consequential
Amendments and Repeals)
Order (SI 2001/3649) *38–058*
   art.170 .... *38–058*

2002 Carriage by Air Acts (Imple-
mentation of the Montreal
Convention 1999) Order
(SI 2002/263)—
   Art.1(3) *35–021, 35–048*
   Art.12(1), (2), (4) *35–064*
   Art.13(1) *35–064, 35–065*
   Art.13(2) *35–065*
   Art.13(3) *35–068, 35–069*
   Art.19 .... *35–072*
   Art.20 .... *35–072*
   Art.22(2) *35–056, 35–063*
   Art.26 .... *35–068*
   Art.27 .... *35–031*
   Art.29 ....*35–022, 35–069, 35–070*
   Art.31(2) *35–056, 35–067*
   Art.31(4) *35–056, 35–067*
   Art.33(4) *35–025*
   Art.35(1) *35–026*
   Art.35(2) *35–026*
   Art.36(1), (2) *35–048*
   Art.51 .... *35–030*
   Art.52 .... *35–056, 35–067*

2002 Financial Services and Markets
Act 2000 (Regulated Ac-
tivities) (Amendment)
Order (SI 2002/682) 38–011

2002 Electronic Money (Miscellaneous Amendments) Regula-
tions (SI 2002/765) 38–011

2002 Electronic Commerce Directive
(Financial Services and
Markets) Regulations (SI
2002/1775) 38–011

2002 Electronic Commerce (EC Directive) Regulations (SI
2002/2013) 38–012B, 43–134

2002 Fixed-term Employees
(Prevention of Less
Favourable Treatment)
Regulations (SI
2002/2034)—
   reg.3 39–149

2002 Sale and Supply of Goods to
Consumers' Regulations
(SI 2002/3045)
   reg.6(1) *43–005*
   reg.6(2) *43–005*

2003 Enterprise Act 2002 (Super-
complaints to Regulators)
Order (SI 2003/1368) *43–157*

2003 Enterprise Act 2002 (Part 8
Community Infringements
Specified UK Laws) Order
(SI 2003/1374) *30–100, 43–157*

2003 Enterprise Act 2002 (Part 8 Request for Consultation)
Order (SI 2003/1375) *43–157*

2003 Enterprise Act 2002 (Part 9 Restrictions on Disclosure of Information) (Amendment and Specification) Order (SI 2003/1400) *43–136*

2003 Financial Services and Markets Act 2000 (Regulated Activities) (Amendment) (No.1) Order (SI 2003/1475) 38–214, 38–493

2003 Enterprise Act 2002 (Part 8 Domestic Infringements) Order (SI 2003/1593) 230–100, 243–157

2003 Race Relations Act 1976 (Amendment) Regulations (SI 2003/1626)—
reg.11 .... *30–109*

2003 Employment Equality (Religion or Belief) Regulations (SI 2003/1660) *27–072*
reg.9 .... *30–109*
reg.30 .... *27–072*
reg.30(1)(c) *27–072*
reg.30(3) *27–072*

2003 Employment Equality (Sexual Orientation) Regulations (SI 2003/1661) *27–072*
reg.9 .... *30–109*

2003 Disability Discrimination Act 1995 (Amendment) Regulations (SI 2003/1673) *30–109*

2003 Timeshare (Cancellation Information) Order (SI 2003/2579) *14–129*

2003 Money Laundering Regulations (SI 2003/3075) *34–224, 34–249, 34–356*

2003 Control of Misleading Advertisements (Amendment) Regulations (SI 2003/3183) *43–159*

2003 Conduct of Employment Agencies and Employment Businesses Regulations (SI 2003/3319) *39–027*

2004 Price Marking Order (SI 2004/102) *43–159*

2004 Employment Equality (Religion or Belief) (Amendment) Regulations (SI 2004/437) *30–109*

2004 Employment Act 2002 (Dispute Resolution) Regulations (SI 2004/752) *39–259*

2004 Enterprise Act 2002 (Part 8) (Designation of the Financial Services Authority as a Designated Enforcer) Order (SI 2004/935) *43–157*

2004 Competition Act 1998 (Appealable Decisions and Revocation of Notification of Excluded Agreements) Regulations (SI 2004/1078) *42–077*

2004 Education (Student Loans) (Repayment) (Amendment) Regulations (SI 2004/1175) *38–247*

2004 Competition Act 1998 (Determination of Turnover for Penalties) (Amendment) Order (SI 2004/1259) *42–077, 42–139*

2004 Competition Act 1998 (Land Agreements Exclusion and Revocation) Order (SI 2004/1260) *42–077,* 42–091, 42–115
Sch.1, para.49 .... 42–101, 42–102

2004 Competition Act 1998 and Other Enactments (Amendment) Regulations (SI 2004/1261) *42–077, 42–087,* 42–104, *42–118,* 42–132

2004 Air Carrier Liability Regulations (SI 2004/1418) ....35–007—35–010, *35–011, 35–014, 35–035*

2004 Consumer Credit (Disclosure of Information) Regulations (SI 2004/1481) *38–006,* 38–012A, 38–070, 38–494
reg.1(2) 38–070, 43–137

2004 Consumer Credit (Agreements) (Amendment) Regulations (SI 2004/1482) *38–006,* 38–012A, *38–032, 38–048, 38–055,* 38–071, *38–072, 38–083, 38–122, 38–131, 38–135,* 38–168, 38–462

2004 Consumer Credit (Early Settlement) Regulations (SI 2004/1483) .... *38–006,* 38–012A, *38–124,* 38–139—38–140

2004 Consumer Credit (Advertisements) Regulations (SI 2004/1484) *38–006,* 38–012A, *38–014, 38–033,* 38–061, *38–161, 38–220*

2004 Enterprise Act 2002 (Bodies Designated to make Super-complaints) Order (SI 2004/1517) *43–157*

2004 Carriage by Air Acts (Application of Provisions) Order (SI 2004/1899)—
Ch.II (Arts 3–16) 35–074
Art.2 .... *35–073*

2004 Carriage by Air Acts (Application of Provisions) Order—*cont.*

Art.2(2)	35–016
Art.3	35–074
Art.3(1)	*35–073*
Art.4	*35–020*, 35–073
Art.5(1)	*35–015*
Art.5(2)	*35–015*
Art.6(1)	*35–020*
Art.6(2)	*35–015*
Art.8	*35–016*
Art.8(2)	*35–016*
Art.24(1)	*35–022*
Sch.1	*35–016*, 35–073
Sch.1, Art.2(2)	*35–074*
Sch.1, Art.21	35–074
Sch.2	35–002, 35–073
Sch.2, Art.1(2), (3)	*35–021*
Sch.2, Art.1(3)	*35–048*
Sch.2, Art.3(1)	*35–028*
Sch.2, Art.3(2)	*35–030*
Sch.2, Art.4	*35–053*
Sch.2, Art.4(4)	*35–053*
Sch.2, Art.5(1)	*35–057*
Sch.2, Art.6(1), (2), (5)	*35–057*
Sch.2, Art.7	*35–046*, 35–057
Sch.2, Art.9	*35–059*
Sch.2, Art.10(1)	*35–057*
Sch.2, Art.11(2)	*35–058*
Sch.2, Art.12(1), (2)	*35–064*
Sch.2, Art.12(4)	*35–064*
Sch.2, Art.13(1)	*35–064*, 35–065
Sch.2, Art.13(2)	*35–065*
Sch.2, Art.13(3)	*35–068*, 35–069
Sch.2, Art.17	*35–032*
Sch.2, Art.18(1), (2)	*35–054*, *35–062*
Sch.2, Art.19	*35–072*
Sch.2, Art.20	*35–072*
Sch.2, Art.20(1)	*35–035*
Sch.2, Art.20(2)	*35–072*
Sch.2, Art.21	*35–036*, 35–072
Sch.2, Art.22	35–036
Sch.2, Art.22(2)	*35–055*, 35–063
Sch.2, Art.22(3)	*35–052*, 35–055
Sch.2, Art.23	*35–068*
Sch.2, Art.24(1)	*35–022*, 35–069, *35–070*
Sch.2, Art.24(2)	*35–070*
Sch.2, Art.25	35–036
Sch.2, Art.26(2)	*35–056*, 35–067
Sch.2, Art.26(4)	*35–056*, 35–067
Sch.2, Art.28(1)	*35–024*

2004 Carriage by Air Acts (Application of Provisions) Order—*cont.*

Sch.2, Art.28(2)	*35–025*
Sch.2, Art.29(1)	*35–026*
Sch.2, Art.29(2)	*35–026*
Sch.2, Art.30(1), (2)	*35–048*
Sch.2, Art.33	*35–031*
Sch.2, Art.34	*35–030*
Sch.2, Art.35	*35–056*, 35–067
Sch.3	35–002, 35–073
Sch.3, Art.22(2), (3)	*35–055*

2004 Air Carrier Liability (No.2) Regulations (SI 2004/1974) *35–011*, 35–073

2004 Competition Appeal Tribunal (Amendment and Communications Act Appeal) Rules (SI 2004/2068) *42–145*

2004 Financial Services (Distance Marketing) Regulations (SI 2004/2095) *2–062, 14–129, 30–063, 30–100, 34–222, 38–012B, 38–094A, 43–157*

reg.14	38–475
reg.25	38–094, 43–137

2004 Employment Equality (Sexual Orientation) Regulations 2003 (Amendment) Regulations (SI 2004/2519) *30–109*

2004 Employment Equality (Religion or Belief) Regulations 2003 (Amendment) (No.2) Regulations (SI 2004/2520) *30–109*

2004 Consumer Credit (Miscellaneous Amendments) Regulations (SI 2004/2619) ......*38–006, 38–012, 38–014, 38–032, 38–033, 38–048, 38–055, 38–061, 38–071, 38–072, 38–077, 38–079, 38–083, 38–118, 38–120, 38–122, 38–124, 38–131, 38–135, 38–139—38–140, 38–154, 38–161, 38–166, 38–168, 38–220, 38–462, 38–496*

2004 Competition Act 1998 (Office of Fair Trading's Rules) Order (SI 2004/2751) 42–077

2004 Education (Student Loans) (Repayment) (Amendment) (No 2) Regulations (SI 2004/2752) *38–247*

2004 Air Navigation (Dangerous Goods) Regulations (SI 2004/3214) *35–061*

2004 Consumer Credit Act 1974 (Electronic Communications) Order (SI 2004/3236) 38–012, *38–032, 38–048, 38–055*, 38–055A, *38–058*, 38–071, *38–072*, 38–077, 38–079, *38–083, 38–098, 38–118, 38–120, 38–131, 38–154, 38–166, 38–168, 38–176, 38–462, 38–496*

art.2(2) *38–496*
art.2(3) *38–075*
art.2(4) *38–080*
art.5 .... *38–164*
art.7 .... *38–106*
art.12 .... *38–119*

2004 Consumer Credit (Enforcement, Default and Termination Notices) (Amendment) Regulations (SI 2004/3237) *38–006*, 38–012, *38–144, 38–148, 38–153*

2004 Electronic Commerce Directive (Financial Services and Markets) (Amendment) Regulations (SI 2004/3378) 38–011

2004 Life Assurance Consolidation Directive (Consequential Amendments) Regulations (SI 2004/3379) *30–044*

2004 Contracts (Applicable Law) Act 1990 (Commencement No.2) Order (SI 2004/3448) *30–016, 30–019*

2005 Supply of Extended Warranties on Domestic Electrical Goods Order (SI 2005/37) ....43–135—43–137, 43–155

2005 Regulatory Reform (Unsolicited Goods and Services Act 1971) (Directory Entries and Demands for Payment) Order (SI 2005/55) *2–004*, 43–137

2005 Unsolicited Goods and Services Act 1971 (Electronic Commerce) (Amendment) Regulations (SI 2005/148) *2–004*

2005 Insolvency (Amendment) Rules (SI 2005/527) *34–313*

2005 Consumer Protection (Distance Selling) Regulations (SI 2005/689) *2–062, 14–129, 14–154, 30–063, 30–100,* 38–094, 38–475, 43–137

2005 Regulatory Reform (Trading Stamps) Order (SI 2005/871) 13–030, 14–127, *38–354, 38–423, 38–424, 38–435, 43–013, 43–062, 43–082, 43–159*

2005 Enterprise Act 2002 (Part 8) (Designation of the Consumers' Association) Order (SI 2005/917) *43–157*

2005 Civil Aviation (Denied Boarding, Compensation and Assistance) Regulations (SI 2005/975) *35–047*

2005 Civil Aviation (Insurance) Regulations (SI 2005/1089)—
reg.3 .... *35–012*
reg.4 .... *35–012*
reg.5 .... *35–012*
reg.12 .... *35–012*

2005 Prospectus Regulations (SI 2005/1433) *6–027*, 6–149
reg.2(1) *6–017*, 6–089
Sch.1 para.5 .... *6–089*
Sch.1 para.6(1) *6–017*
Sch.1 para.6(2) *6–017*

2005 General Product Safety Regulations (SI 2005/1803) *43–153*

2005 Regulatory Reform (Execution of Deeds and Documents) Order (SI 2005/1906) ....1–077, 1–077—1–082, 1–077A, 1–082A, 1–082C, 1–082F, *9–010*
art.1(1) *1–077A*
art.1(2) ....1–077—1–082, *1–077A*
art.3 .... *1–082G*
art.4 .... *1–077A, 1–082F*
art.5 .... *1–082F*
art.6 .... *1–077A, 1–082F*
art.7(1) *1–082C*
art.7(2) *1–082C*
art.7(3) .... *1–082A—1–082C*
art.7(4) *1–082C*
art.8 .... *1–082B*
art.9 .... *1–082E*
art.10(1) *1–082G*
Sch.1 para.10 .... *1–082G*
Sch.1 para.14 .... *1–082D*
Sch.2 ....*1–082B, 1–082D*

2005 Air Navigation Order (SI 2005/1970)—
art.155(1) *35–016*

2005 Railways (Convention on International Carriage by Rail) Regulations (SI 2005/2092) 36–080
reg.5 36–106
reg.7 36–094

2005 Consumer Protection (Code of
      Practice for Traders on
      Price Indications) Ap-
      proval   Order   (SI
      2005/2705) 43–154
2005 Financial Services and Markets
      Act 2000 (Consequential
      Amendments) Order (SI
      2005/2967) 38–039,
             38–129—38–132, 38–131,
                                   38–493
      art.3 38–214
2006 Public Contracts Regulations
      (SI 2006/5) 10–026
      reg.47 10–028
      reg.47(9) 10–028
      reg.47(10) 10–011
      Sch.7 Pt 2 10–026
2006 Utilities Contracts Regulations
      (SI 2006/6) 10–026
      reg.45 10–028
      reg.45(7) 10–028
      reg.45(10) 10–011
      reg.47 10–026
2006 Working Time (Amendment)
      Regulations   (SI
      2006/99) 39–108
2006 Transfer of Undertakings (Pro-
      tection of Employment)
      Regulations   (SI
      2006/246) 39–171, 39–216,
                          39–255, 39–256
      reg.3(1)(b) 39–171
      reg.3(3) 39–171
      reg.4(4)—(5) 39–171
      reg.4(9) 39–171
      reg.11 39–355

2006 Unfair Terms in Consumer
      Contracts   (Amendment)
      and Water Act 2003 (Tran-
      sitional Provisions) Regu-
      lations (SI 2006/523)—
      reg.2 15–098
2006 Employment Equality (Age)
      Regulations   (SI
      2006/1031) 39–034, 39–166A,
                                   39–216A
      reg.47 ....39–166A
      Sch.6 ....39–166A
      Sch.6 paras 2–4 ....39–166A
      Sch.6 paras 5–7 ....39–166A
      Sch.6 para.8 ....39–166A
      Sch.6 para.11 ....39–166A
      Sch.8 paras 21–23 ....39–216A
      Sch.8 para.25 39–208
      Sch.8 para.30 .... 39–248, 39–252
      Sch.8 para.32 39–248
      Sch.8 para.35 .... 39–232, 39–248
2006 Consumer   Credit   (Exempt
      Agreements)   (Amend-
      ment)   Order   (SI
      2006/1273) 38–006, 38–037
2006 Credit Unions (Maximum In-
      terest Rate on Loans)
      Order (SI 2006/1276) 38–256
2006 Consumer Credit Act 2006
      (Commencement)   Order
      (SI 2006/1508) 38–012A,
                      38–041A, 38–041B,
                      38–117A, 38–119,
                      38–143B, 38–143C,
                 38–143E, 38–148, 38–150,
                      38–0186A, 38–208
      art.3(2) 38–148
      Sch.2 38–148

TABLE OF NON-UK STATUTORY MATERIAL

Where a reference indicates significant discussion of the statute in the text, it is in **bold**. Where a reference is to a footnote, it is *italic*.

European Community Treaties and Conventions

1957 Rome. Treaty establishing the European Economic Community (March 25) U.N.T.S. 11 (EU Treaty)—

    Art.81 ....*16–153*, *16–199*, 42–037, 42–066, 42–067

    Art.81(1) 42–027, 42–059

    Art.81(3) 42–032

    Art.82 42–067

1968 Brussels. Convention on Jurisdiction and Enforcement of Judgments in Civil and Commercial Matters (September 27) [1978] O.J. L 304/77—

    Art.39 .... *36–147*

1980 Rome. Convention on the Law Applicable to Contracual Obligations (June 19) [1980] O.J. 1266/1—

    Art.4(2) *30–088*

    Art.4(5) *30–088*

    Art.5 15–093

2004 Brussels Protocol 30–016, 30–019

2005 Convention for the accession of the Czech Republic, Estonia, Cyprus, Latvia, Lithuania, Hungary, Malta, Poland, Slovenia and the Slovak Republic [2005] O.J. C334/1 30–016

European Community Regulations

1991 Reg.295/91 35–047

1997 Reg.2027/97 [1997] O.J. L285/1 ... 35–007–35–010, 35–035, 35–036

    Art.3a 35–014

    Art.6 35–014

2002 Reg.889/2002 [2002] O.J. L140 .... 35–007—35–010, 35–035, 35–036, 35–054, 35–073

2004 Reg.44/2004 .... *36–147*

2004 Reg.139/2004 [2004] O.J. L24/1 42–037

2004 Reg.261/2004 [2004] O.J. L46/1 35–047

2004 Reg.772/2004 [2004] O.J. L123/11 .... 42–034, 42–056

2004 Reg.773/2004 [2004] O.J. L123/18 42–074

2004 Reg.785/2004 [2004] O.J. L 138/1 35–012

    Art.1(2) *35–012*

    Art.4(1) *35–012*

2005 Reg.2111/2005 34–049

European Community Directives

1972 Dir.72/166 .... *41–093*

1984 Dir.84/5 .... *41–093*

1984 Dir.84/374 .... *28–009*

    Art.7 ....*15–032A*

1990 Dir.90/232 .... *41–093*

1993 Dir.93/13 [1993] O.J. L95/21 ....15–014–15–017, 15–032A, *15–092*

    Art.2(c) *15–021*

    Art.3 ....15–048A

1993 Dir.93/13—*cont.*
    Art.3(1) *15–032A*, 15–048A
    Art.3(2) *15–032A*
    Art.5(1) *15–092*
    Art.5(2) *15–092*
    Art.6(2) 15–093
    Art.7 .... *15–092*
1997 Dir.97/7 38–094
    Art.3(2) 38–094
1998 Dir.98/27 .... *15–092*
    Art.1(2) *15–092*
    Annex 9 .... *15–092*
1999 Dir.99/44 [1999] O.J. L
    171/7—
    Recital 16 .... *15–060*
2002 Dir.2002/65 ...*30–063, 30–100, 34–222,*
    36–094A
2002 Dir.2002/83 .... *30–044*
2004 Dir.2004/17 [2004] O.J.
    L134/1 10–026
2004 Dir.2004/18 [2004] O.J.
    L134/114 10–026
    Art.82 10–026
2004 Dir.2004/36—
    Art.9 35–049
    Arts 10–13 35–049
2005 Dir.2005/29 [2005] O.J. L
    149/22 .... 6–001, 7–001
    Art.3(1) 6–001, 7–001
    Art.6 6–001
    Art.7 6–001
    Art.8 7–001
    Art.9 7–001

International Conventions

1929 Warsaw Convention *35–030*
1950 European Convention on
    Human Rights and Funda-
    mental Freedoms—
    Art.6 .... *1–039*, 1–042, 11–003,
    32–142
    Art.6(1) 32–144
    Arts 8, 14 1–041
    Protocol 1, Art.1 .... 1–039, 1–041,
    1–042, **10–015A**
1956 Geneva. Convention on the
    Contract for the Interna-
    tional Carriage of Goods
    by Road (CMR) (May
    19) 36–086, *36–134*
    Art.2(1) *36–085*
    Art.17(2) *36–129*
    Art.27 .... *36–134*
    Art.36 .... *36–141*
1958 New York Convention on the
    Recognition and Enforce-
    ment of Foreign Arbitral
    Awards 32–019
    Art.IV.1 32–019

1968 Brussels. Protocol to the Hague
    Rules (Hague-Visby
    Rules)—
    Art.III, r.2 14–117
1973 Athens. Convention relating to
    the Carriage of Passengers
    and their Luggage on
    Board Ships (December
    13) 13–034
1974 Athens Convention relating to
    the Carriage of Passengers
    and their Luggage by
    Sea 36–101
1975 Montreal Additional Protocol
    No.1 amending the War-
    saw Convention ... 35–002, 35–073
1980 Berne. Convention relating to
    the International Carriage
    by Rail (COTIF) (Cmnd.
    8535) (May 9)—
    Art.9(1) *36–094*
    Art.9(2) *36–094*
    Art.9(3) *36–094*
    Art.9(4) *36–094*
    Art.24(1) *36–092*, 36–100, 36–101
    App.A (CIV) ....**36–099—36–116**
    App.Art.1(1) *36–100*
    App.Art.1(2) *36–100*
    App.Art.1(3) *36–100*, 36–101
    App.Art.1(4) *36–100*
    App.Art.1(5) *36–100*
    App.Art.3(c) *36–104*
    App.Art.5 .... *36–100*
    App.Art.6(1) *36–102*
    App.Art.6(2) *36–104*
    App.Art.6(3) *36–104*
    App.Art.7(1) *36–104*
    App.Art.7(2) *36–104*
    App.Art.7(3) *36–104*
    App.Art.7(4) *36–104*
    App.Art.7(5) *36–104*
    App.Art.8(1) *36–102*
    App.Art.9 .... *36–104*
    App.Art.9(1) *36–103*
    App.Art.9(2) *36–103*
    App.Art.12(1) *36–103*
    App.Art.12(2) *36–111*
    App.Art.15 .... *36–103*
    App.Art.16(1) *36–111*
    App.Art.16(2) *36–111*
    App.Art.16(3) *36–111*
    App.Art.16(4) *36–112*
    App.Art.17(1) *36–111*
    App.Art.17(2) *36–111*
    App.Art.17(3) *36–111*
    App.Art.19 .... *36–112*
    App.Art.22(1) *36–112*
    App.Art.24 .... *36–111*
    App.Art.25 ....*36–102*, 36–111
    App.Art.26(1) *36–105*

1980   Berne. Convention relating to
       the International Carriage
       by Rail—*cont.*
       App.Art.26(2)(a) *36–107*
       App.Art.26(2)(b) *36–107*
       App.Art.26(2)(c) *36–107*
       App.Art.26(3) *36–107*
       App.Art.26(5) *36–114*
       App.Art.27 .... *36–105*
       App.Art.27(1) *36–105*
       App.Art.27(2) *36–105*
       App.Art.28 .... *36–105*
       App.Art.29 .... *36–105*
       App.Art.30(2) *36–110*
       App.Art.32(1) *36–108*
       App.Art.32(2) *36–108*
       App.Art.32(3) *36–108*
       App.Art.33(1) *36–109*
       App.Art.33(2) *36–109*
       App.Art.34 .... *36–110*
       App.Art.36(1) *36–112*
       App.Art.36(2) *36–112*
       App.Art.36(3) *36–112*
       App.Art.37(1) *36–112*
       App.Art.37(2) *36–112*
       App.Art.38 .... *36–111*
       App.Art.39 .... *36–111*
       App.Art.40(1) *36–112*
       App.Art.41(1) *36–113*
       App.Art.41(2) *36–113*
       App.Art.42 .... *36–113*
       App.Art.43(1) *36–113*
       App.Art.44 .... *36–113*
       App.Art.45 .... *36–113*
       App.Art.48 .... *36–113*
       App.Art.47 .... *36–112*
       App.Art.48 .... *36–110*
       App.Art.54 .... *36–115*
       App.Art.55(1) *36–114*
       App.Art.55(2) *36–114*
       App.Art.56(1) *36–114*
       App.Art.56(2) *36–114*
       App.Art.56(3) *36–114*
       App.Art.57(1) *36–114*
       App.Art.58(1) *36–115*
       App.Art.58(2) *36–115*
       App.Art.59(1) *36–115*
       App.Art.59(2)(a) *36–115*
       App.Art.59(2)(b) *36–115*
       App.Art.59(2)(c) *36–115*
       App.Art.59(2)(d) *36–115*
       App.Art.60(1) *36–116*
       App.Art.60(2) *36–116*
       App.Art.60(3) *36–116*
       App.Art.60(4) *36–116*
       App.B (CIM) ....**36–084—36–098**
       App.Art.1(1) *36–085*
       App.Art.1(2) *36–085*
       App.Art.1(3) *36–085*
       App.Art.1(4) *36–085*

1980   Berne. Convention relating to
       the International Carriage
       by Rail—*cont.*
       App.Art.1(6) *36–085*
       App.Art.5 .... *36–085*
       App.Art.6(1) *36–087*
       App.Art.6(2) *36–088*
       App.Art.6(4) *36–088*
       App.Art.6(5) *36–088*
       App.Art.6(6) *36–088*
       App.Art.6(8) *36–088*
       App.Art.7 .... *36–088*
       App.Art.8 .... *36–088*
       App.Art.10(1) *36–087*
       App.Art.12(1) *36–088*
       App.Art.13(1) *36–089*
       App.Art.14 .... *36–089*
       App.Art.15 .... *36–092, 36–094*
       App.Art.16 .... *36–092*
       App.Art.17(1) *36–089*
       App.Art.17(2) *36–089*
       App.Art.17(4) *36–093*
       App.Art.18(1) *36–090*
       App.Art.18(2) *36–090*
       App.Art.18(3) *36–090*
       App.Art.18(4) *36–090*
       App.Art.18(5) *36–090*
       App.Art.19(1) *36–090*
       App.Art.19(3) *36–090*
       App.Art.19(4) *36–090*
       App.Art.19(6) *36–092*
       App.Art.19(7) *36–090*
       App.Art.20(1) *36–091*
       App.Art.20(2) *36–091*
       App.Art.21(1) *36–091*
       App.Art.21(2) *36–091*
       App.Art.21(3) *36–091*
       App.Art.21(4) *36–091*
       App.Art.22(3) *36–091*
       App.Art.22(4) *36–091*
       App.Art.23(2) *36–091, 36–092*
       App.Art.23(3) *36–092*
       App.Art.24 .... *36–085, 36–092*
       App.Art.25(1) *36–092*
       App.Art.25(2) *36–092*
       App.Art.25(3) *36–092*
       App.Art.26 .... *36–095*
       App.Art.27(1) *36–095*
       App.Art.27(2) *36–095*
       App.Art.29(1) *36–092*
       App.Art.30(1) *36–094*
       App.Art.30(2) *36–094*
       App.Art.30(4) *36–094*
       App.Art.31 .... *36–092*
       App.Art.32 .... *36–094*
       App.Art.32(1) *36–094*
       App.Art.32(2) *36–094*
       App.Art.33(1) *36–094*
       App.Art.33(2) *36–094*
       App.Art.33(3) *36–094*

1980 Berne. Convention relating to
the International Carriage
by Rail—*cont.*
App.Art.33(4) 36–094
App.Art.34 36–094
App.Art.35 36–094
App.Art.36 36–094
App.Art.37(2) 36–094
App.Art.37(3) 36–094
App.Art.40 36–092
App.Art.42(1) 36–093
App.Art.42(3) 36–093
App.Art.43 36–094
App.Art.43(1) 36–096
App.Art.43(2) 36–096
App.Art.43(3)–(6) 36–096
App.Art.44(1)(a) 36–096
App.Art.44(1)(b) 36–096
App.Art.44(2) 36–096
App.Art.45(1) 36–095
App.Art.45(2) 36–095

1980 Berne. Convention relating to
the International Carriage
by Rail—*cont.*
App.Art.46(1) 36–096
App.Art.47(1) 36–097
App.Art.47(2)(a) 36–097
App.Art.47(2)(b) 36–097
App.Art.47(2)(c) 36–097
App.Art.47(2)(d) 36–097, 36–115
App.Art.48(1) 36–098
App.Art.48(2) 36–098
App.Art.48(3) 36–098
1999 Protocol for the modification of
the Convention Concern-
ing International Carriage
by Rail (Vilnius
Protocol) 36–080
Art.42 36–080
1999 Montreal
Convention ....35–007—35–010,
35–035, 35–036, 35–037,
35–054, 35–073

TABLE OF CASES

Where a reference indicates significant discussion of the case in the text, it is in **bold**. Where a reference is to a footnote, it is *italic*.

1 Pump Court Chambers v Horton; sub nom. Higham v Horton; Horton v 1 Pump Court Chambers; Horton v Higham [2004] EWCA Civ 941; [2004] 3 All E.R. 852; [2005] I.C.R. 292; (2004) 101(33) L.S.G. 34; (2004) 148 S.J.L.B. 911; *The Times*, July 21, 2004; *Independent*, July 28, 2004, CA (Civ Div) *3–038*
21st Century Logistic Solutions Ltd v Madysen Ltd [2004] EWHC 231; [2004] S.T.I. 497; (2004) 101(12) L.S.G. 35; [2004] 2 Lloyd's Rep. 92 .... *16–017*
24 Seven Utility Services Ltd v Rosekey Ltd (t/a Atwasl Builders) [2003] EWHC 3415, QBD *16–057*

A v Lord Grey School Governors; sub nom. A v Headteacher and Governors of Lord Grey School [2004] EWCA Civ 382; [2004] Q.B. 1231; [2004] 2 W.L.R. 1442; [2004] 4 All E.R. 628; [2005] B.L.G.R. 212; [2004] E.L.R. 169; (2004) 101(14) L.S.G. 25; (2004) 148 S.J.L.B. 417; *The Times*, April 9, 2004; *Independent*, April 1, 2004, CA (Civ Div) *27–023*
A&S Enterprises Ltd v Kema Holdings Ltd [2005] EWHC 3365; [2005] B.L.R. 76, QBD (TCC) *37–260*
ABB AG v Hochtief Airport GmbH [2006] EWHC 388; [2006] 1 All E.R. (Comm) 529; [2006] 2 Lloyd's Rep. 1, QBD (Comm) *32–137, 32–138*
ABB Lummus Global Ltd v Keppel Fels Ltd (formerly Far East Levingston Shipbuilding Ltd) [1999] 2 Lloyd's Rep. 24, QBD (Comm) *32–132*
AIC Ltd v ITS Testing Services (UK) Ltd [2005] EWHC 2122; [2006] 1 Lloyd's Rep. 1; [2005] 2 C.L.C. 490, QBD (Comm) *28–086*
AIG Capital Partners Inc v Kazakhstan [2005] EWHC 2239; [2006] 1 W.L.R. 1420; [2006] 1 All E.R. 284; [2006] 1 All E.R. (Comm) 1; [2006] 1 Lloyd's Rep. 45, QBD (Comm) 11–003, *11–004, 32–160*
AMB Imballaggi Plastici Srl v Pacflex Ltd [1999] 2 All E.R. (Comm) 249; [1999] C.L.C. 1391; [2000] E.C.C. 381; [1999] Eu. L.R. 930; (1999) 18 Tr. L.R. 153; (1999) 96(27) L.S.G. 34, CA (Civ Div) *31–005, 31–006*
AMEC Civil Engineering Ltd v Secretary of State for Transport [2005] EWCA Civ 291; [2005] 12 E.G.C.S. 219; *The Times*, March 22, 2005, CA (Civ Div) *32–025, 32–029, 32–166, 32–169, 37–247, 37–260*
AMP (UK) Plc v Barker [2001] O.P.L.R. 197; [2001] Pens. L.R. 77; [2001] W.T.L.R. 1237; (2000–01) 3 I.T.E.L.R. 414, Ch D *5–095*
ASM Shipping Ltd of India v TTMI Ltd of England [2005] EWHC 2238; [2006] 2 All E.R. (Comm) 122; [2006] 1 Lloyd's Rep. 375, QBD (Comm) *32–073, 32–137, 32–138, 32–149*
AWG Construction Services Ltd v Rockingham Motor Speedway Ltd [2004] EWHC 888; [2004] T.C.L.R. 6, QBD (TCC) *37–260*
AY Bank Ltd (In Liquidation), Re; sub nom. AY Bank Ltd (In Liquidation) v Bosnia and Herzegovina [2006] EWHC 830, Ch D (Companies Ct) *11–007*

Abbey National Plc v JSF Finance & Currency Exchange Co Ltd; sub nom. Abbey National
Plc v JSF Financial & Currency Exchange Co Ltd [2006] EWCA Civ 328, CA (Civ
Div) *34–035, 34–083, 34–164*
Abbott v Condici Ltd [2005] 2 Lloyd's Rep. 450, CC (Central London) *31–147*
Abou-Rahmah v Abacha [2005] EWHC 2662; [2006] 1 All E.R. (Comm) 247; [2006] 1
Lloyd's Rep. 484; [2006] W.T.L.R. 377, QBD *18–031, 29–174, 34–255,* 34–290, *34–396A*
Absalom v TCRU Ltd (formerly Monument Insurance Brokers Ltd) [2005] EWCA Civ
1586; [2006] 1 All E.R. (Comm) 375; [2006] 1 C.L.C. 648, CA (Civ Div) *12–050, 12–057,*
12–119
Ackinclose v Gateshead MBC [2005] I.R.L.R. 79, EAT *39–046*
Actionstrength Ltd v International Glass Engineering IN.GL.EN SpA [2003] UKHL 17;
[2003] 2 A.C. 541; [2003] 2 W.L.R. 1060; [2003] 2 All E.R. 615; [2003] 2 All E.R.
(Comm.) 331; [2003] B.L.R. 207; 88 Con. L.R. 208; (2003) 153 N.L.J. 563; (2003) 147
S.J.L.B. 418 ....*4–078, 37–169*
Aer Lingus Plc v Gildacroft Ltd [2006] EWCA Civ 4; [2006] 1 W.L.R. 1173; [2006] 2 All
E.R. 290; [2006] C.P. Rep. 21; [2006] P.I.Q.R. P16; (2006) 103(6) L.S.G. 32; (2006)
156 N.L.J. 147; (2006) 150 S.J.L.B. 129; [2006] N.P.C. 4· CA (Civ Div) *28–051*
Agip (Africa) Ltd v Jackson [1991] Ch. 547; [1991] 3 W.L.R. 116; [1992] 4 All E.R. 451;
(1991) 135 S.J. 117; *The Times*, January 9, 1991; *Financial Times*, January 18, 1991,
CA (Civ Div) 5–100
Agtrack (NT) Pty Ltd v Hatfield [2005] HCA 38 .... *35–026*
Ahmed Amin v Brown [2005] EWHC 1670; [2006] I.L.Pr. 5; [2005] A.C.D. 95; (2005) 155
N.L.J. 1278; [2005] N.P.C. 104, Ch D *11–024, 11–028*
Air France v Saks, 470 U.S. 392 (1985), US Ct *35–020*
Air Link Pty Ltd v Paterson [2005] HCA 39 .... *35–026*
Al-Fayed v Advocate General for Scotland (Forward Tax Agreements); sub nom. Al-Fayed
v Inland Revenue Commissioners; Ali Fayed v Advocate General for Scotland; Fayed
v Inland Revenue Commissioners [2004] S.T.C. 1703; 2004 S.C. 745; 2004 S.L.T. 798;
[2004] S.T.I. 1723; 2004 G.W.D. 22–491, IH (1 Div) *10–015A*
Al-Kadhimi v Government of Saudi Arabia [2003] EWCA Civ 1689 .... *11–005*
Al-Naimi (t/a Buildmaster Construction Services) v Islamic Press Agency Inc; sub nom.
Al-Naimi (t/a Buildmaster Construction Services) v Islamic Press Services Inc [2000]
1 Lloyd's Rep. 522; [2000] C.L.C. 647; [2000] B.L.R. 150; (2000) 2 T.C.L.R. 499; 70
Con. L.R. 21; *The Times*, March 16, 2000, CA (Civ Div) *32–046, 32–048*
Alawiye v Mahmood (t/a Amsons) [2006] EWHC 277; [2006] 3 All E.R. 668, Ch D *34–324*
Alfred McAlpine Capital Projects Ltd v Tilebox Ltd [2005] EWHC 281; [2005] B.L.R. 271;
104 Con. L.R. 39; (2005) 21 Const. L.J. 539, QBD (TCC) *26–109, 26–111, 26–117*
Alfred McAlpine Construction Ltd v Panatown Ltd (No.1); sub nom. Panatown Ltd v Alfred
McAlpine Construction Ltd [2001] 1 A.C. 518; [2000] 3 W.L.R. 946; [2000] 4 All E.R.
97; [2000] C.L.C. 1604; [2000] B.L.R. 331; (2000) 2 T.C.L.R. 547; 71 Con. L.R. 1;
[2000] E.G.C.S. 102; (2000) 97(38) L.S.G. 43; (2000) 150 N.L.J. 1299; (2000) 144
S.J.L.B. 240; [2000] N.P.C. 89; *The Times*, August 15, 2000, HL *18–055*
Alfred McAlpine Plc v BAI (Run-Off) Ltd [2000] 1 All E.R. (Comm) 545; [2000] 1 Lloyd's
Rep. 437; [2000] C.L.C. 812; (2001) 3 T.C.L.R. 5; 69 Con. L.R. 87; [2000] Lloyd's
Rep. I.R. 352, CA (Civ Div) *41–054, 41–064*
Allan Janes LLP v Johal [2006] EWHC 286; [2006] I.C.R. 742; [2006] I.R.L.R. 599; (2006)
156 N.L.J. 373, Ch D *16–103*
Allardyce v Roebuck; sub nom. Gray (Deceased), Re [2004] EWHC 1538; [2005] 1 W.L.R.
815; [2004] 3 All E.R. 754; [2004] W.T.L.R. 779; (2004–05) 7 I.T.E.L.R. 232; [2004]
N.P.C. 109, Ch D *2–125, 3–170*
Allen J Panozza & Co Pty Ltd v Allied Interstate (Qld) Pty Ltd [1976] 2 N.S.W.L.R. 192 ..... *30–150*
Alphapoint Shipping Ltd v Rotem Amfert Negev Ltd (The Agios Dimitrios) [2004] EWHC
2232; [2005] 1 Lloyd's Rep. 23, QBD (Comm) *32–137, 32–138, 32–141, 32–142, 32–143A,*
32–145
Alstom Signalling Ltd (t/a Alstom Transport Information Solutions) v Jarvis Facilities Ltd
[2004] EWHC 1232; 95 Con. L.R. 55, QBD (TCC) *2–129, 2–135*
Amalgamated Investment & Property Co Ltd (In Liquidation) v Texas Commerce International Bank Ltd [1982] Q.B. 84; [1981] 3 W.L.R. 565; [1981] 3 All E.R. 577; [1982]
1 Lloyd's Rep. 27; [1981] Com. L.R. 236; 125 S.J. 623 ....*3–103, 3–113, 44–057*

Amec Developments Ltd v Jury's Hotel Management (UK) Ltd [2002] T.C.L.R. 13; (2001)
82 P. & C.R. 22; [2001] 1 E.G.L.R. 81; [2001] 07 E.G. 163; [2000] E.G.C.S. 138;
[2000] N.P.C. 125 .... *26–024, 29–151*
American Express Co v British Airways Board [1983] 1 W.L.R. 701; [1983] 1 All E.R. 557;
(1983) 133 N.L.J. 65; (1983) 127 S.J. 70 .... *35–074*
American Express International Banking Corp v Hurley [1985] 3 All E.R. 564; [1986]
B.C.L.C. 52; [1985] F.L.R. 350; (1985) 135 N.L.J. 1034, QBD *44–104*
American International Marine Agency v Dandridge [2005] EWHC 829, QBD (Comm) *41–094*
Andrea Merzario Ltd v Internationale Spedition Leitner Gesellschaft GmbH [2001] EWCA
Civ 61; [2001] 1 All E.R. (Comm) 883; [2001] 1 Lloyd's Rep. 490; [2001] C.L.C. 643;
[2002] I.L.Pr. 26; (2001) 98(9) L.S.G. 41; (2001) 145 S.J.L.B. 54; *The Times*, February
27, 2001; *Daily Telegraph*, February 13, 2001, CA (Civ Div) *36–147*
Andrewes v Garstin (1861) 10 C.B.N.S. 444 .... *6–157*
Anon., unreported, January 28, 1975, Cass. Paris *36–094*
Anon. (1976) 11 E.T.L. 787 .... *36–094*
Anon. (1994) 29 E.T.L. 360 .... *36–094*
Anon. (2003) 38 E.T.L. 512 .... *36–127*
Anon. (2003) 38 E.T.L. 656 .... *36–147*
Anon. (2004) 39 E.T.L. 93 .... *36–094, 36–132*
Anon. (2004) 39 E.T.L. 244 .... *36–129*
Anon. (2004) 39 E.T.L. 400 .... *36–144*
Anon. (2004) 39 E.T.L. 517 .... *36–134*
Anon. (2005) 40 E.T.L. 395 .... *36–098*
Anon. (2005) 40 E.T.L. 729 .... *36–132*
Anon. (2005) 40 E.T.L. 878 .... *36–145*
Anon. (2006) 41 E.T.L. 228 .... *36–121*
Anton Durbeck GmbH v Den Norske Bank ASA [2005] EWHC 2497; [2006] 1 Lloyd's
Rep. 93; [2005] 2 C.L.C. 783, QBD (Comm) *18–134, 18–136*
Apple Corps Ltd v Apple Computer Inc. [2004] EWHC 768 .... *30–020, 30–074, 30–087*
Aqua Design Ltd v Kier Regional Ltd [2002] EWCA Civ 797; [2003] B.L.R. 111; 82 Con.
L.R. 107 .... *37–064*
Arab National Bank v El-Abdali [2004] EWHC 2381; [2005] 1 Lloyd's Rep. 541, QBD
(Comm) *32–007, 32–123*
Archibald v Fife Council [2004] UKHL 32; [2004] I.R.L.R. 197; 2004 G.W.D. 11–247 .... *39–131*
Architype Projects Ltd v Dewhurst Macfarlane & Partners [2003] EWHC 3341; 96 Con.
L.R. 35; [2004] P.N.L.R. 38, QBD (TCC) *18–032*
Argo Fund Ltd v Essar Steel Ltd; sub nom. Essar Steel Ltd v Argo Fund Ltd [2006] EWCA
Civ 241; [2006] 2 All E.R. (Comm) 104; [2006] 1 C.L.C. 546, CA (Civ Div); affirming
[2005] EWHC 600; [2006] 1 All E.R. (Comm) 56; [2005] 2 Lloyd's Rep. 203; [2005]
2 C.L.C. 209, QBD (Comm) *2–045, 3–077*
Argos Ltd v Office of Fair Trading (Case Management: New Material) [2003] CAT 24;
[2004] Comp. A.R. 212, CAT *42–089*
Ark Therapeutics Plc v True North Capital Ltd [2005] EWHC 1585; [2006] 1 All E.R.
(Comm) 138, QBD (Comm) *30–073, 30–075, 30–127, 30–128*
Armitage v Staveley Industries Plc [2005] EWCA Civ 792, CA (Civ Div); reversing [2004]
EWHC 2320; [2004] Pens. L.R. 385, Ch D *12–055, 12–080, 13–009*
Armlea plc v Gov & Co of the Bank of Scotland, unreported, June 14, 2004 .... *34–490*
Arup (Ove) & Partners International Ltd v Mirant Asia-Pacific Construction (Hong Kong)
Ltd [2003] EWCA Civ 1729; [2004] B.L.R. 49; 92 Con. L.R. 1 .... *37–039*
Asghar v Legal Services Commission, The Times, August 5, 2004 .... *32–025*
Aspin v Metric Group Ltd [2004] EWHC 1265, QBD *39–142*
Assicurazioni Generali SpA v CGU International Insurance plc [2004] EWCA Civ 429;
[2004] 2 Lloyd's Rep. I.R. 457; (2004) 148 S.J.L.B. 475 .... *41–095*
Assimina Maritime Ltd v Pakistan National Shipping Corp [2004] EWHC 3005; [2005] 1
All E.R. (Comm) 460; [2005] 1 Lloyd's Rep. 525, QBD (Comm) *32–100, 32–101*
Astea (UK) Ltd v Time Group Ltd [2003] EWHC 725; [2005] All E.R. (D) 212, QBD
(TCC) *21–020*

Aston Cantlow and Wilmcote with Billesley Parochial Church Council v Wallbank; sub nom. Wallbank v Aston Cantlow and Wilmcote with Billesley Parochial Church Council [2003] UKHL 37; [2004] 1 A.C. 546; [2003] 3 W.L.R. 283; [2003] 3 All E.R. 1213; [2003] H.R.L.R. 28; [2003] U.K.H.R.R. 919; [2003] 27 E.G.C.S. 137; (2003) 100(33) L.S.G. 28; (2003) 153 N.L.J. 1030; (2003) 147 S.J.L.B. 812; [2003] N.P.C. 80; *The Times*, June 27, 2003, HL 1–042

Atlanska Plovidba v Consignaciones Asturianas SA [2004] EWHC Comm 1273; [2004] 2 Lloyd's Rep.109 .... 32–059, 32–061, *32–065*

Atlantic Telecom GmbH, Noter, 2004 S.L.T. 1031; 2004 G.W.D. 30–623, OH *30–020, 30–031, 30–040, 30–075*

Att.-Gen. of Hong Kong v Humphreys Estate (Queen's Gardens) Ltd [1987] A.C. 114; [1987] 2 W.L.R. 343; [1987] 2 All E.R. 387; (1987) 54 P. & C.R. 96; (1987) 84 L.S.G. 574; (1987) 131 S.J. 194, PC (HK) *3–143*

Att.-Gen. of Hong Kong v Reid [1994] 1 A.C. 324; [1993] 3 W.L.R. 1143; [1994] 1 All E.R. 1; (1993) 143 N.L.J. 1569; (1993) 137 S.J.L.B. 251; [1993] N.P.C. 144 .... *29–156, 31–126*

Autologic Holdings Plc v Inland Revenue Commissioners; sub nom. Test Claimants in Loss Relief Group Litigation v Inland Revenue Commissioners; Loss Relief Group Litigation Order Claimants v Inland Revenue Commissioners [2005] UKHL 54; [2006] 1 A.C. 118; [2005] 3 W.L.R. 339; [2005] 4 All E.R. 1141; [2005] S.T.C. 1357; [2005] 3 C.M.L.R. 2; [2006] Eu. L.R. 131; [2005] B.T.C. 402; [2005] S.T.I. 1336; (2005) 155 N.L.J. 1277, HL *29–084*

Axa General Insurance Ltd v Gottlieb; sub nom. Gottleib v Axa General Insurance Ltd [2005] EWCA Civ 112; [2005] 1 All E.R. (Comm) 445; [2005] 1 C.L.C. 62; [2005] N.P.C. 20; *The Times*, March 3, 2005, CA (Civ Div) *41–069*

Axiom Business Computers Ltd v Frederick, unreported, November 10, 2003, OH *16–105*

Azienda Autonoma Ferrovie dello Stato v La Pace (1976) 11 E.T.L. 137 .... *36–085*

Aziz v Yemen [2005] EWCA Civ 745; [2005] I.C.R. 1391; *The Times*, June 22, 2005; *Independent*, June 23, 2005, CA (Civ Div) *11–004, 11–005, 11–021*

Azov Shipping Co v Baltic Shipping Co (No.1) [1999] 1 All E.R. 476; [1999] 1 Lloyd's Rep. 68; [1998] C.L.C. 1240, QBD (Comm) *32–081*

BMW Financial Services (GB) Ltd v Taylor [2006] 1 C.L. 113 .... *38–306*

BP Exploration Operating Co Ltd v Kvaerner Oilfield Products Ltd [2004] EWHC 999; [2004] 2 All E.R. (Comm) 266; [2005] 1 Lloyd's Rep. 307, QBD (Comm) *12–050, 12–051, 12–055, 12–080, 41–008*

BP Plc v AON Ltd (No.2) [2006] EWHC 424; [2006] 1 All E.R. (Comm) 789; (2006) 103 L.S.G. 31, QBD (Comm) *18–022, 18–031, 31–112, 31–124*

Bacon v Cooper [1982] 1 All E.R. 397 .... *26–095C*

Baden v Societe Generale pour Favoriser le Developpement du Commerce et de l'Industrie en France SA [1993] 1 W.L.R. 509; [1992] 4 All E.R. 161, Ch D 5–100

Bailey v Warren [2006] EWCA Civ 51; [2006] W.T.L.R. 753; *The Times* February 20, 2006, CA (Civ Div *8–072, 8–077*

Baines & Ernst Ltd v Customs and Excise Commissioners [2006] EWCA Civ 1040; [2006] S.T.I. 1987, CA (Civ Div) *29–084, 29–086*

Baird Textile Holdings Ltd v Marks & Spencer Plc; sub nom. Baird Textiles Holdings Ltd v Marks & Spencer Plc [2001] EWCA Civ 274; [2002] 1 All E.R. (Comm) 737; [2001] C.L.C. 999, CA (Civ Div) *2–155*

Bairstow Eves London Central Ltd v Darlingtons [2004] EWHC 263; [2004] W.L. 1054905 .... *15–036A*

Balfour Beatty Civil Engineering v Technical & General Guarantee Co Ltd [2000] C.L.C. 252; 68 Con. L.R. 180 .... *34–489*

Balkis Consolidated Co, Re (1888) 58 L.T. 300 .... *1–082H*

Balmoral Group Ltd v Borealis (UK) Ltd [2006] EWHC 1900, QBD (Comm) *12–011, 12–012, 14–094, 30–007, 30–047, 30–066, 43–108, 43–110*

Bank of America v Arnell [1999] Lloyd's Rep. Bank. 399 .... *34–138*

Bank of Credit and Commerce International SA (In Liquidation) v Ali (No.1) [2001] UKHL 8; [2002] 1 A.C. 251; [2001] 2 W.L.R. 735; [2001] 1 All E.R. 961; [2001] I.C.R. 337; [2001] I.R.L.R. 292; [2001] Emp. L.R. 359; (2001) 98(15) L.S.G. 32; (2001) 151 N.L.J. 351; (2001) 145 S.J.L.B. 67; (2001) 145 S.J.L.B. 70 .... *5–042*

Bank of India v Morris [2005] EWCA Civ 693, CA (Civ Div) *9–006*

Bank of Scotland v Alfred Truman (A Firm) [2005] EWHC 583, QBD *38–029, 38–454*

Bank of Scotland v Henry Butcher & Co [2003] EWCA Civ 67; [2003] 2 All E.R. (Comm.) 557; [2003] 1 B.C.L.C. 575; (2003) 100(13) L.S.G. 29 .... *44–099*

Bank of Scotland v Singh, unreported, June 17, 2005, QBD *34–222*

Banner Homes Holdings Ltd (formerly Banner Homes Group Plc) v Luff Developments Ltd (No.2) [2000] Ch. 372; [2000] 2 W.L.R. 772, CA (Civ Div) *4–073*

Banque Financiere de la Cite SA (formerly Banque Keyser Ullmann SA) v Westgate Insurance Co (formerly Hodge General & Mercantile Co Ltd); sub nom. Banque Keyser Ullmann SA v Skandia (UK) Insurance Co; Skandia (UK) Insurance Co v Chemical Bank; Skandia (UK) Insurance Co v Credit Lyonnais Bank Nederland NV [1991] 2 A.C. 249, HL; affirming [1990] 1 Q.B. 665; [1989] 3 W.L.R. 25; [1989] 2 All E.R. 952; [1988] 2 Lloyd's Rep. 513; [1989] Fin. L.R. 1; (1989) 133 S.J. 817, CA (Civ Div) *6–139*

Banque Saudi Fransi v Lear Siegler Services Inc [2005] EWHC 2395; [2006] 1 Lloyd's Rep. 273, QBD (Comm) *34–486, 44–014*

Barbados Trust Co Ltd (formerly CI Trustees (Asia Pacific) Ltd) v Bank of Zambia [2006] EWHC 222; [2006] 1 Lloyd's Rep. 723; [2006] 1 C.L.C. 311; (2005–06) 8 I.T.E.L.R. 739, QBD (Comm) *18–019, 18–079, 18–087, 19–045*

Barber v Somerset County Council [2004] UKHL 13; [2004] 1 W.L.R. 1089; [2004] 2 All E.R. 385; [2004] I.C.R. 457; [2004] I.R.L.R. 475; (2004) 101(18) L.S.G. 34; (2004) 148 S.J.L.B. 419 ....*26–074, 39–100*

Barclays Bank Plc v Kingston [2006] EWHC 533; [2006] 1 All E.R. (Comm) 519; [2006] 2 Lloyd's Rep. 59; [2006] 12 E.G.C.S. 223, QBD *12–118, 44–089, 44–104*

Barlow Clowes International Ltd (In Liquidation) v Eurotrust International Ltd [2005] UKPC 37; [2006] 1 W.L.R. 1476; [2006] 1 All E.R. 333; [2006] 1 All E.R. (Comm) 478; [2006] 1 Lloyd's Rep. 225; [2005] W.T.L.R. 1453; (2005–06) 8 I.T.E.L.R. 347; (2005) 102(44) L.S.G. 32; [2006] 1 P. & C.R. DG16, PC (IoM) *29–174, 34–290*

Barrett v Universal-Island Records Ltd [2006] EWHC 1009, Ch D; [2006] E.M.L.R. 21 .... *21–049*

Barros Mattos Junior v MacDaniels Ltd; Barros Mattos Junior v General Securities & Finance Co Ltd; sub nom. Mattos Junior v MacDaniels Ltd [2004] EWHC 1188; [2005] 1 W.L.R. 247; [2004] 3 All E.R. 299; [2004] 2 All E.R. (Comm) 501; [2004] 2 Lloyd's Rep. 475, Ch D *29–179, 29–183, 30–141, 30–159, 30–169, 30–174, 34–137*

Base Metal Trading Ltd v Shamurin [2004] EWCA Civ 1316; [2005] 1 W.L.R. 1157; [2005] 1 All E.R. (Comm) 17; [2005] B.C.C. 325; [2004] 2 C.L.C. 916; (2004) 148 S.J.L.B. 1281; *The Times*, November 1, 2004, CA (Civ Div) *30–020, 30–031, 30–032, 30–040, 30–107, 30–113*

Bath and North East Somerset DC v Mowlem Plc [2004] EWCA Civ 115; [2004] B.L.R. 153; (2004) 148 S.J.L.B. 265, CA (Civ Div) *32–111*

Batooneh v Asombang [2003] EWHC 2111; [2004] B.P.I.R. 1 .... *38–198*

Bayoumi v Women's Total Abstinence Educational Union Ltd [2003] EWCA Civ 1548; [2004] Ch. 46; [2004] 2 W.L.R. 181; [2004] W.T.L.R. 133; (2003) 100(47) L.S.G. 21; (2003) 147 S.J.L.B. 1307; [2003] N.P.C. 135; [2004] 1 P. & C.R. D9 .... *3–019*

Beam Technology (Mfg) Pte Ltd v Standard Chartered Bank [2003] 1 S.L.R. 597 .... *34–489*

Beesly v Hallwood Estates Ltd [1961] Ch. 105; [1961] 2 W.L.R. 36; [1961] 1 All E.R. 90; 105 S.J. 61, CA *1–082E*

Belgravia Property Co Ltd v S&R (London) Ltd [2001] C.L.C. 1626; [2001] B.L.R. 424; 93 Con. L.R. 59; (2003) 19 Const. L.J. 36, QBD (TCC) *32–081*

Bell v Lever Brothers Ltd; sub nom. Lever Bros Ltd v Bell [1932] A.C. 161, HL *6–157*

Bell Electric Ltd v Aweco Appliance Systems GmbH & Co KG (Application to Stay Appeal) [2002] EWCA Civ 1501; [2003] 1 All E.R. 344; [2003] C.P. Rep. 18CA (Civ Div) *31–147*

Benaim (UK) Ltd v Davies Middleton & Davies Ltd (No.2) [2005] EWHC 1370; 102 Con. L.R. 1, QBD (TCC) *32–137, 32–142*

Benford Ltd v Lopecan SL (No.2) [2004] EWHC 1897; [2004] 2 Lloyd's Rep. 618, QBD (Comm) *32–025, 32–026A, 43–203*

Benhams Ltd v Kythira Investments Ltd [2004] EWHC 2973; [2004] All E.R. (D) 313, QBD *31–132*

Bernhard Schulte GmbH & Co KG v Nile Holdings Ltd [2004] EWHC 977; [2004] 2 Lloyd's Rep. 352, QBD (Comm) *1–020, 32–166*

Bernuth Lines Ltd v High Seas Shipping Ltd (The Eastern Navigator) [2005] EWHC 3020;
[2006] 1 All E.R. (Comm) 359; [2006] 1 Lloyd's Rep. 537; [2006] 1 C.L.C. 403;
[2006] C.I.L.L. 2343; (2006) 156 N.L.J. 64, QBD (Comm) 2–049, 2–089, 32–041, 32–059A, 32–137, 32–138
Beyeler v Italy (33202/96) (No.1) (2001) 33 E.H.R.R. 52, ECHR 10–015A
Bielecki v Suffolk Coastal CC [2004] EWHC 3142, QBD 10–017
Bim Kemi AB v Blackburn Chemicals Ltd [2004] EWHC Comm 166 16–199
Bishopsgate Investment Management Ltd v Homan [1995] Ch. 211; [1994] 3 W.L.R. 1270;
[1995] 1 All E.R. 347; [1994] B.C.C. 868; (1994) 91(36) L.S.G. 37; (1994) 138
S.J.L.B. 176, CA 34–138
Black v Davies [2005] EWCA Civ 531, CA (Civ Div) 6–064
Blackburn Rovers Football and Athletic Club Plc v Avon Insurance Plc [2005] EWCA Civ
423, CA (Civ Div) 41–051A
Blackpool and Fylde Aero Club v Blackpool BC [1990] 1 W.L.R. 1195; [1990] 3 All E.R.
25; 88 L.G.R. 864; (1991) 3 Admin. L.R. 322; (1991) 155 L.G. Rev. 246, CA (Civ
Div) 10–025
BLCT (13096) Ltd v J Sainsbury Plc [2003] EWCA Civ 884; [2004] 1 C.L.C. 24; [2004]
2 P. & C.R. 3; (2003) 147 S.J.L.B. 815, CA (Civ Div) 32–015, 32–016, 32–142
Blue Haven Enterprises Ltd v Tully [2006] UKPC 17, PC (Jam) 3–138
Blue Water Shipping A/S v Melship Eesti OÜ (2000) 35 E.T.L. 772 36–147
BNP Paribas v Deloitte and Touche LLP [2003] EWHC 2874; [2004] 1 Lloyd's Rep. 233;
[2004] B.L.R. 90; (2003) 153 N.L.J. 1841 32–100
Bolton MBC v Municipal Mutual Insurance Ltd [2006] EWCA Civ 50; [2006] 1 W.L.R.
1492; [2006] 1 C.L.C. 242; (2006) 103(9) L.S.G. 31; (2006) 150 S.J.L.B. 226, CA (Civ
Div) 41–023
Bolton MBC v Torkington [2003] EWCA Civ 1634; [2004] 2 W.L.R. 426; [2004] 1 P. &
C.R. 9; [2004] 07 E.G. 132; [2003] 46 E.G.C.S. 130; (2003) 100(43) L.S.G. 33; (2003)
147 S.J.L.B. 1304, CA 1–082, 1–082F, 2–117
Bonner v Cox Dedicated Corporate Member Ltd [2005] EWCA Civ 1512; [2006] 1 All E.R.
(Comm) 565; [2006] 6 Lloyd's Rep. 385; [2006] 1 C.L.C. 126, CA (Civ Div);
affirming [2004] EWHC 2963, QBD (Comm) 41–045
Boomer v Muir, 24 P. 2d 570 (1933) 29–068
Booth v Phillips [2004] EWHC 1437; [2004] 1 W.L.R. 3292; [2004] 2 Lloyd's Rep. 457;
(2004) 101(30) L.S.G. 29; (2004) 154 N.L.J. 1050; The Times, July 27, 2004, QBD
(Comm) .... 30–032, 30–112—30–114
Boral Formwork v Action Motors [2002] N.S.W.S.C. 713 .... 34–491B
Borders (UK) Ltd v Commissioner of Police for the Metropolis [2005] EWCA Civ 197;
(2005) 149 S.J.L.B. 301; The Times, April 15, 2005, CA (Civ Div) 26–019, 26–022
Boston Deep Sea Fishing & Ice Co v Ansell (1888) L.R. 39 Ch. D. 339, CA 21–030
Bottiglieri di Navigazione Spa v Cosco Qingado Ocean Shipping Co [2005] EWHC 244;
[2005] 1 Lloyd's Rep. 1, QBD (Comm) 3–083, 3–094, 3–095, 3–097, 3–132, 32–137, 32–141
Bradford & Bingley Plc v Rashid [2006] UKHL 37; [2006] 1 W.L.R. 2066; (2006) 103(30)
L.S.G. 30; (2006) 156 N.L.J. 1172; (2006) 150 S.J.L.B. 983, HL 28–094, 28–095
Brake Bros Ltd v Ungless [2004] EWHC 2799; [2004] All E.R. (D) 586, QBD 16–107
Bramhill v Edwards [2004] EWCA Civ 403 43–086
Brennan v Bolt Burden (a firm) [2004] EWCA Civ 1017[2005] Q.B. 303; [2004] 3 W.L.R.
1321; [2004] C.P. Rep. 43; (2004) 101(34) L.S.G. 31; (2004) 148 S.J.L.B. 972; [2004]
N.P.C. 133 ....5–042, 22–021, 29–047, 29–04, 28–187, 29–189
Bretton v Hancock [2005] EWCA Civ 404; Independent, April 20, 2005, CA (Civ Div) 41–091
Brickenden v London Loan & Savings Co [1934] 3 D.L.R. 465, PC (Can) 31–127
Britvic Case [2003] C.L.J. 260 43–096
Brocket v DGS Retail Ltd [2004] C.L. 322 43–097
Brook Street Bureau v Dacas [2004] EWCA Civ 217; [2004] I.R.L.R. 358, The Times,
March 19, 2004 18–005
Brownlie v Campbell (1879–80) L.R. 5 App. Cas. 925, HL 6–139
Bryen & Langley Ltd v Boston [2005] EWCA Civ 973; [2005] B.L.R. 508, CA (Civ Div);
reversing [2004] EWHC 2450; [2005] B.L.R. 28; 98 Con. L.R. 82; [2004] N.P.C. 165,
QBD (TCC) 2–114, 15–032A, 15–054, 15–060
Buchanan v Alba Diagnostics Ltd [2004] UKHL 5; 2004 S.L.T. 255; 2004 S.C.L.R. 273;
(2004) 27(4) I.P.D. 27034; (2004) 148 S.J.L.B. 183; 2004 G.W.D. 5–95 16–119

Bulfracht (Cyprus) Ltd v Boneset Shipping Co Ltd [2002] EWHC Comm 2292; [2002] 2
Lloyd's Rep.681 ....*32–137, 32–143A*
Bunce v Postworth Ltd (t/a Skyblue) [2005] EWCA Civ 490; [2005] I.R.L.R. 557, CA (Civ
Div) *39–023, 39–027*
Bunning v GT Bunning & Sons Ltd (No.2) [2005] EWCA Civ 104, CA (Civ Div) *39–146, 39–187*
Burney v London Mews Co Ltd [2003] EWCA Civ 766, CA (Civ Div) *31–142*
Burton Marsden Douglas, Re [2004] EWHC 593; [2004] 3 All E.R. 222; (2004) 154 N.L.J.
618 .... *3–173*
Burchall v Gowrie & Blockhouse Collieries [1910] A.C. 614 .... *29–068*
Byblos Bank SAL v Rushingdale SA; Byblos Bank SAL v Khudhairy; Byblos Bank SAL
v Barrett; sub nom. Rushingdale SA v Byblos Bank SAL [1987] B.C.L.C. 232; [1986]
P.C.C. 249, CA (Civ Div); affirming [1985] P.C.C. 342 .... *1–082H*

CGU International Insurance Plc v Astrazeneca Insurance Co Ltd [2005] EWHC 2755;
[2006] 6 Lloyd's Rep. 409; [2006] 1 C.L.C. 162, QBD (Comm) *30–069, 41–095*
CIB Properties Ltd v Birse [2005] 1 W.L.R. 2252; [2005] B.L.R. 173, QBD (TCC) *37–260*
CIBC Mellon Trust Co v Stolzenberg (Costs) [2005] EWCA Civ 628; *The Times*, June 8,
2005, CA (Civ Div) *16–053*
Cable & Wireless plc v IBM UK Ltd [2002] EWHC 2059; [2002] 2 All E.R. (Comm.) 1041;
[2002] C.L.C. 1319; [2003] B.L.R. 89; [2002] Masons C.L.R. 58; (2002) 152 N.L.J.
1652 ....*37–254A*
Cable & Wireless Plc v Muscat; sub nom. Muscat v Cable & Wireless Plc [2006] EWCA
Civ 220; [2006] I.C.R. 975; [2006] I.R.L.R. 354; (2006) 103(12) L.S.G. 30; (2006) 150
S.J.L.B. 362; *The Times*, April 10, 2006; *Independent*, March 15, 2006, CA (Civ Div) *18–005,*
39–023, 39–027
Cadogan Estates Ltd v McMahon [2001] 1 A.C. 378; [2000] 3 W.L.R. 1555; [2000] 4 All
E.R. 897; [2001] B.P.I.R. 17; (2001) 33 H.L.R. 42; [2001] L. & T.R. 2; [2001] 1
E.G.L.R. 47; [2001] 06 E.G. 164; [2000] E.G.C.S. 119; (2000) 97(43) L.S.G. 39;
(2000) 97(44) L.S.G. 45; (2000) 150 N.L.J. 1625; (2000) 144 S.J.L.B. 281; [2000]
N.P.C. 110; (2001) 81 P. & C.R. DG11; *The Times*, November 1, 2000, HL *20–033*
Cadre SA v Astra Asigurari [2005] EWHC 2504, QBD (Comm) *30–053*
Cambridge Display Technology Ltd v EI Dupont de Nemours & Co [2005] EWCA Civ 224,
CA (Civ Div) *12–076*
Cambridge Antibody Technology Ltd v Abbott Biotechnology Ltd [2004] EWHC 2974;
[2005] F.S.R. 27, Ch D (Patents Ct) *5–095*
Cameroon Airlines v Transnet Ltd [2004] EWHC 1829; [2006] T.C.L.R. 1, QBD (Comm) *32–137,*
32–138
Campden Hill Ltd v Chakrani [2005] EWHC 911; [2005] N.P.C. 65, Ch D *29–167, 34–137*
Campion Investments Ltd v Ahmed [2004] All E.R. (D) 28 .... *22–021*
Can-Dive Services Ltd v Pacific Coast Energy Corp (2000) 74 B.C.L.R. (3d) 30 .... *5–064*
Canelhas Comercio Importacao e Exportacao Ltd v Wooldridge; sub nom. Wooldridge v
Canelhas Comercio Importacao e Exportacao Ltda [2004] EWCA Civ 984; [2005] 1
All E.R. (Comm) 43; [2004] 2 C.L.C. 469; [2004] Lloyd's Rep. I.R. 915; (2004) 148
S.J.L.B. 943, CA (Civ Div) *41–051A*
Canmer International Inc v UK Mutual Steamship Assurance Association (Bermuda) Ltd
(The Rays) [2005] EWHC 1694; [2005] 2 Lloyd's Rep. 479, QBD (Comm) *3–107, 12–050,*
12–055, 12–118, 21–084
Cantrell v Wright and Fuller Ltd [2003] EWHC 1545; [2003] B.L.R. 412; 91 Con. L.R.
97 .... *37–101*
Caparo group Ltd v Fagor Arrasate Sociedad Cooperative [2000] A.D.R.L.J. 254 .... *32–080*
Caparo Industries Plc v Dickman [1990] 2 A.C. 605; [1990] 2 W.L.R. 358; [1990] 1 All E.R.
568; [1990] B.C.C. 164; [1990] B.C.L.C. 273; [1990] E.C.C. 313; [1955–95] P.N.L.R.
523; (1990) 87(12) L.S.G. 42; (1990) 140 N.L.J. 248; (1990) 134 S.J. 494; *The Times*,
February 12, 1990; *Independent*, February 16, 1990; *Financial Times*, February 13,
1990; *Guardian*, February 15, 1990; *Daily Telegraph*, February 15, 1990, HL *1–157*
Capital Bank Cashflow Finance Ltd v Southall [2004] EWCA Civ 817; [2004] 2 All E.R.
(Comm) 675, CA (Civ Div) *44–060*
Capital Finance Co Ltd v Stokes [1969] 1 Ch. 261; [1968] 3 W.L.R. 899; [1968] 3 All E.R.
625; 19 P. & C.R. 791; 112 S.J. 746 .... *29–173*

[xxxiii]

Capital Structures Plc v Time & Tide Construction Ltd [2006] EWHC 591; [2006] B.L.R. 226; [2006] C.I.L.L. 2345, QBD (TCC) *37–260*

Carmichael v National Power Plc [1999] 1 W.L.R. 2042; [1999] 4 All E.R. 897; [1999] I.C.R. 1226; [2000] I.R.L.R. 43; (1999) 96(46) L.S.G. 38; (1999) 143 S.J.L.B. 281; *The Times*, November 23, 1999; *Independent*, November 25, 1999, HL *2–169, 12–126*

Carnegie v Giessen [2005] EWCA Civ 191; [2005] C.P. Rep. 24; *The Times*, March 14, 2005; *Independent*, March 18, 2005, CA *30–183*

Carson v Tazaki Foods Ltd [2006] 2 C.L. 106 .... *38–090*

Carter (t/a Michael Carter Partnership) v Harold Simpson Associates (Architects) Ltd [2004] UKPC 29; [2005] 1 W.L.R. 919; [2004] 2 Lloyd's Rep. 512; [2004] 2 C.L.C. 1053; (2004) 101(27) L.S.G. 29; (2004) 148 S.J.L.B. 759; *The Times*, June 25, 2004, PC (Jam) *32–124*

Carvill America Inc v Camperdown UK Ltd; Carvill America Inc v XL Speciality Insurance Co Ltd [2005] EWCA Civ 645, CA (Civ Div) *41–042*

Caterpillar Financial Services Corp. v SNC Passion [2004] EWHC Comm 569 ... *30–033, 30–059, 30–141*

Caulfield v Marshalls Clay Products Ltd [2004] EWCA Civ 422; [2004] 2 C.M.L.R. 45 .... *39–108*

Cave v Robinson Jarvis & Rolf [2002] UKHL 18; [2003] 1 A.C. 384; [2002] 2 W.L.R. 1107; [2002] 2 All E.R. 641; 81 Con. L.R. 25; [2002] P.N.L.R. 25; [2002] 19 E.G.C.S. 146; (2002) 99(20) L.S.G. 32; (2002) 152 N.L.J. 671; (2002) 146 S.J.L.B. 109 .... *28–086*

CEL Group Ltd v Nedlloyd Lines UK Ltd [2003] EWCA Civ 1716; [2004] 1 All E.R. (Comm.) 689; [2004] 1 Lloyd's Rep. 381; (2003) 147 S.J.L.B. 1399 .... *2–148, 13–005, 13–012*

Centre Reinsurance International Co v Curzon International Ltd [2004] EWHC 200; [2004] 2 All E.R. (Comm.) 28; (2004) 101(11) L.S.G. 34 .... *18–123, 41–090*

Cetelem SA v Roust Holdings Ltd [2005] EWCA Civ 618; [2005] 1 W.L.R. 3555; [2005] 4 All E.R. 52; [2005] 2 All E.R. (Comm) 203; [2005] 2 Lloyd's Rep. 494; [2005] 1 C.L.C. 821, CA (Civ Div) *32–101*

Charge Card Services Ltd, Re [1989] Ch. 497; [1988] 3 W.L.R. 764; [1988] 3 All E.R. 702; (1988) 4 B.C.C. 524; [1988] B.C.L.C. 711; [1988] P.C.C. 390; [1988] Fin. L.R. 308; (1989) 8 Tr. L.R. 86; (1988) 85(42) L.S.G. 46; (1988) 138 N.L.J. Rep. 201; (1988) 132 S.J. 1458; *The Times*, July 7, 1988; *Independent*, July 6, 1988; *Financial Times*, July 8, 1988; *Guardian*, July 7, 1988; *Daily Telegraph*, July 7, 1988, CA (Civ Div) *21–074*

Chater v Mortgage Agency Services Number Two Ltd; sub nom. Charter v Mortgage Agency Services; Mortgage Agency Services Number Two Ltd v Chater [2003] EWCA Civ 490; [2003] H.L.R. 61; [2004] 1 P. & C.R. 4; [2003] 15 E.G.C.S. 138; (2003) 147 S.J.L.B. 417; [2003] N.P.C. 48; [2003] 2 P. & C.R. DG9, CA (Civ Div) *7–073*

Checkpoint Ltd v Strathclyde Pension Fund [2003] EWCA Civ 84; [2003] L. & T.R. 22; [2003] 1 E.G.L.R. 1; [2003] 14 E.G. 124; [2003] 8 E.G.C.S. 128; (2003) 100(12) L.S.G. 29; (2003) 147 S.J.L.B. 233; [2003] N.P.C. 23; *The Times*, February 12, 2003, CA (Civ Div) *32–073*

Chelsea & Waltham Green Building Society v Armstrong [1951] Ch. 853; [1951] 2 All E.R. 250; [1951] 2 T.L.R. 313, Ch D *18–114*

Cheltenham and Gloucester plc v Appleyard [2004] EWCA Civ 291; [2004] 13 E.G.C.S. 127; (2004) 101(14) L.S.G. 26; (2004) 101(13) L.S.G. 37; (2004) 148 S.J.L.B. 356; [2004] N.P.C. 42 .... *29–173*

Chwee Kin Keong v Digilandmall.com Pte Ltd [2005] S.G.C.A. 2; [2005] 1.S.L.R. 502 .... *5–043*

City & General (Holborn) Ltd v AYH Plc [2005] EWHC 2494; [2006] B.L.R. 55, QBD (TCC) *32–087*

Claire & Co Ltd v Thames Water Utilities Ltd [2005] EWHC 1022; [2005] B.L.R. 366, QBD (TCC) *32–073, 32–137*

Clark v Clark [2006] EWHC 275; [2006] 1 F.C.R. 421; [2006] W.T.L.R. 823, Ch D *3–150, 3–153*

Clarke v Shee and Johnson (1774) 1 Cowp. 197 .... *40–082*

Clifford Harris & Co v Solland International Ltd (No.2) [2005] EWHC 141; [2005] 2 All E.R. 334; *The Times*, March 10, 2005, Ch D *43–351*

Cobbe v Yeomans Row Management Ltd (No.1); sub nom. Yeomans Row Management Ltd v Cobbe [2006] EWCA Civ 1139, CA (Civ Div); affirming [2005] EWHC 266; [2005] W.T.L.R. 625; [2005] N.P.C. 29; [2005] 2 P. & C.R. DG1, Ch D *3–139, 3–140, 3–142, 3–143, 3–155, 4–078*

Cobbold v Bakewell Management Ltd [2003] EWHC 2289 ....*29–034, 29–160, 29–187*

Colchester BC v Smith; Colchester BC v Tillson [1992] Ch. 421; [1992] 2 W.L.R. 728; [1992] 2 All E.R. 561, CA (Civ Div) *6–132*

Colen v Cebrian (U.K.) Ltd [2003] EWCA Civ 1676; [2004] I.R.L.R. 210; (2004) 101(2) L.S.G. 27 .... *16–007, 39–032*

Collins (Contractors) Ltd v Baltic Quay Management (1994) Ltd [2004] EWCA Civ 1757; [2005] B.L.R. 63; [2005] T.C.L.R. 3; (2005) 102(5) L.S.G. 26; *The Times*, January 3, 2005, CA (Civ Div) *32–049, 37–247*

COLT Telecom Group plc, Re [2002] EWHC 2815; [2003] B.P.I.R. 324 .... *30–067, 30–173*

Commercial Credit Services v Knowles [1978] 6 C.L. 64 .... *1–082H*

Commerzbank AG v Gareth Price-Jones [2003] EWCA Civ 1663; [2004] 1 P. & C.R.D. 15 ....*29–179, 29–180, 29–181, 29–183, 34–136, 34–137*

Commerzbank Aktiengesellschaft v IMB Morgan Plc [2004] EWHC 2771; [2005] 1 Lloyd's Rep. 298; [2005] 1 P. & C.R. DG17, Ch D *21–066, 29–160, 29–167*

Commission for the New Towns v Cooper (Great Britain) Ltd (formerly Coopind UK); sub nom. Milton Keynes Development Corp v Cooper (Great Britain) [1995] Ch. 259; [1995] 2 W.L.R. 677; [1995] 2 All E.R. 929; (1996) 72 P. & C.R. 270; [1995] 2 E.G.L.R. 113; [1995] E.G.C.S. 30; (1995) 139 S.J.L.B. 87; [1995] N.P.C. 34; (1995) 69 P. & C.R. D40; *The Times*, March 3, 1995; *Independent*, March 15, 1995, CA (Civ Div) *5–064, 5–100*

Commissioners of Customs & Excise v Barclays Bank plc Customs and Excise Commissioners v Barclays Bank Plc [2006] UKHL 28; [2006] 3 W.L.R. 1; (2006) 103(27) L.S.G. 33; (2006) 156 N.L.J. 1060; (2006) 150 S.J.L.B. 859; *The Times*, June 22, 2006, HL *1–157, 1–162, 34–255*

Compagnie Noga d'Importation et d' Exportation SA v Abacha (No.4) [2003] EWCA Civ 1100; [2003] 2 All E.R. (Comm.) 915 .... *12–123*

Compania Financiera "Soleada" S.A. v Hamoor Tanker Corp. Inc. [1981] 1 W.L.R. 274; [1981] 1 All E.R. 856; [1981] 1 Lloyd's Rep. 483; [1981] Com. L.R. 29; 125 S.J. 185 .... *26–095D*

Computer 2000 Distribution Ltd v ICM Computer Solutions Plc; sub nom. ICM Computer Solutions Plc v Computer 2000 Distribution [2004] EWCA Civ 1634; [2005] Info. T.L.R. 147, CA (Civ Div) *43–270*

Concord Trust v Law Debenture Trust Corp Plc [2005] UKHL 27; [2005] 1 W.L.R. 1591; [2005] 1 All E.R. (Comm) 699; (2005) 155 N.L.J. 692; *The Times*, May 3, 2005; *Independent*, May 6, 2005, HL *13–005, 38–238*

Conlon v Simms [2006] EWHC 401; [2006] 2 All E.R. 1024; (2006) 103(13) L.S.G. 25, Ch D *6–139, 6–157*

Connex South Eastern Ltd v MJ Building Services Group plc [2004] EWHC 1518, TCC *24–048*

Construction Parnership UK Ltd v Leek Developments Ltd [2006] C.I.L.L. 2357, QBD (TCC) ....*37–032—37–033*

Continental Enterprises Ltd v Shandong Zhucheng Foreign Trade Group Co [2005] EWHC 92, QBD (Comm) *30–040, 30–139, 30–171, 30–173, 30–175*

Continental Illinois National Bank & Trust Co of Chicago v Papanicolaou (The Fedora, The Tatiana and The Eretrea II) [1986] 2 Lloyd's Rep. 441; [1986] Fin. L.R. 373; (1986) 83 L.S.G. 2569, CA (Civ Div) *44–104*

Cookson & Clegg Ltd v Ministry of Defence [2005] EWCA Civ 811; (2005) 149 S.J.L.B. 771, CA (Civ Div) *10–019*

Cooper v Pure Fishing (UK) Ltd [2004] EWCA Civ 375 .... *31–147*

Coopers Payne Ltd v Southampton Container Terminal Ltd [2003] EWCA Civ 1223; [2004] 1 Lloyd's Rep.331 .... *33–049*

Cope v Doherty 91858) 2 De G. & J. 614 .... *30–150*

Coral Leisure Group Ltd v Barnett [1981] I.C.R. 503; [1981] I.R.L.R. 204; 125 S.J. 374 .... *16–007*

Cornwall CC v Prater; sub nom. Prater v Cornwall CC [2006] EWCA Civ 102; [2006] 2 All E.R. 1013; [2006] I.C.R. 731; [2006] I.R.L.R. 362; (2006) 156 N.L.J. 372; *Independent*, February 28, 2006, CA (Civ Div) *2–169, 39–023, 39–157*

Cotswold Developments Construction Ltd v Williams [2006] I.R.L.R. 181, EAT *3–025, 39–009*

Cottrell v King; sub nom. TA King (Services) Ltd, Re [2004] EWHC 397; [2004] B.C.C. 307; [2004] 2 B.C.L.C. 413; [2005] W.T.L.R. 63, Ch D *2–125*

Coulter v Chief of Dorset Police [2004] EWCA Civ 1259; [2005] 1 W.L.R. 130; [2005]
B.P.I.R. 62; (2004) 101(40) L.S.G. 28; (2004) 148 S.J.L.B. 1213; *The Times*, October
22, 2004, CA (Civ Div); affirming [2003] EWHC 3391; [2004] 1 W.L.R. 1425 ....*19–025,*
20–018
Country Assured Financial Services Ltd v Deanne Smart [2004] EWHC 1214 .... *16–092*
Coutts & Co v Sebestyen [2005] EWCA Civ 473, CA (Civ Div) *38–092, 38–264*
Credit Suisse (Monaco) SA v Attar [2004] EWHC Comm 374 .... *34–137*
Crehan v Inntrepreneur Pub Co (CPC); sub nom. Inntrepreneur Pub Co (CPC) v Crehan
[2006] UKHL 38; (2006) 150 S.J.L.B. 983; [2006] N.P.C. 85, HL *16–153, 42–071*
Cressman v Coys of Kensington (Sales) Ltd; sub nom. Coys of Kensington (Sales) Ltd v
McDonald; McDonald v Coys of Kensington Holdings Ltd [2004] EWCA Civ 47;
[2004] 1 W.L.R. 2775; (2004) 101(10) L.S.G. 29; (2004) 148 S.J.L.B. 182; *The Times*,
February 13, 2004, CA (Civ Div) *29–017, 29–018, 29–021, 29–022, 29–174, 29–193,*
31–042, 31–006
Crill v Wood (2003–04) 6 I.T.E.L.R. 590, Royal Ct (Jer) *34–348*
Criterion Properties Plc v Stratford UK Properties LLC [2004] UKHL 28; [2004] 1 W.L.R.
1846; [2004] B.C.C. 570; (2004) 101(26) L.S.G. 27; (2004) 148 S.J.L.B. 760; [2004]
N.P.C. 96; *The Times*, June 25, 2004, HL *9–030A, 34–301*
Crossley v Faithful & Gould Holdings Ltd [2004] EWCA Civ 293; [2004] I.R.L.R. 377;
(2004) 101(14) L.S.G. 26; (2004) 154 N.L.J. 653; (2004) 148 S.J.L.B. 356, The Times,
March 29, 2004 ....*13–009,* 13–010, *39–145*
Crown Dilmun v Sutton [2004] EWHC 52; [2004] 1 B.C.L.C. 468; [2004] W.T.L.R. 497;
(2004) 101(7) L.S.G. 34; *The Times*, February 5, 2004, Ch D *29–155, 29–174, 34–301*
Customs and Excise Commissioners v Barclays Bank Plc [2006] UKHL 28; [2006] 3
W.L.R. 1; (2006) 103(27) L.S.G. 33; (2006) 156 N.L.J. 1060; (2006) 150 S.J.L.B. 859;
The Times, June 22, 2006, HL; reversing [2004] EWCA Civ 1555; [2005] 1 W.L.R.
2082; [2005] 1 Lloyd's Rep. 165; (2004) 154 N.L.J. 1831; (2004) 148 S.J.L.B. 1402;
[2004] N.P.C. 175; *Independent*, December 2, 2004, CA (Civ Div) *1–157, 18–031, 34–255*

DFDS Transport A/S v Dieter Mehrholz Internationale Transporte (2004) 39 E.T.L. 74 .... *36–147*
Dacas v Brook Street Bureau (UK) Ltd [2004] EWCA Civ 217; [2004] I.R.L.R. 358 ....*39–023,*
39–027
Dairy Containers Ltd v Tasman Orient Line CV (The Tasman Discoverer) [2004] UKPC 22;
[2005] 1 W.L.R. 215; [2004] 2 All E.R. (Comm) 667; [2004] 2 Lloyd's Rep. 647;
[2004] 2 C.L.C. 794, PC (NZ) *12–050, 14–005, 14–009*
Dale v Hamilton (1846) 5 Hare 369 .... *4–063A*
Dalkia Utilities Services Plc v Celtech International Ltd [2006] EWHC 63; [2006] 1 Lloyd's
Rep. 599, QBD (Comm) *5–092, 21–017, 22–047, 22–048, 24–013, 24–018, 24–019*
Daniel v Drew; sub nom. Daniel v Drew [2005] EWCA Civ 507; [2005] 2 F.C.R. 365;
[2005] W.T.L.R. 807; [2005] 2 P. & C.R. DG14; *The Times*, May 18, 2005, CA (Civ
Div) *7–041, 7–053*
Daniels (A.C.) & Co Ltd v Jungwoo Logic, April 14, 2000, QBD *43–310*
Daraydan Holdings Ltd v Solland [2004] EWHC 622 ....*29–156, 29–160, 31–126*
Datec Electronic Holdings Ltd v United Parcels Service Ltd [2005] EWCA Civ 1418;
[2006] 1 Lloyd's Rep. 279; [2005] 2 C.L.C. 1025, CA (Civ Div) *2–004, 36–129, 36–132,*
36–149
Davidson v Scottish Ministers (No.1); sub nom. Scott v Scottish Ministers; Scott, Petitioner;
Davidson, Petitioner (No.1) [2005] UKHL 74; 2006 S.C. (H.L.) 41; 2006 S.L.T. 110;
2006 S.C.L.R. 249; 2006 G.W.D. 4–72; *The Times*, December 19, 2005, HL *10–002,* 10–011
Days Medical Aids Ltd v Pihsiang Machinery Manufacturing Co Ltd [2004] EWHC 44;
[2004] 1 All E.R. (Comm) 991; [2004] 2 C.L.C. 489; [2004] U.K.C.L.R. 384; [2004]
E.C.C. 21; [2004] Eu. L.R. 477, QBD (Comm) *16–104, 16–120*
De Bernardy v Harding (1853) 8 Ex. 822 .... *29–068*
Deaville v Aeroflot Russian International Airlines [1997] 2 Lloyd's Rep. 67, QBD *35–022*
Debtor (No.50A-SD-1995), Re; sub nom. Jelly v All Type Roofing Co [1997] Ch. 310;
[1997] 2 W.L.R. 57; [1997] 2 All E.R. 789; [1997] B.C.C. 465; [1997] 1 B.C.L.C. 280;
[1996] B.P.I.R. 565, Ch D *28–015*

Decoma UK Ltd (formerly Conix UK Ltd) v Haden Drysys International Ltd; sub nom.
Decoma UK Ltd (formerly Conex UK Ltd) v Haden Drysys International Ltd [2006]
EWCA Civ 723, CA (Civ Div); affirming [2005] EWHC 2948; 103 Con. L.R. 1, QBD
(TCC) 12–082
Deep Vein Thrombosis and Air Travel Group Litigation [2005] UKHL 72; [2006] 1 A.C.
495; [2005] 3 W.L.R. 1320; [2006] 1 All E.R. 786; [2006] 1 All E.R. (Comm) 313;
[2006] 1 Lloyd's Rep. 231; [2005] 2 C.L.C. 1083; [2006] P.I.Q.R. P14; (2006) 87
B.M.L.R. 1; (2006) 103(3) L.S.G. 26; (2005) 155 N.L.J. 1925; (2006) 150 S.J.L.B. 29;
The Times, December 12, 2005; *Independent*, December 13, 2005, HL; affirming
[2003] EWCA Civ 1005; [2004] Q.B. 234; [2003] 3 W.L.R. 956; [2004] 1 All E.R.
445; [2004] 1 All E.R. (Comm.) 459; [2004] 1 Lloyd's Rep. 316; [2003] P.I.Q.R. P35;
(2004) 76 B.M.L.R. 38; (2003) 100(35) L.S.G. 34; (2003) 147 S.J.L.B. 869 ......*18–034*, 35–020,
35–033
Demco Investments & Commercial SA v SE Banken Forsakring Holding AB [2005] EWHC
1398; [2005] 2 Lloyd's Rep. 650, QBD (Comm) *32–141, 32–142*
Den Norske Bank ASA v Acemex Management Co [2003] EWCA Civ 1559; [2004] 1 All
E.R. (Comm.) 904; [2004] 1 Lloyd's Rep. 1 .... *18–134*
Department of Economic Policy and Development of the City of Moscow v Bankers Trust
Co; sub nom. Moscow City Council v Bankers Trust Co; Department of Economics,
Policy and Development of the City of Moscow v Bankers Trust Co [2004] EWCA Civ
314; [2005] Q.B. 207; [2004] 3 W.L.R. 533; [2004] 4 All E.R. 746; [2004] 2 All E.R.
(Comm) 193; [2004] 2 Lloyd's Rep. 179; [2004] 1 C.L.C. 1099; [2004] B.L.R. 229;
(2004) 148 S.J.L.B. 389, CA (Civ Div) *32–015, 32–016, 32–040*
Deutsche Morgan Grenfell Group Plc v Inland Revenue Commissioners; sub nom. Inland
Revenue Commissioners v Deutsche Morgan Grenfell Group Plc [2005] EWCA Civ
78; [2005] S.T.C. 329; [2005] B.T.C. 126; 7 I.T.L. Rep. 476; [2005] S.T.I. 194; (2005)
102(10) L.S.G. 30; [2005] N.P.C. 18; *The Times*, February 15, 2005, CA (Civ Div) *29–042*,
29–046, 29–084, 29–094
Deverne II, The. See Vitesse Yacht Charterers SL v Spiers (The Deverne II).
Dextra Bank & Trust Co Ltd v Bank of Jamaica [2002] 1 All E.R. (Comm.) 193 ....34–083, *34–137*
Diamantides v JP Morgan Chase Bank; JP Morgan Chase Bank v Pollux Holding Ltd [2005]
EWCA Civ 1612, CA (Civ Div) *31–063, 34–251*
Diab v Regent Insurance Co Ltd [2006] UKPC 29, PC (Bze) *41–064*
Dicker v Scammell; sub nom. Scammell v Dicker [2005] EWCA Civ 405; [2005] 3 All E.R.
838; *The Times*, April 27, 2005; *Independent*, April 19, 2005, CA (Civ Div) ... 2–086, 2–113,
2–126, 2–136, 2–137, 2–139, 2–141
Director General of Fair Trading v First National Bank plc [2001] UKHL 52; [2002] 1 A.C.
481; [2001] 3 W.L.R. 1297; [2002] 1 All E.R. 97; [2001] 2 All E.R. (Comm.) 1000;
[2002] 1 Lloyd's Rep. 489; [2002] E.C.C. 22; (2001) 151 N.L.J. 1610 ....15–036A, **15–036B**,
15–048A
Director of the Assets Recovery Agency v Singh [2005] EWCA Civ 580; [2005] 1 W.L.R.
3747; [2005] Crim. L.R. 665, CA (Civ Div) 29–137
Dobson v General Accident Fire and Life Assurance Corp [1990] 1 Q.B. 274; [1989] 3
W.L.R. 1066; [1989] 3 All E.R. 927; [1989] 2 Lloyd's Rep. 549; [1990] Crim. L.R.
271; (1989) 86(40) L.S.G. 43; (1989) 133 S.J. 1445, CA (Civ Div) *41–051A*
Dockpride Pty Ltd v Subiaco Redevelopment Authority [2005] W.A.S.C. 211 .... *10–025*
Doe d. Garnons v Knight (1826) 5 B. & C. 671 .... *1–082E*
Doheny v New India Assurance Co Ltd [2004] EWCA Civ 1705; [2005] 1 All E.R. (Comm)
382; [2005] Lloyd's Rep. I.R. 251, CA (Civ Div) *41–029, 41–030*
Don King Productions Inc v Warren (No.1) [2000] Ch. 291; [1999] 3 W.L.R. 276; [1999]
2 All E.R. 218; [1999] 1 Lloyd's Rep. 588; [2000] 1 B.C.L.C. 607; [1999] E.M.L.R.
402; *The Times*, February 9, 1999; *Independent*, January 25, 1999 (C.S.), CA (Civ
Div) 19–045
Dornoch Ltd v Mauritius Union Assurance Co Ltd [2006] EWCA Civ 389, CA (Civ Div) *30–053*,
30–075
Douglas v Hello! Ltd (No.6); sub nom. Douglas v Hello! Ltd (Trial Action: Breach of
Confidence) (No.3) [2005] EWCA Civ 595; [2006] Q.B. 125; [2005] 3 W.L.R. 881;
[2005] 4 All E.R. 128; [2005] E.M.L.R. 28; [2005] 2 F.C.R. 487; [2005] H.R.L.R. 27;
(2005) 28(8) I.P.D. 28057; (2005) 155 N.L.J. 828; *The Times*, May 24, 2005; *Independent*, May 26, 2005, CA (Civ Div) *18–127*

TABLE OF CASES

Drake Insurance plc v Provident Insurance plc [2003] EWCA Civ 1834; [2004] Q.B. 601;
    [2004] 2 W.L.R. 530; [2004] 1 Lloyd's Rep. 268; [2004] R.T.R. 19; [2004] Lloyd's
    Rep. I.R. 277 ....2–027, 41–035, 41–077
Dubai Aluminium Co Ltd v Salaam; Dubai Aluminium Co Ltd v Amhurst; Dubai Alumin-
    ium Co Ltd v Amhurst Brown Martin & Nicholson [2002] UKHL 48; [2003] 2 A.C.
    366; [2002] 3 W.L.R. 1913; [2003] 1 All E.R. 97; [2003] 2 All E.R. (Comm) 451;
    [2003] 1 Lloyd's Rep. 65; [2003] 1 B.C.L.C. 32; [2003] 1 C.L.C. 1020; [2003] I.R.L.R.
    608; [2003] W.T.L.R. 163; (2003) 100(7) L.S.G. 36; (2002) 146 S.J.L.B. 280; The
    Times, December 6, 2002; Independent, December 10, 2002, HL 29–015
Dumford Trading AG v OAO Atlantrybflot [2005] EWCA Civ 24; [2005] 1 Lloyd's Rep.
    289, CA (Civ Div) 3–113, 12–075, 12–122, 12–124, 44–057
Dungate v Dungate [1965] 1 W.L.R. 1477; [1965] 3 All E.R. 818; 109 S.J. 715, CA 28–095
Dunlop v Lambert (1839) 6 Cl. & F. 600, 626, 627 18–050
Dunnachie v Kingston-upon-Hull City Council [2004] UKHL 36; [2004] 3 W.L.R. 310 26–077,
                                                                                                                                              39–233
Durham CC v Darlington BC [2003] EWHC 2598; [2004] B.L.G.R. 311; [2003] N.P.C.
    136 32–112
Durtnell (R) & Sons Ltd v Secretary of State for Trade and Industry [2001] 1 All E.R.
    (Comm.) 41; [2001] 1 Lloyd's Rep. 275; [2000] C.L.C. 1365; [2000] B.L.R. 321; 74
    Con. L.R. 87; [2000] N.P.C. 64 32–065

EIC Services Ltd v Phipps [2004] EWCA Civ 1069; [2005] 1 W.L.R. 1377; [2005] 1 All
    E.R. 338; [2004] B.C.C. 814; [2004] 2 B.C.L.C. 589; (2004) 148 S.J.L.B. 1118, CA
    (Civ Div) 5–050, 9–031
ERC Frankona Reinsurance v American National Insurance Co [2005] EWHC 1381 41–029,
                                                                                                                                              41–030
ERDC Group Ltd v Brunel University [2006] EWHC 687; [2006] B.L.R. 255; [2006]
    C.I.L.L. 2348, QBD (TCC) 37–050A
Eagle Star Insurance Co Ltd v Cresswell [2004] EWCA Civ 602; [2004] 2 All E.R.
    (Comm.) 244 41–054
Ease Faith Ltd v Leonis Marine Management Ltd [2006] EWHC 232; [2006] 1 Lloyd's Rep.
    673; [2006] 1 C.L.C. 345, QBD (Comm) 3–107, 13–006, 14–006
East v Pantiles (Plant Hire) [1982] 2 E.G.L.R. 111; (1982) 263 E.G. 61, CA (Civ Div) 5–092,
                                                                                                                                              12–075
East West Corp. v DKBS 1912 [2003] EWCA Civ 83; [2003] Q.B. 1509; [2003] 3 W.L.R.
    916; [2003] 2 All E.R. 700; [2003] 1 All E.R. (Comm.) 524; [2003] 1 Lloyd's Rep.
    239; (2003) 100(12) L.S.G. 31 .... 14–033, 14–054
Eastwood v Magnox Electric plc [2004] UKHL 35; [2004] 3 W.L.R. 322 ......1–026, 26–074, 26–077,
                                                                                                                          39–146, 39–196
Ecuador v Occidental Exploration & Production Co; sub nom. Occidental Exploration &
    Production Co v Ecuador [2005] EWCA Civ 1116; [2006] Q.B. 432; [2006] 2 W.L.R.
    70; [2006] 2 All E.R. 225; [2005] 2 All E.R. (Comm) 689; [2005] 2 Lloyd's Rep. 707;
    [2005] 2 C.L.C. 457; (2005) 102(37) L.S.G. 31; The Times, September 23, 2005, CA
    (Civ Div) 11–007, 32–132, 32–137
Edmonds v Lawson; sub nom. Edmunds v Lawson [2000] Q.B. 501; [2000] 2 W.L.R. 1091;
    [2000] I.C.R. 567; [2000] I.R.L.R. 391; (2000) 97(14) L.S.G. 42; (2000) 144 S.J.L.B.
    151; The Times, March 16, 2000; Independent, March 16, 2000, CA (Civ Div) 3–038
Edwards v International Connection (UK) Ltd, unreported, April 27, 2006–09–29 31–005
Edwinton Commercial Corporation v Tsavliriss Russ (Worldwide Salvage and Towage) Ltd
    (The Sea Angel) [2006] EWHC 1713, QBD (Comm) 23–007, 23–034, 23–056, 23–057,
                                                                                                                          23–058, 23–059, 23–063
Ehrlich v American Airlines Inc., 360 F 3d 366 (2nd Cir., 2004) 35–034
El Nasharty v J Sainsbury plc [2003] EWHC 2195; [2004] 1 All E.R. (Comm.) 728; [2004]
    1 Lloyd's Rep. 309 ....32–025, 32–048
Elizabeth Claire Care Management Ltd v Francis [2005] I.R.L.R. 858, EAT 39–093
Eltham v Kingsman (1818) 1 B. & Ald. 683 ....40–A005
Emcor Drake & Scull Ltd v Sir Robert McAlpine Ltd [2004] EWCA Civ 1733; 98 Con. L.R.
    1, CA (Civ Div 2–114
Enfield London Borough Council v Sivaandan [2004] EWHC 672; [2004] All E.R. (D)
    73 24–013

Enterprise Oil Ltd v Strand Insurance Co Ltd [2006] EWHC 58; [2006] 1 Lloyd's Rep. 500;
    [2006] 1 C.L.C. 33, QBD (Comm) *41–088*
Enterprise Plus Ltd v Wagenmann [2003] EWHC Comm 1827 .... *31–101*
Essex Strategic Health Authority v David-John [2004] I.C.R. 112; [2003] Lloyd's Rep.
    Med. 586 .... *2–175*
Essington Investments Pty Ltd v Regency Property Ltd [2004] N.S.W.C.A. 375 .... *31–056*
Estate of Arnandh v Barnet Primary Health Care Trust [2004] EWCA Civ 5, CA (Civ
    Div) *16–146*
Et Plus SA v Welter [2005] EWHC 2115; [2006] 1 Lloyd's Rep. 251; [2006] I.L.Pr. 18,QBD
    (Comm) 32–018, *32–025, 32–043, 32–048*
Euro Cellular (Distribution) plc v Danzas Ltd t/a Danzas AEI Intercontinental [2003]
    EWHC Comm 3161; [2004] 1 Lloyd's Rep. 521 ....*14–018, 14–019, 33–049*
Euro London Appointments Ltd v Claessens International Ltd [2006] EWCA Civ 385; *The
    Times*, June 2, 2006, CA (Civ Div) *26–118, 26–119*
European Bank of Reconstruction & Development v Tekoglu [2004] EWHC Comm 846 ....*30–020,*
    30–050
European International Reinsurance Co Ltd v Curzon Insurance Ltd [2003] EWCA Civ
    1074; [2003] Lloyd's Rep. I.R. 793; (2003) 100(36) L.S.G. 43; (2003) 147 S.J.L.B.
    906 ....*1–162, 41–042*
Evans v Amicus Healthcare Ltd; sub nom. Hadley v Midland Fertility Services Ltd [2004]
    EWCA Civ 727; [2005] Fam. 1; [2004] 3 W.L.R. 681; [2004] 3 All E.R. 1025; [2004]
    2 F.L.R. 766; [2004] 2 F.C.R. 530; (2004) 78 B.M.L.R. 181; [2004] Fam. Law 647;
    (2004) 148 S.J.L.B. 823; *The Times*, June 30, 2004; *Independent*, June 29, 2004, CA
    (Civ Div) *3–088, 3–090, 3–096, 3–098, 3–101*
Evans v HSBC Trust Co (UK) Ltd [2005] W.T.L.R. 1289, Ch D *3–140, 3–147, 3–153, 3–155,*
    3–157
Evans v Motor Insurers' Bureau [1999] 1 C.M.L.R. 1251; [1999] Eu. L.R. 389; [1999]
    Lloyd's Rep. I.R. 30; [1999] P.I.Q.R. P101 .... *41–093*
Evans v Secretary of State for the Environment, Transport and the Regions [2001] EWCA
    Civ 32; [2001] 2 C.M.L.R. 10; [2002] Lloyd's Rep. I.R. 1 .... *41–093*
Evialis S.A. v S.I.A.T. [2003] EWHC 863; [2003] 2 Lloyd's Rep. 377; [2003] I.L.Pr. 43;
    [2004] Lloyd's Rep. I.R. 187 .... *30–050*
Explora Group Plc v Hesco Bastion Ltd; Explora Group Ltd v Trading Force Ltd [2005]
    EWCA Civ 646; (2005) 149 S.J.L.B. 924, CA (Civ Div) *31–145, 31–150*
Expo Fabrics (UK) Ltd v Martin [2003] EWCA Civ 1165, CA (Civ Div) *14–092*

Fairclough Building Ltd v Port Talbot BC, 62 B.L.R. 82; 33 Con. L.R. 24, CA (Civ Div) *10–025*
Farrell Matthews & Weir v Hansen [2005] I.C.R. 509; [2005] I.R.L.R. 160, EAT *39–093*
Favermead Ltd v FPD Savills Ltd [2005] EWHC 626; [2005] All E.R. (D) 30, Ch D *31–142*
Fawcett v Whitehouse (1829) 1 Russ. & M. 132 .... *6–157*
Feldarol Foundry Plc v Hermes Leasing (London) Ltd; Feldarol Foundry Plc v Amari Sant
    Agata Classics; sub nom. Feldaroll Foundry Plc v Hermes Leasing (London) Ltd
    [2004] EWCA Civ 747; (2004) 101(24) L.S.G. 32; (2004) 148 S.J.L.B. 630, CA (Civ
    Div) *14–066, 43–106*
Fibrenetix Storage Ltd v Davis [2004] EWHC 1359 .... *16–107*
Fidelity Management SA v Myriad International Holdings BV [2005] EWHC 1193; [2005]
    2 All E.R. (Comm) 312; [2005] 2 Lloyd's Rep. 508, QBD (Comm) *32–137, 32–138*
Fielding v Mansi [1974] 1 All E.R. 1035; [1974] I.C.R. 347; [1974] I.R.L.R. 79; [1974]
    I.T.R. 208, NIRC *39–172*
Filby v Mortgage Express (No.2) Ltd [2004] EWCA Civ 759 .... *29–173*
Financial Institutions Services Ltd v Negril Negril Holdings Ltd [2004] UKPC 40 .....*34–312, 34–334*
Financial Services Authority v Fitt [2004] EWHC 1669 .... *34–236*
Financial Services Compensation Scheme Ltd v Larnell (Insurances) Ltd (In Creditors
    Voluntary Liquidation); sub nom. Financial Services Compensation Scheme v Larnell
    Insurance [2005] EWCA Civ 1408; [2006] 2 W.L.R. 751; [2006] 6 Lloyd's Rep. 448;
    [2006] C.P. Rep. 14; [2006] P.N.L.R. 13, CA (Civ Div) *28–012*
Fiorentino Comm Giuseppe Srl v Farnesi [2005] EWHC 160; [2005] 2 All E.R. 737; [2005]
    1 All E.R. (Comm) 575; *The Times*, March 3, 2005, Ch D *9–008, 34–046*
First Energy v Hungarian International Bank [1993] 2 Lloyd's Rep. 194; [1993] B.C.C. 533;
    [1993] B.C.L.C. 1409; [1993] N.P.C. 34 .... *6–020*

First National Bank plc v Achampong [2003] EWCA Civ 487; [2004] 1 F.C.R. 18; (2003)
147 S.J.L.B. 419; [2003] N.P.C. 46; [2003] 2 P. & C.R. D11 .... 7–108, 34–271
First National Securities Ltd v Jones [1978] Ch. 109; [1978] 2 W.L.R. 475; [1978] 2 All
E.R. 221; 121 S.J. 760; *The Times*, November 9, 1977, CA (Civ Div) 1–082B, 1–082H
Fitzgerald v University of Kent at Canterbury [2004] EWCA Civ 143; [2004] I.R.L.R. 300;
(2004) 101(11) L.S.G. 34; (2004) 148 S.J.L.B. 237 39–213
Fleming & Wendeln GmbH & Co v Sanofi SA/AG [2003] EWHC 561; [2003] 2 Lloyd's
Rep. 473 43–275
Flett v Matheson [2006] EWCA Civ 53; [2006] I.C.R. 673; [2006] I.R.L.R. 277, CA (Civ
Div) 39–005
Flight Training International Inc v International Fire Training Equipment Ltd [2004] EWHC
721; [2004] 2 All E.R. (Comm) 568, QBD (Comm) 32–014, 32–018
Forster v Hale (1800) 5 Ves. Jr. 308 .... 4–063A
Fortisbank SA v Trenwick International Ltd [2005] EWHC 399; [2005] Lloyd's Rep. I.R.
464, QBD (Comm) 3–090, 3–094, 3–104, 3–109, 41–057
Foskett v McKeown [2001] 1 A.C. 102; [2000] 2 W.L.R. 1299; [2000] 3 All E.R. 97; [2000]
Lloyd's Rep. I.R. 627; [2000] W.T.L.R. 667; (1999–2000) 2 I.T.E.L.R. 711; (2000)
97(23) L.S.G. 44 34–136
Four Seasons Healthcare Ltd (formerly Cotswold Spa Retirement Hotels Ltd) v Maughan
[2005] I.R.L.R. 324, EAT 39–167
Foxtons Ltd v Thesleff [2005] EWCA Civ 514; [2005] 2 E.G.L.R. 29; [2005] 21 E.G. 140;
[2005] 17 E.G.C.S. 122, CA (Civ Div) 31–083, 31–139
Frans Maas (UK) Ltd v Samsung Electronics (UK) Ltd [2004] EWHC 1502; [2004] 2
Lloyd's Rep. 251, QBD (Comm) ... 14–010, 14–011, 14–016, 14–085, 14–087, 14–096, 14–099,
36–028, 36–044
Freakley v Centre Reinsurance International Co [2004] EWHC 2740; [2005] Lloyd's Rep.
I.R. 264, Ch D 41–088
Freeman v Walker [2001] EWCA Civ 923, CA (Civ Div) 38–374
Friarwood Ltd v Champagne Cattier SA [2006] EWCA Civ 1105, CA (Civ Div) 43–086
Friends' Provident Life Office v Hillier Parker May and Rowden [1997] Q.B. 85; [1996] 2
W.L.R. 123; [1995] 4 All E.R. 260; (1996) 71 P. & C.R. 286; [1995] E.G.C.S. 64;
[1995] N.P.C. 63 29–121
Frigo Express Bvba v Frigo Traffic Company NV (2004) 39 E.T.L. 521 36–145
Frontier International Shipping Corp v Swissmarine Corp Inc (The Cape Equinox) [2005]
EWHC 8; [2005] 1 All E.R. (Comm) 528; [2005] 1 Lloyd's Rep. 390; [2005] 1 C.L.C.
1, QBD (Comm) 14–138
Fuji Seal Europe Ltd v Catalytic Combustion Corp [2005] EWHC 1659; 102 Con. L.R. 47,
QBD (TCC) 18–009
Fujitsu Computer Products Corp v Bax Global Inc [2005] EWHC 2289; [2006] 1 All E.R.
(Comm) 211; [2006] 1 Lloyd's Rep. 367; [2005] 2 C.L.C. 760; (2005) 102(48) L.S.G.
18, QBD (Comm) 35–028, 35–059
Fusion Interactive Communication Solutions Ltd v Venture Investment Placement Ltd
(No.2) [2005] EWHC 736; [2005] All E.R. (D) 111, Ch D 21–074

G Scammell and Nephew Ltd v HC&JG Ouston [1941] A.C. 251, HL 2–136
GE Capital Bank Ltd v Rushton [2005] EWCA Civ 1556; [2006] 1 W.L.R. 899; [2006]
R.T.R. 17, CA (Civ Div) 38–367, 38–372, 43–006
GE Commercial Finance Ltd v Gee [2005] EWHC 2056; [2006] 1 Lloyd's Rep. 337,
QBD 6–048
GMAC Commercial Credit Development Ltd v Sandhu (No.1) [2004] EWHC 716; [2006]
1 All E.R. (Comm) 268, QBD (Comm) 44–049A
Gafford v Graham (1999) 77 P. & C.R. 73; [1999] 3 E.G.L.R. 75; [1999] 41 E.G. 159;
(1999) 96(40) L.S.G. 44; (1998) 95(21) L.S.G. 36; (1998) 142 S.J.L.B. 155; [1998]
N.P.C. 66 26–024
Gailey v Environmental Waste Controls [2004] Eu. L.R. 423; 2003 G.W.D. 40–1068, OH 31–005
Gallaher Ltd v Gallaher Pensions Ltd [2005] EWHC 42; [2005] O.P.L.R. 57; [2005] Pens.
L.R. 103, Ch D 5–095
General Legal Council (on the application of Whitter) v Frankson [2006] UKPC 42, PC
(Jam) 31–001

George Wimpey UK Ltd (formerly Wimpey Homes Holdings Ltd) v VI Construction Ltd
(formerly VI Components Ltd); sub nom. George Wimpey UK Ltd (formerly Wimpey
Homes Holdings Ltd) v VIC Construction Ltd (formerly Vic Components Ltd) [2005]
EWCA Civ 77; [2005] B.L.R. 135; (2005) 102(9) L.S.G. 28; (2005) 149 S.J.L.B. 182;
The Times, February 16, 2005, CA (Civ Div) 5–100
Ghaidan v Godin Mendoza [2004] UKHL 30, HL; affirming [2002] EWCA Civ 1533;
[2003] Ch. 380; [2003] 2 W.L.R. 478; [2002] 4 All E.R. 1162; [2002] 3 F.C.R. 591;
[2003] U.K.H.R.R. 254; 13 B.H.R.C. 608; [2003] H.L.R. 35; [2003] L. & T.R. 14;
[2003] A.C.D. 12; [2003] Fam. Law 87; [2002] 46 E.G.C.S. 197; (2003) 100(1) L.S.G.
24; (2002) 152 N.L.J. 1718; (2002) 146 S.J.L.B. 253; [2002] N.P.C. 138; [2003] 1 P.
& C.R. D14; [2004] 3 W.L.R. 113 .... 1–041, 32–016
Glasbrook Bros Ltd v Glamorgan CC; sub nom. Glamorgan CC v Glasbrook Bros Ltd
[1925] A.C. 270, HL 3–063
Glidepath BV v Thompson [2005] EWHC 818; [2005] 2 All E.R. (Comm) 833; [2005] 2
Lloyd's Rep. 549; [2005] 1 C.L.C. 1090, QBD (Comm) 32–040
Global Multimedia International Ltd v ARA Media Services, *The Times*, August 1, 2006, Ch
D 30–047
Golden Strait Corp v Nippon Yusen Kubishika Kaisha (The Golden Victory) [2005] EWHC
161; [2005] 1 All E.R. (Comm) 467; [2005] 1 Lloyd's Rep. 443; [2005] 1 C.L.C. 138;
The Times, March 4, 2005, QBD (Comm) 26–041
Goldsworthy v Brickell [1987] Ch. 378; [1987] 2 W.L.R. 133; [1987] 1 All E.R. 853; (1987)
84 L.S.G. 654; (1987) 131 S.J. 102, CA (Civ Div) 7–083
Good v Elliott (1790) 3 Tr. 693 .... 40–A005
Good Challenger Navegante SA v Metalexportimport SA [2003] EWCA Civ 1668; [2004]
1 Lloyd's Rep. 67; (2004) 101(2) L.S.G. 27 32–164
Goodway v Zurich Insurance Co [2004] EWHC 137; 96 Con. L.R. 49, QBD (TCC) 13–011
Goshawk Dedicated Ltd v Tyser & Co Ltd [2006] EWCA Civ 54; [2006] 1 All E.R.
(Comm) 501; [2006] 1 Lloyd's Rep. 566; [2006] 1 C.L.C. 198; *The Times*, April 4,
2006; *Independent* February 16, 2006, CA (Civ Div); reversing [2005] EWHC 461;
[2005] All E.R. (Comm.) 115, QBD (Comm) 2–155, 13–006, 31–018, 31–038, 31–046,
41–042, 41–043
Goshawk Dedicated (No.2) Ltd v Bank of Scotland [2005] EWHC 2906; [2006] 2 All E.R.
610, Ch D 38–021, 38–044, 38–079, 38–099
Gotham v Doodes; sub nom. Doodes v Gotham [2006] EWCA Civ 1080; [2006] N.P.C. 89;
The Times, August 14, 2006, CA (Civ Div) 28–003
Gravgaard v Aldridge & Brownlee (A Firm) [2004] EWCA Civ 1529; [2005] P.N.L.R. 19;
(2005) 149 S.J.L.B. 27; [2004] N.P.C. 187, CA (Civ Div) 28–011, 28–033
Gray (Deceased), Re. *See* Allardyce v Roebuck.
Gray v New Augarita Porcupine Mines Ltd [1952] 3 D.L.R. 1 31–127
Great Peace Shipping Ltd v Tsavliris Salvage (International) Ltd [2002] EWCA Civ 1407;
[2003] Q.B. 679; [2002] 3 W.L.R. 1617; [2002] 4 All E.R. 689; [2002] 2 All E.R.
(Comm) 999; [2002] 2 Lloyd's Rep. 653; [2003] 2 C.L.C. 16; (2002) 99(43) L.S.G. 34;
(2002) 152 N.L.J. 1616; [2002] N.P.C. 127; *The Times*, October 17, 2002; *Independent*,
October 22, 2002, CA (Civ Div) 5–043, 5–064
Grecoair Inc v Tilling [2004] EWHC 2851; [2005] Lloyd's Rep. I.R. 151, QBD (Comm) 18–004
Green v Gaul; sub nom. Loftus (Deceased), Re [2005] EWHC 406; [2005] 1 W.L.R. 1890;
[2005] 2 All E.R. 700; (2004–05) 7 I.T.E.L.R. 640; *The Times*, March 28, 2005, Ch
D 28–134
Greenhof v Barnsley MBC [2006] I.R.L.R. 98, EAT 39–146
Griffiths v Salisbury DC [2004] EWCA Civ 162; [2004] B.L.G.R. 454, CA (Civ Div) 39–046
Grosvenor Casinos Ltd v National Bank of Abu Dhabi [2006] EWHC 784 .... 34–366, 34–392,
34–397
Group Josi Re v Walbrook Insurance Co Ltd [1996] 1 W.L.R. 1152; [1996] 1 All E.R. 791;
[1996] 1 Lloyd's Rep. 345; [1996] 5 Re. L.R. 91 34–487
Grovit v De Nederlandsche Bank; Thorncroft v De Nederlandsche Bank [2005] EWHC
2944; [2006] 1 All E.R. (Comm) 397; [2006] 1 Lloyd's Rep. 636; [2006] Eu. L.R. 731;
[2006] I.L.Pr. 22, QBD 11–003, 11–004
Gryf-Lowczowski v Hinchingbrooke Healthcare NHS Trust [2005] EWHC 2407; [2006]
I.C.R. 425; [2006] I.R.L.R. 100; [2006] Lloyd's Rep. Med. 199; (2006) 87 B.M.L.R.
46, QBD 27–022

Guildford BC v Hein [2005] EWCA 979 .... *29–130*

H v M (Property Occupied by Wife's Parents); sub nom. JH v AM [2004] EWHC 625;
[2004] 2 F.L.R. 16; [2004] Fam. Law 485, Fam Div *3–146*
HF Pension Trustees Ltd v Ellison [1999] Lloyd's Rep. P.N. 489; [1999] P.N.L.R. 894;
[1999] O.P.L.R. 67; (1999) 96(8) L.S.G. 30, Ch D *28–011*
HSBC Rail (UK) Ltd v Network Rail Infrastructure Ltd (formerly Railtrack Plc) [2005]
EWHC 403; [2005] 1 All E.R. (Comm) 689, QBD (Comm) *18–053, 33–021, 36–044*
Habib Bank Ltd v Central Bank of Sudan (formerly Bank of Sudan) [2006] EWHC 1767,
QBD (Comm) *30–002, 30–011, 30–075, 30–088*
Habib Bank Ltd v Tufail [2006] EWCA Civ 374, CA (Civ Div) *6–123, 7–083*
Hackwood Ltd v Areen Design Services Ltd [2005] EWHC 2322; (2006) 22 Const. L.J. 68,
QBD (TCC) *32–041, 32–133*
Hadley Design Associates Ltd v Westminster City Council [2003] EWHC 1617; [2004]
T.C.L.R. 1; [2004] Masons C.L.R. 3 ....*13–009, 14–072, 14–074*
Hadley v Baxendale 156 E.R. 145; (1854) 9 Ex. 341 ....*26–054, 26–095B, 26–095C*
Hallam-Eames v Merrett Syndicates Ltd (No.1) [1995] C.L.C. 173; [1996] 5 Re. L.R. 110;
[1996] 7 Med. L.R. 122; [2001] Lloyd's Rep. P.N. 178; [1955–95] P.N.L.R. 672, CA
(Civ Div) *28–011*
Halley v Law Society [2003] EWCA Civ 97; [2003] W.T.L.R. 845; (2003–04) 6 I.T.E.L.R.
40; (2003) 153 N.L.J. 262 .... *16–172*
Halpern v Halpern [2006] EWHC 603; [2006] 2 Lloyd's Rep. 83, QBD (Comm) *2–137, 7–045A,
29–019, 29–088, 30–008, 30–026, 30–029, 30–039, 30–047, 30–053, 30–069,
30–073, 30–075, 30–127, 32–009, 32–109*
Halton International Inc (Holdings) Sarl v Guernroy Ltd; sub nom. Halton International Inc
(Holdings) Sarl v Guernroy Ltd (No.1) [2006] EWCA Civ 801, CA (Civ Div) *31–116*
Hamilton-Jones v David & Snape [2003] EWHC 3147; [2004] 1 W.L.R. 924; [2004] 1 All
E.R. 657; [2004] 1 F.L.R. 774; [2004] 1 F.C.R. 243; [2004] P.N.L.R. 21; [2004] Fam.
Law 246; (2004) 101(4) L.S.G. 31; (2004) 154 N.L.J. 55 .... *26–074*
Harb v Aziz (No.1); sub nom. Harb v King Fahd Bin Abdul Aziz (No.1) [2005] EWCA Civ
632; [2005] 2 F.L.R. 1108; [2005] 2 F.C.R. 342; [2005] Fam. Law 778; *The Times*, June
6, 2005, CA (Civ Div) *11–004*
Hardie Polymers Ltd v Polymerland Ltd, 2002 S.C.L.R. 64; 2001 G.W.D. 35–1338, OH *31–148*
Harding v Wealands [2006] UKHL 32; [2006] 3 W.L.R. 83; (2006) 156 N.L.J. 1136; (2006)
150 S.J.L.B. 917, HL *30–150, 30–151*
Hardy v Polk Ltd [2005] I.C.R. 557; [2004] I.R.L.R. 420, EAT *39–163*
Harper v Virgin Net Ltd [2004] EWCA Civ 271; [2004] I.R.L.R. 390; (2004) 101(14)
L.S.G. 25; (2004) 148 S.J.L.B. 353 ....*39–193, 39–216*
Harvey Shopfitters Ltd v ADI Ltd [2003] EWCA Civ 1757; [2004] 2 All E.R. 982; 91 Con.
L.R. 71; (2003) 100(48) L.S.G. 18 .... *2–114*
Hasan v Willson [1977] 1 Lloyd's Rep. 431, QBD 34–083
Hasbro UK Ltd v Director General of Fair Trading (Application for Time Extension) [2003]
CAT 1; [2003] Comp. A.R. 47, CCAT 42–089
Haugland Tankers AS v RMK Marine Gemi Yapim Sanayii ve Deniz Tasimaciligi Isletmesi
AS [2005] EWHC 321; [2005] 1 All E.R. (Comm) 679; [2005] 1 Lloyd's Rep. 573,
QBD (Comm) *12–027, 12–039*
Haward v Fawcetts (A Firm) [2006] UKHL 9; [2006] 1 W.L.R. 682; [2006] 3 All E.R. 497;
[2006] P.N.L.R. 25; [2006] 10 E.G.C.S. 154; [2006] N.P.C. 25, HL *28–011*
Hawkins v C.D. Bramall plc [2004] C.L. 94 .... *43–310*
Hazel (for Lloyd's Syndicate 260) v Whitlam; sub nom. Whitlam v Lloyds Syndicate 260
(t/a KGM Motor Policies at Lloyds) [2004] EWCA Civ 1600; [2005] Lloyd's Rep. I.R.
168, CA (Civ Div) *41–029, 41–034*
Heath Lambert Ltd v Sociedad de Corretaje de Seguros [2004] EWCA Civ 792; [2004] 1
W.L.R. 2820; [2005] 1 All E.R. 225; [2004] 2 All E.R. (Comm) 656; [2005] 1 Lloyd's
Rep. 597; [2004] Lloyd's Rep. I.R. 905; (2004) 101(28) L.S.G. 34; (2004) 148 S.J.L.B.
793; *The Times*, July 2, 2004, CA (Civ Div) *31–040, 41–043, 41–050*
Hedley Byrne & Co Ltd v Heller & Partners Ltd [1964] A.C. 465; [1963] 3 W.L.R. 101;
[1963] 2 All E.R. 575; [1963] 1 Lloyd's Rep. 485; 107 S.J. 454, HL *6–080*
Henderson v Merrett Syndicates [1995] 2 A.C. 145; [1994] 3 W.L.R. 761; [1994] 3 All E.R.
506; [1994] 2 Lloyd's Rep. 468; (1994) 144 N.L.J. 1204 .... *1–120*

Henry Boot Construction Ltd v Alstom Combined Cycles Ltd [2005] EWCA Civ 814; [2005] 1 W.L.R. 3850; [2005] 3 All E.R. 832; [2005] 2 C.L.C. 63; [2005] B.L.R. 437; 101 Con. L.R. 52; (2005) 102(30) L.S.G. 28, CA (Civ Div) *12–053, 32–150*

Hick v Raymond & Reid; sub nom. Hick v Rodocanachi; Pantland Hick v Raymond & Reid [1893] A.C. 22; [1891–4] All E.R. Rep. 491, HL *43–272*

Hickinbotham Developments Pty Ltd v Woods [2005] S.A.S.C. 215 .... *10–025*

HIH Casualty & General Insurance Ltd v Chase Manhattan Bank; Chase Manhattan Bank v HIH Casualty & General Insurance Ltd [2003] UKHL 6; [2003] 1 All E.R. (Comm) 349, HL; reversing in part [2001] EWCA Civ 1250; [2001] 2 Lloyd's Rep. 483; [2001] C.L.C. 1853; [2001] Lloyd's Rep. I.R. 703, CA (Civ Div) *6–139*

Hill v Secretary of State for the Environment, Food and Rural Affairs [2005] EWHC 696; [2006] 1 B.C.L.C. 601; [2005] B.P.I.R. 1330, Ch D *16–005*

Hilton v Barker Booth & Eastwood; sub nom. Hilton v Baker Booth & Eastwood; Hilton v Bariker Booth & Eastwood [2005] UKHL 8; [2005] 1 W.L.R. 567; [2005] 1 All E.R. 651; [2005] P.N.L.R. 23; [2006] Pens. L.R. 1; [2005] 6 E.G.C.S. 141; (2005) 102(14) L.S.G. 27; (2005) 155 N.L.J. 219; (2005) 149 S.J.L.B. 179; [2005] N.P.C. 14, HL *31–038, 31–116, 31–122*

Hindcastle Ltd v Barbara Attenborough Associates Ltd [1997] A.C. 70; [1996] 2 W.L.R. 262; [1996] 1 All E.R. 737; [1996] B.C.C. 636; [1996] 2 B.C.L.C. 234; [1996] B.P.I.R. 595; [1996] 1 E.G.L.R. 94; [1996] 15 E.G. 103; [1996] E.G.C.S. 32; (1996) 93(12) L.S.G. 29; (1996) 140 S.J.L.B. 84; [1996] N.P.C. 28 .... *44–088*

Hiscox Underwriting Ltd v Dickson Manchester & Co Ltd [2004] EWHC 49; [2004] 1 All E.R. (Comm.) 753; [2004] 2 Lloyd's Rep. 438 .... *32–101*

HL Estates Ltd v Parker-Lake Homes Ltd [2003] EWHC 604 .... *4–056*

Hok Sport Ltd v Aintree Racecourse Co Ltd [2002] EWHC 3094; [2003] B.L.R. 155; 86 Con. L.R. 165; [2003] Lloyd's Rep. P.N. 148 .... *26–070*

Holding & Barnes Plc v Hill House Hammond Ltd (Preliminary Issue) [2001] EWCA Civ 1334; [2002] 2 P. & C.R. 11; [2002] L. & T.R. 7, CA (Civ Div) *12–075*

Holding & Management (Solitaire) Ltd v Ideal Homes North West Ltd (formerly Broseley Estates Ltd) [2005] EWCA Civ 59, CA (Civ Div); affirming [2004] EWHC 2408; 96 Con. L.R. 114; [2005] P.N.L.R. 16, QBD (TCC) *13–009, 18–033*

Holladay v East Kent Hospitals NHS Trust [2003] EWCA Civ 1696; (2004) 76 B.M.L.R. 201; (2003) 147 S.J.L.B. 1398, CA (Civ Div) *39–146*

Holland v Lampen-Wolfe [2000] 1 W.L.R. 1573; [2000] 3 All E.R. 833; [2001] I.L.Pr. 49; [2000] U.K.H.R.R. 734; (2000) 97(32) L.S.G. 37; (2000) 144 S.J.L.B. 223; *The Times*, July 27, 2000; Independent, October 23, 2000 (C.S), HL *11–003*

Holme v Brunskill (1877–78) L.R. 3 Q.B.D. 495, CA *44–012, 44–096*

Holmes v Bangladesh Biman Corp. [1989] A.C. 1112; [1989] 2 W.L.R. 481; [1989] 1 All E.R. 852; [1989] 1 Lloyd's Rep. 444; (1989) 133 S.J. 291 .... *35–073*

Homburg Houtimport BV v Agrosin Private Ltd (The Starsin); Hunter Timber Ltd v Agrosin Private Ltd; sub nom. Owners of Cargo Lately Laden on Board the Starsin v Owners of the Starsin [2003] UKHL 12; [2004] 1 A.C. 715; [2003] 2 W.L.R. 711; [2003] 2 All E.R. 785; [2003] 1 All E.R. (Comm) 625; [2003] 1 Lloyd's Rep. 571; [2003] 1 C.L.C. 921; 2003 A.M.C. 913; (2003) 100(19) L.S.G. 31; *The Times*, March 17, 2003, HL *14–009*

Home of Homes Ltd v Hammersmith and Fulham LBC [2003] EWHC 807; 92 Con. L.R. 48, QBD (TCC) *32–073, 32–137*

Hopkins v TL Dallas Group Ltd; Hopkins v TL Dallas & Co Ltd [2004] EWHC 1379; [2005] 1 B.C.L.C. 543, Ch D *9–030A, 31–042*

Horbury Building Systems Ltd v Hampden Insurance NV [2004] EWCA Civ 418; [2004] All E.R. (D) 124; (2004) 148 S.J.L.B. 477 .... *41–025*

Horkulak v Cantor Fitzgerald International; sub nom. Cantor Fitzgerald International v Horkulak [2004] EWCA Civ 1287; [2005] I.C.R. 402; [2004] I.R.L.R. 942; (2004) 148 S.J.L.B. 1218, CA (Civ Div) *2–129, 2–169, 39–074, 39–145, 39–195*

Horn Linie GmbH & Co v Panamericana Formas e Impresos SA (The Hornbay) [2006] EWHC 373; [2006] 2 Lloyd's Rep. 44, QBD (Comm) *30–125*

Horsford v Bird; sub nom. Horsfold v Bird [2006] UKPC 3; [2006] 1 E.G.L.R. 75; [2006] 15 E.G. 136; (2006) 22 Const. L.J. 187; (2006) 103(6) L.S.G. 34, PC (Ant) *29–144*

Horton v Higham. *See* 1 Pump Court Chambers v Horton.

Hunt v Power Resources Ltd [2005] All E.R. (D) 23, EAT *16–161*

Hunter v Lex Vehicle Finance Ltd [2005] EWHC 223; [2005] B.P.I.R. 586, Ch D *38–328*

Hurst Stores & Interiors Ltd v ML Europe Property Ltd [2004] EWCA Civ 490; [2004] B.L.R. 249; 94 Con. L.R. 66; (2004) 148 S.J.L.B. 421, CA (Civ Div) *5–100*

Hyundai Engineering & Construction Co Ltd v Vigour Ltd [2005] B.L.R. 416, CA (HK) *37–050A*

Inchbold v Western Neilgherry Coffee, etc (1864) 17 C.B. (N.S.) 733 .... *29–068*

Independent Broadcasting Authority v EMI Electronics Ltd; sub nom. IBA v EMI Electronics Ltd and BICC Construction Ltd, 14 B.L.R. 1; [1955–95] P.N.L.R. 179, HL *18–009*

Indescon Ltd v Ogden [2004] EWHC 2326; [2005] 1 Lloyd's Rep. 31; [2005] B.L.R. 152, QBD *2–005*

Ing Re (UK) Ltd v R&V Versicherung AG [2006] EWHC 1544, QBD (Comm) *31–027, 31–031, 31–056*

Inland Revenue Commissioners v Deutsche Morgan Grenfell Group Plc. *See* Deutsche Morgan Grenfell Group Plc v Inland Revenue Commissioners.

Intense Investments Ltd v Development Ventures Ltd [2006] EWHC 1628, QBD (TCC) *22–025*

Interleasing (UK) Ltd v Morris [2002] EWHC 1086; [2002] 2 Lloyd's Rep. 563; (2002) 99(30) L.S.G. 37 .... *13–010*

Internaut Shipping GmbH v Fercometal SARL [2003] EWCA Civ 812; [2003] 2 All E.R. (Comm.) 760; [2003] 2 Lloyd's Rep. 430 .... *12–075, 12–114*

Interpart Comerciao e Gestao SA v Lexington Insurance Co [2004] Lloyd's Rep. I.R. 690, QBD (Comm) *41–069*

Investors Compensation Scheme Ltd v West Bromwich Building Society [1998] 1 W.L.R. 896; [1998] 1 All E.R. 98; [1998] 1 B.C.L.C. 531; [1997] C.L.C. 1243; [1997] P.N.L.R. 541; (1997) 147 N.L.J. 989 .... *44–057*

IPCO (Nigeria) Ltd v Nigerian National Petroleum Corp [2005] EWHC 726; [2005] 2 Lloyd's Rep. 326; [2005] 1 C.L.C. 613, QBD (Comm) *32–160*

Islington LBC v Uckac [2006] EWCA Civ 340; [2006] 1 W.L.R. 1303; [2006] 1 F.C.R. 668; [2006] N.P.C. 39; *The Times*, April 19, 2006; *Independent*, April 7, 2006, CA (Civ Div) *5–044, 6–108*

Item Software (UK) Ltd v Fassihi; sub nom. Fassihi v Item Software (UK) Ltd [2004] EWCA Civ 1244; [2004] B.C.C. 994; [2005] I.C.R. 450; [2004] I.R.L.R. 928; (2004) 101(39) L.S.G. 34; (2004) 148 S.J.L.B. 1153; *The Times*, October 21, 2004, CA (Civ Div) *21–030, 29–070, 31–114*

I-way Ltd v World Online Telecom Ltd [2002] EWCA Civ 413, CA *22–044A*

Izzard v Universal Insurance Co Ltd [1937] A.C. 773; (1937) 58 Ll. L. Rep. 121, HL *12–079*

J Pereira Fernandes SA v Mehta; sub nom. Metha v J Pereira Fernandes SA [2006] EWHC 813; [2006] 1 W.L.R. 1543; [2006] 2 All E.R. 891; [2006] 1 All E.R. (Comm) 885; *The Times*, May 16, 2006, Ch D *4–006, 4–027, 44–049, 44–051*

JA Pye (Oxford) Ltd v United Kingdom (44302/02) (2006) 43 E.H.R.R. 3; 19 B.H.R.C. 705; [2005] 3 E.G.L.R. 1; [2005] 49 E.G. 90; [2006] R.V.R. 188; [2005] 47 E.G.C.S. 145; [2005] N.P.C. 135; *The Times*, November 23, 2005, ECHR *1–039*

J&H Ritchie Ltd v Lloyd Ltd, 2005 S.L.T. 64; 2005 G.W.D. 2–38, IH (Ex Div) ... *43–053, 43–311*

JIS (1974) Ltd v MCP Investment Nominees I Ltd (Construction of Lease) [2003] EWCA Civ 721; (2003) 100(24) L.S.G. 36, CA (Civ Div) *5–095*

JJB Sports Plc v Office of Fair Trading; Allsports Ltd v Office of Fair Trading [2004] CAT 17; [2005] Comp. A.R. 29, CAT *42–089*

JSC Zestafoni G Nikoladze Ferroalloy Plant v Ronly Holdings Ltd [2004] EWHC 245; [2004] 2 Lloyd's Rep. 335; [2004] 1 C.L.C. 1146, QBD (Comm) *2–049, 16–031, 32–079, 32–134, 32–141, 32–149*

JT Mackley & Co Ltd v Gosport Marina Ltd [2002] EWHC 1315; [2002] B.L.R. 367; [2002] T.C.L.R. 26, QBD (TCC) *32–132*

Jackson v Royal Bank of Scotland [2005] UKHL 3; [2005] 1 W.L.R. 377; [2005] 2 All E.R. 71; [2005] 1 All E.R. (Comm) 337; [2005] 1 Lloyd's Rep. 366; (2005) 102(11) L.S.G. 29; (2005) 149 S.J.L.B. 146; *The Times*, February 2, 2005, HL *26–040, 26–047, 26–054, 26–055, 26–062A, 26–078, 34–465, 43–430, 43–452*

James Buchanan & Co Ltd v Babco Forwarding & Shipping (UK) Ltd [1978] A.C. 141; [1977] 3 W.L.R. 907; [1977] 3 All E.R. 1048; [1978] 1 Lloyd's Rep. 119; [1978] R.T.R. 59; [1978] 1 C.M.L.R. 156; 121 S.J. 811, HL *36–094*

James E McCabe Ltd v Scottish Courage Ltd [2006] EWHC 538, QBD (Comm) *16–192*

Jeancharm Ltd v Barnet Football Club Ltd [2003] EWCA Civ 58; (2003) 92 Con. L.R. 26 .....*26–110,*
38–258

Jelson Ltd v Derby City Council [1999] 4 P.L.R. 11; [1999] 3 E.G.L.R. 91; [1999] 39 E.G.
149; [2000] J.P.L. 203; [1999] E.G.C.S. 88; (1999) 96(26) L.S.G. 30; [1999] N.P.C.
68 4–060

Jewsons Ltd v Boykan [2003] EWCA Civ 1030; [2004] 1 Lloyd's Rep. 505; [2004] B.L.R.
31 .... *37–077*

Jimenez v Inland Revenue Commissioners [2004] S.T.C. (S.C.D.) 371; [2004] S.T.I. 1939,
Sp Comm *11–014*

Jindal Iron & Steel Co Ltd v Islamic Solidarity Shipping Co Jordan Inc; TCI Trans
Commodities AG v Islamic Solidarity Shipping Co Jordan Inc [2004] UKHL 49;
[2005] 1 W.L.R. 1363; [2005] 1 All E.R. 175; [2005] 1 All E.R. (Comm) 1; [2005] 1
Lloyd's Rep. 57; [2004] 2 C.L.C. 1172; 2005 A.M.C. 1; (2004) 148 S.J.L.B. 1405; *The
Times*, November 26, 2004, HL 14–117

John Doyle Construction Ltd v Laing Management (Scotland) Ltd; sub nom. Laing Management (Scotland) Ltd v John Doyle Construction Ltd, 2004 S.C. 713; 2004 S.C.L.R.
872; [2004] B.L.R. 295; (2004) 20 Const. L.J. 477; [2004] C.I.L.L. 2135; 2004 G.W.D.
20–434; *The Times*, June 18, 2004, IH (Ex Div) *37–254*

John Roberts Architects Ltd v Parkcare Homes (No.2) Ltd [2006] EWCA Civ 64; [2006] 1
C.L.C. 333; [2006] B.L.R. 106; 105 Con. L.R. 36; (2006) 22 Const. L.J. 343; [2006]
C.I.L.L. 2323; [2006] 7 E.G.C.S. 134; [2006] N.P.C. 13, CA (Civ Div) *37–260*

Johnsey Estates (1990) Ltd v Newport Marketworld [1996] N.P.C. 81, Ch D *1–082B*

Johnson v Gore Wood & Co (No.1); sub nom. Johnson v Gore Woods & Co [2002] 2 A.C.
1; [2001] 2 W.L.R. 72; [2001] 1 All E.R. 481; [2001] C.P.L.R. 49; [2001] B.C.C. 820;
[2001] 1 B.C.L.C. 313; [2001] P.N.L.R. 18; 98(1) L.S.G. 24; 98(8) L.S.G. 46; 150
N.L.J. 1889; 145 S.J.L.B. 29; The Times, December 22, 2000, HL 3–103

Johnson v Unisys Ltd [2001] UKHL 13; [2003] 1 A.C. 518; [2001] 2 W.L.R. 1076; [2001]
2 All E.R. 801; [2001] I.C.R. 480; [2001] I.R.L.R. 279; [2001] Emp. L.R. 469, HL *39–187*

Jones v Callagher (t/a Gallery Kitchens & Bathrooms); sub nom. Jones v Gallagher (t/a
Gallery Kitchens & Bathrooms) [2004] EWCA Civ 10; [2005] 1 Lloyd's Rep. 377, CA
(Civ Div) *43–305*

Jones v Saudi Arabia; Mitchell v Al-Dali; sub nom. Jones v Minister of the Interior
Al-Mamlaka Al-Arabiya AS Saudiya [2006] UKHL 26; [2006] 2 W.L.R. 1424; (2006)
156 N.L.J. 1025; (2006) 150 S.J.L.B. 811; *The Times*, June 15, 2006; *Independent*,
June 22, 2006, HL *11–003, 11–004*

Joscelyne v Nissen [1970] 2 Q.B. 86; [1970] 2 W.L.R. 509; [1970] 1 All E.R. 1213; (1969)
114 S.J. 55, CA (Civ Div) 5–095

Joyce v Rigolli [2004] EWCA Civ 79; (2004) 148 S.J.L.B. 234; [2004] 1 P. & C.R. D22 ...... 4–056A

Judge v Crown Leisure Ltd [2005] EWCA Civ 571; [2005] I.R.L.R. 823, CA (Civ Div) *2–136,*
2–176, 39–074

K Ltd v National Westminster Bank Plc [2006] EWCA Civ 1039; (2006) 103(31) L.S.G. 24;
(2006) 150 S.J.L.B. 982CA (Civ Div) 34–317

Kanoria v Guinness [2006] EWCA Civ 222; [2006] 1 Lloyd's Rep. 701, CA (Civ Div) *32–160*

Kastner v Jason, unreported, March 23, 2004 ....*32–093, 32–111*

Kastor Navigation Co Ltd v Axa Global Risks (UK) Ltd [2002] EWHC Comm 2601; [2003]
Lloyd's Rep. I.R. 262; affirmed [2004] EWCA Civ 277; [2004] Lloyd's Rep. I.R. 481 ....*41–025,*
41–070

Kaur v MG Rover Group Ltd [2004] EWCA Civ 1507; [2005] I.C.R. 625; [2005] I.R.L.R.
40; *The Times*, December 6, 2004, CA (Civ Div) *2–171, 39–048, 39–203*

Kazakhstan v Istil Group Inc [2005] EWCA Civ 1468; [2006] 1 W.L.R. 596; [2006] 2 All
E.R. (Comm) 26; [2006] C.P. Rep. 12, CA (Civ Div) *32–150*

Kellar v Williams [2004] UKPC 30 ....*16–004, 16–049*

Kellog Brown & Root Services Inc v Aerotech Herman Nelson Inc (2004) 238 D.L.R. (4th)
595 .... *43–059*

Kempson v Ashbee (1874–75) L.R. 10 Ch. App. 15 .... *7–064*

Kerry Foods Ltd v Lynch [2005] I.R.L.R. 681, EAT *39–187*

Kilcarne Holdings Ltd v Targetfollow (Birmingham) Ltd [2004] EWHC 2547; [2004]
N.P.C. 167, Ch D *4–063A, 4–064, 4–073*

Kinane v Mackie-Conteh; Kinane v Almack Marketing Services Ltd [2005] EWCA Civ 45; [2005] W.T.L.R. 345; [2005] 6 E.G.C.S. 140; (2005) 149 S.J.L.B. 177; [2005] 2 P. & C.R. DG3, CA (Civ Div) *3–114, 3–139, 3–143, 3–146, 3–150,* 4–073, 4–078

King v Brandywine Reinsurance Co (UK) Ltd (formerly Cigna RE Co (UK) Ltd) [2005] EWCA Civ 235; [2005] 2 All E.R. (Comm) 1; [2005] 1 Lloyd's Rep. 655, CA (Civ Div) *30–002, 30–010*

King v Lewis; sub nom. Lewis v King [2004] EWCA Civ 1329; [2005] I.L.Pr. 16; [2005] E.M.L.R. 4; (2004) 148 S.J.L.B. 1248; *The Times,* October 26, 2004; *Independent,* November 11, 2004, CA (Civ Div) *30–094*

King v Telegraph Group Ltd [2004] EWCA Civ 613; [2004] C.P. Rep. 35; [2004] 3 Costs L.R. 449; [2004] E.M.L.R. 23; (2004) 101(25) L.S.G. 27; (2004) 154 N.L.J. 823; (2004) 148 S.J.L.B. 664; *The Times,* May 21, 2004, CA (Civ Div) *16–056*

Kleinwort Benson Ltd v Glasgow City Council (No.2) [1999] 1 A.C. 153; [1997] 3 W.L.R. 923; [1997] 4 All E.R. 641; [1998] Lloyd's Rep. Bank. 10; [1997] C.L.C. 1609; [1998] I.L.Pr. 350; (1997) 9 Admin. L.R. 721; (1997) 94(44) L.S.G. 36; (1997) 147 N.L.J. 1617; (1997) 141 S.J.L.B. 237 5–042

Korbetis v Transgrain Shipping BV [2005] EWHC 1345, QBD 2–049, 2–056, *2–058, 2–094*

Kronos Worldwide Ltd v Sempra Oil Trading Sarl [2004] EWCA Civ 3; [2004] 1 All E.R. (Comm.) 915; [2004] 1 Lloyd's Rep. 260 .... *34–470*

Kuwait Oil Tanker Co SAK v Qabazard [2003] UKHL 31; [2004] 1 A.C. 300; [2003] 3 W.L.R. 14; [2003] 3 All E.R. 501; [2003] 2 All E.R. (Comm.) 101; [2003] I.L.Pr. 45; (2003) 100(28) L.S.G. 32; (2003) 147 S.J.L.B. 750 .... *34–324*

Kyle Bay Ltd (t/a Astons Nightclub) v Underwriters; sub nom. Kyle Bay Ltd (t/a Astons Nightclub) v Underwriters Subscribing under Policy No. 019057/08/01 [2006] EWHC 607; *The Times,* May 29, 2006, QBD (Comm) 6–007

Lady Archer v Williams [2003] EWHC 1670; [2003] E.M.L.R. 38 .... *1–056*

Laemthong International Lines Co Ltd v Artis (The Laemthong Glory) (No.2); sub nom. Laemthong International Lines Co Ltd v Abdullah Mohammed Fahem & Co [2005] EWCA Civ 519; [2005] 1 Lloyd's Rep. 688, CA (Civ Div) 18–087, 27–008, *30–162, 31–083*

Laemthong International Lines Co Ltd v Artis (The Laemthong Glory) (No.3) [2005] EWHC 1595, QBD (Comm) *30–139*

Lafarge (Aggregates) Ltd v Newham LBC [2005] EWHC 1337; [2005] 2 Lloyd's Rep. 577, QBD (Comm) *12–075, 21–022*

Lagden v O'Connor; Burdis v Livsey; Clark v Ardington Electrical Services; Dennard v Plant; Sen v Steelform Engineering Co Ltd; sub nom. Clark v Tull (t/a Ardington Electrical Services) [2003] UKHL 64; [2004] 1 A.C. 1067; [2003] 3 W.L.R. 1571; [2004] 1 All E.R. 277; [2004] R.T.R. 24; [2004] Lloyd's Rep. I.R. 315; (2003) 153 N.L.J. 1869; (2003) 147 S.J.L.B. 1430, HL 26–095A, *38–033, 38–037,* 38–044

Lakin v Exe Haulage Ltd [2006] 2 C.L. 105 .... *38–090*

Lamarra v Capital Bank Plc, 2005 S.L.T. (Sh Ct) 21; 2004 G.W.D. 40–817, Sh Pr *43–053, 43–310, 43–311*

Lambeth LBC v O'Kane; Helena Housing Ltd v Pinder [2005] EWCA Civ 1010; [2006] H.L.R. 2; [2005] 32 E.G.C.S. 67; [2005] N.P.C. 110; *The Times,* September 22, 2005, CA (Civ Div) *3–087*

Land Rover Group Ltd v UPF (UK) Ltd [2002] EWHC 3183; [2003] B.C.L.C. 222 ....*27–014, 27–017, 27–059*

Lane v O'Brien Homes [2004] EWHC 303 .... 26–024, *29–151*

LauritzenCool AB v Lady Navigation Inc; sub nom. Lady Navigation Inc v LauritzenCool AB [2005] EWCA Civ 579; [2005] 1 W.L.R. 3686; [2006] 1 All E.R. 866; [2005] 2 All E.R. (Comm) 183; [2005] 2 Lloyd's Rep. 63, CA (Civ Div) ...*27–022, 27–024, 27–065, 27–068, 27–069, 31–160, 32–101*

Law Debenture Trust Corp Plc v Elektrim Finance BV [2005] EWHC 1412; [2005] 2 All E.R. 476; [2005] 2 Lloyd's Rep. 755, Ch D *32–046, 32–079, 32–080, 32–133*

Law Society v Sephton & Co [2006] UKHL 22; [2006] 2 W.L.R. 1091; [2006] 3 All E.R. 401; [2006] P.N.L.R. 31; (2006) 156 N.L.J. 844; (2006) 150 S.J.L.B. 669; [2006] N.P.C. 56; *The Times,* May 11, 2006, HL *28–033*

Laws v Society of Lloyds [2003] EWCA Civ 1887, The Times, January 23, 2004 ....6–067, *28–010, 28–118*

Lawson v Serco Ltd; Crofts v Veta Ltd; Botham v Ministry of Defence; sub nom. Serco Ltd
   v Lawson [2006] UKHL 3; [2006] 1 All E.R. 823; [2006] I.C.R. 250; [2006] I.R.L.R.
   289; (2006) 103(6) L.S.G. 36; (2006) 156 N.L.J. 184; (2006) 150 S.J.L.B. 131, HL *39–208*
Lee v Airtours Holidays Ltd [2004] 1 Lloyd's Rep. 683 13–034
Leeds Rugby Ltd v Harris [2005] EWHC 1591; [2005] All E.R. (D) 286 .... *16–103*
Legends Surf Shops Plc (In Administrative Receivership) v Sun Life Assurance Society Plc;
   sub nom. Sun Life Assurance Society Plc v Legends Surf Shops Plc [2005] EWHC
   1438; [2006] B.C.C. 204; [2005] B.P.I.R. 1145; [2005] 3 E.G.L.R. 43; [2005] 46 E.G.
   178; [2005] N.P.C. 94; [2006] 1 P. & C.R. DG1, Ch D *44–008*
Lennon v Commissioner of Police of the Metropolis; sub nom. Commissioner of Police of
   the Metropolis v Lennon [2004] EWCA Civ 130; [2004] 1 W.L.R. 2594; [2004] 2 All
   E.R. 266; [2004] I.C.R. 1114; [2004] I.R.L.R. 385; (2004) 101(11) L.S.G. 36; (2004)
   148 S.J.L.B. 264; *The Times*, February 25, 2004, CA (Civ Div) *1–120, 3–177, 39–145*
Les Affreteurs Reunis SA v Leopold Walford (London) Ltd [1919] A.C. 801 .... *31–132*
Lesotho Highlands Development Authority v Impregilo SpA [2005] UKHL 43; [2006] 1
   A.C. 221; [2005] 3 W.L.R. 129; [2005] 3 All E.R. 789; [2005] 2 All E.R. (Comm) 265;
   [2005] 2 Lloyd's Rep. 310; [2005] 2 C.L.C. 1; [2005] B.L.R. 351; 101 Con. L.R. 1;
   [2005] 27 E.G.C.S. 220; (2005) 155 N.L.J. 1046, HL *30–152, 30–183, 32–003, 32–023,*
                                                                          32–111, 32–112, 32–137
Lever v Koffler [1901] 1 Ch. 543, Ch D *44–049*
Liberty Mutual Insurance Co (UK) Ltd v HSBC Bank Plc (Subrogation) [2001] Lloyd's
   Rep. Bank. 224, Ch D *44–104*
Lichtenstein v Clube Atletico Mineiro [2005] EWHC 1300; [2005] All E.R. (D) 341,
   QBD *31–039, 31–142*
Liesbosch Case, The [1933] A.C. 449; [1933] All E.R. Rep. 144; (1933) 45 Ll. L. Rep.
   123 ....26–095A
Lincoln National Life Insurance Co v Sun Life Assurance Co of Canada; sub nom. Sun Life
   Assurance Co of Canada v Lincoln National Life Insurance Co [2004] EWCA Civ
   1660; [2005] 1 Lloyd's Rep. 606, CA (Civ Div) *12–046, 21–013, 32–123, 41–088*
Linden Gardens Trust Ltd v Lenesta Sludge Disposals Ltd [1994] 1 A.C. 85; [1993] 3
   W.L.R. 408; [1993] 3 All E.R. 417; 63 B.L.R. 1; 36 Con. L.R. 1; [1993] E.G.C.S. 139;
   (1993) 143 N.L.J. 1152; (1993) 137 S.J.L.B. 183 .... *18–051, 18–059*
Linklaters (a firm) v HKSB Bank plc [2003] EWHC Comm 1113; [2003] 1 Lloyd's Rep.
   545 .... *34–171*
Lipkin Gorman (a firm) v Karpnale Ltd [1991] 2 A.C. 548; [1991] 3 W.L.R. 10; [1992] 4
   All E.R. 512; (1991) 88(26) L.S.G. 31; (1991) 141 N.L.J. 815; (1991) 135 S.J.L.B. 36 ......*3–008,*
                                                                          3–016, 3–017, 34–136, 40–083
Littman v Aspen Oil (Broking) Ltd [2005] EWCA Civ 1579; [2006] 2 P. & C.R. 2; (2006)
   103(5) L.S.G. 29; [2005] N.P.C. 150, CA (Civ Div) *12–075*
Lloyds Bank Plc v Independent Insurance Co Ltd [2000] Q.B. 110; [1999] 2 W.L.R. 986;
   [1999] 1 All E.R. (Comm.) 8; [1999] Lloyd's Rep. Bank. 1; [1999] C.L.C. 510; (1999)
   96(3) L.S.G. 31, CA (Civ Div) *31–056*
Lloyds TSB Bank Plc v Hayward [2005] EWCA Civ 466, CA (Civ Div) *44–096*
Locker & Woolf Ltd v Western Australian Insurance Co Ltd [1936] 1 K.B. 408; (1936) 54
   Ll. L. Rep. 211, CA *40–A003*
Lodgepower Ltd v Taylor; sub nom. Taylor v Lodgepower Ltd [2004] EWCA Civ 1367;
   [2005] 08 E.G. 192; [2004] 44 E.G.C.S. 152; [2004] N.P.C. 156; *The Times*, November
   3, 2004, CA (Civ Div) *31–160*
Loftus (Deceased), Re. *See* Green v Gaul.
London Borough of Newham v Khatun [2004] EWCA Civ 55; [2004] 3 W.L.R. 417; (2004)
   148 S.J.L.B. 268; [2004] N.P.C. 28 .... 15–014–15–017, *15–021*, 27–056
London North Securities Ltd v Meadows [2005] EWCA Civ 956; [2005] C.C.L.R. 7, CA
   (Civ Div) *38–020, 38–039*, 38–044
Lonsdale (t/a Lonsdale Agencies) v Howard & Hallam Ltd [2006] EWCA Civ 63; [2006]
   1 W.L.R. 1281; [2006] 1 Lloyd's Rep. 760; [2006] 1 C.L.C. 219; [2006] Eu. L.R. 804;
   [2006] I.C.R. 584; [2006] I.R.L.R. 481; (2006) 103(9) L.S.G. 30, CA (Civ Div) *31–149*
Louis Dreyfus Trading Ltd v Reliance Trading Ltd [2004] EWHC 525; [2004] 2 Lloyd's
   Rep. 243, QBD (Comm) *26–052, 43–440, 43–442, 43–460, 43–461*
Lovell and Christmas v Wall (1911) 104 L.T. 84 5–095
Lovell Projects Ltd v Legg [2003] B.L.R. 452, TCC *15–072*

Lowsley v Forbes (t/a LE Design Services) [1999] 1 A.C. 329; [1998] 3 W.L.R. 501; [1998] 3 All E.R. 897; [1998] 2 Lloyd's Rep. 577; (1998) 95(35) L.S.G. 37; (1998) 148 N.L.J. 1268; (1998) 142 S.J.L.B. 247; *The Times*, August 24, 1998, HL *28–015*

Lucas Laureys v Graham Earl, unreported, November 3, 2005 .... *31–083*, 43–046

Luck t/a Luck Arboricultural & Horticultural v London Borough of Tower Hamlets [2003] EWCA Civ 52; [2003] 2 C.M.L.R. 12; [2003] Eu. L.R. 143; [2003] A.C.D. 59 .... *10–026*

Lumbermans Mutual Casualty Co v Bovis Lend Lease Ltd (Preliminary Issues); sub nom. Lumbermens Mutual Casualty Co v Bovis Lend Lease Ltd (Preliminary Issues) [2004] EWHC 2197; [2005] 1 Lloyd's Rep. 494; [2005] B.L.R. 47; 98 Con. L.R. 21; [2005] Lloyd's Rep. I.R. 74; [2004] 42 E.G.C.S. 160, QBD (Comm) *41–088*

Lymington Marina Ltd v Macnamara [2006] EWHC 704; [2006] 2 All E.R. (Comm) 200; [2006] N.P.C. 43, Ch D *2–129, 2–149*

M v Home Office [1994] 1 A.C. 377; [1993] 3 W.L.R. 433; [1993] 3 All E.R. 537; (1995) 7 Admin. L.R. 113; (1993) 90(37) L.S.G. 50; (1993) 143 N.L.J. 1099; (1993) 137 S.J.L.B. 199; *The Times*, July 28, 1993; *Independent*, July 28, 1993, HL 10–011

M/V Nord Cloud (2006) 41 E.T.L. 79 .... *36–129*

McAdam v Boxpak Ltd, 2005 S.L.T. (Sh Ct) 47; 2005 G.W.D. 9–127, Sh Pr *31–005*

McAlpine PPS Pipeline Systems Joint Venture v Transco Plc [2004] EWHC 2030; [2004] B.L.R. 352; 96 Con. L.R. 69, QBD (TCC) 37–260

McCarthy v McCarthy and Stone Plc (Application for Summary Judgment) [2006] EWHC 1851, Ch D *29–107*

McConnell Dowell Construction (Aust) Pty Ltd v Semcorp Engineering and Constructions Pte Ltd [2002] B.L.R. 450 ....*34–491B*

McDonald v Coys of Kensington Holdings Ltd. *See* Cressman v Coys of Kensington (Sales) Ltd.

McFarlane v Tayside Health Board [2000] 2 A.C. 59 .... *18–039*

Macklin v Dowsett [2004] EWCA Civ 904; [2004] 2 E.G.L.R. 75; [2004] 34 E.G. 68; [2005] W.T.L.R. 1561; [2004] 26 E.G.C.S. 193, CA (Civ Div) *7–049, 7–070A*

McMillan Williams v Range [2004] EWCA Civ 294; [2004] 1 W.L.R. 1858 .... *38–017*

McNicholas Construction Holdings v Endemol UK plc [2003] EWHC 2472; [2003] 43 E.G.C.S. 136; (2003) 100(40) L.S.G. 32 .... *2–006*

Macedo v Stroud [1922] 2 A.C. 330, PC (Trin) *1–082E*

Maden v Clifford Coppock & Carter [2004] EWCA Civ 1037; [2005] 2 All E.R. 43; [2005] P.N.L.R. 7; (2004) 101(38) L.S.G. 29; (2004) 154 N.L.J. 1218, CA (Civ Div) *26–039*

Mahonia Ltd v J.P. Morgan Chase Bank [2003] 2 Lloyd's Rep. 911 ....*16–031, 16–175, 34–402, 34–487*

Mahonia Ltd v West LB AG [2004] EWHC Comm 1938 .... *16–031*

Mainstream Properties Ltd v Young [2005] EWCA Civ 861; [2005] I.R.L.R. 964; (2005) 102(30) L.S.G. 31; *The Times*, July 28, 2005, CA (Civ Div) *18–127*

Mamidoil-Jetoil Greek Petroleum Co SA v Okta Crude Oil Refinery AD [2003] 1 Lloyd's Rep.1; [2003] EWCA Civ 1031; [2003] 2 Lloyd's Rep. 635 .... *14–141*

Man (ED&F) v Societe Anonyme Tripolitaine des Usines de Raffinage de Sucre [1970] 2 Lloyd's Rep. 416, QBD (Comm) *32–026A*

Manifest Shipping Co Ltd v Uni-Polaris Insurance Co Ltd (The Star Sea); sub nom. Manifest Shipping Co Ltd v Uni-Polaris Shipping Co Ltd (The Star Sea) [2001] UKHL 1; [2003] 1 A.C. 469; [2001] 2 W.L.R. 170; [2001] 1 All E.R. 743; [2001] 1 All E.R. (Comm) 193; [2001] 1 Lloyd's Rep. 389; [2001] C.L.C. 608; [2001] Lloyd's Rep. I.R. 247; *The Times*, January 23, 2001, HL 6–139

Mann v Coutts & Co [2003] EWHC 2138; [2004] 1 All E.R. (Comm.) 1 .... *34–350*

Manx Electricity Authority v JP Morgan Chase Bank [2003] EWCA Civ 1324; (2003) 147 S.J.L.B. 1205; 2003 W.L. 22187638 44–085

Marc Rich Agriculture Trading SA v Fortis Corporate Insurance NV [2004] EWHC 2632, QBD (Comm) *41–069*

Marconi Communications International Ltd v PT Pan Indonesia Bank Ltd Tbk [2005] EWCA Civ 422; [2005] 2 All E.R. (Comm) 325, CA (Civ Div) *30–075, 30–088, 34–486*

Marcq v Christie Manson & Woods Ltd (t/a Christie's); sub nom. Christie Manson & Woods
Ltd (t/a Christies) v Marcq [2003] EWCA Civ 731; [2004] Q.B. 286; [2003] 3 W.L.R.
980; [2003] 3 All E.R. 561; (2003) 100(27) L.S.G. 38; (2003) 147 S.J.L.B. 662; *The
Times*, May 30, 2003; *Independent*, June 6, 2003, CA (Civ Div) *33–001, 33–006, 33–014,
33–118*
Margulead Ltd v Exide Technologies [2004] EWHC 1019; [2004] 2 All E.R. (Comm) 727;
[2005] 1 Lloyd's Rep. 324, QBD (Comm) *32–137, 32–145, 32–149*
Mark v Mark; sub nom. Marks v Marks (Divorce: Jurisdiction) [2005] UKHL 42; [2006] 1
A.C. 98; [2005] 3 W.L.R. 111; [2005] 3 All E.R. 912; [2005] 2 F.L.R. 1193; [2005] 2
F.C.R. 467; [2005] I.N.L.R. 614; [2005] W.T.L.R. 1223; [2005] Fam. Law 857; (2005)
102(28) L.S.G. 32, HL *30–077*
Market Investigations Ltd v Minister of Social Security [1969] 2 Q.B. 173; [1969] 2 W.L.R.
1; [1968] 3 All E.R. 732; 112 S.J. 905, QBD *39–025*
Marklands Ltd v Virgin Retail Ltd [2003] EWHC 3428; [2004] 2 E.G.L.R. 43; [2004] 27
E.G. 130, Ch D *32–137, 32–141*
Marks and Spencer plc v Customs and Excise Commissioners [2005] UKHL 53, HL; [2005]
C.M.L.R. 3 ....*29–026, 29–086*
Marks & Spencer plc v Fresfields Bruckhaus Deringer [2004] EWCA Civ 741 .....*31–038, 31–120*
Marplace (Number 512) Ltd v Chaffe Street (A Firm) [2006] EWHC 1919, Ch D *24–023*
Marubeni Hong Kong and South China Ltd v Government of Mongolia [2005] EWCA Civ
395; [2005] 1 W.L.R. 2497; [2005] 2 All E.R. (Comm) 288; [2005] 2 Lloyd's Rep. 231;
[2005] 1 C.L.C. 540, CA (Civ Div); affirming [2004] EWHC Comm 472; [2004] 2
Lloyd's Rep.198 ....*10–009, 10–017, 30–139, 31–060, 44–012—44–014, 44–089*
Masterman-Lister v Jewell; Masterman-Lister v Brutton & Co [2002] EWCA Civ 1889;
[2003] 1 W.L.R. 1511; [2003] 3 All E.R. 162; [2003] C.P. Rep. 29; (2004) 7 C.C.L.
Rep. 5; [2003] P.I.Q.R. P20; [2003] Lloyd's Rep. Med. 244; (2003) 73 B.M.L.R. 1;
[2003] W.T.L.R. 259; (2003) 147 S.J.L.B. 60; *The Times*, December 28, 2002, CA (Civ
Div) *8–072*
Matthews v Kent and Medway Towns Fire Authority; sub nom. Mathews v Kent and
Medway Towns Fire Authority [2006] UKHL 8; [2006] 2 All E.R. 171; [2006] I.C.R.
365; [2006] I.R.L.R. 367; [2006] Pens. L.R. 61, HL *39–148*
MCI Worldcom International Inc. v Primus Telecommunications plc [2004] EWCA Civ
957; [2004] All E.R. (D) 418 ....*6–020, 6–036*
Meikle v Nottinghamshire CC; sub nom. Nottinghamshire CC v Meikle [2004] EWCA Civ
859; [2004] 4 All E.R. 97; [2005] I.C.R. 1; [2004] I.R.L.R. 703; (2004) 80 B.M.L.R.
129; (2004) 148 S.J.L.B. 908; *The Times*, July 15, 2004; *Independent*, July 14, 2004,
CA (Civ Div) *39–145*
Melhuish v Redbridge Citizens Advice Bureau [2005] I.R.L.R. 419, EAT *3–008, 39–023*
Metal Distributors (UK) Ltd v ZCCM Investment Holdings Plc [2005] EWHC 156; *The
Times*, March 9, 2005, QBD (Comm) *32–026A, 32–132*
Micro Anvika Ltd v TNT Express Worldwide (Euro Hub) NV [2006] EWHC 230, QBD
(Comm) *36–132*
Midland Mainline Ltd v Eagle Star Insurance Co Ltd [2004] EWCA Civ 1042; [2004] All
E.R. (D) 499 .... *41–073*
Military Affairs Office of the Embassy of the State of Kuwait v Caramba-Coker (EAT/
1054/02/RN, April 10, 2003) *11–004, 11–005*
Millar v Bassey [1994] E.M.L.R. 44; *Independent*, August 26, 1993, CA (Civ Div) *18–127*
Minermet SpA Milan v Luckyfield Shipping Corp SA [2004] EWHC 729; [2004] 2 Lloyd's
Rep. 348; [2004] 2 C.L.C. 421, QBD (Comm) *32–063, 32–106, 32–137*
Mingeley v Pennock and Ivory [2004] EWCA Civ 328; [2004] I.R.L.R. 373; (2004) 101(11)
L.S.G. 33 ....*39–009, 39–023*
Ministry of Sound (Ireland) Ltd v World On-line Ltd [2003] EWHC 2178; [2003] 2 All E.R.
(Comm.) 823 .... *26–107*
Mint Security Ltd v Blair [1982] 1 Lloyd's Rep. 188 .... *41–036*
Minter v Julius Baer Investment Management Inc London; Minter v Julius Baer Investments
Ltd [2004] EWHC 2472; [2005] Pens. L.R. 73, Ch D *2–124*
Mirant Asia-Pacific Construction (Hong Kong) Ltd v Ove Arup & Partners International Ltd
(OAPIL) (No.2) [2004] EWHC 1750; 97 Con. L.R. 1; [2005] P.N.L.R. 10, QBD
(TCC) *2–074*
Mitchell v Al-Dali [2005] EWCA Civ 720, CA (Civ Div) *11–021*

Mitsubishi Corp v Eastwind Transport Ltd (The Irbenskiy Proliv) [2004] EWHC 2924;
    [2005] 1 All E.R. (Comm) 328; [2005] 1 Lloyd's Rep. 383, QBD (Comm) *14–007*
Mohsin v Commonwealth Secretariat [2002] EWHC Comm 377 .... *11–019*
Monarch Steamship Co Ltd v A/B Karlshamns Oljefabriker [1949] A.C. 196; [1949] 1 All
    E.R. 1; (1948–49) 82 Ll. L. Rep. 137; 1949 S.C. 1; 1949 S.C. (H.L.) 1; 1949 S.L.T. 51;
    65 T.L.R. 217; [1949] L.J.R. 772; 93 S.J. 117 ....26–095A
Montrod Ltd v Grundkotter Fleischvertriebs [2001] EWCA Civ 1954; [2002] 1 W.L.R.
    1975; [2002] 3 All E.R. 697; [2002] 1 All E.R. (Comm.) 257; [2002] C.L.C. 499 ....*34–491B*
Moody v Condor Insurance Ltd [2006] EWHC 100; [2006] 1 W.L.R. 1847; [2006] 1 All
    E.R. 934; [2006] 1 All E.R. (Comm) 419; [2006] 1 C.L.C. 263; *The Times*, February
    27, 2006, Ch D 1–088, 18–005, *18–102, 18–114, 44–030*
Mora Shipping Inc v Axa Corporate Solutions Assurance SA [2005] EWCA Civ 1069;
    [2005] 2 Lloyd's Rep. 769; [2005] 2 C.L.C. 349; [2006] I.L.Pr. 10, CA (Civ Div) *12–057,*
                                                                                                                    21–006
More OG Romsdal Fylkesbatar AS v Demise Charterers of the Jotunheim [2004] EWHC
    671; [2005] 1 Lloyd's Rep. 181, QBD (Comm) *22–047, 38–308*
Morgan v Ashcroft [1938] 1 K.B. 49, CA *40–030*
Morgan Est (Scotland) Ltd v Hanson Concrete Products Ltd [2005] EWCA Civ 134; [2005]
    3 All E.R. 135; [2005] C.P. Rep. 23; [2005] B.L.R. 218; *The Times*, February 28, 2005,
    CA (Civ Div) *28–119*
Morin v Bonhams & Brooks Ltd [2003] EWCA Civ 1802; [2004] 1 All E.R. (Comm.)
    880 .... *18–005*
Mortgage Agency Services Number Two Ltd v Chater [2003] EWCA Civ 490; [2003]
    H.L.R. 61; [2004] 1 P. & C.R. 4; [2003] 15 E.G.C.S. 138; (2003) 147 S.J.L.B. 417;
    [2003] N.P.C. 48; [2003] 2 P. & C.R. D9 ....*7–073, 7–099, 34–266*
Mortimer v Bailey [2004] EWCA Civ 1514; [2005] B.L.R. 85; [2005] 2 P. & C.R. 9; [2005]
    1 E.G.L.R. 75; [2005] 02 E.G. 102; [2004] N.P.C. 162, CA (Civ Div) *27–059*
Moussavi-Azad v Sky Properties Ltd [2003] EWHC 2669; [2003] All E.R. (D) 38 .....*25–020, 25–023*
Mowlem Plc (t/a Mowlem Marine) v Stena Line Ports Ltd [2004] EWHC 2206, QBD
    (TCC) *29–002, 29–054, 29–068*
Muhammad Issa el Sheikh Ahmad v Ali [1947] A.C. 427, PC 26–095A
Munchener Ruckversicherungs Gesellschaft (t/a Munich Reinsurance Co) v Commonwealth
    Insurance Co [2004] EWHC 914; [2004] 2 C.L.C. 665; [2005] Lloyd's Rep. I.R. 99,
    QBD (Comm) *30–050*
Munkenbeck & Marshall v Harold [2005] EWHC 356; [2005] All E.R. (D) 227, QBD
    (TCC) *15–076, 15–086*
Munt v Beasley [2006] EWCA Civ 370, CA (Civ Div) *5–095*
Murad v Al-Saraj; Murad v Westwood Business Inc [2005] EWCA Civ 959; [2005]
    W.T.L.R. 1573; (2005) 102(32) L.S.G. 31, CA (Civ Div *29–139, 29–155, 29–157, 31–127*
Myrto, The [1978] 1 Lloyd's Rep. 11, CA (Civ Div); reversing [1977] 2 Lloyd's Rep. 243,
    QBD (Admlty) *18–134*

NB Three Shipping Ltd v Harebell Shipping Ltd [2004] EWHC 2001; [2005] 1 All E.R.
    (Comm) 200; [2005] 1 Lloyd's Rep. 509, QBD (Comm) *32–018*
NBTY Europe Ltd (formerly Holland & Barrett Europe Ltd) v Nutricia International BV
    [2005] EWHC 734; [2005] 2 Lloyd's Rep. 350, QBD (Comm) *5–060, 12–050, 12–119*
NEC Semi Conductors Ltd v Inland Revenue Commissioners; sub nom. Boake Allen Ltd v
    Revenue and Customs Commissioners [2006] EWCA Civ 25; [2006] S.T.C. 606;
    [2006] Eu. L.R. 755; [2006] B.T.C. 266; 8 I.T.L. Rep. 819; [2006] S.T.I. 321; (2006)
    156 N.L.J. 240; *The Times*, February 10, 2006; *Independent* February 8, 2006, CA (Civ
    Div) *29–002, 29–016, 29–018, 29–084*
NMBS v NV Fonciere Carner (1976) 11 E.T.L. 780 .... *36–092*
NV Optitrade EA v NV Cat Benelux (2004) 39 E.T.L. 407 .... *36–145*
NV Valkeniersnaite (2006) 41 E.T.L. 272 .... *36–132*
National Car Parks Ltd v Baird (Valuation Officer) [2004] EWCA Civ 967; [2005] 1 All
    E.R. 53; [2004] R.A. 245; (2004) 148 S.J.L.B. 942; [2004] N.P.C. 126; *The Times*,
    September 9, 2004, CA (Civ Div) *21–020*
National Commercial Bank (Jamaica) Ltd v Hew's Executors; sub nom. National Commer-
    cial Bank (Jamaica) Ltd v Hew [2003] UKPC 51, PC (Jam) *29–137*

National Insurance & Guarantee Corp Ltd v M Young Legal Services Ltd [2004] EWHC 2972; [2005] 2 Lloyd's Rep. 46, QBD *32–101*

National Justice Compania Naviera SA v Prudential Assurance Co Ltd (The Ikarian Reefer) (No.2); sub nom. Comninos v Prudential Assurance Co Ltd [2000] 1 W.L.R. 603; [2000] 1 All E.R. 37; [1999] 2 All E.R. (Comm) 673; [2000] 1 Lloyd's Rep. 129; [2000] C.P. Rep. 13; [2000] C.L.C. 22; [2000] 1 Costs L.R. 37; [2000] I.L.Pr. 490; [2000] Lloyd's Rep. I.R. 230; (1999) 96(41) L.S.G. 35; (1999) 96(42) L.S.G. 40; (1999) 149 N.L.J. 1561; (1999) 143 S.J.L.B. 255, CA (Civ Div) *32–009*

National Provincial Bank of England v Jackson (1886) L.R. 33 Ch. D. 1, CA *1–082H*

National Westminster Bank Plc v Morgan [1985] A.C. 686; [1985] 2 W.L.R. 588; [1985] 1 All E.R. 821; [1985] F.L.R. 266; (1985) 17 H.L.R. 360; (1985) 82 L.S.G. 1485; (1985) 135 N.L.J. 254; (1985) 129 S.J. 205, HL *7–073*

Navigation Maritime Bulgare v Rustal Trading Ltd [2002] 1 Lloyd's Rep.106 .... *32–042*

Neilson v Poole (1969) 20 P. & C.R. 909 .... *4–056A*

Nejad v City Index Ltd [2000] C.C.L.R. 7, CA *38–017*

Nelson v Nelson (1995) 132 A.L.R. 133 .... *31–099*

Newell v Tarrant [2004] EWHC 772; (2004) 148 S.J.L.B. 509, Ch D *4–069, 4–070*

Newfield Construction Ltd v Tomlinson [2004] EWHC 3051; 97 Con. L.R. 148, QBD (TCC) *32–138, 32–, 32–143A*

Newgate Stud Co v Penfold [2004] EWHC 2993, Ch D *31–126*

Newton Woodhouse v Trevor Toys Ltd, unreported, December 20, 1991, CA *29–068*

Nigel Upchurch Associates v Aldridge Estates Investment Co Ltd [1993] 1 Lloyd's Rep. 535 .... *18–123*

Niru Battery Manufacturing Co v Milestone Trading Ltd (No.1) [2003] EWCA Civ 1446; [2004] 1 All E.R. (Comm.) 193; [2004] 1 Lloyd's Rep. 344; (2003) 100(44) L.S.G. 33 .... *18–022, 34–137*

Niru Battery Manufacturing Co v Milestone Trading Ltd (No.2) [2004] EWCA Civ 487; [2004] 2 All E.R. (Comm.) 289; [2004] 2 Lloyd's Rep. 319 ....*29–099, 29–102, 29–121, 29–173, 29–184*

Nisshin Shipping Co Ltd v Cleaves & Co Ltd [2003] EWHC 2602; [2004] 1 All E.R. (Comm.) 481; [2004] 1 Lloyd's Rep. 38; (2003) 153 N.L.J. 1705 ...*18–003, 18–074, 18–087, 18–091, 18–108, 31–132*

Norfolk Southern Ry Co v James Kirby Pty Ltd, 125 S. Ct 385 (2004) *31–110*

Norsk Hydro ASA v State Property Fund of Ukraine [2002] EWHC Comm 2120 .... *11–006*

North Ocean Shipping Co v Hyundai Construction Co (The Atlantic Baron) [1979] Q.B. 705; [1979] 3 W.L.R. 419; [1978] 3 All E.R. 1170; [1979] 1 Lloyd's Rep. 89; 123 S.J. 352, QBD (Comm) *7–045A*

North Star Shipping Ltd v Sphere Drake Insurance Plc [2006] EWCA Civ 378; [2006] 2 All E.R. (Comm) 65; [2006] 1 C.L.C. 606, CA (Civ Div); affirming [2005] EWHC 665, QBD (Comm) *41–029*

Nottinghamshire Healthcare Trust v Prison Officers Association [2003] I.C.R. 1192, EAT *31–032*

NPower Direct Ltd v South of Scotland Power Ltd [2005] EWHC 2123; (2005) 102(43) L.S.G. 29, QBD (Comm) *22–048, 31–147*

Nweze v Nwoko [2004] EWCA Civ 379; [2004] 2 P. & C.R. D1; (2004) 101(17) L.S.G. 30; (2004) 148 S.J.L.B. 472; [2004] N.P.C. 50, The Times, may 6, 2004 .... *4–060, 4–063*

OBG Ltd v Allan [2005] EWCA Civ 106; [2005] 2 W.L.R. 1174; [2005] 2 All E.R. 602; [2005] 1 All E.R. (Comm) 639; [2005] P.N.L.R. 27; (2005) 102(14) L.S.G. 27; *The Times*, February 24, 2005; *Independent*, February 18, 2005, CA (Civ Div) *18–127, 31–115*

OEM Plc v Schneider [2005] EWHC 1072, Ch D *29–159, 29–174*

OT Africa Line Ltd v Magic Sportswear Corp [2005] EWCA Civ 710; *The Times*, June 21, 2005; *Independent*, June 16, 2005, CA (Civ Div) *30–144*

Oakley v Ultra Vehicle Design Ltd. *See* Ultra Motorhomes International Ltd, Re.

O'Byrne v Sanofi Pasteur MSD Ltd (formerly Aventis Pasteur MSD Ltd) (C127/04) [2006] 1 W.L.R. 1606; [2006] All E.R. (EC) 674; [2006] 2 C.M.L.R. 24; [2006] C.E.C. 493; *The Times*, February 15, 2006, ECJ (1st Chamber) *28–009*

Ocwen v Hughes [2004] C.C.L.R. 4 .... *38–039, 38–044*

Odfjell Seachem A/S v Continentale des Petroles et d'Investissements; sub nom. Odfjfell Seachem A/S v Continentale des Petroles et d'Investissements [2004] EWHC 2929; [2005] 1 All E.R. (Comm) 421; [2005] 1 Lloyd's Rep. 275, QBD (Comm) *24–051*

Office of Fair Trading v Lloyds TSB Bank Plc [2006] EWCA Civ 268; [2006] 2 All E.R.
821; [2006] 1 All E.R. (Comm) 629; (2006) 103 L.S.G. 28; (2006) 156 N.L.J. 553, CA
(Civ Div); reversing [2004] EWHC 2600; [2005] 1 All E.R. 843; [2005] 1 All E.R.
(Comm) 354; [2005] E.C.C. 27; (2004) 154 N.L.J. 1728, QBD (Comm) *30–082, 30–099,
38–025, 38–029, 38–454*
O'Hagan v Wright [2001] NICA 26; [2003] C.C.L.R. 6 .... *38–037, 38–082*
O'Kane v Jones [2004] 1 Lloyd's Rep. 389 ....*41–004, 41–005, 41–012, 41–014, 41–029, 41–030,
41–086*
Olex Focas Pty Ltd v Skodaexport Co Ltd [1998] 3 V.R. 380 .... *34–491B*
Olympic Airways v Husain 124 S Ct 1221 (2004) *35–033*
Omilaju v Waltham Forest LBC (No.2); sub nom. Waltham Forest LBC v Omilaju (No.2)
[2004] EWCA Civ 1493; [2005] 1 All E.R. 75; [2005] I.C.R. 481; [2005] I.R.L.R. 35;
(2004) 148 S.J.L.B. 1370; *The Times*, November 26, 2004, CA (Civ Div) *39–145, 39–187*
Ophthalmic Innovations International (UK) Ltd v Ophthalmic Innovations International Inc
[2004] EWHC 2948; [2005] I.L.Pr. 10, Ch D *30–020, 30–073, 30–075, 30–088*
OT Computers Ltd (in administration), Re [2004] EWCA Civ 653; [2004] 2 All E.R.
(Comm.) 331 .... *41–090*
Oxley v Hiscock; sub nom. Hiscock v Oxley [2004] EWCA Civ 546; [2005] Fam. 211;
[2004] 3 W.L.R. 715; [2004] 3 All E.R. 703; [2004] 2 F.L.R. 669; [2004] 2 F.C.R. 295;
[2004] W.T.L.R. 709; (2003–04) 6 I.T.E.L.R. 1091; [2004] Fam. Law 569; [2004] 20
E.G.C.S. 166; (2004) 101(21) L.S.G. 35; (2004) 148 S.J.L.B. 571; [2004] N.P.C. 70;
[2004] 2 P. & C.R. DG14; *The Times*, July 14, 2004, CA (Civ Div) *3–141, 29–160*

P1 International Ltd v Llewellyn [2005] EWHC 407; [2005] U.K.C.L.R. 530, QBD *27–060*
P&O Nedlloyd BV v Arab Metals Co (The UB Tiger) [2005] EWHC 1276; [2005] 1 W.L.R.
3733; [2006] 1 Lloyd's Rep. 111, QBD (Comm) *28–118, 28–134, 28–135*
P & S Platt Ltd v Crouch [2003] EWCA Civ 1110; [2004] 1 P. & C.R. 18; [2003] 32
E.G.C.S. 67; (2003) 147 S.J.L.B. 934; [2003] N.P.C. 97; [2003] 2 P. & C.R. D19, The
Times, August 27, 2003 .... *12–119*
P & V Industries Pty Ltd v Porto [2005] VSC 131 .... *31–114*
PJ Pipe & Valve Co Ltd v Audco India Ltd [2005] EWHC 1904; [2006] Eu. L.R. 368,
QBD *31–005, 31–132*
PT Pan Indonesia Bank TBK v Marconi Communications International Ltd. *See* Marconi
Communications International Ltd v PT Pan Indonesia Bank TBK.
Pacific Carriers Ltd v BNP Paribas [2004] H.C.A.35, High Court of Australia *31–056*
Pacific Carriers Corp v Tradax Export SA (The North King) [1971] 2 Lloyd's Rep. 460,
QBD (Comm) *31–056*
Palfrey v Transco Plc [2004] I.R.L.R. 916, EAT *39–213*
Pallant v Morgan [1953] Ch. 43; [1952] 2 All E.R. 951; [1952] 2 T.L.R. 813, Ch D *4–073*
Papamichael v National Westminster Bank [2003] EWHC 164; [2003] 1 Lloyd's Rep. 341 ....*34–136,
34–301*

Paragon Finance Plc (formerly National Home Loans Corp) v Nash; Paragon Finance Plc
v Staunton; sub nom. Nash v Paragon Finance Plc; Staunton v Paragon Finance Plc
[2001] EWCA Civ 1466; [2002] 1 W.L.R. 685; [2002] 2 All E.R. 248; [2001] 2 All
E.R. (Comm) 1025; [2002] 2 P. & C.R. 20; (2001) 98(44) L.S.G. 36; (2001) 145
S.J.L.B. 244; [2002] 1 P. & C.R. DG13; *The Times*, October 25, 2001, CA (Civ Div) *1–026*
Paragon Finance Plc (formerly National Home Loans Corp Ltd) v Pender [2005] EWCA
Civ 760; [2005] All E.R. (D) 307, CA (Civ Div) *1–026, 22–039, 38–198, 38–257*
Parker v Clark [1960] 1 W.L.R. 286; [1960] 1 All E.R. 93; 104 S.J. 251, Assizes (Exeter) *4–027*
Parsons v George [2004] EWCA Civ 912; [2004] 1 W.L.R. 3264; [2004] 3 All E.R. 633;
[2005] C.P. Rep. 3; [2004] 3 E.G.L.R. 49; [2004] 40 E.G. 150; [2004] 31 E.G.C.S. 93;
(2004) 101(33) L.S.G. 36; (2004) 148 S.J.L.B. 879; [2004] N.P.C. 117; [2005] 1 P. &
C.R. DG1; *The Times*, July 28, 2004, CA (Civ Div) *28–119*
Paul v Speirway Ltd (in liquidation) [1976] 1 W.L.R. 220 .... *29–173*
Pauling's Settlement Trusts (No.1), Re; sub nom. Younghusband v Coutts & Co (No.1)
[1964] Ch. 303; [1963] 3 W.L.R. 742; [1963] 3 All E.R. 1; 107 S.J. 492, CA *28–134*
Peekay Intermark Ltd v Australia & New Zealand Banking Group Ltd [2006] EWCA Civ
386; [2006] 1 C.L.C. 582, CA (Civ Div) *6–039, 6–132*

Peer International Corp v Termidor Music Publishers Ltd (No.1); sub nom. Peer International Corp v Termidor Music Publishers Co Inc [2003] EWCA Civ 1156; [2004] Ch. 212; [2004] 2 W.L.R. 849; [2003] E.M.L.R. 34; [2004] R.P.C. 23; (2003) 26(11) I.P.D. 26070; (2003) 100(37) L.S.G. 31; *The Times*, September 11, 2003, CA (Civ Div) 30–117, 30–174
Pegler Ltd v Wang (UK) Ltd (No.1) [2000] B.L.R. 218; 70 Con. L.R. 68; [2000] I.T.C.L.R. 617; [2000] Masons C.L.R. 19, QBD (TCC) 14–087
Pegram Shopfitters Ltd v Tally Weijl (UK) Ltd [2003] EWCA Civ 1750; [2004] 1 All E.R. 818; [2004] 1 All E.R. (Comm.) 593; [2004] B.L.R. 65; 91 Con. L.R. 173 32–169
Pena v Dale [2003] EWHC 1065; [2004] 2 B.C.L.C. 508, Ch D 2–176, 27–011, 27–023
Peninsula Business Services Ltd v Sweeney [2004] I.R.L.R. 49, EAT 39–205
Pennycook v Shaws (EAL) Ltd; sub nom. Pennycook v Shuns (EAL) Ltd; Shaws (EAL) Ltd v Pennycook [2004] EWCA Civ 100; [2004] Ch. 296; [2004] 2 W.L.R. 1331; [2004] 2 All E.R. 665; [2004] L. & T.R. 34; [2004] 2 E.G.L.R. 55; [2004] 18 E.G. 102; [2004] 8 E.G.C.S. 135; (2004) 101(11) L.S.G. 35; (2004) 148 S.J.L.B. 235; [2004] N.P.C. 21; [2004] 1 P. & C.R. DG25; *The Times*, February 20, 2004; *Independent*, February 19, 2004, CA (Civ Div) 1–039
Peoples Insurance Co of China v Vysanthi Shipping Co Ltd [2003] EWHC Comm 1655; [2003] 2 Lloyd's Rep.617 32–132
Percy v Church of Scotland Board of National Mission [2005] UKHL 73; [2006] 2 A.C. 28; [2006] 2 W.L.R. 353; 2006 S.C. (H.L.) 1; 2006 S.L.T. 11; [2006] I.C.R. 134; [2006] I.R.L.R. 195; (2006) 150 S.J.L.B. 30; *The Times*, December 16, 2005; *Independent*, December 20, 2005, HL 2–175, 18–004
Peregrine Systems Ltd v Steria Ltd [2005] EWCA Civ 239; [2005] All E.R. (D) 215, CA (Civ Div) 21–013, 21–020
Pesticcio v Huet [2004] EWCA Civ 372; (2004) 154 N.L.J. 653; (2004) 148 S.J.L.B. 420; [2004] N.P.C. 55 7–049
Peterson Farms Inc. v C & M Farming Ltd [2004] EWHC 121; [2004] 1 Lloyd's Rep. 603; [2004] N.P.C. 13 .... 31–063, 32–035, 32–043, 32–109, 32–132, 32–149, 32–150
Petromec Inc v Petroleo Brasileiro SA Petrobras (No.3) [2005] EWCA Civ 891; [2006] 1 Lloyd's Rep. 121, CA (Civ Div) 1–020, 2–114, 2–135, 18–087, 43–187
Phillips v Rafiq [2006] EWHC 1461 41–093
Phillips v Syndicate 992 Gunner [2003] EWHC 1084 ; [2004] Lloyd's Rep. I.R. 426 41–077
Phillipson v Indus Realty Pty Ltd (2004) 8 V.L.R. 446 31–136
Picardi v Cuniberti [2002] EWHC 2923; [2003] B.L.R. 487; (2003) 19 Const. L.J. 350 15–072
Pickett v Motor Insurers Bureau [2004] EWCA Civ 6; [2004] 2 All E.R. 685; [2004] P.I.Q.R. P24; (2004) 148 S.J.L.B. 117, CA 41–093
Pilkington UK Ltd v CGU Insurance Plc [2004] EWCA Civ 23; [2005] 1 All E.R. (Comm) 283; [2004] 1 C.L.C. 1059; [2004] B.L.R. 97; [2004] T.C.L.R. 5; [2004] Lloyd's Rep. I.R. 891; [2004] N.P.C. 10, CA (Civ Div) 41–096
Pine Valley Developments v Ireland (A/222) (1992) 14 E.H.R.R. 319; *The Times*, December 11, 1991, ECHR 10–015A
Pirtek (UK) Ltd v Deanswood Ltd [2005] EWHC 2301; [2005] 2 Lloyd's Rep. 728, QBD (Comm) 32–106, 32–119
Portman Building Society v Hamlyn Taylor Neck [1998] 4 All E.R. 202; [1998] P.N.L.R. 664; (1999) 77 P. & C.R. 66; [1998] 2 E.G.L.R. 113; [1998] 31 E.G. 102; (1998) 76 P. & C.R. D16, CA (Civ Div) 29–019
Post Office v British World Airlines Ltd [2000] 1 All E.R. (Comm.) 532; [2000] 1 Lloyd's Rep. 378; [2000] C.L.C. 581 35–074
Potomek Construction Ltd v Zurich Securities Ltd [2003] EWHC 2827; [2004] 1 All E.R. (Comm.) 672 .... 21–061, 21–067
Potter v RJ Temple [2003] All E.R. (D) 327 24–013
Povey v Quantas Airways Ltd [2005] H.C.A. 33 35–033
Powell v Wiltshire; sub nom. Wiltshire v Powell [2004] EWCA Civ 534; [2005] Q.B. 117; [2004] 3 W.L.R. 666; [2004] 3 All E.R. 235; (2004) 148 S.J.L.B. 573; *The Times*, June 3, 2004, CA (Civ Div) 43–229A
Practice Note (QBD: Indorsements for Interest on Claims for Debts or Liquidated Sums); sub nom. Practice Direction (QBD: Interest: Pleading) [1983] 1 W.L.R. 377; [1983] 1 All E.R. 924, QBD 34–120
Prater v Cornwall County Council. *See* Cornwall CC v Prater.

Pratt Contractors Ltd v Transit New Zealand [2003] UKPC 83; [2004] B.L.R. 143 .....10–025, *37–053*

Prenn v Simmonds [1971] 1 W.L.R. 1381; [1971] 3 All E.R. 237; 115 S.J. 654, HL 44–057

President of India v La Pintada Compania Navigacion SA (The La Pintada) [1985] A.C. 104; [1984] 3 W.L.R. 10; [1984] 2 All E.R. 773; [1984] 2 Lloyd's Rep. 9; [1984] C.I.L.L. 110; (1984) 81 L.S.G. 1999; (1984) 128 S.J. 414, HL 6–064

President of the Methodist Conference v Parfitt [1984] Q.B. 368; [1984] 2 W.L.R. 84; [1983] 3 All E.R. 747; [1984] I.C.R. 176; [1984] I.R.L.R. 141, CA (Civ Div) 2–175

Primetrade AG v Ythan Ltd [2005] EWHC 2399; [2006] 1 All E.R. 367; [2006] 1 All E.R. (Comm) 157; [2006] 1 Lloyd's Rep. 457; [2005] 2 C.L.C. 911, QBD (Comm) *30–064, 32–132, 32–134, 32–149*

Prince Blucher Ex p. Debtor, Re [1931] 2 Ch. 70, CA *31–001*

Prison Service v Bewley [2004] I.C.R. 422, EAT *39–108*

Protech Projects Construction (Pty) Ltd v Al-Kharafi & Sons; Mohammed Abdulmohsin Al-Kharafi & Sons WLL v Big Dig Construction (Proprietary) Ltd (In Liquidation) [2005] EWHC 2165; [2005] 2 Lloyd's Rep. 779, QBD (Comm) *32–137*

PW & Co v Milton Gate Investment Ltd [2003] EWHC 1994; [2003] All E.R. (D) 58; [2004] 2 W.L.R. 443; [2004] L. & T.R. 8; (2003) 100(38) L.S.G. 36; (2003) 153 N.L.J. 1347 .... 1–032, 1–041

Quarter Master UK Ltd, Re, July 15, 2004 ....*29–155, 29–157*

R v Attorney General of England and Wales [2003] UKPC 22; [2003] E.M.L.R. 24; (2003) 147 S.J.L.B. 354, PC (NZ) *29–088*

R. v Ministry of Defence Ex p. Cookson & Clegg Ltd. *See* Cookson & Clegg Ltd v Ministry of Defence.

R. v Secretary of State for the Environment, Transport and the Regions Ex p. International Air Transport Association (No.2) [2000] 1 Lloyd's Rep. 242; [1999] 2 C.M.L.R. 1385; [1999] Eu. L.R. 811; [1999] C.O.D. 315QBD *35–022*

R. (on the application of Abassi) v Secretary of State for Foreign and Commonwealth Affairs [2002] EWCA Civ 1598; [2003] U.K.H.R.R. 76; (2002) 99(47) L.S.G. 29 .... *11–007*

R. (on the application of Alamieyeseigha) v Crown Prosecution Service [2005] EWHC 2704; [2006] Crim. L.R. 669; *The Times*, January 16, 2006, QBD (Admin) *11–006*

R. (on the application of Geologistics Ltd) v Financial Services Compensation Scheme [2003] EWCA Civ 1877; [2004] Lloyd's Rep. I.R. 336 .... *41–089*

R. (on the application of Kemp) v Denbighshire Local Health Board [2006] EWHC 181; [2006] 3 All E.R. 141; (2006) 9 C.C.L. Rep. 354, QBD (Admin) *26–149*

R. (on the application of Wandsworth LBC) v Secretary of State for Transport, Local Government and the Regions [2003] EWHC Admin 622; [2004] 1 P. & C.R. 32 ...... *10–017*

R. (on the application of West) v Lloyd's of London [2004] EWCA Civ 506; [2004] 3 All E.R. 251; [2004] 2 All E.R. (Comm) 1; [2004] 2 C.L.C. 649; [2004] H.R.L.R. 27; [2004] Lloyd's Rep. I.R. 755; (2004) 148 S.J.L.B. 537, CA (Civ Div) 1–042

R. (Verner) v Derby City Council [2003] EWHC Admin 2708; [2004] I.C.R. 535 ......*23–037, 23–056*

Rahman v Sterling Credit Ltd; sub nom. Sterling Credit Ltd v Rahman [2002] EWHC 3008, Ch D 38–257

Rai v Somerfield Stores Ltd [2004] I.C.R. 656, EAT *39–152*

Raiffeisen Zentralbank Osterreich Ag v Crossseas Shipping Ltd [2000] 1 W.L.R. 1135; [2000] 3 All E.R. 274; [2000] 1 All E.R. (Comm.) 76; [2000] Lloyd's Rep. Bank. 108; [2000] C.L.C. 553 .... *44–099*

Ramco (UK) Ltd v International Insurance Co of Hanover; sub nom. Ramco (UK) Ltd v International Insurance Co of Hannover Ltd [2004] EWCA Civ 675; [2004] 2 All E.R. (Comm) 866; [2004] 2 Lloyd's Rep. 595; [2004] 1 C.L.C. 1013; [2004] Lloyd's Rep. I.R. 606; (2004) 148 S.J.L.B. 695, CA (Civ Div) *18–002, 18–047, 18–120, 33–025, 33–050, 41–008*

Ratiu v Conway; sub nom. Conway v Ratiu [2005] EWCA Civ 1302; [2006] 1 All E.R. 571; [2006] 1 E.G.L.R. 125; [2006] W.T.L.R. 101; [2005] 46 E.G.C.S. 177, CA (Civ Div) *31–116*

Re-Source America International Ltd v Platt Site Services Ltd (Damages); sub nom. Barkin Construction Ltd v Re-Source America International Ltd [2005] EWCA Civ 97; [2005] 2 Lloyd's Rep. 50; 105 Con. L.R. 30; [2005] N.P.C. 19, CA (Civ Div) *26–101*

Reading Festival Ltd v West Yorkshire Police Authority; sub nom. West Yorkshire Police Authority v Reading Festival Ltd [2006] EWCA Civ 524; [2006] 1 W.L.R. 2005; (2006) 103(20) L.S.G. 28; (2006) 150 S.J.L.B. 607; *The Times*, May 15, 2006; *Independent*, May 10, 2006, CA (Civ Div) 3–063

Redrow Homes (Yorkshire) Ltd v Wright; Redrow Homes (North West) Ltd v Roberts; sub nom. Wright v Redrow Homes (Yorkshire) Ltd; Roberts v Redrow Homes (North West) Ltd [2004] EWCA Civ 469; [2004] 3 All E.R. 98; [2004] I.C.R. 1126; [2004] I.R.L.R. 720; (2004) 148 S.J.L.B. 666; *Independent*, April 27, 2004, CA (Civ Div) *39–009*

Regent International Hotels (UK) v Pageguide, *The Times*, May 13, 1985, CA (Civ Div) *31–160*

Regina (Reprotech (Pebsham) Ltd) v East Sussex County Council [2002] UKHL 8; [2003] 1 W.L.R. 348; [2002] 4 All E.R. 58; [2003] 1 P. & C.R. 5; [2002] J.P.L. 821; [2002] 10 E.G.C.S. 158; [2002] N.P.C. 32 10–017

Rendall v Combined Insurance Co of America [2005] EWHC 678, QBD (Comm) *41–032*

Reynard Construction (ME) Pty Ltd v Minister of Public Works (1992) 26 N.S.W.L.R. 234 .... *29–068*

RG Kensington Management Co v Hutchinson [2002] EWHC 1180; [2003] 2 P. & C.R. 13 .... *4–069*

Richards (t/a Colin Richards & Co) v Hughes; sub nom. Hughes v Richards (t/a Colin Richards & Co) [2004] EWCA Civ 266; [2004] P.N.L.R. 35; (2004) 148 S.J.L.B. 353, CA (Civ Div) *18–012, 18–037, 18–038*

Ridgeway Motors (Isleworth) Ltd v ALTS Ltd; sub nom. Ridgeway Motors (Isleworth) Ltd v Altis Ltd [2005] EWCA Civ 92; [2005] 2 All E.R. 304; [2005] B.C.C. 496; [2005] B.P.I.R. 423; [2005] R.V.R. 173; [2005] N.P.C. 27; *The Times*, February 24, 2005, CA (Civ Div) *28–015*

Riyad Bank v Ahli United Bank (UK) Plc [2006] EWCA Civ 780, CA (Civ Div); [2005] EWHC 279; [2005] 2 Lloyd's Rep. 409; [2006] 1 B.C.L.C. 311, QBD (Comm) *18–055, 34–255*

Robbins of Putney Ltd v Meek [1971] R.T.R. 345 ....*26–095C*, 26–097

Robertson v Department for the Environment, Food and Rural Affairs; sub nom. Department for the Environment, Food and Rural Affairs v Robertson [2005] EWCA Civ 138; [2005] I.C.R. 750; [2005] I.R.L.R. 363; (2005) 102(15) L.S.G. 33, CA (Civ Div) *39–122*

Rodaro v Royal Bank of Canada (2002) 59 O.R. (3d) 74 (Ont. CA) *34–304*

Rogers v Markel Corp (formerly Market Holdings Inc) (Liability) [2004] EWHC 2046, QBD *30–152, 30–153, 30–180*

Rolls Royce Power Engineering plc v Ricardo Consulting Engineers Ltd [2003] EWHC 2871; [2004] 2 All E.R. (Comm.) 129 ...... *12–014, 12–114, 18–050, 18–059, 31–063, 31–065*

Ronly Holdings Ltd v JSC Zestafoni G Nikoladze Ferroalloy Plant [2004] EWHC 1354; [2004] 1 C.L.C. 1168; [2004] B.L.R. 323, QBD (Comm) *32–026A, 32–137*

Rosewood Trucking Ltd v Balaam [2005] EWCA Civ 1461; [2006] 1 Lloyd's Rep. 429; [2005] 2 C.L.C. 959; [2006] R.T.R. 23, CA (Civ Div) *36–134, 36–141*

Rotary Watches Ltd v Rotary Watches (USA) Inc (2005) 71 *Arbitration* (2) 172 .... *32–126*

Rover International Ltd v Cannon Film Sales Ltd (No.3) [1989] 1 W.L.R. 912; [1989] 3 All E.R. 423; [1988] B.C.L.C. 710, CA (Civ Div) *29–068*

Rowland v Environment Agency [2003] EWCA Civ 1885; [2005] Ch. 1; [2004] 3 W.L.R. 249; [2004] 2 Lloyd's Rep. 55; (2004) 101(8) L.S.G. 30; [2003] N.P.C. 165; *The Times*, January 20, 2004, CA (Civ Div) *10–015A*

Royal & Sun Alliance Insurance Plc v Dornoch Ltd [2005] EWCA Civ 238; [2005] 1 All E.R. (Comm) 590, CA (Civ Div) *41–051A, 41–054, 41–064*

Royal & Sun Alliance Insurance Plc v MK Digital FZE (Cyprus) Ltd [2006] EWCA Civ 629; [2006] 2 All E.R. (Comm) 145; [2006] 2 Lloyd's Rep. 110, CA (Civ Div); reversing [2005] EWHC 1408, QBD (Comm) *36–145, 36–147*

Royal Bank of Canada v Stangl (1992) 32 A.C.W.S. (3d) 17 ....*34–396A*

Royal Bank of Scotland Plc v Etridge (No.2); Barclays Bank Plc v Coleman; Barclays Bank Plc v Harris; Midland Bank Plc v Wallace; National Westminster Bank Plc v Gill; UCB Home Loans Corp Ltd v Moore; Bank of Scotland v Bennett; Kenyon-Brown v Desmond Banks & Co (Undue Influence) (No.2) [2001] UKHL 44; [2002] 2 A.C. 773; [2001] 3 W.L.R. 1021; [2001] 4 All E.R. 449; [2001] 2 All E.R. (Comm) 1061; [2002] 1 Lloyd's Rep. 343; [2001] 2 F.L.R. 1364; [2001] 3 F.C.R. 481; [2002] H.L.R. 4; [2001] Fam. Law 880; [2001] 43 E.G.C.S. 184; (2001) 151 N.L.J. 1538; [2001] N.P.C. 147; [2002] 1 P. & C.R. DG14; *The Times*, October 17, 2001; *Daily Telegraph*, October 23, 2001, HL *7–073*
Royal Bank of Scotland plc v Fielding [2003] EWHC 986; affirmed [2004] EWCA Civ 64 ....*34–312, 34–334*
Royal National Lifeboat Institution v Bushaway [2005] I.R.L.R. 675, EAT *39–025, 39–027*
Rugby Group Ltd v ProForce Recruit Ltd [2006] EWCA Civ 69, CA (Civ Div) *12–104, 12–119*
Rupert Morgan Building Services (LLC) Ltd v Jervis [2003] EWCA Civ 1563; [2004] 1 W.L.R. 1867; [2004] 1 All E.R. 529; [2004] B.L.R. 18; [2004] T.C.L.R. 3; 91 Con. L.R. 81; (2003) 153 N.L.J. 1761; *The Times*, November 26, 2003; *Independent*, November 20, 2003, CA (Civ Div) *37–260*

S v S [2002] EWHC 223; [2003] Fam. 1; [2002] 3 W.L.R. 1372; [2002] 1 F.L.R. 992; [2002] Fam. Law 422; (2002) 99(15) L.S.G. 34; (2002) 152 N.L.J. 398; (2002) 146 S.J.L.B. 78 .... *5–042*
S & W Process Engineering Ltd v Cauldron Foods Ltd [2005] EWHC 153, QBD (TCC) *29–002, 29–021*
SA Nicolas Corman v SNCF (1976) 11 E.T.L. 120 .... *36–090*
SEB Trygg Holding AB v Manches; sub nom. AMB Generali Holding AG v SEB Trygg Liv Holding AB; AMB Generali Holding AG v Manches [2005] EWCA Civ 1237; [2006] 1 All E.R. 437; [2006] 2 All E.R. (Comm) 38; [2006] 1 Lloyd's Rep. 318; (2005) 102(45) L.S.G. 28; (2005) 155 N.L.J. 1781, CA (Civ Div) *31–029, 31–056, 31–099, 31–163*
SHV Gas Supply & Trading SAS v Naftomar Shipping & Trading Co Ltd Inc (The Azur Gaz) [2005] EWHC 2528; [2006] 1 Lloyd's Rep. 163; [2005] 2 C.L.C. 815, QBD (Comm) *14–140, 14–150, 43–272*
Saggar v Ministry of Defence; Lucas v Ministry of Defence; Ministry of Defence v Gandiya [2005] EWCA Civ 413; [2005] I.C.R. 1073; *The Times*, May 9, 2005, CA (Civ Div) *30–109*
Samwoh Asphalt Premix Pte Ltd v Sum Cheong Piling Pte Ltd [2002] B.L.R. 459 .... *34–491B*
Sandilands, Ex p. (1871) L.R. 6 C.P. 411 .... *1–082H*
Saudi Arabian Monetary Agency v Dresdner Bank AG [2003] EWHC 3271; [2004] 2 Lloyd's Rep.19; affirmed [2004] EWCA Civ 1074 .... *34–314*
Scammell v Dicker. *See* Dicker v Scammell.
Scandinavian Trading Tanker Co AB v Flota Petrolera Ecuatoriana (The Scaptrade) [1983] 2 A.C. 694; [1983] 3 W.L.R. 203; [1983] 2 All E.R. 763; [1983] 2 Lloyd's Rep. 253, HL *27–024, 27–068*
Scheldebouw BV v St James Homes (Grosvenor Dock) Ltd [2006] EWHC 89; [2006] B.L.R. 113; 105 Con. L.R. 90, QBD (TCC) *37–186*
Scottish Equitable plc v Derby [2001] EWCA Civ 369; [2001] 3 All E.R. 818; [2001] 2 All E.R. (Comm.) 274; [2001] O.P.L.R. 181; [2001] Pens. L.R. 163; (2001) 151 N.L.J. 418 ....*3–103, 34–137*
Scottish Widows plc v Tripipatkal [2003] EWHC 1874; [2003] B.P.I.R. 1413; [2004] 1 P. & C.R. 29; [2004] L. & T.R. 12; [2003] N.P.C. 106; [2004] 1 P. & C.R. D4 .... *44–088*
Secretary of State for Transport v Christos [2003] EWCA Civ 1073; [2004] 1 P. & C.R. 17; [2004] 10 E.G. 186; [2003] R.V.R. 307; [2003] 31 E.G.C.S. 68; [2003] N.P.C. 96 ....*2–117, 3–143*
Selvas Pty Ltd v Hansen Yuncken (SA) Pty Ltd (1987) 6 Australian Construction Law Rep. 36 ....*34–491B*
Sempra Metals Ltd (formerly Metallgesellschaft Ltd) v Inland Revenue Commissioners [2005] EWCA Civ 389; [2006] Q.B. 37; [2005] 3 W.L.R. 521; [2005] S.T.C. 687; [2005] 2 C.M.L.R. 30; [2005] Eu. L.R. 773; [2005] B.T.C. 202; [2005] S.T.I. 831; [2005] N.P.C. 52, CA (Civ Div) *29–083, 29–084*
Serco Ltd v Lawson [2004] EWCA Civ 12; [2004] 2 All E.R. 200; [2004] I.C.R. 204; [2004] I.R.L.R. 206; (2004) 148 S.J.L.B. 148 ....*30–109, 39–208*
Severn Trent Water Ltd v Barnes [2004] EWCA Civ 570 .... *29–142, 29–144*

Seymour, Re; sub nom. Fielding v Seymour [1913] 1 Ch. 475, CA *1–082E*

Shaker v Al-Bedrawi; Shaker v Masry; Shaker v Steggles Palmer (A Firm) [2002] EWCA
    Civ 1452; [2003] Ch. 350; [2003] 2 W.L.R. 922; [2002] 4 All E.R. 835; [2003] B.C.C.
    465; [2003] 1 B.C.L.C. 157; [2003] W.T.L.R. 105; (2002–03) 5 I.T.E.L.R. 429;
    Independent, October 25, 2002, CA (Civ Div) *30–048*

Shalson v Russo [2005] Ch. 281; [2003] EWHC 1637; [2003] W.T.L.R. 1165; (2003)
    100(35) L.S.G. 37 .... *29–162, 34–138*

Shamil Bank of Bahrain v Beximco Pharmaceuticals Ltd [2004] EWCA Civ 19; [2004] 1
    W.L.R. 1784; (2004) 101(8) L.S.G. 29 ....*30–008, 30–029, 30–047*

Sharp v Pereira [1999] 1 W.L.R. 195; [1998] 4 All E.R. 145; [1999] R.T.R. 125; [1999]
    Lloyd's Rep. I.R. 242; [1998] P.I.Q.R. Q129 .... *41–093*

Sharratt v London Central Bus Co Ltd [2003] EWCA Civ 718; [2003] 4 All E.R. 590 .... *16–056*

Shawton Engineering Ltd v DGP International Ltd (t/a Design Group Partnership) [2005]
    EWCA Civ 1359; [2006] B.L.R. 1; (2006) 22 Const. L.J. 129, CA (Civ Div) *12–038, 21–014*

Shearson Lehman Hutton Inc v Maclaine Watson & Co Ltd (Damages and Interest) [1990]
    3 All E.R. 723; [1990] 1 Lloyd's Rep. 441QBD (Comm) *34–120*

Shinedean Ltd v Alldown Demolition (London) Ltd (In Liquidation) [2006] EWCA Civ
    939; *The Times*, July 26, 2006, CA (Civ Div) *41–064*

Shirayama Shokusan Co Ltd v Danovo Ltd (No.1) [2003] EWHC 3306; [2004] B.L.R. 207,
    Ch D *32–048, 37–254A*

Shogun Finance Ltd v Hudson [2003] UKHL 62; [2004] 1 A.C. 919; [2003] 3 W.L.R. 1371;
    [2004] 1 All E.R. 215; [2004] 1 All E.R. (Comm.) 332; [2004] 1 Lloyd's Rep. 532;
    [2004] R.T.R. 12; (2003) 100(46) L.S.G. 25; (2003) 153 N.L.J. 1790; (2003) 147
    S.J.L.B. 1368 .... *5–078—5–082A, 12–122*

Simoco Digital UK Ltd; Thunderbird Industries LLC v Simoco Digital UK Ltd [2004]
    EWHC 209; [2004] 1 B.C.L.C. 541 .... *21–013, 24–030*

Simpson v Grant & Bowman Ltd [2006] Eu. L.R. 933, QBD *31–131*

Sinclair v Woods of Winchester Ltd [2005] EWHC 1631; 102 Con. L.R. 127, QBD *32–073,
                                                    32–119, 32–137, 32–148, 32–149*

Sinclair Investment Holdings SA v Versailles Trade Finance Ltd (In Administrative Receiv-
    ership) [2005] EWCA Civ 722; [2006] 1 B.C.L.C. 60, CA (Civ Div) *29–160*

Sinochem International Oil (London) Co Ltd v Fortune Oil Co Ltd [2000] 1 Lloyd's Rep.
    682, QBD (Comm) *32–065*

Sirius International Insurance Co (Publ) v FAI General Insurance Ltd; sub nom. Sirius
    International Insurance Corp Ltd v FAI General Insurance Co Ltd [2004] UKHL 54;
    [2004] 1 W.L.R. 3251; [2005] 1 All E.R. 191; [2005] 1 All E.R. (Comm) 117; [2005]
    1 Lloyd's Rep. 461; [2005] Lloyd's Rep. I.R. 294; (2004) 101(48) L.S.G. 25; (2004)
    148 S.J.L.B. 1435; *The Times*, December 3, 2004, HL *12–050, 12–057, 12–118, **34–491A**,
                                                    34–491B, 41–051A, 41–054, 41–064*

Slater v Buckinghamshire County Council [2004] EWHC 77; [2004] Lloyd's Rep. I.R.
    432 .... *41–091*

Slowey v Lodder [1904] A.C. 442, PC (NZ); affirming (1900) N.Z.L.R. 321 .... *29–068*

Smith, Re (1892) 67 L.T. 64 .... *1–082H*

Smith v Reliance Water Controls Ltd [2003] EWCA Civ 1153; [2004] E.C.C. 38; [2003] Eu.
    L.R. 874, CA (Civ Div) *31–005, 39–025*

SmithKline Beecham Plc v Apotex Europe Ltd [2006] EWCA Civ 658; (2006) 103(23)
    L.S.G. 32; (2006) 156 N.L.J. 952; *The Times*, June 9, 2006, CA (Civ Div) *3–107, 3–113,
                                                    18–051, 18–056*

Sobelgra NV v Nationale Maatschappij der Belgische Spoorwegen (NMBS) (1997) 33
    E.T.L. 714 .... *36–089*

Societa Esplosivi Industriali SpA v Ordnance Technologies (UK) Ltd (formerly SEI (UK)
    Ltd) [2004] EWHC 48; [2004] 1 All E.R. (Comm) 619, Ch D *13–006, 16–083*

Solectron Scotland Ltd v Roper [2004] I.R.L.R. 4, EAT *39–166*

Sookraj v Samaroo [2004] UKPC 50; (2004) 148 S.J.L.B. 1244; [2005] 1 P. & C.R. DG11,
    PC (Trin) *22–028, 24–013*

South Buckinghamshire DC v Flanagan; sub nom. Flanagan v South Bucks DC [2002]
    EWCA Civ 690; [2002] 1 W.L.R. 2601; [2002] J.P.L. 1465; (2002) 99(25) L.S.G. 35;
    (2002) 146 S.J.L.B. 136; [2002] N.P.C. 71, CA (Civ Div) *10–017*

South Caribbean Trading Ltd v Trafigura Beheer BV [2004] EWHC 2676; [2005] 1 Lloyd's
Rep. 128, QBD (Comm) *3–066, 3–069, 3–076, 3–079, 3–096, 24–013, 24–014, 43–274A,*
43–275
South East Sheffield Citizens Advice Bureau v Grayson [2004] I.R.L.R. 353, EAT *39–009*
Specialist Ceiling Services Northern Ltd v ZVI Construction (UK) Ltd [2004] B.L.R. 403,
QBD (TCC) *37–260*
Spectrum Plus Ltd (In Liquidation), Re; sub nom. National Westminster Bank Plc v
Spectrum Plus Ltd (In Creditors Voluntary Liquidation) [2005] UKHL 41; [2005] 2
A.C. 680; [2005] 3 W.L.R. 58; [2005] 4 All E.R. 209; [2005] 2 Lloyd's Rep. 275;
[2005] B.C.C. 694; [2005] 2 B.C.L.C. 269; (2005) 155 N.L.J. 1045, HL *29–048*
Sphere Drake Insurance Ltd v Euro International Underwriting Ltd [2003] EWHC 2376,
QBD (Comm) *31–042*
Sport International Bussum BV v Inter-Footwear [1984] 1 W.L.R. 776; [1984] 2 All E.R.
321; (1984) 81 L.S.G. 1992; (1984) 134 N.L.J. 568; (1984) 128 S.J. 383, HL *38–308*
Squirrell Ltd v National Westminster Bank Plc [2005] EWHC 664; [2005] 2 All E.R. 784;
[2005] 1 All E.R. (Comm) 749; *The Times,* May 25, 2005, Ch D *34–317*
St George Soccer Football Association Inc v Soccer NSW Ltd [2005] N.S.W.S.C. 1288 .... *10–025*
St George's Investment Co v Gemini Consulting Ltd [2004] EWHC 2353; [2005] 01 E.G.
96; [2005] 1 P. & C.R. DG12, Ch D *32–073, 32–137, 32–138*
Staffordshire Sentinel Newspapers Ltd v Potter [2004] I.R.L.R. 752, EAT *39–022*
Stancliffe Stone Co Ltd v Peak District National Park Authority [2004] EWHC 1475;
[2004] All E.R. (D) 232 .... *10–017*
Standard Chartered Bank v Banque Marocaine du Commerce Exterieur [2006] EWHC 413;
[2006] All E.R. (D) 213 (Feb), Ch D *5–015*
Standard Chartered Bank v Pakistan National Shipping Corp. (No.2) [2002] UKHL 43;
[2003] 1 A.C. 959; [2002] 3 W.L.R. 1547; [2003] 1 All E.R. 173; [2002] 2 All E.R.
(Comm.) 931; [2003] 1 Lloyd's Rep. 227; [2002] B.C.C. 846; [2003] 1 B.C.L.C. 244;
[2002] C.L.C. 1330; (2003) 100(1) L.S.G. 26; (2002) 146 S.J.L.B. 258 ......*6–036, 6–063*
State Securities plc v Initial Industry Ltd [2004] All E.R. (D) 317 ......*21–015, 22–044A, 24–003*
Static Control Components (Europe) Ltd v Egan; sub nom. Egan v Static Control Compo-
nents (Europe) Ltd [2004] EWCA Civ 392; [2004] 2 Lloyd's Rep. 429; (2004) 148
S.J.L.B. 507, CA (Civ Div) *12–050, 12–118, 44–057*
Stevens v Bower; sub nom. Bower v Stevens [2004] EWCA Civ 496; [2004] I.C.R. 1582;
[2004] I.R.L.R. 957; (2004) 148 S.J.L.B. 475; *The Times,* May 24, 2004, CA (Civ
Div) *39–172*
Stevens v Head, 176 C.L.R. 433, HC (Aus) *30–150*
Stevenson v Dudley Social Services [2006] 3 C.L. 90 .... *38–037*
Stilk v Myrick (1809) 2 Camp. 317 .... *3–069*
Strachan v Universal Stock Exchange Ltd (No.1); sub nom. Universal Stock Exchange Ltd
v Strachan (No.1) [1896] A.C. 166, HL *40–032*
Stretch v United Kingdom (2004) 38 E.H.R.R. 12; [2004] 03 E.G. 100; [2003] 29 E.G.C.S.
118; [2003] N.P.C. 125 ....*10–015A*
Stromdale & Ball Ltd v Burden [1952] Ch. 223; [1952] 1 All E.R. 59; [1951] 2 T.L.R. 1192,
Ch D *1–082H*
Strover v Strover [2005] EWHC 860; [2005] N.P.C. 64; *The Times,* May 30, 2005, Ch D *3–145*
Sukuman Ltd v Commonwealth Secretariat [2006] EWHC 304; [2006] 1 All E.R. (Comm)
621; [2006] 2 Lloyd's Rep. 53; [2006] 1 C.L.C. 394, QBD (Comm) *1–039, 12–014, 32–016,*
32–144
Super Chem Products Ltd v American Life & General Insurance Co Ltd [2004] UKPC 2;
[2004] 2 All E.R. 358; [2004] 1 All E.R. (Comm.) 713; (2004) 148 S.J.L.B. 113 ....*3–090,*
28–109, 41–065
Surefire Systems Ltd v Guardian ECL Ltd [2005] EWHC 1860; [2005] B.L.R. 534, QBD
(TCC) *32–141, 32–142*
Susie Radin Ltd v GMB [2004] EWCA Civ 180; [2004] 2 All E.R. 279; [2004] I.R.L.R.
400; (2004) 101(11) L.S.G. 34; (2004) 148 S.J.L.B. 266 .... *39–256*
Sutherland Shire Council v Heyman [1955–95] P.N.L.R. 238; 157 C.L.R. 424; (1985) 60
A.L.R. 1; (1985) 59 A.L.J.R. 564; (1986) 2 Const. L.J. 161, HC (Aus) *1–157*
Sutton v Hutchinson [2005] EWCA Civ 1773CA (Civ Div) *16–161*
Sutton v Mishcon Reya [2003] EWHC 3166; [2004] 1 F.L.R. 837; [2004] Fam. Law 247 ..... *2–178*

Svenska Petroleum Exploration AB v Lithuania [2005] EWHC 9; [2005] 1 All E.R.
  (Comm) 515; [2005] 1 Lloyd's Rep. 515, QBD (Comm) *11–005*, *32–160*
Svenska Petroleum Exploration AB v Lithuania (No.2) [2005] EWHC 2437; [2006] 1 All
  E.R. (Comm) 731; [2006] 1 Lloyd's Rep. 181; [2005] 2 C.L.C. 965; (2005) 102(47)
  L.S.G. 26, QBD (Comm) *11–004*, *11–005*, *11–020*, *11–021*
Sweeney v Boylan Nominees Pty Ltd [2006] HCS 19, (2006) 80 A.L.J.R. 900 .... *31–074*
Swiss Reinsurance Co v United India Insurance Co Ltd [2005] EWHC 237; [2005] 1 C.L.C.
  203; [2005] Lloyd's Rep. I.R. 341, QBD (Comm) *41–031*, *41–051*

T&N Ltd, Re [2005] EWHC 2870; [2006] 1 W.L.R. 1728; [2006] B.P.I.R. 532, Ch D
  (Companies Ct) 1–039
TCB Ltd v Gray [1987] Ch. 458; [1987] 3 W.L.R. 1144; [1988] 1 All E.R. 108; (1987) 3
  B.C.C. 503; [1988] B.C.L.C. 281; [1988] Fin. L.R. 116, CA (Civ Div) ... *1–082H*
TFS Derivatives Ltd v Morgan [2004] EWHC 3181; [2005] I.R.L.R. 246, QBD *16–114*
Tajik Aluminium Plant v Hydro Aluminium AS [2005] EWCA Civ 1218; [2006] 1 W.L.R.
  767; [2005] 4 All E.R. 1232; [2006] 1 Lloyd's Rep. 155; [2006] C.P. Rep. 7; [2005]
  2 C.L.C. 604, CA (Civ Div) *32–100*
Talbot v Von Boris [1911] 1 K.B. 854, CA 34–083
Talbot Underwriting Ltd v Nausch Hogan & Murray Inc [2006] EWCA Civ 889, CA (Civ
  Div) *31–065*, *41–008*
Tamarind International Ltd v Eastern Natural Gas (Retail) Ltd [2000] C.L.C. 1397; [2000]
  Eu. L.R. 708; (2000) 97(26) L.S.G. 35, QBD (Comm) *31–005*
Tame Shipping Ltd v Easy Navigation Ltd (The Easy Rider) [2004] EWHC 1862; [2004]
  2 All E.R. (Comm) 521; [2004] 2 Lloyd's Rep. 626; [2004] 2 C.L.C. 1155; *The Times*,
  November 8, 2004, QBD (Comm) *32–115*, *32–137*, 32–145
Targe Towing Ltd v Marine Blast ltd [2004] EWCA Civ 346; [2004] 1 Lloyd's Rep.721 ....*31–044*,
                                                                                            33–026
Tayeb v HSBC Bank plc [2004] EWHC Comm 1529 ...*34–304*, *34–317*, *34–379*, 34–402, *34–406*
Taylor v Motability Finance Ltd [2004] EWHC 2619, QBD (Comm) *29–002*
Taylor v Rive Droite Music Ltd [2005] EWCA Civ 1300; [2006] E.M.L.R. 4, CA (Civ
  Div) *12–078*, *13–012*
Tektrol Ltd (formerly Atto Power Controls Ltd) v International Insurance Co of Hanover
  Ltd [2005] EWCA Civ 845; [2006] 1 All E.R. (Comm) 780; [2005] 2 Lloyd's Rep.
  701; [2005] 2 C.L.C. 339; [2006] Lloyd's Rep. I.R. 38, CA (Civ Div); reversing [2004]
  EWHC 2473; [2005] 1 All E.R. (Comm) 132; [2005] Lloyd's Rep. I.R. 358, QBD
  (Comm) *12–083*, *12–085*, *41–051A*, *41–054*
Tekron Resources Ltd v Guinea Investment Co Ltd [2003] EWHC Comm 2577; [2004] 2
  Lloyd's Rep.26 ....*16–028*, *30–067*, *30–141*, *30–174*
Tennaro Ltd v Majorarch Ltd; sub nom. Tennero Ltd v Majorarch Ltd [2003] EWHC 2601;
  [2003] 47 E.G.C.S. 154; [2004] 1 P. & C.R. DG13, Ch D *21–013*
Tesco Stores Ltd v Pook [2003] EWHC 823; [2004] I.R.L.R. 618, Ch D *39–060*
Thames Valley Power Ltd v Total Gas & Power Ltd [2005] EWHC 2208; [2006] 1 Lloyd's
  Rep. 441, QBD (Comm) *12–051*, *14–140*, *27–008*, *27–011*, *27–017*, *27–025*, 32–166
Thew v Cole [2003] EWCA Civ 1828, The Times, January 15, 2004 .... *38–037*
Thompson Monella v Pizza Express (Restaurants) Ltd [2003] EWHC 2966; [2004] 12 E.G.
  172 .... *32–054*
Thompson v Christie Manson & Woods Ltd [2004] EWHC 1101 .... *43–046*
Thor Navigation Inc v Ingosstrakh Insurance Co Ltd [2005] EWHC 19; [2005] 1 Lloyd's
  Rep. 547; [2005] 1 C.L.C. 12, QBD (Comm) *3–107*, *3–109*, *12–079*, *41–074*
Thoresen & Co (Bangkok) Ltd v Fathom Marine Co [2004] EWHC 167; [2004] 1 All E.R.
  (Comm.) 935; [2004] 1 Lloyd's Rep. 622 .... *2–114*
Through Transport Mutual Insurance Association (Eurasia) Ltd v New India Assurance Co
  Ltd (The Hari Bhum) [2004] EWCA Civ 1598; [2005] 1 All E.R. (Comm) 715; [2005]
  1 Lloyd's Rep. 67; [2004] 2 C.L.C. 1189; [2005] I.L.Pr. 30; (2004) 148 S.J.L.B. 1435,
  CA (Civ Div) *32–042*, *32–065*
Thyssen Canada Ltd v Mariana Maritime SA [2005] EWHC 219; [2005] 1 Lloyd's Rep.
  640, QBD (Comm) *32–137*, *32–148*, *32–149*
Tiffany Investments Ltd v Bircham & Co Nominees (No.2) Ltd [2003] EWCA Civ 1759;
  [2004] 2 P. & C.R. 10; [2004] L. & T.R. 22; [2004] 2 E.G.L.R. 31; [2004] 21 E.G. 152,
  CA (Civ Div) *2–125*

Tilby v Perfect Pizza Ltd (2002) 152 N.L.J. 397, Sup Ct Costs Office *38–017*
Tinsley v Milligan [1994] 1 A.C. 340 16–175
Tioxide Europe Ltd v Commercial Union Assurance Co Plc [2005] EWCA Civ 928; [2005]
    All E.R. (D) 281 .... *41–064*
Tonicstar Ltd (t/a Lloyds Syndicate 1861) v American Home Assurance Co [2004] EWHC
    1234; [2005] Lloyd's Rep. I.R. 32, QBD (Comm) *30–050, 30–075, 32–007*
Toomey v Banco Vitalicio de Espana SA de Seguros y Reaseguros [2004] EWCA Civ 622;
    [2004] 1 C.L.C. 965; (2004) 148 S.J.L.B. 633, CA (Civ Div) *41–053, 41–094*
Tootal Clothing Ltd v Guinea Properties Management Ltd (1992) 64 P. & C.R. 452; [1992]
    41 E.G. 117; [1992] E.G.C.S. 80; [1992] N.P.C. 75; *The Times*, June 8, 1992;
    Independent, June 8, 1992, CA (Civ Div) *4–064*
Torch Offshore LLC v Cable Shipping Inc [2004] EWHC 787; [2004] 2 All E.R. (Comm)
    365; [2004] 2 Lloyd's Rep. 446; [2004] 2 C.L.C. 433, QBD (Comm) *32–119, 32–137,*
                                                               32–138, 32–148
Total Spares & Supplies Ltd v Antares SRL [2004] EWHC 2626, Ch D *24–015*
Townends Group Ltd v Cobb (2005) 102(4) L.S.G. 30; *The Times*, December 1, 2004, Ch
    D *16–104, 27–060*
Tradigrain SA v State Trading Corp of India [2005] EWHC 2206; [2006] 1 All E.R.
    (Comm) 197; [2006] 1 Lloyd's Rep. 216; [2005] 2 C.L.C. 589, QBD (Comm) *44–014*
Trans Trust S.P.R.L. v Danubian Trading Co Ltd [1952] 2 Q.B. 297; [1952] 1 All E.R. 970;
    [1952] 1 Lloyd's Rep. 348; [1952] 1 T.L.R. 1066; 96 S.J. 312 ....26–095C
Transports Collomb Muret auto SA v Panini France SA (2004) 39 E.T.L. 531 .... *36–145*
Travelers Casualty & Surety Co of Europe Ltd v Sun Life Assurance Co of Canada (UK)
    Ltd [2004] EWHC 1704; [2004] I.L.Pr. 50; [2004] Lloyd's Rep. I.R. 846, QBD
    (Comm) *30–050, 30–054, 30–069, 41–068*
Triodos Bank NV v Dobbs; sub nom. Triodosbank NV v Dobbs [2005] EWCA Civ 630;
    [2005] 2 Lloyd's Rep. 588; [2005] 2 C.L.C. 95; *The Times*, May 30, 2005, CA (Civ
    Div) *3–107, 44–096*
Tryg Baltica International (UK) Ltd v Boston Compania de Seguros SA [2004] EWHC
    1186; [2005] Lloyd's Rep. I.R. 40, QBD (Comm) *30–050, 30–053*
TTI Team Telecom International Ltd v Hutchinson 3G UK Ltd [2003] EWHC 762; [2003]
    1 All E.R. (Comm.) 914 ....*34–489, 34–491B*
Tupper v Foulkes, 142 E.R. 314; (1861) 9 C.B. N.S. 797 .... *1–082E*
Turcan, Re (1889) L.R. 40 Ch. D. 5, CA 19–045
Turkey v Awadh [2005] EWCA Civ 382; [2005] 2 F.C.R. 7; [2005] 2 P. & C.R. 29; [2006]
    W.T.L.R. 553, CA (Civ Div) *7–049, 7–070A, 7–073*
Turner v Steinhoff UK Furniture Ltd [2006] Eu. L.R. 50, CC (Taunton) *31–131*
Twinsectra Ltd v Yardley [2002] UKHL 12; [2002] 2 A.C. 164; [2002] 2 W.L.R. 802;
    [2002] 2 All E.R. 377; [2002] P.N.L.R. 30; [2002] W.T.L.R. 423; [2002] 38 E.G.C.S.
    204; (2002) 99(19) L.S.G. 32; (2002) 152 N.L.J. 469; (2002) 146 S.J.L.B. 84; [2002]
    N.P.C. 47, HL 34–290

UCB Group Ltd v Hedworth [2003] EWCA Civ 1717; [2003] 3 F.C.R. 739; (2004) 101(4)
    L.S.G. 30; (2003) 147 S.J.L.B. 1428; [2004] 1 P. & C.R. D21 .... *34–271*
UCB Corporate Services Ltd v Kohli [2004] EWHC 1126; [2004] 2 All E.R. (Comm) 422,
    Ch D *28–100, 28–103*
UCB Corporate Services Ltd v Thomason [2005] EWCA Civ 225; [2005] 1 All E.R.
    (Comm) 601, CA (Civ Div); affirming [2004] EWHC 1164; [2004] 2 All E.R. (Comm)
    774, Ch D *6–099, 12–118*
Ultra Motorhomes International Ltd, Re; sub nom. Oakley v Ultra Vehicle Design Ltd (In
    Liquidation) [2005] EWHC 872, Ch D *30–049*
Ultraframe (UK) Ltd v Fielding; Northstar Systems Ltd (In Liquidation) v Fielding;
    Burnden Group Plc v Northstar Systems Ltd (In Liquidation) [2005] EWHC 1638;
    [2006] F.S.R. 17; (2005) 28(9) I.P.D. 28069, Ch D *31–073*
Ultraframe (UK) Ltd v Tailored Roofing Systems Ltd [2004] EWCA Civ 585; [2004] 2 All
    E.R. (Comm) 692; [2004] B.L.R. 341, CA (Civ Div) *13–010, 37–067*
Unique Pub Properties Ltd v Beer Barrels & Minerals (Wales) Ltd [2004] EWCA Civ 586;
    [2005] 1 All E.R. (Comm) 181; [2004] N.P.C. 77, CA (Civ Div) *18–127*
United States v Motor Trucks Ltd [1924] A.C. 196, PC (Can) 44–049A
United Trading Corp. v Allied Arab Bank Ltd [1985] 2 Lloyd's Rep. 554 .... *34–402*

University of Edinburgh v Onifade, 2005 S.L.T. (Sh Ct) 63; 2005 G.W.D. 5–60, Sh Pr *2–014*,
2–025, 2–028
Uren v First National Home Finance Ltd [2005] EWHC 2529; *The Times*, November 17,
2005, Ch D *29–015, 29–016, 29–018, 29–024, 29–025*
US International Marketing Ltd v National Bank of New Zealand Ltd, CA 144/02, October
28, 2003 .... *34–288*

Vakante v Addey & Stanhope School [2004] EWCA Civ 1065; [2004] I.C.R. 279, CA *16–161*,
39–032
Vale do Rio doce Navegacao SA v Shanghai Bao Steel Ocean Shipping Co Ltd (t/a Bao
Steel Ocean Shipping Co); sub nom. Vale do Rio doce Navegacao SA v Shanghai Bao
Steel Ocean Shipping Co Ltd (t/a Baosteel Ocean Shipping Co) [2000] 2 All E.R.
(Comm) 70; [2000] 2 Lloyd's Rep. 1; [2000] C.L.C. 1200; *The Times*, May 16, 2000,
QBD (Comm) *32–065, 32–081, 32–112*, 32–132
Van Laethem v Brooker [2005] EWHC 1478; [2006] 1 F.C.R. 697; [2006] Fam. Law 537;
[2005] N.P.C. 91, Ch D *3–139, 3–146*
Vee Networks Ltd v Econet Wireless International Ltd [2004] EWHC 2909; [2005] 1 All
E.R. (Comm) 303; [2005] 1 Lloyd's Rep. 192, QBD (Comm) *32–023, 32–079, 32–134*,
32–137, 32–138, 32–149
Vick v Vogle-Gapes Ltd [2006] EWHC 1665; (2006) 150 S.J.L.B. 917, QBD *31–131, 31–147*,
31–149
Vincent v Premo Enterprises (Voucher Sales) [1969] 2 Q.B. 609; [1969] 2 W.L.R. 1256;
[1969] 2 All E.R. 941; (1969) 20 P. & C.R. 591; (1969) 113 S.J. 266, CA (Civ Div) *1–082E*
Virani Ltd v Manuel Revert y Cia SA [2003] EWCA Civ 1651; [2004] 2 Lloyd's Rep. 14,
CA (Civ Div) *30–180*
Vitesse Yacht Charterers SL v Spiers (The Deverne II) [2003] EWHC 2426; [2004] 1
Lloyd's Rep.179 .... *18–012*
Vodafone Ltd v GNT Holdings (UK) Ltd [2004] All E.R. (D) 194 44–057
Vrinera Marine Co Ltd v Eastern Rich Operations Inc (The Vakis T) [2004] EWHC 1752;
[2004] 2 Lloyd's Rep. 465; [2004] 2 C.L.C. 1148, QBD (Comm) *32–143*

WPP Holdings Italy SRL v Benatti [2006] EWHC 1641, QBD (Comm) *30–107*
WWF World Wide Fund for Nature (formerly World Wildlife Fund) v World Wrestling
Federation Entertainment Inc [2006] EWHC 184; [2006] F.S.R. 38; (2006) 150
S.J.L.B. 263, Ch D 29–154
Wadsworth v Lydell [1981] 1 W.L.R. 598; [1981] 2 All E.R. 401; 125 S.J. 309 ....26–095C
Waldwiese Sftung v Lewis [2004] EWHC 2589, Ch D *30–036, 30–073, 30–075, 30–088, 30–116*,
30–117
Walford v Miles [1992] 2 A.C. 128; [1992] 2 W.L.R. 174; [1992] 1 All E.R. 453; (1992) 64
P. & C.R. 166; [1992] 1 E.G.L.R. 207; [1992] 11 E.G. 115; [1992] N.P.C. 4; *The Times*,
January 27, 1992; *Independent*, January 29, 1992, HL 1–020, *2–135, 37–050A*
Wall v British Compressed Air Society [2003] EWCA Civ 1762; [2004] I.C.R. 408; [2004]
I.R.L.R. 147; [2004] Pens. L.R. 87; (2004) 101(5) L.S.G. 28; (2003) 153 N.L.J.
1903 .... *39–208*
Warborough Investments Ltd v S Robinson & Sons (Holdings) Ltd [2003] EWCA Civ 751;
[2004] 2 P. & C.R. 6; [2003] 2 E.G.L.R. 149; (2003) 100(24) L.S.G. 38; (2003) 147
S.J.L.B. 748; [2003] N.P.C. 75; *The Times*, July 9, 2003, CA (Civ Div) *32–073, 32–137*
Warnborough Ltd v Garmite Ltd [2006] EWHC 10; [2006] 3 E.G.C.S. 121, Ch D 21–056
Waters v Monarch Fire & Life Assurance Co [1834–60] All E.R. Rep. 654; (1856) 5 El. &
Bl. 870, QBD *18–120*
Wethered Estate Ltd v Davis [2005] EWHC 1903; [2006] B.L.R. 86; (2005) 102(39) L.S.G.
29, Ch D 37–254A
Webley v Department for Work and Pensions; sub nom. Department for Work and Pensions
v Webley [2004] EWCA Civ 1745; [2005] I.C.R. 577; [2005] I.R.L.R. 288; (2005)
102(8) L.S.G. 30; *The Times*, January 17, 2005; *Independent*, January 13, 2005, CA
(Civ Div) 39–149
Weill v Mean Fiddler Holdings Ltd [2003] EWCA Civ 1058, CA (Civ Div) 18–046, *27–039*
Well Barn Farming Ltd v Backhouse [2005] EWHC 1520; [2005] 3 E.G.L.R. 109, Ch D *3–015*,
3–024

Wessex Reserve Forces and Cadets Association v White [2005] EWHC 983; [2005] 22
E.G.C.S. 132, QBD 22–045
West Bromwich Albion Football Club Ltd v El-Safty [2005] EWHC 2866; [2006] Lloyd's
Rep. Med. 139; (2006) 88 B.M.L.R. 196; [2006] P.N.L.R. 18, QBD 18–031
West Tankers Inc v RAS Riunione Adriatica di Sicurta (The Front Comor) [2005] EWHC
454; [2005] 1 C.L.C. 347, QBD (Comm) 30–119, 30–120, 32–042
Westdeutsche Landesbank Girozentrale v Islington LBC; Kleinwort Benson Ltd v Sandwell
BC; sub nom. Islington LBC v Westdeutsche Landesbank Girozentrale [1996] A.C.
669; [1996] 2 W.L.R. 802; [1996] 2 All E.R. 961; [1996] 5 Bank. L.R. 341; [1996]
C.L.C. 990; 95 L.G.R. 1; (1996) 160 J.P. Rep. 1130; (1996) 146 N.L.J. 877; (1996) 140
S.J.L.B. 136; *The Times*, May 30, 1996, HL 6–064
Western Power Investments Ltd v Teeside Power Ltd, unreported, February 18, 2005, Ch
D 16–199
Westland Helicopters Ltd v Al-Hejailan [2004] EWHC 1625; [2004] 2 Lloyd's Rep. 523,
QBD (Comm) 32–079, 32–112, 32–134, 32–137, 32–148, 32–149
Westminster Building Co Ltd v Beckingham [2004] EWHC 138; [2004] B.L.R. 163; [2004]
B.L.R. 265; [2004] T.C.L.R. 8; 94 Con. L.R. 107, QBD (TCC) 2–074, 15–072
Wheeler v Quality Deep Ltd (t/a Thai Royale Restaurant); sub nom. Wheeler v Qualitydeep
Ltd (t/a Thai Royale Restaurant) [2004] EWCA Civ 1085; [2005] I.C.R. 265; (2004)
101(35) L.S.G. 33; *The Times*, August 30, 2004, CA (Civ Div) 16–161, 39–032
White v Baycorp Information Services Ltd [2006] N.S.W.S.C. 441 31–065
Wight v Eckhardt Marine GmbH; sub nom. Wight v Eckhardt GmbH [2003] UKPC 37;
[2004] 1 A.C. 147; [2003] 3 W.L.R. 414; [2003] B.C.C. 702; [2004] 2 B.C.L.C. 539;
The Times, June 6, 2003, PC (CI) 30–158
Wilkinson v West Bromwich Building Society; sub nom. West Bromwich Building Society
v Wilkinson [2005] UKHL 44; [2005] 1 W.L.R. 2303; *The Times*, July 4, 2005;
Independent, July 7, 2005, HL 28–003
Williams v Fanshaw Porter 7 Hazelhurst [2004] EWCA Civ 157; [2004] 2 All E.R. 616 28–086
Williams v Roffey Bros & Nicholls (Contractors) Ltd [1991] 1 Q.B. 1; [1990] 2 W.L.R.
1153; [1990] 1 All E.R. 512; 48 B.L.R. 69; (1991) 10 Tr. L.R. 12; (1990) 87(12) L.S.G.
36; (1989) 139 N.L.J. 1712, CA (Civ Div) 3–069
Willis Management (Isle of Man) Ltd v Cable & Wireless Plc; sub nom. Cable & Wireless
Plc v Valentine [2005] EWCA Civ 806; [2005] 2 Lloyd's Rep. 597, CA (Civ Div) 2–124,
2–128, 2–134, 2–139
Wilson v Circular Distributors Ltd [2006] I.R.L.R. 38, EAT 39–023
Wilson v First County Trust (No.2) [2003] UKHL 40; [2004] 1 A.C. 816; [2003] 3 W.L.R.
568; [2003] 4 All E.R. 97; [2003] 2 All E.R. (Comm.) 491; [2003] H.R.L.R. 33; [2003]
U.K.H.R.R. 1085; (2003) 100(35) L.S.G. 39; (2003) 147 S.J.L.B. 872 ......1–032, 1–039, 38–044
Wilson v Robertsons (London) Ltd [2005] EWHC 1425; [2006] 1 W.L.R. 1248; [2005] 3
All E.R. 873; (2005) 102(30) L.S.G. 29; *The Times*, July 28, 2005, Ch D 14–125, 38–008,
38–020
Wise Group v Mitchell [2005] I.C.R. 896, EAT 39–193
WISE (Underwriting Agency) Ltd v Grupo Nacional Provincial SA [2004] EWCA Civ 962;
[2004] All E.R. (D) 356 .... 41–030, 41–036
Woolwich Building Society (formerly Woolwich Equitable Building Society) v Inland
Revenue Commissioners [1993] A.C. 70; [1992] 3 W.L.R. 366; [1992] 3 All E.R. 737;
[1992] S.T.C. 657; (1993) 5 Admin. L.R. 265; 65 T.C. 265; (1992) 142 N.L.J. 1196;
(1992) 136 S.J.L.B. 230; *The Times*, July 22, 1992; *Independent*, August 13, 1992;
Guardian, August 19, 1992, HL 29–094
World Trade Corp Ltd v C Czarnikow Sugar Ltd [2004] EWHC 2332; [2004] 2 All E.R.
(Comm) 813; [2005] 1 Lloyd's Rep. 422, QBD (Comm) 32–119, 32–137, 32–148
Wrexham Associated Football Club Ltd (In Administration) v Crucialmove Ltd [2006]
EWCA Civ 237, CA (Civ Div) 31–042
Wroth v Tyler [1974] Ch. 30; [1973] 2 W.L.R. 405; [1973] 1 All E.R. 897; 25 P. & C.R. 138;
(1972) 117 S.J. 90 ....26–098A

X v Y (Employment: Sex Offender) [2004] EWCA Civ 662; [2004] I.R.L.R. 625 39–215
X Ltd v Y Ltd [2005] EWHC 769; [2005] B.L.R. 341; [2005] T.C.L.R. 5, QBD (TCC) 32–025
Xenos v Wickman (1863) 14 C.B. (N.S.) 435 .... 1–082E

Yarmouth (Isle of Wight) Harbour Commissioners v Harold Hayles (Yarmouth Isle of
   Wight) Ltd [2004] EWHC 3375, Ch D 10–017
Yaxley v Gotts; sub nom. Yaxley v Gott [2000] Ch. 162; [1999] 3 W.L.R. 1217; [2000] 1
   All E.R. 711; [1999] 2 F.L.R. 941; (2000) 32 H.L.R. 547; (2000) 79 P. & C.R. 91;
   [1999] 2 E.G.L.R. 181; [1999] Fam. Law 700; [1999] E.G.C.S. 92; (1999) 96(28)
   L.S.G. 25; (1999) 143 S.J.L.B. 198; [1999] N.P.C. 76; (1999) 78 P. & C.R. D33; *The
   Times*, July 8, 1999; *Independent*, July 6, 1999, CA (Civ Div) *3–139*
Yorkshire Bank plc v Tinsley [2004] EWCA Civ 816; [2004] 3 All E.R. 463 ...... *7–106A*, *29–137*,
                                                                                      34–271

Zaporozhyve production Society v Ashly Ltd [2002] EWHC Comm 1410 .... *32–123, 32–132, 32–133*
Zebrarise Ltd v De Nieffe [2004] EWHC 1842; [2005] 2 All E.R. (Comm) 816; [2005] 1
   Lloyd's Rep. 154, QBD (Comm) *30–002, 30–010, 30–037, 30–152, 30–159*

TABLE OF EUROPEAN CASES

Where a reference indicates significant discussion of the case in the text, it is in **bold**. Where a reference is to a footnote, it is *italic*.

Allonby v Accrington & Rossendale College (C–256/01) [2004] 1 C.M.L.R. 35; [2004]
I.R.L.R. 224; [2004] Pens. L.R. 199, ECJ *39–122*

Commission of the European Communities v Spain (C70/03), unreported, September 9,
2004, ECJ *15–092*, 15–093, *30–100*

Criminal Proceedings against Arblade (C369/96); Criminal Proceedings against Leloup
(C376/96) [1999] E.C.R. I–8453; [2001] I.C.R. 434, ECJ *30–061*

DaimlerChrysler v Commission of the European Communities (T325/01), unreported,
September 15, 2005, CFI 42–059

easyCar (UK) Ltd v Office of Fair Trading (C336/03) [2005] 2 C.M.L.R. 2; *The Times*,
March 15, 2005, ECJ (1st Chamber) 38–094

Engler v Janus Versand GmbH (C27/02) [2005] E.C.R. I–481; [2005] C.E.C. 187; [2005]
I.L.Pr. 8, ECJ (2nd Chamber) *30–090*

Evans v Secretary of State for the Environment, Transport and the Regions (C–63/01)
[2004] Lloyd's Rep. I.R. 391, ECJ *41–093*

Federacion Nacional de Empresas de Instrumentacion Cientifica Medica Tecnica y Dental
(FENIN) v Commission of the European Communities (C–205/03), unreported, July
11, 2006, ECJ *42–013*

Freiburger Kommunalbauten GmbH Baugesellschaft & Co KG v Hofstetter (C–237/02)
[2004] 2 C.M.L.R. 13 .... 15–014–15–017, 15–048A

Gaillard v Chekili (C518/99) [2001] E.C.R. I–2771; [2001] I.L.Pr. 33, ECJ (6th
Chamber) *30–080*

Gruber v Baywa AG (C464/01); sub nom. Gruber v Bay Wa AG [2006] Q.B. 204; [2006]
2 W.L.R. 205; [2005] E.C.R. I–439; [2005] I.L.Pr. 12, ECJ (2nd Chamber) *30–090*

Heininger v Bayerische Hypo-und Vereinsbank AG (C–481/99) [2004] All E.R. (EC) 1;
[2001] E.C.R. I–9945; [2003] 2 C.M.L.R. 42; [2004] C.E.C. 202 .... *38–093*

Klein v Rhodos Management Ltd (C73/04) [2005] E.C.R. I–8667; [2006] I.L.Pr. 2 ECJ (1st
Chamber) *30–082*

Lawrence v Regent Office Care Ltd (C320/00) [2002] E.C.R. I–7325; [2002] 3 C.M.L.R.
27; [2003] I.C.R. 1092; [2002] I.R.L.R. 822; [2002] Emp. L.R. 1248, ECJ *39–122*

Manfredi v Lloyd Adriatico Assicurazioni SpA (C295/04), unreported, July 13, 2006,
ECJ 42–066
Martin v South Bank University (C–4/01) [2004] 1 C.M.L.R. 15; [2004] C.E.C. 90; [2004]
I.R.L.R. 74; [2003] Pens. L.R. 329, ECJ 39–171
Microsoft Corp v Commission of the European Communities (T201/04 R 1) [2004] 5
C.M.L.R. 21, CFI 42–063, 42–064

O'Byrne v Sanofi Pasteur MSD Ltd (formerly Aventis Pasteur MSD Ltd) (C127/04) [2006]
1 W.L.R. 1606; [2006] All E.R. (EC) 674; [2006] 2 C.M.L.R. 24; [2006] C.E.C. 493,
ECJ (1st Chamber) 43–148
Océano Grupo Editorial SA v Murciano Quintero (C–240/98 to C–244/98) [2000] E.C.R.
I–4941; [2002] 1 C.M.L.R. 43 .... 15–048A

Poseidon Chartering BV v Marianne Zeeschip Vof (C3/04) [2006] 2 Lloyd's Rep. 105,
ECJ 31–001

Robinson-Steele v RD Retail Services Ltd (C131/04); Clarke v Frank Staddon Ltd
(C257/04); Caulfield v Hanson Clay Products Ltd (C257/04) [2006] 2 C.M.L.R. 34;
[2006] I.C.R. 932; [2006] I.R.L.R. 386, ECJ (1st Chamber) 39–108

Schulte v Deutsche Bausparkasse Badenia AG (C350/03) [2006] All E.R. (EC) 420; [2005]
E.C.R. I–9215; [2006] 1 C.M.L.R. 11; [2006] C.E.C. 115, ECJ 30–100, 38–093

Veedfald v Arhus Amtskommune (C203/99) [2001] E.C.R. I–3569; [2003] 1 C.M.L.R. 41;
(2002) 66 B.M.L.R. 1; The Times, June 4, 2001, ECJ (5th Chamber) 15–032A

Weber's Wine World Handels GmbH v Abgabenberufungskommission Wien (C147/01)
[2005] All E.R. (EC) 224; [2003] E.C.R. I–11365; [2004] 1 C.M.L.R. 7; [2003] C.E.C.
501; [2004] B.T.C. 8019, ECJ (5th Chamber) 29–084

VOLUME I

GENERAL PRINCIPLES

Part One

INTRODUCTION

Chapter 1

INTRODUCTORY

			PARA.
	1.	Definitions of contract	1–001
■	2.	Central principles of contract law	1–010
		(a) Freedom of contract	1–011
		(b) The binding force of contract	1–017
□		(c) A principle of good faith or of contractual fairness?	1–020
■	3.	The Human Rights Act 1998 and contracts	1–029
■		(a) Contracts made before October 2, 2000	1–031
■		(i) The construction and review of legislation governing contracts	1–031
		(ii) Contracts made by "public authorities"	1–033
		(iii) The duty of courts as "public authorities" in relation to contracts	1–037
■		(b) Contracts made on or after October 2, 2000	1–038
□		(i) The construction and review of legislation governing contracts	1–038
■		(ii) Contracts made by "public authorities"	1–042
		(iii) The duty of courts as "public authorities" in relation to contracts	1–048
■		(iv) Contractual confidentiality and section 12 of the 1998 Act	1–055
	4.	Classification of contracts	1–057
		(a) Classification of contracts according to their subject matter	1–058
		(b) Classification of contracts according to their parties	1–063
		(c) Classification of contracts according to their form or means of formation	1–064
		(d) Classification of contracts according to their effect	1–068
■	5.	Contracts contained in deeds	1–075
■		(a) Form and delivery	1–075
■		(i) Deeds executed on or before September 14, 2005	1–080
■		(ii) Deeds executed on or after September 15, 2005	1–082A
		(b) Consideration	1–087
□		(c) Other aspects	1–088
■	6.	The relationship between contract and tort	1–096
		(a) The classification of the forms of action at common law	1–097
		(b) Differences of substance between contract and tort	1–098
		(c) Concurrence of actions in contract and tort	1–105
■		(i) Pre-contractual liability	1–110

[1]

■   (ii) Torts committed in the course of performance of a
                contract   1–116
□   (d) The influence of contract on tort beyond privity   1–148
    7.   Contract and other legal categories   1–166

2. CENTRAL PRINCIPLES OF CONTRACT LAW

(c) *A principle of good faith or of contractual fairness?*

No general principle of good faith

1–020   [*Add new text to note 152: page* [19]]
See similarly *Bernhard Schulte GHBH & Co KG v Nile Holdings Ltd* [2004]
EWHC 977; [2005] 1 A.C. 503 at [113].

However, in *Petromec Inc v Petroleo Brasiliero SA Petrobras (No.3)* [2005]
EWCA Civ 891; [2006] 1 Lloyd's Rep. 121 the Court of Appeal considered that
Lord Ackner's observations regarding duties to negotiate in good faith in *Walford
v Miles* [1992] 2 A.C. 128 at 138, quoted in the text, were not appropriate (nor
binding on it) as regards an express obligation to negotiate in good faith
contained in a complex concluded contract which had been drafted by City of
London solicitors. In *Petromeo,* the question arose as to the enforceability of a
term in a contract supplementing a complex series of contractual arrangements
relating to the purchase, "upgrading" and hire (by bareboat charter) of an oil
production platform, this term providing for the negotiation in good faith of the
cost of the upgrading of the platform for use on a particular oil-field. On the loss
by fire of the platform, a number of preliminary questions arose as to the proper
allocation of the insurance monies, including as to whether earlier "global"
settlement negotiations among the parties fell within this express term and, if so,
whether the term was enforceable. Longmore L.J. (with whom Pill and Mance
L.JJ. agreed at [45] and [124]) held first that the settlement negotiations did *not*
fall within the express term, since it provided for various elements which were
inconsistent with such a global approach and given that the problems of the
enforceability of the obligation to negotiate in good faith would mean that it
would be "restrictively construed in accordance with its exact wording": at
[112]–[113].

However, Longmore L.J. nevertheless considered (though *obiter*) whether the
term would have been enforceable if the negotiations which took place had fallen
within its ambit. In this respect, he considered that there were three traditional
objections to enforcing an obligation to negotiate in good faith: "(1) that the
obligation is an agreement to agree and thus too uncertain to enforce, (2) that it
is difficult, if not impossible, to say where, if negotiations are brought to an end,
the termination is brought about in good or in bad faith, and (3) that, since it can
never be known whether good faith negotiations would have produced an
agreement at all or what the terms of any agreement would have been if it would
have been reached, it is impossible to assess any loss caused by breach of the
obligation" (at [117]). In the context of the contract before him, in the view of
the learned Lord Justice, the first of these objections carried little weight as the
express obligation to negotiate in good faith was contained in a contract which

it was accepted was generally enforceable; and the third objection could be overcome as the obligation to negotiate in question related to a limited aspect of the extra costs involved in the upgrade of the platform and so, if agreement were not reached, the court could itself ascertain the losses arising, these being likely to be the same as the reasonable cost of the upgrade: at [117]. However, Longmore L.J. accepted that "[i]t is the second objection that is likely to give rise to the greatest problem viz that the concept of bringing negotiations to an end in bad faith is somewhat elusive. But the difficulty of a problem should not be an excuse for the court to withhold relevant assistance from the parties by declaring a blanket unenforceability of the obligation"(at [119]), though he then added that he thought that in the absence of fraud, it would be unlikely that there would be a finding of bad faith. Overall, therefore, given the inclusion of a term of "comparatively narrow scope" which had been "deliberately and expressly" entered by the parties to a professionally drafted commercial contract, Longmore L.J. concluded that it would be "a strong thing to declare [it] unenforceable" as this would "defeat the reasonable expectations of honest men" (at [121]). While the Court of Appeal could not reconsider *Walford v Miles*, the learned Lord Justices considered that this decision did not bind them "to hold that the express obligation to negotiate as contained in [the clause in question] is completely without legal substance": at [121].

Fairness relevant: (2) Implied terms

[Add to note 178: page [23]]   **1–026**
    Eastwood v Magnox Electric plc [2004] UKHL 35; [2005] 1 A.C. 503 at [4]–[6].

[Add new text after note 185: page [24]]
    On the other hand, while in *Paragon Finance plc v Plender*[185a] the parties accepted that a mortgagee's contractual power to vary the interest rates was subject to an implied qualification that it would not be exercised improperly, capriciously or arbitrarily, or in a way which no reasonable mortgagee, acting reasonably as Dyson L.J. had earlier held in *Paragon Finance plc v Nash,*[185b] Jonathan Parker L.J. did not understand Dyson L.J. to be saying

> "that a lender may not, *for a genuine commercial reason*, adopt a policy of raising interest rates to levels at which its borrows generally, or a particular category of its borrowers, may be expected to consider refinancing their borrowings at more favourable rates of interest offered by other commercial lenders. Save as otherwise expressly agreed with its borrowers, a commercial lender is in my judgment free to conduct its business in what it genuinely believes to be its best commercial interest".[185c]

Jonathan Parker L.J. (with whom Carnwath and Ward L.JJ. agreed,[185d] then held that on the facts the mortgagee had not acted for other than a legitimate commercial reason, there being no evidence that it had embarked on a policy of forcing its borrowers to redeem their mortgages, still less that the mortgagors before the court had been singled out for special treatment in this respect.[185e]

[185a] [2005] EWCA Civ 760; [2005] 1 W.L.R. 3412 at [118].
[185b] [2002] 1 W.L.R. 685.
[185c] [2005] EWCA Civ 760 at [120].

185d *ibid.*, at [131], [132].
185e *ibid.*, at [121].

3. THE HUMAN RIGHTS ACT 1998 AND CONTRACTS

(a) *Contracts made before October 2, 2000*

(i) *The construction and review of legislation governing contracts*

The impact of sections 3 and 4 of the 1998 Act on accrued contractual rights

1–032
[*Add to text at end of paragraph: page* [27]]
On the other hand, in *PW & Co v Milton Gate Investments Ltd*215a Neuberger
J. was prepared to accept that s.3 of the Human Rights Act could apply to an
issue arising from a lease made before its coming into force. There, the learned
judge had held that, apart from the operation of s.3, the exercise of a "break
clause" in a head tenancy did not determine the sub-tenancies entered into by the
tenant as permitted under the head-lease even though the head-landlord was
unable to recover rent under the sub-tenancy covenants.215b Having referred to a
number of passages in the speeches of their lordships in *Wilson v First County
Trust (No.2)*,215c Neuberger J. concluded that their reasoning did not preclude the
application of ss.3 or 4 of the 1998 Act to issues arising out of contracts made
before its coming into force as long as this did not impair "vested rights" or
otherwise create unfairness.215d In particular, he noted as "very much in point"
Lord Scott of Foscote's reference in *Wilson's* case to the example of the impact
of legislation intervening between the creation of a lease and its expiry where the
legislation could affect the rights and obligations arising under the transac-
tion.215e On the facts before him, Neuberger J. considered that "the earliest that
any 'vested rights' could be said to have arisen under [the break clause in the
head-lease], was the date of the service of the Notice under that clause. Unless
and until [the break clause] was operated, the rights and obligations of any of the
parties as a result of the exercise were merely contingent and not vested."215f
Since this notice had been served after the coming into force of s.3 of the 1998
Act there were no vested rights at the relevant time so as to prevent its operation
on the legislative provisions whose application allegedly prejudiced the head-
landlord's right to property under Art.1 of the First Protocol of the European
Convention. Moreover, in the learned judge's view, it was not more generally
unfair to apply s.3 in this way even though the notice had been served only four
days after its coming into force given, in particular, that the 1998 Act had been
on the Statute Book for around two years before it came into force.215g

215a [2003] EWHC 1994 (Ch); [2003] All E.R. (D) 58 (Aug.).
215b *ibid.*, at [103]–[104].
215c [2003] UKHL 40; [2004] 1 A.C. 816.
215d *ibid.*, at [107]–[115].
215e [2003] UKHL 40 at [161]; [2003] EWHC 1994 (Ch) at [110] and [114].
215f [2003] EWHC 1994 (Ch) at [114].
215g *ibid.*, at [115].

(b) *Contracts made on or after October 2, 2000*

(i) *The construction and review of legislation governing contracts*

Unenforceable contractual rights and engaging Article 1 of the First Protocol

In *Pennycook v Shaws (EAL) Ltd* [2004] EWCA Civ 100; [2004] 2 W.L.R. **1–039** 1331 at [30]–[42], the Court of Appeal considered the difference of view in the House of Lords in *Wilson v First County Trust Ltd (No.2)* [2003] UKHL 40; [2004] 1 A.C. 816, between Lord Nicholls on the one hand and Lords Scott of Foscote and Hope on the other, as to the engagement of Art.1 of the First Protocol to the European Convention on Human Rights in relation to a lender's rights under a consumer credit contract (described in this paragraph of the Main Work), in the context of the question whether a tenant's statutory right to renew a business tenancy conferred by Pt II of the Landlord and Tenant Act 1954 is a "possession" for the purposes of Art.1. Arden L.J. (with whom Thorpe L.J. and Sir Martin Nourse agreed) found "the most detailed guidance" as to how to approach this question in Lord Nicholl's speech in the *Wilson* case ([2004] EWCA Civ 100 at [34]), the court needing to look "at the substance of the claimed right to see whether the bar to the exercise of the tenant's right is a delimination of the right or whether it represents a deprivation of right": *ibid.*, at [35]. According to Arden L.J., Lord Hope in the *Wilson* case took the opposite view to Lord Nicholls as to how this test applied in relation to the impact of the Consumer Credit Act to the facts before the House: *ibid.*, at [37]. On the facts before her, Arden L.J. held that the 1954 Act deprived the tenant of a right rather than merely deliminating it: *ibid.*, at [38].

The engagement of Art.1 was the subject of further discussion by David Richards J. in *Re T & N Ltd* [2005] EWHC 2870 (Ch); [2006] 1 W.L.R. 1728 in the context of the question whether a future claim for damages in respect of asbestos contamination attracted protection as a "possession" within the meaning of Art.1 of the First Protocol to the Convention. In the course of this discussion, the learned judge referred to the (then unreported) decision of the European Court of Human Rights in *JA Pye (Oxford) Ltd v United Kingdom (44302/02)* (2006) 43 E.H.R.R. 3 at [52]. The European Court had referred to the House of Lords' decision in *Wilson* where, in its words, "the majority held that the relevant legislation regulating the enforceability of loan agreements 'bit' at the moment the transaction was concluded and that the lender accordingly had no right to enforce repayment of the loan of which he could be deprived under Art.1." The European Court then contrasted this position with the position applicable to the question before it, namely, whether provisions of the Land Registration Act 1925 and Limitation Act 1980 attracted the application of Art.1 in that they permitted the acquisition of title to land by adverse possession. In this respect, the European court took the view that these provisions are "to be seen as 'biting' on the applicants' property rights only at the point at which the [would-be acquirer] had completed 12 years' adverse possession of the applicants' land and not as delimiting the right at the moment of its acquisition" (at [52]). In the view of David Richards J. in *Re T & N Ltd*, the view taken by the European Court involved "no criticism of the majority view in [*Wilson*] but appears to endorse it": [2005] EWHC 2870 (Ch) at [171].

Other examples

1–041   *[Add new footnote 252a at the end of the first sentence of paragraph 1–041: page [32]]*

252a On the possible impact of the Human Rights Act on arbitral proceedings see Vol.II, paras 32–015—32–017, and this Supplement para.32–144 referring to *Sukuman Ltd v Commonwealth Secretariat* [2006] EWHC 304 (Comm.); [2006] 1 All E.R. (Comm.) 621, where it was held that an express exclusion agreement of the right to appeal from an arbitral award under s.69(1) of the Arbitration Act 1996 was not incompatible with Art.6 of the European Convention of Human Rights.

[Add to text at end of paragraph: page [32]]

   Moreover, in *PW & Co v Milton Gate Investments Ltd*[255a] Neuberger J. accepted the argument of a head-landlord that the effect of ss.139 or 141 of the Law of Property Act 1925 should and could be interpreted so as to prevent the head-landlord from being deprived of rent under the covenants of sub-tenancies which had not determined by the exercise of a "break clause" by the head-tenant. In these circumstances, Art.1 of the First Protocol to the European Convention was engaged: if the underleases would survive the determination of the headlease without the tenant's covenants being enforceable, the head-landlord would be kept out of the premises in question for the remainder of the sub-leases without being able to recover any rent whatever. "That is scarcely 'peaceful enjoyment of [its] possessions'."[255b]

   In *Ghaidan v Godin Mendoza*[255c] a majority of the House of Lords relied on s.3 of the Human Rights Act 1998 to "read and give effect" to the provisions of the Rent Act 1977[255d] which grants a statutory tenancy to "[t]he surviving spouse (if any) of the original tenant if residing in the dwelling-house immediately before the death of the original tenant" so as to include homosexual cohabitees so as to give effect to their Convention right not to be discriminated against on the ground of sexual orientation in respect of their right to respect for a person's home.[255e] In doing so, their Lordships made a number of important observations on the ambit of the obligation imposed by s.3 of the 1998 Act.[255f]

255a [2003] EWHC 1994 (Ch); [2004] Ch. 142.
255b *ibid.*, at [126] *per* Neuberger J.
255c [2004] UKHL 30; [2004] 2 A.C. 557.
255d Rent Act 1977, Sch.I, paras 2 and 3 (as amended).
255e European Convention on Human Rights Arts 8 and 14.
255f [2004] UKHL 30 esp. at [25]–[35] *per* Lord Nicholls of Birkenhead; [38]–[51] *per* Lord Steyn; [104]–[124] *per* Lord Rodger of Earlsferry; *cf.* at [57]–[72] *per* Lord Millett (dissenting).

(ii) *Contracts made by "public authorities"*

"Public authorities" within the meaning of section 6 of the 1998 Act

1–042   In *Aston Cantlow and Wilmcote with Billesley Parochial Church Council v Wallbank* [2003] UKHL 37; [2004] 1 A.C. 546 the House of Lords considered what is meant by "public authority" and "functions of a public nature" within the meaning of s.6(1) and 6(3) of the Human Rights Act 1998 respectively. It held that the purpose of s.6(1) is that those bodies for whose acts the state is answerable before the European Court of Human Rights shall in future be subject to a domestic law obligation not to act incompatibly with Convention rights ([2003] UKHL 37 at [6], [7], [52], [88]) and that the phrase "a public authority" for the purpose of s.6(1) is therefore "essentially a reference to a body whose nature is governmental in the broad sense of the expression:" *ibid.*, at [7], [88], [171]. The House of Lords futhermore accepted the distinction between " 'core' or 'standard' public authorities" and " 'hybrid' public authorities" for the purposes of s.6: [2003] UKHL 37 at [8]–[11], [35], [85]. " 'Core' public authorities" were persons all of whose functions are of a public character, it being important to recall for this purpose that such persons are not themselves able to *claim* the benefit of Convention rights: *ibid.*, at [85] and [8] respectively. As regards " 'hybrid' public authorities", which exercise both public functions and non-public functions, there is no single test as to determining whether or not a particular function is "public" within the meaning of s.6(3)(b), though factors to be taken into account include "the extent to which in carrying out the relevant function the body is publicly funded, or is exercising statutory powers, or is taking the place of central government or local authorities, or is providing a public service": *ibid.*, at [12]. In this respect, although the domestic case law on judicial review may provide some assistance as to what does and does not constitute a "function of a public nature" within the meaning of s.6(3)(b), this case law must be examined in the light of the jurisprudence of the European Court of Human Rights as to those bodies which engage the responsibility of the state for the purposes of the Convention: *ibid.*, at [52].

In *R. (West) v Lloyd's of London* [2004] EWCA Civ 506; [2004] 3 All E.R. 251, the Court of Appeal held that decisions by Lloyd's of London under powers contained in its byelaws to approve minority buy-outs of four syndicates of which the applicant was a member (and which he complained were prejudicial to his rights of due process and of possession of this property under Art.6 of the Convention and under Art.1 to its First Protocol) were not subject to challenge by way of judicial review, whether by virtue of s.6 of the 1998 Act or more generally. In the view of the Court of Appeal, the relationship between Lloyd's and its members was entirely voluntary and contractual and their rights to participate in a syndicate governed exclusively by the terms of their contracts with their managing agents: [2004] EWCA Civ 506 at [8]–[9]. As regards judicial review generally, the decisions were solely concerned with the commercial relationship between the applicant and the relevant managing agents and were therefore of a private and not of a public nature, a position not affected by the fact that Lloyd's was constituted by private Act of Parliament: *ibid.*, at [30]–[31]. And applying the approach of the House of Lords in *Wallbank*, the Court of Appeal held for the purposes of s.6 of the 1998 Act that the objectives of Lloyd's were "wholly commercial" and "not governmental even in the broad sense of that expression": it was rather the Financial Services Authority acting under the Financial Services and Markets Act 2000 "which is the governmental organisation which will be answerable to the Strasbourg court": *ibid.*, at [38] *per* Brooke L.J.

(iv) *Contractual confidentiality and section 12 of the 1998 Act*

Its impact on duties of confidentiality

[*note 307: page* [40]]   **1–056**
Lady Archer v Williams [2003] EWHC 1670 is reported at [2003] E.M.L.R. 38.

5. Contracts Contained In Deeds

(a) *Form and Delivery*

Legislative reform of the requirements for the due execution and delivery of deeds

1–077—
1–082

The legislative provisions described in the Main Work at paras 1–077—1–082 relating to contracts contained in deeds were themselves reformed by the Regulatory Reform (Execution of Deeds and Documents) Order 2005 ((SI 2005/1906), made under the Regulatory Reform Act 2001, s.1, "the 2005 Order") so as to give effect to the principal recommendations of the Law Commission in its report *The Execution of Deeds and Documents by or on behalf of Bodies Corporate*, Law Com. No.253 (1998). These amendments came into force as regards instruments executed on or after September 15, 2005, but leave unaffected any instrument executed before this date: 2005 Order, art.1(2). As a result, the law described in the Main Work still applies to contracts contained in deeds made up to and including September 14, 2005, but applies only as amended by the 2005 Order as regards contracts contained in deeds made on or after September 15, 2005. For this reason, this Supplement will first set out any amendments made to the existing paragraphs of the Main Text which govern instruments made on or before September 14, 2005, and then in the following paragraphs (which will be numbered as 1–082A *et seq.*) will describe the amended law in the present tense, this law governing instruments made on or after September 15, 2005.

The general abolition of the requirement of sealing

[Delete paragraph 1–077 and replace with new paragraphs 1–077 and 1–077A: pages [49]–[50]]

1–077 **Recent legislative history.** In 1989, legislation was introduced which abolished the ancient requirement of sealing for the execution of the deeds in many situations.[397] As regards deeds executed by an individual, the requirement of sealing was replaced with requirements that the intention of the party making a deed should make this intention clear on its face, of signature[398] by that party and of attestation.[399] As regards companies incorporated under the Companies Acts, the requirement of sealing for the execution of *documents*[400] was supplemented by an alternative method of execution of a document which required signature by a director and the secretary of the company or by two directors and the expression "in whatever form of words" that it was executed by the company; and it was further provided that where a document made clear on its face that it was intended to be a *deed* it should take effect on delivery as a deed, delivery being rebuttably presumed where it was so executed.[401] In the case of deeds executed by other persons (including other corporations aggregate and corporations sole), the common law requirement of sealing was left unaffected. However, in 2005 further (prospective) amendments were made to this position by an order ("the

2005 Order") made under the Regulatory Reform Act 2001.[401a] The main changes concern: (i) the creation of standard requirements for companies incorporated under the Companies Act 1985 (companies) and corporations aggregate[401b] (but not corporations sole[401c]) for the due execution of instruments in general and of deeds in particular[401d]; (ii) the making of specific provision for the execution of documents by persons (including companies and corporations aggregate) by or on behalf of another person (whether the latter is an individual, a company within the meaning of the Companies Act or a corporation)[401e]; and (iii) the clarification that the mere sealing of a document by a person (whether an individual or another corporate body) does not in itself satisfy the so-called "face-value requirement" that "an instrument shall not be a deed unless . . . it makes clear on its face that it is intended to be a deed by the person making it".[401f]

[397] On the ancient requirement see Sheppard's *Touchstone of Common Assurances* (7th ed., 1820), p.56.
[398] This requirement had been imposed by the Law of Property Act 1925, s.73.
[399] Law of Property (Miscellaneous Provisions) Act 1989, s.1.
[400] Companies Act 1985, s.36A(2).
[401] Companies Act 1985, s.36A(4) and (5).
[401a] Regulatory Reform (Execution of Deeds and Documents) Order 2005 (SI 2005/1906).
[401b] A corporation aggregate may be defined as consisting of "a body of persons which is recognised by the law as having a personality which is distinct from the separate personalities of the members of the body or the personality of the individual holder of the office in question for the time being": Law Com. No.253 para.4.1, n.1 referring to *Halsbury's Laws of England* (4th ed., reissue, 1998) Vol.9(2), para.1005.
[401c] A corporation sole may be defined as consisting of "one person and his or her successors in some particular office or status, who are incorporated in law in order to give them certain legal capacities and advantages which they would not have in their natural person": Law Com. No.253 para.4.23 referring to *Halsbury's Laws of England* (4th ed., reissue, 1998) Vol.9(2), para.1007.
[401d] Below, para.1–082E.
[401e] Below, para.1–082C.
[401f] Law of Property (Miscellaneous Provisions) Act 1989, s.1(2)(a) and see below, para.1–082B.

The prospective effect of the 2005 changes. The 2005 Order provides that it **1–077A** shall come into force on September 15, 2005.[401g] The Order further provides that its provisions "shall not apply to any *instrument executed* before the date on which this Order comes into force."[401h] This raises the question as to how this provision applies to changes contained in the Order to the law governing the making of *deeds*.[401i] It could be thought that a deed (the "instrument") is "executed" only after its delivery and not merely after the making of the document as only on delivery is the deed a valid instrument. However, it is submitted that the Order (following the Law Commission's recommendation[401j]) distinguishes clearly between the formal requirements required for the execution of an instrument (or document) and the further requirement for the execution of an instrument *as a deed* of delivery[401k] and that this argues for the temporal application of the new amendments contained in the Order to apply only to *documents executed* on or after September 15, 2005, and not also to documents executed as deeds on or before September 14, 2005, but delivered as deeds only after this date. This interpretation also has the practical advantage of not applying the amendments contained in the Order governing the execution of documents retrospectively to this albeit limited category of case.

[401g] The 2005 Order, art.1(1) (this being 12 weeks from June 23, 2005, the day on which the Order was made).
[401h] *ibid.*, art.1(2) (emphasis added).
[401i] *cf.* the discussion in Law Com. No.253, paras 3.6–3.12 as to the confusion over whether the term "executed" in the Companies Act 1985, s.36A, the Law of Property Act 1925, s.74 and the Law of Property (Miscellaneous Provisions) Act 1989, s.1 included "delivery".
[401j] Law Com. No.253, para.3.12.
[401k] See notably, the 2005 Order, arts 4, 6 and below, para.1–082E.

[*Insert new heading before paragraph 1–080: page* [51]]

(i) Deeds executed on or before September 14, 2005

Deeds executed by companies incorporated under the Companies Acts

1–080   [*Delete first sentence and replace text at the beginning of the paragraph: page* [51]]
In 1989, the law governing the execution of documents and deeds by companies incorporated under the Companies Acts was amended so as to create a "dual system".[410a] So, while it preserved the possibility for a company to execute a document (including a deed) by the affixing of its common seal,[411] it also provided that a document signed by a director and secretary, or by two directors, of a company incorporated under the Act and expressed to be executed by the company has the same effect as if executed under the common seal of the company and notwithstanding that the company has no common seal.[412] In either case, it is provided that a "document executed by a company which makes clear on its face that it is intended by the person or persons making it to be a deed has effect, upon delivery, as a deed".[413]

[410a] Law Commission, *The Execution of Deeds and Documents by or on behalf of Bodies Corporate*, Law Com. No.253 (1998), para.3.3.
[411] Companies Act 1985, s.36A(4) as inserted by Companies Act 1989, s.130(2).
[412] Companies Act 1985, s.36A(3) as inserted by Companies Act 1989, s.130(2).
[413] *ibid.*, s.36A(5).

Delivery

1–082   [*Delete text of note 430 from "Once a document" to the end and insert new text: page* [52]]
In *Bolton Metropolitan B.C. v Torkington* [2003] EWCA Civ 1634; [2004] Ch. 66 the Court of Appeal held that while s.74(1) of the Law of Property Act 1925 deemed a deed "duly executed" where a corporation's seal is affixed in the presence of and attested by its designated officers, it created no presumption as to its delivery: *ibid.* at [22], [45]. Moreover, while it was not necessary on the facts to decide the point, in Peter Gibson L.J.'s view, at common law "to describe the sealing by a corporation as giving rise to a rebuttable presumption may go too far, implying, as that does, that the burden is on the corporation affixing the seal": *ibid.* at [46]. Where, as on the facts before the court, negotiations were undertaken towards a lease expressly subject to contract, a court should not infer an intention to be bound from the mere sealing of a deed of execution of a lease: *ibid.*, at [53]. On the other hand, in the case of a company incorporated under the

Companies Act 1985, where a document makes it clear on its face that "it is intended by the person or persons making it to be a deed . . . it shall be presumed, unless a contrary intention is proved, to be delivered upon its being so executed": Companies Act 1985 s.36A(5) as inserted by the Companies Act 1989, s.130(2).

[Insert new heading after paragraph 1–082, and new paragraphs 1–082A—1–082H: page [52]]

(ii) *Deeds executed on or after September 15, 2005*

The new general requirements for all deeds after the 2005 Order. Under   **1–082A** s.1(2) of the Law of Property (Miscellaneous Provisions) Act 1989 (as amended by the 2005 Order[431a]), an instrument shall not be a deed unless—

(a) it makes clear on its face that it is intended to be a deed by the person making it or, as the case may be, by the parties to it (whether by describing itself as a deed or expressing itself to be executed to be signed as a deed or otherwise); and

(b) it is validly executed as a deed

    (i) by that person or a person authorised to execute it in the name or on behalf of that person, or

    (ii) by one or more of those parties or a person authorised to execute it in the name or on behalf of one or more of those parties.

These requirements apply to *all* instruments whether executed by an individual, by a company incorporated under the Companies Act 1985, by a corporation aggregate, or by a corporate sole. However, even after the reforms of 2005, the significance and impact of these provisions differ somewhat according to these different categories of person. In this respect, a distinction is to be drawn between the condition contained in s.1(2)(a) (the so-called "face value requirement") and the condition in s.1(2)(b) of "valid execution".

[431a] Regulatory Reform (Execution of Deeds and Documents) Order 2005 (SI 2005/1906), art.7(3).

The "face value requirement" for deeds. The reforms of 1989 introduced   **1–082B** the idea that an instrument should qualify as a deed by reference to the intention of the party or parties to it as made clear on its face.[431b] This change itself reflected earlier developments in judicial attitudes to the common law requirement of sealing, the courts adopting an approach which saw this requirement as satisfied where any evidence on the face of an instrument showed that it was intended to be executed as a deed.[431c] Following the Law Commission's recommendations,[431d] this face-value requirement was retained in 2005, though its formulation was clarified and standardised for instruments executed by individuals and companies.[431e] In particular, it is now expressly provided that "an instrument shall not be taken to make it clear on its face that it is intended to be a deed merely because it is executed under seal."[431f]

[431b] Law of Property (Miscellaneous Provisions) Act 1989, s.1(2) (as enacted); Companies Act 1985, s.36A(5).

[431c] *First National Securities v Jones* [1978] Ch. 109 and *Chitty on Contracts* (26th ed., 1989) para.23.

[431d] Law Com. No.253, paras 2.29–2.34.

[431e] 2005 Order, art.7(3) (individuals); Sch.2, repealing Companies Act 1985, s.36A(5) (companies); Law Com. No.253, paras 2.50, 2.54.

[431f] Law of Property (Miscellaneous Provisions) Act 1989, s.1(2A) as inserted by the 2005 Order, art.8. This statutory clarification also casts doubt on the contrary approach taken by the unreported decision at first instance in *Johnsey Estates (1900) Ltd v Newport Marketworld Ltd*, unreported, May 10, 1996, Judge Moseley Q.C.), noted and criticised by Law Com. No.253, paras 2.17–2.18.

1–082C   **Execution on behalf of one or more of the parties to the instrument.** Following the Law Commission's recommendations,[431g] the 2005 Order introduced new clarifying provisions so as to provide expressly for execution in the name or on behalf of another person. So, it is provided that as regards individuals, a document may be executed by a person on behalf of another, and that it is the person who executes the document (whether or not on behalf of the other) who must comply with the formalities[431h]; as regards companies, the provisions of the Companies Act 1985 which state how a company may execute a document and provide for deemed execution in favour of a purchaser, apply where a company executes a document on behalf of another person[431i]; and as regards corporations aggregate, the Law of Property Act 1925 is amended so as to provide that deemed execution in favour of a purchaser applies where the corporation executes an instrument on behalf of another person.[431j]

[431g] Law Com. No.253, Pt 7.

[431h] Law of Property (Miscellaneous Provisions) Act 1989, s.1(2)(b) and (4A), as amended and inserted by the 2005 Order, art.7(3) and 7(4) respectively.

[431i] Companies Act 1985 s.36A(7) as inserted by the 2005 Order, art.7(2).

[431j] Law of Property Act 1925 s.74(1A) as inserted by the 2005 Order, art.7(1).

1–082D   **"Valid execution": individuals.** By s.1(3) of the Law of Property (Miscellaneous Provisions) Act 1989, for an instrument to be validly executed as a deed by an individual, it must be "signed (i) by him in the presence of a witness who attests the signature; or (ii) at his direction and in his presence and the presence of two witnesses who each attest the signature". "Signature" is defined later in the section to include making one's mark.[431k] The Act specifically preserved the further common law requirement that for an instrument to be validly executed as a deed it must be "delivered" as a deed.[431l]

[431k] Law of Property (Miscellaneous Provisions) Act 1989, s.1(4)(b) as amended by the 2005 Order, Sch.1, para.14.

[431l] Law of Property (Miscellaneous Provisions) Act 1989, s.1(3)(b) as amended by the 2005 Order, Sch.2 and see below, para.1–082D.

1–082E   **Delivery.** At common law, "[w]here a contract is to be by deed, there must be a delivery to perfect it".[431m] "Delivered", however, in this connection does not mean "handed over" to the other party. It means delivered in the old legal sense,[431n] namely, an act done so as to evince an intention to be bound.[431o] Any act of the party which shows that he intended to deliver the deed as an instrument binding on him is enough. He must make it his deed[431p] and recognise it as presently binding on him.[431q] Delivery is effective even though the grantor retains the deed in his own possession: there need be no actual transfer of possession to the other party.[431r] Moreover, where a solicitor, duly certified notary public or licensed conveyancer (or their agent) in the course of a transaction purports to deliver an instrument as a deed on behalf of a party to the instrument, it shall be conclusively presumed in favour of a purchaser that he is authorised so to deliver the instrument.[431s] Unlike the position as regards corporations,[431t] the execution of a document intended to be executed as a deed by an individual does not give rise to a presumption of delivery either at common law or by statute.

[431m] *Xenos v Wickham* (1863) 14 C.B.(N.S.) 435 at 473; *Termes de la Ley*, s.v. Fait; Co.Litt. 171b.

[431n] But see *Yale* [1970] C.L.J. 52.

[431o] *Vincent v Premo Enterprises Ltd* [1969] 2 Q.B. 609 at 619.

[431p] *Tupper v Foulkes* (1861) 9 C.B.(N.S.) 797; *Xenos v Wickham* (1867) L.R. 2 H.L. 296 at 312; *Re Seymour* [1913] 1 Ch. 475.

[431q] *Xenos v Wickham*, above.

[431r] *Xenos v Wickham*, above, *per* Lord Cranworth at 323; *cf. per* Pigott B. at 309; *Doe d. Garnons v Knight* (1826) 5 B. & C. 671; *Macedo v Stroud* [1922] 2 A.C. 330; *Beesly v Hallwood Estates Ltd* [1960] 1 W.L.R. 549, affd. [1961] Ch. 105; *Vincent v Premo Enterprises Ltd* [1969] 2 Q.B. 609.

[431s] Law of Property (Miscellaneous Provisions) Act 1989, s.1(5) as amended by the 2005 Order, art.9 which therefore extended the presumption beyond its earlier restriction to transactions involving the disposition or creation of an interest in land.

[431t] Below, para.1–082F.

"Valid execution": companies and corporations aggregate. One of the   **1–082F** purpose of the 2005 Order was to harmonise the law governing the execution of instruments as deeds by corporate bodies.[431u] So, it is now provided that a document is validly executed *as a deed* by both companies and corporations aggregate so as to satisfy the general requirements imposed by the 1989 Act[431v] "if and only if" it is "duly executed" by the corporate body *and* if it is delivered as a deed.[431w] As regards delivery, it is provided for both types of corporate body that an instrument shall be presumed to be delivered for these purposes "upon its being executed, unless a contrary intention is proved".[431x] As regards companies, this provision marked a change from the previous law where the presumption of delivery was irrebuttable in these circumstances[431y]; as regards corporations aggregate, it clarified the position given that the existence of a rebuttable presumption at common law had been recently judicially doubted.[431z]

[431u] Law Com. No.153, Pt 4.

[431v] Law of Property (Miscellaneous Provisions) Act 1989, s.1(2)(b), para.1–082A, above.

[431w] Law of Property Act 1925, s.74A(1) as inserted by the 2005 Order, art.4 (corporations aggregate); Companies Act 1985, s.36AA(1) as inserted by the 2005 Order, art.6.

[431x] Law of Property Act 1925, s.74A(2) as inserted by the 2005 Order, art.4 (corporations aggregate); Companies Act 1985, s.36AA(2) (companies) as inserted by 2005 Order, art.6.

[431y] As a result, the 2005 Order, art.5 amended the Companies Act 1985, s.36A(6) and see Law Com. No.253, paras 6.37–6.43.

[431z] *Bolton Metropolitan B.C. v Torkington* [2003] EWCA Civ 1634; [2004] Ch. 66 at [46], above para.1–082, differing from the position taken by the Law Commission, which took the view that at common law, the sealing of a deed raises a rebuttable presumption of delivery: Law Com. No.253, para.6.1.

1–082G   However, the conditions for "due execution" of a document still differ somewhat as between companies and corporations aggregate. In the case of companies, there are alternative requirements: a document may be executed either by the affixing of its common seal[431aa] or by being signed "by a director and the secretary of the company, or by two directors of a company, and expressed (in whatever form of words) to be executed by the company."[431ab] Where a document is to be signed by a person as a director or the secretary of more than one company, it shall not be taken to be duly signed by that person for these purposes unless the person signs it separately in each capacity.[431ac] In the case of corporations aggregate, the common law requirement of affixing the corporation's seal still applies in principle,[431ad] but it is provided that "in favour of a purchaser an instrument shall be deemed to have been duly executed . . . if a seal purporting to be the corporation's seal purports to be affixed to the instrument in the presence of and attested by (a) two members of the board of directors, council or other governing body of the corporation, or (b) one such member and the clerk, secretary or other permanent officer of the corporation or his deputy".[431ae]

[431aa] Companies Act 1985, s.36A(1) as inserted by the Companies Act 1989, s.130(2).
[431ab] Companies Act 1985, s.36A(4) as inserted by the Companies Act 1989, s.130(2).
[431ac] Companies Act 1985, s.36A(4A) as inserted by 2005 Order, art.10(1), Sch.1, para.10.
[431ad] Law Com. No.253, para.4.5.
[431ae] Law of Property Act 1925, s.74(1) as substituted by the 2005 Order, art.3. s.74(1B) of the 1925 Act as inserted by the 2005 Order, art.10(1), Sch.1, para.2 provides that for these purposes "a seal purports to be affixed in the presence of and attested by an officer of the corporation, in the case of an officer which is not an individual, if it is affixed in the presence of and attested by an individual authorised by the officer to attest on its behalf". And see Law Com. No.253, paras 4.6–4.9.

1–082H   **"Valid execution": corporations sole.** Where a deed is executed by a corporation sole (such as a government minister or Church of England bishop[431af]), the common law requirement of sealing still applies.[431ag] However, as has been noted,[431ah] this requirement has been interpreted by the courts very liberally: "to constitute a sealing neither wax nor wafer nor a piece of paper nor even an impression is necessary".[431ai] Pieces of green ribbon[431aj] or a circle printed on the document containing the letters "L.S." (*locus sigilli*)[431ak] or even a document bearing no indication of a seal at all[431al] will suffice, if there is evidence (*e.g.* attestation) that the document was intended to be executed as a deed.[431am] In the absence of such evidence, a signatory of a document expressed to have been "signed, sealed and delivered" by him may be estopped from denying that it was sealed.[431an]

[431af] Law. Com. No.253, para.4.23 and see above, for a definition of corporations sole.
[431ag] Law of Property (Miscellaneous Provisions) Act 1989, s.1(10) specifically provides that s.1's provisions governing "individuals" do not apply to corporations sole. Note also that s.1(9) specifically reserves the requirement of sealing at common law in relation to deeds required or authorised to be made under the seals of the county palatine of Lancaster, the Duchy of Lancaster or the Duchy of Cornwall.
[431ah] Above, para.1–082B.
[431ai] *Ex p. Sandilands* (1871) L.R. 6 C.P. 411 at 413.
[431aj] *Ex p. Sandilands*, above, see also *Stromdale & Ball Ltd v Burden* [1952] Ch. 233 at 230.
[431ak] *First National Securities Ltd v Jones* [1978] Ch. 109.
[431al] *First National Securities Ltd v Jones*, above; *Commercial Credit Services v Knowles* [1978] 6 C.L. 64.

431am *cf. National Provincial Bank v Jackson* (1886) 33 Ch.D. 1; *Re Balkis Consolidated Ltd* (1888) 58 L.T. 300; *Re Smith* (1892) 67 L.T. 64 (these cases were explained in *First National Securities Ltd v Jones*, above): *cf. TCB v Gray* [1986] 1 Ch. 621 at 633.

431an *TCB v Gray*, above, *cf. Rushingdale Ltd v Byblos Bank* (1985) P.C.C. 342 at 346–347.

(c) Other Aspects

Benefit of person not a party

[*Add new text to note 451 on page*: [55]]

1–088

cf. Moody v Condor Insurance Ltd [2006] EWHC 100 (Ch); [2006] 1 W.L.R. 1847, where this significance of the distinction between deeds poll and indentures ("deeds *inter partes*") was accepted, but where it was held that the mere fact that a deed was executed by a guarantor and a principal debtor and expressed as being made "between" them did not conclude the issue whether the document was a deed poll or a deed *inter partes,* as it is "necessary to examine what the parties . . . set out to do by it": *ibid.*, at [18], *per* Park J. According to the learned judge:

> "[t]he rational distinction must surely be between (i) a deed which as respects the operative contents of it purports to have effect between the parties to it (a deed *inter partes*) and (ii) a deed which as respects the operative contents of it purports to have effect between a party to it and a non-party (not truly a deed *inter partes*, even if there happens also to be some other person who is a party to the deed, but to whom the rights-creating provisions in the deed are not directed)": *ibid.*, at [26].

6. The Relationship Between Contract And Tort

(c) Concurrence of Actions in Contract and Tort

(ii) Torts Committed in the Course of Performance of a Contract

Assumption of responsibility

[*Add new note 659a at end of paragraph: page* [75]]

1–120

659a *cf. Lennon v Metropolitan Police Commissioner* [2004] EWCA Civ 130; [2004] 1 W.L.R. 2594 where the principle in *Henderson v Merrett Syndicates* was applied so as to impose liability on a police authority vicariously in respect of its agent's express assumption of responsibility towards one of its constables (technically not being a contractual employee) in respect of the task of transferring him without loss of allowance to another police force.

(d) The Influence of Contract on Tort beyond Privity

Assumption of responsibility

The more eclectic approach to deciding whether or not a duty of care should be imposed in the tort of negligence (especially as regards pure economic loss) which looks in turn at "assumption of responsibility", the "three-fold test" in

1–157

Caparo Industries plc v Dickman [1990] 2 A.C. 605 at 618 and the "incremental approach" advocated by Brennan J. in *Sutherland Shire Council v Heyman* (1985) 157 C.L.R. 424 at 481 (noted at n.899 on p.[103] of Vol.I of the Main Work) was taken by the House of Lords in *Customs and Excise Commissioners v Barclays Bank plc* [2006] UKHL 28; [2006] 3 W.L.R. 1, though the third approach was seen as "of little value as a test in itself" (at [7] *per* Lord Rodger of Earlsferry) and as "an important cross-check" (at [93] *per* Lord Mance). In this case, the House of Lords unanimously held that a third party (here, the bank) with notice of a "freezing order" (formerly, a *Mareva* injunction) which nevertheless released the property subject to the order did not owe a duty of care to the person for whose benefit the order had been made (here, the Customs and Excise). While the grounds of the decisions of the five members of the House differed, the principal points can be summarised as follows. First, the involuntary nature of the position of the bank as recipient of the order was inconsistent with any assumption of responsibility, even if this were understood to mean the undertaking of a task for another person: [2006] UKHL 28 at [14] (Lord Bingham of Cornhill); [65] *per* Lord Rodger; and [74] *per* Lord Walker of Gestingthorpe. Secondly, the courts had developed a very powerful means for protecting those who fear that their legitimate claims are to be thwarted by disposal of available assets by the development of freezing orders and these are buttressed by the sanction of contempt of court. In this respect, a distinction is drawn between the strict liability of the person against whom an order has been made, and the requirement that a third party with notice of an order is liable for contempt only if he knowingly takes a step to frustrate the court's purpose. It would be inconsistent with this to impose the higher standard of reasonable care by means of a duty of care in tort: at [61]–[64] *per* Lord Rodger. Thirdly, their Lordships were concerned with the practical effects of the imposition of liability in damages for negligence by third parties with notice of a freezing order. While it may appear reasonable in this respect to impose liability for negligence in a business such as a bank, the new duty of care would also apply to any non-business with notice of such an order which would be unreasonable: at [23] *per* Lord Bingham, who expressed concern with the potential extent of a third party's expose to liability; [61] *per* Lord Rodger; [77] *per* Lord Walker; and [102] *per* Lord Mance, who drew attention in this respect with the different likely insurance positions in this respect.

Subsequent cases

1–162   *[Add at end of note 925: page [108]]*
European International Reinsurance Co Ltd v Curzon Insurance Ltd [2003] EWCA Civ 1074; [2003] Lloyd's Rep. I.R. 793. *cf. Customs and Excise Commissioners v Barclays Bank plc* [2006] UKHL 28; [2006] 3 W.L.R. 1, noted above, para.1–157.

Part Two

FORMATION OF CONTRACT

<small>CHAPTER 2</small>

THE AGREEMENT

			PARA.
	1.	Introduction	2–001
☐	2.	The offer	2–002
■	3.	The acceptance	2–025
■		(a) Definition	2–025
☐		(b) Communication of acceptance	2–043
☐		(c) Posted acceptance	2–046
		(d) Prescribed mode of acceptance	2–063
■		(e) Silence	2–068
		(f) Unilateral contracts	2–076
■	4.	Termination of the offer	2–085
☐		(a) Withdrawal	2–086
		(b) Rejection	2–090
☐		(c) Lapse of time	2–093
		(d) Occurrence of condition	2–096
		(e) Death	2–097
■		(f) Supervening personal incapacity	2–100
		(g) Supervening corporate incapacity	2–101
	5.	Special cases	2–108
☐	6.	Incomplete agreement	2–110
☐	7.	Certainty of terms	2–136
■	8.	Conditional agreements	2–142
		(a) Classification	2–142
☐		(b) Degrees of obligation	2–145
☐	9.	Contractual intention	2–153

2. THE OFFER

Conduct as offer

[Add to note 21: page [124]]

2–004

For further amendments of the Unsolicited Goods and Services Act 1971, see Regulatory Reform (Unsolicited Goods and Services Act 1971) (Directory Entries and Demands for Payment) Order 2005 (SI 2005/55) and Unsolicited Goods and Services Act 1971 (Electronic Commerce) (Amendment) Regulations 2005 (SI 2005/148).

[Add new text at end of paragraph: page [124]]

An offer by a consignor to enter into a contract for the carriage of goods may be made by his tendering the goods to the carrier and by the latter's accepting them for this purpose.[21a]

²¹ª *Datec Electronic Holdings Ltd v United Parcels Service Ltd* [2005] EWCA Civ 1418; [2006] 1 Lloyd's Rep. 16. The carriers' standard terms provided that they did not "offer carriage of packages" except subject to certain restrictions; but it was held that "offer" was not here used in its technical legal sense (see at [15] and [16]). The word was interpreted instead to refer to the *terms* of the contract made by the conduct of the parties, described above.

Inactivity as an offer

2–005   [*Add to note 30: page* [125]]
   cf. Indescon Ltd v Ogden [2004] EWHC 2326 (TCC); [2005] 1 Lloyd's Rep. 31 (right to appoint arbitrator not lost by lapse of time).

Offer and invitation to treat

2–006   [*Add new text at end: page* [126]]
   It has been held that a draft document sent in the course of contractual negotiations with the clear intention of inviting further comment from the recipient was not an offer.³⁵ª

   ³⁵ª *McNicholas Construction Holdings v Endemol UK plc* [2003] EWHC 2472; [2003] E.G.C.S. 136.

2–007   [*Add to note 37: page* [126]]
   For another sense of "offer", see this Supplement para.2–004 note 21a.

Other displays

2–014   [*Add to note 59: page* [129]]
   See also *University of Edinburgh v Onifade* 2005 S.L.T. (Sh Ct) 63 where landowners displayed a notice on the land to the effect that persons parking their cars there without permit would be subject to a "fine" of £30 per day. It was held that a person who had so parked his car was liable for the specified amount. The judgment is mainly concerned with the question whether the motorist's conduct could be regarded as an acceptance (see below, para.2–025); but to reach this question the court must have made the assumption that the notice amounted to an offer. This is perhaps a questionable interpretation of the landowners' intention (even objectively ascertained) in putting up the notice. This could be said to have been rather to deter unauthorised parking than to invite it with a view to earning the specified amount.

3. THE ACCEPTANCE

(a) *Definition*

Acceptance defined

2–025   [*Add to note 100: page* [134]]
   For the application of the objective test to an acceptance, see also *University of Edinburgh v Onifade* 2005 S.L.T. (Sh Ct) 63, where landowners displayed a

notice on the land stating that persons who parked their car there without a permit would be liable to a "fine" of £30 per day. The defender, who was aware of the notice, repeatedly parked on the land without permit and was held liable for the stipulated amount on the ground that a contract had arisen between him and the owner. It was "nothing to the purpose that he did not intend to pay" as the landowners were "entitled to conclude that the defender, by parking without permit with knowledge of the notice, had accepted liability for the payment to them of £30" (at [6]).

Negotiation after apparent agreement

[Add to note 109: page [135]]   **2–027**
For an application of the principle of looking at the whole correspondence in order to determine whether a contract has been rescinded, see *Drake Insurance plc v Provident Insurance plc* [2003] EWCA Civ 1834; [2004] Q.B. 601 at [100].

Acceptance by conduct

[Add to note 115: page [135]]   **2–028**
By reason of the objective principle, the offeree could not escape liability merely on the ground that he had no subjective intention to accept: see *University of Edinburgh v Onifade* 2005 S.L.T. (Sh Ct) 63, above, para.2–014 of this Supplement.

(b) *Communication of Acceptance*

Exception to the requirement of communication of acceptance

[Add to paragraph after note 190: page [144]]   **2–045**
Another situation, in which communication of acceptance was said to be unnecessary in the case of a unilateral contract, arose in *Argo Fund Ltd v Essar Steel Ltd.*[190a] In that case, an arrangement was made between a debtor and its creditor bank, by which each creditor was empowered to transfer its rights to a transferee by delivery of a transfer certificate to an agent (as defined by the loan agreement). This arrangement was described as a unilateral contract[190b] by which the debtor made a standing offer (a) to the creditor to terminate the old contract and (b) to the transferee to enter into a new contract.[190c] The former offer was accepted by the creditor's delivery of the transfer certificate to the agent,[190d] and the latter by the fact of the transferee's agreeing to the transfer with the transferor (*i.e.* the creditor) on the terms of the agreement as set out in the certificate.[190e] Notification of these acts of acceptance was not necessary (though in fact the offeror had notice of them) since no such requirement was stated in the original agreement; and this was apparently regarded as a waiver of the requirement of communication of acceptance.[190f] The effect of these acts of acceptance was to novate the original agreement.[190g]

[190a] [2005] EWHC 600 (Comm); [2006] 1 All E. R. (Comm.) 56; affd. on other grounds [2006] EWCA Civ 241; [2006] 2 All E.R. (Comm.) 104.

[190b] [2005] EWHC 600; [2006] 1 All E.R. (Comm.) 56 at [51].

[190c] *ibid.*

[190d] *ibid.*

[190e] *ibid.*, at [52].

[190f] *ibid.*, at [53], where the explanation is rather cautiously stated ("perhaps this is the correct analysis").

[190g] *ibid.*, at [50], [51].

(c) *Posted Acceptance*

Dictated telegrams, faxes, emails and web-site trading

2–049 [*Add new footnote 209a at "circumstances", line 8: page* [147]].

[209a] In *JSC Zestafoni Nikoladze Ferroalloy Plant v Ronly Holdings Ltd* [2004] EWHC 245 (Comm) [2004] 2 Lloyd's Rep. 335 an acceptance by fax was classified as an "instantaneous communication" [at 75] and held to take effect on receipt as the sender's machine would generally indicate whether the message had been received "effectively" (as distinct from having been received only in part). The further possibility of the message's having been wholly received, but of its being wholly or partly illegible, is not discussed.

[*Add to text in line 6, after "acceptance": page* [147]]

A fax message was likewise held not to be an effective acceptance in *Korbetis v Transgrain Shipping BV*,[209b] where the message was misdirected in the sense of having been sent to a telephone number other than that of the offeror.

[209b] [2005] EWHC 1345 (QB), discussed below in para.2–056 of this Supplement.

[*Add to note 210*]

cf. *Bernuth Lines Ltd v High Seas Shipping Ltd (The Eastern Navigator)* [2005] EWHC 3020 (Comm); [2006] 1 Lloyd's Rep. 537 at [29]–[31] (email notice of arbitration regarded as effective on receipt).

Misdirected letter of acceptance

2–056 [*Add to text: page* [149]]

Paragraph 2–056 of the Main Work was cited with approval in *L.J. Korbetis v Transgrain Shipping BV*,[226a] where Toulson J. said: "I agree with that general approach because it seems to me to correspond with principle and justice."[226b] In that case a dispute about demurrage had arisen under a charterparty and the question before the court was whether the parties had agreed on the appointment of X as the sole arbitrator to whom the dispute was to be referred. An original nomination faxed by the shipowners was rejected by the charterers, who, in a further fax, made a counter-proposal inviting the owners to choose one of three other names. A third fax agreeing to one of these names was sent from the owners' office in Piraeus to the charterers in the Netherlands but this was never received by the charterers because the appropriate international dialling code had not been entered, so that the fax went, not to the charterers, but to a recipient in the Piraeus area who had no connection with the transaction. It was held that this misdirected acceptance was not effective to conclude an agreement between owner and charter for the appointment of X as sole arbitrator of the dispute between them.

[226a] [2005] EWHC 1345 (QB) at [15].

[226b] *ibid.*

Revocation of posted acceptance

[Add new note 231a at "acceptance." in line 15: page [150]]   **2–058**
[231a] For similar reasoning in the case of a misdirected acceptance, see *L.J. Korbetis v Transgrains Shipping BV* [2005] EWHC 1345 (QB) at [11]; this case is discussed above, in para.2–056 of this Supplement.

Consumer's right to cancel distance contracts

[Add to note 246: page [152]]   **2–062**
For amendment of the Consumer Protection (Distance Selling) Regulations 2000, affecting the consumer's right to cancel distance contracts, see Financial Services (Distance Marketing) Regulations 2004 (SI 2004/2095); Consumer Protection (Distance Selling) (Amendment) Regulations 2005 (SI 2005/689).

(e) *Silence*

Silence and conduct

[Add to note 296: page [158]]   **2–074**
See also *Westminster Building Co Ltd v Beckingham* [2004] EWHC 138; [2004] B.L.R. 163 (terms of building contractor's offer to refurbish property accepted by owner's conduct in allowing the stipulated work to proceed); contrast *Mirant Asia-Pacific Construction (Hong Kong) Ltd v Ove Arup & Partners International OAPIL (No.2)* [2004] EWHC 1750; 97 Con. L.R. 1, where on the facts no inference of the owner's assent to the terms of a draft contract which had not been signed by the owner could be drawn merely from his allowing the work to proceed. In both cases the point at issue related to the terms, rather than to the existence, of the contract.

4. Termination of the Offer

(a) *Withdrawal*

General rule

[Add to note 335, line 4 after "Pt 36": page [163]]   **2–086**
For further proceedings in *Scammell v Dicker* see [2005] EWCA Civ 405; [2005] 3 All E.R. 838, below paras 2–113, 2–126, 2–136, 2–137, 2–139 and 2–141 of this Supplement.

Exceptions to the requirement of communication

[Add to note 347: page [165]]   **2–089**
See also *Bernuth Lines Ltd v High Seas Shipping Ltd (The Eastern Navigator)* [2005] EWHC 3020 (Comm); [2006] 1 Lloyd's Rep. 537 at [30], [31] (email notice of arbitration).

(c) *Lapse of Time*

Reasonable time

2–094   [*Add to note 364: page* [167]]

See also *L.J. Korbetis v Transgrain Shipping BV* [2005] EWHC 1345 (QB) (offer to appoint an arbitrator to whom disputes under a charterparty were to be referred held to have lapsed after eight months). Toulson J. at [18] stressed "the contractual context" in which the offer was made and in particular the fact that the charterparty required the parties to agree on the appointment of the arbitrator "forthwith", an expression which connoted "some urgency".

(f) *Supervening Personal Incapacity*

Mental patients

2–100   [*Page* [169]]

References in this paragraph to "mental patients" should now be to persons who lack mental capacity as defined in ss.1 and 2 of the Mental Capacity Act 2005. The substantive rules stated in Main Work, para.2–100 are not affected by this change in terminology.

6. Incomplete Agreement

Agreement required for continued operation of contract

2–113   [*Add to note 425: page* [175]]

See also *Scammell v Dicker* [2005] EWCA Civ 405; [2005] 3 All E.R. 838 at [40] *per* Rix L.J. ("The world is full of perfectly sound contracts which require further agreement for the purpose of their implementation.")

Stipulation for the execution of a formal document

2–114   [*Add to note 427: page* [175]]

; *Emcor Drake & Scull Ltd v Sir Robert McAlpine Ltd* [2004] EWCA Civ 1733; 98 Con. L.R. 1. See also *Petromec Inc v Petroleo Brasileiro SA Petrobras* [2005] EWCA Civ 891; [2006] 1 Lloyd's Rep. 121 at [74]–[77], where a Memorandum of Agreement (MOA) stated that "The Transactions contemplated in this MOA shall be governed by Transaction Documents referred to herein . . . ". It was held that "The MOA was not legally binding as it contemplated the execution of a complex series of interlocking contractual agreements to be made in the future (as in fact happened)."

[*Add to note 428*]

Thoresen & Co (Bangkok) Ltd v Fathom Marine Co [2004] EWHC 167 (Comm); [2004] 1 All E.R. (Comm.) 935 (agreement for the sale of a ship "sub details" held not to be a binding contract).

[*Add to note 429, line 9 after reference to The Kurnia Dewi: page* [176]]
Harvey Shopfitters Ltd v ADI Ltd [2003] EWCA Civ 1752; [2004] 2 All E.R.
982; *Bryen & Langley Ltd v Boston* [2005] EWCA Civ 973; [2005] B.L.R.
508.

General requirement of "exchange of contracts"

[*Add to note 444: page* [177]]   **2–117**
Secretary of State for Transport v Christos [2003] EWCA Civ 1073 is reported
in [2004] 1 P.&C.R. 17; *Bolton MBC v Torkington* [2003] EWCA Civ 1634;
[2004] Ch. 66 at [53], where the mere sealing (without delivery) of a counterpart
lease by a local authority was held not to give rise to a contract binding the
authority: see above, para.1–082 of this Supplement.

Acting on agreement subsequently completed

[*Add at end of paragraph: page* [180]]   **2–122**
Similarly, when an agreement for the supply of services provided that specified
terms should, "subject to contract", apply, and the parties then acted on that
agreement without executing any further document, it was held that an implied
binding contract on those terms had come into existence between the parties.[471a]

[471a] *Proforce Ltd v Rugby Group Ltd* [2006] EWCA Civ 69.

Terms "to be agreed"

[*Add to note 477: page* [181]]   **2–124**
Minter v Julius Baer Investments Ltd [2004] EWHC 2472; [2005] Pens. L.R.
73 (letter stating that "the remaining terms of service shall be worked out" held
to be no more than an agreement to agree and therefore to have no contractual
force).

[*In line 14 at "them" add new note 479a*]
[479a] *cf. Willis Management (Isle of Man) Ltd v Cable and Wireless plc* [2005] EWCA Civ 806;
[2005] 2 Lloyd's Rep. 597 at [33].

Options and rights of pre-emption

[*Add to note 485: page* [182]]   **2–125**
And see *Re Gray* [2004] EWHC 1538 (Ch); [2005] 1 W.L.R. 815 at [25]. On
the exercise of a right of pre-emption, the right may acquire the characteristics of
an option: see *Cottrell v King* [2004] EWHC 397; [2004] B.C.C. 307.

[*Add to note 486*]
For the distinction between options and rights of pre-emption, see also *Tiffany
Investments Ltd v Bircham & Co Nominees (No.2) Ltd* [2003] EWCA Civ 1759;
[2004] 2 P.&C.R. 10.

Agreement not incomplete merely because further agreement is required

2–126 [*Add to note 490: page* [182]]
See also *Scammell v Dicker* [2005] EWCA Civ 405; [2005] 3 All E.R. 838 at [31], [40].

Criteria laid down in the agreement

2–128 [*Add to text at end: page* [185]]
An agreement may also lack contractual force where, though it lays down a criterion for resolving matters which are left open, it also states that the principles for determining the application of that criterion are to be settled by further negotiations between the parties.[509a]

> [509a] *Willis Management (Isle of Man) Ltd v Cable and Wireless plc* [2005] EWCA Civ 806; [2005] 2 Lloyd's Rep. 597, below para.2–139 of this Supplement.

Machinery laid down in the agreement

2–129 [*Add to note 511: page* [185]]
See also *Horkulak v Cantor Fitzgerald International* [2004] EWCA Civ 1287; [2005] I.C.R. 402 at [48], below, para.2–169 of this Supplement. *cf. Lymington Marina Ltd v Macnamara* [2006] EWHC 704 (Ch); [2006] 2 All E.R. (Comm.) 200.

[*Add to note 514*]
Alstom Signalling Ltd v Jarvis Facilities Ltd [2004] EWHC 1232; 95 Con. L.R. 55 (power to determine differences between the parties given by them to Technology and Construction Court).

Agreement to negotiate

2–134 [*Add to note 535: page* [187]]
Willis Management (Isle of Man) Ltd v Cable and Wireless plc [2005] EWCA Civ 806; [2005] 2 Lloyd's Rep. 597 at [24], [26].

2–135 [*Add to text at end of paragraph: page* [189]]
An express term, in an agreement that is intended to be legally binding, to negotiate outstanding matters in good faith may likewise have contractual force.[553a]

> [553a] See *Petromec Inc v Petroleo Brasileiro SA Petrobras* [2005] EWCA Civ 891; [2006] 1 Lloyd's Rep. 121 at [115]–[121], distinguishing *Walford v Miles* [1992] 2 A.C. 128 on the grounds that in the latter case there was "no concluded agreement at all since everything was subject to contract" and that there was "no express agreement to negotiate in good faith" (at [120]). In the *Petromec* case, the point was "not essential to the disposition of this appeal" (at [115]). (See also above, para.1–020).

7. CERTAINTY OF TERMS

Requirement of certainty

2–136 [*Add to note 554: page* [190]]
See also *Scammell v Dicker* [2005] EWCA Civ 405; [2005] 3 All E.R. 838 at [41], describing *Scammell v Ouston* as "a rare case of uncertainty". *cf. Judge v*

Crown Leisure Ltd [2005] EWCA Civ 571; [2005] I.R.L.R. 823 at [23] (promise to increase an employee's salary "eventually" or "in due course" held to be "too vague to amount to a binding contractual promise").

Qualification of the requirement of certainty

[Add to note 556: page [190]]
; *Alstom Signalling Ltd v Jarvis Facilities Ltd* [2004] EWHC 1232; 95 Con. L.R. 55.

2–137

[Add to note 557]
See also *Scammell v Dicker* [2005] EWCA Civ 405; [2005] 3 All E.R. 838, *per* Rix L.J. ("the courts should strain to be the preserver and not the destroyer of bargains"). See also *Halpern v Halpern* [2006] EWHC (Comm) 603; [2006] 2 Lloyd's Rep. 83 at [115] ("A court strives to give effect to agreements, unless not intended to create legal relations, particularly when the agreement is a compromise of an existing dispute and when it has been acted on"). For further proceedings in this case, see [2006] EWHC 1728, see para.7–045A of this Supplement.

Reasonableness

[Add to note 563: page [191]]
See also *Scammell v Dicker* [2005] EWCA Civ 405; [2005] 3 All E.R. 838 at [42], below para.2–141 of this Supplement where the agreement (in a consent order settling a boundary dispute) was "capable of being made definite without further agreement. It was reasonably certain."

2–139

[Add to text at end of paragraph: page [191]]
An agreement to pay a "fair" sum may also lack contractual force where it states that the principles for determining what amounts to such a sum are to be settled by further negotiations between the parties. In one such case,[564a] A accepted liability for a "fair" share of losses suffered by B as a result of the acts of one of A's employees; but the compromise agreement to this effect added that the parties would draw up a statement of principles by which that "fair" share was to be determined. The description of the share to be paid by A as a "fair" one was said to be "simply the label which the parties put on the outcome which they hoped to achieve. There was no unqualified commitment [by A] to pay a fair share."[564b] The compromise agreement was therefore merely an agreement to negotiate and had no contractual force.

[564a] *Willis Management (Isle of Man) Ltd v Cable and Wireless plc* [2005] EWCA Civ 806; [2005] 2 Lloyd's Rep. 597.
[564b] *ibid.,* at [24].

Meaningless or self contradictory phrases

[Add new text: page [192]]
An agreement is not too uncertain to amount to a contract merely because of a conflict between two of its terms if, as is often the case, the conflict can be resolved by the court in the course of the normal adjudication of a contractual

2–141

dispute. In *Scammell v Dicker*[569a] a consent order relating to a boundary dispute was alleged to be ineffective by reason of an alleged conflict between the terms of the order and a plan annexed to it. The Court of Appeal held that the order was not vitiated by uncertainty since it was "for the parties to resolve any disagreement as to interpretation" and if they failed to do so they would "go to tribunals to find the answer."[569b] The ordinary processes of construction can in such cases resolve the uncertainty.

[569a] [2005] EWCA Civ 405; [2005] 3 All E.R. 838.
[569b] *ibid.*, at [31].

8. Conditional Agreements

(b) *Degrees of Obligation*

Duty not to prevent occurrence of the event

2–148   [*Add to note 584: page* [195]]
      cf. CEL Group Ltd v Nedlloyd Lines UK Ltd [2003] EWCA Civ 1716; [2004] 1 All E.R. (Comm.) 689 at [11] (where the contract was not in terms conditional but the court applied a similar principle to that stated in Main Work, para.2–148 by virtue of the rule stated in Main Work, para.13–012.)

Condition of "satisfaction"

2–149   [*Add to note 597: page* [196]]
      See also *Lymington Marina Ltd v Macnamara* [2006] EWHC 704 (Ch); [2006] 2 All E.R. (Comm.) 200 at [86]–[88].

Duty of reasonable diligence to bring about the event

2–150   [*Note 602: page* [197]]
      Update reference to Benjamin to (7th ed., 2006), paras 18–309—18–311.

      [*Note 604*]
      Update reference to Benjamin to (7th ed., 2006), paras 18–313—18–318.

      [*Note 605*]
      Update reference to Benjamin to (7th ed., 2006), paras 21–022—21–027.

      [*Note 607*]
      Update reference to Benjamin to (7th ed., 2006), para.18–328.

9. CONTRACTUAL INTENTION

Burden of proof: agreements inferred from conduct

[*Add to note 622: page* [199]]   2–155
Contrast *Goshawk Dedicated Ltd v Tyser & Co Ltd* [2006] EWCA Civ 54;
[2006] 1 All E.R. (Comm.) 501 at [66], apparently rejecting the argument, based
(at [46]) on the *Baird Textile* case [2001] EWCA Civ 274; [2002] 1 All E.R.
(Comm.) 737, that there was no implied contract.

Agreements giving discretion to one party whether to perform

[*Add to note 696: page* [208]]   2–169
Carmichael v National Power plc [1999] 1 W.L.R. 2042 was also distinguished in *Prater v Cornwall County Council* [2006] EWCA Civ 102; [2006] 2
All E.R. 1013. In the latter case, C was engaged by D as a home tutor for pupils
who were unable to attend school. D was under no contractual obligation to offer
pupils to C, nor was C under any contractual obligation to accept any pupils that
might be offered to her; but once C had agreed to accept a particular pupil she
was obliged to fulfil her commitment to that pupil and D was obliged to continue
to provide work in relation to that pupil until the engagement in relation to him
or her had run its course. It was held that there had been a succession of
individual contracts (relating to each of the pupils offered to and accepted by C)
as there was "mutuality of obligation" in each of these contracts. This gave rise
to a contract of service between C and D even though there was no obligation on
D to offer further work, or on C to accept any such offer.

[*Add to note 697*]
See also *Horkulak v Cantor Fitzgerald International* [2004] EWCA Civ 1287;
[2005] I.C.R. 402 where a "discretionary bonus on dismissal" clause in a
contract of employment was held not to give the employer an unfettered discretion but one which had to be exercised "rationally and in good faith" (at [48]);
cf. ibid., at [46]: "bona fide and rationally".

Collective agreements

[*Add to note 699: page* [208]]   2–171
See also *Kaur v MG Rover Group Ltd* [2004] EWCA Civ 1507; [2005] I.C.R.
625, where a term of a collective agreement to the effect that there would be no
compulsory redundancies was held not to have been incorporated in individual
employment contracts as it was merely of an "aspirational nature" (at [33]) and
not intended to constitute a binding contractual commitment.

Nature of relationship between the parties

[*Add to text after note 715: page* [210]]   2–175
President of the Methodist Conference v Parfitt[715a] and the other cases cited in
Main Work, para.2–175, note 715, must be contrasted with *Percy v Board of*

National Mission of the Church of Scotland.[715b] The issue in the former group of cases was whether the claimants were entitled to remedies for unfair dismissal from their posts as ministers of a church, or similar posts in other religious institutions. Such remedies were, under the relevant legislation, available only to a person between whom and the institution there was a "contract of service".[715c] The claim in *Percy's* case, by contrast, was based on sex discrimination in employment contrary to the Sex Discrimination Act 1975. The "statutory prerequisite" for such a claim was "expressed in wider terms"[715d] than those applicable to an unfair dismissal claim. The prerequisite for a sex discrimination claim was that there should be a "contract of employment" and this expression was defined by s.82(1) of the 1975 Act to include "a contract personally to execute any work or labour", a phrase that was wide enough to cover a contract for services even where there was no contract of service. Ms Percy had been appointed for a five-year term as an associate minister in a Church of Scotland parish. She had applied for the post in response to a publication by the Board inviting applications; been invited by the General Secretary of the Board to accept the appointment; been sent a copy of the "terms and conditions" on which it was to be held; and had then written to the General Secretary formally accepting the appointment.[715g] The "terms and conditions" specified the duration of the appointment and the salary; they stated that a manse would be supplied and that travelling expenses would be paid; and they referred to the duties that she would be expected to perform. The House of Lords, by a majority, held (1) that there was a contract between Ms Percy and the Board and (2) that this contract was one "personally to execute any work or labour" within s.82(1) of the 1975 Act, and hence a "contract of employment" within that subsection. Lord Nicholls accepted that "many arrangements . . . in church matters" were such that "viewed objectively on ordinary principles, the parties [could] not be taken to have intended to enter into a legally binding contract" because of the "breadth and looseness [of the arrangements] and the circumstances in which they were undertaken".[715h] But this principle "could not be carried into arrangements which on their face were intended to give rise to legally binding obligations. The offer and acceptance of a church post for a specified period, with specific provisions for the appointee's duties and remuneration and travelling expenses and holidays [fell] firmly into this latter category."[715i] On the facts of *Percy's* case, the requirements of contractual intention was therefore satisfied. Moreover, the view (expressed at the end of note 715 on page 210 of the Main Work), that the attitude of the courts to cases of this kind is changing, is supported by Lord Nicholls' further observations that "in this regard there seems to be no cogent reason to-day to draw a distinction between a post whose duties are primarily religious and a post within the church where this is not so"; and that, in the context of statutory protection for employees, "it is time to recognise that employment arrangements between a church and its ministers should not lightly be taken as intended to have no legal effect and, in consequence, its ministers denied this protection".[715k]

[715a] [1984] Q.B. 368.
[715b] [2005] UKHL 73; [2006] 2 W.L.R. 353.
[715c] See Employment Rights Act 1996, ss.94(1), 230(1) and (2).
[715d] *Percy's* case, above n.715b, at [13].
[715e] *ibid.*

[715f] *ibid.*, at [3].
[715g] *ibid.*, at [31]; *cf.* at [96].
[715h] *ibid.*, at [23].
[715i] *ibid.*, [24]; *cf.* at [112], [137].
[715j] *ibid.*, at [25]; *cf. ibid.*, at [151].
[715k] *ibid.*, at [26]; *cf. ibid.*, at [152].

[*Add to note 719: page* [210]]
    cf. Essex Strategic Health Authority v David-John [2003] Lloyd's Rep. Med. 586 (relationship between general practitioner and Health Authority not contractual).

Vague agreements

[*Add to note 729: page* [211]]   **2–176**
    See also *Judge v Crown Leisure Ltd* [2005] EWCA Civ 571; [2005] I.R.L.R. 823, above, para.2–136 of this Supplement. The judgment at [23] states that the issue was not one of intention to create legal relations but one of vagueness; but passages at [9] and [24] show that the two issues are related.

[*Add at end*]
    The fact that some terms of an agreement are too vague to have contractual force does not preclude the enforcement of other terms which are, in themselves, sufficiently certain. This is, in particular, the case where the parties have acted in reliance on the latter term.[731a]

[731a] *Pena v Dale* [2003] EWHC 1065; [2004] 2 B.C.L.C. 508 at [95].

Other cases

[*Add to note 735: page* [212]]   **2–178**
    cf. Sutton v Mishcon Reya [2003] EWHC 3166 (Ch); [2004] F.L.R. 837: cohabitation agreement by which one man was to be "slave" to another arguably "just an act or a role-play" (at [26]).

CHAPTER 3

CONSIDERATION

			PARA.
	1.	Introduction	3–001
■	2.	Definitions	3–004
□	3.	Adequacy of consideration	3–014
□	4.	The concept of "valuable" consideration	3–022
	5.	Past consideration	3–026
■	6.	Consideration must move from the promisee	3–036
■	7.	Compromise and forbearance to sue	3–046
		(a) Valid claims	3–047
■		(b) Invalid or doubtful claims	3–050
		(c) Actual forbearance	3–057
■	8.	Existing duties as consideration	3–061
□		(a) Public duty	3–062
□		(b) Duty imposed by contract with promisor	3–065
■		(c) Duty imposed by contract with a third party	3–072
■	9.	Discharge and variation of contractual duties	3–076
□		(a) Rescission	3–077
■		(b) Variation	3–079
■		(i) Requirement of consideration	3–079
■		(ii) Common law mitigations	3–081
□		(iii) Equitable mitigations	3–085
■	10.	Part payment of a debt	3–115
		(a) General rule	3–115
		(b) Limitations at common law	3–118
■		(c) Limitations in equity	3–128
■	11.	Proprietary estoppel	3–137
□		(a) Nature of the doctrine	3–137
□		(b) Bases of liability	3–139
□		(c) Conditions giving rise to liability	3–143
□		(d) Effects of the doctrine	3–148
		(e) Comparison with other doctrines	3–158
□	12.	Special cases	3–163

2. DEFINITIONS

Performances and promises as consideration

3–008   *[Add to note 33: page* [219]]

See also *Melhuish v Redbridge Citizens Advice Bureau* [2005] I.R.L.R. 419, where a voluntary worker agreed to work (without pay) for two days a week; his expenses were to be reimbursed and he had the benefit of being allowed to take part in training courses. It was held that there was no "mutuality of obligation" (and hence no contract of employment) but at most "a limited unilateral contract" (at [18]).

3. ADEQUACY OF CONSIDERATION

Illustrations

[*Add new text at end of paragraph: page* [225]]   **3–015**
  The grant of permission to cut back undergrowth has been held to constitute consideration for the grant of a contractual licence to occupy land, in spite of "the temporary nature of the arrangement".[78a]

[78a] *Well Barn Farming Ltd v Backhouse* [2005] EWHC 1520 at [45].

Objects of trifling value

[*Add to note 80: page* [225]]   **3–016**
  By virtue of s.335(1) of the Gambling Act 2005, consideration for money paid by a member of the club will be provided, on facts such as those of *Lipkin Gorman v Karpnale Ltd* [1991] 2 A.C. 548, by reason of the fact that the club's promise to the member will be legally enforceable: see below, Vol.II, paras 40–001D and 40–083 of this Supplement.

[*Add to note 90: page* [226]]   **3–017**
  For the effect of the Gambling Act 2005 on the reasoning of *Lipkin Gorman v Karpnale Ltd* [1991] 2 A.C. 548, see above, para.3–016 of this Supplement.

Nominal consideration

[*Add to note 94: page* [228]]   **3–019**
  See also Charities Act 1993, s.65(1)(a), requiring "full consideration in money or money's worth", a requirement not satisfied in *Bayoumi v Women's Total Abstinence Educational Union Ltd* [2003] EWCA Civ 1548; [2004] Ch. 40 at [46]–[47].

4. THE CONCEPT OF "VALUABLE" CONSIDERATION

Promisee would have performed anyway

[*Add to note 119: page* [230]]   **3–024**
  For a case in which the promisor failed to discharge the burden of proof on the issue that the promisee would have done the act alleged to constitute consideration anyway (*i.e.* even if the promise had not been made): see *Well Barn Farming Ltd v Backhouse* [2005] EWHC 1520 at [47], [48].

Discretionary promise

3–025   [*Add to note 124: page* [231]]
See also the discussion in *Cotswold Development Construction Ltd v Williams* [2006] I.R.L.R. 181 of the requirement of "mutuality of obligation", which must be satisfied to give a casual worker the status of an "employee".

6. CONSIDERATION MUST MOVE FROM THE PROMISEE

Bar pupillage contracts

3–038   [*Add to note 180: page* [238]]
But an application for pupillage is not one for "membership" of chambers within the Disability Discrimination Act 1995, s.13(1)(c): *Horton v Higham* [2004] EWCA Civ 941; [2004] 3 All E.R. 863, where *Edmonds v Lawson* [2000] Q.B. 501 (discussed in Main Work, para.3–038) is cited at [21].

7. COMPROMISE AND FORBEARANCE TO SUE

(b) *Invalid or Doubtful Claims*

Claims known to be invalid

3–050   [*Add to note 229: page* [244]]
Under s.335(1) of the Gambling Act 2005, contracts relating to gambling will, as a general rule, become legally enforceable: see below, Vol.II, para.40–001D. It follows that a promise not to sue a client for the amount of a lost bet will, in general, be good consideration for a promise made in return by the client. Such a case will fall within the principle stated in Main Work, para.3–047.

8. EXISTING DUTIES AS CONSIDERATION

(a) *Public Duty*

Promisee doing more than public duty

3–063   [*Add to text after note 277: page* [249]]
The requirements of s.25(1) of the Police Act 1996 were further considered in *Reading Festival Ltd v West Yorkshire Police Authority*.[277a] A claim under the subsection was there made by a police authority against the promoters of a music festival to recover the costs incurred by the authority in deploying a considerable police force, not on the site of the festival, but in the surrounding area, so as to be ready to intervene if serious disorder broke out. The promoters had not made

any express request for this deployment[277b] and were by the terms of their licence for the event made responsible for providing, on the site, "security in sufficient numbers deployed to an agreed specification as acceptable to the Chief Officer of Police"[277c] and to other listed public authorities. The promoters' view was that the police authority would "not be policing this event"[277d]; they had hired security staff[277e]; and, as the occasion "went off more calmly that in previous years",[277f] the police did not have to intervene. The Court of Appeal held that the police authority had no claim under s.25(1) of the 1996 Act. The main reason for this conclusion was that, in the circumstances described above, the promoters had not made any "request" at all for special police services[277g]; another possible reason for it was that some such request had been made, but that assuming (in spite of the evidence referred to above)[277h] that this request was for a police presence *on* the festival site,[277i] the services provided differed from those requested, consisting merely of an *off*-site deployment.[277j] This appears to be the significance of the trial judge's finding that "a claim in contract could not have succeeded because there was no meeting of the minds as to how the police services were to be deployed . . . ".[277k] In the Court of Appeal it was said that this finding was "fatal to the claim", the reference at this stage being[277l] to one under s.25(1); and this reasoning raises the question of the nature of such a claim. It was said that the subsection had not "added anything to or altered the common law position [as stated in *Glasbrook Brothers Ltd v Glamorgan County Council*][277m] except possibly to clarify that the police authority had the last word on charges"[277n]; and that, although "the section does not speak of a contract as such", yet, to give rise to liability to pay, "there would ordinarily need to be agreement between the promoter and the police—at least in broad terms",[277o] the qualification in the last phrase here quoted reflecting the point that "how the police provide the services requested must ultimately always be a matter for them".[277p] It is respectfully submitted that an agreement for services which left such a broad discretion to the provider of the services as to what was to be provided, and what the recipient was to pay for the services provided, would not normally be sufficiently certain to satisfy the requirements of a binding contract.[277q] The subsection is satisfied if there is a request and if services of the general kind requested are rendered; there is no further legislative requirement of a binding contract.

In view of the conclusion that the services provided had not been requested, it was not strictly necessary to decide whether the services provided were "special police services" within the subjection.[277r] But Scott Baker L.J. expressed (apparently with some reluctance)[277s] the view that the services were not of this nature. Two factors seem to have led to this conclusion: the fact that the "predominant purpose" of the police deployment was "the protection of the public at large"[277t]; and the fact that the deployment was not something that the promoters of the festival had requested.[277u] In this respect, the requirement that the services must be "special" is linked with that of a "request" for them.[277v]

[277a] [2006] EWCA Civ 524; *The Times*, May 15, 2006.

[277b] *ibid.*, at [37]; a request had been made for traffic management and the police authority was paid for this service: *ibid.*, at [14], [41], [44].

[277c] *ibid.*, at [35].

[277d] *ibid.*, at [43].

[277e] *ibid.*, at [44].

277f *ibid.*
277g See *ibid.*, at [12], heading before [34], [58], [67] and [72].
277h At n.277d, above.
277i [2006] EWCA Civ 524 at [53].
277j *ibid.*, at [55].
277k *ibid.*, at [54].
277l *ibid.*, at [55].
277m [1925] A.C. 270, discussed in Main Work, para.3–063.
277n [2006] EWCA Civ 524 at [20].
277o *ibid.*, at [21].
277p *ibid.*
277q See Main Work, paras 2–110 *et seq.*
277r [2006] EWCA Civ 524 at [58].
277s See *ibid.*, at [67], [72].
277t *ibid.*, at [63].
277u *ibid.*, at [67].
277v *ibid.*, at [65].

(b) *Duties Imposed by Contract with Promisor*

Cases in which there was no consideration

3–066   *[Add to note 287: page* [251]]
See also *South Caribbean Trading v Trafigura Beheer BV* [2004] EWHC 2676
(Comm); [2005] 1 Lloyd's Rep. 128 at [107], as to which see also below, paras
3–069 and 3–079 of this Supplement.

Factual benefit to the promisor

3–069   *[Add to note 305: page* [253]]
For the difficulty of reconciling *Williams v Roffey Bros & Nicholls (Contractors) Ltd* [1991] 1 Q.B. 1 with *Stilk v Myrick* (1809) 2 Camp. 317 and the
cases that have followed it, see also *South Caribbean Trading v Trafigura Beheer
BV* [2004] EWHC 2676 (Comm); [2005] 1 Lloyd's Rep. 128 at [107], [108].
Colman J. there accepted that the *Williams* case "appears to have introduced
some amelioration" (at [107]), but said that he would not have followed the
reasoning of that case if it had not been a decision of the Court of Appeal. The
learned judge criticised the reasoning of the case as being "inconsistent with
the . . . rule that consideration must move from the promisee" (*i.e.* the carpentry
sub-contractor in that case). It is, however, respectfully submitted that the
requirement that consideration must move from the promisee can be satisfied by
the promisee's conferring a benefit on the promisor even though the promisee, in
doing so, suffers no detriment (see Main Work, para.3–037) and that the carpentry sub-contractor had conferred such a benefit on the promisor by doing the
agreed work (see *ibid.*, at n.176). Colman J.'s refusal to apply the reasoning of
the *Williams* case is, however, with respect justifiable on the different ground
(given by him in the *South Caribbean* case at [109]) that the promisee's "threat
of non-compliance of its delivery obligation" under the original contract was in
the latter case "analogous to economic duress." In the *Williams* case, there was
no such threat (see Main Work, para.3–068 after n.302) and it is clear that, where
the new promise is obtained by duress, it cannot be enforced by virtue of the
principle enunciated in that case (see Main Work, para.3–069).

(c) *Duty imposed by Contract with a Third Party*

Performance of the duty

[Add to note 325: page [256]]   **3–073**
A "civil partnership agreement" likewise does not have contractual force:
Civil Partnership Act 2004, s.73.

9. DISCHARGE AND VARIATION OF CONTRACTUAL DUTIES

Introduction

[Add new note 344a in line 11, after "originally undertaken by A": page [258]]   **3–076**
[344a] The issue discussed in *South Caribbean Trading v Trafigura Beheer BV* [2004] EWHC 2676
(Comm); [2005] 1 Lloyd's Rep. 128 at [107]–[112] appears to have been of this kind: it was whether
a seller of oil had provided consideration for the buyer's promise to take delivery after the originally
agreed date by promising to perform his (the seller's) duties with respect to delivery by a specified
later date: see below, para.3–079 of this Supplement.

(a) *Rescission*

Agreements to rescind where each party has outstanding rights

[Add to note 346: page [258]]   **3–077**
cf. Argo Fund Ltd v Essar Steel Ltd [2005] EWHC 600 (Comm); [2006] 1 All
E.R. (Comm.) 56 at [51] (consideration for the termination of a contract which
is novated said to be that "each side [to the original contract] agrees to give up
all rights and obligations as against the other"); affd. on other grounds [2006]
EWCA Civ 241; [2006] 2 All E.R. (Comm.) 104.

(b) *Variation*

(i) *Requirement of Consideration*

Agreements to vary contracts

[Add new text at end of paragraph: page [260]]   **3–079**
An agreement for the sale of goods can likewise be varied by mutual promises
(made before the delivery date originally specified) on the part of the buyer to
accept delivery and of the seller to perform his obligations with respect to
delivery, on a different (later) date. This was held to be the position where a seller
of fuel oil, to be produced by blending components to be provided by the buyer,
had encountered "apparently insuperable"[353a] problems in completing the blending process by the originally agreed delivery date. An agreement was then made
by which the seller promised to complete that process by a later date and the
buyer promised to accept delivery on that date. The price remained fixed at a
level which was below the market price on the date of the variation agreement

but which "might exceed"[353b] the market price on the extended delivery date. It was held that the variation amounted to "a new agreement supported by mutual promises"[353c] and that "sufficient consideration [for the buyer's promise to accept delivery on the later date] moved from the promisee"[353d] (*i.e.* the seller).

[353a] *South Caribbean Trading v Trafigura Beheer BV* [2004] EWHC 2676 (Comm); [2005] 1 Lloyd's Rep. 128 at [105]. It does not appear that these difficulties were treated by the buyer as a breach of the contract.
[353b] *ibid.*
[353c] *ibid.*; for mutual promises as consideration for each other, see Main Work, para.3–008A.
[353d] *South Caribbean Trading* case, above n.353a, at [105].

(ii) *Common Law Mitigations*

Forbearance may become irrevocable

3–083   [*Add to note 369: page* [262]]
See also *Bottiglieri di Navagazione SpA v Cosco Quindao Ocean Shipping Co (The Bunge Saga Lima)* [2005] EWHC 244 (Comm); [2005] 2 Lloyd's Rep. 1 at [31], below para.3–097 n.438 of this Supplement.

(iii) *Equitable Mitigations*

Relationships within the doctrine

3–087   [*Add to note 377: page* [264]]
See also *Lambeth LBC v O'Kane Holdings Ltd* [2005] EWCA Civ 1010; [2006] H.L.R. 2: in absence of special circumstances, there was no new tenancy between a former landlord and a tolerated trespasser.

Requirement of pre-existing legal relationship

3–088   [*Add to note 378: page* [264]]
Evans v Amicus Healthcare Ltd has been affirmed ([2004] EWCA Civ 727; [2005] Fam. 1) on the ground that estoppel or waiver could not preclude a man from withdrawing his consent to the use of his genetic material since the right to withdraw such consent was expressly given by the Human Fertilisation and Embryology Act 1990, Sch.3 para.4(1), so that the application of waiver or estoppel "would conflict with the Parliamentary scheme" (at [37]; see also at [36] and [120]).

The promise or representation must be "clear" or "unequivocal"

3–090   [*Add to note 386, line 12: page* [266]]
Super Chem Products Ltd v American Life & General Insurance Co Ltd [2004] UKPC 2; [2004] 2 All E.R. 358 at [23], where the present requirement was not satisfied.

[*Add to note 386, line 12, after* "689"]
Fortisbank SA v Trenwick International Ltd [2005] EWHC 339; [2005] Lloyd's Rep. I.R. 464 at [32], [35].

[Add to note 387: page [266]]
Evans v Amicus Healthcare Ltd has been affirmed [2004] EWCA Civ 727;
[2005] Fam. 1: see above, para.3–088 of this Supplement.

Whether "detriment" is required

[Add to note 421: page [269]]   3–094
See also *Fortisbank SA v Trenwick International Ltd* [2005] EWHC 339;
[2005] Lloyd's Rep. I.R. at [31] ("has altered its [the promisee's] position to its
detriment or otherwise relied on the promise so that it would be inequitable or
unconscionable for [the promisor] not to be held to the promise").

[Add to note 422: page [269]]
See also *Bottiglieri di Navigazione SpA v Cosco Quindao Ocean Shipping Co
(The Bunge Saga Lima)* [2005] EWHC 244; [2005] 2 Lloyd's Rep. 1, the facts
of which are stated in para.3–097 of this Supplement. Gloster J. said (at [31]) that
"a failure to act by the representee may give rise to a waiver . . . ; it is
unnecessary that the conduct of the representee should be to his detriment
provided that there is some conduct which differs from that which would have
occurred in the absence of the representation".

Inequitable

[Add to note 424: page [270]]   3–095
See also *Bottiglieri di Navigazione SpA v Cosco Quindao Ocean Shipping Co
(The Bunge Saga Lima)* [2005] EWHC 244; [2005] 2 Lloyd's Rep. 1 at [31],
quoted below in para.3–097, n.438 of this Supplement.

[Add to note 428]
Evans v Amicus Healthcare Ltd has been affirmed [2004] EWCA Civ 727;
[2005] Fam. 1: see above, para.3–088 of this Supplement.

[Add to note 429]
See also *South Caribbean Trading v Trafigura Beheer BV* [2004] EWHC 2676
(Comm); [2005] 1 Lloyd's Rep. 128 at [112], holding that the "estoppel" (see
Main Work, para.3–103) does not prevent the promisor from going back on a
promise obtained by economic duress in the form of a refusal on the promisee's
part to perform the original contract.

Extinctive effect in exceptional cases

[Add to note 438: page [271]]   3–097
In *Bottiglieri di Navigazione SpA v Cosco Quindao Ocean Shipping Co (The
Bunge Saga Lima)* [2005] EWHC 244 (Comm); [2005] 2 Lloyd's Rep. 1, a time
charter contained a "cleaning clause" requiring the vessel to be clean and
suitable for the charterer's cargo at the first loadport. The charterer loaded cargo
there in spite of the fact that the clause had not been complied with but later
claimed damages in respect of contamination caused to further cargo loaded at
the second loadport by reason of the original failure to comply with the cleaning

clause. The claim failed as the charterer had waived the clause. Gloster J. said at [31]:

"Although a waiver of this kind may be retracted, no revocation can be retrospective; thus waiver may have permanent effect where it would be inequitable to permit retraction (for example because the representee can no longer resume his former position)."

Defensive nature of the doctrine

3–098   [*Add to note 455: page* [273]]
Evans v Amicus Healthcare Ltd has been affirmed ([2004] EWCA Civ 727; [2005] Fam. 1) on the ground stated in para.3–088 of this Supplement and without reference to the point discussed in para.3–098 of the Main Work.

Doctrine may deprive promisor of certain defences

3–101   [*Add to note 471a: page* [275]]
Evans v Amicus Healthcare Ltd has been affirmed ([2004] EWCA Civ 727; [2005] Fam. 1) on the ground stated in para.3–088 of this Supplement and without reference to the point discussed in para.3–101 of the Main Work.

Analogy with waiver

3–104   [*Add to note 494 line 8, after* "2003": *page* [278]]
See also *Fortisbank SA v Trenwick International Ltd* [2005] EWHC 339; [2005] Lloyd's Rep. I.R. 464 at [29].

Distinguished from estoppel by convention

3–107   [*Add to note 514: page* [281]]
See also *Thor Navigation Inc v Ingosstrakh Insurance* [2005] EWHC 19 (Comm); [2005] 1 Lloyd's Rep. 547 at [66], [67]; *Triodos Bank NV v Dobbs* [2005] EWCA Civ 630; [2005] 2 Lloyd's Rep. 588 at [22]; *Canmer International Insurance v UK Mutual Assurance* [2005] EWHC 1694; [2005] 2 Lloyd's Rep. 479 at [41], where there was no common assumption and hence no estoppel by convention.

[*Add to note 515*]
See also the *Thor Navigation* case, above n.514, at [66]; and *Ease Faith Ltd v Leonis Marine Management Ltd* [2006] EWHC 232 (Comm); [2006] 1 Lloyd's Rep. 673 at [171], where the requirements of estoppel by convention were not satisfied.

[*Add to note 518: page* [282]]
Although no representation is required to give rise to estoppel by convention, it seems that the assumption on which such an estoppel is based must (like the representation required to give rise to an estoppel by representation) be "unambiguous and unequivocal": see *Smithkline Beecham plc v Apotex Europe Ltd* [2006] EWCA Civ 658; *The Times*, June 9, 2006 at [102], where this point was "not disputed" and the concession was apparently approved by the court.

"Communication" passing "across the line"

[*Add to note 528: page* [283]]   **3–109**
See also *Thor Navigation Inc v Ingosstrakh Insurance* [2005] EWHC 19
(Comm); [2005] 1 Lloyd's Rep. 547 at [66] for the requirement that "both parties
must have conducted themselves on the basis of such shared assumption"; and
Fortisbank SA v Trenwick International [2005] EWHC 339; [2005] Lloyd's Rep.
I.R. 464 at [43] (no estoppel by convention as no conduct on the basis of the
alleged assumption).

Whether estoppel by convention creates new rights

[*Add to note 557 line 1, after "132": page* [286]]   **3–113**
    cf. *Dunford Trading A-G v OAO Atlantrybflot* [2005] EWCA Civ 24; [2005] 1
Lloyd's Rep. 289 at [39], referring to Brandon L.J.'s view in the *Amalgamated
Investment* case [1982] Q.B. 84 at [131]–[132] as the likely answer to the
argument that the estoppel was being used "as a sword rather than as a shield"
(*per* Rix L.J.).

[*Add to note 566: page* [287]]
The view that estoppel by convention cannot create new rights is supposed by
Smithkline Beecham plc v Apotex Europe Ltd [2006] EWCA Civ 658; *The Times*,
June 9, 2006. A claim based on estoppel by convention and on estoppel by
representation (see at [102]) was there rejected. Counsel's argument that "An
estoppel cannot be used as a key element of a claim (sword not shield)" was
accepted by the court, Jacob L.J. saying "I think he [counsel] was right" (at
[103]); that "an estoppel cannot create an agreement" (at [107]) and that "an
estoppel inherently must be raised by way of riposte" (at [110]).

Invalidity of assumed term

[*Add to note 568: page* [287]]   **3–114**
A party may, however, be liable on an agreement which does not comply with
the formal requirements of s.2(1) of the Law of Property (Miscellaneous Provisions) Act 1989 on the basis of a *proprietary* estoppel amounting, or giving rise
also, to a constructive trust: see *Kinane v Mackie-Conteh* [2005] EWCA Civ 45;
[2005] W.T.L.R. 345, below paras 3–139 and 4–078 of this Supplement. Such
liability arises by virtue of s.2(5) of the 1989 Act. On the question whether a
defendant would be so liable if his conduct gave rise to a proprietary estoppel,
but not to a constructive trust, there may be a difference of judicial opinion in the
Kinane case. The judgment of Arden L.J. at one point [28] may support an
affirmative answer to this question, while Neuberger L.J. was "content to
assume" that the defendant would not be so liable "if he could only establish a
proprietary estoppel, and not a trust", (at [46] and see [45]). All the members of
the court, however, based their judgments in favour of the claimant on the
conclusion that the case was one of both proprietary estoppel and constructive
trust: see [31], [49], [52]. For the relationship between these two concepts, see
Main Work, para.3–139 and below, para.3–139 of this Supplement.

10. PART PAYMENT OF A DEBT

(c) *Limitations in Equity*

Extinctive effects in exceptional cases

3–132   [*Add to note 658: page* [297]]
The statement in *Bottiglieri di Navigazione SpA v Cosco Quindao Ocean Shipping Co (The Bunge Saga Lima)* [2005] EWHC 244 (Comm); [2005] 2 Lloyd's Rep. 1 at [31] that "no revocation can be retrospective" is made in the context of a situation in which "it would be inequitable to permit retraction": see the account of this case given above in para.3–097, n.438 of this Supplement. The case was not concerned with "waiver" of an obligation to pay money.

11. PROPRIETARY ESTOPPEL

(a) *Nature of the Doctrine*

Scope of proprietary estoppel

3–138   [*Add to note 685: page* [300]]
Blue Haven Enterprises Ltd v Tully [2006] UKPC 17 appears likewise to be a case in which proprietary estoppel was alleged to have arisen from acquiescence (of the kind described at this note in the Main Work) so that no issue arose as to the enforceability of any promise. The claim failed as the defendant had drawn the claimant's attention to his (the defendant's) interest in time and so had not acted unconscionably in asserting that interest against the claimant.

(b) *Bases of Liability*

Expenditure on another's land in reliance on the promise

3–139   [*Add to note 696: page* [301]]
See also *Van Laethen v Brooker* [2005] EWHC 1478; [2006] 1 F.C.R. 697, below, para.3–146 of this Supplement.

[*Add to note 698: page* [302]]
For the relationship between proprietary estoppel and constructive trust, see also *Kinane v Mackie-Conteh* [2005] EWCA Civ 45; [2005] W.T.L.R. 345 at [26], [29], [31] and [47]–[51], discussing the question whether these concepts could be invoked by a party seeking to enforce an agreement which failed to comply with the formal requirements of Law of Property (Miscellaneous Provisions) Act 1989, s.2(1). A distinction was there drawn between cases in which proprietary estoppel does not, and those in which it can, also give rise to a constructive trust. An example of the former situation would be that in which "a landowner stands by while his neighbour mistakenly builds on the former's land"

(at [47], citing *Yaxley v Gotts* [2000] Ch. 162 at 176), while the latter was based on "the element of agreement, or at least expression of common understanding, exchanged between the parties, as to the existence, or intended existence, of a proprietary interest . . . ". In a case of the latter kind, the estoppel can (where the requirements stated in paras 3–143—3–147 of the Main Work are satisfied) "*also* give rise to a constructive trust*" (at [51], italics supplied; *cf. ibid.*, at [31]: "proprietary estoppel overlapping with constructive trust"). The distinction between the two situations reflects that between cases of "acquiescence" and those of "encouragement" drawn in para.3–138 of the Main Work, where it is pointed out that our concern in the present Chapter is with cases of the latter kind.

The relationship between proprietary estoppel and constructive trust is further discussed in *Cobbe v Yeomans Row Management Ltd* [2005] EWHC 266; [2006] W.T.L.R. 625 at [226] *et seq.* The discussion is there said not to be necessary for the decision, which was based on proprietary estoppel alone.

Other acts done in reliance on the promise

[Add to note 700, in line 8 after "657;": page [302]]   **3–140**
cf. Cobbe v Yeomans Row Management Ltd [2005] EWHC 266; [2005] W.T.L.R. 625 (work done and expense incurred by promise in obtaining planning permission to develop promisor's land).

[Add to note 703: page [303]]
See also *Evans v HSBC Trust Co (UK) Ltd* [2005] W.T.L.R. 1289; but this case gives rise to the further difficulty discussed in para.3–147 of this Supplement.

Alternative explanation: contract

[Add to note 709: page [303]]   **3–141**
See also *Oxley v Hiscock* [2004] EWCA Civ 546; [2005] Fam. 211 at [35]–[36], distinguishing between cases of proprietary estoppel and those in which parties *before* acquiring property reach "an agreement, arrangement or understanding . . . that each is to have a beneficial share in the property".

[Add to note 714: page [304]]   **3–142**
The explanation of proprietary estoppel as based on contract also fails to account for the fact that the promisee's remedy may fall short of awarding him his full expectation interest: see *Cobbe v Yeoman's Row Management Ltd* [2005] EWHC 266; [2005] W.T.L.R. 625 at [168] and [169] ("not remedies for breach of contract"). For the remedy in this case, see below, para.3–155 of this Supplement.

(c) *Conditions giving rise to Liability*

Kinds of promises capable of giving rise to proprietary estoppel

[Add to note 719–720: page [305]]   **3–143**
Secretary of State for Transport v Christos [2003] EWCA Civ 1073 is reported in [2004] 1 P. & C.R. 17.

[Add new note 720a in line 2, after "favour": page [305]]
[720a] See *Kinane v Mackie-Conteh* [2005] EWCA Civ 45; [2005] W.T.L.R. 345 at [29] (requirement of a representation "that the agreement created an enforceable obligation").

[Add to note 725: page [305]].
See also *Cobbe v Yeomans Row Management Ltd* [2005] EWHC 266; [2005] W.T.L.R. 625. The agreement in pursuance of which work had there been done, and expense incurred by the promise, in securing planning permission to develop the promisor's land, though not expressly "subject to contract" was not thought by either party to be a legally binding contract. But a proprietary estoppel nevertheless arose because the promisee had been induced to act in pursuance of the agreement by his belief, encouraged by the promisor, that the latter would not withdraw from the agreement (at [122]). *Att.-Gen. of Hong Kong v Humphreys Estates (Queen's Gardens)* [1987] 1 A.C. 113 was said at [98] to depend on its "precise facts" and distinguished on the ground that in that case no such belief had been encouraged by the promisor.

Subject-matter of the promise

3–145   *[Add to note 734: page [307]]*
In *Strover v Strover* [2005] EWHC 860 "proprietary estoppel" (at [39]) operated in relation to a life insurance policy; the case was one in which the estoppel arose, not from an "assurance" but from a "mistake" (at [42]); *cf.* Main Work, para.3–138 for the distinction between the two lines of cases; our concern in this Chapter is with the "assurance" (or "encouragement") cases (*ibid.*).

Detrimental reliance

3–146   *[Add to note 737: page [307]]*
See also *H v M (Property Occupied by Wife's Parents)* [2004] EWHC 625; [2004] 2 F.L.R. 16, where a claim alleging proprietary estoppel failed for want of detrimental reliance; *Van Laethem v Brooker* [2005] EWHC 1478; [2006] 1 F.C.R. 697, where the detrimental reliance took the form (1) of the promisee's first mortgaging and then selling her home to enable her to make a financial contribution to the purchase of the property to which the promise related; and (2) herself doing some of the work of restoring that property.

[Add to note 739]
Kinane v Mackie-Conteh [2005] EWCA Civ 45; [2005] W.T.L.R. 345 at [29].

Whether reliance must relate to a specific property

3–147   *[Add to note 749: page [308]]*
In *Evans v HSBC Trust Co (UK) Ltd* [2005] W.T.L.R. 1289 the promise (that the promisees would inherit the whole of the promisor's estate) did indeed identify, at least in general terms, the relevant property. But the acts done in reliance on the promise did not in any way relate to the property, nor did they benefit the promisor in any way. While the latter of these factors is not decisive (see Main Work, para.3–140), the combination of both of them seems to reduce

the case to one of mere action in reliance on a (gratuitous) promise. The judgment recognises (at [73]) that mere change of position by the promisee does not suffice to give rise to proprietary estoppel but does not make it clear what additional factors in the case justified the application of the doctrine.

(d) *Effects of the Doctrine*

Extent of the equity

[*Add to note 763: page* [310]]   **3–150**
  cf. *Kinane v Mackie-Conteh* [2005] EWCA Civ 45; [2005] W.T.L.R. 345 at [33] (declaration that promisee was equitable chargee of the land in question).

[*Add to note 765*]
  See also *Clark v Clark* [2006] EWHC 275; [2006] 1 F.C.R. 421 (proprietary estoppel arising in respect of land owned by one of two brothers who used the land for joint business purposes, and in respect of an access way to the business across that land, held to take effect only temporarily: *i.e.* for so long as the land was used for the business and the access way was needed for the purposes of the business by one of the brothers after the other had retired from it).

Remedy: principled discretion

[*Add to note 771: page* [311]]   **3–153**
  For the flexibility of the remedy in cases of proprietary estoppel, see also *Clark v Clark* [2006] EWHC 275; [2006] 1 F.C.R. 241, above, para.3–150 of this Supplement.

[*Add to note 780*]
  See also *Evans v HSBC Trust Co (UK) Ltd* [2005] W.T.LR 1289, where the promise was that the promisees would inherit the whole of the promisor's estate, valued at £340,000, and the remedy was to award one of the promisees £100,000 and the other £80,000, taking into account life-time gifts of £20,000 made by the promisor to the latter promisee. For this case, see also above, para.3–147 of this Supplement.

Compensation in money

[*Add to note 789: page* [312]]   **3–155**
  See also *Evans v HSBC Trust Co. (UK) Ltd* [2005] W.T.L.R. 1299 (as to which see above, para.3–147 of this Supplement); *Cobbe v Yeomans Row Management Ltd* [2005] EWHC 266; [2005] W.T.L.R. 625, where the value of the promisor's property had been increased as a result of the promisee's incurring trouble and expense to obtain planning permission to develop the property, in circumstances giving rise to a proprietary estoppel in his favour. The remedy awarded by the court was a lien on the property for half the increase in the value of the property as a result of the grant of the planning permission: see at [139], [170], [229].

Balance of hardship

3–157   [*Add to note 802: page* [313]]

See also *Evans v HSBC Trust Co. (UK) Ltd* [2005] W.T.L.R. 1289, where, in deciding on the amount to be awarded to the promisees (see above, para.3–153), the court took account, not only the extent of their reliance on the promise that they would inherit the whole of the promisor's estate, but also the interests of one of the promisor's blood relatives, the relationship between one of whom and the promisor had been very close. The case gives rise to the difficulty discussed in para.3–147 of this Supplement.

12. SPECIAL CASES

Both promises defective by statute

3–167   [*Add to note 850: page* [319]]

For the repeal of s.18 of the Gaming Act 1845 by the Gambling Act 2005 ss.334(1)(c), 356(3)(d) and s.356(4) and Sch.17, see below Vol.II, para.40–001A.

Firm offers

3–170   [*Add to note 870: page* [321]]

For the description of an option as "an irrevocable offer that only matures into a bilateral contract upon its exercise", see *Re Gray* [2004] EWHC (Ch); [2005] 1 W.L.R. 815 at [25].

Novation of partnership debts

3–173   [*Add new text at end: page* [324]]

In *Re Burton Marsden Douglas*[892a] A practised as a solicitor and was instructed by X to act in the administration of an estate of which X was executor. After liabilities were incurred by A to X, A went into partnership with B and C. A then disappeared, and it was held that B and C were not responsible for liabilities incurred by A before they had joined the partnership. There had been no novation of A's liabilities incurred before that time since (a) there had been no agreement to novate those liabilities; and (b) there would be no consideration for any promise by B and C to discharge those liabilities since there was no promise by X to release A.

[892a] [2004] EWHC 593 (Ch); [2004] 3 All E.R. 222.

Non-feasance and misfeasance

3–177   [*Add new text at end: page* [326]]

There appears to be an exception to the position stated at the end of this paragraph of the Main Work. The exception is said to arise where A's representation to B that A will take certain steps to safeguard some specific financial interest of B's amounts to an "express assumption of responsibility for a particular matter".[908a] A's failure to exercise due care in discharging that responsibility may then make him liable to B in tort and such liability has been said to cover "acts of omission".[908b]

[908a] *Lennon v Metropolitan Police Commissioner* [2004] EWCA Civ 130; [2004] 1 W.L.R. 2594 at [34].

[908b] *ibid.*, at [20]. *Quaere*, however, whether the wrongful conduct in *Lennon's* case did not amount to misfeasance in the sense in which that expression is used in para.3–177 of the Main Work (*i.e.* "failure to achieve a *promised result*").

CHAPTER 4

FORM

			PARA.
☐	1.	In general	4–001
■	2.	Contracts for the sale or other disposition of an interest in land	4–009
☐		(a) The old law: contracts made on or before September 26, 1989	4–010
☐		(i) Contracts within section 40 of the Law of Property Act 1925	4–011
☐		(ii) Formal requirements	4–022
		(iii) The effect of failure to comply with the formal requirements	4–041
■		(b) The new law: contracts made on or after September 27, 1989	4–052
■		(i) Contracts within section 2 of the Law of Property (Miscellaneous Provisions) Act 1989	4–054
■		(ii) Formal requirements	4–066
☐		(iii) The effect of failure to comply with the formal requirements	4–071

1. IN GENERAL

Impact on formality requirements

4–006   *[Add new note 38a after "occurs automatically" on line 14 of page* [333]*]*
[38a] In *J Pereira Fernandes SA v Mehta* [2006] EWHC 813 (Ch); [2006] 2 All E.R. 881 at [25]–[30], it was held that the automatic insertion of an email address in a message by an internet service provider did not constitute a signature by the writer of the message as it did not represent any intention to authenticate the message by the writer. However, Judge Pelling Q.C. accepted that "if a party or a party's agent sending an e-mail types his or her or his or her principal's name to the extent required or permitted by existing case law in the body of an e-mail, then . . . that would be sufficient signature for the purposes of section 4 [of the Statute of Frauds]" (*ibid.*, at [31]), the learned judge noting the position of the Law Commission to this effect.

[Add new note 42a after "to be bound thereby" on line 1 of page [334]*]*
[42a] *cf. J Pereira Fernandes SA v Mehta* [2006] EWHC 813 (Ch); [2006] 2 All E.R. 881 at [31], where the Law Commission's broad approach was approved (and see above, n.38a).

[46]

2. Contracts For The Sale Or Other Disposition Of An Interest In Land

(a) *The Old Law: Contracts made on or before September 26, 1989*

(i) *Contracts within Section 40 of the Law of Property Act 1925*
Other things to be detached from land

[*Note 94: page* [339]]
Update reference to Benjamin to (7th ed., 2006), para.1–092.

4–019

(ii) *Formal Requirements*
Memorandum need not be prepared as such

[*Add to note 126 after "Parker v Clarke [1960] 1 W.L.R. 286": page* [341]]
J Pereira Fernandes SA v Mehta [2006] EWHC 813 (Ch); [2006] 2 All E.R.
881 at [11]–[17] (s.4 of the Statute of Frauds 1677).

4–027

(b) *The New Law: Contracts made on or after September 27, 1989*

(i) *Contracts within Section 2 of the Law of Property (Miscellaneous Provisions) Act 1989*
Variations

[*Add new note 262a at end of paragraph: page* [354]]
²⁶²ᵃ *cf. HL Estates Ltd v Parker-Lake Homes Ltd* [2003] EWHD 604 (Ch).

4–056

[*Add new paragraph: page* [354]]
Boundary agreements between neighbours. In *Joyce v Rigolli*²⁶²ᵇ the Court of Appeal considered whether a boundary agreement between neighbouring landowners constituted "a contract for the sale or other disposition of an interest in land" within the meaning of s.2 of the Law of Property (Miscellaneous Provisions) Act 1989. In this respect, the court adopted the distinction drawn by Megarry J. in *Neilson v Poole*,²⁶²ᶜ in the context of the requirement of registration of such an agreement as an "estate contract" within s.10(1) of the Land Charges Act 1925, between agreements which constitute an exchange of land and those by which the parties merely intend to "demarcate" an unclear boundary referred to in title documents, "a contract merely to demarcate and confirm [not being] a contract to convey".²⁶²ᵈ According to the Court of Appeal, for a contract to be one "for" selling or disposing of land within the meaning of s.2 of the 1989 Act, "it must have been part of the parties' purposes, or the purposes to be attributed to them, in entering into such a contract that the contract should achieve a sale or other disposition of land. The fact that the effect of their contract is that land or an interest in land is actually conveyed, when that effect was

4–056A

neither foreseen nor intended nor was it something which ought to have been foreseen or intended, is not the acid test."[262e] However, on the facts before them it had been found that while the agreement to establish the boundary did not purport to be a contract to convey any land, one of its parties consciously thought that he was giving up a small amount of land.[262f] Nevertheless, the Court of Appeal held s.2 inapplicable: the important public policy in upholding informal boundary agreements which are "act[s] of peace, quieting strife and averting litigation"[262g] led the court to hold that Parliament could not have intended s.2 to apply to transfers of land pursuant to demarcating boundary agreements simply because a trivial transfer or transfers of land were consciously involved, and it should be presumed, until the contrary is shown, that any transfer of land effected by such an agreement is trivial for this purpose.[262h]

[262b] [2004] EWCA Civ 79; [2004] All E.R. (D) 203 (Feb.).
[262c] (1969) 20 P. & C.R. 909.
[262d] *ibid.*, at [918]–[920].
[262e] [2004] EWCA Civ 79 at [31] *per* Arden L.J.
[262f] *ibid.*, at [30], [32].
[262g] *Nielson v Poole* (1969) 20 P. & C.R. 909 at 919 *per* Megarry J.
[262h] [2004] EWCA Civ 79 at [32]–[34]. cf. *ibid.*, at [45] Sir Martin Nourse referring to "the de minimis principle".

Conditions in planning agreements

4–060

[*Page* [356]]
Criticism by *Emmet and Farrand on Title* (19th ed.) para.2–047 of the decision in *Jelson Ltd v Derby City Council*, which required the signature of the housing association, on the basis that s.2 of the 1989 Act requires only the signature of the contracting parties was said to seem valid by Waller L.J. in *Nweze v Nwoko* [2004] EWCA Civ 379; [2004] 2 P. & C.R. D1, *The Times,* May 6, 2004.

Compromises

4–063

[*Add to text at end of paragraph*: *page* [358]]
Similarly, in *Nweze v Nwoko*[295a] the Court of Appeal held that a compromise agreement between two parties to an executed contract of sale of land under which, *inter alia,* the buyer agreed to sell the property with vacant possession at the best price available on the open market (so as to be in a position to pay the price of the earlier purchase to the sellers) was not a contract *for* the sale or other disposition of an interest in land within the meaning of s.2 of the Law of Property (Miscellaneous Provisions) Act 1989. In doing so, Waller L.J. relied on the Law Commission's Report, *Formalities for Contracts for Sale, etc. of Land,*[295b] which "is clearly concerned with contracts or dispositions under which land or an interest in land is actually sold or disposed of".[295c] While the compromise agreement required the buyer to sell the property (to a third party), it did not itself effect a sale of the property.[295d]

[295a] [2004] EWCA Civ 379; [2004] 2 P. & C.R. 33.
[295b] (1987) No. 164.
[295c] [2004] EWCA Civ 379 at [25].
[295d] *ibid.*, at [31].

[Add new paragraph 4-063A: page [358]]

Partnerships. In *Kilcarne Holdings Ltd v Targetfollow (Birmingham) Ltd*[295a] **4-063A**
it was held that an overall bargain for the creation of a joint venture involving the
development of premises which consisted of a number of individual contracts
could include contracts falling within and attracting the formal requirements of
s.2 of the Law of Property (Miscellaneous Provisions) Act 1989 and that this
remained the case even though the contract was expressed as a partnership. In so
holding, the court rejected the argument based on nineteenth century authority[295b] that an oral partnership agreement can be validly made but that if the
partnership assets include land, then the land is held on a constructive trust for
the partnership[295c]: unlike the Statute of Frauds, the 1989 Act created a "substantive rule of law which prohibits the making of an oral contract for the sale or
disposition of an interest in land" even if "it is wrapped up in an alleged partnership".[295d]

[295a] [2004] EWHC 2547 at [193]–[195], [200]–[204]
[295b] *Forster v Hale* (1800) 5 Ves. Jr. 308; *Dale v Hamilton* (1846) 5 Hare 369.
[295c] [2004] EWHC 2547 at [200]–[204].
[295d] *ibid.,* at [203], *per* Lewison J.

Composite agreements

[Add new text at end of note 303: page [359]]   **4-064**
See also the criticisms of the approach of Scott L.J. in *Tootal Clothing Ltd v
Guinea Properties Ltd* (1992) 64 P. & C.R. 3513 in *Kilcarne Holdings Ltd v
Targetfollow (Birmingham) Ltd* [2004] EWHC 2547 at [197]–[198].

(ii) *Formal Requirements*

Signature

[Add at the beginning of note 320: page [361]]   **4-069**
RG Kensington Management Co v Hutchinson [2002] EWHC 1180; [2003] 2
P. & C.R. 13 (signature by each party to the contract, not each party to the
prospective conveyance or transfer).

[Add new text at end of paragraph: page [362]]
However, it has been held that a party can sign a document by writing only his
initials, provided that it is clear that he intended to authenticate the full terms of
the document.[325a]

[325a] *Newell v Tarrant* [2004] EWHC 772 at [47].

[Add new text at end of paragraph: page [362]]   **4-070**
Similarly, while a manuscript initialling of a document may constitute its
"signature", the mere initialling of corrections at the margins of a document does
not constitute its signing for the purposes of s.2 of the 1989 Act, as it does not
evidence assent to the whole document.[328a]

[328a] *Newell v Tarrant* [2004] EWHC 772 at [48].

(iii) *The Effect of Failure to Comply with the Formal Requirements*

Constructive trust

4–073   *[Add new text at the end of the paragraph: page* [364]]

Similarly, in *Kinane v Mackie-Conteh*[350a] the claimant had loaned money to a company of which one of the defendants was managing director, this loan being intended to be secured by a charge on a house in the form of a "security agreement" signed by himself and his wife. The question arose whether the security agreement came within the formal requirements found in s.2 of the 1989 Act. The Court of Appeal held that on the facts "an estoppel overlapping with a constructive trust" was established so as to come within the exception found in s.2(5) of the 1989 Act, in that the defendants had encouraged the claimant in his erroneous belief that the agreement created an enforceable obligation. A further illustration of the way in which a constructive trust may avoid the formal requirements imposed by s.2 of the 1989 Act may be found in the application of the so-called *Pallant v Morgan* equity.[350b] Where A and B agree that A will acquire some specific property for the joint benefit of A and B, and B, in reliance on A's agreement, refrains from attempting to acquire the property, then equity will not permit A, when he acquires the property, to keep it for his own benefit, to the exclusion of B. It has been said that because this equity is in the nature of a constructive trust, it is unaffected by s.2(1) the 1989 Act.[350c]

[350a] [2005] EWCA Civ 45; [2005] W.T.L.R. 345.
[350b] *Pallant v Morgan* [1953] Ch. 43; *Banner Homes Group plc v Luff Developments Ltd* [2000] Ch. 372.
[350c] *Kilcarne Holdings Ltd v Targetfollow (Birmingham) Ltd* [2004] EWHC 2547 at [219] (where it was held inapplicable on the facts).

Estoppel generally

4–074   *[Add to note 356: on page* [365]]

And see further below, para.4–078 of this Supplement.

Proprietary estoppel

4–078   *[Add new text after "by the Act itself" on last line of page* [366]]

Although not arising on the facts, in *Kinane v Mackie-Conteh*[369a] Arden L.J. and Neuberger L.J. expressed contrasting views as to whether or not a proprietary estoppel "unassociated with a constructive trust" would avoid the formal requirements found in s.2. According to Neuberger L.J. "one must ... avoid regarding [subsection 2(5)] as an automatically available statutory escape route from the rigours of section 2(1) of the 1989 Act, simply because fairness appears to demand it. A provision such as section 2 ... was enacted for policy reasons which, no doubt, appeared sensible to the legislature ... the Court should not allow its desire to avoid what might appear a rather harsh result in a particular case to undermine the statutory policy."[369b] He concluded, therefore, that a "mere estoppel, unassociated with a constructive trust" might not avoid the formal requirements of s.2, especially given the decision of the House of Lords in *Actionstrength Ltd v International Glass Engineering SpA*.[369c] However, here Arden L.J. did not agree, and emphasised that the latter decision was concerned with s.4 of the Statute of Frauds 1677 which contains no exception to its formal requirements equivalent to s.2(5) of the 1989 Act. In her view, proprietary estoppel could form the basis of disapplying s.2(1): "the cause of action in proprietary estoppel is . . . not founded on the unenforceable agreement but upon the defendant's conduct which, when viewed in all relevant aspects, is unconscionable".[369d]

[369a] [2005] EWCA Civ 45; [2005] W.T.L.R. 345.
[369b] at [40].
[369c] [2003] UKHL 17; [2003] 2 A.C. 541, noted at para.44–053 of Vol.II of the Main Work.
[369d] at [29].

[On the last line of page [366]]
Replace "On the other hand," with "Moreover,".

[Add new text at end of paragraph 4–078: page [367]]
This remedial flexibility was of central importance to the decision of the Court of Appeal in *Yeoman's Row Management Ltd v Cobbe*.[370a] There a company which owned a building had orally agreed in principle with a property developer that it would sell the building to him if he obtained planning permission for its redevelopment, this agreement fixing a price and specifying an "overage" payment if the gross resale of the building exceeded a certain sum. The director of the company encouraged the developer to expect that her company would fulfil this agreement even after she had decided not to do so but to renegotiate for more money, and then (acting for the company) reneged on the agreement on the same day on which planning permission was granted. Mummery L.J. (with whom Dyson L.J. and Sir Martin Nourse agreed) held that s.2 of the 1989 did not prevent the application of proprietary estoppel.[370b] He noted that the Law Commission had contemplated the availability of proprietary estoppel after the enactment of s.2[370c] and continued that:

"Its availability does not infringe the public policy underlying section 2(1) of the 1989 Act by either directly or indirectly enforcing the [agreement] so as to frustrate the purpose of section 2. The estoppel here did not rest merely on the existence of the [agreement]. It was founded on the fact that [the developer] was induced and encouraged to believe that [the company] regarded the [agreement] as binding in honour and would not withdraw from its terms if [he] obtained planning permission; that [he] relied on that inducement and encouragement; and that it was unconscionable for [the company] to rely on its strict legal rights."[370d]

Rather than making an award for a reasonable sum to cover the cost of the work done by the developer towards winning planning permission (which would not have done justice to the developer's equity as it would not have reflected his expectation of profit from the increased value of the property with planning permission[370e]), the Court of Appeal confirmed the judge's award at first instance which had given the developer a half interest in the increase in value of the property after planning permission.[370f] In this respect, Dyson L.J. observed that:

"the fundamental question for the court in each case is to decide what relief justice requires to satisfy the equity. Relevant factors include the nature of the expectation created by the defendant's conduct; the detriment suffered by the claimant in reliance on the defendant's representations; the degree to which the defendant's conduct can properly be said to be unconscionable; and the need for some proportionality between the claimant's expectation and his or her detriment."[370g]

[370a] [2006] EWCA Civ 1139.

[370b] *ibid.*, at [62]–[68], [120], [141].

[370c] *ibid.*, at [66]. The Law Commission's views are noted at para.4–076 of the Main Work.

[370d] *ibid.*, at [66]–[67].

[370e] *ibid.* at [90], [132].

[370f] *ibid.*, at [90]–[95] (Mummery L.J. seeing this as "least unsatisfactory" solution); [135]–[138].

[370g] *ibid.*, at [126].

CHAPTER 5

MISTAKE

			PARA.
☐	1.	Introduction	5–001
■	2.	Common mistake	5–016
		(a) Introduction	5–016
		(b) Different approaches before *Bell v Lever Bros*	5–017
■		(c) Mistake at common law	5–026
		(i) *Bell v Lever Bros*	5–026
■		(ii) Situations in which contract may be void for Common Mistake	5–030
☐		(d) No separate Rule in Equity	5–043
☐		(e) Summary of Common Mistake	5–050
■	3.	Mistakes in "communication"	5–055
		(a) Underlying principles	5–055
☐		(b) Mutual misunderstanding	5–060
■		(c) Unilateral mistake as to terms	5–063
■		(i) When mistake will affect contract	5–063
■		(ii) Mistaken identity	5–076
	4.	*Non est factum*	5–086
☐	5.	Rectification of written agreements	5–092

1. INTRODUCTION

Common mistake and construction of the contract

For a recent case on which the judge reached the conclusion that the contract was binding on the alternative grounds that the mistake did not make the agreement essentially different and that the risk was clearly allocated to one party, see *Standard Chartered Bank v Banque Marocaine De Commerce Exterieur* [2006] EWHC 413 (Comm); [2006] All E.R. (D) 213 (Feb.) **5–015**

2. COMMON MISTAKE

(c) *Mistake at Common Law*

(ii) *Situations in which contract may be void for Common Mistake*

Section 6 cases

[*Note 121: page* [388]] **5–034**
Update reference to Atiyah, *Sale of Goods* to (11th ed., 2005), pp.106–107.

Mistakes as to law

5–042   [*Note 163, page* [393]]

The decision of Morland J. in *Brennan v Bolt Burdon* (which in the Main Work is stated incorrectly: Morland J. held that the compromise agreement was invalidated by the mistake of law) was reversed on appeal, [2004] EWCA Civ 1017; [2005] Q.B. 303. The Court of Appeal accepted that a mistake of law may render a contract void; the principle underlying the decision in *Kleinwort Benson Ltd v Glasgow City Council (No.2)* [1999] 1 A.C. 153 is not confined to restitution (at [12] and [26]). However, there is not a mistake of law if the relevant law was merely in doubt. The majority held that in this case the law was merely in doubt; the parties could have discovered that the relevant decision was under appeal.

In addition, when combined with the "declaratory theory of law" espoused in the *Kleinwort* case that when a decision is overturned the previous view of the law was mistaken, the mistake of law rule would threaten the finality of compromise agreements. In the view of Maurice Kay L.J. and Bodey J., a compromise agreement is one under which each party should be treated as accepting the risk that their view of the law might subsequently turn out to be mistaken (at [31] and [39]; *cf.* Main Work, para.5–015). Bodey J. would imply a term to that effect (at [42]). If the parties want to be able to withdraw from the compromise agreement should their view of the law turn out to have been mistaken, they should provide for that expressly (at [22] and [42]).

Sedley L.J. agreed that the appeal should be allowed: "a shift in the law cannot be allowed to undo a compromise of litigation entered into in the knowledge of both of how the law now stood and of the fact—for it is always a fact—that it might not remain so" (at [64]), though he preferred not to base this on an implied term but on the factual matrix of the agreement.

The court left open the question whether a mistake of law could ever invalidate a compromise agreement if, as a matter of construction, the compromise applies (*cf. Bank of Credit and Commerce International SA (In Liquidation) v Ali (No.1)* [2001] UKHL 8; [2002] 1 A.C. 251, in which the House of Lords held that a general release was not effective to release a claim for "stigma" damages that neither party could have known about: see Main Work, para.5–012.) To exempt compromises altogether from the mistake of law rule might not be inconsistent with the *Kleinwort* case, as Lord Goff (at p.382G) and Lord Hope (at p.412F–G) had suggested that in a restitution case there might be a defence of "settlement of an honest claim" (at [14], [23] and [30]).

Maurice Kay L.J. doubted if a mistake of law would ever render performance impossible (at [22]). Sedley L.J. considered that in mistake of law cases the test of impossibility was too narrow; he would apply a test of whether the mistake destroyed the subject matter (at [60]).

In *S v S* [2003] Fam 1 it was held that a mistake of law was not a sufficient ground to set aside a consent order made in ancillary relief proceedings, though there was no such mistake on the facts. One ground for the decision, that the *Kleinwort* principle was confined to restitution cases, was rejected in *Brennan v Bolt Burdon* but Maurice Kay L.J. (at [12]) expressed sympathy with the other ground, that public policy favouring an end to litigation must prevail. On consent orders see Main Work, para.5–048, n.200.

(d) *No separate Rule in Equity*

No separate doctrine of common mistake in equity

The Court of Appeal in Singapore has hinted that it might not follow *The Great Peace*. See *Chwee Kin Keong v Digilandmall.com Pte Ltd* [2005] SGCA 2; [2005] 1 S.L.R. 502 at [66]–[73]. The case was one of unilateral mistake (see below, para.5–064). It is noted by Yeo in (2005) 121 L.Q.R. 393.

5–043

Previous authority on common mistake in equity

[*Add to note 174, line 5, after the reference to* The Great Peace*: page* [395]] *Islington London Borough Council v UCKAC* [2006] EWCA Civ 340; [2006] All E.R. (D) 441 (Mar.) at [19]–[21].

5–044

(e) *Summary of Common Mistake*

Other common mistakes

In *EIC Services Ltd v Phipps* [2004] EWCA Civ 1069; [2005] 1 W.L.R. 1377 the doctrine of common mistake in contract was applied by analogy to an issue of bonus shares. The issue had proceeded on the false assumption that all the relevant shares were fully paid up and would have the right to participate.

5–052

Mistake and construction

See above, para.5–015.

5–054

3. Mistakes in "Communication"

(b) *Mutual Misunderstanding*

Parties at cross-purposes

This paragraph was cited in *NBTY Europe Ltd (formerly Holland & Barrett Europe Ltd) v Nutricia International BV* [2005] EWHC 734; [2005] 2 Lloyd's Rep. 350, but it was held on the facts that there was no ambiguity in the agreement, nor indeed were the parties at cross-purposes.

5–060

(c) *Unilateral Mistake as to Terms*

(i) *When mistake will affect contract*

Mistakes which ought to have been apparent

In *Chwee Kin Keong v Digilandmall.com Pte Ltd* [2005] SGCA 2; [2005] 1 S.L.R. 502 the Singapore Court of Appeal held that the common law doctrine of

5–064

mistake applies only when the non-mistaken party had actual knowledge of the other's mistake (at [53]). It appears that this would include cases of " 'Nelsonian knowledge', namely, wilful blindness or shutting one's eyes to the obvious" (*ibid.*, at [42]). The court considered that there is also an equitable jurisdiction to set aside a contract for unilateral mistake in cases in which there is "sharp practice" or "unconscionable conduct" (at [76]–[77]). However, it indicated that it would not follow the view of the Canadian court in *Can-Dive Services v Pacific Coast Energy Corp* (2000) 74 B.C.L.R. (3d) 30 that constructive knowledge alone would suffice to "invoke equity's conscience" (at [78]–[80]). The practical difference between what the Court of Appeal envisaged would suffice and actual knowledge is not clear, but perhaps it would include the type of conduct described by Stuart-Smith L.J. in *Commission for New Towns v Cooper* [1995] Ch. 259, 280, quoted below, para.5–100. The *Chwee Kin Keong* case is noted by Yeo in (2005) 121 L.Q.R. 393.

(ii) *Mistaken Identity*

5–078—
5–082A   *Shogun Finance Ltd v Hudson* is now reported at [2004] 1 A.C. 919.

5. RECTIFICATION OF WRITTEN AGREEMENTS

Common mistake

5–092   It should be noted that where a mistake is obvious, *e.g.* because the literal meaning of the words would be absurd (see Main Work, para.12–055), and it is clear what is meant, rectification is not necessary; the matter will be dealt with as one of construction. See *Dalkia Utilities Services Plc v Celtech International Ltd* [2006] EWHC 63; [2006] 1 Lloyd's Rep. 599, quoting (at [109]) the words of Brightman L.J. in *East v Pantiles Plant Hire Ltd* [1982] 2 E.G.L.R. 111:

> "It is clear on the authorities that a mistake in a written instrument can, in limited circumstances, be corrected as a matter of construction without obtaining a decree in an action for rectification. Two conditions must be satisfied: first, there must be a clear mistake on the face of the instrument; secondly, it must be clear what correction ought to be made in order to cure the mistake. If those conditions are satisfied, then the correction is made as a matter of construction. If they are not satisfied, then either the Claimant must pursue an action for rectification or he must leave it to a court of construction to reach what answer it can on the basis that the uncorrected wording represents the manner in which the parties decided to express their intention."

Concluded agreement

5–095   It seems that the requirement of an "outward expression of accord" is not an absolute one, but one of evidence that the parties shared a common intention even if they had not put it into words. The requirement of outward accord was first relaxed in a series of cases involving pension schemes (in particular *AMP v Barker* [2001] P.L.R. 77 and *Gallaher v Gallaher Pensions Ltd* [2005] EWHC 42 (Ch); [2005] All E.R. (D) 177 (Jan.)). However, in *Munt v Beasley* [2006] EWCA

Civ 370; [2006] All E.R. (D) 29 (Apr.), which involved rectification of a lease, Mummery L.J., with whom the other members of the court agreed, said (at [36]):

> "I would also accept . . . that the recorder was wrong to treat 'an outward expression of accord' as a strict legal requirement for rectification in a case such as this, where the party resisting rectification has in fact admitted . . . that his true state of belief when he entered into the transaction was the same as that of the other party and there was therefore a continuing common intention which, by mistake, was not given effect in the relevant legal document. I agree with the trend in recent cases to treat the expression 'outward expression of accord' more as an evidential factor rather than a strict legal requirement in all cases of rectification."

Earlier cases had tended to suggest that the parties must have reached an informal agreement on what they intended. Thus in *Joscelyne v Nissen* [1970] 2 Q.B. 86 the Court of Appeal had cited with approval its previous decision, *Lovell and Christmas Ltd v Wall* (1911) 104 L.T. 85 and, in particular, the following passage from the judgment of Buckley L.J.:

> "In ordering rectification the court does not rectify contracts, but what it rectifies is the erroneous expression of contracts in documents. For rectification it is not enough to set about to find out what one or even both of the parties to the contract intended. What you have got to find out is what intention was communicated by one side to the other, and with what common intention and common agreement they made their bargain."

It is submitted that the "recent trend" does not mean that rectification can be based on intentions that were never expressed to the other party in any form, even if the unexpressed intentions of each party happened to coincide. Rectification is to make the document conform to the agreement and in English law some outward manifestation is required for there to be an agreement. However, as Carnwath L.J. suggested in *JIS (1974) Ltd v MCP Investment Nominees Ltd* [2003] EWCA Civ 721 at [33]–[34], it might cover understandings that the parties thought so obvious as to go without saying, or that were reached without being spelled out in so many words. See also *Cambridge Antibody Technology v Abbott Biotechnology Ltd* [2004] EWHC 2974 (Pat) at [105]–[112].

Unilateral mistake

In *Hurst Stores & Interiors Ltd v ML Property Europe Ltd* [2004] EWCA 490; **5–100**
[2004] Building L.R. 249 at [19], the Court of Appeal applied the dicta of Stuart-Smith L.J. in *Commission for New Towns v Cooper* [1995] Ch. 259 at 280:

> " . . . were it necessary to do so in this case, I would hold that where A intends B to be mistaken as to the construction of the agreement, so conducts himself that he diverts B's attention from discovering the mistake by making false and misleading statements, and B in fact makes the very mistake that A intends, then notwithstanding that A does not actually know, but merely suspects, that B is mistaken, and it cannot be shown that the mistake was induced by any misrepresentation, rectification may be granted. A's conduct is unconscionable and he cannot insist on performance in accordance to the strict letter of the contract; that is sufficient for rescission."

and of Evans L.J. (*ibid.*, at [292]) that " 'knowledge' in this context includes 'shut-eye' knowledge".

The nature of the knowledge that A must be shown to have of B's mistake if rectification is to be granted was discussed in detail by the Court of Appeal in *George Wimpey UK Ltd v VI Construction Ltd* [2005] EWCA Civ 77; [2005] B.L.R. 135. It must be (i) actual knowledge; (ii) wilfully shutting one's eyes to the obvious; or (iii) wilfully and recklessly failing to make such inquiries as an honest and reasonable man would make. See the analysis of the various forms of knowledge made by Peter Gibson J. in *Baden v Société Générale pour Favoriser le Développement du Commerce et de l'Industrie en France SA (Note)* [1993] 1 W.L.R. 509 and cited by Millett J. in *Agip (Africa) Ltd v Jackson* [1990] Ch. 265 at 293. Millett J. said that the true distinction is between honesty and dishonesty. In cases within (i)–(iii) A would not be acting honestly. The implication is that the same would not be true if A had merely (again using the categories of Peter Gibson J.) (iv) knowledge of circumstances which would indicate the facts to an honest and reasonable man or (v) knowledge of circumstances which would put an honest and reasonable man on inquiry, though it might depend on the comparative competence and resources of the parties (see the judgment of Sedley L.J., [2005] EWCA Civ 77 at [65]). The type of conduct described by Stuart-Smith L.J. in *Commission for New Towns v Cooper* [1995] Ch. 259 at 280 (above) would clearly not be honest.

CHAPTER 6

MISREPRESENTATION

			PARA.
■	1.	In general	6–001
■	2.	What constitutes effective misrepresentation	6–004
□		(a) False statement of fact	6–004
■		(b) Statement by or known to other party	6–020
□		(c) Other requirements	6–027
■	3.	Damages for misrepresentation	6–041
□		(a) Fraudulent misrepresentation	6–042
□		(b) Negligent misrepresentation	6–066
□		(c) Innocent misrepresentation	6–092
□	4.	Rescission for misrepresentation	6–100
□		(a) General	6–100
□		(b) *Restitutio in integrum*	6–112
□		(c) Other bars to remedy of rescission	6–120
□	5.	Exclusion of liability for misrepresentation	6–131
□	6.	Contracts *uberrimae fidei*	6–139

1. IN GENERAL

Preliminary

The Unfair Commercial Practices Directive (2005/29/EC of May 11, 2005, OJ   **6–001**
L 149/22), which must be implemented by December 12, 2007, requires Member
States to prohibit, and to provide "adequate and effective" means to combat
unfair commercial practices. These are defined so as to include misleading
actions (Art.6) and misleading omissions (Art.7). However it seems that unfair
commercial practices within the meaning of the Directive will not give rise to
civil remedies for individual consumers, as the Directive is "without prejudice to
contract law and, in particular, to the rules of validity, formation or effect of a
contract" (Art.3(1)). A useful summary of the Directive and its likely impact will
be found in Twigg-Flesner (2005) 121 L.Q.R. 386.

2. WHAT CONSTITUTES EFFECTIVE MISREPRESENTATION

(a) *False Statement of Fact*

Statement of opinion may carry implication that grounds for belief

Although a settlement agreement may be rescinded on the ground of mis-   **6–007**
representation like any other contract, "care is needed in examining what was

said in the course of negotiations, whether it truly amounted to a representation as opposed to an argument or a contention, and if so what the representation was. In the course of settlement negotiations, parties are likely to make a number of assertions. The Court should guard against misrepresentation being used—or rather abused—as an improper means of re-opening a compromise agreement." Propositions put forward by either side are likely to be treated as mere statements of opinion and—at least when the negotiations are conducted by experienced professionals in good faith—are unlikely to be treated as including a representation that they are based on reasonable grounds: *Kyle Bay Ltd (trading as Astons Nightclub) v Underwriters subscribing under policy 019057/08/01* [2006] EWHC 607 (Comm); [2006] All E.R. (D) 433 (Mar.), Jonathan Hirst Q.C., at [45]–[47], [52]–[54].

Statements of law

6–011   [*Note 45a, page* [435]]
See this Supplement, para.5–042, above.

Representation ceases to be true

6–017   [*Note 77: page* [439]]
Formerly Financial Services and Markets Act 2000, s.86 extended the provision on supplementary listing particulars (s.81) to a prospectus required by the listing rules. The issue of supplementary prospectuses is now governed by s.87G, inserted by the Prospectus Regulations 2005 (SI 2005/1443), reg.2(1), Sch.1 para.6(1), (2)). This applies to both listed and unlisted securities; the Public Offer of Securities Regulations 1995 have been revoked. See further below, para.6–027.

(b) *Statement By or Known to Other Party*

The representor

6–020   [*Add to note 88, page* [440]]
An agent may have authority to make representations in relation to a particular transaction even though he has no authority to conclude the transaction: *First Energy v HIB* [1993] 2 Lloyd's Rep. 194, 204; *MCI Worldcom International Inc v Primus Telecommunications plc* [2004] EWCA Civ 957; [2004] 2 All E.R. (Comm.) 833 at [25]. For examples see Main Work, Vol.II, para.31–015.

(c) *Other Requirements*

The representee or person intended to act on the representation

6–027   [*Note 119: page* [444]]
The Public Offer of Securities Regulations 1995 have been revoked and replaced by new provisions inserted into the Financial Services and Markets Act

2000 by the Prospectus Regulations 2005 (SI 2005/1443). The effect of the Regulations is that unlisted securities are now within the definition of "transferable securities" in new s.102A, and the rules of the amended Pt VI of the Act apply to both listed and unlisted securities: see s.73A(4) (rules relating to transferable securities are known as the "prospectus rules") and ss.84–87R.

Intention

[Note 130: page [446]]
Update reference to *Clerk & Lindsell* to (19th ed., 2006), para.18–28.

6–029

No requirement of materiality

In *MCI Worldcom International Inc v Primus Telecommunications plc* [2004] EWCA Civ 957; [2004] All E.R. (Comm.) 833 Mance L.J., delivering the judgment of the court, said that this paragraph appears "to put the position too cautiously". As he saw the position, "whether there is a representation and what its nature is must be judged objectively according to the impact that whatever is said may be expected to have on a reasonable representee in the position and with the known characteristics of the actual representee . . . The position in the case of a fraudulent misrepresentation may of course be different" (at [30]).

6–036

[Note 166: page [450]]
The decision of the House of Lords in *Standard Chartered Bank v Pakistan National Shipping Corp (No.2)* is now reported at [2003] 1 A.C. 959.

Representee could have discovered truth: rescission

[Add to text after note 173: page [451]]
Thus it is irrelevant that the true position is stated in the contract signed by the misrepresentee unless he was actually aware of the "correction" in the contract document.[173a]

6–039

[173a] *Peekay Intermark Ltd v Australia & New Zealand Banking Group Ltd* [2006] EWCA Civ 386; [2006] All E.R. (D) 70 (Apr.). However, the misrepresentee must still prove inducement and if the misrepresentation was in very "rough and ready terms", while the contract was a detailed financial instrument which the investor would be expected to read in order to discover the details which he claimed were of importance to him, but he signed the contract without reading it, he may be held not to have relied on the misrepresentation: *ibid.*

3. DAMAGES FOR MISREPRESENTATION

Preliminary

[Amend note 182, line 3: page [452]]
The reference to Lord Tenterden's Act should be to "Statute of Frauds Amendment Act 1828".

6–041

(a) *Fraudulent Misrepresentation*

Principal and agent

6–048   The position of a junior employee, for instance one who passes on information given to him by a more senior officer and, though he has doubts about its accuracy, puts his name to it because he does not like to question it, is discussed by Tugendhat J. in *GE Commercial Finance Ltd v Gee* [2006] 1 Lloyd's Rep. 337 at [96]–[112].

Contributory negligence

6–063   [*Note 257: page* [462]]
    Standard Chartered Bank v Pakistan National Shipping Corp (No.2) is now reported at [2003] 1 A.C. 959.

Compound interest

6–064   In *Black v Davies* [2005] EWCA Civ 531; [2005] All E.R. (D) 78 (May) the Court of Appeal held that compound interest cannot be awarded on damages for fraud. Waller L.J., giving the judgment of the court, said that compound interest will be awarded in equity in the two cases referred to by Lord Brandon in *President of India v LaPintada Compania Navigacion SA* [1985] A.C. 104 at 116A, HL.

> "[(1)] where money had been obtained and retained by fraud, or [(2)] where it had been withheld or misapplied by a trustee or anyone else in a fiduciary position."

This was the view of the majority in *Westdeutsche Landesbank Girozentrale v Islington LBC* [1996] A.C. 669, HL. The first case covered only cases in which money has been obtained and retained by fraud; in other words, where the fraudster has had in hand a fund which he has, or is deemed to have, made use of for his own benefit. It does not apply when the fraud has caused the misrepresentee to lose money by, as in *Black v Davies*, trading in markets (at [87]). The fact that there may be a cause of action in equity for fraud which is concurrent with the cause of action in deceit, irrespective of whether money has been obtained and retained by fraud, is in the light of the *Westdeutsche Landesbank* case irrelevant (at [89]).

(b) *Negligent Misrepresentation*

Misrepresentation Act, section 2(1)

6–067   An action under s.2(1) is not an action for negligence within the meaning of the Limitation Act 1980, s.14A, since it is not necessary for the claimant to aver any negligent act or omission: *Laws v Society of Lloyd's* [2003] EWCA Civ 1887; *The Times*, January 23, 2004, at [91]. Whether it is an action in tort within s.2 of that Act was left open (see at [92]).

Liability for negligence at common law

[Note 305: page [468]]
Update reference to *Clerk & Lindsell* to (19th ed., 2006), paras 8–83—8–107, and especially 8–102—8–104.

6–077

Hedley Byrne & Co Ltd v Heller and Partners Ltd

[Note 321: page [470]]
Update reference to *Clerk & Lindsell* to (19th ed., 2006), paras 8–83—8–101.

6–080

Other legislative provisions creating liability for negligent misrepresentations: financial services

[Notes 362 and 363: page [475]]
The Public Offer of Securities Regulations 1995 have been revoked: see above, para.6–027. The Financial Services and Markets Act 2000 s.86(1), which extended the provisions on listing particulars to a prospectus required by the listing rules, has been replaced by a new s.90(11), inserted by the Prospectus Regulations 2005 (SI 2005/1443), reg.2(1), Sch.1, para.5). This extends s.90 to prospectuses. A new s.90(12) provides that a person is not to be subject to civil liability solely on the basis of a summary in a prospectus unless the summary is misleading, inaccurate or inconsistent when read with the rest of the prospectus; and, for this purpose, a summary includes any translation of it.

6–089

(c) *Innocent Misrepresentation*

Exercise of court's discretion

The court may also exercise its discretion where to permit rescission would expose the misrepresentor to a large liability, even if that might in practice not be enforceable, whereas to maintain it would result in little additional loss to the misrepresentee. In *UCB Corporate Services Ltd v Thomason* [2005] EWCA Civ 225; [2005] 1 All E.R. (Comm.) 601 the respondents were liable for large sums under two guarantees. As the result of misrepresentation, the appellants entered an agreement to waive their rights under the guarantees in exchange for payment of a much smaller sum. The trial judge refused to permit rescission and the Court of Appeal affirmed the decision. The judge was entitled to conclude that, had the misrepresentations not been made, the appellants would have recovered little or no more (at [37] and [52]), whereas if rescission were permitted the respondents would have faced "massive liability" (Brooke L.J. at [50]). "Loss" in s.2(2) includes financial loss and "what may loosely be described as detriment" (Latham L.J. at [37]). The damages that might be awarded to the appellants under s.2(2) were not the full sums due under the guarantees but only compensation for any loss of the chance to recover more than the appellants gave up when they entered the waiver agreement (at [38] and [51]).

6–099

4. RESCISSION FOR MISREPRESENTATION

(a) *General*

Preliminary

6–100   The right to rescind particular types of contract may be excluded by statute: see below, para.6–108.

Court order not required

6–108   In *Islington London Borough Council v UCKAC* [2006] EWCA Civ 340; [2006] All E.R (D) 441 (Mar.) it was held that a tenancy to which the Act applies can be brought to an end only on the grounds stated in the Act on which the landlord may obtain possession, which include a false statement made knowingly or recklessly by the tenant (s.84 and Sch.2, ground 5). It may not be rescinded for misrepresentation by a person who later assigned the tenancy to the tenant against whom possession is sought. In reaching this conclusion, Dyson L.J. adopted the opposing theory that a contract is only rescinded for misrepresentation by a court order. He said (at [26]):

> "A contract may be voidable inter alia for misrepresentation. A contract which is voidable exists until and unless it is set aside by an order of rescission made by the court at the instance of a party seeking to terminate it or bring it to an end. A representee who has been induced by misrepresentation, whether fraudulent, negligent or innocent, to enter into a contract with the representor has, on discovery of the true facts, a right of election: he may affirm or disaffirm the contract: Halsbury's Laws Vol 31 para 784. If the representee affirms the contract, then he loses his right to rescind and the contract continues to have full force and effect. If he disaffirms and seeks to bring the contract to an end, the court may make an order of rescission, but in some circumstances will refuse to do so. If the contract is rescinded, then the contract is avoided ab initio: it is treated as if it never had effect. But that is not to say that, until it is rescinded, it does not have effect. None of this is controversial law."

Housing Act 1985, s.82, which provides that a landlord can only bring a tenancy to an end, to which the section applies, by obtaining an order for possession, means that the landlord cannot bring it to an end in any other way, *e.g.* by obtaining an order for rescission on the ground of misrepresentation (at [27]).

Dyson L.J.'s analysis seems to be inconsistent with the cases referred to in this paragraph of the Main Work. Furthermore, if it were correct, s.2(2) of the Misrepresentation Act 1967 would be inaptly drafted. That subsection refers to claims that " the contract has been rescinded", which seems to be a clear indication that it is the misrepresentee who rescinds by giving notice, not the court by ordering it. It is submitted that the court's conclusion that, as Mummery L.J. put it " . . . the relevant provisions of the 1985 provide a complete code for the termination of a secure tenancy, the private law remedy of rescission of the tenancy for fraudulent representation is not available to the council" (at [46]), can be supported as a matter of statutory construction without resorting to the notion that a court order is needed for rescission. There would be little point in including ground 5 within the Act if the right to rescind for misrepresentation were not affected.

(c) Other Bars to Remedy of Rescission

Estoppel

In *Habib Bank Ltd v Tufail* [2006] EWCA Civ 374; [2006] All E.R. (D) 92 **6–123** (Apr.) the Court of Appeal distinguished between estoppel and acquiescence: see below, para.7–083. The right to avoid a contract for misrepresentation may be lost by acquiescence if the misrepresentee indicates that he will not avoid it and the other party acts on this to its detriment, at least if the representation was made after the misrepresentee knew of the facts giving him the right to avoid (at [22]).

5. Exclusion of Liability for Misrepresentation

"No reliance" clauses

[*Add new text at end of paragraph: page* [497]] **6–132**
; or if the parties have in fact agreed to conduct their affairs on the basis that there has been no reliance, so that an estoppel arises by convention.[524a]

[524a] *Peekay Intermark Ltd v Australia & New Zealand Banking Group Ltd* [2006] EWCA Civ 386; [2006] All E.R. (D) 70 (Apr.), at [54]–[60], referring to *Colchester Borough Council v Smith* [1991] Ch. 448, affd. on appeal [1992] Ch. 421. See above, paras 3–107 *et seq.*

6. Contracts Uberrimae Fidei

Non-disclosure

In *Conlon v Simms* [2006] EWHC 401 (Ch); [2006] 2 All E.R. 1024, Laurence **6–139** Collins J. held (in the context of negotiations for a partnership agreement: see below, para.6–157) that where the non-disclosure is not only in breach of a duty to disclose but also fraudulent, it gives rise to an action for damages. This, with respect, is very doubtful. It is well-established that breach of the duty of disclosure in insurance does not of itself give rise to an action for damages: see Main Work, para.1–113 and this paragraph at n.550. A negligent failure to speak may give rise to liability in damages but only if there is a "voluntary assumption of responsibility" (*Banque Keyser Ullmann SA v Skandia (UK) Insurance Co Ltd* [1990] 1 Q.B. 665 at 794). It is almost certain that without a voluntary assumption of responsibility there is no liability for merely keeping silent, even with an intention to deceive.

Liability in damages for fraudulent non-disclosure had been mooted as a possibility by Rix L.J. in *HIH Casualty & General Insurance Ltd v Chase Manhattan Bank* [2001] EWCA Civ 1250; [2001] 2 Lloyd's Rep. 483 at [48], [164] and [168] but the point was neither argued nor decided. In the House of Lords, as Laurence Collins J. points out, Lord Bingham said that the deliberate withholding of information which the person knows or believes to be material, if done dishonestly or recklessly, may amount to a fraudulent misrepresentation: [2003] UKHL 6; [2003] 1 All E.R. (Comm.) 349 at [21]. However this appears to refer to cases where in the circumstances a failure to disclose amounts to a positive misrepresentation. The judge also relied on Lord Hoffmann, who said that where there is a duty or an obligation to speak, and the person holds his tongue and does not speak, and does not say the thing he was bound to say, if that was done with the intention of inducing the other party to act upon the belief that the reason why he did not speak was because he had nothing to say, that was fraud also (at [72], citing *Brownlie v Campbell* (1880) 5 App. Cas. 925 at 950). However Lord Hoffmann's dictum was not directed to the question of damages for non-disclosure but to whether a clause of agreement in the *HIH* case excluded remedies for fraudulent non-disclosure. In fact Lord Hoffmann said that "nondisclosure (whether dishonest or otherwise) does not as such give rise to a claim in damages" (at [75]). Lord Hoffmann referred to the judgments in *Banque Keyser Ullmann SA v Skandia (UK) Insurance Co Ltd* [1990] 1 Q.B. 665 at 777–781 and 788 ("without a misrepresentation there can be no fraud in the sense of giving rise to a claim for damages in tort") and [1991] 2 A.C. 249 at 280 (*per* Lord Templeman) and at 281 (*per* Lord Jauncey of Tullichettle). Moreover, in *Manifest Shipping Co v Uni-Polaris Insurance Co, The Star Sea* [2001] UKHL 1; [2003] 1 A.C. 469 at [46], Lord Hobhouse regarded the *Banque Keyser Ullman* case as deciding authoritatively that a breach of duty to disclose does not give rise to damages. Damages may be recovered in tort for deceit but even deliberate non-disclosure does not give rise to an action for deceit. See *Clerk & Lindsell on Torts* (19th ed., 2006), para.18–05.

Companies

6–149   The Public Offer of Securities Regulations 1995 have been revoked and replaced by new provisions inserted into the Financial Services and Markets Act 2000 by the Prospectus Regulations 2005 (SI 2005/1443): see above, paras 6–027 and 6–089.

Partnership

6–157   In *Conlon v Simms* [2006] EWHC 401 (Ch); [2006] 2 All E.R. 1024, Laurence Collins J. held that, although the case cited in n.628 of this paragraph, *Fawcett v Whitehouse* (1829) 1 Russ. & M. 132, does not really support the proposition, there is a duty of disclosure in negotiating a partnership agreement. (In *Fawcett v Whitehouse* the defendant had negotiated a lease on behalf of the partnership formed for the purpose of taking the lease and had taken a secret profit from the lessor. It was held that he held it on trust for the other partners.) However *Andrewes v Garstin* (1861) 10 C.B.N.S. 444 supports the existence of such a duty, as does a dictum of Lord Atkin in *Bell v Lever Bros Ltd* [1932] A.C. 161 at 227, HL.

CHAPTER 7

DURESS AND UNDUE INFLUENCE

				PARA.
■	1.	Duress		7–001
		(a) Introduction		7–001
		(b) Nature of duress		7–002
		(c) Types of illegitimate pressure		7–007
			(i) Duress of the person	7–008
			(ii) Duress of goods	7–009
			(iii) Economic duress	7–011
		(d) Causation		7–019
		(e) Other factors in economic duress		7–025
			(i) Reasonable alternative	7–025
□		(f) Legitimacy of the demand		7–028
		(g) Parties to duress		7–043
□		(h) General effect of duress		7–045
■	2.	Undue influence		7–047
□		(a) Introduction		7–047
■		(b) "Actual" undue influence		7–053
■		(c) Presumed undue influence		7–058
■			(i) Relationships giving rise to presumption of influence	7–060
□			(ii) Confidential relationship shown on facts in earlier decisions	7–067
□			(iii) A transaction not explicable by ordinary motives	7–073
		(d) Rebutting the presumption		7–079
□		(e) Remedies for undue influence		7–083
□		(f) Undue influence by a third party		7–090
□	3.	Unconscionable bargains and inequality of bargaining power		7–111

The Unfair Commercial Practices Directive (2005/29/EC of May 11, 2005, OJ L 149/22), which must be implemented by December 12, 2007, requires Member States to prohibit, and to provide "adequate and effective" means to combat unfair commercial practices. These are defined so as to include "aggressive commercial practices" (Art.8) and "harassment, coercion and undue influence" (Art.9). However it seems that unfair commercial practices within the meaning of the Directive will not give rise to civil remedies for individual consumers, as the Directive is "without prejudice to contract law and, in particular, to the rules of validity, formation or effect of a contract" (Art.3(1)). A useful summary of the Directive and its likely impact will be found in Twigg-Flesner (2005) 121 L.Q.R. 386.

1. Duress

(f) *Legitimacy of the Demand*

Threat to institute civil proceedings

7–041   An example of a threat to take legal proceedings which in the circumstances amounted to improper pressure, and thus actual undue influence, is *Drew v Daniel* [2005] EWCA Civ 507; [2005] 2 F.C.R. 365.

(h) *General Effect of Duress*

Contract under duress is voidable

7–045   Acquiescence is presumably also a bar, as it is in cases of misrepresentation and undue influence: see below, para.7–083.

[Add new paragraph 7–045A: page [533]]

7–045A   **Restitution of benefits may be necessary.** It has been held that a person cannot avoid a contract he has entered into under duress unless he is able to restore the benefits he has received under the contract, at least in substantially the same form, or make an adequate monetary allowance. The position is the same as in cases of misrepresentation or undue influence.[187a] Thus where the agreement was a compromise under which all documents relating to the agreement were to be and had been destroyed, which would benefit the party seeking to avoid and prejudice the other parties if the agreement were avoided, and pecuniary relief could not adequately restore the other parties' position, it was no longer possible to avoid the contract for alleged duress.[187b] It is submitted that this is correct where the transaction to be set aside involved an exchange.[187c] However, where the promise that it is sought to avoid was merely one to pay an additional sum for a benefit already due under an existing contract,[187d] there should be no requirement of counter-restitution.[187e]

[187a] See Main Work, paras 6–112—6–117 and 7–084—7–089.
[187b] *Halpern v Halpern (No.2)* [2006] EWHC 1728 (Comm); [2006] 3 All E.R. 1139.
[187c] It may be that counter-restitution is not required if criminal fraud is used merely as a defence: see Main Work, para.6–106, n.425. It is possible that the same approach, which seems to be based on the *ex turpi causa* rule (see Main Work, paras 16–159 and 16–163), would be applied in cases of duress were the duress to amount to a crime.
[187d] As in, *e.g. North Ocean Shipping Co Ltd v Hyundai Construction Co Ltd* [1979] Q.B. 705, see Main Work, para.7–102.
[187e] See Burrows, *Law of Restitution* (2nd ed., 2002), p.218. In *Halpern v Halpern* the judge did not accept the submission made to him on the basis of Professor Burrows's argument, but it was not noted that Professor Burrows is addressing this different type of case.

2. Undue Influence

(a) Introduction

Unconscionable conduct

[*Add to note 215: page* [536]]   **7–049**
See also *Pesticcio v Huet* [2004] EWCA Civ 372; [2004] All E.R. (D) 36
(Apr.), also a case of a gift; *Macklin v Dowsett* [2004] EWCA Civ 904; [2004]
All E.R. (D) 95 (Jun.) at [10]; *Turkey v Awadh* [2005] EWCA Civ 382; [2005]
2 F.C.R. 7 at [11] ("no need to show . . . either misconduct or that the deal was
disadvantageous").

Manifest disadvantage not essential

[*Note 234: page* [538]]   **7–052**
Update reference to Snell to (31st ed., 2005), para.38–26.

(b) "Actual" Undue Influence

Express influence

[*Add to note 243: page* [540]]   **7–053**
An example of actual undue influence that seems to have amounted to illegit-
imate pressure is *Drew v Daniel* [2005] EWCA Civ 507; [2005] 2 F.C.R. 365.
Ward L.J. pointed out that whether a vulnerable person has been exploited is not
relevant only in cases of presumed undue influence. In all cases of undue
influence, "the critical question is whether or not the influence has invaded the
free volition of the donor to accept or reject the persuasion or withstand the
influence" (at [36]).

(c) Presumed Undue Influence

(i) Relationships giving rise to presumption of influence

Guardian and ward

[*Correct note 315: page* [546]]   **7–064**
Kempson v Ashbee (1874) L.R. 10 Ch. App. 15

(ii) Confidential relationship shown on facts in earlier decisions

[*Add new paragraph 7–070A: page* [550]]
Relationship may arise from transaction. It has been held that a confidential   **7–070A**
relationship may arise from the circumstances of the very transaction in question,

e.g. if the defendant has advised and assisted the claimant over it and the claimant has relied on the defendant for that.[347a]

[347a] *Turkey v Awadh* [2005] EWCA Civ 382; [2005] 2 F.C.R. 7, referring to *Macklin v Dowsett* [2004] EWCA Civ 904; [2004] All E.R. (D) 95 (Jun.). In that case the defendant, who was impecunious, had made an arrangement to give up his rights to land for a small sum unless he completed building a bungalow on the land within three years, which he was very unlikely to be able to do.

(iii) *A Transaction not explicable by Ordinary Motives*

Transaction not explicable by ordinary motives

7–073   [*Note 361: page* [552]]

Mortgage Agency Services Number Two Ltd v Chater is now reported at [2004] 1 P. & C.R. 4. In that case the court had said [at 30]:

> "In our judgment the correct legal test is that set out by Lord Nicholls at paragraph [14] in *Etridge (No.2)*. In so far as the passage cited from Lord Scarman's speech in *Morgan* suggests a higher test, we prefer the reformulated test given by Lord Nicholls. We detect a possible distinction between a transaction explicable *only* on the basis that undue influence had been exercised to procure it (Lord Scarman) and one which called for an explanation, which if not given would enable the court to infer that it could only have been procured by undue influence (Lord Nicholls)."

However in *Turkey v Awadh* [2005] EWCA Civ 382; [2005] 2 F.C.R. 7, in which *Mortgage Agency Services Number Two Ltd v Chater* does not appear to have been cited, the Court of Appeal held to the contrary. A presumption of undue influence does not arise merely because the transaction called for an explanation. It must be one that cannot be explained by ordinary motives (as had been said by Lord Scott in *Etridge's* case at [220]); or, as the trial judge (Judge Cooke Q.C.) had put it: " . . . whether, given the circumstances and the nature of the transaction, it says to the unbiased observer that absent explanation it must represent the beneficiary taking advantage of his position": [2005] EWCA Civ 382 at [20]–[22]. The transaction must be looked at in its context and to see what its general nature was and what it was trying to achieve for the parties (at [32]). The judge's decision that, although neither party had given thought to the value of the property, the transaction was otherwise explicable by the circumstances was upheld.

(e) *Remedies for Undue Influence*

Affirmation

7–083   In *Habib Bank Ltd v Tufail* [2006] EWCA Civ 374; [2006] All E.R. (D) 92 (Apr.) Lloyd L.J. drew a distinction between affirmation, which requires knowledge of the right to rescind (at [19]) and acquiescence. Acquiescence can operate rather like promissory estoppel, though in *Goldsworthy v Brickell* [1987] Ch. 378 at 409, Nourse L.J. had pointed out that promissory estoppel is normally concerned with the giving up of rights under a contract, whose validity is not in dispute and its requirements are more formalised than those of acquiescence.

Thus if before she seeks to avoid the contract the victim of undue influence or misrepresentation indicates that she will perform it, and the other party acts on that representation to its detriment, the victim will lose the right to avoid the contract, at least if the representation was made after she knew of the facts giving her the right to avoid (at [22]; Lloyd L.J. doubted whether the supposed further requirement that her representation be intended to be acted on added anything). If, as on the facts of the case, the other party cannot show that the representation, that solicitors had been instructed to sell the mortgaged property, led it to act differently, it cannot rely on acquiescence (at [25]) and the victim may still be entitled to avoid the contract. The case was one in which a mortgage to a bank had been entered into as the result of misrepresentation by a third party of which the bank had constructive notice (see Main Work, paras 7–090 *et seq.*) but the same principle applies in a two-party case like *Goldsworthy v Brickell*.

(f) *Undue Influence by Third Party*

Constructive notice: *Barclays Bank v O'Brien*

[*Note 434: page* [560]]   **7–094**
See now the *Banking Code* of March 2005, para.13.4.

Transaction not on its face to the advantage of the surety

[*Note 456: page* [562]]   **7–099**
Mortgage Agency Services Number Two Ltd v Chater is now reported at [2004] 1 P. & C.R. 4.

[*Add new paragraph, page* [565]]
Replacement mortgages. Where a mortgage granted by a wife to a bank was   **7–106A**
voidable against the bank because the bank had constructive notice of undue influence by the husband, a replacement mortgage may also be voidable against the bank even if when the replacement was given there was no undue influence, at least where the replacement mortgage is taken as a condition of discharging the original mortgage.[473a] It does not matter that the new agreement is a fresh contract rather than a variation of the old one, provided that the replacement mortgage is between the same parties.[473b] However, it seems that the replacement mortgage must be inseparable from the original mortgage, in the sense that the replacement mortgage was granted before the grantor became aware that she had a right to avoid the original one and in order to discharge it.[473c]

[473a] *Yorkshire Bank plc v Tinsley* [2004] EWCA Civ 816; [2004] 1 W.L.R. 2380 at [19].
[473b] *ibid.*, at [19]–[20].
[473c] *ibid.*, at [24], [32] and [39].

Loss of right to avoid by inconsistent action

The right may also be lost be acquiescence, which is a form of inconsistent   **7–107**
action: see above, para.7–083.

Jointly-owned homes

7–108 *[Note 478: page [566]]*
First National Bank plc v Achampong is now reported at [2004] 1 F.C.R.
18.

3. UNCONSCIONABLE BARGAINS AND INEQUALITY OF BARGAINING POWER

Equitable relief against unconscionable bargains

7–111 *[Note 487: page [567]]*
Consumer Credit Act 1974, ss.137–140 will be repealed by s.70 and Sch.4 of
the Consumer Credit Act 2006. They are to be replaced by ss.140A–140D
(inserted by ss.19–22 of the 2006 Act): see below, para.38–192.

Statutory provisions

7–123 See above, para.7–111.

Part Three

CAPACITY OF PARTIES

CHAPTER 8

PERSONAL INCAPACITY

		PARA.
1.	In general	8–001
2.	Minors	8–002
	(a) Generally	8–002
	(b) Contracts binding on a minor	8–007
	(i) Liability for necessaries	8–007
	(ii) Apprenticeship, service and other beneficial contracts	8–021
	(c) Contracts binding on a minor unless repudiated	8–030
	(d) Contracts unenforceable against a minor unless ratified	8–042
	(e) Third parties and incapacity	8–045
	(f) Liability of minor in tort and contract	8–046
	(g) Liability of minor to make restitution	8–048
	(h) Agency and membership of societies	8–058
	(i) Liability of parent or guardian	8–061
	(j) Procedure in actions	8–062
	(k) Disposition of property by minors	8–065
3.	Married women	8–068
□ 4.	Mentally disordered persons	8–070
5.	Drunken persons	8–080

4. MENTALLY DISORDERED PERSONS

The Mental Capacity Act 2005 ("the 2005 Act") has given effect to the recommendations of the Law Commission's Report No.231, *Mental Incapacity* (1995) and will have important effects on the making of contracts and deeds and the disposition of property by incapable adults (and incapable minors whom the court considers are likely still to lack capacity to make decisions in respect of the matter in question on attaining 18): 2005 Act, ss.2(5) and 18(3). It will replace the provisions governing mental patients found in Pt 7 of the Mental Health Act 1983 (and discussed at para.8–077 of the Main Work). While the Act was given Royal Assent in April 2005, its provisions are expected to be brought into force only in April 2007. Until the relevant provisions are brought into force, the law governing the making of contracts and deeds by mentally disordered persons will remain as stated in the Main Work. This Supplement will therefore note only the four most significant aspects of the Act for the making of contracts by incapable adults.

First, the 2005 Act provides that "a person lacks capacity in relation to a matter if at the material time he is unable to make a decision for himself in relation to the matter because of an impairment of, or a disturbance in the

[73]

functioning of, the mind or brain": s.2(1). The Act then explains various considerations which are and are not to be taken into account for this purpose: s.2(2)–(4) and s.3. In relation to contracts, the 2005 Act removes the reference to mental incapacity in the Sale of Goods Act 1979, s.3(2), and instead provides that a person who lacks capacity to contract for the supply of goods or services must pay a reasonable price for necessary goods or services supplied to him, defining "necessary" as "suitable to a person's condition in life and to his actual requirements at the time when the goods or services are supplied": 2005 Act, s.7. This provision reflects the existing terms of the 1979 Act and clarifies the common law position as regards liability for necessary services.

Secondly, the 2005 Act makes provision for a new separate Court of Protection, with wide powers in relation to those lacking mental capacity: 2005 Act, ss.15–19, Pt 2. The new court will have a power to make declarations as to a person's capacity in relation to specified decisions or matters and on the lawfulness of any act done or to be done in relation to such a person: *ibid.*, s.15. It may itself make decisions on behalf of a person lacking capacity in relation to a matter either concerning that person's personal welfare or his property and affairs (*ibid.*, s.16(1) and 16(2)(a), 17 and 18) or appoint another person (a "deputy") to make decisions on that person's behalf in relation to such a matter: *ibid.*, s.16(2)(b). In coming to its decisions, the court must follow new statutory principles and give effect to the best interests of the person affected by the lack of capacity: *ibid.*, ss.1, 4 and 16(3).

Thirdly, the Act makes general provision to empower and to protect from liability (except for negligence) persons who "act in connection with the care or treatment of another person", which it terms "deputies": 2005 Act, ss.5–6, 19–20. As has been noted, such a deputy is to be treated as the agent of the incapable person (s.19(6)) and may be authorised to act in relation to many (but not all) of the property and affairs over which the court itself has power: *ibid.*, ss.16(2)(b), 18. Such a deputy must also follow the new statutory principles and give effect to the best interests of the person affected by the lack of capacity: *ibid.*, s.20(6).

Fourthly, the 2005 Act makes new provision for "lasting powers of attorney" which will replace the "enduring powers of attorney" provided for by the Enduring Powers of Attorney Act 1985: 2005 Act, ss.9–14.

Nature of understanding required

8–072   [*Add to end of note 308: page* [609]]
This approach has been adopted for the test of mental capacity for the purposes of the conduct of litigation (including the making of any settlement) under CPR Pt 21: *Masterman-Lister v Jewell* [2002] EWCA Civ 1889; [2003] 1 W.L.R. 1511, esp. at [62]; *Bailey v Warren* [2006] EWCA Civ 51; [2006] C.P. Rep. 26.

The Mental Health Acts 1959 and 1983

8–077   [*Add to end of note 324: page* [611]]
Where a person is found to be a "patient" within the meaning of the Mental Health Act 1983 as "incapable of managing and administrating his own property

or affairs", then in any litigation to which he is party he must have a "litigation friend" to conduct proceedings on his behalf: CRP Pt 21(1)(2)(b); 21(2). Where a claim is made by such a patient "no settlement, compromise or payment . . . shall be valid, so far as it relates to the claim, by or on behalf of or against the patient, without the approval of the court": CPR 21(10)(1); *Bailey v Warren* [2006] EWCA Civ 51; [2006] C.P. Rep. 26.

CHAPTER 9

CORPORATIONS AND UNINCORPORATED ASSOCIATIONS

			PARA.
■	1.	Corporations	9–001
		(a) Kinds of corporations	9–001
		(b) Corporations in general	9–003
■		(c) Attribution of acts to a company	9–006
■		(d) Registered companies	9–011
□		(i) Contracts between companies and third parties	9–012
		(ii) Contracts between companies and promoters or directors	9–057
		(iii) Contracts between companies and their members	9–063
		(iv) Contracts between companies and their auditors	9–066
	2.	Unincorporated associations	9–068
		(a) Generally	9–068
		(b) Clubs	9–076
		(i) Members' clubs	9–077
		(ii) Proprietary clubs	9–084
		(c) Trade unions	9–085

1. CORPORATIONS

(c) *Attribution of acts to a company*

9–006   [*Add to note 21: page* [617]]
Bank of India v Morris [2005] EWCA Civ 693; *The Times*, July 19, 2005.

Personal liability: estoppel

9–008   [*Add to note 32: page* [618]]
Fiorentino Comm Guiseppe SRL v Farnesi [2005] EWHC 160 (Ch); [2005] 2 All E.R. 737.

Deeds

9–010   [*Add to note 42: page* [619]]
The Regulatory Reform (Execution of Deeds and Documents) Order 2005 (SI 2005/1906): see above, Supplement to paras 1–077—1–082.

(d) *Registered Companies*

(i) *Contracts between Companies and Third Parties*

Ultra vires **contracts**

[*Add new footnote 95a at end of first sentence of the paragraph: page* [625]]   **9–020**
[95a] Payne and Prentice, "Company Contracts and vitiating factors: developments in the law on directors' duties" [2005] L.M.C.L.Q. 447.

[*Add new paragraph 9–030A: page* [631]]
An agent only has authority to act for the benefit of his principal unless the   **9–030A**
parties otherwise agree.[146a] The same rule applies to directors. As was stated by
Lord Nicholls in *Criterion Properties Plc v Stratford UK Properties Ltd*[146b]:

> "If a company (A) enters into an agreement with B under which B acquires benefits
> from A, A's ability to recover these benefits from B depends essentially on whether
> the agreement is binding on A. If the directors of A were acting for an improper
> purpose when they entered into the agreement, A's ability to have the agreement set
> aside depends upon the application of familiar principles of agency and company
> law. If, applying these principles, the agreement is found to be valid and is therefore
> not set aside, questions of 'knowing receipt' by B do not arise. So far as B is
> concerned there can be no question of A's assets having been misapplied. B acquired
> the assets from A, the legal and beneficial owner of the assets, under a valid
> agreement made between him and A. If, however, the agreement is set aside, B will
> be accountable for any benefits he may have received from A under the agreement.
> A will have a proprietary claim, if B still has the assets. Additionally, and irrespective
> of whether B still has the assets in question, A will have the personal claim against
> B for unjust enrichment, subject always to the defence of change of position. B's
> personal accountability will not be dependent upon proof of fault or 'unconscionable'
> conduct on his part. B's accountability, in this regard, will be 'strict'."[146c]

[146a] *Bowstead and Reynolds on Agency* (17th ed.), art.23 cited with approval in *Hopkins v T L Dallas Group Ltd* [2004] EWHC 1379 (Ch); [2005] 1 B.C.L.C. 543.
[146b] [2004] UKHL 28; [2004] 1 W.L.R. 1846.
[146c] [2004] UKHL 28 at [4].

Ultra vires **and director's authority**

[*Replace last sentence of paragraph: page* [632]]   **9–031**
In *EIC Services Ltd v Phipps*[153] the Court of Appeal held that in the case of a
bonus issue of shares, which is an internal corporate arrangement with no
alteration in the assets of liabilities of the company, a shareholder could not be
held as dealing with the company within the terms of s.35A.

[153] [2004] EWCA Civ 1069; [2005] 1 All E.R. 325.

CHAPTER 10

THE CROWN, PUBLIC AUTHORITIES AND THE EUROPEAN COMMUNITY

			PARA.
☐	1.	The Crown: Status and Special Rules	10–001
☐	2.	The Ultra Vires Rule	10–013
	3.	Agency	10–016
■	4.	Estoppel and Legitimate Expectations	10–017
☐	5.	Judicial Review and other "Public Law" Obligations	10–018
☐	6.	Fettering of Discretion by Contract	10–022
☐	7.	Public Procurement	10–024
	8.	Public Employment	10–031
	9.	European Community	10–038

[*Note 1: page* [663]]
Update reference to Wade and Forsyth, *Administrative Law* to (9th ed., 2004), Chs 20 and 21.

1. THE CROWN: STATUS AND SPECIAL RULES

Contracts between Crown and subject

10–001   [*Note 1: page* [663]]
Update reference to Wade and Forsyth, *Administrative Law* to (9th ed., 2004), Chs 20 and 21.

Update reference to Hogg, *Liability of the Crown* (1989) to Hogg and Monahan, *Liability of the Crown* (2000).

Update reference to Arrowsmith, *The Law of Public and Utilities Procurement* (2nd ed., 2005).

Crown Proceedings Act

10–002   [*Add new footnote 7a to heading of paragraph: page* [664]]
[7a] A detailed and authoritative account of the genesis, purpose and effects of the Act is given in *Davidson v Scottish Ministers* [2005] UKHL 74; 2006 S.L.T. 110 at [8]–[21], *per* Lord Nicholls.
[*Add to note 9: page* [664]]
S.39(1) and Sch.2, Crown Proceedings Act 1947 were repealed by Statute Law Revision Act 1950, s.1; but the 1950 Act did not reinstate those provisions

repealed by s.39(1) and Sch.2 (see the proviso to Statute Law Revision Act 1950, s.1).

Fettering of discretion by contract

[*Note 35: page* [667]]
Delete reference to paras 10–007 *et seq.* and substitute para.10–017.

10–006

Exercise of discretionary power in relation to a valid contract

[*Note 41: page* [667]]
Delete reference to para.10–001 and substitute para.10–011.

10–008

Crown contracting through agents

[*Add to end of note 43: page* [668]]
Marubeni Hong Kong and South China Ltd v Government of Mongolia [2004]
EWHC 472 (Comm); [2004] 2 Lloyd's Rep. 198.

10–009

Remedies against the Crown

[*Add to note 49: page* [668]]
For two exceptions relating to procurement contracts see SI 2006/5, reg.47(10) and SI 2006/6, reg.45(10).

10–011

[*Add text after footnote 50: page* [668]]
This provision has been described as being "of Delphic opaqueness".[50a] In *M v Home Office* the House of Lords interpreted it to mean that if an injunction or order for specific performance had been available against an individual officer before the 1947 Act was passed, it would continue to be available.[50b] In other words, the Act preserved the previous position, where individual officers could be subject to any remedy that was available against an ordinary individual. However, in *Davidson v Scottish Ministers* Lord Rodger cast doubt on this interpretation:

> "There are, however, no words in subsection (2) which refer to the position before the passing of the 1947 Act. If, as seems likely, Lord Woolf was thinking of the closing words of the subsection, I would respectfully prefer to interpret them as referring to the hypothetical situation where the claimant or pursuer has brought proceedings against the Crown rather than against an officer of the Crown. The purpose of the subsection seems to be to prevent the claimant or pursuer from circumventing the ban on an injunction, interdict or order for specific performance against the Crown in subsection (1)(a) by seeking a similar remedy against an officer of the Crown."[50c]

He did not feel it appropriate to advance a concluded view. Lord Mance agreed that s.21(2) did not expressly refer to the position before 1947, but continued:

> "However, even without that phrase, the purpose of subsection (2) can hardly have been to remove or preclude a right on the part of a claimant to injunctive relief

against an officer of the Crown threatening to commit a tortious act against the claimant."[50d]

This disagreement has significant implications for the Crown's contractual position. For instance, if an injunction is available against a Crown officer to restrain him from inducing a breach of contract by the Crown, there is, in effect, a remedy of injunction to prevent a threatened breach of contract. The meaning of s.21(2) should be clarified when the House of Lords hears the appeal in *Beggs v Scottish Ministers*,[50e] in which the Court of Session seems to have assumed that the interpretation advanced in *M v Home Office* was correct.[60f] The House of Lords' speeches in *Davidson* were delivered in December 2005 and referred to the appeal being heard "in due course", but the appeal is not expected to be heard in Trinity Term 2006.

[50a] *Davidson v Scottish Ministers* [2005] UKHL 74; 2006 S.L.T. 110 at [13].
[50b] [1994] 1 A.C. 377 at 412–413.
[50c] [2005] UKHL 74 at [93].
[50d] *ibid.*, at [102].
[50e] 2005 1 S.C. 342.
[50f] See particularly at [22].

[*Add to note 51: page* [668]]
The same result has been reached in Scotland: *Davidson v Scottish Ministers* [2005] UKHL 74; 2006 S.L.T. 110, reversing 2002 S.C. 205.

2. THE *ULTRA VIRES* RULE

Statutory Modification of *ultra vires* rule

10–015

[*Add to note 70: page* [670]]
Davies (2006) 122 L.Q.R. 98 at 104–110.

[*Add new paragraph 10–015A: page* [671]]

10–015A
Impact of human rights on *ultra vires*. Where a public body makes an ultra vires agreement conferring a right to property, the intended recipient of that property right may have a remedy for breach of his human rights.[70a] According to European human rights jurisprudence, an ultra vires transaction purporting to confer a property right gives rise to a legitimate expectation of receiving that right; the legitimate expectation is, in itself, a possession for the purposes of Art.1, Protocol 1.[70b] The right expected to be conferred may be an interest in property,[70c] or it may relate to a component of the property, such as the existence of planning permission,[70d] or the absence of any public navigation right over a stretch of river.[70e] What is recognised as a legitimate expectation for these purposes is not dependent on domestic law definitions or classifications.[70f] Any interference with the right must be for a legitimate aim[70g] and proportionate.[70h] The mere fact that the public authority is reverting to its statutory mandate does not automatically satisfy the tests of justification and proportionality; some form of compensation may be required.[70i] The remedy for infringement of the right to

property cannot require the defendant to confer the property interest which the claimant expected.[70j] If it takes the form of compensation, the European Court of Human Rights has held that the sum awarded should reflect the proportion of the initial consideration paid that can be attributed to the ultra vires element of the transaction.[70k] Such an award has been said to be based on unjust enrichment[70l]; as such, it transcends the usual requirement that restitution is only available for a total failure of consideration.[70m]

[70a] Art.1 of Protocol No.1, European Convention for the Protection of Human Rights and Fundamental Freedoms. *Stretch v United Kingdom* (2004) 38 E.H.R.R. 12; (2003) 5 E.H.R.L.R. 554.

[70b] *Pine Valley Developments Ltd v Ireland* (1991) 14 E.H.R.R. 319. *cf. Al Fayed v Advocate General for Scotland* [2004] S.T.C. 1703 at [120], where it was conceded that a forward taxation agreement, under which the taxpayer paid a set sum per year, instead of being subject to assessment on actual transactions, created an expectation that engaged Art.1. It is difficult to reconcile this concession with the requirement that there should be the expectation of a property right.

[70c] *Stretch v United Kingdom* (2004) 38 E.H.R.R. 12; (2003) 5 E.H.R.L.R. 554.

[70d] *Pine Valley Developments Ltd v Ireland* (1991) 14 E.H.R.R. 319.

[70e] *Rowland v Environment Agency* [2003] EWCA Civ 1885; [2004] 2 Lloyd's Rep. 55.

[70f] *Beyeler v Italy* (2001) 33 E.H.R.R. 1224 at [100]. *cf. Al Fayed v Advocate General for Scotland* [2004] S.T.C. 1703 at [120], where counsel for the defender reserved the right to argue "if the case went further" that an expectation under an ultra vires agreement was a nullity and could not, therefore, give rise to a legitimate expectation. Although an appeal to the House of Lords was lodged, it is not being pursued.

[70g] e.g. *Al Fayed v Advocate General for Scotland* [2004] S.T.C. 1703; *Eden* [2005] B.T.R. 21 (forward taxation agreement repudiated in order to apply the taxation system equally to all taxpayers). *Pine Valley Developments Ltd v Ireland* (1991) 14 E.H.R.R. 319 (annulment of outline planning permission in order to protect the environment). Quaere, whether the aim of ceasing to act outside statutory powers should not automatically be regarded as a legitimate aim.

[70h] e.g. *Rowland v Environment Agency* [2003] EWCA Civ 1885; [2004] 2 Lloyd's Rep. 55 (reinstatement of public navigation right carried out so as to cause minimal interference to riparian owner).

[70i] *Stretch v United Kingdom* (2004) 38 E.H.R.R. 12; *cf. Pine Valley Developments Ltd v Ireland* (1991) 14 E.H.R.R. 319 (inherently risky nature of property development justified awarding no compensation where claimant deprived of planning permission).

[70j] *Rowland v Environment Agency* [2002] EWHC 2785; [2003] 1 Lloyd's Rep 427 at [80] (Lightman J.); expressly approved by the Court of Appeal, [2003] EWCA Civ 1885; [2004] 2 Lloyd's Rep. 55 at [85] (Peter Gibson L.J.) and [140] (Mance L.J.).

[70k] *Stretch v United Kingdom* (2004) 38 E.H.R.R. 12 at [47]–[50].

[70l] *Rowland v Environment Agency* [2003] EWCA Civ 1885; [2004] 2 Lloyd's Rep. 55 at [88].

[70m] See Main Work, para.29–054.

4. ESTOPPEL AND LEGITIMATE EXPECTATIONS

Estoppel and legitimate expectations

[*Add to text after "contrary to statute", 7 lines from end: page* [672]]   **10–017**

That there would be a substantive change is confirmed by a subsequent case, applying *Reprotech*, where it was observed that finding a legitimate expectation was "a task that is very different from an attempt to decide whether or not there is an estoppel in private law".[80a]

[80a] *R. (on the application of Wandsworth LBC) v Secretary of State for Transport, Local Government and the Regions* [2003] EWHC 622 (Admin); [2004] 1 P. & C.R. 32 at [22].

[Note 80: page [672]]
Update references to *Wade and Forsyth* to (9th ed., 2004), pp.372–376, 500–505.

[Add to text at end of paragraph]
Where an authority is exercising the kind of public function that prevents it from being bound by an estoppel, it is also precluded from asserting an estoppel against an applicant.[81a]

[81a] *Stancliffe Stone Co Ltd v Peak District National Park Authority* [2004] EWHC 1475 (QB); [2004] All E.R. (D) 232 at [35].

10–017   *[Page [672]]*
This paragraph must now be treated with caution in the light of recent cases applying the decision in *Regina (Reprotech (Pebsham) Ltd) v East Sussex County Council* [2002] UKHL 8; [2003] 1 W.L.R. 348. Since there can be no contract for planning permission (*Bielecki v Suffolk Coastal County Council* [2004] EWHC 342 (QB)), Lord Hoffmann's analysis can only be applicable to contracts where the factual matrix is analogous to a planning determination. Several important features of the planning context have been emphasised: planning determinations concern the general public interest (*South Bucks District Council v Flanagan* [2002] 1 W.L.R. 2601 at [16]); they bind the general public; and they involve participation by other planning authorities, the Secretary of State and the general public itself. (*R. (on the application of Wandsworth LBC) v Secretary of State for Transport Local Government and the Regions* [2003] EWHC 622 (Admin); [2004] 1 P. & C.R. 32 at [10]–[13]; *Stancliffe Stone Co Ltd v Peak District National Park Authority* [2004] EWHC 1475 (QB); [2005] Env.L.R. 4 at [32].) Some of these features were present in *Yarmouth (Isle of Wight) Harbour Commissioners v Harold Hayles (Yarmouth Isle of Wight) Ltd* [2004] EWHC 3375 (Ch), [2004] All E.R. (D) 66 (Dec.), where it was held that an estoppel could not be relied upon against a statutory harbour authority in respect of its decision not to renew mooring licences. But many contracts made by public authorities are unlikely to share these features, and there seems to be no good reason to deny an estoppel where such features are absent. That there is still a role for estoppel in government contracts is confirmed by *Marubeni Hong Kong and South China Ltd v Government of Mongolia* [2004] EWHC 472 (Comm); [2004] 2 Lloyd's Rep. 198, which concerned a commercial guarantee issued by the Mongolian Minister of Finance. There counsel for the defendant cited *Reprotech* in support of a submission that the Minister's authority to issue the guarantee could not be determined using estoppel, but had to be analysed in terms of public law concepts (at [97]–[102]). Cresswell J. rejected the submission, and proceeded to apply the orthodox principles of ostensible authority, which, as he acknowledged (at [124]), is a species of estoppel. His analysis was not challenged on appeal: *Marubeni Hong Kong and South China Ltd v The Mongolian Government* [2005] EWCA Civ 395 at [6].

5. JUDICIAL REVIEW AND OTHER "PUBLIC LAW" OBLIGATIONS

Judicial review and misfeasance in public office

[*Add to note 83: page* [672]]   **10–019**
On the relationship between judicial review and the statutory scheme of
procurement regulations, see *R. v Ministry of Defence Ex p. Cookson & Clegg
Ltd* [2005] EWCA Civ 811.

6. FETTERING OF DISCRETION BY CONTRACT

Fettering of discretion by contract

[*Add to note 96: page* [674]]   **10–022**
Davies (2006) 122 L.Q.R. 98 at 115–122.

7. PUBLIC PROCUREMENT

Implied contract governing public tendering

[*Page* [675]]   **10–025**
This paragraph should now be read in the light of the Privy Council's decision
in *Pratt Contractors Ltd v Transit New Zealand* [2003] UKPC 83; [2004] B.L.R.
143 (see Arrowsmith, (2004) 13 P.P.L.R. NA125), where (at [2]) it was conceded
"in the light of modern authority" that submitting a tender in response to a
request for tenders created a preliminary contract, which obliged the procuring
authority to act fairly and in good faith in the selection process. This implied duty
required any evaluation of the tenders to express honestly the views of the
selectors. It also precluded selectors from taking steps to avoid receiving relevant
information which they strongly suspected would show their opinion to be
mistaken. However, there was no obligation on the procuring authority to
eliminate any appearance of bias from the process, nor to avoid acting in other
ways that, in different contexts, would be grounds for judicial review (at [47]).
Whether the same analysis will be adopted by English courts will depend on their
willingness to follow the Commonwealth authorities establishing the implied
duty; they may be reluctant to go as far one Australian decision, which saw the
implied duty relating to tenders as part of a more general implied obligation of
good faith (at [45]: "a somewhat controversial question").

[*Add to line 6, after "late": page* [675]]
The necessary contractual agreement may be identified in at least three
ways.[110a] First, the invitation to tender may be an offer, which is accepted by the
submission of a tender. Secondly, the submission of a tender may be an offer,
which is accepted by the procuring authority's receipt of the tender or other
subsequent conduct. Thirdly, an agreement may be deduced from the conduct of
the parties "without the formalities of offer and acceptance".[110b]

[110a] *Dockpride Pty Ltd v Subiaco Redevelopment Authority* [2005] WASC 211 (Supreme Court of Western Australia, September 22, 2005) at [121].
[110b] *ibid.*

[Add to note 111]
See also *Hickinbotham Developments Pty Ltd v Woods* [2005] SASC 215, where the Supreme Court of South Australia distinguished *Blackpool Aero Club* on the basis that the facts of the case before it did not involve either a public body or a formal tender process ([2005] SASC 215 at [57]); *cf. St George Soccer Football Association Inc v Soccer NSW Ltd* [2005] NSWSC 1288 (New South Wales Supreme Court), where there was no suggestion that the status of the defendant as a private corporation precluded the existence of an implied contract arising from the tender process.

[Add to text after footnote 111]
In any event, it must be consistent with the relationship between the parties.[111a]

[111a] *St George Soccer Football Association Inc v Soccer NSW Ltd* [2005] NSWSC 1288 (implied contract inconsistent with claimant's status as member of defendant corporation: liability regulated exclusively by provisions of defendant's constitution).

[Note 113: page [675]]
Fairclough Building Ltd v Port Talbot BC is reported at (1991) 62 B.L.R. 82.

[Add to third line from end, after "however": page [676]]
In Western Australia, for instance, the general observations of Bingham L.J. in the *Blackpool* case have been used as the foundation for a contract imposing implied obligations of good faith and fair dealing on the procuring authority.[115a]

[115a] *Dockpride Pty Ltd v Subiaco Redevelopment Authority* [2005] WASC 211. The observations of Bingham L.J. are cited at [128].

EC procurement law

10–026 *[Note 116: page [676]]*
Arrowsmith, *The Law of Public and Utilities Procurement* is now in a second edition (2005).

[Delete note 119: page [676] and substitute]
Directive 2004/18 on the co-ordination of procedures for the award of public works contracts, public supply contracts and public service contracts [2004] OJ L 134/114, supplemented by Directive 2004/17 co-ordinating the procurement procedures of entities operating in the water, energy, transport and postal services sectors [2004] OJ L 134/1. The previous Directives have been repealed (Directive 2004/18, art.82). The major change in the new legislation is the introduction of a procedure for competitive dialogue: Arrowsmith (2004) 41 C.M.L.Rev. 1277.

[Delete note 120 and substitute: page [676]]
Public Contracts Regulations 2006 (SI 2006/5); Utilities Contracts Regulations 2006 (SI 2006/6). All the previous regulations on the subject are repealed: see

Public Contracts Regulations 2006, Sch.7, Pt 2 and Utilities Contracts Regulations 2006, reg.47.

[*Add to text at end of paragraph: page* [677]]
These detailed express obligations concerning transparency of process may also give rise to a general implied obligation not to act in bad faith.[120a]

[120a] *Luck t/a Luck Arboricultural & Horticultural v London Borough of Tower Hamlets* [2003] EWCA Civ 52; [2003] 2 C.M.L.R. 12 at [59]–[60].

Contractual consequences: domestic proceedings

[*Delete following passage, beginning on line 2, and footnote 128: page* [677]]   **10–028**
"The directives state that is for national law to determine the impact of a violation on a concluded contract[128] and"

[*Delete note 127 and substitute: page* [677]]
SI 2006/5, reg.47; SI 2006/6, reg.45.

[*Delete text of note 129 and substitute: page* [677]]
SI 2006/5, reg.47(9); SI 2006/6, reg.45(7).

CHAPTER 11

POLITICAL IMMUNITY AND INCAPACITY

			PARA.
☐	1.	Foreign states, sovereigns, ambassadors and international organisations	11–001
☐	2.	Alien enemies	11–024

1. FOREIGN STATES, SOVEREIGNS, AMBASSADORS AND INTERNATIONAL ORGANISATIONS

Sovereign immunity and human rights

11–003   [*Add at end of note 12: page* [688]]
Voyiakis (2003) 52 I.C.L.Q. 297; Lloyd Jones (2003) 52 I.C.L.Q. 463; *Yang* (2003) 74 B.Y.I.L. 333; *Garnett* [2005] 54 I.C.L.Q. 705.

[*Add at end of the paragraph*]
In *Jones v Ministry of Interior of the Kingdom of Saudi Arabia*[12a] the House of Lords assumed that Art.6 of the Convention was engaged, as decided by the European Court of Human Rights in the above cases, but held that according sovereign immunity to the state and its servants, agents, officials or functionaries in respect of civil claims arising out of alleged acts of torture committed in the state was not disproportionate as inconsistent with a peremptory norm of international law. Lord Bingham of Cornhill, however, had reservations as to whether Art.6 was engaged at all, since the rule of international law is not that a state should not exercise over another state a jurisdiction which it has, but that save in cases recognised by international law, of which this case was not an example, a state has no jurisdiction over another state and it was therefore difficult to accept that a state had denied access to its court if it had no access to give.[12b]

[12a] [2006] UKHL 26; [2006] 2 W.L.R. 1424.
[12b] *ibid.* at [14]. See, to the same effect, Lord Hoffmann at [64] and *Holland v Lampen-Wolfe* [2000] 1 W.L.R. 1573 at 1588, *per* Lord Millett. See also *AIG Partners Inc v Republic of Kazakhstan* [2005] EWHC 2239 (Comm); [2006] 1 Lloyd's Rep. 45 (restriction on the right of a party to enforce a judgment against a central bank (see State Immunity Act 1978, s.14(4)) is legitimate and proportionate); *Grovit v Nederlandsche Bank* [2005] EWHC 2944 (QB); [2006] 1 All E.R. (Comm.) 397 (according immunity to employees of immune central bank legitimate and proportionate).

State Immunity Act 1978

[*Add to note 13: page* [688]]   **11–004**
See also United Nations Convention on Jurisdictional Immunities of States and
Their Property (December 2004, not yet in force). For the text of the Convention
see (2005) 44 Int. Leg. Mat. 803. Although not in force, the Convention has been
regarded as a strong indicator of international thinking on questions of sovereign
immunity: see *AIG Capital Partners Inc. v Republic of Kazakhstan* [2005]
EWHC 2239 (Comm); [2006] 1 W.L.R. 1420; *Jones v Ministry of the Interior of
the Kingdom of Saudi Arabia* [2006] UKHL 26. For comment on the Convention,
see Denza (2006) 55 I.C.L.Q. 395; Fox (2006) 55 I.C.L.Q. 399; Gardiner (2006)
55 I.C.L.Q. 407; Hall (2006) 55 I.C.L.Q. 411; Dickinson (2006) 55 I.C.L.Q. 427;
McGregor (2006) 55 I.C.L.Q. 437.

[*Note 13*]
Update the reference to *Dicey and Morris on the Conflict of Laws* to *Dicey,
Morris and Collins on the Conflict of Laws* (14th ed., 2006), paras
10–002—10–058.

[*Add to note 16: page* [689]]
Military Affairs Office of the Embassy of the State of Kuwait v Caramba-Coker
(E.A.T./1054/02/RN, April 10, 2003).

[*Add to note 17*]
Aziz v Republic of Yemen [2005] EWCA Civ 754; [2005] I.C.R. 1391. A claim
to immunity should be heard in public: *Harb v King Fahd Bin Abdul Aziz* [2005]
EWCA Civ 632; [2006] 1 W.L.R. 578.

[*Add to note 18*]
The immunity extends to servants or agents, officials and functionaries of a
foreign state in respect of acts done by them as such in the foreign state: *Jones
v Ministry of the Interior of the Kingdom of Saudi Arabia* [2006] UKHL 26;
[2006] 2 W.L.R. 1424. See also *Grovit v Nederlandsche Bank* [2005] EWHC
2944 (QB); [2006] 1 All E.R. (Comm.) 2944.

[*Add to note 19*]
For the position of a state's central bank or other monetary authority, see State
Immunity Act 1978, s.14(3), (4); *AIC Ltd v Federal Government of Nigeria*
[2003] EWHC 1357 (QB); *AIG Capital Partners Inc. v Republic of Kazakhstan*
[2005] EWHC 2239 (Comm); [2006] 1 W.L.R. 1420.

[*Add to note 21*]
The same principle applies in respect of proceedings for permission to enforce
a foreign arbitration award under Arbitration Act 1996, s.101: *Svenska Petroleum
Exploration AB v Government of the Republic of Lithuania (No.2)* [2005] EWHC
2437 (Comm); [2006] 1 Lloyd's Rep. 181.

[*Add in line 10 of note 22*]
*Svenska Petroleum Exploration AB v Government of the Republic of Lithuania
(No.2)*, above.

11-005   [*Add in penultimate line of note 25: page* [690]]
Al-Kadhimi v Government of Saudi Arabia [2003] EWCA Civ 1689; *Aziz v*
Republic of Yemen [2005] EWCA Civ 754; [2005] I.C.R. 1391; Garnett (2005)
54 I.C.L.Q. 705.

[*Add to note 26*]
cf. *Military Affairs Office of the Embassy of the State of Kuwait v Caramba-*
Coker (E.A.T./1054/02/RN, April 10, 2003).

[*Add at end of note 34*]
See *Svenska Petroleum Exploration AB v Government of the Republic of*
Lithuania [2005] EWHC 9 (Comm); [2005] 1 Lloyd's Rep. 515; *Svenska Petro-*
leum Exploration AB v Government of the Republic of Lithuania (No.2) [2005]
EWHC 2437 (Comm); [2006] 1 Lloyd's Rep. 181.

11-006   [*Add at end of note 35: page* [691]]
Norsk Hydro ASA v State Property Fund of Ukraine [2002] EWHC 2120
(Comm).

[*Add to note 38*]
On the importance of the certificate, see *R. (on the application of Alamieye-*
seigha) v Crown Prosecution Service [2005] EWHC 2704 (Admin).

Acts of sovereign states

11-007   [*Note 39: page* [691]]
Update the reference to *Dicey and Morris on the Conflict of Laws* to *Dicey,*
Morris and Collins on the Conflict of Laws (14th ed., 2006), paras
5–041—5–050.

[*Add at end of note 44*]
R. (on the Application of Abassi) v Secretary of State for Foreign and Com-
monwealth Affairs [2002] EWCA Civ 1598; [2003] U.K.H.R.R. 76; *Republic of*
Ecuador v Occidental Exploration and Production Co [2005] EWCA Civ 116;
[2006] 2 W.L.R. 70; *AY Bank Ltd v Bosnia and Herzegovina* [2006] EWHC 830
(Ch).

[*Add at end of note 45*]
Republic of Ecuador v Occidental Exploration and Production Co, above; *AY*
Bank Ltd v Bosnia and Herzegovina, above. See Briggs (2002) 6 Sing. J. Int. &
Comp. L. 953; Carruthers and Crawford (2003) 52 I.C.L.Q. 761.

[*Add to note 46: page* [692]]
See also *Republic of Ecuador v Occidental Exploration and Production Co*,
above.

[*Add to note 47*]
Republic of Ecuador v Occidental Exploration and Production Co, above; *AY*
Bank v Bosnia and Herzegovina, above.

Period of immunity

[Add in penultimate line of note 65: page [694]]
Jimenez v Inland Revenue Commissioners [2004] S.T.C. 371.

11–014

[Note 65]
Update the reference to *Dicey and Morris on the Conflict of Laws* to *Dicey, Morris and Collins on the Conflict of Laws* (14th ed., 2006), para.10–070.

International organisations

[Note 85: page [695]]
International Organisations Act 1968 is further amended by International Organisations Act 2005.

11–018

Other persons entitled to immunity

[First line of note 103: page [697]]
Although immunity is conferred on the Commonwealth Secretariat, that immunity does not extend to the Commonwealth Secretariat Arbitration Tribunal, decisions of which may be reviewed under the Arbitration Act 1996: *Mohsin v Commonwealth Secretariat* [2002] EWHC 377 (Comm). The Commonwealth Secretariat Act 1966 is amended by International Organisations Act 2005, ss.1–3.

11–019

Waiver of immunity: common law

[Note 111: page [698]]
Update the reference to *Dicey and Morris on the Conflict of Laws* to *Dicey, Morris and Collins on the Conflict of Laws* (14th ed., 2006), para.10–051.

11–020

[Delete final sentence and add]
It has been held that State Immunity Act 1978, s.9, extends to enforcement of an arbitration award: *Svenska Petroleum Exploration AB v Government of the Republic of Lithuania (No.2)* [2005] EWHC 2437 (Comm); [2006] 1 Lloyd's Rep. 181.

Submission to jurisdiction

[Add to note 116]
State Immunity Act 1978, s.2 is a complete statement of the circumstances in which a state submits for the purposes of the Act: *Svenska Petroleum Exploration AB v Government of the Republic of Lithuania (No.2)*, above.

11–021

[Add to note 119]
Aziz v Republic of Yemen [2005] EWCA Civ 745; [2005] I.C.R. 1391.

[Add to note 121]
It has been held that a contractual waiver of immunity, without any submission to the jurisdiction of the court, is not a submission for the purposes of State Immunity Act 1978, s.2(2): *Svenska Petroleum Exploration AB v Government of the Republic of Lithuania (No.2)*, above.

[Add to note 125: page [699]]
See *Mitchell v Ibrahim Al-Dali* [2005] EWCA Civ 720 (undertaking by foreign state not to appeal a costs order made against it does not imply waiver of immunity should enforcement of the costs order be sought).

Waiver of diplomatic or consular immunity

11–022   *[Note 130: page* [699]]
Update the reference to *Dicey and Morris on the Conflict of Laws* to *Dicey, Morris and Collins on the Conflict of Laws* (14th ed., 2006), para.10–074.

2. ALIEN ENEMIES

[Note 137: page [700]]
In *Ahmed Amin v Brown* [2005] EWHC 1670 (Ch); [2006] I.L.Pr. 67, it was held that the procedural incapacity of an alien enemy only came into existence if a technical state of war existed as between the United Kingdom and the relevant country and that there was no warrant for extending the disability to modern armed conflict which did not involve war in this sense. Accordingly, an Iraqi citizen resident in Iraq was entitled to proceed in the English court as claimant since the court was satisfied, on the basis of Ministerial statements, that Her Majesty's government position was that there is not, and has not been, a state of war between the United Kingdom and Iraq.

Who is an alien enemy

11–024   *[Add to note 139: page* [700]]
Ahmed Amin v Brown, above.

Alien enemy as claimant

11–028   *[Add to notes 161 and 162: page* [702]]
Ahmed Amin v Brown, above.

Part Four

THE TERMS OF THE CONTRACT

CHAPTER 12

EXPRESS TERMS

			PARA.
☐	1.	Proof of terms	12–002
		(a) Contractual undertakings and representations	12–003
☐		(b) Standard form contracts	12–008
■	2.	Classification of terms	12–019
■		(a) Conditions	12–025
		(b) Warranties	12–031
☐		(c) Intermediate terms	12–034
■	3.	Construction of terms	12–041
■		(a) General rules of construction	12–041
☐		(b) Ordinary meaning to be adopted	12–050
☐		(c) Whole contract to be considered	12–063
☐		(d) Effecting the intention of the parties	12–072
☐		(e) Construction against grantor	12–083
		(f) *Ejusdem generis* rule	12–087
		(g) Restriction by express provisions	12–091
		(h) Stipulations as to time	12–093
■	4.	Admissibility of extrinsic evidence	12–095
☐		(a) The parol evidence rule	12–096
		(b) Evidence as to the validity or effectiveness of the written agreement	12–106
☐		(c) Evidence as to the true nature of the agreement	12–113
☐		(d) Evidence to interpret or explain the written agreement	12–117
		(e) Evidence of custom or mercantile usage	12–127

1. PROOF OF TERMS

(b) *Standard Form Contracts*

Course of dealing

[*Add to note 53: page* [713]]
Balmoral Group Ltd v Borealis UK Ltd [2006] EWHC (Comm) 1900 at [357]–[366].

12–011

Usual trade conditions

[*Add at end of note 56*]
Balmoral Group Ltd v Borealis UK Ltd, above, at [357]–[366].

12–012

Reasonable sufficiency of notice

12–014　　[*Add to note 60: page* [714]]
　　cf. Rolls Royce Power Engineering plc v Ricardo Consulting Engineers Ltd [2003] EWHC 2871 (TCC); [2004] 2 All E.R. (Comm.) 129.

　　[*Add to note 64*]
　　Sukuman Ltd v Commonwealth Secretariat [2006] EWHC 304 (Comm); [2006] 2 Lloyd's Rep. 53.

2. Classification of Terms

(a) *Conditions*

Promissory and contingent conditions

12–027　　[*Add at end of note 104: page* [719]]
　　cf. Haugland Tankers AS v RMK Marine Gemi Yapim Sanayii ve Dentz Tasimaciligi Isletmesi AS [2005] EWHC 321 (Comm); [2005] 1 Lloyd's Rep. 573 (payment of commitment fee condition precedent to exercise of option).

(c) *Intermediate Terms*

Classification of time stipulations

12–037　　This paragraph was approved by Langley J. in *Haugland Tankers AS v RMK Marine Gemi Yapim Sanayii ve Dentz Tasimiciligi Isletmesi AS*, above, at [31]. See also *Dalkia Utilities Services plc v Celtech International Ltd* [2006] EWHC 63 (Comm); [2006] 1 Lloyd's Rep. 599 at [130].

Effect of failure to perform on time

12–038　　[*Add to note 182: page* [727]]
　　Dalkia Utilities Services plc v Celtech International Ltd, above, at [131]; *Shawton Engineering Ltd v DGP International Ltd* [2005] EWCA Civ 1359; [2006] Build. L.R. 1. Contrast Stannard (2004) 120 L.Q.R. 137, 155.

3. Construction of Terms

(a) *General Rules of Construction*

Law and fact

12–046　　[*Add to note 208: page* [731]]
　　Sun Life Assurance Co of Canada v Lincoln National Life Insurance Co [2004] EWCA Civ 1660; [2005] 1 Lloyd's Rep. 606 at [15].

(b) *Ordinary Meaning to be Adopted*

Meaning of words

[*Add to note 221; page* [732]]   **12–050**
Static Control Components (Europe) Ltd v Egan [2004] EWCA Civ 392;
[2004] 2 Lloyd's Rep. 429 at [12]–[14]; *BP Exploration Operating Co Ltd v
Kvaerner Oilfield Products Ltd* [2004] EWHC 999 (Comm); [2005] 1 Lloyd's
Rep 307 at [47]–[48]; *Sirius International Insurance (Publ) v FAI General
Insurance Ltd* [2004] UKHL 54; [2004] 1 W.L.R. 3251 at [19]; *Dairy Containers
Ltd v Tasman Orient Line CV* [2004] UKPC 22; [2005] 1 W.L.R. 215 at [12];
NBTY Europe Ltd v Nutricia International BV [2005] EWHC 734 (Comm);
[2005] 2 Lloyd's Rep. 350 at [31]; *Canmer International Inc v UK Mutual
Steamship Assurance Assn (Bermuda) Ltd* [2005] EWHC 1694 (Comm); [2005]
2 Lloyd's Rep. 479 at [22]; *Absalom v TCRU Ltd* [2005] EWHC 1090 (Comm);
[2005] 2 Lloyd's Rep. 735 at [25].

[*Add to note 227; page* [733]]
Sirius International Insurance (Publ) v FAI General Insurance Ltd, above, at
[19].

Adoption of the ordinary meaning of words

[*Add to note 228: page* [733]]   **12–051**
BP Exploration Operating Co Ltd v Kvaerner Oilfield Products Ltd [2004]
EWHC 999 (Comm); [2005] 1 Lloyd's Rep. 307 at [93]; *Thames Valley Power
Ltd v Total Gas & Power Ltd* [2005] EWHC 2208 (Comm); [2006] 1 Lloyd's
Rep. 441 at [25].

Established judicial construction

[*Add to note 235: page* [734]]   **12–053**
Henry Boot Construction Ltd v Alstom Combined Cycles Ltd [2005] EWCA
Civ 814; [2005] 1 W.L.R. 3850 at [29].

Absurdity, inconsistency, etc.

[*Add to note 238: page* [734]]   **12–055**
BP Exploration Operating Co Ltd v Kvaerner Oilfield Products Ltd [2004]
EWHC 999 (Comm); [2005] 1 Lloyd's Rep. 307 at [95]. cf. *Armitage v Staveley
Industries plc* [2004] EWHC 2320 (Comm); [2004] Pens. L.R. 385; *Canmer
International Inc v UK Mutual Steamship Assurance Assn. (Bermuda) Ltd* [2005]
EWHC 1694 (Comm); [2005] 2 Lloyd's Rep. 479 at [24]–[29].

Mercantile contracts

[*Add to note 248: page* [736]]   **12–057**
Sirius International Insurance (Publ) v FAI General Insurance Ltd [2004]
UKHL 54; [2004] 1 W.L.R. 3251 at [19]; *Mora Shipping Inc v Axa Corporate*

Solutions Assurance SA [2005] EWCA Civ 1069; [2005] 2 Lloyd's Rep. 769 at [32]; *Absalom v TCRU Ltd* [2005] EWHC 1090 (Comm); [2005] 2 Lloyd's Rep. 735 at [25].

(d) *Effecting the Intention of the Parties*

Modifying

12–075   The law relating to misnomer was explored by Rix L.J. in *Dumford Trading AG v OAO Atlantrybflot* [2005] EWCA Civ 24; [2005] 1 Lloyd's Rep. 289, where this paragraph was cited (at [27]); but see below, para.12–124.

[Add at end of paragraph: page [743]]
An obvious mistake in a written instrument can also be corrected as a matter of construction without obtaining a decree in an action for rectification,[307a] but there must be a clear mistake on the face of the instrument and it must be clear what correction ought to be made in order to cure the mistake.[307b]

[307a] *East v Pantiles Plant Hire Ltd* [1982] 2 E.G.L.R. 111 at 112; *Holding & Barnes plc v Hill House Hammond Ltd* [2002] L. & T.R. 7 at 103; *Lafarge (Aggregates) Ltd v London Borough of Newham* [2005] EWHC 1337 (Comm); [2005] 2 Lloyd's Rep. 577 at [25]; *Dalkia Utilities Services plc v Celtech International Ltd* [2006] EWHC 63 (Comm); [2006] 1 Lloyd's Rep. 599 at [109]; *Littman v Aspen Oil Broking Ltd* [2005] EWCA Civ 1579; [2006] 2 P. & C.R. 2.
[307b] *East v Pantiles Plant Hire Ltd*, above, at 112.

[Add to note 305: page [743]]
Contrast *Internaut Shipping GmbH v Fercometal SARL* [2003] EWCA Civ 812; [2003] 2 Lloyd's Rep. 430 (mistake beyond misnomer).

Supplying

12–076   *[Add to note 308: page* [743]]
Cambridge Display Technology Ltd v EI Dupont de Nemours [2004] EWHC 1415 (Ch); [2005] F.S.R. 14.

Inconsistent or repugnant clauses

12–078   *[Add to note 318: page* [744]]
cf. Taylor v Rive Droite Music Ltd [2005] EWCA Civ 1300; [2006] E.M.L.R. 4.

Clauses incorporated by reference

12–079   *[Add at end of paragraph: page* [745]]
A term in a proposal for insurance which conflicts with a term of the policy will be overriden by the term of the policy.[327a]

[327a] *Thor Navigation Inc v Ingosstrakh Insurance* [2005] EWHC 19; [2005] 1 Lloyd's Rep. 547 (applying *Izzard v Universal Insurance* [1937] A.C. 773 at 780).

Grammatical errors

[*Add at end of note 330: page* [745]]
See also *BP Exploration Operating Co Ltd v Kvaerner Oilfield Products Ltd* [2004] EWHC 999 (Comm); [2005] 1 Lloyd's Rep. 307 at [95]. *cf. Armitage v Staveley Industries plc* [2004] EWHC 2320 (Comm); [2004] Pens. L.R. 385.

12–080

Party cannot rely on his own breach

[*Add at end of note 341: page* [747]]
Decoma UK Ltd v Haden Drysys International Ltd [2005] EWHC 3427.

12–082

(e) *Construction against Grantor*

Construction against grantor

[*Add at end of note 343: page* [747]]
Tektrol Ltd v International Insurance Co of Hanover Ltd [2005] EWCA Civ 845; [2005] 2 Lloyd's Rep. 701 at [8].

12–083

[*Add at end of note 354: page* [748]]
Tektrol Ltd v International Insurance Co of Hanover Ltd, above, at [8].

12–085

4. Admissibility of Extrinsic Evidence

(a) *The Parol Evidence Rule*

"Entire agreement" clauses

[*Add to note 443: page* [758]]
See also *Proforce Recruit Ltd v Rugby Group Ltd* [2006] EWCA Civ 69 at [41] (clause does not prevent use of pre-contract materials to ascertain meaning of term in contract).

12–104

(c) *Evidence as to the True Nature of the Agreement*

Evidence of agency

[*Add to note 488: page* [762]]
See also *Internaut Shipping v Fercometal SARL* [2003] EWCA Civ 812; [2003] 2 Lloyd's Rep. 430 (evidence of no agency).

12–114

[*Add to note 494*]
Rolls Royce Power Engineering plc v Ricardo Consulting Engineers Ltd [2004] EWHC 2871 (TCC); [2004] 2 All E.R. (Comm.) 129.

(d) *Evidence to Interpret or Explain the Written Agreement*

Evidence of surrounding circumstances

12–118   [*Add to end of note 503: page* [765]]
Static Control Components (Europe) Ltd v Egan [2004] EWCA 392; [2004] 2 Lloyd's Rep. 429; *UCB Corporate Services Ltd v Thomason* [2004] 2 All E.R. (Comm.) 774; *Sirius International Insurance (Publ) v FAI General Insurance Ltd* [2004] UKHL 54; [2004] 1 W.L.R. 3251 at [20]; *Canmer International Inc v Mutual Steamship Assurance Assn. (Bermuda) Ltd* [2005] EWHC 1694 (Comm); [2005] 2 Lloyd's Rep. 479 at [22]; *Barclays Bank plc v Kingston* [2006] EWHC 533 (QB); [2066] 2 Lloyd's Rep. 59 at [29].

12–119   [*Add in line 7, after reference to Aqua Design & Play International Ltd v Kier Regional Ltd in note 507*]
P&S Platt Ltd v Crouch [2003] EWCA Civ 1110; [2004] 1 P. & C.R. 18; *NBTY Europe Ltd v Nutricia International BV* [2005] EWHC 734 (Comm); [2005] 2 Lloyd's Rep. 350 at [29]–[32]; *Absalom v TCRU Ltd* [2005] EWHC 1090 (Comm); [2005] 2 Lloyd's Rep. 735 at [25].

[*Add at end of note 507*]
Lord Nicholls (2005) 121 L.Q.R. 577 at 582–588; *Proforce Recruit Ltd v Rugby Group Ltd* [2006] EWCA Civ 69 at [33]–[35].

[*Add to note 510: page* [766]]
Proforce Recruit Ltd v Rugby Group Ltd, above, at [31].

Identity of parties

12–122   [*Add to note 528: page* [767]]
But contrast *Shogun Finance Ltd v Hudson* [2003] UKHL 62; [2004] 1 A.C. 919 at [49]; *Dumford Trading AG v OAO Atlantrybflot* [2005] EWCA Civ 24; [2005] 1 Lloyd's Rep. 289 at [32]; see below, para.12–124.

Subject-matter

12–123   [*Add to note 530: page* [767]]
cf. *Compagnie Noga d'Importation et d'Exportation SA v Abacha (No.4)* [2003] EWCA Civ 1100; [2003] 2 All E.R. (Comm.) 915 (where no intention to conclude binding contract).

Equivocations

12–124   [*Add at end of paragraph: page* [768]]
However, in *Dumford Trading AG v OAO Atlantrybflot,*[537a] Rix L.J. explored the law relating to misnomer and suggested that where there are two possible entities intrinsic evidence would not be admissible to identify the entity referred to, but if there is only one possible entity then it would be possible to use extrinsic evidence to identify a misdescribed party.
[537a] [2005] EWCA Civ 24; [2005] 1 Lloyd's Rep. 289 at [32].

Subsequent acts

12–126   [*Add at end of note 547: page* [769]]
Carmichael v National Power plc [1999] 1 W.L.R. 2042 at 2051.

CHAPTER 13

IMPLIED TERMS

Intention of parties

[*Add to note 5: page* [774]]   **13–004**
cf. Kramer [2004] C.L.J. 384.

Efficacy to contract

[*Add to note 10: page* [775]]   **13–005**
CEL Group Ltd v Nedlloyd Lines UK Ltd [2003] EWCA Civ 1716; [2004] 1
Lloyd's Rep. 381 at [20]–[21]; *Concord Trust v Law Debenture Trust Corp plc*
[2005] UKHL 27; [2005] 1 W.L.R. 1591 at [37].

[*Add at end of paragraph: page* [775]]   **13–006**
; into a contract which provided that one party should not offer design services
to any third person without the consent of the other that the consent would not
unreasonably be withheld[21a]; into insurance contracts between underwriters and
insureds that documents previously shown to the underwriters by the insureds'
brokers, and in the possession of the brokers, should be made available to the
underwriters[21b]; into a towage contract that the tug would proceed with all
reasonable despatch.[21c]

[21a] *Societa Explosivi Industriale SpA v Ordnance Technologies (VIC) Ltd* [2004] EWHC 48
(Comm); [2004] 1 All E.R. (Comm.) 619.
[21b] *Goshawk Dedicated Ltd v Tyser & Co Ltd* [2006] EWCA Civ 54; [2006] 1 Lloyd's
Rep. 566.
[21c] *Ease Faith Ltd v Leonis Marine Management Ltd* [2006] EWHC 232.

Where term not implied

[*Add to note 36: page* [777]]   **13–009**
Holding and Management (Solitaire) Ltd v Ideal Homes Northwest Ltd [2004]
EWHC 2408; (2004) 96 Const.L.R. 114.

[*Add to note 39: page* [778]]
But in *Crossley v Faithful & Gould Holdings Ltd* [2004] EWCA Civ 293;
[2004] I.R.L.R. 377, Morritt V.C. expressed the view that, in the case of a
contract of employment, it was better to focus on questions of reasonableness,

fairness and the balance of competing policy considerations rather than on the elusive concept of "necessity".

[*Add to note 40*]
Armitage v Staveley Industries plc [2004] EWHC 2320; [2004] Pens. L.R. 385.

[*Add to note 42*]
Hadley Design Associates Ltd v Westminster City Council [2003] EWHC 1617; [2004] T.C.L.R. 1.

13–010   [*Page* [778]]
In *Interleasing (UK) Ltd v Morris* [2002] EWHC 1086 (Ch), where a contract made provision for obtaining counsel's opinion, no term was implied that the opinion would only be valid if given on the basis of true facts or proper instructions. In *Crossley v Faithful & Gould Holdings Ltd* [2004] EWCA Civ 293; [2004] I.R.L.R. 377, no term was implied into a contract of employment that an employer ought to take reasonable care of an employee's economic well-being by advising him of the financial consequences under an insurance scheme of his early retirement. In *Ultraframe (UK) Ltd v Tailored Roofing Systems Ltd* [2004] EWCA Civ 585; [2004] 2 All E.R. (Comm.) 692, no term was implied into an exclusive purchasing agreement that the seller would not act in a way that was prejudicial to the buyer by selling directly to customers.

[*Add to note 48*]
But see the doubts expressed in *Crossley v Faithful & Gould Holdings Ltd*, above.

Co-operation

13–011   [*Add to note 66: page* [780]]
Goodway v Zurich Insurance Co [2004] EWHC 137; (2004) 96 Const.L.R. 49.

Prevention of performance

13–012   [*Add after reference to Martin-Smith v Williams in note 69: page* [780]]
CEL Group Ltd v Nedlloyd Lines UK Ltd [2003] EWCA Civ 1716; [2004] 1 Lloyd's Rep. 381 at [11], [22] and [23].

[*Add at end of note 71*]
Taylor v Rive Droite Music Ltd [2005] EWCA Civ 1300; [2006] E.M.L.R. 4.

Export and import licences

13–013   [*Note 76: page* [781]]
Update reference to *Benjamin's Sale of Goods* to (7th ed.), paras 18–308—18–322.

Trading Stamps

The Trading Stamps Act 1964 has been repealed by the Regulatory Reform **13–030**
(Trading Stamps) Order 2005 (SI 2005/871).

Package travel, etc.

For the relationship between the Regulations and the (Athens) International **13–034**
Convention on the Carriage of Passengers and their Luggage by Sea (see below,
paras 14–117 and 36–063), see *Lee v Airtours Holidays Ltd* [2004] 1 Lloyd's
Rep. 683.

[*Add to note 162: page* [790]]
Chapman [2004] I.T.L.J. (3) 129.

CHAPTER 14

EXEMPTION CLAUSES

			PARA.
	1.	In general	14–001
☐	2.	Rules of construction	14–005
	3.	Fundamental breach	14–020
☐	4.	Application of rules of construction to particular contracts	14–025
☐	5.	Exemption clauses and third parties	14–039
■	6.	Statutory control of exemption clauses	14–059
☐		(a) Unfair Contract Terms Act 1977	14–059
		(b) Misrepresentation Act 1967	14–114
☐		(c) Other statutes	14–115
	7.	Common law qualifications	14–132
☐	8.	*Force majeure* clauses	14–137

2. RULES OF CONSTRUCTION

General principles

14–005 [*Add to note 19: page* [793]]
Dairy Containers Ltd v Tasman Orient Line CV [2004] UKPC 22; [2005] 1
W.L.R. 215 at [12].

Clause must extend to event

14–006 [*Note 30: page* [794]]
Update reference to Benjamin to (7th ed., 2006), paras 13–026 *et seq.*

[*Add to note 31 after "Watford Electronics Ltd v Sanderson CFL Ltd": page* [795]]
Ease Faith Ltd v Leonis Marine Management Ltd [2006] EWHC 232.

Inconsistency with main purpose of contract

14–007 [*Add to note 37: page* [795]]
See *Mitsubishi Corp v Eastwind Transport Ltd* [2004] EWHC 2924 (Comm);
[2005] 1 Lloyd's Rep. 383 at [29].

[*Add to note 44: page* [796]]
Mitsubishi Corp v Eastwind Transport Ltd, above.

Construction contra proferentem

[*Add to note 58: page* [797]]   14–009
Homburg Houtimport BV v Agrosin Private Ltd [2004] 1 A.C. 715 at 779;
Dairy Containers Ltd v Tasman Orient Line CV [2004] UKPC 22; [2005] 1
W.L.R. 215 at [12].

Liability for negligence

[*Add to note 61: page* [798]]   14–010
Frans Maas (UK) Ltd v Samsung Electronics (UK) Ltd [2004] EWHC 1502
(Comm); [2004] 2 Lloyd's Rep. 251 at [131]–[139].

Words wide enough to cover negligence

[*Add to note 80: page* [800]]   14–011
Frans Maas (UK) Ltd v Samsung Electronics (UK) Ltd, above, at
[139]–[152]

Deliberate breaches

[*Add to note 110: page* [803]]   14–016
Frans Maas (UK) Ltd v Samsung Electronics (UK) Ltd [2004] EWHC 1502
(Comm); [2004] 2 Lloyd's Rep. 251 at [139]–[152]

Burden of proof

[*Add at end of note 125: page* [805]]   14–018
followed in *Euro Cellular (Distribution) plc v Danzas Ltd* [2003] EWHC 3161
(Comm); [2004] 1 Lloyd's Rep. 521.

[*Add at end of note 127: page* [805]]   14–019
Euro Cellular (Distribution) plc v Danzas Ltd, above.

4. Application of Rules of Construction to Particular Contracts

Sale of goods: terms as to quality, etc.

[*Note 169: page* [811]]   14–027
Update reference to Benjamin to (7th ed., 2006), paras 13–028, 13–029,
13–031 and 13–032.

Misdelivery by carrier

[*Add at end of note 198: page* [814]]   14–033
East West Corporation v DKBS 1912 [2003] EWCA Civ 83; [2003] Q.B. 1509
at [65]–[68].

5. Exemption Clauses and Third Parties

Contracts excluded from the 1999 Act

14–044   [*Note 240: page* [819]]
Update reference to Benjamin to (7th ed., 2006), Ch.18.

Bailment

14–054   [*Add to note 274: page* [824]]
East West Corporation v DKBS 1912 [2003] EWCA Civ 83; [2003] Q.B. 1509
at [25]–[27].

[*Add to note 279: page* [825]]
East West Corporation v DKBS 1912, above, at [30], [69].

14–055   [*Note 284: page* [825]]
Update reference to Benjamin to (7th ed., 2006), para.18–029.

[*Note 285: page* [826]]
Update reference to Benjamin to (7th ed., 2006), paras 18–022—18–028.

[*Note 286*]
Update reference to Benjamin to (7th ed., 2006), paras 18–102—18–122.

6. Statutory Control of Exemption Clauses

(a) *Unfair Contract Terms Act 1977*

Dealing as consumer

14–066   [*Add to note 343: page* [832]]
The *R&B* case was followed in *Feldaroll Foundry plc v Hermes Leasing
(London) Ltd* [2004] EWCA Civ 747; see para.43–106, below.

Liability arising in contract

14–072   [*Add to note 365: page* [834]]
Hadley Design Associates Ltd v Westminster City Council [2003] EWHC
1617; [2004] T.C.L.R. 1.

14–074   [*Add to note 377: page* [835]]
Contrast *Hadley Design Associates Ltd v Westminster City Council*, above
(one month's termination clause in architects' contract not unreasonable).

Guidelines

[*Add to note 425: page* [840]]   **14–085**
Frans Maas (UK) Ltd v Samsung Electronics (UK) Ltd [2004] EWHC 1502
(Comm); [2004] 2 Lloyd's Rep. 251 at [159]; *Balmoral Group Ltd v Borealis UK
Ltd* [2006] EWHC (Comm) 1900 at [405]–[416].

[*Add to note 426*]
Frans Maas (UK) Ltd v Samsung Electronics (UK) Ltd, above, at [159];
Balmoral Group Ltd v Borealis UK Ltd, above, at [405]–[416].

[*Add to note 427*]
Frans Maas (UK) Ltd v Samsung Electronics (UK) Ltd, above, at [159];
Balmoral Group Ltd v Borealis UK Ltd, above, at [405]–[416].

Limits on amount

[*Add in note 432 after Pegler Ltd v Wang: page* [841]]   **14–087**
Frans Maas (UK) Ltd v Samsung Electronics (UK) Ltd [2004] EWHC 1502
(Comm); [2004] 2 Lloyd's Rep. 251 at [159]; *Balmoral Group Ltd v Borealis UK
Ltd* [2006] EWHC (Comm) 1900 at [405]–[416].

Reasonableness under Unfair Contract Terms Act 1977

[*Add to note 454: page* [844]]   **14–092**
Contrast *Expo Fabrics (UK) Ltd v Martin* [2003] EWCA Civ 1165 (textiles:
20-day time limit held reasonable).

[*Add to note 456*]   **14–094**
See also *Balmoral Group Ltd v Borealis UK Ltd* [2006] EWHC (Comm) 1900
at [418].

In *Frans Maas (UK) Ltd v Samsung Electronics (UK) Ltd* [2004] EWHC 1502   **14–096**
(Comm); [2004] 2 Lloyd's Rep. 251, a clause in the BIFA (freight forwarders)
contract limiting the damages recoverable in respect of the loss by theft of mobile
telephones from the bailee's warehouse was upheld as reasonable.

[*Add to note 482: page* [847]]   **14–099**
Frans Maas (UK) Ltd v Samsung Electronics (UK) Ltd, above, at [158].

(c) *Other Statutes*

Carriage by sea

In *Jindal Iron and Steel Co Ltd v Islamic Solidarity Shipping Co Jordan Inc*   **14–117**
[2004] UKHL 49; [2005] 1 W.L.R. 1363, a term in a charterparty transferring
responsibility for loading, stowage and discharge of cargo from the owner to the
cargo owner was held to be valid notwithstanding art, III, r.2, of the Hague-Visby
rules.

Consumer protection

14-125   [*Add to note 542: page* [855]]
Final proposals have now been made by the two Law Commissions in a joint report (Law Com. No. 292, Scot Law Com. No. 199) published in February 2005.

[*Add to note 548: page* [855]]
See *Wilson v Robertsons (London) Ltd* [2005] EWHC 1425 (Ch); [2006] 1 W.L.R. 1248.

14-127   The Trading Stamps Act 1964 has been repealed by the Regulatory Reform (Trading Stamps) Order 2005 (SI 2005/871).

14-129   [*Add to note 554: page* [856]]
Amended by SI 2005/689. See also the Financial Services (Distant Marketing) Regulations 2004 (SI 2004/2095).

[*Add to note 555*]
Amended by SI 2003/2579.

Enterprise Act 2002

14-131   [*Add to notes 571 and 575: page* [857]]
See para.43–157, below, for Orders and Regulations made.

8. *FORCE MAJEURE* CLAUSES

Force majeure clauses

14-137   [*Add to note 602: page* [860]]
See Allen (2003) 147 S.J. 1416–1417.

14-138   [*Add at the end of note 608: page* [861]]
The words "beyond our control" will be construed to apply to the specific as well as to the non-specific events: *Frontier International Shipping Corp v Swissmarine Corporation Inc* [2004] EWHC 8 (Comm); [2005] 1 Lloyd's Rep. 390 at [27]–[28].

Burden of proof

14-140   [*Add to note 621: page* [862]]
SHV Gas Supply & Trading SAS v Naftomar Shipping and Trading Co Ltd Inc [2005] EWHC 2528 (Comm); [2006] 1 Lloyd's Rep. 163 at [29].

"Prevented" clauses

[Add to note 622: page [862]]   **14–141**
Thames Valley Power Ltd v Total Gas & Power Ltd [2005] EWHC 2208
(Comm); [2006] 1 Lloyd's Rep. 441 at [50].

[Note 625: page [863]]
Update reference to Benjamin to (7th ed., 2006), para.18–350.

[Add to end of note 627: page [864]]
Contrast *Mamidoil-Jetoil Greek Petroleum Co SA v Okta Crude Oil Refinery
AD* [2003] 1 Lloyd's Rep. 1 (Comm Ct.); [2003] EWCA Civ 1031; [2003] 2
Lloyd's Rep. 635.

Specified events

[Note 651: page [866]]   **14–146**
Update reference to Benjamin to (7th ed., 2006), paras 18–342 *et seq.*

Conditions precedent

[Add after Bunge SA v Kruse in note 682: page [869]]   **14–150**
SHV Gas Supply & Trading SAS v Naftomar Shipping and Trading Co Ltd Inc,
above, at [39].

[Note 682]
Update reference to Benjamin to (7th ed., 2006), para.18–356.

[Note 683]
Update reference to Benjamin to (7th ed., 2006), para.18–357.

Insufficiency of goods

[Note 686: page [870]]   **14–151**
Update reference to Benjamin to (7th ed., 2006), paras 6–053, 8–103 and
18–353.

Distance Selling Regulations 2000

[Add to note 697: page [871]]   **14–154**
amended by SI 2005/689.

CHAPTER 15

UNFAIR TERMS IN CONSUMER CONTRACTS

			PARA.
	1.	Introduction	15–001
■	2.	The Unfair Terms in Consumer Contracts Regulations 1999	15–004
■		(a) The contracts governed by the Regulations	15–011
□		(b) Contract terms governed by the Regulations	15–030
■		(c) The requirement of fairness	15–043
□		(i) The test of unfairness	15–045
□		(ii) The "indicative list" of terms	15–069
		(iii) The effect of failure to comply with the requirement of fairness	15–087
■		(d) The requirement of plain and intelligible language	15–089
		(i) The test	15–089
■		(ii) The effects of failure to comply with the requirement of plain and intelligible language	15–091
□		(e) Choice of law clauses	15–093
		(f) The prevention of unfair terms	15–094

2. THE UNFAIR TERMS IN CONSUMER CONTRACTS REGULATIONS 1999

[Add new paragraph 15–010A: page [879]]

15–010A   **Proposals for reform.** The Law Commissions have published a joint report on proposed reforms to the legislation on unfair terms in contracts.[46a] The proposals include the creation of a unified regime for the control of unfair terms in consumer contracts, putting together the controls at present found in the Unfair Contract Terms Act 1977 and the Unfair Terms in Consumer Contracts Regulations 1999; preserving the protection given by the Unfair Contract Terms Act 1977 in business contracts; and extending existing protection against unfair contract terms for consumers to small businesses.

[46a] Law Commission, Scottish Law Commission, *Unfair Terms in Contracts,* Law Com. No.292, Scot Law Com. No.199 (2005).

(a) *The Contracts Governed by the Regulations*

Contracts for the sale, etc. of an interest in land

15–014—   *[Pages [880]–[882]]*
15–017   Paragraphs 15–014—15–017 need to be read in the light of the decision of the Court of Appeal in *London Borough of Newham v Khatun* [2004] EWCA Civ 55;

[2005] Q.B. 37. In that case, the question arose whether the 1993 Directive (and therefore the 1999 Regulations) applies to the terms on which accommodation is let by a local authority pursuant to its duty under the homeless persons legislation contained in Pt VII of the Housing Act 1996. Having looked at the *travaux préparatoires* of the Directive, the Court of Appeal noted the differences of terminology used by some of its different language versions to describe its subject matter (*e.g.* "seller of goods" and "*vendeur des biens*", as identified in para.15–014 of the Main Text) and considered that these "effectively demolish" the textual argument that the English version's reference to "seller of goods" point to the exclusion of contracts relating to land: [2004] EWCA Civ 55, at [78]–[83]. The Court of Appeal therefore held that the 1999 Regulations apply equally to contracts relating to land. Moreover, a few weeks after this decision, the European Court of Justice in *Freiburger Kommunalbauten GMbH Baugesellschaft & Co KG v Hofstetter* Case C-237/02 [2004] 2 C.M.L.R. 13 was apparently content to assume that a contract for the purchase of a building to be constructed falls within the ambit of the 1993 Directive, although the issue of the application of the 1993 Directive to contracts relating to land was not before the court.

"Sellers or suppliers"

[Add to text after note 82: page [884]]
    In *London Borough of Newham v Khatun*[82a] the Court of Appeal held that the provision of accommodation by a local authority under a contract of tenancy, pursuant to its duty under the homeless persons legislation contained in Pt VII of the Housing Act 1996, falls within the scope of the 1993 Directive, as this activity comes within the words "trade, business or profession" under Art.2(c) of the Directive, despite the statutory context of this provision.

[82a] [2004] EWCA Civ 55; [2005] Q.B. 37.

15–021

(b) *Contract Terms Governed by the Regulations*

[Add new paragraph 15–032A: page [892]]
    Standard terms put forward by the consumer and "individual negotiation". In *Bryen & Langley Ltd v Boston* the question arose as to how, if at all, the 1999 Regulations would affect standard terms put forward by a consumer (or rather by his professional advisers) and incorporated into a consumer contract, on the facts the standard terms stemming from one of the JCT standard building contracts.[150a] At first instance it had been seen as "at least arguable that where the 'consumer' has been able to influence the substance of the relevant term because he chose to use the standard form of contract in which it is contained, the term does not fall to be regarded as not having been individually negotiated".[150b] In the Court of Appeal Rimer J. noted that the consumer before him had had "the opportunity to influence the terms on which the contractors were being invited to tender, even though he may not have taken it up; and [that] there is therefore at least an argument" that the terms were not therefore "not individually negotiated", but as the point had not been argued before the court, he specifically expressed no view on it.[150c] Instead, the Court of Appeal held that in these circumstances any term contained in the standard contract would not fail the test

15–032A

of fairness found in reg.5 of the 1999 Regulations as it would not cause a significant imbalance in the rights and obligations of the parties to the detriment of the consumer *contrary to the requirement of good faith*.[150d] It is submitted that the provisions of the 1999 Regulations and the 1993 Directive governing the exclusion of individually negotiated terms from the ambit of their control do not bear out the argument that standard terms put forward by a consumer fall or always fall within the exclusion, particularly bearing in mind that this exclusion is to be interpreted strictly following the general approach of the European Court of Justice to exceptions.[150e] For while a consumer who proposes a set of standard terms may sometimes be thought to have "been able to influence the substance of the term" (by amending or deleting the standard terms which he himself proposes), this will not always be the case. Moreover, the exclusion found in reg.5(1) of the 1999 Regulations is for contract terms which have been the object of "individual negotiation", whereas a term in a set of standard terms proposed by the consumer remains standard (and often unknown to, or not understood by, the consumer and possibly even his professional advisers) and cannot easily be said to be "*individually* negotiated".[150f] For this reason, it is respectfully submitted that the putting forward of standard terms by a consumer should be dealt with in terms of the requirement of good faith, rather than in terms of the question of their "individual negotiation".[150g]

[150a] [2005] EWCA Civ 973; [2005] All E.R. (D) 507 (Jul.) on appeal from [2004] EWHC 2450 (TCC); 98 Con. L.R. 82.
[150b] [2004] EWHC 2450 (TCC) at [43], *per* Judge Richard Seymour Q.C.
[150c] [2005] EWCA Civ 973 at [46].
[150d] *ibid.*, and see below, Supplement to para.15–060.
[150e] 1993 Directive, Art.3(1) and 3(2); 1999 Regulations, regs 5(1)–(4). On the strict interpretation of exceptions see, *e.g.* Case C-203/99, *Veedfald v Århus Amtskommune,* para.15 in the context of Dir. 84/374 concerning liability for defective products, Art.7.
[150f] *cf.* the condition for the application of the controls found in the Unfair Contract Terms Act 1977, s.3(1) that the term be on the written standard terms of the business relying on a particular term ("the *other's* written standard terms of business"): see Main Work, para.14–073.
[150g] Below, Supplement to para.15–060.

[*Add new paragraphs 15–036A and 15–036B after paragraph 15–036: page* [895]]

15–036A   **The relevance of construction of the contract.** In *Bairstow Eves London Central Ltd v Darlingtons*,[165a] the House of Lords' approach to reg.6(2) of the 1999 Regulations in the *First National Bank plc* case[165b] was applied to clauses setting the contract price in an estate agency contract. There a vendor of a flat (the "consumer") had entered a contract with an estate agent by which the latter undertook the sole agency to sell the flat on their behalf. Under its standard terms, the "standard commission" payable to the estate agent was set at 3 per cent of the sale price of the property, but "early payment" attracted a "discount rate" of 1.5 per cent of the sale price, early payment being defined as payment of the full sum payable within 10 working days of completion of the sale. It was further expressly specified that if such a full sum was not paid within this time, the "standard commission" would become payable together with interest at 3 per cent above base rate. After completing a sale, the vendor's solicitors did not pay the agent the *full* sum of the "discount rate" within the 10 day period (falling short by a mere £387) even though they were in funds to do so, and so the estate agent claimed the "standard rate" plus interest. It was then claimed that the terms of the contract setting the 3 per cent commission rate were unfair within the meaning of the 1999 Regulations, but to this the estate agents countered that these terms fell within the exclusion from the requirement of fairness contained in reg.6(2) of terms which relate to the "adequacy of the price or remuneration, as against the goods or services supplied in exchange."

165a [2004] EWHC 263; [2004] 2 E.G.L.R. 25.
165b *Director General of Fair Trading v First National Bank plc* [2001] UKHL 52; [2002] 1 A.C. 481.

Having looked at the treatment of this provision by the House of Lords in the **15–036B** *First National Bank plc* case as described in para.15–036 of the Main Text, Gross J. held that the applicability of reg.6(2) turned on an issue of construction of the contract, *viz* whether the agreement provided for a 3 per cent commission rate (or price) with the vendors having an option (but no obligation) to pay 1.5 per cent (in which case reg.6(2) *would* apply) or an obligation to pay a price of 1.5 per cent, with a "default" provision exercisable at the estate agents' option to insist on payment of 3 per cent (in which case reg.6(2) *would not* apply).165c In his view, the prevailing market, the pre-contractual negotiations between the parties, and their expectation that the 1.5 per cent commission would be paid within 10 days all indicated that *both* the parties to the contract contemplated an agreed operative price of 1.5 per cent with a default provision of 3 per cent.165d This view of the parties' intention was not precluded by the language used by the agreement as set in its contractual matrix, even though "at first blush" the reference to the higher price as the "standard commission rate" and the lower as the "early payment discounted rate" suggested the opposite conclusion165e: the idea that there was merely an option in the consumer (not an obligation) to pay the lower rate was "simply fanciful".165f As a result, reg.6(2) did not exclude this "default provision" from the requirement of fairness. Given that the view of the judge below that the clauses in question were unfair had not been appealed, the estate agent's claim to the higher commission rate failed.

165c [2004] EWHC 263 at [26].
165d *ibid.*, at [27].
165e *ibid.*, at [29].
165f *ibid.*, at [30].

(c) *The Requirement of Fairness*

(i) *The Test of Unfairness*

[Add new paragraph after paragraph 15–047: page [903]]
The relative roles of the European Court of Justice and national courts. In **15–047A** *Freiburger Kommunalbauten GmbH Baugesellschaft & Co KG v Hofstetter*207a the European Court of Justice was asked by a national court to decide whether a clause in a particular consumer contract before it was unfair within the meaning of the 1993 Directive. This the European Court refused to do, noting that "in referring to concepts of good faith and significant imbalance between the rights

and obligations of the parties, Art.3 of the [1993] Directive merely defines in a general way the factors that render unfair a contractual term that has not been individually negotiated."[207b] Given the range of factors which the Directive requires to be taken into account in assessing the fairness of a contract term, "the consequences of the term under the law applicable to the contract must also be taken into account. This requires that consideration be given to the national law."[207c] So, while the European Court "may interpret general criteria used by the Community legislation in order to define the concept of unfair terms . . . it should not rule on the application of these general criteria to a particular term, which must be considered in the light of the particular circumstances of the case in question."[207d] As a result, it is generally for a national court to decide whether a contract term satisfies the requirements for it to be regarded as unfair within the meaning of Art.3(1) of the 1993 Directive.[207e]

[207a] Case C-237/02 of April 1, 2004 [2004] 2 C.M.L.R. 13.

[207b] *ibid.*, at paras 19–21.

[207c] *ibid.*, at para.21. For an example of this, see *Director General of Fair Trading plc v First National Bank plc* [2001] UKHL 52; [2002] 1 A.C. 481, discussed in the Main Text, para.15–061.

[207d] Case C-237/02 at para.22, "distinguishing" (at para.23) its earlier decision in *Océano Grupo Editorial SA v Murciano Quintero*, Joined Cases C-240/98 to C-244/98 of June 27, 2000 [2000] E.C.R. 1–4941, Main Text, para.15–063, where it had held an internal territorial jurisdiction clause unfair on the basis that such a clause satisfied all the criteria necessary for it to be judged unfair for the purposes of the 1993 Directive without consideration of all the circumstances in which the contract was concluded or the advantages and disadvantages which the term would have under the applicable national law.

[207e] Case C-237/02, para.25.

"The nature of the goods or services"

15–054   [*Add new text at end of paragraph: page* [906]]
Furthermore, in *Bryen & Langley Ltd v Boston*[225a] it was considered material to the issue of fairness of a term that the transaction was not of a "normal 'consumer' type, like buying a television set", but, for the individual or individuals concerned, a major project such as the costly construction of a building which would be undertaken only with the benefit of appropriate professional advice.

[225a] [2004] EWHC 2450 (TCC) at [45]; 98 Con L.R. 82; [2005] EWCA Civ 973; [2005] All E.R. (D.) 507 (Jul.) (appeal allowed on other grounds).

Other factors in the assessment of good faith or fairness

15–060   [*Add new text: page* [909]]
Where a consumer's professional agent put forward a standard set of terms which were held to have been incorporated into the contract, and thereby "imposed these terms" on the supplier of a service, the Court of Appeal has regarded "the suggestion that there was any lack of good faith or fair dealing by [the supplier] with regard to the ultimate incorporation of these terms into the contract as repugnant to common sense . . . It was not for [the suppliers] to take the matter up with [the consumer] and ensure that he know what he was doing: they knew that he had the benefit of the services of a professional . . . to advise

him on the effects of the terms."[247a] In this way, even if a particular contract term (here, an arbitration clause) were found to cause a "significant imbalance in the parties' rights and obligations under the contract, to the detriment of the consumer" as envisaged by reg.5(1) of the 1999 Regulations, this would not be "contrary to the requirement of good faith", with the result that the contract term would not be unfair within the meaning of the Regulations. On the other hand, if a business supplier were to agree to a set of standard terms (perhaps promulgated by a trade association) proposed by a consumer which the supplier knows to be very prejudicial to the consumer's interests in circumstances where he also knows that the consumer is ignorant of this effect (especially where the consumer is not professionally advised), then the mere fact that the terms were proposed by the consumer should not be allowed to determine the issue of the fairness of the terms: in these circumstances, the supplier may be acting "contrary to the requirement of good faith" and one or more of the terms may be "unfair" given their effect on the relative rights and obligations of the parties and taking into account the other circumstances specified by the 1999 Regulations for this purpose.[247b]

[247a] *Bryen & Langley Ltd v Boston* [2005] EWCA Civ 973 at [46], *per* Rimer J. (with whom Clarke and Pill L.JJ. agreed (at [56] and [64] respectively); [2005] All E.R. (D.) 507 (Jul.).
[247b] Main Work, paras 15–050—15–057.

(ii) *The "Indicative List" of terms*

Arbitration and adjudication clauses

[*Note 289: page* [917]]   **15–072**
   Picardi v Cuniberti [2002] EWHC 2923 is reported at (2003) 19 Const. L.J. 350.

[*Add to text at end of paragraph: page* [917]]
   On the other hand, in *Westminster Building Co Ltd v Beckingham*[291a] a private individual (the "consumer") who had commissioned a firm of builders to renovate his property under a contract falling outside the Housing Grants, Regeneration and Construction Act 1996 was held bound by an adjudication clause which it contained since this clause was not unfair in the circumstances: its terms were couched in plain and intelligible language and had been decided upon by the consumer's professional agents, chartered surveyors, who could have given him competent and objective advice as to its existence and effect.

[291a] [2004] EWHC 138 (TCC) esp. at [31]. See similarly *Lovell Projects Ltd v Legg* (TCC) [2003] B.L.R. 452. *cf. Bryen & Langley Ltd v Boston* [2005] EWCA Civ 973; [2005] All E.R. (D) 507 (Jul.) (arbitration clause in JCT standard contract held binding where the *consumer* imposed it on the supplier) and see above, paras 15–032A and 15–060.

Penalty clauses

[*Add new text at end of paragraph: page* [919]]   **15–076**
   So, for example, it has been held that a clause which requires a consumer to pay interest at 8 per cent over the Bank of England current base rate on sums due to the business under the contract 30 days after the issue of an account is unfair within the meaning of the 1999 Regulations, even though it constituted a genuine

pre-estimate of damage likely to be suffered by the claimant in the event of non-payment and therefore not a penalty clause at common law,[301a] this decision on the unfairness of the term resting principally on the grounds that the term was unusual and not balanced by a similar term governing unpaid monies such as damages which may fall due *to* the consumer.[301b]

[301a] *Munkenbeck & Marshall v Harold* [2005] EWHC 356 (TCC); [2005] All E.R. (D) 227.
[301b] *ibid.*, [12] and [15]

Other potentially unfair terms

15–086   *[Add new text at end of paragraph: page* [925]]

It has also been held that a contract term which provides that the consumer must indemnify the business in respect of its legal or other costs in any action or proceedings and pay it a reasonable sum in respect of time spent in connection with such an action or proceedings was unfair within the meaning of the 1999 Regulations, even though the court saw the force of the argument that such a term could protect the business against unfair treatment of the business by the customer who could use the business's unrecoverable costs to negotiate a discount on the unpaid contract price: the term remained unbalanced by any similar provision for the benefit of the consumer.[338a]

[338a] *Munkenbeck & Marshall v Harold* [2005] EWHC 356 (TCC) at [12]–[15]; [2005] All E.R. (D) 227.

(d) *The requirement of Plain and Intelligible Language*

(ii) *The Effects of Failure to Comply with the Requirement of Plain and Intelligible Language*

Other possible effects

15–092   *[Note 353: page* [928]].

The argument in this note that a failure of a written contract to conform to the requirement of plainness and intelligibility can in itself attract the preventative measures foreseen by Art.7 of the 1993 Directive appears to run contrary to the approach of the European Court of Justice in Case C-70/03, *Commission v Spain* of September 9, 2004, on the effect of Art.5(2) of the Directive, as the court there held that the reason why the rule of interpretation *contra proferentem* of ambiguous terms should not apply in proceedings under Art.7 was to be found in the need to enhance the effectiveness of preventive proceedings against *unfair* terms (*ibid.*, at paras 16 and 17) as otherwise a potentially unfair term could be rescued by interpretation. This reasoning appears to assume, therefore, that proceedings under Art.7 can not be founded *merely* on a failure of term to be plain and intelligible. On the other hand, the European Court in this case did not consider the impact of the Consumer Injunctions Directive (Dir. 98/27 of the European Parliament and of the Council of May 19, 1998, on injunctions for the protection of consumers' interests), a list which required the introduction of injunctions aimed at the protection of the collective interests of consumers where there is "any act contrary" to the directives listed in its annex, which includes the 1993

Directive *in toto*: Dir. 98/27, Art.1(2); Annex, No.9. This suggests that the measures provided in English law for the implementation of the Consumer Injunctions Directive (which are explained at para.15–099 of the Main Text) could be used for a mere failure of plainness or intelligibility of a term of a consumer contract, on the basis that this would appear to be an "act contrary" to Art.5(1) of the 1993 Directive.

(e) *Choice of Law Clauses*

Choice of law clauses ineffective

[Add new text at end of paragraph: page [929]]   **15–093**
In Case C-70/03, *Commission v Spain* of September 9, 2004 the European Court of Justice noted that Art.6(2) of the Unfair Terms in Consumer Contracts Directive 1993 (implemented in English law by reg.9 of the 1999 Regulations) "merely states that the contract is to have a close connection with the territory of the Member States" in order to attract the application of the 1993 Directive's provisions.[356a] This "deliberately vague" "general expression seeks to make it possible to take account of various ties depending on the circumstances of the case" and so while the legislature of a Member State may properly seek to give it concrete effect by the use of presumptions, it cannot circumscribe it by "a combination of predetermined criteria for ties such as the cumulative conditions as to residence and conclusion of the contract referred to in Article 5 of the Rome Convention".[356b]

[356a] Case C-70/03, para.32.
[356b] *ibid.*, paras 32, 33.

(f) *The Prevention of Unfair Terms*

"Qualifying bodies"

[Note 374: page [932]]   **15–098**
The "Director General of Water Services" should be replaced by the "Water Services Regulation Authority": the Unfair Terms in Consumer Contracts (Amendment) and Water Act 2003 (Transitional Provision) Regulations 2006 (SI 2006/523), reg.2.

Part Five

ILLEGALITY AND PUBLIC POLICY

CHAPTER 16

ILLEGALITY AND PUBLIC POLICY

			PARA.
	1.	Introduction	16–001
■	2.	The position at common law	16–003
□		(a) Generally	16–003
■		(b) Objects which are illegal by common law or by statute	16–014
■		(c) Objects injurious to good government	16–019
		(i) Domestic affairs	16–019
■		(ii) Foreign affairs	16–026
■		(d) Objects injurious to the proper working of justice	16–035
		(i) Agreements to conceal offences and compromises	16–035
		(ii) Other contracts affecting the course of justice	16–039
		(iii) Ouster of jurisdiction	16–044
■		(iv) Maintenance and champerty	16–048
		(e) Objects injurious to morality and marriage	16–067
		(i) Immorality	16–067
		(ii) Interference with marriage	16–070
■		(f) Contracts in restraint of trade	16–075
■		(i) Scope of the doctrine	16–075
□		(ii) Employer and employee	16–103
		(iii) Vendor and purchaser of business	16–115
■		(iv) Partners	16–118
■		(v) Supply and acquisition of goods: restraints in vertical agreements	16–120
		(vi) Restraints on the use of land or chattels	16–127
		(vii) Supply and acquisition of goods: restraints in horizontal agreements	16–131
		(viii) Labour and services: restraints in horizontal agreements	16–135
		(ix) Invalidating and regulatory statutory provisions	16–140
■	3.	Contracts unenforceable by statute	16–141
■		(a) General principles	16–141
		(b) Statutory regulation of trading with the enemy	16–157
■	4.	Enforcement of collateral and proprietary rights	16–159
□		(a) The maxim *ex turpi causa non oritur actio* and related rules	16–159
		(b) Collateral transactions	16–170
■		(c) Recovery of money paid or property transferred under illegal contracts	16–171
□	5.	Severance	16–188
■	6.	Pleading and practice	16–198

2. The Position at Common Law

(a) *Generally*

Public policy

[Add to note 12: page [939]]
Kellar v Williams [2004] UKPC 30.

16–004

Scope of public policy

[Add new text at end of paragraph: page [941]]

16–005

Although a contract may be associated with a particular illegality, the public policy underlying the illegality may be such that it results in the contract being enforceable. In *Hill v Secretary of State for the Environment, Food and Rural Affairs*[24a] the defendant argued that the contract that it had entered into with the claimant was illegal as the director, who had acted for the claimant, had been declared a bankrupt and had therefore committed an offence under s.11 of the Company Directors Disqualification Act 1986 which prohibits an undischarged bankrupt from taking part in the management of a company. As the court pointed out, this proscription had been introduced to protect persons dealing with companies and, were the argument of the defendant to prevail, it would have the effect of prejudicing creditors since it would prevent the company from enforcing the contract. Accordingly, public policy favoured the claimant's right of enforcement and the defendant's defence of illegality failed.[24b]

[24a] [2005] EWHC 696 (Ch).
[24b] See also para.16–162. The company could probably have enforced the contract without relying on any illegality.

How illegality may affect a contract

[Add to text at end of paragraph: page [942]]

16–007

The Law Commission has stated that "Generally, it seems that the commission of a legal wrong, or acting otherwise contrary to public policy, in the course of performing a contract does not, at common law, affect enforcement".[35a] Illegality will only preclude the enforcement of the contract where it has been "entered into with the purpose of doing [an] . . . unlawful or immoral act or the contract itself (as opposed to the mode of . . . performance) is prohibited by law."[35b]

[35a] *Illegal Transactions: The Effect Of Illegality On Contracts And Trusts* (LC CP No. 154, para.2.29) cited with approval in *Colen v Cebrian (U.K.) Ltd.* [2003] EWCA Civ 1676 at [44].
[35b] *Coral Leisure Group Ltd v Barnett* [1981] I.C.R. 503 at 509.

(b) *Objects which are Illegal by Common Law or Statute*

Fraud

[Add to the text at end of the paragraph: page [949]]

16–017

However, where the contract in question is remote from the illegality, the court will enforce the contract.[92a]

[92a] *21st Century Logistic Solutions Ltd v Madysen Ltd* [2004] EWHC 231 (QB); [2004] 2 Lloyd's Rep. 92. (In this case a company that intended to evade the payment of VAT could nevertheless enforce a contract for the supply of goods, the avoidance of VAT not being an integral part of the contract.)

(c) *Objects Injurious to good Government*

(ii) *Foreign Affairs*

Performance contrary to public policy in place for performance

16–028　　[*Add to note 138: page* [953]]
　　　　Tekron Resources Ltd v Guinea Investment Co Ltd [2004] 2 Lloyd's Rep. 26.

Illegality under foreign applicable law to contract

16–031　　[*Add to note 149: page* [954]]
　　　　See also *Mahonia Ltd v J.P. Morgan Chase Bank* [2003] 2 Lloyd's Rep. 911; *Mahonia Ltd v West LB AG* [2004] EWHC 1938 (Comm); *JSC Zestafoni G Nikoladze Ferroalloy Plant v Ronly Holdings Ltd* [2004] EWHC 245 (Comm); [2004] 2 Lloyd's Rep. 335.

(d) *Objects Injurious to the Proper Working of Justice*

(iv) *Maintenance and Champerty*

Public policy today respecting maintenance and champerty

16–049　　[*Add at end of paragraph; page* [964]]
　　　　In *Kellar v Williams*[237a] Lord Carswell stated *obiter* that the "content of public policy can change over the years, and it may now be time to reconsider the accepted [common law] prohibition [on conditional fees] in the light of modern practising conditions".[237b]

[237a] [2004] UKPC 30.
[237b] *ibid.*, at [21].

Effect of maintenance

16–053　　[*Add to note 267: page* [966]]
　　　　The court could make an order under s.51 against a shareholder of a company as a shareholder who, unlike directors, was under no duty as regards the conduct of litigation on behalf of a company and thus the principle of limited liability would not be undermined by such an order: see *CIBC Mellon Trust Co v Stolzenberg* [2005] EWCA Civ 628; *The Times*, June 8, 2005.

Non-champertous agreements between solicitor and client

[*Add to note 293: page* [968]]   **16–056**
For techniques available to the court to regulate costs in an action involving a conditional fee agreement: see *King v Telegraph Group Ltd* [2004] EWCA Civ 613; [2005] 1 W.L.R. 2282.

[*Replace note 295: page* [968]]
²⁹⁵ *ibid.*, s.58(3). Various statutory instruments have been made with respect to conditional fee orders: see *Sharratt v London Central Bus Co Ltd* [2003] EWCA Civ 718; [2003] 4 All E.R. 590 where the law is fully analysed.

Agreements savouring of champerty: assignment of the right to litigate

[*Add to note 307: page* [969]]   **16–057**
24 Seven Utility Services Ltd v Rosekey Ltd [2003] EWHC 3415 (QB); [2004] All E.R. (D) 288 (Feb.).

(f) *Contracts in Restraint of Trade*

(i) *Scope of the Doctrine*

Criteria for application of doctrine

[*Add at end of paragraph: page* [984]]   **16–083**
However, the absence of reciprocal obligation may be a factor in determining whether a restraint is reasonable.[447a]

[447a] *Societa Explosivi Industriali SpA v Ordnance Technologies (U.K.) Ltd* [2004] EWHC 48 (Ch); [2004] 1 All E.R. (Comm.) 619.

Legitimate interests of the parties

[*Add to note 481: page* [988]]   **16–092**
Countryside Assured Financial Services Ltd v Deanne Smart [2004] EWHC 1214.

(ii) *Employer and Employee*

Employee's activities after determination of employment

[*Add to text after note 539: page* [995]]   **16–103**
Post termination restraints if reasonable are enforceable.[539a]

[539a] *Leeds Rugby Ltd v Harris* [2005] EWHC 1591 (QB); [2005] All E.R. (D) 286 (Jul.).

[*Add to text after note 545: page* [996]]
What is reasonable in one type of relationship may not be reasonable in another.[545a]

[545a] *Allan Janes LLP v Jahal* [2006] EWHC 286 (Ch); [2006] I.C.R. 742 (a covenant unreasonable for a milk roundsman may not be unreasonable for a solicitor).

16–104   [*Add to text at end of paragraph: page* [997]]
The court will not imply a term in order to save a covenant restraining an employee's post-employment conduct.[557a] Nor will the court re-write a covenant in restraint of trade where the contract provides that the covenant, if unenforceable, should be rewritten with such minimum amendment as renders it enforceable.[557b] A provision that the restraint should apply "for as long as permitted by law" was too uncertain to have effect.[557c]

[557a] *Townends Group Ltd v Cobb* [2004] All E.R. (D) 421 (Nov.).
[557b] *Townends Group Ltd v Cobb* [2004] All E.R. (D) 421 (Nov.).
[557c] *Days Medical Aids Ltd v Pihsiang Machinery Manufacturing Co Ltd* [2004] EWHC 44 (Comm); [2004] All E.R. (Comm.) 95.

Competition

16–105   [*Add to note 560: page* [997]]
Axiom Business Computers Ltd v Jeannie Frederick (November 20, 2003, Court of Session).

Protection by general law and by covenant

16–106   [*Add new text at end of paragraph 16–106: page* [999]]
It may be that a person possesses a particular status and this precludes competition by that person. For example, a director must act in the best interests of the company and must not enter into a transaction in which his interests conflict with those of the company. Where these duties are applicable, thus restricting the competitive activities of the director against the company, the rules of public policy as to restraint of trade do not "trump" these duties.[571a]

[571a] *Shepherds Investments Ltd v Walters* [2006] EWHC 836 (Ch).

Trade secrets and connection with customers

16–107   [*Add to note 574: page* [999]]
Brake Bros Ltd v Ungless [2004] EWHC 2799 (QB); [2004] All E.R. (D) 586 (Jul.).

[*Add to note 577: page* [999]]
Fibrenetix Storage Ltd v Davis [2004] EWHC 1359 (QB) (protection of pricing policies).

Restraints during currency of employment

16–114   [*Add to note 645: page* [1005]]
TFS Derivatives Ltd v Morgan [2004] EWHC (QB) 3181; [2005] I.R.L.R. 246.

(iv) *Partners*

Analogous Agreements

16–119   [*Add to text at end of paragraph: page* [1010]]
In *Buchanan v Alba Diagnostics Ltd*[680a] Lord Hoffmann upheld as valid a perpetual restraint in the assignment of a patent entitling the assignee to the rights

of any improvement in the patent. He considered that it was in the public interest for inventors to be able to borrow money on the security of future rights,[680b] and a clear implication of his reasoning is that the agreement was treated as being analogous to the sale of the goodwill of a business.

[680a] [2004] UKHL 5; 2004 S.C.(H.L.) 9.
[680b] *ibid.*, at [29].

(v) *Supply and Acquisition of Goods: Restraints in Vertical Agreements*

Application of doctrine

[Add to note 681 at end: page [1010]]   **16–120**
The court held in *Days Medical Aids Ltd v Pihsiang Machinery Co Ltd* [2004] EWHC 44 (Comm) that an agreement not invalidated by Art.81 of the EU Treaty could not be subject to the common law restraint of trade doctrine.

3. CONTRACTS UNENFORCEABLE BY STATUTE

(a) *General principles*

Aids to statutory interpretation

[Add to note 773, page [1023]]   **16–146**
See also *Estate of Anandh v Barnet Primary Health Care Trust* [2004] EWCA Civ 5; [2004] All E.R. (D) 242 (Jan.).

Statute: one party only affected

[Add to note 798: page [1026]]   **16–153**
Crehan v Inntrepreneur Pub Company CPC [2004] EWCA Civ 637; [2004] E.C.C. 28, the claimant, as a matter of Community Law, could claim damages from his co-contractor with respect to an agreement which breached Art.81 of the EU Treaty. The claimant in *Crehan* was not significantly responsible for any distortion of competition.

4. ENFORCEMENT OF COLLATERAL AND PROPRIETARY RIGHTS

(a) *The Maxim Ex Turpi Causa Non Oritur Actio and Related Rules*

Tainting

[Delete note 825 and replace: page [1030]]   **16–161**
[825] *Vakante v Addey & Stanhope School* [2004] EWCA Civ 1065; [2004] 4 All E.R. 1056 where the Court of Appeal (Civil Division) upheld the decision of the Employment Appeal Tribunal that

illegality precluded the claimant from pursuing his racial discrimination claim. See also *Wheeler v Quality Deep Ltd* [2004] EWCA Civ 1085 where the lack of English and limited knowledge of tax and national insurance provisions were considered relevant in determining the extent to which the employee participated in an illegality.

[*Add to note 826: page* [1030]]
Hunt v Power Resources Ltd [2005] All E.R. (D) 23 (Apr.).

[*Add to note 828: page* [1031]]
Sutton v Hutchinson [2005] EWCA Civ 1773.

(c) *Recovery of Money Paid or Property Transferred under Illegal Contracts*

Transfer of property under illegal transactions

16–172   [*Add to note 901: page* [1039]]
The court will not enforce a claim by a person claiming funds held by a person in the position of trustee (in this case a solicitor) where the claimant has to rely on his fraud: see *Halley v Law Society* [2003] EWCA Civ 97.

Determination of limited interests created by illegal transactions

16–173   [*Note 904: page* [1040]]
Update the reference to *Treitel* to (11th ed., 2003), p.496.

16–174   [*Note 914: page* [1041]
Update reference to *Treitel* to (11th ed., 2003), p.496.

[*Note 916*]
Update reference to *Treitel, op. cit.*, at p.496.

16–175   [*Add at end of paragraph: page* [1042]]
Although collateral rights, as in *Tinsley v Milligan*,[919a] may arise out of an illegal contract, a collateral right normally involves a proprietary right and does not include a right of action on the contract itself.[919b]

[919a] *ibid.*
[919b] *Mahonia Ltd v J P Morgan Chase Bank* [2003] 2 Lloyd's Rep. 911, at [27]. See also *Mahonia Ltd v West LB AG* [2004] EWHC 1938 (Comm).

Oppression and fraud

16–180   [*Note 942: page* [1045]]
Update reference to *Treitel* to (11th ed., 2003), pp.492–493.

Mistake

16–181   [*Note 943: page* [1045]]
Update reference to *Treitel, op. cit.*, at p.493.

5. SEVERANCE

Scope of agreement to be left unchanged

[Add to note 987: page [1051]]
; *James E McCabe Ltd v Scottish Courage Ltd* [2006] EWHC 538 (Comm).

16–192

6. PLEADING AND PRACTICE

Pleading of illegality

[Add at end of note 1029: page [1055]]
   Bim Kemi AB v Blackburn Chemicals Ltd [2004] EWHC 166 (Comm); [2004]
EWCA Civ 1490 (court could take notice that agreement was illegal under Art.81
of the EU Treaty); *Western Power Investments Ltd v Teeside Power Ltd* (February
18, 2005) (unreported).

16–199

Part Six

JOINT OBLIGATIONS, THIRD PARTIES AND ASSIGNMENT

CHAPTER 17

JOINT OBLIGATIONS

Effect of judgment or compromise

17–032   The Civil Liability (Contribution) Act 1978 does apply—so that contribution can be claimed—even where a settlement requires a party to carry out work for, rather than to make a payment to, the person who has suffered the damage. That is, the word "payment" in, *e.g.* s.1(4) of the 1978 Act includes a payment in kind.

CHAPTER 18

THIRD PARTIES

PARA.
- 1. Introduction 18–001
- 2. The common law doctrine 18–003
  - □ (a) Parties to the agreement 18–004
  - □ (b) Party to the consideration 18–016
  - □ (c) Development of the common law doctrine 18–019
- 3. Scope 18–021
  - □ (a) Liability in negligence to third parties 18–022
  - (b) Liability to third parties for intimidation 18–040
  - (c) Liability to third parties in restitution? 18–041
- 4. Contracts for the benefit of third parties 18–042
  - (a) Effects of a contract for the benefit of a third party 18–042
  - □ (i) Promisee's remedies 18–043
  - (ii) Position between promisee and third party 18–068
  - (b) Exceptions to the doctrine 18–073
  - □ (i) Equitable exceptions 18–074
  - □ (ii) Contracts (Rights of Third parties) Act 1999 18–084
  - □ (iii) Other statutory exceptions 18–113
- 5. Enforcement against third parties 18–125

1. INTRODUCTION

Preliminary

[*Add to note 1: page* [1073]]
Furmston, *Third Party Rights* (2005).

18–001

Present structure of the subject

[*Add to note 7: page* [1073]]
For the nature of the right of enforcement created by the Contracts (Rights of Third Parties) Act 1999 as an exception to the common law doctrine of privity of contract, see also *Ramco (UK) Ltd v International Insurance Co of Hanover* [2004] EWCA Civ 675; [2004] 2 All E.R. (Comm.) 866 at [32].

18–002

2. THE COMMON LAW DOCTRINE

(a) *Parties to the Agreement*

Who are the parties?

18–004   *[Add to note 20: page* [1076]]
See also *Percy v Board of National Mission of the Church of Scotland* [2005] UKHL 73; [2006] 2 W.L.R. 353, discussed above in para.2–175 of this Supplement. The contract in that case was between the person appointed as associate minister in a parish and the Board to which the Church of Scotland had delegated responsibility for making such appointments: see at [27]–[28], [116]–[118]; and *Grecoair Inc v Tilling* [2004] EWHC 2851; [2005] Lloyd's Rep. I.R. 151, where the issue was whether negotiations involving an insured person and the reinsurer had led to a direct contract between these parties.

Collateral contracts

18–005   *[Add to note 24: page* [1076]]
Morin v Bonhams & Brooks Ltd has been affirmed on the ground that the governing law was that of Monaco: [2003] EWCA Civ 1802; [2004] 1 All E.R. (Comm.) 880. For similar reasoning, leading to the formation of a contract "in the context of an associated and simultaneous set of transactions" see *Moody v Condor Insurance Ltd* [2006] EWHC 100 (Ch); [2006] 1 All E.R. 934 at [39] (offer by guarantor to seller of a business to guarantee loan notes issued by the buyer held to give rise to a contract between guarantor and seller on the seller's entering into the main agreement and so becoming loan creditors).

[Add to text at end of paragraph: page [1077]]
Similarly, in *Brook Street Bureau v Dacas*[31a] an employment agency entered into contracts with workers whom it supplied to a local authority. It was held that there was not only an express contract between the workers and the agency, but also an implied contract between the workers and the authority.

[31a] [2004] EWCA Civ 217; [2004] I.C.R 1437; followed in *Muscat v Cable and Wireless plc* [2006] EWCA Civ 220; [2006] I.R.L.R. 354.

Contractual intention in collateral contracts

18–009   *[Add to note 49: page* [1079]]
A fortiori there will be no collateral contract between A and C where these parties have deliberately chosen not to enter into a direct contract with each other: see *Fuji Seal Europe Ltd v Catalytic Combustion Corp* [2005] EWHC 1649; 102 Con. L.R. 47 (where, as in *Independent Broadcasting Authority v EMI Electronics* (1980) 14 Build. L.R. 1 (discussed in Main Work, para.18–009), C was held liable in tort).

Agency

18–012   *[Add to note 60: page* [1080]]
Vitesse Yacht Charterers SL v Spiers (The Deverne II) [2003] EWHC 2426 (Admlty); [2004] 1 Lloyd's Rep. 179 (contract to charter yacht for holiday to be taken by two persons together made by one of them on behalf of both).

[*Add to note 61: page* [1080]]
cf. Richards v Hughes [2004] EWCA Civ 266; [2004] P.N.L.R. 35 (arguable that accountant advising parent about the setting up of a trust fund for the education of children owed a contractual duty, not only to the parent, but also to the children).

(c) *Development of the Common Law Doctrine*

The doctrine established

[*Add to note 85: page* [1083]]   **18–019**
See also *Barbados Trust Company Ltd v Bank of Zambia* [2006] EWHC 222 (Comm); [2006] 1 Lloyd's Rep. 723 at [59], referring to "days when that principle [of privity of contract] was more 'fundamental' than it is perhaps today".

3. SCOPE

(a) *Liability in Negligence to Third Parties*

Duty of care may be owed to third party

[*Add to note 115: page* [1087]]   **18–022**
See also *BP plc v Aon Ltd* [2006] EWHC 424; [2006] 1 All E.R. (Comm.) 789 (insurance brokers held liable in tort to insureds, with whom the brokers were not in any contractual relationship, in respect of failure to make declarations under an open cover agreement).

[*Add to note 117, line 6: page* [1087]]
Niru Battery Manufacturing Co v Milestone Trading Ltd [2003] EWCA Civ 1446 is now reported in [2004] 1 Lloyd's Rep. 344.

Economic loss and physical harm

[*Add to note 154: page* [1092]]   **18–031**
For liability in tort based on assumption of responsibility, in respect of failure by the defendant to render professional services to a claimant with whom the defendant was not in any contractual relationship, see also *BP plc v Aon Ltd* [2006] EWHC 424; [2006] 1 All E.R. (Comm.) 789.
For a discussion of the tests to be applied to determine whether a defendant owed a duty of care not to cause economic loss to the claimant, see *Customs and Excise Commissioners v Barclays Bank plc* [2006] UKHL 28; [2006] 3 W.L.R. 1. In that case, the claimant's loss arose because the defendant bank failed to comply with an injunction obtained by the claimant freezing an account held by one of the bank's customers. The bank was held not to owe any duty of care to the claimant. The case does not directly affect the subject-matter of the present Chapter since the claimant's loss was not the result of any breach of contract between the bank and its customer.

[Add to note 155, line 5 after "137": page [1092]]
; *Abou-Rahmah v Abacha* [2005] EWHC 2662 (QB); [2006] 1 All E.R.
(Comm.) 268 at [67] (bank not liable in negligence to persons who had paid
money into an account, not their own, for parting with the money to a payee other
than the one named in their instructions as the intended payee). See also *West
Bromwich Albion Football Club v El Safty* [2005] EWHC 2868; [2006] 1 Lloyd's
Rep. Med. 139 (consultant surgeon not liable in tort to a football club, with which
he was not in any contractual relationship, for giving negligent advice to one of
the club's injured players, as a result of which the player had to retire from
professional football so that the club suffered economic loss).

Requirement of "proximity"

18–032   *[Add to note 161: page* [1093]]
See also *Architype Projects Ltd v Dewhurst MacFarlane & Partners* [2003]
EWHC 3341; [2004] P.N.L.R. 38 (subcontractor not liable in tort to building
owner).

Defects in the very thing supplied insufficient

18–033   *[Add to note 166: page* [1094]]
See also *Holding Management (Solitaire) Ltd v Ideal Homes Northwest Ltd*
[2004] EWHC 2408; 96 Con. L.R. 114 (T&CC).

Claimant having no title to thing damaged

18–034   *[Add to note 179, after "Conventions" in line 8: page* [1096]]
See also *Re Deep Vein Thrombosis and Air Travel Group Litigation* [2005]
UKHL 72; [2006] 1 All E.R. 786 at [3], [27], [29] and [62].

Damages in "disappointed beneficiary" cases

18–037   *[Add to note 201: page* [1099]]
But a claim by a person in a position analogous to that of a disappointed
beneficiary may be available where the consequences of the adviser's negligence
do not become apparent for many years after the transaction in question:
Richards v Hughes [2004] EWCA Civ 266; [2004] P.N.L.R. 35.

Analogous situations

18–038   *[Add to note 209: page* [1100]]
For a further possible extension of the principle of the "disappointed beneficiary" cases, see *Richards v Hughes* [2004] EWCA Civ 266; [2004] P.N.L.R. 35
(accountant advising client about the setting up of a trust fund to pay for the
education of client's children).

4. CONTRACTS FOR THE BENEFIT OF THIRD PARTIES

(a) *Effects of a Contract for the Benefit of a Third Party*

(i) *Promisee's Remedies*

Damages in respect of promisee's loss

[*Add new text at end of paragraph: page* [1107]]   **18–046**
The question whether the loss had been suffered by the promisee or by a third
party was discussed in *De Jongh Weill v Mean Fiddler Holdings*.[239b] The
claimant in that case had been engaged as a financial consultant by the defendant
company; he was to be remunerated partly by a specified fee, but the main
element of his remuneration was that "in addition warrants to purchase shares in
the [defendant company] will be granted to a company representing my family
interests."[239c] The antecedent negotiations made it clear that the grant of those
warrants was to be the claimant's (own) principal remuneration[239d] and that "it
was *he* who was to benefit in reality and the idea of a nominated company was
just the way that *he* was to be paid".[239e] Judge Bruce Coles Q.C., after referring
to paras 18–042—18–047 above,[239f] held that the loss resulting from the defendant's failure to issue the warrants had been suffered by the claimant himself and
that damages in respect of it were therefore recoverable by him under the
principle stated in para.18–046.

[239b] [2005] All E.R. (D) 331 (Jul.).
[239c] *ibid.*, at [2], [25].
[239d] *ibid.*, at [30].
[239e] *ibid.*
[239f] *ibid.*, at [26].

Damages in respect of third party's loss: general rule

[*Add to note 242: page* [1107]]   **18–047**
See also *Ramco (UK) Ltd v International Insurance Co of Hanover* [2004]
EWCA Civ 675; [2004] 2 All E.R. (Comm.) 866 at [32] where the actual
decision (that an insurance policy issued to a bailee of goods did not cover loss
suffered by the bailor in circumstances in which the bailee was not liable to the
bailor in respect of that loss) turned on the wording of the policy.

Damages in respect of third party's loss: exceptions in general

[*Add to note 269: page* [1109]]   **18–050**
In *Rolls Royce Power Engineering plc v Ricardo Consulting Engineers Ltd*
[2003] EWHC 2871 (TCC); [2004] 2 All E.R. (Comm.) 129 it was held that a
contracting party could not recover damages in respect of a third party's loss as
trustee for the third party where the other contracting party at the time of the
contract did not know or have reason to know that the former party was
contracting as trustee.

[*Add to note 272, line 10, after reference to [1977] C.L.J. 24: page* [1110]]

In the *Rolls Royce Power* case, above, n.269, it was held that the "rule in *Dunlop v Lambert*" ((1839) 2 Cl. & F. 626 at 627) applied only if at the time of the contract it was "in the actual contemplation of the parties that an identified third party or a third party who was a member of an identified class might suffer damage in the event of a breach of the contract" (at [124]).

Further exceptions: building contracts

18–051   [*Add to note 280: page* [1111]]

The principle of the *Linden Gardens* case does not apply where, as a condition of obtaining an interim injunction against A, B gives an undertaking to the court to comply with any order which the court may later in the proceedings make requiring B to compensate A for any loss that the injunction has caused to A: see *SmithKline Beecham plc v Apotex Europe Ltd* [2006] EWCA Civ 658; *The Times*, June 9, 2006. It was accordingly held in that case that A, who had been restrained by the injunction granted to B from dealing in the United Kingdom with a pharmaceutical product, could not recover damages from B in respect of loss suffered as a result of the injunction by A's supplier, C. One reason for this conclusion was that the principle of cases such as the *Linden Gardens* case was "only about what damages [could] be recovered following a breach of contract" (at [88]); and that principle did not apply in the *SmithKline* case since in that case "there [was] in fact no contract between the parties. The undertaking [was] given to the court" (at [86]). A second reason for the decision in the *SmithKline* case was that, even if there had been a contract between A and B and a breach of it, A's only interest in the performance of the hypothetical contract was in A's not being restrained from dealing with the product and that there was "no 'legal black hole' of the sort contemplated in *Linden Gardens*" (at [94]). In the latter case, if A could not have recovered damages in respect of C's loss, B would be under no liability in respect of a proved or of an admitted breach. In the *SmithKline* case, damages could have been recovered by A in respect of B's breach of the hypothetical contract.

The "narrower ground": loss suffered by third party to whom the subject-matter was to be transferred

18–053   [*Add to note 290: page* [1112]]

HSBC Rail (UK) Ltd v Network Rail Infrastructure Ltd [2005] EWCA Civ 1437; [2006] 1 All E.R. 343 at [23].

Third party having independent contractual rights against promisor

18–055   [*Add to note 307: page* [1114]]

The reasoning of the *Panatown* case [2001] 1 A.C. 518 (discussed in para.18–055 of the Main Work), by which the promise cannot recover damages in respect of the third party's loss where the third party has its own independent contractual right in respect of that loss against the promisor, has been said to apply also where the third party's right against the promisor arises in tort: *Riyad Bank v Ali United Arab Bank (UK) plc* [2005] EWHC 279 (Comm); [2005] 2 Lloyd's Rep. 409 at [173].

[Add to note 312: page [1115]]   **18–056**
For another situation in which the promisee could not recover damages in respect of the third party's loss because there was no "legal black hole", see the reasoning of *SmithKline Beecham plc v Apotex Europe Ltd* [2006] EWCA Civ 658; *The Times*, June 9, 2006 at [94], above, para.18–051 of this Supplement. In that case the reason why there was no "legal black hole" was that full effect would be given to the (hypothetical) promise by awarding damages to the promisee for the loss it had suffered as a result of the (hypothetical) breach.

Scope of the "broader ground"

[Add to note 324: page [1116]]   **18–059**
In *Rolls Royce Power Engineering plc v Ricardo Consulting Engineers Ltd* [2003] EWHC 2871 (TCC); [2004] 2 All E.R. (Comm.) 129, Judge Seymour Q.C. said (at [128]) that the "broader ground" for the decision in the *Linden Gardens* case ([1994] 1 A.C. 85) was not easy to apply "where the alleged damage is damage to, or failure to repair, property and there is no suggestion of consequential loss".

(b) *Exceptions to the Doctrine*

(i) *Equitable Exceptions*

Effects of the trust

[Add to note 429: page [1129]]   **18–079**
In *Barbados Trust Company Ltd v Bank of Zambia* [2006] EWHC 222 (Comm); [2006] 1 Lloyd's Rep. 723 at [57] Langley J. pointed out that a trust of the kind considered in paras 18–074—18–082 of the Main Work "does not make the beneficiary a party to the contract nor *necessarily* entitle him to claim the benefit from the obligor in his own name" (italics supplied). The point is illustrated by the facts of the *Barbados Trust* case itself where a group of banks and financial institutions agreed to make available to the defendant bank a facility for the issue of letters of credit. The contract provided that each member of the group of creditor banks was to be entitled to assign its rights to "banks or other financial institutions" with the consent of the debtor bank. A bank to which rights under the contract had been effectively assigned then purported to make a further assignment of those rights to the claimant and this assignment was ineffective as the claimant was not itself a "bank" or "other financial institution". It was held that a declaration of trust by this bank of its rights under the contract in favour of the claimant likewise did not entitle the claimant to enforce the contract against the debtor bank since, to give it this effect, would be "inconsistent with the terms of the facility", *i.e.* (in particular) with the term which defined and restricted the categories of bodies to which rights under the facility against the debtor bank could be assigned (at [73]).

(ii) *Contracts (Rights of Third Parties) Act 1999*

Term conferring benefit on third party

[Add new note 471b in line 18 at "property owned by C.": page [1133]]   **18–087**
[471b] A similar problem arose, apparently under Brazilian law, in *Petromec Inc v Petroleo Brasileiro SA Petrobras* [2004] EWHC 1180 (Comm); [2005] 1 Lloyd's Rep. 219. A, a sub-bareboat charterer

of an oil production platform, took out a policy of insurance with B, relating to the platform. It was held that no claim could be brought on the policy in his own right by C, a subcontractor engaged to do upgrading work on the platform, as A had not purported to insure for the benefit of C. In a case governed by English law, similar reasoning could be applied, on such facts, to a claim brought by C under s.1(1)(b) of the Contracts (Rights of Third Parties) Act 1999. On appeal, the decision in the *Petromec* case was affirmed without further reference to the point of Brazilian law discussed in this note: see [2005] EWCA Civ 891; [2006] 1 Lloyd's Rep. 121.

[Add new note 471c after "year" in: line 3: page [1134]]
471c Section 1(4) of the Contracts (Rights of Third Parties) Act 1999 would also prevent a third party from enforcing a term of the contract on facts such as those of *Barbados Trust Company Ltd v Bank of Zambia* [2006] EWHC 222 (Comm); [2006] 1 Lloyd's Rep. 723, discussed in para.18–079 of this Supplement. The 1999 Act did not apply in that case as the contract had been made in 1985.

[Add new text at end of paragraph: page [1134]]
The operation of ss.1(1)(b) and 1(2) is illustrated by *The Laemthong Glory (No.2)*[473b] where goods had been carried on a voyage chartered ship and difficulties had arisen with regard to their delivery at the end of the transit as the bill of lading had not reached the prospective receiver by the time of the arrival of the ship at the contractual destination. The shipowners delivered the goods to the receiver against letters of indemnity one of which was addressed by the receiver to the charterer and so amounted to a contract between these parties. It contained a promise by the receiver to indemnify "you [*i.e.* the charterer], your servants or agents" in respect of liability which might be incurred by reason of delivery of the goods at the receiver's request without production of the bill of lading. The Court of Appeal held that this promise on its true construction purported to confer a benefit on the shipowner within s.1(1)(b) of the 1999 Act since the shipowner had acted as one of the charter's "agents" in delivering the goods to the receiver and that the receiver had failed to discharge the burden imposed on him by s.1(2) of proving that letter of indemnity was not intended by the parties to it (*i.e.* the receiver and the charterer) to be enforceable by the shipowner. The receiver's promise in that letter was accordingly enforceable by the shipowner against the receiver under the 1999 Act.

473b *Laemthong International Lines Co Ltd v Artis (The Laemthong Glory) (No.2)* [2005] EWCA Civ 519; [2005] 1 Lloyd's Rep. 632.

Promisor's defences against third party

18–102 *[Add new note 520a after "misrepresentation." in line 7 of sub-paragraph headed "(1) General principle": page* [1141]]
520a See *Moody v Condor Insurance Ltd* [2006] EWHC 100 (Ch); [2006] 1 All E.R. 934 at [30].

(iii) *Other Statutory Exceptions*

Law of Property Act 1925, section 56(1)

18–114 *[Add to note 575: page* [1149]]
See also *Moody v Condor Insurance Ltd* [2006] EWHC 100 (Ch); [2006] 1 All E.R. 934 (below, note 576) at [24]–[27], discussing the *Chelsea and Walham Green* case ([1951] Ch. 853), cited in this note in the Main Work.

[*Add to note 576: page* [1149]]

See also *Moody v Condor Insurance Ltd* [2006] EWHC 100 (Ch); [2006] 1 All E.R. 934 where it was said (at [16]) that the distinction between deeds which could (at common law), and those which could not, confer rights on persons not parties to them was "not to be made in [a] purely mechanistic way" and that the distinction was "commonly equated with that between deeds poll and deeds *inter partes*". The question was not whether the deed was executed by one party or by two parties; it was whether "one or more of them in fact make promises to the other" or whether the parties who execute the document "seek to use the document as a means for each of them to make unilateral promises to a person who is not a party to it" (at [18]). In the former case, the document is (in the traditional terminology) a deed *inter partes*, not enforceable at common law by the person who is not a party to it; in the latter it is (in that terminology) a deed poll, enforceable by such a party. A deed of guarantee of instalments due under a contract for the sale of a company was held in that case to fall into the latter category.

Life Insurance

[*Add to note 601: page* [1151]]   **18–118**

Section 70 of the Civil Partnership Act 2004 applies s.11 of the Married Women's Property Act 1882 to "a policy of assurance (a) effected by a civil partner on his own life, and (b) expressed to be for the benefit of his civil partner, or of his children, or of his civil partner and children, or any of them".

Insurance by persons with limited interests

[*Add to note 608: page* [1152]]   **18–120**

For the possibility of displacing the principle of *Waters v Monarch Insurance Co* (1856) 5 E. & B. 870 by the terms of the policy, see *Ramco (UK) Ltd v International Insurance Co of Hanover* [2004] EWCA Civ 675; [2004] 2 All E.R. (Comm.) 866 at [32].

Third parties' rights against insurers

[*Note 615, line 14: page* [1153]]   **18–123**

In *Centre Reinsurance International Co v Curzon International Ltd* [2004] EWHC 200 (Ch); [2004] 2 All E.R. (Comm.) 28 it was held that a transfer of rights under the Third Parties (Rights against Insurers) Act 1930 could occur "notwithstanding that the insured's liability to the third party has yet to be established" (at [29]). The contrary view in *Nigel Upchurch Associates v Aldridge Estates Investment Co Ltd* [1993] 1 Lloyd's Rep. 533 (cited in Main Work, p.1153, n.615) was rejected. The decision in the *Centre Reinsurance* case, above, was varied, but not on the point here under discussion, on appeal [2005] EWCA Civ 115; [2005] 2 All E.R. (Comm.) 65, where the Court of Appeal also held that s.1(3) of the 1930 Act was not intended to strike down provisions in the insurance contract itself designed to put the third party in a better position than that in which the insured would have been immediately before the statutory transfer of the insured's rights to the third party (at [83]).

5. ENFORCEMENT AGAINST THIRD PARTIES

Scope of the rule

18-127   [*Add to note 635: page* [1156]]

For the requirements of knowledge of the contract and intention to procure its breach, see also *Unique Pub Properties Ltd v Beer Barrels & Mineral Waters Ltd* [2004] EWCA Civ 586; [2005] 1 All E.R. (Comm.) 181.

For discussion of the mental element required for the tort of interference with contractual rights, see also *Douglas v Hello! Ltd (No.2)* [2005] EWCA Civ 596; [2005] 4 All E.R. 129. Although "malice" is not required, there must be intentional wrongdoing (at [195], [222], [223]); mere foresight of such interference does not suffice. As Lord Phillips M.R. said in that case [at 220]: "It is often the case that failure to perform a contract [*e.g.* between C and B] will lead to a series of consequent breaches of contracts [*e.g.* between B and A] to which the original contract breaker [C] is not a party. To render him liable [to A] for these breaches simply because they are consequences which he foresaw would be to undermine the doctrine of privity of contract." *cf.* his reference, with apparent approval, to the criticism by Weir, *Economic Torts* (1997), p.19, of *Millar v Bassey* [1994] E.M.L.R. 44, also described at [200] as "somewhat out of step with the authorities". For the requirement of a "specific subjective intention" for the tort, see also *Mainstream Properties Ltd v Young* [2005] EWCA Civ 861; [2005] I.R.L.R. 964 at [72].

[*Add to note 636*]

For the requirement of "wrongfulness", see also *OBG Ltd v Allan* [2005] EWCA Civ 106; [2005] 2 All E.R. 602.

Lack of causal connection

18-134   [*Add to note 667: page* [1160]]

The mortgagee of a ship is not obliged to defer the exercise of his power of sale under the mortgage even though such exercise interferes with contracts made by the mortgagor for the carriage of goods in the ship with the shippers of those goods: *Den Norske Bank ASA v Acemex Management Co* [2003] EWCA Civ 1559; [2004] All E.R. (Comm.) 904 at [22].

The Myrto [1977] 2 Lloyd's Rep. 243 was followed in *Anton Durbeck GmbH v Den Norske Bank ASA* [2005] EWHC 2497 (Comm); [2006] 1 Lloyd's Rep. 93 at [50]–[64], though in a part of the judgment said at [50] to be "*obiter*".

Third party's state of mind

18-136   [*Add to note 676: page* [1161]

See also *Anton Durbeck GmbH v Den Norske Bank ASA* [2005] EWHC 2497 (Comm); [2006] 1 Lloyd's Rep. 93, esp. at [68], [71]: bank not liable to cargo-owner, who had contracted with shipowner for the carriage of goods, for arresting and detaining the ship in order to safeguard the bank's security, with the result that the goods so deteriorated that they had to be thrown overboard.

CHAPTER 19

ASSIGNMENT

			PARA.
■	1.	Assignment	19–001
		(a) Statutory assignments	19–006
■		(b) Equitable assignments	19–020
■		(c) Principles applicable to statutory and equitable assignments	19–042
□		(i) What rights are assignable	19–042
		(ii) Validity of assignments against assignor's creditors and successors in title	19–057
		(iii) Priorities between successive assignees	19–067
		(iv) Assignments "subject to equities"	19–069
		(v) No assignment of liabilities	19–076
	2.	Vicarious performance	19–080
	3.	Assignment and negotiability	19–084
	4.	Assignment, novation and acknowledgment	19–085

1. ASSIGNMENT

(b) *Equitable Assignments*

Formalities for equitable assignments

[*Add to note 98; page* [1173]]   **19–025**

In *Coulter v Chief of Dorset Police* [2003] EWHC 3391 (Ch); [2004] 1 W.L.R. 1425 it was held that the benefit of a judgment (for costs) had been assigned in equity by a retiring chief constable to his successor. Patten J., after referring to the need for there to be "a sufficient expression of an intention to assign" for an equitable assignment, said (at [16]): "What, in my judgment, acts as the trigger, if trigger is needed, is the manifest event of the resignation or retirement of the existing office holder, and the assumption of office by his successor. That is, as I see it, a sufficient outward manifestation of an intention that the successor office holder should obtain the benefits held on trust by a predecessor, for there to be an equitable assignment of the benefit of the judgment."

(c) *Principles Applicable to Statutory and Equitable Assignments*

(i) *What Rights are Assignable*

Rights declared by contract to be incapable of assignment

19–043   [*Add to note 159; page* [1182]]
Thomas, "Contractual Prohibitions on the Assignment of Copyright" (2004) 120 L.Q.R. 222.

19–045   In *Barbados Trust Company Ltd v Bank of Zambia* [2006] EWHC 222 (Comm); [2006] 1 Lloyd's Rep 723, a clause in a loan facility prevented assignment by the lender other than to a bank or financial institution unless the borrower (the Bank of Zambia) gave its written consent. There was an assignment to a bank. That bank, without the borrower's consent, declared itself a trustee of its rights under the loan for the claimant, who was neither a bank nor a financial institution. It was held that that declaration of trust did not transfer the lender's rights under the loan to the claimant because to allow that would undermine the prohibition on assignment to such a claimant. In Langley J.'s words (at [73]): "By its terms . . . the Facility . . . decrees that, at least absent express consent, a claimant such as the present claimant shall not be entitled to claim payment from Bank of Zambia as assignee of the Asset. To permit such a claim to be made as the beneficiary of a declaration of trust of the Asset would in my judgment be to permit the use of [the law on such a trust] in a commercial context in which it has no place because it would achieve a result which would be inconsistent with the terms of the Facility." Langley J. reasoned that *Re Turcan* (1888) 40 Ch.D. 5 and *Don King Productions Inc v Warren* [2000] Ch. 291 (cited in the main text at notes 167–168) did not dictate a contrary result. He also reasoned—but with respect this seems incorrect—that, in any event, the claimant, even though a beneficiary under the trust, could not itself enforce the contractual rights despite the fact that it had joined the trustee as defendant.

[*Add to note 168: page* [1183]]
For criticism of this decision, making the argument that one cannot have a trust of, or charge over, unassignable rights, see Turner, "Charges of Unassignable Rights" (2004) 20 J.C.L. 97.

CHAPTER 20

DEATH AND BANKRUPTCY

			PARA.
	1.	Death	20–001
□	2.	Bankruptcy	20–015
□		(a) Contracts made prior to bankruptcy	20–018
□		(b) Vesting of property in trustee	20–024
□		(c) Trustee takes "subject to equities"	20–039
		(d) Discharge of bankrupt	20–045
		(e) Schemes of arrangement	20–050
		(f) Contracts made after adjudication	20–053
		(g) Second bankruptcies	20–057

2. BANKRUPTCY

(a) *Contracts made Prior to Bankruptcy*

Grounds for creditor's bankruptcy petition

[Add to note 63 after Re Patel, etc.: page [1209]]   **20–018**
   Coulter v Chief Constable of Dorset Police [2004] EWCA 1259; [2005]
B.P.I.R. 62.

Assignments by bankrupt

[Note 82: page [1211]]   **20–021**
   Update reference to *Bowstead and Reynolds on the Law of Agency* to (18th ed.,
2006).

(b) *Vesting of Property in Trustee*

Effect on contractual rights

[Note 140: page [1217]]   **20–033**
   Update reference to Benjamin to (7th ed, 2006), para.15–037.

[Add to note 143]
   There is no need to have recourse to s.345 if the contract provides that
bankruptcy is a terminating event: see *Cadogan Estates v McMahon* [2001]
B.P.I.R.

(c) *Trustee takes "subject to equities"*

Set-off and mutual dealings

20–041   *[Note 198: page* [1222]]
Update reference to Goode to (3rd ed.), pp.235–237.

Part Seven

PERFORMANCE AND DISCHARGE

CHAPTER 21

PERFORMANCE

			PARA.
☐	1.	In general	21–001
☐	2.	Time of performance	21–011
■	3.	Partial performance of an entire obligation	21–027
■	4.	Payment	21–039
☐		(a) In general	21–039
■		(b) Appropriation of payments	21–059
■		(c) Revalorisation: gold clauses and index-linking	21–068
■		(d) Payment by negotiable instrument or documentary credit	21–073
		(e) Payment by credit or charge card	21–082
☐	5.	Tender	21–083

1. IN GENERAL

Promises in the alternative

[*Add to note 22: page* [1235]]   **21–006**
However there is no rule of law to the effect that the right to elect the alternative is impliedly invested in the promisor. In all cases it is a question of construction of the contract: *Mora Shipping Inc v AXA Corporate Solutions Assurance SA* [2005] EWCA Civ 1069; [2005] 2 Lloyd's Rep. 769 at [44], albeit that the natural meaning of a clause which imposes an obligation on a party to do A or B is likely to be that it is for the promisor to choose whether to do A or B.

2. TIME OF PERFORMANCE

Time made expressly or implicitly "of the essence"

[*Add to note 82: page* [1241]]   **21–013**
 Re Simoco Digital UK Ltd: Thunderbird Industries LLC v Simoco Digital UK Ltd [2004] EWHC 209 (Ch); [2004] 1 B.C.L.C. 541 at [14]; *Haugland Tankers AS v RMK Marine Gemi Yapim Sanayii ve Deniz Taşimaciliii Işletmesi AS* [2005] EWHC 321 (Comm); [2005] 1 Lloyd's Rep. 573; *Peregrine Systems Ltd v Steria Ltd* [2005] EWCA Civ 239; [2005] All E.R. (D) 215 (Mar.) at [15].

[*Add to end of note 83: page* [1241]]
Tennara Ltd v Majorarch Ltd [2003] EWHC 2601 (Ch) (on the facts it was held that time was not expressly or impliedly of the essence). Where time is not of the essence and there has been unreasonable delay in performance, a court may be able to infer that the delay nevertheless amounts to a repudiation of the contract where the consequences of the delay are sufficiently serious. When deciding whether or not the delay amounts to a repudiation of the contract, the court will have regard to all the facts and circumstances of the case: *ibid.*

Notice making time "of the essence"

21–014   [*Add to the end of note 87: page* [1242]]
The notice must make it sufficiently clear that time has been made of the essence: *Shawton Engineering Ltd v DGP International Ltd* [2006] 1 B.L.R. 1 at [44].

Consequences of time being "of the essence"

21–015   [*Add to note 101: page* [1243]]
State Securities plc v Initial Industry Ltd [2004] All E.R. (D) 317 (Jan.).

Consequences of "time being made of essence"

21–017   [*Add to the end of note 111: page* [1244]]
Dalkia Utilities Services plc v Celtech International Ltd [2006] EWHC 63 (Comm); [2006] 1 Lloyd's Rep. 599 at [131].

[*Add to the end of note 112: page* [1245]]
Dalkia Utilities Services plc v Celtech International Ltd [2006] EWHC 63 (Comm); [2006] 1 Lloyd's Rep. 599 at [131].

Where no precise time for performance is specified

21–020   [*Add to note 128 after reference to Jolley v Carmel Ltd: page* [1246]]
National Car Parks Ltd v Baird (Valuation Officer) [2004] EWCA Civ 967; [2005] 1 All E.R. 53 at [58].

[*Add to text at the end of the paragraph*]
When deciding whether or not performance has taken place within a reasonable time, a court is not limited to what the parties contemplated or ought to have foreseen at the time of entry into the contract but can, with the benefit of hindsight, take account of a broad range of factors, including any estimate given by the performing party of the time which it would take for it to perform, whether the party for whose benefit the relevant obligation was to be performed needed to participate in the performance, whether it was necessary for a third party to collaborate with the performing party in order to enable it to perform, and the nature of the cause or causes of any delay in performance.[130a]

[130a] *Peregrine Systems Ltd v Steria Ltd* [2005] EWCA Civ 239; [2005] All E.R. (D) 215 (Mar.) at [15]; *Astea (UK) Ltd v Time Group Ltd* [2003] EWHC 725 (TCC); [2003] All E.R. (D) 212 (Apr.) at [144].

Meaning of "day"

[Insert new note 138a after "ordinarily done" in line 7: page [1247]]   **21–022**
138a In *Lafarge (Aggregates) Ltd v London Borough of Newham* [2005] EWHC 1377 (Comm); [2005] 2 Lloyd's Rep. 577, Cooke J. stated that "in ordinary parlance in the UK, 'working days' are Mondays to Friday, excluding Christmas, Easter and Bank Holidays" (at [57]).

3. Partial Performance Of An Entire Obligation

Partial performance of entire obligations

[In note 180, delete text after first sentence and substitute: page [1252]]   **21–030**
  The Court of Appeal in *Item Software (UK) Ltd v Fassihi* [2004] EWCA Civ 1244; [2004] I.R.L.R. 928 held that the effect of s.2 of the Act is that, unless the parties agree otherwise, the salary of an employee whose employment terminates part way through a pay period shall be apportioned and paid in respect of the period actually worked (with payment only becoming due and payable at the end of the relevant pay period). The decision of the Court of Appeal in *Boston Deep Sea Fishing and Ice Co Ltd v Ansell* (1888) 39 Ch. D. 339 was held not to stand in the way of this conclusion because the Act was not mentioned at any point in the case: it is therefore not an authority on the construction, scope or effect of the Apportionment Act.

4. Payment

(a) *In General*

Payment

[Add to end of note 234: page [1257]]   **21–039**
  The current edition of Mann (6th ed., 2005) at paras 3.04–3.05 does, however, recognise that frustration may have a limited role to play in such cases.

Payment to joint creditors, partners, trustees, etc.

[Add to note 282: page [1262]]   **21–049**
  Barrett v Universal Island Records Ltd [2006] EWHC 1009 (Ch); [2006] E.M.L.R. 21 at [214].

Loss in post

[Add to note 318: page [1265]]   **21–056**
  Warnborough Ltd v Garmite Ltd [2006] EWHC 10 (Ch) at [84], [93]. The fact that payment is usually made through the post is insufficient of itself to show that the creditor has assumed the risk of loss in the post.

(b) Appropriation of Payments

Creditor's right to appropriate

21–061 [*In note 344, insert after reference to Lowther v Heaver: page* [1267]]
Potomek Construction Ltd v Zurich Securities Ltd [2003] EWHC 2827 (Ch);
[2004] 1 All E.R. (Comm.) 672 at [69].

Current account: Clayton's Case

21–066 [*Add to note 363: page* [1269]]
Commerzbank Aktiengesellschaft v IMB Morgan plc [2004] EWHC 2771 (Ch);
[2005] 1 Lloyd's Rep. 298 at [42]–[48].

Appropriation as between principal and interest

21–067 [*Add to note 364: page* [1270]]
Potomek Construction Ltd v Zurich Securities Ltd [2003] EWHC 2827 (Ch);
[2004] 1 All E.R. (Comm.) 672 at [69].

(c) Revalorisation: Gold Clauses and Index-Linking

The nominalistic principle

21–068 [*Note 365: page* [1270]]
Update reference to Mann, *The Legal Aspect of Money* to (6th ed., 2005), Chs
9–13.

Gold clauses

21–070 [*Note 379: page* [1271]]
Update reference to Mann, *The Legal Aspect of Money* to (6th ed., 2005), paras
11.19 *et seq.*

Index-linking in domestic contracts

21–072 [*Note 396: page* [1273]]
Update reference to Mann, *The Legal Aspect of Money* to (6th ed., 2005), paras
11.38–11.46.

(d) Payment by Negotiable Instrument or Documentary Credit

Conditional payment

21–074 [*Add to note 404 after reference to Re Charge Card Services Ltd: page* [1274]]
Fusion Interactive Communication Solutions Ltd v Venture Investment Placement Ltd [2005] EWHC 736 (Ch); [2005] All E.R. (D) 111 (May) at [91].

5. TENDER

Tender of money

[*Add new note 437a in line 2 after "does not discharge the debt": page* [1278]]   **21–084**
[437a] *Canmer International Inc v UK Mutual Steamship Assurance Association (Bermuda) Ltd (The "Rays")* [2005] EWHC 1694 (Comm); [2005] 2 Lloyd's Rep. 479 at [53], citing R. Goode, *Payment Obligations in Commercial and Financial Transactions* (1983), pp.14–16.

Time of tender

[*Note 475: page* [1281]]   **21–090**
Update reference to *Benjamin's Sale of Goods* to (7th ed., 2006), para.12–031.

CHAPTER 22

DISCHARGE BY AGREEMENT

			PARA.
	1.	In general	22–001
	2.	Release	22–003
■	3.	Accord and satisfaction	22–012
□	4.	Rescission	22–025
■	5.	Variation	22–032
□	6.	Waiver	22–040
□	7.	Provision for discharge in the contract itself	22–047

3. ACCORD AND SATISFACTION

Ineffective accord

22–021   [*Add to note 75 at end: page* [1292]]
     This is likely to be a difficult hurdle to overcome (see, for example, *Champion Investments Ltd v Ahmed* [2004] All E.R. (D) 28 (Aug.)). In the rare case in which it is overcome, compromise may be vitiated by a mistake of law as well as a mistake of fact: *Brennan v Bolt Burden (a firm)* [2004] EWCA Civ 1017; [2004] 1 All E.R. (D) 551 (Jul.) at [17].

4. RESCISSION

Rescission by agreement

22–025   [*Insert footnote 91a at end of the paragraph: page* [1294]]
     [91a] *Intense Investments Ltd v Development Ventures Ltd* [2006] EWHC 1628 (TCC); [2006] All E.R. (D) 346 (Jun.) at [117].

Substituted contract

22–028   [*Add to note 101: page* [1295]]
     Sookraj v Samaroo [2004] UKPC 50.

5. Variation

Unilateral power of variation

[Add to end of note 154: page [1300]]   **22–039**
See also *Paragon Finance plc v Pender* [2005] EWCA Civ 760; [2005] All
E.R. (D) 307 (Jun.).

6. Waiver

[Insert new paragraph: page [1303]]
Contracting out of waiver. It would appear that there is no general principle   **22–044A**
of law that parties to a contract cannot restrict the operation of the doctrine of
waiver by the terms of their contract.[182a] In *State Securities plc v Initial Industry
Ltd*[182b] Jonathan Gaunt Q.C., sitting as a Deputy Judge of the High Court,
stated,

> "I can, however, see no reason in principle why the parties to an equipment lease . . .
> or other commercial contract, should not be free to stipulate that a particular act, such
> as payment of a rental instalment should not be taken to waive a right to terminate
> for an earlier breach. After all, such a provision may be very convenient and operate
> to the benefit of both parties. The finance company may want to encourage the lessee
> to correct the breach but not want him to fall behind with his payments while he does
> so. It may be in the interests of the lessee that the finance company should not have
> to take an early decision whether to terminate."[182c]

However it cannot be assumed that the courts in all cases will give effect to a
term of the contract which purports to exclude or limit the operation of the
doctrine of waiver; in some circumstances the term of the contract may not
suffice to deny effect to a clear and unequivocal representation made by one party
to the contract.[182d]

[182a] *State Securities plc v Initial Industry Ltd* [2004] All E.R. (D) 317 (Jan.).
[182b] [2004] All E.R. (D) 317 (Jan.).
[182c] At [57].
[182d] *I-Way Ltd v World Online Telecom Ltd* [2002] EWCA Civ 413 (Court of Appeal refused to give
summary judgment in a case in which the court was asked, in effect, to enforce a term of the contract
which provided that "no addition, amendment or modification of this Agreement shall be effective
unless it is in writing and signed by or on behalf of both parties".)

Waiver of condition for benefit of one party

[Add to end of note 184: page [1304]]   **22–045**
Wessex Reserve Forces and Cadets Association v White [2005] EWHC 983
(QB); [2005] All E.R. (D) 310 (May).

Waiver of breach

[Note 188: page [1304]]   **22–046**
Update reference to *Benjamin's Sale of Goods* to (7th ed, 2006), paras
12–034—12–036.

7. Provision for Discharge in the Contract Itself

Express provision

22-047   *[Add to note 192 after "[2001] EWCA Civ 1235" in line 17: page* [1305]]
    Dalkia Utilities Services plc v Celtech International Ltd [2006] EWHC 63
(Comm); [2006] 1 Lloyd's Rep. 599 at [90]–[102].

   [Add to end of note 195]
    *More OG Romsdal Fylkesbatar AS v The Demise Charterers of the Ship
"Jotunheim"* [2004] EWHC 671 (Comm); [2005] 1 Lloyd's Rep. 181.

22-048   *[Insert note 200a in line 5 after "exercise of the contractual right": page* [1306]
    200a *Npower Direct Ltd v South of Scotland Power Ltd* [2005] EWHC 2123 (Comm) at [177].

   [Add to note 210: page [1307]]
    For further discussion of the case, see *Dalkia Utilities Services plc v Celtech
International Ltd* [2006] EWHC 63 (Comm); [2006] 1 Lloyd's Rep. 599 at
[139]–[142].

CHAPTER 23

DISCHARGE BY FRUSTRATION

				PARA.
■	1.	Introduction		23–001
□	2.	The test for frustration		23–007
■	3.	Illustrations of the doctrine		23–019
		(a) General		23–019
■		(b) Common types of frustrating events		23–021
□			(i) Subsequent legal changes and supervening illegality	23–021
■			(ii) Cancellation of an expected event	23–032
□			(iii) Delay	23–034
■		(c) Application of the doctrine to common types of contracts .		23–036
■			(i) Personal contracts	23–036
■			(ii) Charterparties	23–040
□			(iii) Sale and carriage of goods	23–045
			(iv) Building contracts	23–047
■			(v) Leases and tenancies	23–050
			(vi) Contracts for the sale of land	23–055
□	4.	The limits of frustration		23–056
■	5.	The legal consequences of frustration		23–068

1. INTRODUCTION

Introduction

[Note 1: page [1311]]   **23–001**
Update reference to Treitel, *Frustration and Force Majeure* to (2nd. ed., 2004).

Historical development

[Note 10: page [1312]]   **23–004**
Update reference to Treitel to (2nd. ed., 2004), Chap.2.

2. THE TEST FOR FRUSTRATION

Introduction

[Note 24: page [1314]]   **23–007**
Update reference to Treitel, *Frustration and Force Majeure* to (2nd. ed., 2004), paras 16–006—16–016.

[Add to the end of note 29: page [1315]]
See also *Edwinton Commercial Corp v Tsavliris Russ (Worldwide Salvage and Towage) Ltd (The Sea Angel)* [2006] EWHC 1713 (Comm); [2006] All E.R. (D) 396 (Jul.).

Practical differences between the tests

23–018   *[Note 76: page [1321]]*
Update reference to Treitel, *Frustration and Force Majeure* to (2nd. ed., 2004), paras 16–013—16–016.

3. ILLUSTRATIONS OF THE DOCTRINE

(b) *Common Types of Frustrating Events*

(i) *Subsequent Legal Changes and Supervening Illegality*

Changes affecting employment

23–022   *[Note 104: page [1324]]*
Update reference to Treitel to (2nd. ed., 2004), Chap.8.

Supervening illegality under a foreign law

23–026   *[Note 114: page [1325]]*
Update reference to *Benjamin's Sale of Goods* to (7th ed., 2006), paras 18–348—18–355.

(ii) *Cancellation of an Expected Event*

The "coronation cases"

23–032   *[Note 130: page [1327]]*
Update reference to Treitel to (2nd. ed., 2004), paras 7–006—7–014.

(iii) *Delay*

Delay

23–034   *[Note 142: page [1329]]*
Update reference to Treitel to (2nd. ed., 2004), paras 5–036—5–056.

[Add to note 144 after "[1998] 2 Lloyd's Rep. 209, 222"]
Edwinton Commercial Corp v Tsavliris Russ (Worldwide Salvage and Towage) Ltd (The Sea Angel) [2006] EWHC 1713 (Comm); [2006] All E.R. (D) 396 (Jul.) at [83].

[Add to note 150 after "[1978] 2 Lloyd's Rep. 509, 514, 515–516": page [1330]]
Edwinton Commercial Corp v Tsavliris Russ (Worldwide Salvage and Towage) Ltd (The Sea Angel) [2006] EWHC 1713 (Comm); [2006] All E.R. (D) 396 (Jul.) at [83].

(c) *Application of the Doctrine to Common Types of Contracts*

(i) *Personal Contracts*

Death

[*Note 162: page* [1330]]   **23–036**
Update reference to Treitel to (2nd. ed., 2004), para.2–015.

Illness or incapacity

[*Add to note 168: page* [1331]]   **23–037**
It may be that permanent incapacity alone will not suffice to frustrate a
contract of employment, on the basis that the contract itself may, exceptionally,
envisage the possibility that the employee will continue to be employed notwithstanding the fact that he or she is suffering a permanent incapacity: see *R.
(Verner) v Derby City Council* [2003] EWHC 2708 (Admin); [2004] I.C.R. 535
at [66]. Lindsay J. concluded (at [68]) that in such a case the contract of
employment continues to exist "in an entirely shadowy form in which, by reason
of the employee's incapacity and retirement, the employer cannot require any
performance and the employee cannot offer it".

(ii) *Charterparties*

[*Note 184: page* [1333]]
Update reference to Treitel to (2nd. ed., 2004), paras 5–052—5–054.

(iii) *Sale and Carriage of Goods*

Sale and carriage of goods

[*Note 202: page* [1336]]   **23–045**
Update reference to Atiyah, *The Sale of Goods* to (11th ed., 2005),
pp.360–365.
Update reference to *Benjamin's Sale of Goods* to (7th ed., 2006), paras 6–035
et seq.

[*Note 208: page* [1337]]
Update reference to *Benjamin's Sale of Goods* to (7th ed, 2006), paras
18–318—18–341.

(v) *Leases and Tenancies*

[*Note 220: page* [1339]]
Update reference to Treitel to (2nd. ed., 2004), Chap.11.

Prohibition on intended use

[*Note 234: page* 1340]]   **23–052**
Update reference to Treitel to (2nd. ed., 2004), paras 7–023—7–0024 and
11–022.

4. THE LIMITS OF FRUSTRATION

Express provision

23–056   *[Note 253: page* [1343]]
Update reference to Treitel to (2nd. ed., 2004), Chap.12.

[Add to the end of note 254]
cf. *R. (Verner) v Derby City Council* [2003] EWHC 2708 (Admin); [2004]
I.C.R. 535 at [66].

[Note 256: page [1343]
Update reference to *Benjamin's Sale of Goods* to (7th ed., 2006), paras
8–095—8–097, 18–330—18–331, 19–124—19–126.

[Add to note 259 after "[1983] 1 A.C. 736": page [1343]]
*Edwinton Commercial Corp v Tsavliris Russ (Worldwide Salvage and Towage)
Ltd (The Sea Angel)* [2006] EWHC 1713 (Comm); [2006] All E.R. (D) 396 (Jul.)
at [84].

Significance of a foreseen event

23–057   *[Note 264: page* [1344]]
Update reference to Treitel, *Frustration and Force Majeure* to (2nd. ed.,
2004), Chap.13.

[Add to note 270 after "[1913] 1 Ch. 274": page [1345]]
*Edwinton Commercial Corp v Tsavliris Russ (Worldwide Salvage and Towage)
Ltd (The Sea Angel)* [2006] EWHC 1713 (Comm); [2006] All E.R. (D) 396 (Jul.)
at [84].

Event foreseeable but not foreseen

23–058   *[Insert note 271a in line 3 after "held to be inapplicable": page* [1345]]
[271a] *Edwinton Commercial Corp v Tsavliris Russ (Worldwide Salvage and Towage) Ltd (The Sea
Angel)* [2006] EWHC 1713 (Comm); [2006] All E.R. (D) 396 (Jul.) at [84].

[Note 273]
Update reference to Treitel to (2nd. ed., 2004), para.13–012.

Self-induced frustration

23–059   *[Note 274: page* [1345]]
Update reference to Treitel to (2nd. ed., 2004), Chap.14.

[Add to note 275]
*Edwinton Commercial Corp v Tsavliris Russ (Worldwide Salvage and Towage)
Ltd (The Sea Angel)* [2006] EWHC 1713 (Comm); [2006] All E.R. (D) 396 (Jul.)
at [85].

Allocation of available supplies

[*Note 293: page* [1347]]   **23–062**
Update reference to *Benjamin's Sale of Goods* to (7th ed., 2006), paras
18–353—18–354.

Onus of proof

[*Add to note 296 after "[1987] Q.B. 301": page* [1348]]   **23–063**
*Edwinton Commercial Corp v Tsavliris Russ (Worldwide Salvage and Towage)
Ltd (The Sea Angel)* [2006] EWHC 1713 (Comm); [2006] All E.R. (D) 396 (Jul.)
at [85].

Partial excuse at common law

[*Note 311: page* [1350]]   **23–066**
Update reference to Treitel, *Frustration and Force Majeure* to (2nd. ed.,
2004), para.5–060.
Update reference to *Benjamin's Sale of Goods* to (7th ed., 2006), paras
18–353—18–354.

5. THE LEGAL CONSEQUENCES OF FRUSTRATION

[*Note 318: page* [1351]]   **23–068**
Update reference to Treitel to (2nd. ed., 2004), Chap.15.

Law Reform (Frustrated Contracts) Act 1943

[*Note 329: page* [1353]]   **23–072**
Update reference to Treitel to (2nd. ed., 2004), paras 15–049—15–096.

Contracts excluded from the Act

[*Note 398: page* [1363]]   **23–094**
Update reference to Atiyah, *The Sale of Goods* to (11th ed., 2005),
pp.365–368.

Chapter 24

DISCHARGE BY BREACH

			PARA.
□	1.	In general	24–001
□	2.	Renunciation	24–018
□	3.	Impossibility created by one party	24–028
□	4.	Failure of performance	24–034
□	5.	Consequences of discharge	24–047

1. In General

Affirmation

24–003   *[Add to note 19: page* [1368]]
State Securities plc v Initial Industry Ltd [2004] All E.R. (D) 317 (Jan.) (acceptance of rental payment held not to have amounted to an election to continue with the contract).

Sale of goods

24–005   *[Note 33: page* [1370]]
Update reference to *Benjamin's Sale of Goods* to (7th ed., 2006), para.12–038.

Other waivers

24–009   *[Note 64: page* [1373]]
Update reference to *Benjamin's Sale of Goods* to (7th ed., 2006), paras 12–034—12–036.

Effect if repudiation not accepted

24–011   *[Note 79: page* [1375]]
Update reference to *Benjamin's Sale of Goods* to (7th ed., 2006), paras 19–167—19–171.

[Note 81]
Update reference to *Benjamin's Sale of Goods* to (7th ed., 2006), paras 9–011—9–016, 19–167—19–171.

Acceptance of repudiation

[*Add to note 91: page* [1377]]   **24-013**
When deciding whether or not inconsistent actions amount to an acceptance of
a repudiation, the courts apply an objective test: *Enfield London Borough Council
v Sivanandan* [2004] EWHC 672 (QB); [2004] All E.R. (D) 73 (Apr.) at
[38]–[39].

[*Insert into text after note 91: page* [1377]]
In an appropriate case an acceptance of a repudiation may take the form of
reliance on a contractual term which entitles the innocent party to terminate the
contract. Where the conduct of the party in breach is such as to entitle the
innocent party to terminate the contract either pursuant to a term of the contract
or under the general law, the innocent party is not required to elect between its
two rights to terminate and so can be treated as having terminated the contract
both under the appropriate term of the contract and in accordance with its rights
at common law.[91a]

[91a] *Dalkia Utilities Services plc v Celtech International Ltd* [2006] EWHC 63 (Comm); [2006] 1
Lloyd's Rep. 599 at [135]–[144].

[*Add to note 93: page* [1377]]
Sookraj v Samaroo [2004] UKPC 50 at [17]; *South Caribbean Trading Ltd v
Trafigura Beheer BV* [2004] EWHC 2676 (Comm); [2005] 1 Lloyd's Rep. 128
at [129]–[130].

[*Add to note 95*]
In such a case the contractor may be absolved from his contractual obligation
before he communicates his acceptance: *Potter v RJ Temple* [2003] All E.R. (D)
327 (Dec.).

No reason or bad reason given

[*Add to note 100 after reference to Sheffield v Conrad: page* [1378]]   **24-014**
South Caribbean Trading Ltd v Trafigura Beheer BV [2004] EWHC 2676
(Comm); [2005] 1 Lloyd's Rep. 128 at [133]–[134].

Both parties in breach

[*Add to note 108: page* [1379]]   **24-015**
Total Spares & Supplies Ltd v Antares SRL [2004] EWHC 2626 (Ch) at
[147].

2. RENUNCIATION

Renunciation

[*Add to note 126 after "[105]": page* [1382]]   **24-018**
Dalkia Utilities Services plc v Celtech International Ltd [2006] EWHC 63
(Comm); [2006] 1 Lloyd's Rep. 599 at [133].

Unequivocal

24–019   [Add to note 134: page [1383]]
See also *Dalkia Utilities Services plc v Celtech International Ltd* [2006] EWHC 63 (Comm); [2006] 1 Lloyd's Rep. 599 at [145]–[149].

Breach not accepted

24–023   [Add to note 150 after "January 16 2001": page [1385]]
Marplace (Number 512) Ltd v Chaffe Street (a firm) [2006] EWHC 1919; [2006] All E.R. (D) 413 (Jul.) at [321].

3. Impossibility Created by One Party

Anticipatory breach

24–030   [Add to note 174 after [1957] 2 Q.B. 401, 449–450: page [1389]]
Re Simoco Digital UK Ltd: Thunderbird Industries LLC v Simoco Digital UK Ltd [2004] EWHC 209 (Ch); [2004] 1 B.C.L.C. 541 at [22]–[23].

Impossibility and frustration

24–033   [Note 182: page [1390]]
Update reference to *Benjamin's Sale of Goods* to (7th ed., 2006), para.16–023.

4. Failure of Performance

Divisible or severable obligations

24–044   [Note 233: page [1396]]
Update reference to *Benjamin's Sale of Goods* to (7th ed., 2006), para.8–064.

5. Consequences of Discharge

Effect on contract

24–048   [Add to note 258: page [1399]]
Similarly, an adjudication provision in a contract will survive the discharge of the contract: *Connex South Eastern Ltd v MJ Building Services Group plc* [2004] EWHC 1518 (TCC) at [25].

Rights acquired before discharge

24–051   [Add to note 274: page [1401]]
Odfjfell Seachem A/S v Continental des Petroles et D'Investissements [2004] EWHC 2929 (Comm); [2005] 1 Lloyd's Rep. 275 at [35].

[Note 281: page [1402]]
Update reference to *Benjamin's Sale of Goods* to (7th ed., 2006), para.15–107.

CHAPTER 25

OTHER MODES OF DISCHARGE

		PARA.
■ 1.	Merger	25–001
■ 2.	Alteration or cancellation of a written instrument	25–020
3.	Miscellaneous modes of discharge	25–028

1. MERGER

Estoppel by judgment

[*Note 44: page* [1409]]
Update reference to *Cross and Tapper on Evidence* to (10th ed., 2005), p.95.

25–011

Requirements

[*Note 55: page* [1411]]
Update reference to *Cross and Tapper on Evidence* to (10th ed., 2005), pp.106–108.

25–012

2. ALTERATION OR CANCELLATION OF A WRITTEN INSTRUMENT

Material alteration

[*Insert new note 111a after "alteration" at the beginning of line 12: page* [1417]]
[111a] It may be necessary in certain cases to distinguish between an "alteration" to a document and an "appendage" to the contract. Thus the addition of an incorrect date after the document has been signed may amount to an "appendage" rather than an alteration: *Moussavi-Azad v Sky Properties Ltd* [2003] EWHC 2669 (QB); [2003] All E.R. (D) 38 (Dec.) at [49]. This may be thought to introduce an unnecessary element of sophistry into the rule and that the better view is that such an addition is an "alteration" and the vital question then becomes whether that alteration is "material".

25–020

Immaterial alteration

[*Add to note 128: page* [1418]]
Moussavi-Azad v Sky Properties Ltd [2003] EWHC 2669 (QB); [2003] All E.R. (D) 38 (Dec.) at [48]–[51].

25–023

Part Eight

REMEDIES FOR BREACH OF CONTRACT

CHAPTER 26

DAMAGES

			PARA.
■	1.	Nature and kinds of damages	26–001
		(a) In general	26–001
		(b) Nominal damages	26–008
		(c) Claims for an agreed sum	26–009
		(d) Liquidated and unliquidated damages	26–010
		(e) Prospective loss and continuing breaches	26–013
		(f) Substitute performance (cost of completion or repairs)	26–016
■		(g) Exemplary damages and depriving the defendant of his profit	26–019
		(h) Appeals against the assessment of damages	26–027
		(i) Third party beneficiaries	26–028
☐	2.	Causation and contributory negligence	26–029
■	3.	Remoteness of damage	26–044
■		(a) General rules	26–044
		(b) Timing of the assessment of damages	26–057
■		(c) Loss of profits	26–059
■		(d) Expenditure wasted or incurred as a result of the breach	26–063
■		(e) Non-pecuniary losses	26–073
	4.	Illustrations of the remoteness of damage and the assessment of damages	26–079
		(a) Sale of goods	26–079
		(b) Carriage of goods	26–080
		(c) Contracts concerning land	26–082
		(d) Contracts to pay or lend money	26–089
		(e) Sale of shares	26–091
☐	5.	Mitigation of damage	26–092
☐	6.	Penalty or liquidated damages	26–109
	7.	The tax element in damages	26–134
☐	8.	Interest and rate of exchange	26–144

1. NATURE AND KINDS OF DAMAGES

(g) *Exemplary Damages and Depriving the Defendant of his Profit*

Exemplary damages

26–019   [*Add to note 94 at end: page* [1433]]
and in *Borders (UK) Ltd v Metropolitan Police Commissioner* [2005] EWCA Civ 197 (see below, para.26–022, n.128).

The extension made by *Att-Gen v Blake*

[Add to note 128 at end; page [1436]]   **26–022**
In *Borders (UK) Ltd v Metropolitan Police Commissioner*, above, *Blake* was
used to justify the extension of exemplary damages to cover disgorgement of
some of the profits made by D through tortious activity.

Partial disgorgement on the *Wrotham Park* basis

[Add to note 139 at end: page [1437]]   **26–024**
A substantial level of damages has been awarded on the *Wrotham Park* basis:
Lane v O'Brien Homes [2004] EWHC 303 (QB). The claimant had lost "the
value of [her] bargaining position"; damages of £150,000 were awarded against
a builder whose profit was at least £280,000 (case noted by Campbell, (2004) 67
M.L.R. 817). See also *Gafford v Graham* (1999) 77 P. & C.R. 73; *Amec
Developments Ltd v Jury's Hotel Management (UK) Ltd* [2001] 1 E.G.L.R. 81.

2. Causation and Contributory Negligence

The claimant's lost opportunities: hypothetical consequences

[Add to note 208 after the Bank of Credit and Commerce case: page [1445]]   **26–039**
Maden v Clifford Coppock & Carter (a firm) [2004] EWCA Civ 1037; [2005]
2 All E.R. 43 (80 per cent chance of obtaining a particular level of damages in
an out of court settlement).

[Add to the text at the end of the paragraph: page [1446]]   **26–040**
or where, but for the breach, there was a real or substantial chance that the
claimant would have continued to make profits from "repeat orders" from
customers.[215a]

[215a] *Jackson v Bank of Scotland* [2005] UKHL 3; [2005] 1 W.L.R. 377 (see below,
para.26–062A).

The contract-breaker's opportunity to minimise the cost of performance

[Add to text after note 220: page [1446]]   **26–041**
Where after a breach of contract the contract-breaker could have relied on a
war clause to terminate the period of the contract, the assessment of damages
took this into account.[220a]

[220a] *The Golden Victory* [2005] EWCA Civ 1190; [2005] 2 Lloyd's Rep. 747.

3. Remoteness of Damage

(a) *General rules*

Modern statement of the rule

[Add to note 248 at end: page [1450]]   **26–047**
On the time when the test is applied, see *Jackson v Bank of Scotland*, above,
at [35]–[36].

Actual and imputed knowledge

26–052 [*Add to note 278 after "The Heron II": page* [1453]]
Louis Dreyfus Trading Ltd v Reliance Trading Ltd [2004] EWHC 525 (Comm); [2004] 2 Lloyd's Rep. 243 (see Vol.II, para.43–442, n.1999).

Actual knowledge of special circumstances

26–054 [*Add to note 288 after the Victoria Laundry case: page* [1454]]
See *Jackson v Bank of Scotland*, above, at [35]–[36].

[*Add to note 289 after "Wroth v Tyler": page* [1454]]
See *Jackson v Bank of Scotland*, above, at [36].

[*Add to the end of the text of the paragraph: page* [1454]]
There is now authority in the House of Lords that the two rules in *Hadley v Baxendale* are not mutually exclusive.[289a]

[289a] *Jackson v Bank of Scotland*, above, at [46]–[49].

Knowledge and assumption of risk

26–055 [*Add to the text of the paragraph after note 293: page* [1455]]
"Where knowledge of special circumstances is relied on, the assumption is that the defendant undertook to bear any special loss which was referable to those special circumstances".[293a]

[293a] *Jackson v Bank of Scotland*, above, at [26].

(c) *Loss of Profits*

[*Add new paragraph after paragraph 26–062: page* [1460]]
26–062A **Loss of future business.** Subject to the rules on causation and remoteness, the contract-breaker may be liable for the claimant's loss of future profits from "repeat orders" from his previous customers which loss was caused by the particular breach of contract.[336a] When loss of future profits is not too remote, the period of time for which the loss should be assessed is until the question whether any loss has been sustained has become "too speculative to permit the making of any award".[336b]

[336a] *Jackson v Bank of Scotland*, above (breach of obligation to maintain confidence). See above, para.26–040; and Vol.II, paras 43–430, 43–452.
[336b] *Jackson v Bank of Scotland*, above, at [37].

(d) *Expenditure Wasted or Incurred as a Result of the Breach*

Damages assessed on a "no transaction" basis

26–070 [*Add to note 383: page* [1466]]
(followed in *Hok Sport Ltd v Aintree Racecourse Co Ltd* [2002] EWHC 3094; [2003] Lloyd's Rep. P.N. 148).

(e) *Non-pecuniary Losses*

Mental distress and disappointment: nervous shock

[*Add to note 409 after the reference to Malik's case: page* [1468]]
In *Eastwood v Magnox Electric plc* [2004] UKHL 35; [2005] 1 A.C. 503, Lord
Nicholls said (at [11]) that if the facts of *Addis* occurred today, the claimant
would have a remedy at common law for breach of contract: see para.26–077,
below.

[*Add to note 412*]
On *Johnson v Unisys*, see the text added to para.26–077, below.

[*Add to text after note 417: page* [1469]]
Damages for breach of contract may be awarded to a mother for the mental
distress caused by the loss of the company of her child.[417a]

[417a] *Hamilton-Jones v David & Snape* (a firm) [2003] EWHC 3147 (Ch); [2004] 1 W.L.R. 924
(solicitor's failure allowed father to remove children from the UK).

[*Add to note 419: page* [1469]]
Barber v Somerset County Council [2004] UKHL 13; [2004] 1 W.L.R. 1089
(employee's psychiatric injury caused by work-related stress).

Loss of reputation

[*Add to text at the end of the paragraph: page* [1470]]
But this case has later been distinguished by the House of Lords, which held
that an employee may have a common law claim for financial loss where his
employer has acted unfairly towards him prior to, and independently of, his
subsequent unfair dismissal.[430a] However, it should be noted that in another case
the House of Lords held that in his unfair dismissal claim an employee cannot
recover compensation for non-economic or non-pecuniary loss, such as distress,
humiliation or loss of reputation.[430b]

[430a] *Eastwood v Magnox Electric plc* [2004] UKHL 35; [2005] 1 A.C. 503.
[430b] *Dunnachie v Kingston upon Hull City Council* [2004] UKHL 36; [2005] 1 A.C. 226 (interpreting s.123 of the Employment Rights Act 1996).

[*Add to note 434: page* [1471]]
Jackson v Bank of Scotland, above (see above, para.26–062A).

5. Mitigation of Damage

"Reasonable steps"

[*Add to note 518: page* [1480]]
See also paras 26–095A—26–095D below.

[*After paragraph 26–095, add new paragraphs: page* [1481]]
Impecuniosity of the claimant. A recent tort case in the House of Lords leads
to the question whether the impecuniosity of the claimant could be relevant in a

contractual claim. In *Lagden v O'Connor*[523a] the House of Lords held that it would not follow the dicta in *The Liesbosch* case[523b] to the effect that the plaintiff's impecuniosity was not relevant to the assessment of damages. *Lagden v O'Connor* was a claim in tort where the claimant's car had been damaged by the defendant's negligence. Since the claimant could not afford simply to hire a replacement car while his was being repaired (the car-hire firm would require him to make an up-front payment) he entered into a more expensive hire arrangement with an "accident hire" insurance company under which he need not pay anything in advance. The majority of their Lordships held that it was reasonably foreseeable that an impecunious claimant might reasonably incur the higher cost of credit hire because he had no other choice in obtaining a replacement car. Thus the claimant's foreseeable impecuniosity resulted in his entitlement to higher damages in tort than would have been awarded to others who could afford to pay for ordinary hire. This rule "requires the wrongdoer to bear the consequences if it was reasonably foreseeable that the injured party would have to borrow money or incur some other kind of expenditure to mitigate his damages".[523c] This language ("wrongdoer", "injured party") is not appropriate to a claim in contract where the main remoteness rule (the first rule in *Hadley v Baxendale*) is different from that in tort: the kind of loss within the reasonable contemplation of the parties at the time of making the contract.[523d] But even in contract the claimant's impecuniosity might be relevant if it prevented him from choosing a cheaper form of mitigation. The rules on mitigation and those on remoteness are entwined in some cases, where what was "within reasonable contemplation" and what was "reasonable" mitigation are treated as interchangeable concepts. In the *Monarch S.S.* case,[523e] Lord Wright said (with reference to the decision of the House of Lords in *Muhammad Issa el Sheikh Ahmad v Ali*[523f]) that "damages consequent on impecuniosity were held not too remote because . . . the loss was such as might reasonably be expected to be in the contemplation of the parties as likely to flow from breach of the obligation undertaken".[523g] This means that the claimant's impecuniosity will be relevant in contract if it falls within the defendant's reasonable contemplation (as at the time of contracting) as not unlikely to affect the claimant's ability to mitigate after a breach of the particular undertaking, *viz.*, that the claimant would be likely to incur greater than usual expense (or higher than normal interest charges) in a reasonable attempt to mitigate. This test will not be easy for the claimant to satisfy if he cannot prove that the defendant actually knew of his impecuniosity (which is the situation examined in the next paragraph.) Thus, there is no reported case holding his impecuniosity to be relevant in relation to the market price rule in the sale of goods[523h] or to the similar market price rule for breach of a contract of hire.[523i]

[523a] [2003] UKHL 64; [2004] 1 A.C. 1067.
[523b] [1933] AC 449, 460.
[523c] *per* Lord Hope, at [61].
[523d] See paras 26–045—26–051.
[523e] [1949] A.C. 196.
[523f] [1947] A.C. 427.

[523g] [1949] A.C. 196 at 224; see para.26–056, n.295.
[523h] See paras 26–097, 43–415.
[523i] See para.26–097, n.530.

Actual knowledge of the claimant's impecuniosity. The claimant's impecu-   **26–095B**
niosity will be relevant in contract if the second rule in *Hadley v Baxendale* is
satisfied *viz.*, if, at the time of contracting, the contract-breaker had actual
knowledge of special circumstances under which a breach was likely to cause the
claimant greater or different loss from that to be normally expected under normal
circumstances.[523j] The claimant's impecuniosity could be a "special circumstance" under this rule if, with his knowledge of it, the defendant could foresee
that the claimant could mitigate his loss caused by the breach only by incurring
greater expense than would be incurred by a financially secure person. The
claimant must act "reasonably" in his mitigating actions but what is reasonable
for a claimant known to be impecunious may be different from the case of a
person with financial resources.[523k] One of the mitigation rules is that the
claimant is entitled to damages for any loss or expense incurred by him in
reasonably attempting to mitigate his loss, even where this attempt was unsuccessful or led to greater loss.[523l]

[523j] See paras 26–054—26–056.
[523k] On the question of actual knowledge, see para.26–089, text at n.495.
[523l] See para.26–105.

Several cases illustrate the position.[523m] In *Wadsworth v Lydall*,[523n] on the   **26–095C**
dissolution of a farming partnership between the parties, the defendant was
obliged to pay £10,000 to the plaintiff on a fixed date. The defendant knew that
the plaintiff needed another farm and would be dependent on payment of that
sum on that date to finance any purchase. When the defendant failed to pay, the
Court of Appeal awarded the plaintiff as special damages the extra interest
charges and legal costs incurred by him as a result of the breach.[523o] In *Bacon v
Cooper*[523p] the rotor of the plaintiff's machine was damaged beyond repair as a
result of the defendant's breach of contract. The only available replacement cost
£41,500 which the plaintiff, a dealer in scrap metal, could not finance out of his
own resources. It was held that the plaintiff had acted reasonably in obtaining it
on hire purchase at a high rate of interest.[523q] A further authority is *Trans Trust
S.P.R.L. v Danubian Trading Co Ltd*.[523r] The buyers undertook that a confirmed
credit was to be opened forthwith in favour of the firm from which the sellers
were obtaining the goods. The buyers knew that the sellers were not in a position
themselves to open the necessary credit. The Court of Appeal held that the loss
due to this impecuniosity of the sellers was not too remote because it was within
the reasonable contemplation of the parties as likely to flow from the buyer's
breach of contract in failing to obtain the credit.

[523m] See also para.26–097, below.
[523n] [1981] 1 W.L.R. 598.
[523o] See para.26–089: the House of Lords approved the decision, *ibid.*, n.490.
[523p] [1982] 1 All E.R. 397; see also para.26–145).
[523q] The case was not explicitly put on the ground of the second rule in *Hadley v Baxendale* but
on the reasonableness of mitigation, as was *Robbins of Putney Ltd v Meek* [1971] R.T.R. 345 (see
para.26–097, below.)
[523r] [1952] 2 Q.B. 297.

26–095D   Another case appears to accept the principle but it was found on the facts that the defendants did not know of the plaintiff's special financial arrangements. In *Compania Financiera "Soleada" S.A. v Hamoor Tanker Corporation Inc.*[523s] the plaintiff's vessel was arrested in breach of contract: since it was reasonably foreseeable that the plaintiff would seek to obtain its release and for that purpose would obtain a guarantee for payment of the debt, the Court of Appeal held that the expense in doing so, if reasonable, would be recoverable either because it was within the remoteness rules, or as the expense of reasonable mitigation.[523t] But because the particular financial arrangements between the plaintiffs and their bank were not known to the defendants, the high interest charges actually incurred by the plaintiffs were held to be "wholly unreasonable" and so not recoverable.

[523s] [1981] 1 W.L.R. 274.
[523t] Although Lord Denning preferred the former, his colleagues seemed to use the two concepts interchangeably.

The time for mitigating action

26–096   *[Note 525: page* [1481]*]*
Update reference to Benjamin to (7th ed., 2006), paras 17–059—17–060.

Sale of goods

26–097   *[Add to text at the end of the paragraph: page* [1482]*]*
The relevance of the claimant's impecuniosity is discussed above.[532a] The market price rule is fundamental to the sale of goods: if the seller fails to deliver, the buyer's damages are *prima facie* the difference between the contract price and the market price at the date of breach.[532b] The rule assumes that the buyer should be able to finance the purchase of substitute goods at the time of the breach, even though he may not receive the damages until much later. The rule works reasonably well if he retains the balance of the price and there has not been a substantial rise in the market price. But the buyer's lack of financial resources could prevent his purchase of a substitute if he had paid the price (or a substantial deposit) in advance, or if the rise in price has been substantial. But to date none of these factors has prevented the application of the prima facie rule.[532c] Actual knowledge of the buyer's lack of resources has been treated as relevant to the purchase of a house[532d]; and the seller's decision to re-sell quickly because he was short of liquid resources was held to be reasonable mitigation in *Robbins of Putney Ltd v Meek.*[532e]

[532a] This Supplement, paras 26–095A—26–095D above.
[532b] See Vol.II, para.43–415.
[532c] See Benjamin's *Sale of Goods* (6th ed.) para.17–008. On the *prima facie* nature of the rule, see Vol.II, 43–416.
[532d] *Wroth v Tyler* [1974] Ch. 30: see this Supplement, para.26–098A below.
[532e] [1917] R.T.R. 345 (sale of goods).

[After paragraph 26–098, add new paragraph: page [1482]*]*

26–098A   **Sale of land.** In *Wroth v Tyler*[536a] the contract-breaker's knowledge of the plaintiffs' lack of resources was treated as relevant to their ability to mitigate.[536b]

Both the seller and the purchasers of a house contemplated at the date of the contract that there would be a rise in house prices after the contract; the seller knew that the purchasers "had no financial resources beyond [the price] that they could have put together for the purchase of [the seller's house] . . . [The purchasers] were therefore to the [seller's] knowledge unable at the time of breach to raise a further £1500 to purchase an equivalent house forthwith, and so . . . mitigate their loss".[536c]

[536a] [1974] Ch. 30 (mentioned in para.26–096, n.527).
[536b] On the relevance of this knowledge, see this Supplement, para.26–095B, above.
[536c] [1974] Ch. 30, 57.

Benefits independent of mitigation

[Add to note 547: page [1484]]
cf. Re-Source America International Ltd v Platt Site Services Ltd [2005] EWCA Civ 97; [2005] 2 Lloyd's Rep.50, CA (the saved cost of refurbishment was deducted from the full cost of replacement).

26–101

Recovery of sum due on performance

[Add to note 572: page [1487]]
The White and Carter case was further distinguished where one party's obligation to pay a definite sum was not dependent on performance by the other party of its own obligations: Ministry of Sound (Ireland) Ltd v World On-line Ltd [2003] EWHC 2178 (Ch); [2003] 2 All E.R. (Comm.) 823.

26–107

[Note 577: page [1488]
Update reference to Benjamin to (7th ed., 2006), paras 16–022—16–059.

6. Penalty or Liquidated Damages

Damages fixed by the parties

[Add to the text after note 592: page [1490]]
The "courts are predisposed . . . to uphold [liquidated damages clauses]. This predisposition is even stronger in the case of commercial contracts freely entered into between parties of comparable bargaining power."[592a]

26–109

[592a] Alfred McAlpine Capital Projects Ltd v Tilebox Ltd [2005] Build. L. R. 271 (TCC) at [48].

Statement of penalty rules

[Add to note 599: page [1490]]
The law laid down in the Dunlop case has not been significantly altered by the Philips Hong Kong case (cited in para.26–109, n.589 above): Jeancharm Ltd v Barnet Football Club Ltd [2003] EWCA Civ 58; [2003] 92 Con. L. R. 26.

26–110

[*Add to note 605: page* [1491]]
cf. Jeancharm Ltd v Barnet Football Club Ltd, above, n.599 (interest rate for late payment of five per cent per week held to be a penalty).

26–111 [*Add to the text after the first sentence: page* [1492]]
It has recently been held that " . . . the test does turn upon the genuineness or honesty of the party or parties who made the pre-estimate. The test is primarily an objective one . . . ". In the same case the judge considered that one strand of the test in the reported cases was "whether the level of damages stipulated was reasonable".[608a]

[608a] *Alfred McAlpine Capital Projects Ltd v Tilebox Ltd* [2005] Build. L. R. 271 (TCC) at [48].

[*Note 612*]
Update reference to Benjamin to (7th ed., 2006), para.13–036.

Graduated damages

26–117 [*Add to note 628: page* [1494]]
Alfred McAlpine Capital Projects Ltd v Tilebox Ltd [2005] Build. L. R. 271 (TCC).

The scope of the law on penalties

26–118 [*Add to the end of note 634: page* [1495]]
Euro London Appointments Ltd v Claessens International Ltd [2006] EWCA Civ 385; [2006] 7 C.L. 113 (a condition precedent imposing no obligation).

Sum payable on event other than breach

26–119 [*Add to note 638: page* [1495]]
Euro London Appointments Ltd v Claessens International Ltd [2006] EWCA Civ 385; [2006] 7 C.L. 113.

8. Interest and Rate of Exchange

Finance charges on particular transaction contemplated

26–145 [*Add to note 788: page* [1511]]
On the relevance of the impecuniosity of the claimant, see paras 26–095A—26–095D, above.

Statutory power to award interest

26–149 [*Add to the end of note 813: page* [1513]]
See also *R. (on the application of Kemp) v Denbighshire Local Health Board* [2006] EWHC 181 (Admin); [2006] 3 All E.R. 141.

CHAPTER 27

SPECIFIC PERFORMANCE AND INJUNCTION

			PARA.
	1.	Introduction	27–001
☐	2.	The "adequacy" of damages	27–005
☐	3.	Contracts not specifically enforceable	27–019
■	4.	Other grounds for refusing specific performance	27–029
	5.	Mutuality of remedy	27–045
	6.	Specific performance and third parties	27–048
		(a) Claim by promisee	27–049
		(b) Claim by third party	27–052
■	7.	Specific performance with compensation	27–053
☐	8.	Injunction	27–059
	9.	Damages and specific performance or injunction	27–075

2. THE "ADEQUACY" OF DAMAGES

Difficulty of quantifying damages

[*Add to note 32: page* [1525]]   **27–008**

In *Laemthong International Lines Co Ltd v Artis (The Laemthong Glory) (No.2)* [2004] EWHC 2738 (Comm); [2005] 1 Lloyd's Rep. 632, goods were delivered from a chartered ship against letters of indemnity, one of which, addressed by the receiver to the character, was held to be enforceable by the shipowner against the receiver under the Contracts (Rights of Third Parties) Act 1999: see above, para.18–087 of this Supplement. One of the terms of this letter provided that, if the ship should be arrested in consequence of the shipowner's delivering the goods without production of the bill of lading, then the receiver would provide bail or other security to secure her release. Cooke J. held that this promise was specifically enforceable as the assessment of damages for detention was "never an entirely straightforward matter" (at [47]) and as the "very purpose" of the letter of indemnity was "to prevent the detention that occurred" (at [49]; *cf.* at [51]). The decision was affirmed, but without any discussion on appeal of the issue of specific enforceability: see [2005] EWCA Civ 519; [2005] 1 Lloyd's Rep. 688, where the shipowner's claim is said at [19] to have been one for a declaration that the promisors under the letters of indemnity were obliged to take the specified steps to secure the release of the ship.

[Add to note 36: page [1526]]
For the difficulty of enforcing a judgment for damages as a ground for ordering specific performance, see also *Laemthong International Lines Co Ltd v Artis (The Laemthong Glory) (No.2)* [2004] EWHC 2738 (Comm); [2005] 1 Lloyd's Rep. 632 at [47]: "the enforcement of judgments in Yemen is a matter of some difficulty"; affirmed without reference to the issue of specific enforceability [2005] EWCA Civ 519; [2005] 1 Lloyd's Rep. 688, above, para.27–008, n.32 of this Supplement. See also *Thames Valley Power Ltd v Total Gas and Power Ltd* [2005] EWHC 2208 (Comm); [2006] 1 Lloyd's Rep. 441, discussed below in para.27–017 of this Supplement.

Availability of substitute

27–011   *[Add to note 41: page* [1526]]
Contrast *Thames Valley Power Ltd v Total Gas and Power Ltd* [2005] EWHC 2208 (Comm); [2006] 1 Lloyd's Rep. 441, discussed below in para.27–017 of this Supplement.

[Add to note 45: page [1527]]
See also *Pena v Dale* [2003] EWHC 1065; [2004] 2 B.C.L.C. 508 at [135] (option to purchase shares in private company specifically enforced).

Sale of goods: non-delivery

27–014   *[Add to note 52, line 6, after reference to Lingen v Simpson: page* [1528]]
cf. Land Rover Group Ltd v UPF (UK) Ltd [2002] EWHC 3183; [2003] B.C.L.C. 222 at [52] (mandatory injunction to enforce obligation to supply chassis to car manufacturer).

"Specific or ascertained" goods

27–016   *[Note 68: page* [1529]]
Update reference to Benjamin to (7th ed., 2006), paras 18–299, 19–204.

Specific enforcement of contracts not within section 52

27–017   *[Add to note 70: page* [1530]]
cf. Land Rover Group Ltd v UPF (UK) Ltd [2002] EWHC 3183; [2003] 2 B.C.L.C. 222, above para.27–014 of this Supplement. For the question whether the goods in that case were indeed specific (as was there agreed: see at [52]) *cf.* Main Work, para.43–031.

[Add to text at end of paragraph: page [1531]]
The view that specific performance may be ordered of a contract for the sale of goods, even though the contract is not within s.52 of the Sale of Goods Act 1979 because the goods are not "specific or ascertained", is further supported by *Thames Valley Power Ltd v Total Gas and Power Ltd.*[77a] In that case A had in 1995 entered into a contract with B by which B agreed to supply A with gas

which A (a "single purpose company")[77b] needed to perform a contract with C to run and operate a heat and power facility at Heathrow Airport; this fact was known to B.[77c] The price of the gas was fixed for about the first two years, after which it was to vary according to an elaborate formula depending on the movement of various indices. In 1995 B purported to invoke a *force majeure* clause in the contract as justifying their refusal to continue to supply gas under the contract, arguing that increases in the market price of gas amounted to *force majeure* within the clause. This argument was rejected by Christopher Clarke J., who further held (though it was "not strictly necessary"[77d] to decide the point) that B's obligation to continue to supply gas under the contract was specifically enforceable. One reason for this view was that the basis of the [contract] was that A "would be assured of a source of supply from a first-rate supplier for a 15 year term", and so would be deprived "of substantially the whole benefit that the contract was intended to give them" if they were confined to "a claim in damages".[77e] This amounts to saying that damages were not an adequate remedy as a satisfactory substitute was not available.[77f] A second reason for the availability of specific performance lay in "the almost impossible task in calculating any damages"[77g]: such a task would involve speculation, not only as to market prices over the remaining five years of the contract, but also as to movements of the indices by reference to which the contract price was to fluctuate from time to time. A third reason why damages were an inadequate remedy lay in the delays likely to be encountered in securing the actual payment of damages. These could result in A's becoming insolvent well before the end of the remaining term of the contract.[77h] No reference is made to s.52 in the judgment; but where, for reasons such as those given above, damages for breach of a contract are not a satisfactory remedy, then it is, with respect, consistent with the principles governing specific relief to hold that such relief is available even in cases not falling squarely within the section.

[77a] [2005] EWHC 2208 (Comm); [2006] 1 Lloyd's Rep. 441.

[77b] *ibid.*, at [49].

[77c] *ibid.*

[77d] *ibid.*, at [63]. B had indicated that, if it were held that they were not protected by the *force majeure* clause, then they would continue to supply gas to A under the terms of the contract between A and B: *ibid.*, at [58].

[77e] *ibid.*, at [63].

[77f] See Main Work, para.27–011.

[77g] *Thames Valley Power Ltd v Total Gas and Power Ltd*, above, n.77a, at [64]; *cf.* Main Work, para.27–008.

[77h] *Thames Valley Power Ltd v Total Gas and Power Ltd*, above, n.77a, at [64]; *cf.* Main Work, para.27–008 at n.36.

3. CONTRACTS NOT SPECIFICALLY ENFORCEABLE

Contracts of Employment

[*Add to note 93: page* [1532]]   **27–021**
Sex Discrimination Act 1975, s.71 has been repealed by Equality Act 2006, s.40 and Sch.3, para.12 and s.91 and Sch.4.

Exceptions

27–022   [*Add to note 103: page* [1534]]
See also Disability Discrimination Act 1995, s.21F(2)(b) (as inserted by
Disability Discrimination Act 2005, s.12), making it unlawful to discriminate
against disabled persons by refusing them admission to private clubs. Enforcement of these provisions appears to be by criminal sanctions rather than by orders
for specific relief.

[*Add to note 107*]
For recognition of the exceptions referred to in the Main Work, para.27–022,
see also *Lauritzencool AB v Lady Navigation Inc* [2005] EWCA Civ 579; [2005]
2 All E.R. (Comm.) 183 at [10].

[*Add to note 108*]
For injunctive relief against an employer who had failed to comply with the
contractual provisions setting out the disciplinary procedures to be followed
before dismissal, see also *Gryf-Lowczowski v Hitchingbroke Healthcare NHS
Trust* [2005] EWHC 2407; [2006] I.R.L.R. 100.

Other contracts involving "personal" service

27–023   [*Add to note 110: page* [1535]]
cf. A v Lord Grey's School [2004] EWCA Civ 382; [2004] Q.B. 1231, where
damages were recovered by a pupil whose expulsion from a state school was
found to amount to a breach of the Human Rights Act 1998, Sch.1 Pt II, Art.2 and
whose requests for *reinstatement* had been denied.

[*Add to note 113*]
In *Pena v Dale* [2003] EWHC 1065; [2004] 2 B.C.L.C. 508 specific performance was ordered of an agreement by which A, a shareholder in a private
company, granted an option to B to acquire a minority shareholding in the
company. The existence of personal animosity between A and B was no bar to
such specific enforcement since B would not, by virtue of exercising the option,
acquire any right to participate in the day to day management of the company:
see *ibid.*, at [136].

Services not of a "personal" nature

27–024   [*Add to note 116: page* [1535]]
Lauritzencool AB v Lady Navigation Inc [2005] EWCA Civ 579; [2005] 2 All
E.R. (Comm.) 183, below n.119.

[*Add to note 119*]
See also *Lauritzencool AB v Lady Navigation Inc* [2005] EWCA Civ 579;
[2005] 2 All E.R. (Comm.) 183, where it was said at [9] to be "common
ground . . . that *The Scaptrade* stands as authority for the proposition that specific
performance will not be ordered of a time charter" though counsel reserved the
right "to ask the House [of Lords] to review this proposition, should that matter
go that far" (*ibid.*). For the injunctive relief granted in the *Lauritzencool* case, see
below, para.27–068 of this Supplement.

Constant supervision

[Note 129: page [1536]]   **27–025**
For "27–016" substitute "27–017".

[Add to note 129]
   In *Thames Valley Power Ltd v Total Gas and Power Ltd* [2005] EWHC 2208 (Comm); [2006] 1 Lloyd's Rep. 441, the court declared that the buyer was "entitled to damages and an order by way of specific performance" (at [65]) to enforce the suppliers' obligation under a long-term contract for the supply of gas. At the time of the order, the contract had nearly five years to run: see this Supplement, above, para.27–017; but no reference was made to any difficulty of supervision, perhaps because the suppliers had indicated their willingness to continue the supply if the decision on the issue of liability went against them (at [58]).

4. OTHER GROUNDS FOR REFUSING SPECIFIC PERFORMANCE

Inutility

[Add new text after note 201: page [1544]]   **27–039**
   Specific performance of a promise to issue share warrants has likewise been refused where "the time for the exercise of the option in any warrants which ought to have been issued" had "long since expired".[201a]

[201a] *De Jongh Weill v Mean Fiddler Holdings* [2005] All E.R. (D) 331 (Jul.) at [75].

7. SPECIFIC PERFORMANCE WITH COMPENSATION

Condition against error or misdescription

[Substitute for note 306: page [1554]]   **27–056**
   The Court of Appeal has held that the Unfair Terms in Consumer Contracts Regulations 1999 (SI 1999/2083), apply to contracts for the sale of an interest in land by a commercial supplier to a consumer: *London Borough of Newham v Khatun* [2004] EWCA Civ 55; [2005] Q.B. 37, see above, para.15–014.

8. INJUNCTION

Negative contracts

[Add to note 323: page [1556]]   **27–059**
   For the application of the "balance of convenience" test to a mandatory injunction to enforce a position obligation (to maintain supplies of components

to the supplier of motor vehicles), see *Land Rover Group Ltd v UPF (UK) Ltd* [2002] EWHC 3183; [2003] B.C.L.C. 222 at [60]. The injunction there granted was an interim injunction (at [65]), so that the "balance of convenience" test was applicable also on the principle stated in Main Work, para.27–060.

[*Add to note 324: page* [1557]]
cf. Mortimer v Bailey [2004] EWCA Civ 1514; [2005] 2 P.&C.R. 9, where a mandatory injunction was granted to order the defendant to pull down an extension built in breach of a restrictive covenant. The point at issue was whether there had been undue delay in applying for this form of relief.

Interim injunctions

27–060   [*Add to note 325 in line 10 after "355": page* [1557]]
Townsends Group Ltd v Cobb [2004] EWHC 3432, December 1, 2004.

[*Add to note 329*]
See also *PI International Ltd v Llewellyn* [2005] EWHC 407; [2005] U.K.C.L.R. 530.

Injunction imposing undue pressure on employee

27–065   [*Add new text at end of paragraph: page* [1560]]
The above discussion is concerned with contracts of employment and reflects the reluctance of the courts to put undue pressure on the employee to render personal service. Where the contract is one for services which are not of a personal nature, an injunction may be available against the party who has promised to provide the services, even though the practical effect of the injunction is to "compel performance". A shipowner who has let him ship out under a time charter may, for example, be restrained by injunction from employing the ship inconsistently with the charterparty.[356a]

[356a] *Lauritzencool AB v Lady Navigation Inc* [2005] EWCA Civ 579; [2005] 2 All E.R. (Comm.) 183, below para.27–068 of this Supplement.

Implied negative promises

27–068   [*Add to note 372: page* [1562]]
In *Lauritzencool AB v Lady Navigation Inc* [2005] EWCA Civ 579; [2005] 2 All E.R. (Comm.) 183 disputes under two time charters were submitted to arbitration and interim injunctions were granted restraining the shipowners from (a) employing the vessels inconsistently with the charterparties, or (b) fixing the vessels with any third party during the period of the charterparties, pending the final award in the arbitration. The contract was not one of personal service, but "a commercial arrangement between two independent companies involving the employment of no named individuals" (at [35]). It was therefore no objection to the grant of an injunction that the "practical effect" of this form of relief would be to "compel performance" (at [19], [20]) in the sense that the "only realistic course" (at [33]) which the injunction left to the owners was to continue to perform the charterparties. A distinction was to be drawn between an injunction

resulting in such practical compulsion to perform and one which was "as a matter of law pregnant with an affirmative obligation to perform the charterparty" (at [6]) such as one "not to break the contract" or "not to take steps to prevent its performance". Such an injunction was "tantamount to" (at [6]) or "juristically indistinguishable from" an order of specific performance (at [10], quoting from *The Scaptrade* [1983] 2 A.C. 694 at 700) and was therefore not available in respect of contracts which were not specifically enforceable: see Main Work para.27–069 and this Supplement para.27–069. An injunction which did not result in such *legal* compulsion to perform the contract was available to restrain breach of a contract of the present kind even though it resulted in practical compulsion of the kind described above. Such practical compulsion was a ground for refusing injunctive relief in personal service cases of the kind described in paras 27–064 and 27–068 at n.371 above, but not where the services were not of a personal nature.

[*Add new text after note 379: page* [1563]]   **27–069**
Similarly, an injunction will not be granted against "taking any step preventing the performance of" a contract.[379a]

[379a] See the decision at first instance in *Lauritzencool AB v Lady Navigation Inc* [2004] EWHC 2607 (Comm); [2005] 1 All E.R. (Comm.) 77, so far as it relates to para.12(a) of the relief claimed. There was no appeal against this aspect of the decision when it was affirmed and injunctions were granted in the more restricted form, "not pregnant with an affirmative obligation to perform", discussed in para.27–068 above: [2005] EWCA Civ 579 at [6].

Statutory provisions against refusal to contract

[*Add to text in line 4, after "sex": page* [1564]]   **27–072**
; religion or belief, sexual orientation[385a]

[385a] Equality Act 2006, Pts 2 and 3. Part 2 contains detailed provisions specifying the situations in which discrimination on grounds of religion or belief is prohibited; refusal to contract could fall within these provisions: *e.g.* under s.46, relating to the provision of goods, facilities and services; or under s.47, relating to the disposal of premises or access to a benefit or facility provided by a manager of premises. Part 3 is an enabling provision under which regulations may be made "about discrimination or harassment on grounds of sexual orientation" (s.81(1)). Regulations, made before the passing of the 2006 Act, which govern discrimination in employment on grounds of religion or belief or sexual orientation, and which remain in force, are cited below in para.27–072 of this Supplement.

[*Add to note 386, line 1, after "s.62;"*]
Race Relations Act 1976, s.62 has been repealed by Equality Act 2006, s.40 and Sch. 3, para.27 and s.91 and Sch. 4. The Equality Act 2006, s.24 empowers the Commission for Equality and Human Rights (created by s.1) to apply for an injunction against a person whom it "thinks . . . likely to commit an unlawful act" restraining that person from committing that act. For this purpose, an act is "unlawful" if it is "contrary to the provisions of the equality enactments" (s.34). These enactments are listed in s.33; the list includes legislation which makes discrimination unlawful on grounds of sex, race, disability, sexual orientation, religion or belief. Where the Commission has entered into an agreement with a person "not to commit an unlawful act of a specified kind" (s.23(1)(a)(i)), the Commission may apply to a county court for an order requiring that person "to comply with his undertaking" (s.24(3)(a): such an order would amount to specific enforcement of the agreement. A claim that a person has done "anything

that is unlawful" by virtue of Pt 2 of the Act (which deals with discrimination on grounds of religion or belief) may be brought (apparently by a person claiming to have been prejudiced by such conduct) "by way of proceedings in tort" (s.66). It is envisaged that such proceedings will normally result in an award of damages but they could also result in a *quia timet* injunction against anticipated or threatened conduct which was "unlawful" within the 2006 Act (*cf.* the reference to s.34, above).

[Add to note 386, line 2, after "ss.4, 5, 12 and 19"]
See also s.21F of the 1995 Act (inserted by Disability Discrimination Act 2005, s.12) making it unlawful for private clubs to discriminate against disabled persons by refusing or deliberately omitting to accept their applications for membership. Enforcement appears to be by criminal prosecution rather than by injunction.

[Add to note 386, line 3, after reference to SI 1996/438]
For the unlawfulness of discrimination on grounds of religion or belief in employment, and for remedies in respect of such discrimination, see Employment Equality (Religion or Belief) Regulations 2003 (SI 2003/1660). Regulation 30 falls short of providing for injunctive relief: it enables an employment tribunal to make a "recommendation" that steps should be taken to obviate or reduce the adverse effect on the complainant of the discrimination (reg.30(1)(c)); but the only effect of failure to comply with the recommendation is to increase the compensation payable to the complainant or to enable him to get compensation where no order for compensation was originally made (reg.30(3)). The position is the same in cases of unlawful discrimination on grounds of sexual orientation: see Employment Equality (Sexual Orientation) Regulations 2003 (SI 2003/1661), reg.30. The two Statutory Instruments discussed in this paragraph of this Supplement (*i.e.* SI 2003/1660 and SI 2003/1661) remain in force after the Equality Act 2006: see s.33(1)(g) and (h) of that Act.

9. DAMAGES AND SPECIFIC PERFORMANCE OR INJUNCTION

No completed cause of action at law

27–076   *[Add to note 402: page [1566]]*
Sex Discrimination Act 1975, s.66 is repealed by Equality Act 2006, s.40 and Sch.3, para.12 and s.91 and Sch.4. For rights to damages in tort under the latter Act, and the possibility of obtaining a *quia timet* injunction in respect of conduct made unlawful by it, see above, para.27–072 of this Supplement.

CHAPTER 28

LIMITATION OF ACTIONS

			PARA.
☐	1.	Periods of limitation	28–001
☐	2.	Accrual of the cause of action	28–031
	3.	Computation of the period	28–062
	4.	The running of time	28–064
■	5.	Extension of the period	28–071
		(a) Disability	28–074
☐		(b) Fraud, concealment or mistake	28–081
☐		(c) Acknowledgment and part payment	28–092
■		(d) Agreement of the parties	28–106
	6.	Abridgement of the period	28–112
☐	7.	Commencement of proceedings	28–116
	8.	The statute bars the remedy, not the right	28–126
☐	9.	Limitation in equity	28–134

1. PERIODS OF LIMITATION

Specialities

[*Add to note 19: page* [1573]]   **28–003**
On s.20, see *West Bromwich Building Society v Wilkinson* [2005] UKHL 44;
[2005] 1 W.L.R. 2303; *Doodes v Gotham* [2006] EWCA Civ 1080.

Product liability

[*Add to note 44: page* [1575]]   **28–009**
A product is supplied, or in the words of Directive 85/374 "put into circula-
tion", when it is taken out of the manufacturing process operated by the producer
and enters a marketing process in the form in which it is offered to the public in
order to be used or consumed: *O'Byrne v Sanofi Pasteur MSD Ltd* [2006] 1
W.L.R. 1606; [2006] 2 C.M.L.R. 24, ECJ.

Latent damage in actions for the tort of negligence

[*Add to note 47: page* [1575]]   **28–010**
It has also been held that the Limitation Act 1980, s.14A does not apply to a
claim for damages under s.2(1) of the Misrepresentation Act 1967 because under

s.2(1) there is no onus on the claimant to prove negligence: *Laws v The Society of Lloyd's* [2003] EWCA Civ 1887; *The Times*, January 23, 2004, at [78]–[93].

28–011   [*Add to note 56: page* [1576]]

In *Haward v Fawcetts* [2006] UKHL 9; [2006] 1 W.L.R. 682, s.14A was examined for the first time by the House of Lords. It was held that a claim against an accountant for negligent advice (or failure to advise), leading to loss-making investment in 1994 and 1995, was statute-barred. The claimant had had the relevant knowledge in December 1998, more than three years before commencing proceedings in December 2001. The case principally turned on the interpretation of s.14A(8)(a): "that the damage was attributable in whole or in part to the act or omission which is alleged to constitute negligence". Their Lordships adverted to the apparent tension between s.14A(8) and s.14A(9). According to the latter: "knowledge that any acts or omissions did or did not, as a matter of law, involve negligence is irrelevant". Their Lordships recognised that knowledge that the defendant had given "flawed" advice was necessary under s.14A(8)(a); and that the courts could safely look for knowledge that, factually, "something had gone wrong" without contravening s.14A(9). The approach to s.14A(8) in *Hallam-Eames v Merrett Syndicates Ltd* [1996] 7 Med. L.R. was approved, while that in *HF Pension Trustees Ltd v Ellison* [1999] P.N.L.R. 894 was disapproved.

[*Add to note 58*]

Section 14A(10) therefore makes clear that constructive knowledge is sufficient. For a consideration of s.14A(10), see *Gravgaard v Aldridge & Brownlee* [2004] EWCA Civ 1529; [2005] P.N.L.R. 19.

28–012   [*Add to note 62: page* [1577]]

The 15-year long-stop under the Limitation Act 1980, s.14B, bars the remedy but does not extinguish the claimant's right of action: *Financial Services Compensation Scheme Ltd v Larnell (Insurances) Ltd* [2005] EWCA Civ 1408; [2006] 2 W.L.R. 751.

Action on a judgment

28–015   [*Add to note 68: page* [1577]]

In *Ridgeway Motors (Isleworth) Ltd v ALTS Ltd* [2005] EWCA Civ 92; [2005] 2 All E.R. 304 it was held that, following *Lowsley v Forbes* [1999] 1 A.C. 329 and impliedly disapproving *Re a Debtor* [1997] Ch. 310, a winding up or bankruptcy petition by a judgement creditor was not "an action upon a judgment" within s.24(1) of the 1980 Act. "An action upon a judgment" had the special meaning of a "fresh action" brought upon a judgment in order to obtain a second judgment, which could be executed. Insolvency proceedings, whether personal or corporate, did not fall within the scope of that special meaning.

2. Accrual of the Cause of Action

Concurrent liability in tort

[Add to note 142: page [1584]]   **28–033**
For consideration of when a cause of action accrues against an accountant in the tort of negligence, see *Law Society v Sephton & Co* [2006] UKHL 22; [2006] 2 W.L.R. 1091. The Law Society brought a claim in the tort of negligence against the defendant accountants who had failed to inspect properly the accounts of a corrupt solicitor. The solicitor over a six-year period had misappropriated over £750,000 from his client account. Subsequently the Law Society had made payments to former clients of the corrupt solicitor from the Solicitors Compensation Fund. It was held that the cause of action in negligence was not time-barred because it accrued only when claims were made for compensation from the Fund. Prior to then, the Law Society had only a contingent liability to pay out compensation. Such a pure contingent liability, which might or might not eventuate, did not count as damage so as to constitute the accrual of a cause of action. This situation was to be distinguished from that dealt with in almost all the prior English cases, which concerned entering into disadvantageous transactions or suffering a diminution in value of an asset.

Civil Liability (Contribution Act) 1978

[Add to note 206: page [1590]]   **28–051**
Where there are separate judgments (or arbitration awards) in relation to liability and quantum, the two-year limitation period for contribution under s.10 of the Civil Liability (Contribution) Act 1978 runs from the judgment on quantum: *Aer Lingus plc v Gildercroft Ltd* [2006] EWCA Civ 4; [2006] 1 W.L.R. 1173.

5. Extension of the Period

(b) *Fraud, Concealment or Mistake*

Concealment

[Add to note 329: page [1602]]   **28–086**
In *Williams v Fanshaw Porter & Hazelhurst* [2004] EWCA Civ 157; [2004] 2 All E.R. 616, the decision in *Cave v Robinson Jarvis & Rolf* [2002] UKHL 18; [2003] 1 A.C. 384 was considered and applied to a professional negligence claim. It was held that a trainee legal executive, employed by the defendants, had deliberately concealed a relevant fact within the meaning of s.32(1)(b) of the Limitation Act 1980. The *Williams* and *Lane* decisions were applied in holding that there had been deliberate concealment of re-tests and their results in *AIC Ltd v ITS Testing Services (UK) Ltd* [2005] EWHC 2122 (Comm); [2006] 1 Lloyd's Rep. 1 (in which one of the claims was for breach of contract).

(c) *Acknowledgement and Part Payment*

Form of the acknowledgement

28–094   [*Add to note 365: page* [1605]]
In *Bradford and Bingley plc v Rashid* [2006] UKHL 37; [2006] 1 W.L.R. 2066 letters were held to be admissible to prove an acknowledgement despite the "without prejudice" rule.

What constitutes acknowledgement

28–095   [*Add to note 378: page* [1606]]
Dungate v Dungate [1965] 1 W.L.R. 1477 was applied in holding that there had been an acknowledgement for the purposes of s.29(5) of the Limitation Act 1980 in *Bradford and Bingley plc v Rashid* [2006] UKHL 37; [2006] 1 W.L.R. 2066.

Parties to the acknowledgement or part payment

28–100   [*Add to note 391: page* [1607]]
In *UCB Corporate Services Ltd v Kohli* [2004] EWHC 1126 (Ch); [2004] 2 All E.R. (Comm.) 422 it was held that the part payments were not made by an agent of the debtor, so that the limitation period did not run afresh under s.29 and s.30(2) of the Limitation Act 1980.

Effect of acknowledgement and part payment on other persons

28–103   [*Add to note 404: page* [1609]]
This sentence in the text was approved in *UCB Corporate Services Ltd v Kohli* [2004] EWHC 1126 (Ch); [2004] 2 All E.R. (Comm.) 422, in which it was held that part payment by a principal debtor bound the surety for the purposes of s.31(7) of the Limitation Act 1980.

(d) *Agreement of the Parties*

Estoppel

28–109   [*Add to note 427; page* [1611]]
Super Chem Products Ltd v American Life and General Insurance Co Ltd [2004] UKPC 2; [2004] 2 All E.R. 358.

7. COMMENCEMENT OF PROCEEDINGS

Amendments to statement of case after the end of the limitation period

28–118   [*Add to note 471: page* [1615]]
Laws v The Society of Lloyd's [2003] EWCA Civ 1887; *The Times,* January 23, 2004; *Furini v Bajwa* [2004] EWCA Civ 412; [2004] 1 W.L.R. 1971; *P&O*

Nedlloyd BV v Arab Metals Co, The UB Tiger [2005] EWHC 1276; [2005] 1 W.L.R. 3733 (in which it was held that a claim for a declaration of different rights than those originally pleaded constituted a new claim under CPR Pt 17, r.4.2).

[*Add to note 474: page* [1616]]   **28–119**
   Parsons v George [2004] EWCA Civ 912; [2004] 1 W.L.R. 3264; *Morgan Est (Scotland) Ltd v Hanson Concrete Products Ltd* [2005] EWCA Civ 134; [2005] 3 All E.R. 135.

9. LIMITATION IN EQUITY

Introductory

[*Add to note 536: page* [1621]]   **28–134**
   The point in *Re Pauling's Settlement Trusts* [1964] Ch. 303 at 353, was applied in *Re Loftus* [2005] EWHC 406 (Ch); [2005] 1 W.L.R. 1890 at [161]–[162].

[*Add to note 537*]
   In *P&O Nedlloyd BV v Arab Metals Co, The UB Tiger* [2005] EWHC 1276; [2005] 1 W.L.R. 3733, Colman J. held that a declaration was not "equitable relief" within s.36(1). Rather it was statutory so that normal time limits within the Limitation Act 1980 apply.

The statute applied by analogy

[*Add to note 543: page* [1622]]   **28–135**
   In *P&O Nedlloyd BV v Arab Metals Co, The UB Tiger* [2005] EWHC 1276; [2005] 1 W.L.R. 3733 the usual contractual limitation period of six years was applied by analogy under s.36(1) to a claim for specific performance, so that it was time-barred.

Part Nine

RESTITUTION

CHAPTER 29

RESTITUTION

			PARA.
■	1.	Introduction	29–001
☐		(a) Nature of restitution	29–001
		(b) Historical introduction	29–005
☐		(c) The theoretical basis of restitution	29–010
■	2.	Unjust enrichment	29–018
☐		(a) The content of the unjust enrichment principle	29–018
☐		(b) Enrichment	29–020
☐		(c) At the expense of the claimant	29–024
		(d) The grounds of restitution	29–027
☐		(e) Mistake	29–028
☐		(f) Failure of consideration	29–054
☐		(g) *Ultra vires* receipts by the Revenue and public authorities	29–083
☐		(h) Compulsion	29–087
☐		(i) Necessity	29–130
■		(j) Exploitation	29–137
☐	3.	Restitution for wrongs	29–139
■		(a) General principles	29–139
☐		(b) Tort	29–141
☐		(c) Breach of Contract	29–151
☐		(d) Equitable wrongdoings	29–155
■	4.	Proprietary restitutionary claims	29–158
☐		(a) Establishing proprietary rights	29–158
☐		(b) Following and tracing	29–162
☐		(c) Proprietary restitutionary claims	29–170
☐	5.	Defences	29–176
☐		(a) Estoppel	29–176
☐		(b) Change of position	29–179
☐		(c) Settlement of an honest claim	29–186
	6.	Miscellaneous restitutionary claims	29–191
		(a) Account stated	29–191
		(b) Account	29–193

[*Note 1: page* [1631]]

Update reference to Virgo, *The Principles of the Law of Restitution* to (2nd ed., 2006).

Update reference to Maddaugh and McCamus, *The Law of Restitution* to (2nd ed., 2004).

1. Introduction

(a) *Nature of Restitution*

Common law

[*Add to note 7: page* [1632]]
  Taylor v Motability Finance Ltd [2004] EWHC 2619 (Comm) at [23] (Cooke J.); *Mowlem plc v Stena Line Ports Ltd* [2004] EWHC 2206; *S and W Process Engineering Ltd v Cauldron Foods Ltd* [2005] EWHC 153 (TCC). See also *Boake Allen Ltd v HM Revenue and Customs* [2006] EWCA Civ 25 at [98] (Sedley L.J.).

29–002

Equity

[*Add to note 15: page* [1633]]
  For the history of the unjust enrichment principle in the United States see Kull [2005] O.J.L.S. 297.

29–003

Classification

[*Note 18, line 3: page* [1634]]
  Update reference to Virgo to pp.6–18.

29–004

(c) *The Theoretical Basis of Restitution*

The principle of unjust enrichment

[*Add to note 47: page* [1638]]
  See Kull [2005] O.J.L.S. 297.

29–012

Statutory recognition

[*Add to line 11, after note 65: page* [1641]]
  It has been recognised that the rationale of the Civil Liability (Contribution) Act 1978 is to ensure that a defendant is not unjustly enriched where the defendant's liability to a third party has been discharged by the claimant.[65a]

29–015

[65a] *Dubai Aluminium Co Ltd v Salaam* [2002] UKHL 48; [2003] 2 A.C. 366 at [76] (Lord Hobhouse).

The state of the unjust enrichment principle

[*Add to the beginning of note 69: page* [1641]]
  In *Uren v First National Home Finance Ltd* [2005] EWHC 2529 (Ch) it was held that English law does not yet recognise a free-standing claim of unjust enrichment such that the claimant can simply plead an enrichment which is unjust. Rather, the claimant needs to establish either that the claim falls within one of the recognised grounds of restitution or within a new ground which is a justifiable extension from the established grounds.

29–016

[*Note 69*]
Update reference to Birks, *Unjust Enrichment* to (2nd ed., 2005). See *Boake Allen Ltd v HM Revenue and Customs* [2006] EWCA Civ 25 at [161] (Mummery L.J.).

Different causes of action within restitution

29–017   [*Add to note 79: page* [1642]]
See also *Criterion Properties Ltd v Stratford UK Properties* [2004] UKHL 28; [2004] 1 W.L.R. 1846 at [4] (Lord Nicholls).

2. UNJUST ENRICHMENT

(a) *The Content of the Unjust Enrichment Principle*

The elements of unjust enrichment

29–018   [*Note 81: page* [1642]]
McDonald v Coys of Kensington is now reported at [2004] 1 W.L.R. 2775.

[*Add to note 83: page* [1642]]
; *Uren v First National Home Finance Ltd* [2005] EWHC 2529 (Ch) at [16] (Mann J.). Restitution will also not be available if the sum was due to the defendant: *Boake Allen Ltd v HM Revenue and Customs* [2006] EWCA Civ 25.

Defences and bars

29–019   [*Add to note 88: page* [1643]]
: see *Halpern v Halpern* [2006] EWHC 1728; [2006] 3 All E.R. 1139 (inability to return documents meant that a contract could not be avoided for duress).

[*Note 92, line 3*]
Portman BS v Hamlyn Taylor Neck is reported at [1998] 4 All E.R. 202.

(b) *Enrichment*

Non-monetary benefits

29–021   [*Note 104: page* [1644]]
Update reference to Virgo to pp.70–72.

[*Note 105*]
McDonald v Coys of Kensington is now reported at [2004] 1 W.L.R. 2775.

[*Add to note 107: page* [1645]]
See *S and W Process Engineering Ltd v Cauldron Foods Ltd* [2005] EWHC 153 (TCC) at [51]–[55].

Service resulting in incontrovertible benefit

[Notes 114 and 116: page [1645]]
McDonald v Coys of Kensington is now reported at [2004] 1 W.L.R. 2775.

[Add to end of note 116]
See Virgo *op cit.* pp.74–81.

(c) *At the expense of the claimant*

Enrichment at the claimant's expense

[Add to note 120: page [1646]]
Uren v First National Home Finance Ltd [2005] EWHC 2529 (Ch) at [22] (Mann J.).

The suggested need for "privity" between the parties

[Note 127: page [1647]]
Update reference to Virgo to pp.108–112.

[Add to the end of the paragraph]
There must be some causal connection between the claimant and the defendant's enrichment: *Uren v First National Home Finance Ltd* [2005] EWHC 2529 (Ch) at [23] (Mann J.).

Rejection of "passing on" defence

[Add to note 128: page [1647]]
However, in *Marks and Spencer plc v Commissioners of Customs and Excise* [2005] UKHL 53; [2005] C.M.L.R. 3, at [25] Lord Walker of Westingthorpe recognised that passing on is recognised as a possible defence to any restitutionary claim. His Lordship cited *Roxborough v Rothmans of Pall Mall Australia Ltd, ibid.*, in support of this conclusion, but that decision expressly rejected the passing on defence in Australia.

(e) *Mistake*

Burden of proof

[Add to note 174, after reference to Kleinwort Benson case: page [1652]]
Cobbold v Bakewell Management Ltd [2003] EWHC 2289 (Ch) at [19] (Rimer J.).

Examples of payments under a mistake of law

29–041   *[Delete last sentence: page* [1657]]

Exceptions to the mistake of law bar

29–042   *[Add to note 221: page* [1658]]
Following the decision of the Court of Appeal in *IRC v Deutsche Morgan Grenfell Group plc* [2005] EWCA Civ 78; [2005] S.T.C. 329 such a claim for restitution against public authorities can only be founded on the *ultra vires* nature of the receipt and not on mistake either of law or fact. See paras. 29–083—29–086. The consequence of this is that the claimant cannot rely on the extended limitation period under s.32(1)(c) of the Limitation Act 1980 which applies to claims involving mistake and for which time does not begin to run until the mistake could reasonably have been discovered. See para.28–088. The decision of the Court of Appeal in *Deutsche Morgan Grenfell* is an appeal to the House of Lords.

Mistake of law: principles governing recovery

29–047   *[Add to note 249: page* [1661]]
In *Brennan v Bolt Burdon* [2004] EWCA Civ 1017; [2005] Q.B. 303 Maurice Kay L.J. stated that he was "reluctant to countenance as a mistake of law a situation in which it is generally known or ought to be known that the law in question is about to be reconsidered on appeal."

[Add new note 249a after "compromise" in line 10: page [1661]]
[249a] See *Brennan v Bolt Burdon* [2004] EWCA Civ 1017.

Changes in the law

29–048   *[Add to note 258: page* [1662]]
Following the decision of the House of Lords in *Spectrum Plus Ltd* [2005] UKHL 41; [2005] A.C. 680 the courts may exceptionally make a decision which is prospective in effect only. If a judgment only operates prospectively it will not be possible to construct a retrospective mistake.

[Add to note 261 in line 3, after reference to Derrick v Williams]
See also *Brennan v Bolt Burdon* [2004] EWCA Civ 1017; [2005] Q.B. 303 especially at [50] (Bodey J.).

Personal and proprietary remedies

29–049   *[Note 262: page* [1662]]
Update reference to Virgo to pp.608–612.

(f) *Failure of Consideration*

General principles

[*Add to note 283: page* [1665]]
cf. *Taylor v Motability Finance Ltd* [2004] EWHC 2619 (Comm) at [25] (Cooke J.), where the judge appears to suggest that the test of whether the consideration has failed totally depends on substantial performance by the claimant, whereas the true position is that it typically depends on whether there has been performance by the other party to the contract.

29–054

Reconsideration of the total failure requirement

[*Note 334: page* [1671]]
Update reference to Virgo to pp.323–326.

29–062

Quantum meruit for work done where the contract is terminated by breach

[*Note 365: page* [1674]]
Update reference to Virgo to p.308.

29–067

[*Note 367, line 2: page* [1675]]
Update reference to Virgo to p.66.

Bad bargains

[*Delete paragraph and replace with the following: page* [1675]]
Bad Bargains. Where the innocent party has made a bad bargain the damages for breach may well be less than the reasonable value of the work he has done. In such circumstances the claimant would wish to obtain a restitutionary remedy rather than damages which would be affected by the contractual limit. It has been unclear whether a restitutionary remedy is available to the innocent party in such circumstances or whether any claim for reasonable remuneration will be limited to a rateable proportion of the contract price. The weight of United States authority favours the view that the *quantum meruit* should not be limited in this way,[369] the Privy Council has held that the measure of relief in a *quantum meruit* is the actual value of the work and that the profitability of the contract is irrelevant[370] and the Law Commission has recommended that a *quantum meruit* granted to an innocent party should not be based on the contract price.[371] Until recently the matter does not appear to have been considered explicitly in England.[372] However, in *Taylor v Motability Finance Ltd*[372a] Cooke J. stated that there is no justification for the award of a restitutionary remedy which is in excess of the contractual limit since the award of such a remedy would put the claimant in a better position than he would have been in had the contract been fulfilled which would be unjust. He emphasised that, when determining the *quantum meruit*, regard should be had to the contract both as a guide to the value which the parties put on the service and to ensure justice between the parties.

29–068

369 The most notable instance is *Boomer v Muir* 24 P. 2d 570 (1933), in which $258,000 was awarded as the value of the work done over and above the price paid although only $20,000 was still due under the contract. See also the authorities cited by Palmer, *The Law of Restitution* (1978), Vol.I, pp.389–390.

370 *Slowey v Lodder* [1904] A.C. 442; affirming (1900) N.Z.L.R. 321; *Reynard Construction (ME) Pty Ltd v Minister of Public Works* (1992) 26 N.S.W.L.R. 234; *Newton Woodhouse v Trevor Toys Ltd*, December 20, 1991, CA; *Rover International Ltd v Cannon Film Sales Ltd (No.3)* [1989] 1 W.L.R. 912 (below, para.29–076; see also above, para.29–055) supports this approach although the contract in that case was void.

371 Law Comm. No.121, para.2.52 on which see Birks *op. cit.* pp.262–263. See in general, Birks [1987] L.M.C.L.Q. 421.

372 *Inchbold v Western Neilgherry Coffee, etc.* (1864) 17 C.B. (N.S.) 733 may suggest the use of the contract price as a ceiling but the judgments make no clear distinction between damages and a *quantum meruit*. See also *Burchall v Gowrie & Blockhouse Collieries* [1910] A.C. 614 (contract price used to value services). *cf. De Bernardy v Harding* (1853) 8 Ex. 822; *Prickett v Badger*, above.

372a [2004] EWHC 2619 (Comm) at [26].

Claim of the party in breach

29–070   *[Add to note 384: page [1676]]*

See also *Item Software v Fassihi* [2004] EWCA Civ 1244; [2005] I.C.R. 450, where the Apportionment Act 1870 was applied to enable an employee who had been dismissed to recover a proportionate part of his monthly salary for the period he had actually worked, despite his breach of the contract of employment.

Absence of consideration

29–075   *[Note 412: page [1679]]*

Update reference to Birks, *Unjust Enrichment* to (2nd ed., 2005).

(g) *Ultra vires Receipts by the Revenue and Public Authorities*

Ultra vires demands

29–083   *[Add to note 452: page [1684]]*

See further *Sempra Metals Ltd v Inland Revenue Commissioners* [2005] EWCA Civ 389.

Scope of right

[Replace the first sentence with the following: page [1684]]

29–084   **Scope of right.** The *Woolwich* principle is applicable when money has been paid to a public authority as a result of a mistake of law.454 In *IRC v Deutsche Morgan Grenfell Group plc*454a the Court of Appeal recognised that claims for restitution of tax paid by mistake can only arise by reference to particular statutory provisions, where the demand for payment was lawful,454b or at common law by virtue of the *Woolwich* principle, where the demand was unlawful. In reaching this decision the Court of Appeal drew a distinction between public and private transactions and recognised that, for the recovery of overpaid taxes at least, restitution occurs by virtue of a specific public law regime which is distinct from the private law regime which governs the bulk of the law of unjust enrichment. The practical consequence of this decision is that the claimant cannot rely on the extended limitation period under s.32(1)(c) of the Limitation Act 1980 which applies to claims involving mistake and for which time does not begin to run until the mistake could reasonably have been discovered.[454c]

[454] [1993] A.C. 70, 177, 205.
[454a] [2005] EWCA Civ 78; [2005] S.T.C. 329. See Virgo [2005] B.T.R. 281. This decision is on appeal to the House of Lords. See also *Boake Allen Ltd v Revenue and Customs Commissioners* [2006] EWCA Civ 25; *Autologic Holdings Plc v Inland Revenue Commissioners* [2005] UKHL 54; [2005] 3 W.L.R. 339; *Sempra Metals Ltd (formerly Metallgesellschaft Ltd) v Inland Revenue Commissioners* [2005] EWCA Civ 389; [2006] Q.B. 37.
[454b] See para.29–085.
[454c] See para.28–088.

Defences

[*Delete note 472: page* [1686], *and replace with*]   **29–086**
As amended by the Finance (No.2) Act 2005, s.3. See *Marks and Spencer plc v Commissioners of Customs and Excise* [2005] UKHL 53, where the House of Lords referred the question of the validity of the unjust enrichment defence to the European Court of Justice. For the present operation of the defence see *Baines and Ernst Ltd v Commissioners For Her Majesty's Revenue and Customs* [2006] EWCA Civ 1040; *Weber's Wine World Handels GmbH v Abgabenberufungskommission Wien* (C147/01) [2005] All E.R. (EC) 224.

(h) *Compulsion*

Unlawful or illegitimate compulsion

[*Add new note 482a, on line 7, after 'act': page* [1687]]   **29–088**
See *R v Attorney-General for England and Wales* [2002] UKPC 22.

[*Add to the end of paragraph: page* [1688]]
Similarly, if the claimant cannot offer the defendant substantial counter-restitution.[494a]

[494a] *Halpern v Halpern* [2006] EWHC 1728 (Comm); [2006] 3 All E.R. 1138.

Extortion colore officii

[*Note 511: page* [1690]]   **29–094**
Update reference to Virgo to pp.190, 405–407.

[*Replace second and third sentences, lines 4–6: pages* [1690]-[1691], *with*]
Following the decision of the Court of Appeal in *IRC v Deutsche Morgan Grenfell Group plc*[513] such a fee is probably only recoverable under the principle laid down in *Woolwich Equitable Building Society v IRC*[514] although the point was not expressly considered.

[513] [2005] EWCA Civ 78; [2005] S.T.C. 329.
[514] [1993] A.C. 70; above para.29–083.

Compulsory payments to a third person

29–099 [*Note 538: page* [1693]]
Update reference to Virgo to pp.220–242.

[*Delete final sentence in note 539,* and replace with:]
See also *Niru Battery Manufacturing Co v Milestone Trading Ltd (No.2)* [2004] EWCA Civ 487; [2004] 2 All E.R. (Comm.) 289 where the "principles of recoupment" were applied, although the effect was to recognise a restitutionary claim founded on the ground of legal compulsion.

The defendant must be primarily or ultimately liable to pay the third person

29–102 [*Add to the end of note 551: page* [1695]]
See also *Niru Battery Manufacturing Co v Milestone Trading Ltd (No.2)* [2004] EWCA Civ 487; [2004] 2 All E.R. (Comm.) 289 where restitution was available even though the claimant and the defendant were not subject to a common demand.

Other illustrations concerning land

29–107 [*Add to note 564, line 7 after "employee": page* [1697]]
In *McCarthy v McCarthy and Stone plc* [2006] EWHC 1851 (Ch) tax paid by an employer under the PAYE system in respect of share options could not be deducted from salary because the employee had left the firm. It was held that the tax could be recovered from the former employee on the ground of legal compulsion because the former employee bore the ultimate liability for the tax.

Voluntary payments

29–109 [*Note 569: page* [1698]]
Update reference to Virgo to pp.39–40, 232–234.

The right to contribution

29–121 [*Note 626, page* [1704]]
Update reference to Virgo to pp.234–240.

[*Delete the final sentence in note 631: page* [1705] *and replace with:*]
However, in *Niru Battery Manufacturing Co v Milestone Trading Ltd (No.2)* [2004] EWCA Civ 487; [2004] 2 All E.R. (Comm.) 289 the Court of Appeal suggested that, if it had been necessary to decide the point, the dicta in *Royal Brompton Hospital Trust* concerning the meaning of "damage" were *obiter* and that it was bound by the earlier decision of the Court of Appeal in *Friends' Provident Life Office v Hillier Parker May and Rowden (a firm)* [1997] Q.B. 85, which held that a claim for restitution could be treated as a claim for compensation for the purposes of the 1978 Act, so that claims for breach of contract or tort and for unjust enrichment could be treated as claims for the same damage.

General average contribution

[Note 659: page [1708]]
Update reference to Virgo to p.303.

(i) *Necessity*

Agency of necessity

[Add to note 661: page [1708]]
See *Guildford Borough Council v Hein* [2005] EWCA Civ 979, at [33] (Clarke
L.J.), and [80] (Waller L.J.).

Necessitous intervention on behalf of the defendant

[Note 666: page [1708]]
Update reference to Virgo to p.297.

Salvage

[Note 683: page [1710]]
Update reference to Virgo to pp.301–303.

(j) *Exploitation*

Undue influence

[Add to note 698: page [1712]]
See *Yorkshire Bank plc v Tinsley* [2004] EWCA Civ 816; [2004] 1 W.L.R.
2380.

[Add to note 699: page [1712]]
See *National Commercial Bank (Jamaica) Ltd v Hew* [2002] UKPC 51 at
[43].

3. Restitution for Wrongs

[Add to the end of note 701: page [1712]]
The Proceeds of Crime Act 2002 creates a new statutory framework for the
confiscation of assets of defendants convicted of crime. Under the Act state
officials can apply to the court to recover the proceeds of crime: see *Asset
Recovery Agency v Singh* [2005] EWCA Civ 580; [2005] 1 W.L.R. 3747.

(a) *General Principles*

Disgorgement for wrongs

[Add to note 702: page [1713]]
See *Murad v Al-Saraj* [2005] EWCA Civ 1235 at [108] (Jonathan Parker
L.J.).

(b) *Tort*

Which torts may give rise to a restitutionary claim

29–142   [*Add to note 732: page* [1715]]
; *Horsford v Bird* [2006] UKPC 3. In *Severn Trent Water Ltd v Barnes* [2004] EWCA Civ 570 damages for trespass to land were awarded to compensate the claimant for the loss of opportunity to bargain with the defendant for the price of interfering with the claimant's land rather than to deprive the defendant of any gain made by committing the tort.

The nature of the benefit

29–144   [*Add to note 751, line 2 after "107": page* [1717]]
; *Horsford v Bird* [2006] UKPC 3.

[*Add to note 751, line 6 after reference to Wrotham Park Estate case*]
Severn Trent Water Ltd v Barnes [2004] EWCA Civ 570.

[*Add new footnote 752a to text, line 17 after "lost"*]
752a See *Horsford v Bird* [2006] UKPC 3, where damages for trespass to land were assessed with reference to the benefit obtained by the defendant from the trespass: at [12]. See Virgo (2006) C.L.J. 272 and Edelman (2006) L.Q.R. 391.

Money obtained by fraud or deceit

29–147   [*Note 771: page* [1719]]
Update reference to Virgo to p.474.

(c) *Breach of Contract*

Restitution for breach of contract

29–151   [*Add to note 796, at end: page* [1721]]
Amec Developments v Jury's Hotel Management [2001] E.G.L.R. 81. See also *O'Brien Homes Ltd v Lane* [2004] EWHC 303 (QB) where damages for breach of a collateral contract not to build more than three houses were assessed by reference to what the defendant would have been prepared to pay the claimant to be released from the contractual obligation.

Subsequent developments

29–154   [*Add to text at end of para: page* [1723]]
In *WWF—World Wide Fund for Nature v World Wrestling Federation Enter-tainment Inc*807a the remedy measured by reference to what the parties would have bargained for to vary a settlement was described as a remedy to compensate the claimant for the absence of a bargain. A variety of principles were identified to assess this hypothetical bargain measure, including that the remedy was available as a matter of judicial discretion, compensatory damages must be

inadequate and it was irrelevant that the claimant would not actually have entered into such a bargain.[807b]

[807a] [2006] EWHC 184 (Ch); [2006] F.S.R. 38.
[807b] See Virgo (2006) C.L.J. 272.

(d) *Equitable Wrongdoing*

Types of equitable wrongdoing

[*Add to note 809: page* [1723]]   **29–155**
Crown Dilmun, Dilmun Investments Ltd v Nicholas Sutton, Fulham River [2004] EWHC 52 (Ch); [2004] 1 B.C.L.C. 468; *Re Quarter Master UK Ltd* (Paul Morgan Q.C.) (July 15, 2004); *Murad v Al-Saraj* [2005] EWCA Civ 1235.

[*Add to text at end of the paragraph: page* [1723]]
A fiduciary who has profited from his breach of duty will be liable to account for all the profits made, even if they would have been made had the defendant not breached his fiduciary duty.[810a]

[810a] *Murad v Al-Saraj* [2005] EWCA Civ 1235. See Conaglen (2006) C.L.J. 281.

Receipt of a bribe, secret profit or commission

[*Text to note 817: page* [1724]]   **29–156**
In *Daraydan Holdings Ltd v Solland* [2004] EWHC 622 (Ch); [2005] Ch. 119 Lawrence Collins J. recognised that a defendant who had received a secret commission from the claimants in breach of fiduciary duty held that commission on constructive trust for the claimants, following the decision of the Privy Council in *Attorney General for Hong Kong v Reid* [1994] 1 A.C. 324.

Equitable allowance

[*Add to note 822: page* [1735]]   **29–157**
Murad v Al-Saraj [2005] EWCA Civ 1235.

[*Add to note 823: page* [1725]]
The award of an equitable allowance was declined in *Re Quarter Master UK Ltd* (July 15, 2004) on the ground that directors should not profit from their breach of fiduciary duty and that the directors concerned had not demonstrated special skills or taken unusual risks.

4. PROPRIETARY RESTITUTIONARY CLAIMS

(a) *Establishing proprietary rights*

Identifying a proprietary interest

[*Add to note 833: page* [1726]]   **29–159**
See also *OEM plc v Schneider* [2005] EWHC 1072 (Ch) at [40] (Peter Clarke J.).

Constructive trusts

29–160 *[Note 836: page [1726]]*
Update the following references:
Snell, *Equity* (31st ed., 2004) pp.190–191, 468, Ch.22.
Hanbury and Martin, *Modern Equity* (17 ed., 2005), Ch.12.
Oakley, *Constructive Trusts* (4th ed.).

[Add to note 837, in line 10, after reference to Att.-Gen. (HK) v Reid]
: approved in *Daraydan Holdings Ltd v Solland International Ltd* [2004] EWHC 622 (Ch) (Lawrence Collins J.).

[Add to note 837, line 16, after 107]
Oxley v Hiscock [2004] EWCA Civ 546; [2005] Fam. 211.

[Add to note 838, line 4, after 'void)']
; *Commerzbank AG v IMB Morgan plc* [2004] EWHC 2771 (Ch); [2005] 1 Lloyd's Rep. 298 at [36] (Lawrence Collins J.); *Sinclair Investment Holdings SA v Versailles Trade Finance Ltd* [2005] EWCA Civ 722; [2006] 1 B.C.L.C. 66.

[Add to note 843: page [1727]]
Cobbold v Bakewell Management Ltd [2003] EWHC 2289 (Ch) at [17] (Rimer J.).

(b) *Following and Tracing*

Following and Tracing

29–162 *[Note 848: page [1727]]*
Update the following references:
Snell, *Equity* to (31st ed., 2004) pp.683–690.
Hanbury and Martin, *Modern Equity* to (17th ed., 2005), pp.684–716.

[Note 853: page [1728]]
Shalson v Russo is reported at [2005] Ch. 281.

Tracing in equity

29–164 *[Note 867: page [1729]*
Update the reference to Snell to pp.65–78.

Withdrawals from a mixed fund in a bank account

29–167 *[Add to note 891: page [1731]]*
Commerzbank AG v IMB Morgan plc [2004] EWHC 2771 (Ch); [2005] 1 Lloyd's Rep. 298 at [50] (Lawrence Collins J.).

[Add to note 894]
Campden Hill Ltd v Chakrani [2005] EWHC 911 (Ch).

(c) *Proprietary Restitutionary Claims*

Subrogation

[*Add to note 919: page* [1734]]
Cheltenham and Gloucester plc v Appleyard [2004] EWCA Civ 291.

[*Add to note 920, after reference to Eagle Star Insurance v Karasiewicz*]
Filby v Mortgage Express (No.2) Ltd [2004] EWCA Civ 759 (where, although the claim was characterised as grounded on unjust enrichment, the court treated it as a claim founded on the vindication of property rights).

[*Add to note 919*]
See also *Niru Battery Manufacturing Co v Milestone Trading Ltd (No.2)* [2004] EWCA Civ 487; [2004] 2 All E.R. (Comm.) 289, where the remedy of subrogation was ordered to prevent the defendant's unjust enrichment arising from the discharge of a liability owed by the defendant. It is unclear, however, why this remedy was sought or obtained since the claimant had a direct restitutionary claim to recover the value of the benefit obtained by the defendant and did not need to step into the shoes of any other party to bring such a claim.

[*In note 925, replace reference to Niru Battery Manufacturing Co v Milestone Trading Ltd (No.2): page* [1735] *with*]
[2004] EWCA Civ 487; [2004] 2 All E.R. (Comm.) 289.

[*Add to note 927*]
See also *Cheltenham and Gloucester plc v Appleyard* [2004] EWCA Civ 291 at [32] (Neuberger L.J.).

[*Add to the end of note 930*]
See also *Filby v Mortgage Express (No.2)* [2004] EWCA Civ 759, where a mortgage was a nullity by virtue of a forged signature; and *Cheltenham and Gloucester plc v Appleyard* [2004] EWCA Civ 291, where a mortgage had not been registered.

[*Add to the end of note 932*]
Compare *Cheltenham and Gloucester plc v Appleyard* [2004] EWCA Civ 291, where the claimant's mortgage had not been registered as required by statute but it was subrogated to another mortgage because, *inter alia*, the claimant had not obtained the legal charge for which it had bargained but only an equitable charge and the failure to register was not the result of the claimant's negligence.

[*Add to note 935, after reference to Banque Financière de la Cité case: page* [1736]]
Cheltenham and Gloucester plc v Appleyard [2004] EWCA Civ 291 at [36] (Neuberger L.J.).

[*Add to the text at the end of the paragraph*]
Principles relating to the award of the equitable remedy of subrogation were usefully summarised by the Court of Appeal in *Cheltenham and Gloucester plc v Appleyard*.[936a] These include that a lender cannot claim subrogation if he

obtains all of the security for which he bargained[936b] or where the lender bargained on the basis that no security would be received.[936c]

[936a] [2004] EWCA Civ 291 at [32]–[44] (Neuberger L.J.).
[936b] *Capital Finance Co Ltd v* Stokes [1969] 1 Ch. 261.
[936c] *Paul v Speirway Ltd (in liquidation)* [1976] 1 W.L.R. 220.

Personal restitutionary remedies

29–174 [*Add to note 937, at the end: page* [1736]]
The House of Lords concluded that the case was not concerned with the question of unconscionability but whether directors had authority to sign an agreement: [2004] UKHL 28; [2004] 1 W.L.R. 1846. On the interpretation of the test of unconscionability see also *Crown Dilmun, Dilmun Investments Ltd v Nicholas Sutton, Fulham River* [2004] EWHC 52 (Ch) at [200]; [2004] 1 B.C.L.C. 468 (Peter Smith J.).

[*Add to note 938: page* [1736]]
Now see *Barlow Clowes International Ltd v Eurotrust International Ltd* [2005] UKPC 37; [2006] 1 All E.R. 333 (objective test of dishonesty), followed in *Abou-Rahmah v City Express Bank of Lagos* [2005] EWHC (QB) 2662.

[*Add to note 939: page* [1736]]
See *OEM plc v Schneider* [2005] EWHC 1072 (Ch).

5. DEFENCES

(a) *Estoppel*

Nature of estoppel

29–176 [*Note 944: page* [1737]]
Update reference to Virgo to pp.675–684.

Reliance by payee

29–178 [*Note 965, line 2: page* [1739]]
Update reference to Virgo to pp.681–682.

(b) *Change of Position*

[*Note 968*]
Update reference to Virgo to pp.689–714.

Change of position as a separate defence

29–179 [*Add to note 972: page* [1740]]
Barros Mattos Jnr v McDaniels Ltd [2004] EWHC 1188 (Ch); [2005] 1 W.L.R. 247 at [16] (Laddie J.).

[*Add to the text after note 973 in line 4*]

In *Commerzbank AG v Gareth Price-Jones*[973a] Mummery L.J. recognised that "the decided cases steer a cautious course, aiming to avoid the dangers of a diffuse discretion and the restrictions of rigid rules." Munby J. stated that the defence was "intended to be a broadly stated concept of practical justice" and that "technicality and black letter law are to be avoided."[973b]

[973a] [2003] EWCA Civ 1663; [2004] 1 P. & C.R. D. 15 at [32].
[973b] *ibid.*, at [48]

Illustrations of change of position

[*Add to note 984: page* [1741]]   **29–180**
The Court of Appeal expressly recognised that an anticipatory change of position is a good defence in *Commerzbank AG v Gareth Price-Jones* [2003] EWCA Civ 1663; [2004] 1 P. & C.R. D. 15 at [38] (Mummery L.J.) and [64] (Munby J.).

Link between receipt and specific expenditure unnecessary

[*Note 992, line 2: page* [1742]]   **29–181**
Update reference to Virgo to pp.699–701.

[*Add to end of paragraph*]
In *Commerzbank AG v Gareth Price-Jones*[992a] the Court of Appeal recognised that a non-pecuniary change of position may be sufficient to establish the defence, although, on the facts of the case, the defendant's change of position in staying in his job rather than seeking more lucrative employment elsewhere was not sufficient for it to be inequitable to require him to make restitution since there was no relevant connection between the anticipated receipt of money and the decision to stay in his job and that decision did not have a significant, precise or substantial impact on the defendant.

[992a] [2003] EWCA Civ 1663; [2004] 1 P. & C.R. D. 15, at [39], [40], [43] (Mummery L.J.) and [59] (Munby J.).

Similar defences

[*Note 994: page* [1742]]   **29–182**
Update reference to Virgo to pp.685–689.

Bad faith

[*Add to note 999: page* [1743]]   **29–183**
See Palmer [2005] R.L.R. 53.

[*Notes 1002 and 1002a*]
McDonald v Coys of Kensington is now reported at [2004] 1 W.L.R. 2775.

[*Add to note 1002a*]
See also *Commerzbank AG v Gareth Price-Jones* [2003] EWCA Civ 1663; [2004] 1 P & C.R. D. 15, para.[53] where Munby J. stated that this was an

exercise in judicial evaluation rather than judicial discretion. Cp. Birks (2004) 120 LQR 373, Burrows (2004) C.L.J. 276.

[*Add to text at end of paragraph*]
The defence is not available where a defendant's change of position is tainted since it involves the commission of an illegal act, other than where the illegality can be characterised as *de minimis*.[1004a]

[1004a] *Barros Mattos Jnr v McDaniels Ltd* [2004] EWHC 1188 (Ch); [2004] 3 All E.R. 299.

Relative fault

29–184 [*Add to text at end of paragraph: page* [1744]]
However, in *Commerzbank AG v Gareth Price-Jones*[1011a] Munby J., whilst acknowledging that relative fault was irrelevant, was clearly influenced by the fact that the defendant changed his position as a result of his own negligent mistake, which was not shared or induced by the claimant, in reaching his conclusion that it was not equitable to allow the defendant to rely on the defence.

[1011a] [2003] EWCA Civ 1663; [2004] 1 P & C.R. D. 15. See also *Niru Battery Manufacturing Co v Milestone Trading Ltd (No.2)* [2004] EWCA Civ 487 at [33] (Clarke L.J.).

(c) *Settlement of an Honest Claim*

Settlement of an honest claim

29–186 [*Note 1017: page* [1745]]
Update reference to Virgo to pp.670–671.

Payer has doubts but nevertheless pays

29–187 [*Add to note 1020: page* [1746]]
Cobbold v Bakewell Management Ltd [2003] EWHC 2289 (Ch) at [19] (Rimer J.); *Brennan v Bolt Burdon* [2004] EWCA Civ 1017; [2005] Q.B. 303.

Compromise

29–189 [*Add to text at end of paragraph: page* [1747]]
A compromise may be invalidated by a mistake, but not where the compromise was agreed on the basis of an erroneous assumption about the law.[1030a]

[1030a] *Brennan v Bolt Burdon* [2004] EWCA Civ 1017; [2005] Q.B. 303.

Part Ten

CONFLICT OF LAWS

Chapter 30

CONFLICT OF LAWS

			PARA.
☐	1.	Preliminary considerations	30–001
☐	2.	Common law: the doctrine of the proper law of a contract	30–004
■	3.	The Rome Convention	30–016
☐		(a) In general	30–016
☐		(b) Exclusions	30–030
☐		(c) Choice of law by the parties	30–046
☐		(d) Applicable law in the absence of choice by the parties	30–069
☐		(e) Certain consumer contracts and individual employment contracts	30–089
☐		(f) Voluntary assignment and subrogation	30–115
■	4.	Scope of the applicable law	30–122
☐		(a) Material validity of the contract	30–123
☐		(b) Formal validity of the contract	30–129
☐		(c) Capacity	30–137
☐		(d) Particular issues: Article 10	30–140
☐		(e) Burden of proof, etc	30–164
☐		(f) Illegality and public policy	30–168
☐		(g) Foreign currency obligations	30–176

1. Preliminary considerations

Introduction

[Note 1: page [1757]]   **30–001**
Update the reference to *Dicey and Morris on the Conflict of Laws* to *Dicey, Morris and Collins on the Conflict of Laws* (14th ed., 2006), Chs 10–13.

Sources of the law

[Note 2: page [1758]]   **30–002**
Update the references to *Dicey and Morris* to *Dicey, Morris and Collins*, Chs 14, 15 and 16.

[Add to note 3]
For an extensive discussion of all aspects of the conflict of laws relating to sale of goods, apart from consumer sales, see Fawcett, Harris and Bridge, *International Sale of Goods in the Conflict of Laws* (2005).

[*Add in line 2 of note 4*]
King v Brandywine Reinsurance Co [2005] EWCA Civ 235; [2005] 1 Lloyd's Rep. 655; *Zebrarise Ltd v De Nieffe*; [2004] EWHC 1842 (Comm); [2005] 1 Lloyd's Rep. 154; *Habib Bank Ltd v Central Bank of Sudan* [2006] EWHC 1767 (Comm).

2. COMMON LAW: THE DOCTRINE OF THE PROPER LAW OF A CONTRACT

Statement of the doctrine

30–004   [*Note 9: page* [1759]]
Update the reference to *Dicey and Morris on the Conflict of Laws* to *Dicey, Morris and Collins on the Conflict of Laws* (14th ed., 2006), paras 32–003—32–007.

Limitations on power to choose: common law

30–006   [*Note 26: page* [1761]]
Update the reference to *Dicey and Morris on the Conflict of Laws* to *Dicey, Morris and Collins on the Conflict of Laws* (14th ed., 2006), paras 5–002—5–016, 32–230—32–241.

Statutory limitations

30–007   [*Note 29: page* [1761]]
Update the reference to *Benjamin's Sale of Goods* to 7th ed., 2006, paras 25–090—25–100, 25–159—25–160. Update the reference to *Dicey and Morris on the Conflict of Laws* to *Dicey, Morris and Collins on the Conflict of Laws* (14th ed., 2006), paras 33–033—33–035, 33–126—33–128.

[*Add to note 34: page* [1762]]
Balmoral Group Ltd v Borealis (UK) Ltd [2006] EWHC 1900 (Comm) at [436]–[448].

[*Note 36*]
Consumer Credit Act 1974 is amended by Consumer Credit Act 2006. See below, Ch.38 of this Supplement.

[*Note 36*]
Update the references to *Dicey and Morris on the Conflict of Laws* to *Dicey, Morris and Collins on the Conflict of Laws* (14th ed., 2006), paras 32–132—32–137, 33–036—33–041.

Incorporation by reference

30–008   [*Note 37: page* [1762]]
Update the reference to *Dicey and Morris* to *Dicey, Morris and Collins*, paras 32–088—32–090.

[Add at end of note 38: page [1763]]
Shamil Bank of Bahrain v Beximco Pharmaceuticals Ltd [2004] EWCA Civ
19; [2004] 1 W.L.R. 1784 (a case on the Rome Convention). See also *Halpern v
Halpern* [2006] EWHC 603 (Comm); [2006] 2 Lloyd's Rep. 83 at [74].

Implied choice of law

[Note 45: page [1764]]   30–009
Update the reference to *Dicey and Morris on the Conflict of Laws* to *Dicey,
Morris and Collins on the Conflict of Laws* (14th ed., 2006), Ch.16.

Relevant factors

[Add at end of note 46: page [1764]]   30–010
King v Brandywine Reinsurance Co [2005] EWCA Civ 235; [2005] 1 Lloyd's
Rep. 655.

[Add to note 52: page [1765]]
cf. King v Brandywine Reinsurance Co, above.

[Add at end of note 60: page [1765]]
Zebrarise Ltd v De Nieffe [2004] EWHC 1842 (Comm); [2005] 1 Lloyd's Rep.
154.

No choice of proper law

[Add to note 61: page [1766]]   30–011
Habib Bank Ltd v Central Bank of Sudan [2006] EWHC 1767 (Comm).

[Add in line 5 of note 73: page [1767]]
Habib Bank Ltd v Central Bank of Sudan, above.

Renvoi

[Note 92: page [1768]]   30–015
Update the reference to *Dicey and Morris on the Conflict of Laws* to *Dicey,
Morris and Collins on the Conflict of Laws* (14th ed., 2006), Ch.4.

3. THE ROME CONVENTION

(a) *In General*

[Add to note 94: page [1769]]
Meeusen, Pertegas and Straetmans (eds.), *Enforcement of International Con-
tracts in the European Union* (2004), Fawcett, Harris and Bridge, *International
Sale of Goods in the Conflict of Laws* (2005), Ch.13.

Update the reference to *Dicey and Morris on the Conflict of Laws* to *Dicey,
Morris and Collins on the Conflict of Laws* (14th ed., 2006), Chs 32 and 33.

[*Note 95*]
Update the reference to *Dicey and Morris* to *Dicey, Morris and Collins,* paras 32–009—32–012.

History and purpose

30–016   [*Text at notes 100 and 101: page* [1769]]
Belgium finally ratified the Brussels Protocol on May 5, 2004. The Protocol entered into force on August 1, 2004, internationally, and is brought into force in UK law by SI 2004/3448 as from March 1, 2005. A Convention was signed on April 14, 2005 providing for the accession of the Czech Republic, Estonia, Cyprus, Latvia, Lithuania, Hungary, Malta, Poland, Slovenia and the Slovak Republic to the Rome Convention and the Brussels Protocol, but is not yet in force. A consolidated version of the Convention and Protocol is printed in [2005] O.J. C334/1.

Revision of the Rome Convention

30–018   [*Add to note 108: page* [1770]]
Meeusen, Pertegas and Straetmans (eds.), *Enforcement of International Contracts in the European Union* (2004).

[*Add at beginning of note 113: page* [1771]]
See the Opinion of the European Economic and Social Committee on the Green Paper at [2004] OJ C108/1.

[*Notes 114–116 and text thereto*]
In December 2005 the Commission presented a proposal for the conversion of the Rome Convention into a Regulation of the European Parliament and the Council: see European Commission, *Proposal for a Regulation of the European Parliament and the Council on the law applicable to contractual obligations (Rome I)* COM(2005) 650 final (hereafter Commission Proposal). Information received from the Department of Constitutional Affairs indicates that the United Kingdom will not, at least at present, participate in the adoption and application of the proposed Regulation: and see Recital 18 of the Commission Proposal. Denmark is not participating: *ibid.,* Recital 19.

[*Note 114*]
On the proposed "Rome II", see House of Lords, European Union Committee, *The Rome II Regulation: Report with Evidence,* HL Paper 66 (2004). See also European Parliament legislative resolution on the proposal for a regulation of the European Parliament and of the Council on the law applicable to non-contractual obligations ("Rome II") (P6_TA-PROV (2005)0284, July 6, 2005). Responding to the latter document the Commission issued an Amended Proposal for a European Parliament and Council Regulation on the law applicable to non-contractual obligations ("Rome II") in February, 2006: see COM(2006) 83 final.

Interpretation: European Court of Justice

[*Text at notes 117 and 118: page* [1771]]   **30-019**
As a result of Belgian ratification of the Protocols on May 5, 2004, the
Protocols entered into force on August 1, 2004. For implementation in UK law
with effect from March 1, 2005, see SI 2004/3448. And see entry at para.30–016,
above.

Uniformity of interpretation and application

[*Add to note 128: page* [1773]]   **30-020**
For the latest text of the Declaration see [2005] O.J. C334/1 at 19.

[*Note 129*]
Update the reference to *Dicey and Morris* to *Dicey, Morris and Collins,*
para.32–020.

[*Add to note 131*]
European Bank of Reconstruction & Development v Tekoglu [2004] EWHC
846 (Comm); *Apple Corps Ltd v Apple Computer Inc* [2004] EWHC 768 (Ch);
[2004] I.L.Pr. 597; *Base Metal Trading Ltd v Shamurin* [2004] EWCA Civ 1316;
[2005] 1 W.L.R. 1157; *Opthalmic Innovations International (United Kingdom)
Ltd v Opthalmic Innovations International Inc* [2004] EWHC 2948 (Ch); [2005]
I.L.Pr. 10; *Atlantic Telecom GmbH, Noter*, 2004 S.L.T. 1031.

Law specified need not be of a Contracting State

[*Note 136: page* [1774]]   **30-023**
Update the reference to *Dicey and Morris* to *Dicey, Morris and Collins,*
para.32–027.

Different parts of UK

[*Notes 142 and 143: page* [1775]]   **30-025**
Update the references to *Dicey and Morris* to *Dicey, Morris and Collins,* paras
32–029—32–030.

Mandatory

[*Add to note 145: page* [1775]]   **30-026**
Halpern v Halpern [2006] EWHC 603 (Comm); [2006] 2 Lloyd's Rep. 83 at
[49].

[*Note 145*]
Update the reference to *Dicey and Morris* to *Dicey, Morris and Collins,*
para.32–044. Update the reference to *Benjamin's Sale of Goods* to 7th ed., 2006,
para.25–027.

Incorporation by reference

[*Add at beginning of note 154: page* [1776]]   **30-029**
Shamil Bank of Bahrain v Beximco Pharmaceuticals Ltd [2004] EWCA Civ
19; [2004] 1 W.L.R. 1784; *Halpern v Halpern*, above.

[*Note 154: page* [1776]]

The principle of incorporation by reference only applies where the parties have sufficiently indicated the provisions of a foreign law or international convention which are apt to be incorporated as terms of the contract. A broad reference to principles of Sharia law is insufficient to incorporate such principles: *Shamil Bank of Bahrain v Beximco Pharmaceuticals Ltd,* above. See also *Halpern v Halpern,* above at [73]–[74].

[*Note 155*]

Update the reference to *Dicey and Morris* to *Dicey, Morris and Collins,* para.32–088.

(b) *Exclusions*

Introduction

30–030   [*Add at end of note 156: page* [1777]]

Fawcett, Harris and Bridge, *International Sale of Goods in the Conflict of Laws* (2005), Ch.18.

Update the reference to *Dicey and Morris* to *Dicey, Morris and Collins,* paras 32–031—32–042.

Meaning of "contractual obligations"

30–031   [*Note 157: page* [1777]]

Update the reference to *Benjamin's Sale of Goods* to 7th ed., 2006, paras 25–121—25–155.

[*Add in first line of note 158*]

Base Metal Trading Ltd v Shamurin [2004] EWCA Civ 1316; [2005] 1 W.L.R. 1157. See also *Atlantic Telecom GmbH, Noter,* 2004 S.L.T. 1031.

[*Note 158*]

Update the reference to *Dicey and Morris* to *Dicey, Morris and Collins,* para.32–023.

[*Add at end of note 159*]

Pertegas in Meeusen, Pertegas and Straetmans (eds.) *Enforcement of International Contracts in the European Union* (2004), pp.175–190; Briggs [2003] L.M.C.L.Q. 12.

[*Add at end of note 160: page* [1778]]

As to unilateral contracts, see Maher, 2002 Jur. Rev. 317.

[*Note 160*]

Update the reference to *Dicey and Morris* to *Dicey, Morris and Collins,* para.32–024.

Concurrent liability

[*Add in first line of note 163: page* [1778]]
Base Metal Trading Ltd v Shamurin [2004] EWCA Civ 1316; [2005] 1 W.L.R. 1157. See also *Booth v Phillips* [2004] EWHC 1437 (Comm); [2004] 1 W.L.R. 3292.

30–032

[*Add in line 2 of note 163: page* [1778]]
Fawcett, Harris and Bridge, *International Sale of Goods in the Conflict of Laws* (2005), Ch.20.

[*Note 164: page* [1778]]
Update the reference to *Dicey and Morris* to *Dicey, Morris and Collins*, para.35–066.

Restitution

[*Add to note 165: page* [1778]]
cf. Fawcett, Harris and Bridge, *International Sale of Goods in the Conflict of Laws*, Ch.19.

30–033

[*Add at end of note 170: page* [1779]]
cf. Caterpillar Financial Services Corporation v SNC Passion [2004] EWHC 569 (Comm); [2004] 2 Lloyd's Rep. 99 at [16].

Wills, succession, etc.

[*Add to note 175: page* [1779]]
Bogdan in Meeusen, Pertegas and Straetmans (eds.), *The Enforcement of International Contracts in the European Union* (2004), pp.211–223.

30–036

[*Add to note 177: page* [1779]]
Waldwiese Stiftung v Lewis [2004] EWHC 2589 (Ch).

[*Note 178: page* [1779]]
Update the reference to *Dicey and Morris* to *Dicey, Morris and Collins*, para.32–033.

Bills of exchange, cheques and promissory notes

[*Add to note 185: page* [1780]]
See *Zebrarise Ltd v De Nieffe* [2004] EWHC 1842 (Comm); [2005] 1 Lloyd's Rep. 154.

30–037

Other negotiable instruments

[*Note 187: page* [1780]]
Update the reference to *Dicey and Morris* to *Dicey, Morris and Collins*, paras 33–323—33–332.

33–038

Arbitration agreements and agreements on the choice of court

30–039   [*Add to note 190; page* [1780]]
Morse in Meeusen, Pertegas and Straetmans (eds.), *The Enforcement of International Contracts in the European Union* (2004), pp.191–209. And see *Halpern v Halpern* [2006] EWHC 603 (Comm); [2006] 2 Lloyd's Rep. 83.

[*Note 190: page* [1780]]
Update the reference to *Dicey and Morris* to *Dicey, Morris and Collins,* paras 32–035—32–037.

[*Note 197: page* [1781]]
Update the reference to *Dicey and Morris* to *Dicey, Morris and Collins,* para.32–037.

[*Note 198*]
Update the reference to *Dicey and Morris* to *Dicey, Morris and Collins,* para.12–090.

[*Note 200*]
Update the reference to *Dicey and Morris* to *Dicey, Morris and Collins,* paras 12–097—12–099, 16–017—16–027, 32–035—32–037.

Questions governed by the law of companies, etc.

30–040   [*Add to note 202: page* [1781]]
Benedetelli in Meeusen, Pertegas and Straetmans (eds.), *The Enforcement of International Contracts in the European Union* (2004), pp.225–254.

[*Note 202*]
Update the reference to *Dicey and Morris* to *Dicey, Morris and Collins,* paras 30–025—30–028.

[*Add to note 205: page* [1782]]
Base Metal Trading Ltd v Shamurin [2004] EWCA Civ 1316; [2005] 1 W.L.R. 1157; *Continental Enterprises Ltd v Shandong Zhucheng Foreign Trade Group Co* [2005] EWHC 92 (Comm); *Atlantic Telecom GmbH, Noter,* 2004 S.L.T. 1031.

Power of agent to bind principal, etc

30–041   [*Add to note 207: page* [1782]]
Contrast Commission Proposal, Art.7.

[*Note 212*]
Update the references to *Dicey and Morris* to *Dicey, Morris and Collins,* paras 33–405—33–425, 33–416—33–425.

[*Note 213: page* [1783]]
Update the reference to *Dicey and Morris* to *Dicey, Morris and Collins,* para.33–243.

[*Note 216*]
Update the reference to *Dicey and Morris* to *Dicey, Morris and Collins*, para.33–430.

Trusts

[*Note 218: page* [1783]]   **33–042**
Update the reference to *Dicey and Morris* to *Dicey and Morris*, Ch.29.

Insurance

[*Note 224: page* [1784]]   **30–044**
Contrast Commission Proposal, Arts 3, 4, 22 and Annex 1.

[*Note 224*]
Update the reference to *Dicey and Morris* to *Dicey, Morris and Collins*, Rule 214, paras 33–137 *et seq.*

[*Add to note 226*]
For amendments to UK legislation consequent on Directive 2002/83/ EC of the European Parliament and of the Council of November 5, 2002, see SI 2004/3379.

[*Note 228*]
Update the reference to *Dicey and Morris* to *Dicey, Morris and Collins*, Rules 215 and 216, paras 33–159 *et seq.*

Identification of *situs*

[*Note 232: page* [1785]]   **30–045**
Update the reference to *Dicey and Morris* to *Dicey, Morris and Collins*, paras 33–144—33–146.

(c) *Choice of Law by the Parties*

[*Note 233: page* [1785]]
Update the reference to *Dicey and Morris on the Conflict of Laws* to *Dicey, Morris and Collins on the Conflict of Laws* (14th ed., 2006), paras 32–062—32–103.

The general principle

[*Note 234: page* [1785]]   **30–046**
Update the reference to *Dicey and Morris* to *Dicey, Morris and Collins*, paras 32–062—32–064.

Choice must be of law of a country

[*Add to note 236: page* [1786]]   **30–047**
Shamil Bank of Bahrain v Beximco Pharmaceuticals Ltd [2004] EWCA Civ 19; [2004] 1 W.L.R. 1784; *Halpern v Halpern* [2006] EWHC 603 (Comm); [2006] 2 Lloyd's Rep. 83.

[Add to note 237]

Shamil Bank of Bahrain v Beximco Pharmaceuticals Ltd, above (choice of principles of Sharia law not a choice of the law of a country). See also *Halpern v Halpern,* above (Jewish law). Contrast Commission Proposal, Art. 3(2): "The parties may also choose as the applicable law the principles and rules of the substantive law of contract recognised internationally or in the Community. However, questions relating to matters governed by such principles or rules which are not expressly settled by them shall be governed by the general principles underlying them or, failing such principles, in accordance with the law applicable in the absence of choice under this Regulation." According to the Explanatory Memorandum accompanying the Proposal, this formula excludes the *lex mercatoria* which is not precise enough.

[Note 237]

Update the reference to *Dicey and Morris* to *Dicey, Morris and Collins,* para.32–081.

Law neither pleaded nor proved

30–048   *[Note 240: page [1786]]*

Update the reference to *Dicey and Morris* to *Dicey, Morris and Collins,* Ch. 9.

[Add to note 244]

See also *Global Multimedia International Ltd v ARA Media Services, The Times*, August 1, 2006; *Balmoral Group Ltd v Borealis (UK) Ltd* [2006] EWHC 1900 (Comm) at [427]–[435].

[Note 244]

Update the reference to *Dicey and Morris* to *Dicey, Morris and Collins,* paras 9–011, 32–060, 32–065.

[Add to note 245: page [1786]]

cf. *Shaker v Al-Bedrawi* [2002] EWCA Civ 1452; [2003] Ch. 350.

Meaning of a "choice" of law: express

30–049   *[Note 248: page [1786]]*

Update the reference to *Dicey and Morris* to *Dicey, Morris and Collins,* para.32–078.

[Add to note 249]

The parties may make an express oral agreement as to the applicable law: *Oakley v Ultra Vehicle Design Ltd* [2005] EWHC 872 (Ch).

"Implied choice"

30–050   *[Note 250: page [1786]]*

Update the reference to *Dicey and Morris* to *Dicey, Morris and Collins,* paras 32–091—32–099.

[Add to note 253: page [1787]]]
*Travelers Casualty & Surety Co of Europe v Sun Life Insurance Co of Canada
(UK) Ltd* [2004] EWHC 1704 (Comm); [2004] I.L.Pr. 50.

[Note 254]
Update the reference to *Dicey and Morris* to *Dicey, Morris and Collins,*
para.32–080.

[Add in line 5 of note 256: page [1787]]]
Evialis S.A. v S.I.A.T. [2003] EWHC 863 (Comm); [2003] 2 Lloyd's Rep. 377;
Tonicstar Ltd v American Home Insurance Co [2004] EWHC 1234 (Comm);
[2005] Lloyd's Rep. I.R. 32; *Munchener Ruckversicherungs Gesellschaft v
Commonwealth Insurance Co* [2004] EWHC 914 (Comm); [2004] C.L.C. 665;
Tryg Baltica International (UK) Ltd v Boston Compania De Seguros SA [2004]
EWHC 1186 (Comm); [2005] Lloyd's Rep. I.R. 40.

[Add to note 258: page [1788]]]
Contrast Commission Proposal, Art. 3(1): "If the parties have agreed to confer
jurisdiction on one or more courts or tribunals of a Member State to hear and
determine disputes that have arisen or may arise out of the contract, they shall
also be presumed to have chosen the law of that Member State."

[Add in line 7 of note 260]
European Bank of Reconstruction & Development v Tekoglu [2004] EWHC
846 (Comm).

[Note 261]
Update the reference to *Dicey and Morris* to *Dicey, Morris and Collins,* paras
32–096—32–098.

[Add at end of note 262: page [1788]]]
See also Morse in Meeusen, Pertegas and Straetmans (eds.), *The Enforcement
of International Contracts in the European Union* (2004), pp.191, 204–206.

[Note 262]
Update the reference to *Dicey and Morris* to *Dicey, Morris and Collins,* paras
32–096—32–097.

[Add to note 264]
The Commission Proposal, Art. 3(1) contains no proposal in respect of arbitration clause, in contrast to the position in relation to jurisdiction clauses.

Subsequent conduct

[Note 273: page [1790]]]   **30–052**
Update the reference to *Dicey and Morris* to *Dicey, Morris and Collins,*
para.32–091.

"Implied" choice or "no" choice

[Add in line 2 of note 274: page [1790]]]   **30–053**
Tryg Baltica International (UK) Ltd v Boston Compania De Seguros SA [2004]
EWHC 1186 (Comm); [2005] Lloyd's Rep. I.R. 40; *Cadre SA v Astra Asigurari*

[2005] EWHC 2504 (Comm); *Halpern v Halpern* [2006] EWHC 603 (Comm); [2006] 2 Lloyd's Rep. 83 at [64]–[66]; *Dornoch v Mauritius Union Assurance Co Ltd* [2006] EWCA Civ 389.

Partial choice of law

30–054   [*Note 279: page* [1790]]
Update the reference to *Dicey and Morris* to *Dicey, Morris and Collins*, paras 32–047—32–053.

[*Add in line 7 of note 283: page* [1790]]
Travelers Casualty & Surety Co v Sun Life Assurance Co of Canada (UK) Ltd [2004] EWHC 1704 (Comm); [2004] I.L.Pr. 50.

Changing the applicable law

30–056   [*Note 290: page* [1791]]
Update the reference to *Dicey and Morris* to *Dicey, Morris and Collins*, paras 32–084—32–085.

[*Note 298: page* [1792]]
Update the reference to *Dicey and Morris* to *Dicey, Morris and Collins*, paras 32–086—32–087.

Validity of choice of law

30–057   [*Note 301: page* [1792]]
Update the reference to *Dicey and Morris* to *Dicey, Morris and Collins*, para.32–103.

Mandatory rules

30–059   [*Add to note 306: page* [1793]]
Chong (2006) 2 Journal of Private International Law 27. See Commission Proposal, Art. 3(4) is virtually identical. Article 3(5) of the Proposal provides that where the parties choose the law of a non-Member State, that choice shall be without prejudice to the application of such mandatory rules of Community law as are applicable to the case.

[*Note 306*]
Update the reference to *Dicey and Morris* to *Dicey, Morris and Collins*, paras 32–070—32–073, 32–132—32–134.

[*Add to note 307*]
For a case where the application of Art.3(3) of the Rome Convention was considered but rejected, see *Caterpillar Financial Services Corporation v SNC Passion* [2004] EWHC 569 (Comm); [2004] 2 Lloyd's Rep. 99.

Connection with one country only

30–060   [*Note 311: page* [1794]]
Update the reference to *Dicey and Morris* to *Dicey, Morris and Collins*, para.32–071.

"Mandatory rules"

[*Note 318: page* [1795]]
Update the reference to *Dicey and Morris* to *Dicey, Morris and Collins,* paras 32–132—32–143.

[*Add to note 320*]
See Commission Proposal, Art. 8(3). Article 8(1) of the Proposal provides a definition of mandatory rules as "rules the respect for which is regarded as crucial by a country for safeguarding its political, social or economic organisation to such an extent that they are applicable to any situation falling within their scope, irrespective of the law otherwise applicable to the contract under this Regulation." *cf.* Case C-396/96 *Arblade* and Case C-376/96 *Leloup* [1999] E.C.R. I-8453. For criticism of Art. 8(3), see Financial Markets Law Committee, *Issue 121 European Commission Final Proposal for a Regulation on the Law Applicable to Contractual Obligations ("Rome I")* (April, 2006), paras 3.1–3.5, available at *http://www.fmlc.org*; Dutson (2006) 122 L.Q.R. 374. *cf.* Chong (2006) 2 Journal of Private International Law 27.

[*Note 320*]
Update the reference to *Dicey and Morris* to *Dicey, Morris and Collins,* para.32–141.

[*Note 321*]
Update the reference to *Dicey and Morris* to *Dicey, Morris and Collins,* para.32–073.

When is a rule mandatory?

[*Note 322: page* [1796]]
Directive 2002/65/EC of the European Parliament and of the Council of September 23, 2002 concerning the distance marketing of consumer financial services is implemented in the UK in Financial Services (Distance Marketing) Regulations 2004 (SI 2004/2095). The anti-avoidance provision is contained in reg.16(3). Consumer Protection (Distance Selling) Regulations 2000 (SI 2000/2334), are amended by SI 2005/689.

Mandatory rules of English law

[*Add to note 326: page* [1796]]
cf. Primetrade AG v Ythan Ltd [2005] EWHC 2399 (Comm); [2006] 1 All E.R. 367 at [14]–[15] (Carriage of Goods by Sea Act 1992 is not mandatory and only applies if the law applicable to the contract is English law).

[*Note 326*]
Update the reference to *Dicey and Morris* to *Dicey, Morris and Collins,* para.32–134.

Mandatory rules of the law of the forum

30–066   *[Add to note 329: page* [1797]]
cf. Commission Proposal, Art. 8(2) which contains slightly different wording.

[Note 329]
Update the reference to *Dicey and Morris* to *Dicey, Morris and Collins*, paras 32–135—32–137.

[Add in line 11 of note 330]
Balmoral Group Ltd v Borealis (UK) Ltd [2006] EWHC 1900 (Comm).

[Note 333: page [1798]]
Update the reference to *Dicey and Morris* to *Dicey Morris and Collins*, paras 1–053—1–061.

Public policy

30–067   *[Add to note 336: page* [1798]]
Chong (2006) 2 Journal of Private International Law 27.

[Note 336]
Update the reference to *Dicey and Morris* to *Dicey, Morris and Collins*, paras 32–230—32–241.

[Add to note 340]
See also *Re COLT Telecom Group plc* [2002] EWHC 2815 (Ch); [2003] B.P.I.R. 324; *Tekron Resources Ltd v Guinea Investment Co Ltd* [2003] EWHC 2577 (Comm); [2004] 2 Lloyd's Rep. 26.

"Community public policy"

30–068   *[Add to note 341: page* [1798]]
Peruzzetto in Meeusen, Pertegas and Straetmans (eds.), *The Enforcement of International Contracts in the European Union* (2004), pp.343–361; Meidanis (2005) 30 E.L.Rev. 95.

(d) *Applicable Law in the Absence of Choice by the Parties*

[Add in line 4 of note 346: page [1799]]
Hill (2004) 53 I.C.L.Q. 325; Atrill (2004) 53 I.C.L.Q. 549.

[Note 346]
Update the reference to *Dicey and Morris on the Conflict of Laws* to *Dicey, Morris and Collins on the Conflict of Laws* (14th ed., 2006), paras 32–108—32–128,   33–113—33–120,   33–150—33–155,   33–217—33–220, 33–229—33–239.

General principle

30–069   *[Add to note 347: page* [1799]]
The law applicable under Art. 4 must be the law of a country and cannot be a non-national body of rules: *Halpern v Halpern* [2006] EWHC 603 (Comm);

[2006] 2 Lloyd's Rep. 83. Article 4 of the Commission Proposal abandons the general principle of application of the law of the country with which the contract is most closely connected. See entry at para.30–070, below.

[Add in last line of note 351]
Travelers Casualty & Surety Co of Europe Ltd v Sun Life Assurance Co of Canada (UK) Ltd [2004] EWHC 1704 (Comm); [2004] I.L.Pr. 50; *CGU International Insurance plc v Astrazeneca Insurance Co Ltd* [2005] EWHC 2755 (Comm); [2006] 1 C.L.C. 162.

Presumptions

[Notes 353–357 and text thereto: page [1800]]   **30–070**
In the absence of a choice of law the Commission Proposal, Art. 4(1) contains fixed rules for determining the applicable law in relation to certain specified contracts such as sale, provision of services, contracts of carriage, contracts relating to immovable property, contracts relating to intellectual property rights, franchise rights and distribution contracts. These rules point for the most part, to the habitual residence of the characteristic performer. The rules cannot be displaced in favour of a more closely connected law. Contracts not so specified are governed by the law of the country in which the party who is to perform the service characterising the contract has his habitual residence. If the characteristic performance cannot be determined, the contract is to be governed by the law of the country with which the contract is most closely connected. For criticism, see Financial Markets Law Committee, above, entry at para.30–061, paras 6.1–6.16; Dutson (2006) 122 L.Q.R. 374.

Characteristic performance

[Add to note 358: page [1801]]   **30–072**
Hill (2004) 53 I.C.L.Q. 325; Atrill (2004) 53 I.C.L.Q. 549.

[Note 358]
Update the reference to *Dicey and Morris* to *Dicey, Morris and Collins,* paras 32–113—32–117.

[Note 360]
Update the reference to *Dicey and Morris* to *Dicey, Morris and Collins,* para.32–124.

Performance for which payment due "characteristic"

[Add to note 364: page [1801]]   **30–073**
See Maher, 2002 Jur. Rev. 317.

[Add to note 365: page [1801]]
See *Waldweise Stiftung v Lewis* [2004] EWHC 2589 (Ch) (gift); *Opthalmic Innovations International (United Kingdom) Ltd v Opthalmic Innovations International Inc* [2004] EWHC 2948 (Ch); [2005] I.L.Pr. 10 (indemnification agreement); *Ark Therapeutics plc v True North Capital Ltd* [2005] EWHC 1585

(Comm); [2006] 1 All E.R. (Comm.) 138 (letter of intent). *cf. Halpern v Halpern* [2006] EWHC 603 (Comm); [2006] 2 Lloyd's Rep. 83 (compromise agreement). See Maher (2002) Jur. Rev. 317.

"Characteristic" performance not determinable

30–074   [*Add to note 367: page* [1802]]
Apple Corps Ltd v Apple Computer Inc [2004] EWHC 768 (Ch); [2004] I.L.Pr. 597 (characteristic performance of an agreement between two companies regulating the use of their respective trade marks cannot be determined).

[*Note 370*]
Update the reference to *Dicey and Morris* to *Dicey, Morris and Collins,* para.32–117.

Specific applications

30–075   [*Note 374: page* [1802]]
Update the reference to *Dicey and Morris* to *Dicey, Morris and Collins,* para.32–116. Update the reference to *Benjamin's Sale of Goods* to 7th ed., 2006, para.25–060.

[*Note 377: page* [1803]]
Update the reference to *Dicey and Morris* to *Dicey, Morris and Collins,* para.33–114.

[*Note 379*]
Update the reference to *Dicey and Morris* to *Dicey, Morris and Collins,* para.33–150.

[*Add to note 380*]
Tonicstar Ltd v American Home Assurance Co [2004] EWHC 1234 (Comm); [2005] Lloyd's Rep. I.R. 32; *Dornoch Ltd v Mauritius Union Assurance Co Ltd* [2006] EWCA Civ 389.

[*Note 380*]
Update the references to *Dicey and Morris* to *Dicey, Morris and Collins,* paras 33–305, 33–298—33–320.

[*Add in line 5 of note 386: page* [1803]]
PT Pan Indonesia Bank Ltd Tbk v Marconi Communications International Ltd [2005] EWCA Civ 235; [2005] 2 All E.R. (Comm.) 325.

[*Add in line 8 of note 386*]
Habib Bank Ltd v Central Bank of Sudan [2006] EWHC 1767 (Comm).

[*Add in first line of note 387*]
PT Pan Indonesia Bank Ltd Tbk v Marconi Communications International Ltd, above.

[*Add to note 389: page* [1804]]
Atlantic Telecom GmbH, Noter, 2004 S.L.T. 1031.

[Note 390: page [1804]]
Update the reference to *Dicey and Morris* to *Dicey, Morris and Collins,* para.32–117.

[Note 391]
Update the reference to *Dicey and Morris* to *Dicey, Morris and Collins,* para.33–140.

[Note 394]
Update the reference to *Dicey and Morris* to *Dicey, Morris and Collins,* para.33–115.

[Note 396]
Update the reference to *Dicey and Morris* to *Dicey, Morris and Collins,* para.33–228.

[Note 397]
Update the reference to *Dicey and Morris* to *Dicey, Morris and Collins,* para.33–454.

[Add in text at end of paragraph: page [1804]]
In a contract of gift, the characteristic performance is that of the donor[398a]; in a contract to provide an indemnity, the characteristic performance is that of the party who is to provide the indemnity;[398b] in a compromise agreement, the characteristic performance is that of the party required to transfer assets.[398c]

[398a] *Waldwiese Stiftung v Lewis* [2004] EWHC 2589 (Ch).
[398b] *Opthalmic Innovations International (United Kingdom) Ltd v Opthalmic Innovations International Inc* [2004] EWHC 2948 (Ch); [2005] I.L.Pr. 10.
[398c] *Halpern v Halpern* [2006] EWHC 603 (Comm); [2006] 2 Lloyd's Rep. 83. See also *Ark Therapeutics plc v True North Capital Ltd* [2005] EWHC 1585 (Comm); [2006] 1 All E.R. (Comm.) 138 (letter of intent).

Applicable law

[Note 401: page [1805]]   **30–076**
Update the reference to *Dicey and Morris* to *Dicey, Morris and Collins,* para.32–120.

Habitual residence

[Note 402: page [1805]]   **30–077**
Update the reference to *Dicey and Morris* to *Dicey, Morris and Collins,* paras 6–125—6–130.

[Add in line 2 of note 403]
Mark v Mark [2005] UKHL 42; [2006] 1 A.C. 98.

[Add in line 4 of note 404]
Mark v Mark, above.

[Note 404]
Update the reference to *Dicey and Morris* to *Dicey, Morris and Collins,* para.6–129.

[*Add in first line of note 406: page* [1806]]
Mark v Mark, above.

Central administration

30–078   [*Note 409: page* [1806]]
Update the reference to *Dicey and Morris* to *Dicey, Morris and Collins,* paras
30–005—30–006.

Principal place of business and place of business

30–079   [*Note 410: page* [1806]]
Update the reference to *Dicey and Morris* to *Dicey, Morris and Collins,* paras
11–115—11–125.

Immovables

30–080   [*Note 414: page* [1807]]
Update the reference to *Dicey and Morris* to *Dicey, Morris and Collins,* paras
33–224—33–247.

[*Add to note 414*]
cf. Commission Proposal, Arts 4(1)(d),(e), 5(3)(c).

[*Add in line 4 of note 417: page* [1807]]
Case C-518/99 *Gaillard v Chekili* [2001] E.C.R. I-2771.

[*Note 417*]
Update the reference to *Dicey and Morris* to *Dicey, Morris and Collins,* paras
23–062—23–074.

Types of contracts for immovables

30–082   [*Add in line 11 of note 421; page* [1808]]
See Case C-73/04 *Klein v Rhodos Management Ltd* [2005] E.C.R. I-867.

[*Add in line 15 of note 421*]
See *Office of Fair Trading v Lloyd's TSB Bank plc* [2006] EWCA Civ 268;
[2006] 1 All E.R. (Comm.) 629.

[*Note 421*]
Update the reference to *Dicey and Morris* to *Dicey, Morris and Collins,* paras
33–233, 33–244—33–247.

[*Note 422*]
Update the reference to *Dicey and Morris* to *Dicey, Morris and Collins,*
para.33–233.

Contracts for the carriage of goods

30–083   [*Note 423*]
Update the reference to *Dicey and Morris* to *Dicey Morris and Collins,* paras
33–264—33–292.

[*Add to note 424*]
cf. Commission Proposal, Art. 4(1)(c).

[*Note 425*]
Update the references to *Dicey and Morris* to *Dicey, Morris and Collins,* paras 33–271—33–272.

[*Note 426: page* [1809]]
Update the reference to *Dicey and Morris* to *Dicey, Morris and Collins,* para.33–273.

[*Note 428*]
Update the references to *Dicey and Morris* to *Dicey, Morris and Collins,* paras 33–274—33–275.

[*Note 429*]
Update the reference to *Dicey and Morris* to *Dicey, Morris and Collins,* para.33–252.

"Other contracts" involving carriage of goods

[*Notes 431, 432, 433*]   **30–084**
Update the references to *Dicey and Morris* to *Dicey, Morris and Collins,* paras 33–265—33–267.

Characteristic performance cannot be determined

[*Add to notes 436 and 437: page* [1810]]   **30–087**
Apple Corps Ltd v Apple Computer Inc [2004] EWHC 768 (Ch); [2004] I.L.Pr. 597.

Rebutting the presumptions

[*Add to note 438: page* [1810]]   **30–088**
Hill (2004) 53 I.C.L.Q. 325; Atrill (2004) 53 I.C.L.Q. 549.

[*Note 438*]
Update the reference to *Dicey and Morris* to *Dicey, Morris and Collins,* paras 32–124—32–128, 33–117—33–120, 33–154—33–155, 33–220, 33–235—33–236, 33–277—33–278, 33–303—33–317, 33–412, 33–454.

[*Add in line 4 of note 447: page* [1811]]
Waldwiese Stiftung v Lewis [2004] EWHC 2589 (Ch); *Opthalmic Innovations International (United Kingdom) Ltd v Opthalmic Innovations International Inc* [2004] EWHC 2948 (Ch); [2005] I.L.Pr. 10.

[*Note 449*]
Update the reference to *Dicey and Morris* to *Dicey, Morris and Collins,* para.33–125.

[Note 454]
Update the references to *Dicey and Morris* to *Dicey, Morris and Collins,* paras 33–235—33–236, 33–277—33–278.

[Note 455]
Update the reference to *Dicey and Morris* to *Dicey, Morris and Collins,* para.32–127.

[Add to note 456: page [1812]*]*
cf. PT Pan Indonesia Bank Ltd Tbk v Marconi Communications International Ltd [2005] EWCA Civ 422; [2005] 2 All E.R. (Comm.) 325 (letter of credit issued by Indonesian bank which became insolvent, confirmed by another Indonesian bank with no place of business in England, the credit to be advised through an English bank which did not confirm credit, documents to be presented in England and payment to be made there, led to conclusion that although presumptively the contract between the beneficiary and the confirming bank was governed by Indonesian law, pursuant to Art.4(2) of the Rome Convention, the above connections with England justified disregarding the presumption, pursuant to Art.4(5). There appear to be no circumstances justifying displacement of the presumption in relation to the contract between the issuing bank and the confirming bank: *ibid.* at [67]).

[Add at end of note 456]
Habib Bank Ltd v Central Bank of Sudan [2006] EWHC 1767 (Comm).

[Add to note 459]
See also *PT Pan Indonesia Bank Ltd Tbk v Marconi Communications International Ltd,* above.

[Note 460]
Update the reference to *Benjamin's Sale of Goods* to 7th ed., 2006, para.25–066.

(e) *Certain Consumer Contracts and Individual Employment Contracts*

"Certain consumer contracts"

30–090   *[Add in line 5 of note 462: page* [1812]*]]*
Basedow in Meeusen, Pertegas and Straetmans (eds.), *The Enforcement of International Contracts in the European Union* (2004), pp.269–288; Straetmans *ibid.* pp.295–322.

[Add at end of note 462]
cf. Commission Proposal, Art.5.

[Note 462]
Update the reference to *Dicey and Morris on the Conflict of Laws* to *Dicey, Morris and Collins on the Conflict of Laws* (14th ed., 2006), paras 33–002—33–054.

[Note 463: page [1813]*]]*
Update the reference to *Dicey and Morris* to *Dicey Morris and Collins,* paras 33–004—33–007.

[Add in line 6 of note 465: page [1813]]
Case C-27/02 *Engler v Janus Versand GmbH* [2005] E.C.R. I-481; [2005]
I.L.Pr. 83; Case C-464/01 *Gruber v Bay Wa AG* [2005] E.C.R. I-439; [2006] Q.B.
204.

Choice of law by the parties

[Note 472: page [1814]]   **30–091**
Update the reference to *Dicey and Morris* to *Dicey, Morris and Collins,* paras
33–009—33–113.

Application to contract concluded "on-line"

[Note 486: page [1815]]   **30–092**
Update the reference to *Benjamin's Sale of Goods* to 7th ed., 2006, paras
25–049—25–053.

[Note 486]
Update the reference to *Dicey and Morris* to *Dicey, Morris and Collins,* paras
33–017—33–023.

Article 5(2): first condition: advertising

[Notes 491 and 492: page [1816]]   **30–094**
Update the references to *Dicey and Morris* to *Dicey, Morris and Collins,*
para.33–019.

[Add to note 495: page [1817]]
cf. *King v Lewis* [2004] EWCA Civ 1329; [2005] I.L.Pr. 185.

Mandatory rules

[Add to note 508: page [1819]]   **30–099**
cf. *Office of Fair Trading v Lloyds TSB Bank plc* [2006] EWCA Civ 268;
[2006] 1 All E.R. (Comm.) 629.

[Note 508]
Consumer Credit Act 1974 is amended by Consumer Credit Act 2006. See
below, Ch.38 of this Supplement.

[Note 508]
Update the reference to *Dicey and Morris* to *Dicey, Morris and Collins,* paras
33–033—33–042.

[Note 509]
Update the reference to *Dicey and Morris* to *Dicey, Morris and Collins,*
para.33–014.

EC consumer protection legislation

[Note 511: page [1820]]   **30–100**
Update the reference to *Dicey and Morris* to *Dicey, Morris and Collins,* paras
33–043—33–054.

Update the reference to *Benjamin's Sale of Goods* to 7th ed., 2006, paras 25–101—25–118.

[*Note 512*]
Stop Now Orders (E.C. Directive) Regulations 2001 (SI 2001/1422) are repealed and replaced by Enterprise Act 2002, Pt 8. See also SI 2003/1374; SI 2003/1593.

[*Add in line 5 of note 512*]
cf. Case C-350/03 *Schulte v Deutsche Bausparkasse Badenia AG* [2005] E.C.R. I-9215.

[*Add to note 512*]
Directive of the European Parliament and of the Council of September 23, 2002, concerning the distance marketing of consumer financial services is implemented in the UK by Financial Services (Distance Marketing) Regulations 2004 (SI 2004/2095). The anti-avoidance provision is contained in reg.16(3).

[*Add to note 514*]
In Case C-70/03 *Commission of the European Communities v Kingdom of Spain* the European Court found that Spain had not properly transposed the anti-avoidance provision in the Directive into national law.

[*Note 514*]
Update the reference to *Benjamin's Sale of Goods* to 7th ed., 2006, paras 25–101—25–106.

[*Add to note 515: page* [1820]]
SI 2000/2334 is amended by SI 2005/689.

[*Note 522: page* [1821]]
Update the reference to *Benjamin's sale of Goods* to 7th ed., 2006, paras 25–111—25–116. See Law Commission, *Unfair Terms in Contracts,* Law Com. No. 292 (2005), paras 7.4–7.6.

Individual employment contracts

30–105   [*Add in line 4 of note 526: page* [1822]]
Polak in Meeusen, Pertegas and Straetmans (eds.), *The Enforcement of International Contracts in the European Union* (2004), pp.323–342.

[*Add at end of note 526*]
cf. Commission Proposal, Art.6.

[*Note 526*]
Update the reference to *Dicey and Morris on the Conflict of Laws* to *Dicey, Morris and Collins on the Conflict of Laws* (14th ed., 2006), paras 33–059—33–102.

"Employment": autonomous meaning

30–107   [*Note 537: page* [1823]]
Update the reference to *Dicey and Morris* to *Dicey, Morris and Collins,* paras 33–063—33–066.

[Note 538: page [1823]]
Base Metal Trading Ltd v Shamurin [2003] EWHC 2419 (Comm) is now reported at [2004] 1 All E.R. (Comm.) 159, rvsd. in part, but not on this point, [2004] EWCA Civ 1316; [2005] 1 W.L.R. 1157.

[Add at end of note 538]
See also *WPP Holdings Italy SRL v Benatti* [2006] EWHC 1641 (Comm). See generally Cavalier and Upex (2006) 55 I.C.L.Q. 587.

Alternative "classification" approach

[Note 539: page [1824]]   **30–108**
Update the reference to *Dicey and Morris* to *Dicey, Morris and Collins,* para.33–065.

Choice of law by the parties and mandatory rules

[Note 541: page [1824]]   **30–109**
See previous entry.

[Note 548: page [1825]]
In *Serco Ltd v Lawson* [2006] UKHL 3; [2006] I.C.R. 250 the House of Lords had to decide on the proper reach of the provisions of the Employment Rights Act 1996, which provide for the right not to be unfairly dismissed, in the light of the repeal of s.196(2) and (3) of that Act. It was held that this depended on the construction of the relevant statutory provisions in the light of the circumstances of the particular case. Primarily, the provisions apply where the employee is working in Great Britain at the time of the dismissal, as opposed to what was contemplated as the place of work at the time of the conclusion of the contract of employment. Where, however, the employee was a peripatetic worker working in several countries, such as an airline pilot, the work would be performed in Great Britain if the employee's base was in Great Britain at the time of the dismissal. As regards expatriate employees working overseas, the relevant provisions apply if a strong connection between the employment and Great Britain at the relevant time can be established. Such may be the case where an employee is posted abroad by a British employer for the purposes of a business carried on in Great Britain, or where an expatriate employee is working in what is in effect an extra-territorial British enclave in a foreign country (*e.g.* a military base).

[Note 548: page [1825]]
Update the reference to *Dicey and Morris* to *Dicey, Morris and Collins,* paras 33–089—33–095.

[Note 549]
Sex Discrimination Act 1975 is amended by Equality Act 2006. Race Relations Act 1976 is amended by Race Relations Act 1976 (Amendment) Regulations 2003 (SI 2003/1626), reg.11, inserting a new s.8(1A) into the principal Act which is further amended by Equality Act 2006. Disability Discrimination Act 1995 is amended by Disability Discrimination Act 1995 (Amendment) Regulations 2003 (SI 2003/1673), inserting a new s.68(1) and (2)–(4A) into the 1995

Act which is further amended by Disability Discrimination Act 2005 and Equality Act 2006.

[Add in line 4 of note 549: page [1825]]
Employment Equality (Religion or Belief) Regulations 2003 (SI 2003/1660, as amended by SI 2004/437 and SI 2004/2520), reg.9; Employment Equality (Sexual Orientation) Regulations 2003 (SI 2003/1661, as amended by SI 2004/2519), reg.9; Equality Act 2006. For consideration of the territorial reach of the Race Relations Act 1976, which may well apply to the other legislation cited in this note, see *Saggar v Ministry of Defence* [2005] EWCA Civ 413; [2005] I.C.R. 1073.

Chosen law more favourable

30–110   *[Note 554: page* [1826]]
Update the reference to *Dicey and Morris* to *Dicey, Morris and Collins,* para.33–071.

Applicable law in absence of choice

30–112   *[Note 558: page* [1826]]
Update the reference to *Dicey and Morris* to *Dicey, Morris and Collins,* paras 33–075—33–076.

[Add at beginning of note 559]
See *Booth v Phillips* [2004] EWHC 1437 (Comm); [2004] 1 W.L.R. 3292.

[Note 559]
Update the reference to *Dicey and Morris* to *Dicey, Morris and Collins,* para.33–077.

[Add to note 560]
Booth v Phillips, above.

30–113   *[Add to note 561: page* [1827]]
cf. Booth v Phillips, above.

[Note 561]
Update the reference to *Dicey and Morris* to *Dicey, Morris and Collins,* para.33–078.

[Note 563]
Base Metal Trading Ltd v Shamurin [2003] EWHC 2419 (Comm) is now reported at [2004] 1 All E.R. (Comm.) 159; rvsd. in part, but not on this point, [2004] EWCA Civ 1316; [2005] 1 W.L.R. 1157.

Contract and tort

30–114   *[Note 564: page* [1827]]
See previous entry.

[*Add in line 4 of note 564: page* [1827]]
Booth v Phillips [2004] EWHC 1437 (Comm); [2004] 1 W.L.R. 3292.

[*Note 565*]
Update the reference to *Dicey and Morris* to *Dicey, Morris and Collins*, paras 32–025—32–026, 33–083—33–085.

[*Note 566*]
Update the reference to *Dicey and Morris* to *Dicey, Morris and Collins*, Ch. 35.

[*Note 569*]
Update the reference to *Dicey and Morris* to *Dicey, Morris and Collins*, paras 32–025—32–026, 33–083—33–085.

(f) *Voluntary Assignments and Subrogation*

Voluntary assignments

[*Add at the end of note 570: page* [1828]]   **30–115**
Kieninger in Meeusen, Pertegas and Stratmans (eds.), *The Enforcement of International Contracts in the European Union* (2004), pp.363–387. *cf.* Commission Proposal, Arts 12, 13, and 14.

[*Note 570*]
Update the references to *Dicey and Morris* (13th ed., 2000) to *Dicey, Morris and Collins*, paras 24–079—24–085, 24–051—24–073.

Assignor and assignee

[*Add to note 573: page* [1828]]   **30–116**
Waldwiese Stiftung v Lewis [2004] EWHC 2589 (Ch).

Assignability, etc.

[*Add at beginning of note 576: page* [1829]]   **30–117**
See *Waldwiese Stiftung v Lewis* [2004] EWHC 2589 (Ch). See also *Peer International Corp v Termidor Music Publishers Ltd* [2003] EWCA Civ 1156; [2004] Ch. 212.

[*Note 578*]
Update the reference to *Dicey and Morris* to *Dicey, Morris and Collins*, para.25–045.

Contract and property

[*Note 579: page* [1829]]   **30–118**
Update the reference to *Dicey and Morris* to *Dicey Morris and Collins*, para.24–064.

[*Note 587: page* [1830]]
Update the reference to *Dicey and Morris* to *Dicey, Morris and Collins,*
para.24–062.

Subrogation

30–119   [*Add to note 588: page* [1830]]
cf. Commission Proposal, Arts 13, 14 and 15.

[*Note 588*]
Update the reference to *Dicey and Morris* to *Dicey, Morris and Collins,*
para.32–211.

[*Add to note 591*]
West Tankers Inc v RAS Riunione Adriatica Di Sicurta [2005] EWHC 454
(Comm); [2005] 1 C.L.C. 347.

Applicable law

30–120   [*Text after note 594: page* [1831]]
See *West Tankers Inc v RAS Riunione Adriatica Di Sicurta,* above.

4. SCOPE OF THE APPLICABLE LAW

(a) *Material Validity of the Contract*

[*Note 601: page* [1832]]
Update the reference to *Dicey and Morris on the Conflict of Laws* to *Dicey,*
Morris and Collins on the Conflict of Laws (14th ed., 2006), paras
32–155—32–173.

Formation of the contract

30–125   [*Add to note 613: page* [1833]]
Horn Linie GmbH & Co v Panamericana Formas E Impresos [2006] EWHC
373 (Comm); [2006] 2 Lloyd's Rep. 44.

[*Add to notes 619 and 620: page* [1834]]
Horn Linie GmbH & Co v Panamericana Formas E Impresos, above.

[*Text after note 621*]
The same views were expressed in *Horn Linie GmbH & Co v Panamericana*
Formas E Impresos, above, in relation to consent to a jurisdiction clause and
choice of law clause.

Validity of consent

30–127   [*Add in line 4 of note 623 page* [1834]]
Halpern v Halpern [2006] EWHC 603 (Comm); [2006] 2 Lloyd's Rep. 83.

[*Note 623*]
Update the reference to *Dicey and Morris* to *Dicey, Morris and Collins,*
para.32–167.

[*Add at beginning of note 624*]
Halpern v Halpern, above.

[*Add in line 2 of note 624*]
See also *Ark Therapeutics Plc v True North Capital Ltd* [2005] EWHC 1585
(Comm); [2006] 1 All E.R. (Comm.) 138.

[*Note 624*]
Update the reference to *Dicey and Morris* to *Dicey, Morris and Collins,* paras
32–166—32–168.

Validity of contract or terms

[*Note 626: page* [1835]]   **30–128**
As to wagering contracts, see now Gambling Act 2005, ss.334 and 335; *Dicey
Morris and Collins,* paras 33–450—33–453.

[*Add to note 628*]
See also *Ark Therapeutics Plc v True North Capital Ltd,* above.

(b) *Formal Validity of the Contract*

[*Note 631: page* [1835]]
Update the reference to *Dicey and Morris on the Conflict of Laws* to *Dicey
Morris and Collins on the Conflict of Laws* (14th ed., 2006), paras
32–176—32–186.

Introduction

[*Add to note 635: page* [1835]]   **30–129**
cf. Commission Proposal, Art.10.

Meaning of formal validity

[*Note 642: page* [1836]]   **30–130**
Update the reference to *Dicey and Morris on the Conflict of Laws* to *Dicey,
Morris and Collins on the Conflict of Laws* (14th ed., 2006), para.32–179.

"Certain consumer contracts"

[*Add to note 649: page* [1837]]   **30–132**
cf. Commission Proposal, Art. 10(3).

Immovables

[*Notes 651, 654, and 655: pages* [1837], [1838]]   **30–133**
Update the references to *Dicey and Morris* to *Dicey, Morris and Collins,* paras
33–240—33–243.

[*Add to note 653: page* [1837]]
cf. Commission Proposal, Art.10(4).

(c) *Capacity*

[*Note 665: page* [1839]]
Update the reference to *Dicey and Morris* to *Dicey, Morris and Collins,* paras 30–021—30–023, 32–217—32–227.

Natural persons

30–138 [*Notes 671 and 672: page* [1839]]
Update the references to *Dicey and Morris* to *Dicey, Morris and Collins,* paras 32–223—32–224.

Corporations

30–139 [*Add to notes 675 and 676: page* [1840]]
Continental Enterprises Ltd v Shandong Zhucheng Foreign Trade Group Co [2005] EWHC 92 (Comm); *Laemthong International Lines Co Ltd v Artis (No. 3)* [2005] EWHC 1595 (Comm). See also *Marubeni Hong Kong and South China Ltd v Government of Mongolia* [2004] EWHC 472 (Comm); [2004] 2 Lloyd's Rep. 198; affd. on other grounds [2005] EWCA Civ 395; [2005] 1 W.L.R. 2497.

[*Note 678*]
Update the reference to *Dicey and Morris* to *Dicey, Morris and Collins,* para.30–022.

[*Note 681*]
Update the reference to *Dicey and Morris* to *Dicey Morris and Collins,* paras 30–025—30–028.

[*Add to note 683*]
cf. Commission Proposal, Arts 1(2)(f), 7.

(d) *Particular Issues: Article 10*

[*Note 684: page* [1841]]
Update the reference to *Dicey and Morris on the Conflict of Laws* to *Dicey, Morris and Collins, on the Conflict of Laws* (14th ed., 2006), paras 32–189—32–210.

Reservation of consequences of nullity

30–141 [*Add in line 7 of note 697: page* [1841]]
cf. Caterpillar Financial Services Corporation v SNC Passion [2004] EWHC 569 (Comm); [2004] 2 Lloyd's Rep. 99 at [16].

[*Note 697: page* [1841]]
Update the references to *Dicey and Morris* to *Dicey, Morris and Collins,*
para.32–210 and Ch. 34.

Overlapping categories

[*Note 698: page* [1842]]
Update the reference to *Dicey and Morris* to *Dicey, Morris and Collins,*
para.32–190.

30–142

Interpretation

[*Add at end of note 702: page* [1842]]
OT Africa Line Ltd v Magic Sportswear Corp [2005] EWCA Civ 710; [2005]
2 Lloyd's Rep. 170.

30–144

[*Note 705*]
Update the reference to *Dicey an Morris* to *Dicey, Morris and Collins,*
para.36–009.

Manner of performance

[*Note 715: page* [1843]]
Update the reference to *Dicey and Morris* to *Dicey, Morris and Collins,*
para.32–197.

30–146

Examples

[*Notes 717 and 718: page* [1844]]
Update the reference to *Dicey and Morris* to *Dicey, Morris and Collins,*
para.32–199.

30–147

[*Note 719*]
Update the reference to *Benjamin's Sale of Goods* to 7th ed., 2006,
para.25–156.

Consequences of breach, etc

[*Note 724: page* [1845]]
Update the reference to *Dicey and Morris* to *Dicey, Morris and Collins,*
para.32–201. Update the reference to *Benjamin's Sale of Goods* to 7th ed., paras
25–178—25–202.

30–149

Damages

[*Notes 725 and 726: page* [1845]]
In *Harding v Wealands* [2006] UKHL 32; [2006] 3 W.L.R. 83 the House of
Lords, reversing the majority decision of the Court of Appeal, held that a
statutory ceiling on damages in tort imposed by a foreign law was procedural

30–150

rather than substantive and that the quantification of damages in tort was a matter exclusively for the law of the forum. It was accepted, however (*ibid.*, at [44]–[46]) that a contractual term which limits the obligation to pay damages for a breach of contract or a statutory provision which is deemed to operate as such a term was substantive. See *Cope v Doherty* (1858) 2 De G. & J. 614 at 626; *Allen J. Panozza & Co Pty Ltd v Allied Interstate (Qld.) Pty Ltd* [1976] 2 N.S.W.L.R. 192 at 196–197. And see *Stevens v Head* (1993) 176 C.L.R. 433 at 458.

[*Note 725*]
Update the reference to *Dicey and Morris* to *Dicey, Morris and Collins*, para.32–202.

[*Note 729: page* [1846]]
See entry at nn.725 and 726 above.

[*Note 730*]
Update the reference to *Dicey and Morris* to *Dicey, Morris and Collins*, para.32–201.

Other remedies

30–151   [*Note 733: page* [1846]]
Update the reference to *Dicey and Morris* to *Dicey Morris and Collins*, para.7–006

[*Note 734*]
Dicta in *Harding v Wealands* [2006] UKHL 32; [2006] 3 W.L.R. 83 at [32] suggest that the nature of the available remedy is a matter of procedure, but this cannot affect the position under the Rome Convention.

[*Note 734*]
Update the reference to *Dicey and Morris* to *Dicey, Morris and Collins*, para.32–201.

Interest

30–152   [*Note 738: page* [1846]]
Update the reference to *Dicey and Morris* to *Dicey, Morris and Collins*, paras 32–200, 33–383.

[*Note 739: page* [1847]]
The House of Lords allowed an appeal from the decision of the Court of Appeal in *Lesotho Highlands Development Authority v Impregilo SpA* [2005] UKHL 43; [2006] 1 A.C. 221. But no view was expressed on the point in the text since the House took the view that the arbitrator's power to award interest under s.49(3) of the Arbitration Act 1996 had not been expressly excluded by the parties. For an earlier, but inconclusive, case on the point see *Zebrarise Ltd v De Nieffe* [2004] EWHC 1842 (Comm); [2005] 1 Lloyd's Rep. 154.

[*Note 739*]
Update the reference to *Dicey and Morris* to *Dicey, Morris and Collins*, paras 33–392—33–393.

THOMSON
™
SWEET & MAXWELL

Thank you for purchasing the third supplement to **Chitty on Contracts**.

☑ **Don't miss important updates**

So that you have all the latest information, **Chitty on Contracts** is supplemented regularly. Sign up today for a Standing Order to ensure you receive the updating supplements as soon as they publish. Setting up a Standing Order with Sweet & Maxwell is hassle-free, simply tick complete and return this FREEPOST card and we'll do the rest.

You may cancel your Standing Order at any time by writing to us at Sweet & Maxwell, PO Box 2000, Andover, SP10 9AF stating the Standing Order you wish to cancel.

Alternatively, if you have purchased your copy of **Chitty on Contracts** from a bookshop or other trade supplier, please ask your supplier to ensure that you are registered to receive your supplements.

Yes, please send me supplements to and / or new editions of **Chitty on Contracts** to be invoiced on publication, unless I cancel the standing order in writing.

☐ All supplements to current edition

☐ All new editions

☐ All new editions and supplements

Name:

Organisation:

Address:

Postcode:

Telephone:

Email:

S&M account number: (if known)

All orders are accepted subject to the terms of this order form, our Terms of Trading (see our website) and relevant Service Terms (available with the product or on request).

By submitting this order form, I confirm that I accept these terms and am authorised to sign on behalf of the customer.

Signed: Date:

Print name: Job Title:

LBU2069

STANDING ORDERS

SWEET & MAXWELL

FREEPOST

PO BOX 2000

ANDOVER

SP10 9AH

UNITED KINGDOM

[Add to note 740: page [1847]]
The view expressed in the text was preferred and applied in *Rogers v Markel Corp* [2004] EWHC 1375 (QBD); [2004] EWHC 2046 (QBD).

[Note 740]
Update the reference to *Dicey and Morris* to *Dicey, Morris and Collins*, paras 33–397—33–399.

[Note 741]
Update the reference to *Dicey and Morris* to *Dicey, Morris and Collins*, para.33–393.

[Notes 741 and 742: page [1847]
See first entry at n.739, above.

[Note 742: page [1847]]
Update the reference to *Dicey and Morris* to *Dicey, Morris and Collins*, para.33–397.

Exchange losses

[Add to note 743: page [1847]]   **30–153**
Rogers v Markel Corp [2004] EWHC 2046 (QBD).

[Note 744]
Update the reference to *Dicey and Morris* to *Dicey, Morris and Collins*, para.36–084.

Extinguishing obligations, etc.

[Note 770: page [1850]]   **30–158**
Update the reference to *Dicey and Morris* to *Dicey, Morris and Collins*, para.32–204.

[Note 772]
Update the reference to *Dicey and Morris* to *Dicey, Morris and Collins*, para.30–011.

[Note 775: page [1851]]
Update the references to *Dicey and Morris* to *Dicey, Morris and Collins*, paras 32–204—32–207, 31–093—31–097, 31–114.

[Note 776]
Wight v Eckhardt Marine GmbH is now reported at [2004] 1 A.C. 147.

[Note 777]
Update the reference to *Dicey and Morris* to *Dicey, Morris and Collins*, paras 7–032, 32–208.

Prescription and limitation of actions

[Notes 778 and 779: page [1851]]   **30–159**
Update the references to *Dicey and Morris* to *Dicey, Morris and Collins*, paras 7–045—7–054.

[*Add at end of note 782: page* [1851]]
See also *Zebrarise Ltd v De Nieffe* [2004] EWHC 1842 (Comm); [2005] 1 Lloyd's Rep. 154. As to restitutionary claims and the Foreign Limitation Periods Act 1984, see *Barros Mattos Junior v MacDaniels Ltd* [2004] EWHC 1323 (Ch); [2005] 1 W.L.R. 247.

[*Note 782: page* [1851]]
Update the reference to *Dicey and Morris* to *Dicey, Morris and Collins,* paras 7–052, 32–209.

[*Note 783: page* [1852]]
Update the references to *Dicey and Morris* to *Dicey, Morris and Collins,* para.7–054.

[*Note 785*]
Update the reference to *Dicey and Morris* to *Dicey, Morris and Collins,* para.32–209.

Other unspecified issues

30–162 [*Note 791: page* [1853]]
Update the reference to *Dicey and Morris* to *Dicey, Morris and Collins,* para.32–190.

[*Add at end of note 792*]
See also *Laemthong International Lines Co Ltd v ARTIS (No.3)* [2005] EWHC 1595 (Comm) (whether a person is party to a contract is a matter for the applicable law).

(e) *Burden of Proof, etc*

[*Note 797: page* [1853]]
Update the reference to *dicey and Morris on the Conflict of Laws* to *Dicey, Morris and Collins on the Conflict of Laws* (14th ed., 2006), paras 7–027—7–028, 32–055—32–056.

Burden of proof and presumptions

30–165 [*Note 800: page* [1854]]
Update the reference to *Dicey and Morris* to *Dicey, Morris and Collins,* para.7–027.

30–166 [*Notes 804 and 805*]
Update the references to *Dicey and Morris* to *Dicey, Morris and Collins,* para.7–029.

(f) *Illegality and Public Policy*

[*Add in line 5 of note 813: page* [1855]]
Peruzzetto in Meeusen, Pertegas and Straetmans (eds.), *The Enforcement of International Contracts in the European Union* (2004), pp.343–361.

[Add at the end of note 813: page [1855]]
Tekron Resources Ltd v Guinea Investment Co Ltd [2004] EWHC 2577
(Comm); [2004] 2 Lloyd's Rep. 26; *Barros Mattos Junior v MacDaniels Ltd*
[2004] EWHC 1188 (Ch); [2005] 1 W.L.R. 247.

[Note 813]
Update the reference to *Dicey and Morris on the Conflict of Laws* to *Dicey,
Morris and Collins on the Conflict of Laws* (14th ed., 2006), paras 5–009,
32–140—32–151, 32–230—32–241.

Illegality under applicable law

[Add in first line of note 815: page [1856]]   **30–169**
Barros Mattos Junior v MacDaniels Ltd, above.

Act illegal under law of country where to be performed

[Add in line 6 of note 823: page [1857]]   **30–171**
Tekron Resources Ltd v Guinea Investment Co Ltd, above. See also *Con-
tinental Enterprises Ltd v Shandong Zhucheng Foreign Trade Group Co* [2005]
EWHC 95 (Comm).

[Note 823: page [1857]]
Update the reference to *Dicey and Morris* to *Dicey, Morris and Collins,* paras
32–144—32–147.

[Add at end of note 828: page [1857]]
Tekron Resources Ltd v Guinea Investment Co Ltd, above.

[Note 828]
Update the reference to *Dicey and Morris* to *Dicey, Morris and Collins,* paras
32–148—32–151.

[Note 830]
Update the reference to *Dicey and Morris* to *Dicey, Morris and Collins,*
para.32–150.

Public policy

[Add to note 838: page [1858]]   **30–173**
Continental Enterprises Ltd v Shandong Zhucheng Foreign Trade Group Co,
above.

[Note 840]
Update the reference to *Dicey and Morris* to *Dicey, Morris and Collins,*
para.32–236.

[Add to start of note 841]
Re COLT Telecom Group plc [2002] EWHC 2815 (Ch); [2003] B.P.I.R. 324;
Continental Enterprises Ltd v Shandong Zhucheng Foreign Trade Group,
above.

30–174   [*Note 847: page* [1860]
Peer International Corp v Termidor Music Publishers Ltd is now reported at [2004] Ch. 212.

[*Add at end of note 847*]
See also *Barros Mattos Junior v MacDaniels Ltd* [2004] EWHC 1188 (Ch); [2005] 1 W.L.R. 247.

[*Note 847*]
Update the references to *Dicey and Morris* to *Dicey, Morris and Collins*, paras 5–020—5–040, 36–062—36–077.

[*Add to note 850*]
See also *Tekron Resources Ltd v Guinea Investment Co Ltd* [2003] EWHC 2577 (Comm); [2004] 2 Lloyd's Rep. 26.

30–175   [*Add in first line of note 851: page* [1860]]
Continental Enterprises Ltd v Shandong Zhucheng Foreign Trade Group Co, above.

[*Add in line last line of note 852*]
Meidanis (2005) 30 Eur. L. Rev. 95.

(g) *Foreign Currency Obligations*

Scope of discussion

30–176   [*Note 853: page* [1861]]
Update the reference to *Dicey and Morris on the Conflict of Laws* to *Dicey, Morris and Collins on the Conflict of Laws* (14th ed., 2006), Ch. 36.
Update the reference to F.A. Mann, *The Legal Aspect of Money* to *Mann on the Legal Aspect of Money* (6th ed., Proctor, 2005).

Principle of nominalism

30–177   [*Note 855: page* [1861]]
Update the references to *Dicey and Morris* to *Dicey, Morris and Collins*, paras 36–011—36–014, 36–036—36–038, 36–041—36–049.

[*Note 859*]
Update the reference to *Dicey and Morris* to *Dicey, Morris and Collins*, para.36–008.

Money of account

30–179   [*Note 863: page* [1862]]
Update the reference to *Dicey and Morris* to *Dicey, Morris and Collins*, para.36–004.

[*Note 867*]
Update the reference to *Dicey and Morris* to *Dicey, Morris and Collins*, paras 30–018—30–022.

Currency of damages

[*Add to note 869: page* [1863]]

30–180

For an example, see *Rogers v Markel Corp* [2004] EWHC 2046 although in this case the contract was governed by the law of Virginia, which seems to be the same on this point as English law.

[*Add to note 870: page* [1863]]

Virani Ltd v Manuel Revert Y Cia SA [2003] EWCA Civ 1651; [2004] 2 Lloyd's Rep. 14.

Money of payment

[*Note 873: page* [1863]]

30–181

Update the reference to *Dicey and Morris* to *Dicey, Morris and Collins,* paras 36–053—36–056.

[*Note 879: page* [1864]]

30–182

Update the reference to *Dicey and Morris* to *Dicey, Morris and Collins,* paras 36–053—36–056.

[*Note 881*]

Update the reference to *Dicey and Morris* to *Dicey, Morris and Collins,* para.36–054.

Judgments in foreign currency

[*Add in line 7 of note 887: page* [1865]]

30–183

Carnegie v Giessen [2005] EWCA Civ 191; [2005] 1 C.L.C. 259 (charging order may be expressed in foreign currency).

[*Note 895 and text thereto: page* [1865]]

Section 48(4) of the Arbitration Act 1996 provides that unless otherwise agreed between the parties (which agreement must be in writing, s.5(1)) an arbitral tribunal may order the payment of a sum of money in any currency. The effect of this provision was considered by the House of Lords in *Lesotho Highlands Development Authority v Impregilo SpA* [2005] UKHL 43; [2006] 1 A.C. 221. In the preferred view of Lord Steyn, the power of the tribunal under s.48(4) was unconstrained by the case law pre-dating the 1996 Act which is referred to in the text: *ibid.* at [22]. In the alternative he held that the fact that the tribunal had rendered the award in a currency other than that of the contract did not constitute a serious irregularity in the award pursuant to s.68 of the 1996 Act which would justify setting the award aside. It was merely an error of law by the tribunal which could not be challenged: *ibid.* at [23]. Lord Scott of Foscote and Lord Rodger of Earlsferry preferred the latter view. Lord Hoffman had reservations in respect of Lord Steyn's preferred view but chose not to express an opinion on the point. Lord Phillips of Worth Matravers dissented. In the light of these opinions it would seem that Lord Steyn's alternative view commands a majority.

[*Add at end of note 896: page* [1865]]

Lesotho Highlands Development Authority v Impregilo SpA, above.

30–184   [*Note 900: page* [1866]]
Update the reference to *Dicey and Morris* to *Dicey, Morris and Collins,*
para.36R–081.

30–185   [*Note 901: page* [1866]]
Update the reference to *Dicey and Morris* to *Dicey, Morris and Collins,*
para.33–400.

VOLUME II

SPECIFIC CONTRACTS

CHAPTER 31

AGENCY

			PARA.
☐	1.	Agency in general	31–001
☐	2.	Examples of types of agent	31–012
■	3.	Creation of agency	31–020
■		(a) Express agreement	31–021
		(b) Implied agreement	31–025
☐		(c) Ratification	31–026
☐		(d) Agency of necessity	31–033
☐		(e) Capacity	31–036
☐		(f) Delegation	31–039
■	4.	Authority	31–041
☐		(a) General principles	31–041
		(b) Examples	31–049
■	5.	Principal's relations with third parties	31–054
		(a) General rule	31–054
☐		(b) Apparent authority	31–056
☐		(c) Undisclosed principal	31–061
☐		(d) Further rules	31–066
☐		(e) Agent's torts	31–074
☐		(f) Disposition of property through agent	31–075
■	6.	Agent's relations with third parties	31–082
☐		(a) On the main contract	31–082
☐		(b) Collateral contracts	31–098
☐		(c) Breach of warranty of authority	31–099
☐		(d) Restitution	31–107
☐		(e) Tort	31–109
■	7.	Obligations of principal and agent *inter se*	31–111
■		(a) Duties of agents	31–111
☐		(i) Obedience	31–111
☐		(ii) Exercise of care and skill	31–112
☐		(iii) Loyalty	31–116
☐		(iv) Remedies	31–124
☐		(v) Estoppel as to principal's title	31–130
☐		(b) Rights of agents	31–131
☐		(i) Remuneration	31–132
☐		(ii) Indemnity	31–156
☐		(iii) Lien	31–158
☐		(iv) Right of stoppage in transit	31–159
☐	8.	Termination of authority	31–160

References to *Bowstead and Reynolds on Agency* (17th ed.) should now be to the 18th ed. (2006). The references within the book remain correct unless otherwise indicated.

1. AGENCY IN GENERAL

Concept of agency

31–001   *[Note 1: page [2]]*
Update reference to *Restatement, Second, Agency* to *Restatement, Third, Agency* (2006), paras 1.01, 6.01.

[Add to note 1]
See now *General Legal Council Ex p. Whitter v Frankson* [2006] UKPC 42 (signature of affidavit alleging professional misconduct can be by agent, disapproving *Re Prince Blücher* [1931] 2 Ch 70).

Commercial agents

31–005   *[Add to note 17: page [4]]*
; Randolph and Davey, above (2nd ed., 2003); Christou, *International Agency, Distribution and Licensing Agreements* (4th ed., 2003); Saintier and Scholes, *Commercial Agents and the Law* (2005).

[Add to note 19]
But see *PJ Pipe and Valve Co Ltd v Audco India Ltd* [2005] EWHC 1904 (QB); [2006] Eu L.R. 368. In *Poseidon Chartering BV v Marianne Zeeschip NOF* Case 3/04 [2006] 2 Lloyd's Rep. 105, the ECJ held that where an agent retained to negotiate a single charterparty negotiates extensions over a period the matter turns on whether he has continuing authority to negotiate extensions.

[Add to note 21]
For an example of change of the agent's status, see *Smith v Reliance Water Controls Ltd* [2003] EWCA Civ 1153; [2003] Eu.L.R. 874.

[Add to note 24]
This definition, inserted by the United Kingdom for itself, has not proved easy to understand: see the *Imballaggi* case, below, n.31, at 254. It seems that the matter must be settled by looking at all the agent's activities, not at the particular transaction: see *Tamarind International Ltd v Eastern Gas (Retail) Ltd* [2000] Eu.L.R. 708 at [28]. Scottish cases have placed the burden of proof on the person alleging that he is such an agent: see *Gailey v Environmental Waste Controls* [2004] Eu.L.R.423; *McAdam v Boxpak Ltd*, 2005 S.L.T.(Sh.Ct.) 147; affd. 2006 S.L.T. 217 (Ex Div); but this was doubted by the English Court of Appeal in *Edwards v International Connection (UK) Ltd*, April 27, 2006.

31–006   *[Add to note 31: page [5]]*
Relevant principles are discussed in the European Commission's *Guidelines on Vertical Restraints* [2000] O.J. C291/1.

[Add to note 32]
A company or partnership can be a commercial agent: see the *Imballaggi* case, above, n.31.

General and special agents

[*Add to note 64: page* [8]]   **31–011**
See on this general topic Brown [2004] J.B.L. 391.

2. Examples of Types of Agent

House, estate and land agents

[*Note 86: page* [10]]   **31–015**
The reference to Murdoch, *Law of Estate Agency and Auctions* (3rd ed.) should
now to Murdoch, *Law of Estate Agency* (4th ed.).
Parts of the 1979 Act are affected by the Enterprise Act 2002.

Insurance agents and brokers

[*Add to note 110: page* [13]]   **31–018**
Goshawk Dedicated Ltd v Tyser & Co Ltd [2006] EWCA Civ 54; [2006] 1
Lloyd's Rep. 566 (broker may provide documents to underwriter).

3. Creation of Agency

(a) *Express Agreement*

Powers of attorney

[*Add to end of note 138: page* [15]]   **31–024**
(including the reference in the Supplement, para.31–165, to the Lasting Power
of Attorney created by the Mental Capacity Act 2005).

(c) *Ratification*

Proof of ratification

[*Add to note 146: page* [16]]   **31–027**
In *Ing Re (UK) Ltd v R & V Versicherung AG* [2006] EWHC 1544 (Comm)
Toulson J. referred to "the only reasonable conclusion to draw in the circum-
stances": at [161].

Knowledge of circumstances

[*Add to note 160: page* [18]]   **31–029**
See discussion in *AMB Generali Holding AG v SEB Trygg Liv Holding
Aktiebolag* [2005] EWCA Civ 1237; [2006] 1 Lloyd's Rep. 318 at [42]–[43]. See
also below, n.173.

Effect of ratification

31–031   [*Add to note 173: page* [19]]
Restatement, Third (2006) now accepts this view: see para.4.02. In *Ing Re (UK) Ltd v R & V Versicherung AG* [2006] EWHC 1544 (Comm) at [138] *et seq.*, it is said that the knowledge required to make the principal bound against the third party may be less than that required to relieve the agent from liability to the principal for breach of duty, which seems correct.

[*Add to note 176*]
The question whether ratification only operates where the third party believed at the time of contracting that the agent was authorised is considered in *Bowstead and Reynolds on Agency* (18th ed., 2006), para.2–050.

Limits on ratification

31–032   [*Add to note 189: page* [20]]
See a further useful discussion by Keith J. (in the context of an originating application issued without authority and ratified after expiry of a three month time limit) in *Nottinghamshire Healthcare Trust v Prisons Officers Assn* [2003] I.C.R. 1192, EAT.

(d) *Agency of Necessity*

Agency of necessity

31–033   The Mental Capacity Act 2005 (not in force at the time of writing) creates by ss.5–8 what may be called a statutory form of agency of necessity for mentally incapacitated persons. Subject to detailed restrictions, it permits a person intervening on behalf of such a person to pledge that person's credit (an example of the first category of agency of necessity mentioned below) in connection with his or her care or treatment, and to use that person's money and/or seek indemnity in respect of acts done for that purpose (the second category). It is separate from operation under a lasting power of attorney (below, substituted note to para 31–165), which if well drawn may more easily avoid controversy.

(e) *Capacity*

Acting for both parties

31–038   [*Add to note 228: page* [24]]
But the point can arise in the context of conflict of interest also: see *Marks & Spencer plc v Freshfields Bruckhaus Deringer* [2004] EWCA Civ 741; [2004] P.N.L.R. 4.

[*Add to note 230*]
cf. Goshawk Dedicated Ltd v Tyser & Co Ltd [2006] EWCA Civ 54; [2006] 1 Lloyd's Rep. 566 (documents held by insurance broker). The duties of solicitors in such cases are authoritatively discussed in *Hilton v Barker Booth &*

Eastwood [2005] UKHL 8; [2005] 1 W.L.R. 567; see Getzler (2006) 122 L.Q.R. 1.

(f) *Delegation*

When delegation permissible

[*Add to note 231: page* [25]]   **31–039**
In *Jacques Lichtenstein v Clube Atletico Mineiro* [2005] EWHC 1300; [2005] All E.R. (D) 341 (Jun.) Jack J. said that a commercial agreement of a general nature could be performed through the actions of another. This seems a useful dictum in the light of more restrictive formulations elsewhere.

Effect of delegation

[*Add to note 236: page* [25]]   **31–040**
See also *Heath Lambert Ltd v Sociedad de Corretaje de Seguros* [2003] EWHC 2269 (Comm); [2004] 1 Lloyd's Rep. 495; affd. [2004] EWCA Civ 792; [2004] 1 W.L.R. 2820.

[*Note 247: page* [26]]
Update reference to *Bowstead and Reynolds* to (18th ed., 2006), Art.68.

4. AUTHORITY

(a) *General Principles*

Express and implied authority

[*Add to note 258: page* [27]]   **31–042**
On the agent's lack of authority to act contrary to the principal's interest see also *Hopkins v T.L.Dallas Group Ltd* [2004] EWHC 1379 (Ch); [2005] 1 B.C.L.C. 543; *Criterion Properties plc v Stratford UK Properties LLC* [2004] UKHL 28; [2004] 1 W.L.R. 1846. See also *Sphere Drake Insurance Co Ltd v Euro International Underwriting* [2003] EWHC 2376 (Comm); [2003] Lloyd's Rep. I.R. 265 at [49]; *Wrexham Association Football Club Ltd v Crucialmove Ltd* [2006] EWCA Civ 237.

Implied authority: incidental authority

[*Add to note 263: page* [28]]   **31–044**
The word "necessarily" is not to be overstressed in this context: implied authority depends on consent, not on the rules for the implication of terms into contracts: *Targe Towing Ltd v Marine Blast Ltd* [2004] EWCA Civ 346; [2004] 1 Lloyd's Rep. 721 at [22].

Customary authority

31–046   [*Add to note 277: page* [29]]
Goshawk Dedicated Ltd v Tyser & Co Ltd [2006] EWCA Civ 54; [2006] 1
Lloyd's Rep. 566 (custom permitting disclosure of insurance documents by
broker).

5. PRINCIPAL'S RELATIONS WITH THIRD PARTIES

(b) *Apparent Authority*

Apparent authority

31–056   [*Add to note 313: page* [33]]
See now *AMB Generali Holding AG v SEB Trygg Liv Holding Aktiebolag*
[2005] EWCA Civ 1237; [2006] 1 Lloyd's Rep. 318 at [31]–[32].

[*Add to note 314*]
The most recent authorities are *Lloyd's Bank Plc v Independent Insurance Co
Ltd* [2000] Q.B. 110 at 122 (Waller L.J.); *AMB Generali Holdings AG v SEB
Trygg Liv Holding Aktiebolag* [2005] EWCA Civ 1237; [2006] 1 Lloyd's Rep.
318 at [31]–[32] (Buxton L.J.); and *Ing Re (UK) Ltd v R & V Versicherung AG*
[2006] EWHC 1544 (Comm) at [99] and [104] (Toulson J.). *Restatement, Third,
Agency* distinguishes between true estoppel and apparent authority: see
para.2.05; *Bowstead and Reynolds on Agency* (18th ed., 2006), Art.21.

[*Note 315*]
Update *Restatement* reference to *Restatement, Third, Agency* (2006), paras
1.03, 2.03. See now also *Ing Re (UK) Ltd v R & V Versicherung AG* [2006]
EWHC 1544 (Comm) at [100] and [117]–[131] (Toulson J.).

[*Add to note 319: page* [34]]
In *Pacific Carriers Ltd v BNP Paribas* [2004] HCA 35; (2004) 218 C.L.R.
451, the High Court of Australia held a bank liable on a letter of indemnity
against delivery without bill of lading which it had signed together with the
shipper, its customer. The document had been stamped and signed by the
Manager of the Documentary Credit Department of its Sydney office. The
Manager intended to authenticate the signature of the shipper but on an objective
interpretation of the document it was held that the signature was to an indemnity.
The Manager had authority to sign authentications of signature but not promises
of indemnity. There was no reason for the third party to know this and to the third
party, who had had no direct dealings with the bank at all, there was just a stamp
accompanied by an illegible signature without description of the signer. The bank
was held liable: its organisational structure and absence of procedures for such
signatures meant that it had placed the signer in a position which equipped her
to deal with letters of indemnity, and on this the third party had relied. See also
Essington Investments Pty Ltd v Regency Property Ltd [2004] N.S.W.C.A. 375;
and for comments on the surprising decision in *Pacific Carriers* Reynolds,
(2005) 121 L.Q.R. 55; Watts, (2005) 26 Aust.Bar Rev. 185.

[*Note 330: page* [35]]
Update reference to *Bowstead and Reynolds* to (18th ed., 2006), Art.73.

[*Note 335*]
The last reference should now be to the same paragraphs in *Restatement, Third, Agency* (2006). The matter is further considered in *Bowstead and Reynolds on Agency* (18th ed., 2006), para.8–031.

Notice of public documents

[*Add to note 348: page* [37]]   **31–059**
See Payne and Prentice [2005] L.M.C.L.Q. 447.

Apparent authority of Crown agents

[*Add to note 353: page* [38]]   **31–060**
But see, for an attribution of apparent authority to an agent of a foreign government, *Marubeni Hong Kong and South China Ltd v Government of Mongolia* [2004] EWHC 472 (Comm); [2004] 2 Lloyd's Rep. 198; point not considered on appeal [2005] EWCA Civ 395; [2005] 2 Lloyd's Rep. 231.

(c) *Undisclosed Principal*

Undisclosed principal

[*Add to note 356: page* [38]]   **31–061**
See in general Tan Cheng-Han (2004) 120 L.Q.R. 480.

Meaning of "undisclosed principal"

[*Add to note 373: page* [40]]   **31–063**
Both the above cases were applied in *Rolls Royce Power Engineering plc v Ricardo Consulting Engineers Ltd* [2004] EWHC 2871; [2004] 2 All E.R. (Comm.) 129.

[*Add to note 374: page* [40]]
The dangers of finding agency between related corporate structures are stressed by Langley J. in *Peterson Farms Inc v C & M Farming Ltd* [2004] EWHC 121 (Comm); [2004] 1 Lloyd's Rep. 603 at [62]; but *cf.* the *Rolls Royce* case, above. As to fiduciary duty owed to a sole shareholder in a company, see *Diamantis Diamantides v JP Morgan Chase Bank* [2005] EWCA Civ 1612.

Exclusion of undisclosed principals

[*Add to note 392: page* [42]]   **31–065**
The *Siu Yin Kwan* case was applied in *Rolls Royce Power Engineering plc v Ricardo Consulting Engineers Ltd* [2004] EWHC 2871; [2004] 2 All E.R. (Comm.) 129, where it was held that the third party did not intend to deal with

anyone on whose behalf the other party might be acting, and hence Rolls Royce as undisclosed principal could not intervene. See also *Talbot Underwriting Ltd v Nausch Hogan & Murray Inc (The Jascon 5)* [2006] EWCA Civ 889; [2006] 2 Lloyd's Rep. 195 (implied exclusion by terms of insurance policy); *White v Baycorp Information Services Ltd* [2006] NSWSC 441 (no exclusion by terms of contract).

(d) Further Rules

Agent acting in fraud of principal

31–066   *[Add to note 398: page* [42]]
See also *Criterion Properties plc v Stratford UK Properties LLC* [2004] UKHL 28; [2004] 1 W.L.R. 1846.

Settlement with and set-off against agent

31–068   *[Note 416: page* [44]]
Update reference to *Bowstead and Reynolds* to (18th ed., 2006), Art.81.

Effect of judgment against agent

31–069   *[Note 421: page* [44]]
Update reference to *Bowstead and Reynolds* to (18th ed., 2006), Art.82.

Election

31–070   *[Note 436: page* [45]]
Update reference to *Bowstead and Reynolds* to (18th ed., 2006), Art.82.

Where principal is discharged by settling with agent

31–071   *[Note 455: page* [47]]
Update reference to *Bowstead and Reynolds* to (18th ed., 2006), Art.80.

Effect of bribery of agent

31–072   *[Note 463: page* [48]]
Update reference to *Bowstead and Reynolds* (18th ed., 2006), para.8–220.

31–073   *[Add to note 471]*
See also *Ultraframe (UK) Ltd v Fielding* [2005] EWHC 1638 (Ch) at [1594].

(e) Agent's torts

Agent's torts

31–074   *[Note 473: page* [49]]
Update reference to *Clerk and Lindsell* to (19th ed., 2006), Ch. 6, esp. Pt 4.

[Add to note 474]

The Australian *Colonial Mutual Life* case is considered by the High Court of Australia in *Sweeney v Boylan Nominees Pty Ltd* [2006] HCA 19; (2006) 80 A.L.J.R. 900.

(f) *Disposition of property through agent*

Dispositions to agent

[Note 515: page [52]]   **31–081**

Update reference to *Bowstead and Reynolds* to (18th ed., 2006), Art.89.

6. AGENT'S RELATIONS WITH THIRD PARTIES

(a) *On the Main Contract*

When agent liable and entitled

[Add to note 528: page [54]]   **31–083**

A recent example is *Foxtons Ltd v Thesleff* [2005] EWCA Civ 514; [2005] 2 E.G.L.R. 29, where a contract to pay estate agent's commission was held also binding on the person "to whom the letter overleaf is addressed", who was an agent for the vendor but did not sign "as agent only". *cf. Lucas Laureys v Graham Earl*, QBD (David Foskett Q.C.), November 3, 2005 (broker not automatically liable on contract he has facilitated).

[Add to text at end of paragraph: page [54]]

And an agent may be entitled as a third party beneficiary of his principal's contract under the Contracts (Rights of Third Parties) Act 1999.[532a]

[532a] See *Laemthong International Lines Co Ltd v Artis (The Laemthong Glory)* [2005] EWCA Civ 519; [2005] 1 Lloyd's Rep. 688 (letter of indemnity given by receiver of goods to charterer against delivery without bill of lading, expressed to be in favour of "you, your servants and agents": owners held agents of charterers to deliver, hence entitled to sue as third parties. But the context in which the owners were held agents is a specialised one, and the decision was largely based on contractual interpretation).

Where "agent" is in fact principal: his liabilities

[Note 573: page [59]]   **31–094**

Update reference to *Bowstead and Reynolds* to (18th ed., 2006), Art.108.

(b) *Collateral contracts*

Collateral contracts

[Note 602: page [61]]   **31–098**

The reference to Murdoch, *Law of Estate Agency and Auctions* should now be to the same writer's *Law of Estate Agency* (4th ed., 2003).

(c) *Breach of Warranty of Authority*

Liability of agent acting without authority

31–099   [*Add to note 607: page* [62]]
        In *SEB Trygg Holding Aktiebolag v Manches* [2005] EWHC 35 (Comm);
    [2005] 2 Lloyd's Rep. 129 Gloster J. regarded *Nelson v Nelson* as establishing
    that a solicitor commencing proceedings for a named party warrants that the
    claimant bears that name and is in existence. But in the Court of Appeal it was
    held that there was no warranty as to the principal's name: merely that the
    solicitor has a client who exists and has authorised proceedings, but not that he
    has a good cause of action or is solvent: *AMB Generali Holdings AG v SEB Trygg
    Liv Holding Aktiebolag* [2005] EWCA Civ 1237; [2006] 1 Lloyd's Rep. 318 at
    [63].

Representation must be of fact and relied on

31–101   [*Add to note 611: page* [63]]
        Enterprise Plus Ltd v Wagenmann [2003] EWHC 1827 (Comm).

(d) *Restitution*

        [*Add to note 631: page* [64]]
        Stevens [2005] L.M.C.L.Q. 101.

(e) *Tort*

Exclusions of liability

31–110   [*Add to note 658: page* [67]]
        An identifiable subcontractor intended to benefit may be able to rely on s.1(6)
    of the Contracts (Rights of Third Parties) Act 1999: see Vol.1, paras 14–039 *et
    seq*. See also a recent decision of the Supreme Court of the United States
    allowing protection to a sub-subcontractor where the principal contract was a
    freight forwarder's bill of lading: *Norfolk Southern Ry Co v James Kirby Pty Ltd*,
    125 S. Ct. 385 (2004).

7. OBLIGATIONS OF PRINCIPAL AND AGENT *INTER SE*

(a) *Duties of Agents*

(i) *Obedience*

Carrying out instructions

31–111   [*Add to note 660: page* [67]]
        See further *Bowstead and Reynolds on Agency* (18th ed., 2006), para.6–009.

(ii) *Exercise of Care and Skill*

Exercise of care and skill

[*Add to note 667: page* [68]]
Action may be brought in tort: see *BP Plc v Aon Ltd (No.2)*[2006] EWHC 424 (Comm); [2006] 1 All E.R. (Comm.) 789, where a claim in contract had been abandoned, perhaps for jurisdictional reasons.

31–112

Disclosure of misdoing

[*Add to note 679: page* [69]]
A director was found liable for such non-disclosure in *Item Software Ltd v Fassihi* [2004] EWCA Civ 1244; [2005] 2 B.C.L.C. 91: *quaere* as to the position of other fiduciaries. For consideration of the case, see *Bowstead and Reynolds on Agency* (18th ed., 2006), para.6–059; Flannigan [2006] Bus. L. Rev. 258 (Canada). It has not been followed in Australia: *P & V Industries Pty Ltd v Porto* [2005] VSC 131.

31–114

Gratuitous agents

[*Add to note 682: page* [69]]
In *OBG Ltd v Allen* [2005] EWCA Civ 106; [2005] Q.B. 762 receivers whose appointment was invalid and who settled claims under contracts without negligence but on less good terms than the debtor (through its liquidator) could have done was by a majority held not liable for the tort of interference with contract: but see a persuasive dissent by Mance L.J.

31–115

(iii) *Loyalty*

Fiduciary duties

[*Add to note 683: page* [70]]
But *cf. Hilton v Barker Booth & Eastwood* [2005] UKHL 8; [2005] 1 W.L.R. 567; *Conway v Ratiu* [2005] EWCA Civ 1302; [2006] 1 All E.R. 571; and see *Halton International Inc v Guernroy Ltd* [2005] EWHC 1968 (Ch).

31–116

[*Note 684*]
Update reference to *Bowstead and Reynolds* to (18th ed., 2006), Arts 43–48.

Duty not to have conflicting interest

[*Add to note 717: page* [72]]
See also *Marks & Spencer Plc v Freshfields Bruckaus Deringer* [2004] EWCA Civ 741; [2004] P.N.L.R. 4, holding that the conflicting interests can arise from different transactions with the same party.

31–120

[*Note 721: page* [73]]
Update reference to *Bowstead and Reynolds* to (18th ed., 2006), Art.45.

Conflict of duty and duty

31–122   [*Substitute for note 732: page* [74]]
See *Hilton v Barker Booth & Eastwood* [2005] UKHL 8; [2005] 1 W.L.R. 567:
see Getzler (2006) 122 L.Q.R. 1.

Exclusion clauses

31–123   [*Add to note 736: page* [74]]
In appropriate cases the Unfair Terms in Consumer Contracts Regulations
1999 might also apply: see Vol.1, paras 15–004 *et seq.*

(iv) *Remedies*

Common law

31–124   [*Add to note 739: page* [75]]
BP Plc v Aon Ltd (No.2) [2006] EWHC 424 (Comm); [2006] 1 All E.R.
(Comm.) 789.

Equity: duty to account and equitable compensation

31–126   [*Add to note 752: page* [76]]
Att-Gen for Hong Kong v Reid (though a Privy Council case: see Bennett
(2005) 121 L.Q.R. 23) was followed on this point by Lawrence Collins J. in
Daraydan Holdings Ltd v Solland International Ltd [2004] EWHC 622 (Ch);
[2005] Ch. 119.

[*Add to note 757: page* [77]]
Newgate Stud Co v Penfold [2004] EWHC 2993 (Ch); [2005] All E.R. (D) 376
(May) (some self-dealing claims time-barred).

Equitable compensation

31–127   [*Add to note 759: page* [77]]
See now *Murad v Al-Saraj* [2005] EWCA Civ 959; [2005] 1 W.T.L.R. 1573,
holding that what might have happened had the act planned been disclosed is not
relevant, following *Brickenden v London Loan and Savings Co* [1934] 3 D.L.R.
465, PC; see also *Gray v New Augarita Porcupine Mines Ltd* [1952] 3
D.L.R.1.

(v) *Estoppel as to Principal's Title*

Whether agent estopped as to title

31–130   [*Note 771: page* [79]]
Update reference to *Clerk and Lindsell* to (19th ed., 2006), paras 17–77 *et
seq.*

(b) *Rights of Agents*

General

[*Add to note 774: page* [79]]
See a useful discussion of the principal's duty under reg.4 to act in good faith, in *Simpson v Grant & Bowman Ltd* [2006] Eu L.R. 933 (Q.B.D., H.H. Judge Alton). The matter is relevant to the agent's right to treat the contract as repudiated under reg.18(b); it was held that the principal's conduct did not justify this. The exercise by the principal of a contractual power to terminate was held justifiable and not contrary to good faith in *Tony Vick v Vogle-Gapes Ltd* [2006] EWHC 1579 (QBD, Richard Seymour Q.C.). But in *Turner v Steinhoff UK Furniture Ltd* [2006] Eu. L.R. 50, Taunton County Court, David Blunt Q.C., the agent was held justifiable in treating the contract as repudiated, and duties of co-operation by the principal are suggested which seem to go beyond the existing authority on implied terms in agency law in general.

(i) *Remuneration*

Right to remuneration

[*Insert new note 774a after "the principal" in line 1: page* [79]]
[774a] The agent's commission may sometimes be provided by the contract which he makes between principal and third party as payable to him. This is often held to create a trust in his favour: see *Les Affreteurs Reunis SA v Leopold Walford (London) Ltd* [1919] A.C. 801; see Main Work, Vol.1, paras 18–074 *et seq*. The agent may now be able to sue directly under the Contracts (Rights of Third Parties) Act 1999: see *ibid.*, paras 18–084 *et seq*. It has been held by Colman J. in such a context that an arbitration clause in the main contract applied to a claim by the agent as third party: *Nisshin Shipping Co Ltd v Cleaves & Co Ltd* [2003] EWHC 2602; [2004] 1 Lloyd's Rep. 38.

[*Add to note 777: page* [79]]
Benhams Ltd v Kythira Investments Ltd [2004] EWHC 2973; [2004] All E.R. (D) 313 (Dec.) (implicit in oral agreement that agent to be remunerated).

[*Add to note 779: page* [80]]
PJ Pipe and Valve Co. Ltd v Audco India Ltd [2005] EWHC 1904 (QB); [2006] Eu. L.R. 368 (parties intended higher commission than usual).

Estate agents

[*Note 788: page* [81]]
The reference to Murdoch, *Law of Estate Agency and Auctions* (3rd ed.) should now be to Murdoch, *Law of Estate Agency* (4th ed., 2003).

Commission on the introduction of a purchaser

[*Add to note 798: page* [81]]
See also *Phillipson v Indus Realty Pty Ltd* (2004) 8 V.L.R. 446 ("subject to completion of sale").

Other types of estate agent's agreement

31–139 *[Add to note 816: page [84]]*
Foxtons Ltd v Thesleff [2005] EWCA Civ 514; [2005] 2 E.G.L.R. 29 (commission due when unconditional contracts exchanged).

Agent must be effective cause of transaction

31–142 *[Add to note 831: page [85]]*
See also *Favermead Ltd v FPD Savills Ltd* [2005] EWHC 626 (Ch); [2005] All E.R. (D) 30 (Mar.) (winding up petition presented by estate agent in respect of commission, restrained on the ground that there was a real and substantial dispute as to whether the effective cause requirement applied).

[Add to note 832]
See also *Jacques Lichtenstein v Clube Atletico Mineiro* [2005] EWHC 1300 (QB); [2005] All E.R. (D) 341 (Jun.) (agent authorised to "interest" clubs in footballer: purchasing club already interested before agent acted).

[Add to note 835: page [86]]
Christie Owen & Davies v Ryelance [2005] 18 E.G.C.S. 148 (sale after authority revoked—commission due); *Burney v London Mews Co* [2003] EWCA Civ 766 (particulars given to estate agent).

Commercial agents

31–144 *[Add to note 844: page [87]]*
For further consideration of the extent to which these provisions may be excluded, see *Bowstead and Reynolds on Agency* (18th ed.), paras 11–025 *et seq.*

Opportunity to earn commission

31–145 *[Note 850: page [87]]*
Update reference to *Bowstead and Reynolds* to (18th ed., 2006), Arts 58 and 123.
[Add to note 857: page [88]]
The implication of such a term is considered in *Explora Group Plc v Hesco Bastion Ltd* [2005] EWCA Civ 646 at [86] and [126].

Where Commercial Agents Regulations applicable

31–147 *[Add to note 868: page [89]]*
Art.16 appears to preserve the common law rules for discharge by breach at the instance of the principal. These might appear to include both general repudiatory conduct (on which see *Decro-Wall International SA v Practitioners in Marketing* [1971] 1 W.L.R. 361) and breach of a specific condition in the contract (as to which see *Wickman Machine Tool Sales v L.Schuler AG* [1974] A.C. 235, where a term on visiting customers in an agency contract was in fact (by a majority)

held not a condition). If however the contract of commercial agency is treated as (in effect) a nominate contract the terms of which arise only from the Regulations, it is not clear that the rule as to the effect of an express condition (for example as to performance targets) would be within the rules preserved by this Article. See *Sté Laboratoires Arkopharma v Mlle Gravier* Cass Com May 28, 2002. The Editors are indebted for this point, which could be of practical importance, to Professor Simon Whittaker.

[Add to note 868: page [89]]
In *Cooper v Pure Fishing (UK) Ltd* [2004] EWCA Civ 375; [2004] 2 Lloyd's Rep. 518 it was held that a principal who had cause for terminating the agency but chose not to renew it at its time of expiry had not "terminated" the contract for the purposes of reg.18(a). See also *NPower Direct Ltd v South of Scotland Power Ltd* [2005] EWHC 2123.

[Add to note 869: page [89]]
For an example see *Tony Vick v Vogle-Gapes Ltd* [2006] EWHC 1579 (QB).

[Add to note 871: page [89]]
(Further proceedings in the *Aweco* case are reported at [2002] EWCA Civ 1501; [2003] 1 All E.R. 344.)

[Add to note 875: page [90]]
It seems this applies also to an agent who retires though his health would permit his continuing: *Abbot v Condici Ltd* [2005] 2 Lloyd's Rep. 450.

Indemnity and compensation: indemnity

[Correct text in line 4: page [90]]   **31–148**
Line 4 of this paragraph contains an error. The words "the principal" should be inserted before "continues". The sentence should read "An indemnity is a sum calculated on an equitable basis with regard to the extent to which the agent has brought the principal new customers or has significantly increased the volume of business with existing customers, and the principal continues to derive substantial benefits from such customers after the cessation of the contract."

[Add to note 883: page [90]]
In a Scottish case a sum described in the contract as compensation was held to be an indemnity: *Hardie Polymers Ltd v Polymerland Ltd*, 2002 S.C.L.R. 54.

Compensation

[Add to note 890: page [91]]   **31–149**
Saintier and Scholes, *Commercial Agents and the Law* (2005), Ch.6.

[Add to note 895: page [91]]
The principal case in England and Wales is now the decision of the Court of Appeal in *Lonsdale v Howard & Hallam Ltd* [2006] EWCA Civ 63; [2006] 1 W.L.R. 1281. The leading judgment of Moore-Bick L.J. discounts most of the earlier cases on this topic as tending to concentrate on likely future loss, and states that the compensation (as opposed to indemnity, or common law damages)

relates to "the loss of goodwill for which a claim would not otherwise arise" (at [28]), or "the value of the goodwill which he has built up and which would otherwise pass to the principal free of charge" (at [48]), which could also be explained as the loss of a quasi-proprietary interest held by the agent in the business. It appears therefore that the specific indications in Art.17(7) of where damage is "deemed to occur particularly" are non-exhaustive. Such an approach can be supported by the fact that compensation is also due when the agent dies, becomes incapable, or (probably) retires, but not where (with the principal's consent) he assigns the agency (and thus receives its value from the buyer). It seems that the quantum to be awarded should be justified by expert evidence except in cases where the sum in dispute is low. Sometimes, however, unamortised expenses mentioned in Art.17(7)(b) are taken into account: the relation between these two heads, and the extent to which special features may in general be taken into account, is not clear. It appears that the state of the principal's business may be relevant: in the case itself this was in decline, which was reflected in the last six annual commissions paid, and led to a reduction of the award; presumably the converse would also be true for a growing business.

Length of service was disregarded in the case and it appears that it should not normally be relevant (though shortness of service, at any rate, might affect the valuation of the goodwill). Where the agent is alleged to have performed unsatisfactorily, there may be a repudiatory breach which would entitle the principal to refuse compensation under Arts 16 and 18(a), though this might not be easy to establish: see this Supplement, addition to n.868, but note also the *Tony Vick* case, below, where compensation was denied under Art.18(b)(i) because the agent had himself repudiated by wrongly reacting to certain actions of the principal. Otherwise the agent may be liable in damages for breach of his obligation, though this will not easily be proved. Moore-Bick L.J. did not think that "the duration of the agency or the quality of the agent's performance are necessarily important factors" (at [57]). Of course unsatisfactory performance might reduce the value of the goodwill generated.

French courts, probably more familiar with the idea of agencies being bought and sold, tend to award (with variations) a sum based on a starting-point of two years' gross commission, but this is rejected by Moore-Bick L.J. even as a guideline (see at [39], [40] and [57]). The result at present is that the English courts, which seem in any case disposed towards net rather than gross commission and have been cautious of sanctioning windfall payments, must work out their own way of assessing the value of the goodwill concerned without the aid of anything like a two-year rule even as a starting point, and the role of those advising parties to potential disputes is not easy. It must be doubtful whether those responsible for adopting the notion of compensation unless indemnity (which is better worked out and normally would yield a lower award) is expressly selected realised that they were choosing a notion only at that time worked out in French law (partly in cases before the introduction of the Directive), and not entirely easy to explain even there (see the judgment at [25]). See *Bowstead and Reynolds on Agency* (18th ed., 2006), paras 11–049 *et seq.*; Saintier and Scholes, this Supplement, addition to n.890, pp.185 *et seq.*; Saintier (2006) 122 L.Q.R. 379. The matter is one on which English and Scottish courts have, as noted by Moore-Bick L.J., expressed different views, and the House of Lords has granted leave to appeal.

The judgment in *Lonsdale* is considered in *Tony Vick v Vogle-Gapes Ltd* [2006] EWHC 1579 (QB) (Richard Seymour QC), where the judge said that he would have only have made a nominal award of £2 on a claim unsupported by evidence, and doubted whether a court should simply "make the best estimate it can". It is not clear that this is entirely consistent with the *Lonsdale* case above (see at [57]), though the sum claimed in *Tony Vick,* at £90/100, 000 was much more substantial than the £19,670 claimed in *Lonsdale,* where £5,000 was in fact awarded.

Commission after cessation of agency

[*Add to note 901: page* [92]]   **31–150**
The whole question is considered by Rix L.J. in *Explora Group Plc v Hesco Bastion Ltd* [2005] EWCA Civ 646 at [59] *et seq.*

Illegality of service

[*Add to note 919: page* [94]]   **31–154**
The Gaming legislation is repealed by s.334 of the Gambling Act 2005 (not in force at the time of writing).

(ii) Indemnity

Where no indemnity available

[*Add to note 946: page* [96]]   **31–157**
The Gaming legislation is repealed by s.334 of the Gambling Act 2005 (not in force at the time of writing).

(iii) Lien

Lien

[*Note 953: page* [96]]   **31–158**
Update reference to *Bowstead and Reynolds* to (18th ed., 2006), Art.65.

[*Note 958: page* [97]]
Update reference to *Bowstead and Reynolds* to (18th ed., 2006), Art.68.

(iv) Right of stoppage in transit

Right of stoppage in transit

[*Note 962: page* [97]]   **31–159**
Update reference to *Bowstead and Reynolds* to (18th ed., 2006), Art.69.

8. Termination of Authority

How authority terminated

31–160   *[Add to note 966: page [97]]*
There is also authority for the approach via equity: see *Regent International Hotels (UK) Ltd v Pageguide Ltd, The Times*, May 13, 1985, CA; *Lauritzencool AB v Lady Navigation Inc* [2005] EWCA Civ 579; [2005] 1 W.L.R. 3686.

[Add to note 968: page [98]]
Lodgepower Ltd v Taylor [2004] EWCA Civ 1367; [2005] 1 E.G.L.R. 1 (notice to remedy served on alleged agent of deceased landlord not valid).

Apparent authority

31–163   *[Add to note 990: page [100]]*
AMB Generali Holding AG v SEB Trygg Liv Holding Aktiebolag [2005] EWCA Civ 1237; [2006] 1 Lloyd's Rep 318 at [30]–[32].

Enduring powers of attorney

31–165   *[Page [101]]*
The Mental Capacity Act 2005 (not yet in force at the time of writing) introduces by ss.9 *et seq.* a new institution, that of the lasting power of attorney. This gives the attorney powers going beyond financial matters and involving decisions about the donor's personal welfare, either generally or in relation to specified issues. Such powers must contain a "certificate of capacity" that the donor acts voluntarily and understands the purpose of the document. The power is invalid unless registered but may be registered before the onset of incapacity. Those acting under such powers will be subject to more regulation by the court (now the Court of Protection, reconstituted by ss.45 *et seq.* of the Act) than is true under the existing scheme. But although the Enduring Powers of Attorney Act 1979 will be repealed, existing enduring powers are unaffected, and remain subject to its provisions (see s.66 and Sch.4) and until the new Act comes into force they may still be created. See Bartlett, *Blackstone's Guide to the Mental Capacity Act 2005* (2005); Bryant (2005) Trusts and Estates Law and Tax J8; Hopkins and Nichols (2006) 150 S.J. 632.

CHAPTER 32

ARBITRATION

			PARA.
☐	1.	Statutory regulation	32–002
☐	2.	The arbitration agreement	32–018
☐	3.	Stay of legal proceedings	32–041
☐	4.	Commencement of arbitral proceedings	32–053
☐	5.	The arbitral tribunal	32–060
☐	6.	Jurisdiction of the arbitral tribunal	32–078
☐	7.	The arbitral proceedings	32–083
☐	8.	Powers of the court	32–100
☐	9.	The award	32–107
■	10.	Costs of the arbitration	32–124
☐	11.	Powers of the court in relation to the award	32–132
☐	12.	Miscellaneous	32–165

1. STATUTORY REGULATION

Arbitration Act 1996

[Add to note 5: page [104]]   **32–003**
   Cited with approval in *Lesotho Highlands Development Authority v Impregilo
SpA* [2005] UKHL 43; [2006] 1 A.C. 221 at [19].

Scope of application of the Act: seat of arbitration in England

[Add to note 16: page [105]]   **32–007**
   Arab National Bank v El-Abdali [2004] EWHC 2381 (Comm); [2005] 1
Lloyd's Rep. 541. See also *Tonicstar Ltd v American Home Assurance Co* [2004]
EWHC 1234 (Comm); [2005] Lloyd's Rep. I.R. 32 (which court is to determine
seat).

Choice of foreign law

[Add to note 25: page [106]]   **32–009**
   But see *Naviera, Amazonica Peruana SA v Compañia Internacional de
Seguros de Peru* [1988] 1 Lloyd's Rep. 116; *Halpern v Halpern* [2006] EWHC
603 (Comm); [2006] 2 Lloyd's Rep. 83 at [62].

ACAS arbitration

32–014   [*Add to note 40: page* [107]]
But see *Flight Training International Inc v International Fire Training Equipment Ltd* [2004] EWHC 721; [2004] 2 All E.R. (Comm.) 568 (ACAS deals only with employment disputes, not commercial).

Human Rights Act 1998

32–015   [*Add to note 41: page* [108]]
Sandy (2004) 20 *Arbitration International* 305; Berkovits (2005) 71 *Arbitration* 189.

[*Add to note 43*]
BLCT (13096) Ltd v J Sainsbury plc [2003] EWCA Civ 884; [2004] 2 P.&.C.R. 3; *Department of Economic Policy and Development of the City of Moscow v Bankers Trust Co* [2004] EWCA Civ 314; [2005] Q.B. 207 at [27].

32–016   [*Add at end of note 49: page* [109]]
Ghaidan v Godin-Mendoza [2004] UKHL 30; [2004] 2 A.C. 557 at [37]–[52] (Lord Steyn); Sandy (2004) 20 *Arbitration International* 305.

[*Add to note 51*]
Contrast *BLCT (13096) Ltd v J Sainsbury plc* [2003] EWCA Civ 884; [2004] 2 P.&C.R. 3 (no right to oral hearing on s.69 application); *Department of Economic Policy and Development of the City of Moscow v Bankers Trust Co* [2004] EWCA Civ 314; [2005] Q.B. 207 (confidentiality of judgment on s.68 application); *Sukuman Ltd v Commonwealth Secretariat* [2006] EWHC 304 (Comm); [2006] 2 Lloyd's Rep. 53 (mutual agreement to exclude right of appeal under s.69).

2. The Arbitration Agreement

Definition of "arbitration agreement"

32–018   [*Add after Eco Swiss China Time Ltd v Benetton International BV in note 60: page* [110]]
; *ET Plus SA v Welter* [2005] EWHC 2115 (Comm); [2006] 1 Lloyd's Rep. 251 at [51].

[*Add at end of note 66: page* [111]]
Flight Training International Inc v International Fire Training Equipment Ltd [2004] EWHC 721; [2004] 2 All E.R. (Comm.) 568 (reference to ACAS mediation not arbitration agreement).

[*Add to note 67*]
NB Three Shipping Ltd v Harebell Shipping Ltd [2004] EWHC 2001; [2005] 1 Lloyd's Rep. 509; see Mulcahy (2004) 70 *Arbitration* 172; Nesbitt and Quinlan (2006) 22 *Arbitration International* 133.

Agreements to be in writing

[Add to note 75: page [112]]

Quaere whether an agreement is in "writing" if concluded by electronic means and whether such an agreement could be enforced under the New York Convention on the Recognition and Enforcement of Foreign Arbitral Awards 1958 (see para.32–160) having regard to Art.IV.1 of the Convention.

32–019

Separability of arbitration agreement

[Add to note 85: page [113]]

Vee Networks Ltd v Econet Wireless International Ltd [2004] EWHC 2909 (Comm); [2005] 1 Lloyd's Rep. 192 at [20]; *Lesotho Highlands Development Authority v Impregilo SpA* [2005] UKHL 43; [2006] 1 A.C. 221 at [21].

32–023

[Add to note 86: page [114]]

Vee Networks Ltd v Econet Wireless International Ltd, above, at [21].

[Add to note 89]

Vee Networks Ltd v Econet Wireless International Ltd, above, at [21].

[Add to note 93]

See s.48(5)(c) (power to order rectification unless parties agree otherwise).

Scope of the arbitration agreement

[Page [114]]

The words "in relation to" a contract include disputes which are related to or connected with it and cover a dispute concerning an alleged variation of the contract: *El Nasharty v J Sainsbury plc* [2003] EWHC 2195 (Comm); [2004] 1 Lloyd's Rep. 308.

32–025

[Add to note 96: page [114]]

Benford Ltd v Lopecan SL [2004] EWHC 1897 (Comm); [2004] 2 Lloyd's Rep. 618 at [26]; *ET Plus SA v Welter* [2005] EWHC 2115 (Comm); [2006] 1 Lloyd's Rep. 251 at [42].

[Add to note 98: page [115]]

See also *Amec Civil Engineering Ltd v Secretary of State for Transport* [2005] EWCA Civ 291; [2005] 1 W.L.R. 2339 ("difference" less hard edged than "dispute").

[Add to note 99]

Amec Civil Engineering Ltd v Secretary of State for Transport, above, at [25]–[31].

[Add to note 101, after reference to Overseas Union Insurance Ltd v AA Mutual International Insurance Ltd]

cf. *X Ltd v Y Ltd* [2005] EWHC 769 (T&CC); [2005] Build. L.R. 341.

[Add in penultimate line of note 102, after reference to Capital Trust Investments Ltd v Radio Design TJAB]

Asghar v Legal Services Commission [2004] EWHC 1803, noted (2005) 71 Arbitration (1) 91; *ET Plus SA v Welter*, above.

[Add new paragraph 32–026A: page [116]]

32–026A   **Set-off and counterclaim.** Subject to the terms of the arbitration clause, a counterclaim by way of set-off arising out of the same or a closely related contract will be within the scope of the clause but not a counterclaim by way of set-off arising out of a separate and unconnected contract.[108a]

> [108a] *Metal Distributors (UK) Ltd v ZCCM Investment Holdings plc* [2005] EWHC 156 (Comm); [2005] 2 Lloyd's Rep. 37. See also *ED&F Man v Société Anonyme Tripolitaine des Usines* [1970] 2 Lloyd's Rep. 416; *Ronly Holdings v JSC Zestafoni Nikoladze Ferroalloy Plant* [2004] EWHC 1354 (Comm); *Benford Ltd v Lopecan SL* [2004] EWHC 1897 (Comm); [2004] 2 Lloyd's Rep. 618.

Pre-conditions

32–029   *[Add at end of note 115: page [116]]*
See also *Amec Civil Engineering Ltd v Secretary of State for Transport* [2005] EWCA Civ 291; [2005] 1 W.L.R. 2339 (reference to engineer under ICE Conditions of Contract).

Third parties

32–035   *[Page [117]]*
In *Peterson Farms Inc v C&M Farming Ltd* [2004] EWHC 121 (Comm); [2004] 1 Lloyd's Rep. 602 at [59]. Langley J. rejected the "group of companies" doctrine applied in ICC arbitrations.

Subrogation

32–036   *[Add to note 128: page [118]]*
See also *West Tankers Inc v RAS Riunione Adriatica di Sicurta* [2005] EWHC 254; [2005] 2 Lloyd's Rep. 257 (duty to arbitrate treated as inseparable component of the subject-matter transferred by subrogation to the insurer) and *Through Transport Mutual Insurance Association (Eurasia) Ltd v New India Assurance Co Ltd (No.2)* [2005] EWHC 455 (Comm); [2005] 2 Lloyd's Rep. 378 (quasi-subrogation rights under foreign statute).

Confidentiality

32–040   *[Add at end of note 137: page [119]]*
Tweeddale (2005) 21 *Arbitration International* 59. See also *Glidepath BV v Thomson* [2005] EWHC 818 (Comm); [2005] 2 Lloyd's Rep. 548 (application by non-party for copies of documents on court record refused on grounds of confidentiality).

[Note 142]
Department of Economics, Policy and Development of the City of Moscow v Bankers Trust Co was affirmed in part and reversed in part by the Court of Appeal: [2004] EWCA Civ 314; [2005] Q.B. 307.

3. STAY OF LEGAL PROCEEDINGS

Resort to legal proceedings

[*Add to note 147: page* [120]]
Contrast *Hackwood Ltd v Areen Design Services Ltd* [2005] EWHC 2322 (TCC); (2006) 22 Const.L.J. 68 (unsuccessful application under s.72), para. 32–133, below.

32–041

Foreign proceedings

[*Add to note 150 in line 10, after reference to The Epsilon Rosa (No.2): page* [120]]
Through Transport Mutual Insurance Association (Eurasia) Ltd v New India Assurance Co Ltd [2004] EWCA Civ 1598; [2005] 1 Lloyd's Rep. 67; *Atlanska Plovibda v Consignaciones Asturianas SA* [2004] EWHC 1273 (Comm); [2004] 2 Lloyd's Rep. 109 at [25]; *West Tankers Inc v RAS Riunione Adriatica di Sicurta* [2005] EWHC 454 (Comm); [2005] 2 Lloyd's Rep. 257.

32–042

[*Add after reference to Toepfer International GmbH v Société Cargill France in note 150, line 3 on page* [121]
Navigation Maritime Bulgare v Rustal Trading Ltd [2002] 1 Lloyd's Rep. 107; *Through Transport Mutual Insurance Association (Eurasia) Ltd v New India Assurance Co Ltd*, above; *West Tankers Inc v RAS Riunione Adriatica di Sicurta*, above.

[*Add at end of note 152*]
Contrast also *West Tankers Inc v RAS Riunione Adriatica di Sicurta*, above, and see *Through Transport Mutual Insurance Association (Eurasia) Ltd v New India Assurance Co Ltd*, above (which court is to decide?).

Stay of legal proceedings

[*Add to note 156: page* [121]]
Contrast *Exeter City Association Football Club Ltd v Football Conference Ltd* [2004] EWHC 2304 (Ch); [2004] 1 W.L.R. 291 (no stay of petition under s.459 of Companies Act 1985).

32–043

[*Add to note 161: page* [122]]
ET Plus SA v Welter [2005] EWHC 2115 (Comm); [2006] 1 Lloyd's Rep. 251 (ICC arbitration in Paris).

Mandatory stay

[*Note 174: page* [123]]
The reference to *Ahmad Al-Naimi v Islamic Press Agency* should be [2000] 1 Lloyd's Rep. 522.

32–046

[*Add to Note 174*]
See Aeberli (2005) 21 *Arbitration International* 253, 278. On an application for a stay, a cross-application may also be made under s.72 of the Act (see

para.32–133, below) by a person who contests the jurisdiction of the arbitrator: *Law Debenture Trust Corp v Elektrim Finance BV* [2005] EWHC 1412 (Ch); [2005] 2 Lloyd's Rep. 755.

Discretionary stay

32–048
[*Page* [123]]
The court also has jurisdiction under CPR, r.11, to direct alternative dispute resolution notwithstanding the unwillingness of one party, but it will not order a stay of proceedings pending the attendance at mediation of a named non-party: *Shirayama Shokusan Co Ltd v Danovo Ltd* [2003] EWHC (Ch); [2004] B.L.R. 207.

[*Note 176: page* [123]]
The reference to *Ahmad Al-Naimi v Islamic Press Agency* should be [2000] 1 Lloyd's Rep. 522.

[*Add at end of note 176*]
Contrast *El Nasharty v J Sainsbury plc* [2003] EWHC 2195 (Comm); [2004] 1 Lloyd's Rep. 309 at [29] (court must be "virtually certain" that there is an arbitration agreement before it grants a stay).

[*Add to note 177: page* [124]]
ET Plus SA v Welter [2005] EWHC 2115 (Comm); [2006] 1 Lloyd's Rep. 251 at [91].

Claims indisputably due

32–049
[*Delete note 178 and substitute: page* [124]]
Now CPR, Pt 24.

[*Add to note 180*]
Collins (Contractors) Ltd v Baltic Quay Management (1994) Ltd [2004] EWCA Civ 1757; *The Times*, January 3, 2005.

4. COMMENCEMENT OF ARBITRAL PROCEEDINGS

Power of the court to extend time for beginning arbitral proceedings

32–054
[*Add to note 203: page* [127]]
See also *Thompson Monella v Pizza Express (Restaurants) Ltd* [2003] EWHC 2966 (Ch); [2004] 12 E.G. 172 (change in the law not outside the reasonable contemplation of the parties and in any event did not contribute to the failure to observe the time-limit).

Commencement of arbitral proceedings

32–059
[*Page* [128]]
In *Atlanska Plovidba v Consignaciones Asturianas SA* [2004] EWHC 1273 (Comm); [2004] 2 Lloyd's Rep. 109 at [17] Moore-Bick J. said:

"If a notice of arbitration is to be effective, it must identify the dispute to which it relates with sufficient particularity and must also make it clear that the person giving it is intending to refer the dispute to arbitration, not merely threatening to do so if his demands are not met. Apart from that, however, I see no need for any further requirements. Whether any particular document meets those requirements will depend on its terms which must be understood in the context in which it was written. The weight of authority supports a broad and flexible approach to this question . . ."

[*Add to note 218: page* [128]]
Bernuth Lines Ltd v High Seas Shipping Ltd [2005] EWHC 3020 (Comm), [2006] 1 Lloyd's Rep. 537 (email notice sufficed).

[*Add new paragraph 32–059A: page* [129]]
Service of notices. Section 76 of the Act deals with the service of notices and **32–059A** subs.(3) of that section provides: "A notice or other document may be served on a person by any effective means." A notice may be sent by email, but it must be despatched to what is, in fact, the email address of the intended recipient and it must not be rejected by the system.[219a]

[219a] *Bernuth Lines Ltd v High Seas Shipping Ltd* [2005] EWHC 3020 (Comm); [2006] 1 Lloyd's Rep. 537 at [28]–[29].

5. THE ARBITRAL TRIBUNAL

Appointment of arbitrators

[*Page* [129]] **32–061**
See *Atlanska Plovidba v Consignaciones Asturianas SA* [2004] EWHC 1273 (Comm); [2004] 2 Lloyd's Rep. 109 at [17]; para.32–059, above.

Power in case of default to appoint sole arbitrator

[*Add to note 233: page* [130]] **32–063**
cf. Minermet SpA Milan v Luckyfield Shipping Corp SA [2004] EWHC 729 (Comm); [2004] 2 Lloyd's Rep. 348 (no need for notice where parties otherwise agree).

Failure of appointment procedure

[*Page* [131]] **32–064**
In *Vale do Rio Doce Navegacao SA v Shanghai Bao Steel Ocean Shipping Co Ltd* [2000] 2 Lloyd's Rep. 1 at [11], Thomas J. suggested that, on an application under s.18, the court could not intervene to determine whether or not there is an arbitration agreement. The respondent in an application under s.18 could (it is submitted) nevertheless make a cross-application under s.72(1) for a declaration that he is not a party to the arbitration agreement: *Sinochem International Oil*

(London) Co Ltd v Fortune Oil Co Ltd [2000] 1 Lloyd's Rep. 682. See also Aeberli (2005) 21 *Arbitration International* 253, 258.

32–065   [*Add to note 242: page* [131]]
Through Transport Mutual Insurance Association (Euroasia) Ltd v New India Assurance Co Ltd (No.2) [2005] EWHC 455 (Comm); [2005] 2 Lloyd's Rep. 378.

[*Note 243*]
The reference for *Durtnell (R) & Sons Ltd v Secretary of State for Trade and Industry* should be [2001] 1 Lloyd's Rep. 275.

[*Add at end of note 243*]
See also *Atlanska Plovidba v Consignaciones Asturianas SA* [2004] EWHC 1273 (Comm); [2004] 2 Lloyd's Rep. 109 (existence of concurrent judicial proceedings in Spain not a ground for refusing appointment).

Removal of arbitrator

32–073   [*Add at end of note 270: page* [134]]
IBA Guidelines on Conflicts of Interest in International Arbitration 2004; Chartered Institute of Arbitrators: Code of Professional and Ethical Conduct (2001, revised 2004); AAA/ABA Code of Ethics for Arbitrators in Commercial Disputes (2004 revision). See also *ASM Shipping Ltd of India v TTMI Ltd of England* [2005] EWHC 2238 (Comm); [2006] 1 Lloyd's Rep. 375 (s.68 application).

[*Add at end of note 272*]
Contrast *Home of Homes Ltd v Hammersmith Fulham LBC* [2003] EWHC 807; [2003] 92 Const.L.R. 48 (arbitrator takes leading counsel's opinion on issues of costs and jurisdiction). On the question of reliance by the arbitrator on his own expertise, see now *Checkpoint Ltd v Strathclyde Pension Fund* [2003] EWCA Civ 84; *Warborough Investment Ltd v S Robinson & Sons (Holdings) Ltd* [2003] EWCA 751; [2003] 2 E.G.L.R. 149; *St George's Investment Co Ltd v Gemini Consulting Ltd* [2004] EWHC 2353 (Ch), noted (2005) 71 *Arbitration* 96; *Claire & Co Ltd v Thames Water Utilities Ltd* [2005] EWHC 1022; [2005] Build. L.R. 366; Altaras (2003) 69 *Arbitration* 216.

[*Add to note 277: page* [135]]
Sinclair v Woods of Winchester Ltd [2005] EWHC 1631 (QB); [2005] 102 Const. L.R. 127.

6. JURISDICTION OF THE ARBITRAL TRIBUNAL

Tribunal can rule on its own jurisdiction

32–078   [*Add to note 300: page* [137]]
See below, para.32–132 (inherent jurisdiction of court).

[*Add to note 302*]
See the Chartered Institute of Arbitrators: Guidelines for Arbitrators dealing with Jurisdictional Problems in International Cases (2004) 70 *Arbitration* 308.

Objection to substantive jurisdiction of tribunal

See Aeberli (2005) 21 *Arbitration International* 253, 264.   **32–079**

[*Add to note 307: page* [137]]
See *Vee Networks Ltd v Econet Wireless International Ltd* [2004] EWHC 2909 (Comm); [2005] 1 Lloyd's Rep. 192; Yang (2004) 70 *Arbitration* 279.

[*Add to note 311, after Athletic Union of Constantinople v National Basketball Association: page* [138]]
; *JSC Zestafoni G Nikoladz Ferroalloy Plant v Ronly Holdings Ltd* [2004] EWHC 245 (Comm); [2004] 2 Lloyd's Rep. 335 at [64]; *Westland Helicopters Ltd v Sheikh Salah al-Hejailan (No.1)* [2004] EWHC 1625 (Comm); [2004] 2 Lloyd's Rep. 523; *Vee Networks Ltd v Econet Wireless International Ltd*, above.

[*Add to note 315: page* [138]]   **32–080**
Caparo Group Ltd v Fagor Arrasate Sociedad Co-operative [2000] A.D.R.L.J. 254; *Law Debenture Trust Corp v Elektrim Finance BV* [2005] EWHC 1412 (Ch); [2005] 2 Lloyd's Rep. 755.

Determination of preliminary point of jurisdiction

See Aeberli (2005) 21 *Arbitration International* 253, 273.   **32–081**

[*Add to note 320 after "s.32(2)": page* [139]]
Belgravia Property Ltd v S&R Ltd [2001] Build L.R. 424

[*Note 320, delete Vale Do Rio Doce Navegacao SA v Shanghai Bao Steel Ocean Shipping Co.* [1999] 2 Lloyd's Rep. 159, 161 *and substitute*]
Azov Shipping Co v Baltic Shipping Co, above, at [161]; *Vale Do Rio Doce Navegacao SA v Shanghai Bao Steel Ocean Shipping Co* [2000] 2 Lloyd's Rep. 1, 10.

7. THE ARBITRAL PROCEEDINGS

Procedural and evidential matters

[*Page* [140]]   **32–085**
See the IBA rules on the taking of evidence in International Commercial Arbitration 1999; Strong and Dries (2005) 21 *Arbitration International* 301.

Consolidation of proceedings and concurrent hearings

See Chartered Institute of Arbitrators: Guideline on Multi-Party Arbitrations   **32–087**
(2006) 7 *Arbitration* 151.

[*Add to note 346: page* [142]]
City & General (Holborn) Ltd v AYH plc [2005] EWHC 2494; [2006] Build.L.R. 55 (JCT form of contract).

[*Add to note 348*]
See Dillon and Limbert (2006) 9 Int. A.L. Rev. 53.

Power to appoint experts etc

32–089   [*Add to note 354: page* [142]]
See the Chartered Institute of Arbitrators' guidelines on the use of tribunal-appointed experts, legal advisers and assessors: (2004) *Arbitration* 70, 45–50.

Provisional relief with agreement of parties

32–093   [*Add to note 369: page* [144]]
Kastner v Jason [2004] EWCA Civ 1599; [2005] 1 Lloyd's Rep. 397 (Lightman J.) (freezing order).

8. Powers of the Court

Court powers in support of arbitral proceedings

32–100   [*Add to note 396: page* [146]]
Assimina Maritime Ltd v Pakistan Shipping Corp [2004] EWHC 3005 (Comm); [2005] 1 Lloyd's Rep. 525; *Tajik Aluminium Plant v Hydro Aluminium AS* [2005] EWCA Civ 1218; [2006] 1 Lloyd's Rep. 155 (witness summons requiring production of documents). But see *ibid.* and *BNP Paribas v Deloitte and Touche LLP* [2003] EWHC 2874 (Comm); [2004] 1 Lloyd's Rep. 233 (no power to order disclosure by non-party).

32–101   [*Add to note 400: page* [147]]
Hiscox Underwriting Ltd v Dickson Manchester & Co Ltd [2004] EWHC 479; [2004] 2 Lloyd's Rep. 438, noted (2005) 71 *Arbitration* 96 (interim order for disclosure). *Assimina Maritime Ltd v Pakistan Shipping Corp*, above (no power to order disclosure by non-party but power to order preservation of documents by non-party); *Lauritzencool AB v Lady Navigation Inc* [2005] EWCA Civ 579; [2005] 2 Lloyd's Rep. 63 (interim injunction pending arbitration); *Cetelem SA v Roust Holdings Ltd* [2005] EWCA Civ 618 (injunction to deliver documentation before arbitration commenced).

[*Add to note 401*]
For the power of the court under s.37 of the Supreme Court Act 1981 to intervene outside of s.44 of the 1996 Act, see *Hiscox Underwriting Ltd v Dickson Manchester & Co*, above; *Cetelem SA v Roust Holdings Ltd*, above.

[*Add to note 402*]
Hiscox Underwriting Ltd v Dickson Manchester & Co Ltd, above (arbitrator newly appointed and unfamiliar with case and so, in effect, unable to act).

[*Add to note 403*]
National Insurance and Guarantee Corp Ltd v M Young Legal Services Ltd
[2004] EWHC 2972 (QB); [2005] 2 Lloyd's Rep. 46.

[*Add to note 405*]
Assimina Maritime Ltd v Pakistan Shipping Corp, above.

Power of court to extend time-limits

[*Add to note 418, after "s.79(3)": page* [148]]   **32–106**
Minermet SpA Milan v Luckyfield Shipping Corp SA [2004] EWHC 729
(Comm); [2004] 2 Lloyd's Rep. 348; *Pirtek (UK) Ltd v Deanswood Ltd* [2005]
EWHC 2301 (Comm); [2005] 2 Lloyd's Rep. 728 at [44, 46].

9. THE AWARD

Conflict of laws

[*Add to note 428: page* [149]]   **32–109**
See *Peterson Farms Inc v C&M Farming Ltd* [2004] EWHC 121 (Comm);
[2004] 1 Lloyd's Rep. 603 at [46]; *Halpern v Halpern* [2006] EWHC 603
(Comm); [2006] 2 Lloyd's Rep. 83 at [46].

Remedies

[*Add at end of note 436: page* [150]]   **32–111**
a freezing order (*Kastner v Jason* [2004] EWCA Civ 1599; [2005] 1 Lloyd's
Rep. 397.

[*Note 438*]
The decision of the Court of Appeal in *Lesotho Highlands Development
Authority v Impregilo SpA* was reversed by the House of Lords [2005] UKHL 43;
[2006] 1 A.C. 221. But there was a difference of opinion in that case as to the
ambit of s.48(4): see paras [22]–[23], [42], [49], [55] and [56].

[*Add to note 441: page* [151]]
Bath and North East Somerset DC v Mowlem [2004] EWCA Civ 115; [2004]
C.I.L.L. 2081; noted (2005) 71 *Arbitration* 161.

Interest

[*Add to note 445: page* [151]]   **32–112**
The provisions of a foreign law applicable to the matrix contract is not such a
contrary agreement: *Lesotho Highlands Development Authority v Impregilo SpA*
[2005] UKHL 43; [2006] 1 A.C. 221 at [37].

[*Add to note 446*]
Lesotho Highlands Development Authority v Impregilo SpA [2005] UKHL 43;
[2006] 1 A.C. 221. *cf. Durham CC v Darlington BC* [2003] EWHC 2598; [2004]

B.L.G.R. 311 (no power to award interest for the period before the principal sum became payable). See Chartered Institute of Arbitrators' Guidelines on the Award of Interest (2004); Altaras (2004) 70 *Arbitration* 108.

[*Note 452*]
The decision of the Court of Appeal in *Lesotho Highlands Development Authority v Impregilo SpA* was reversed by the House of Lords [2005] UKHL 43; [2006] 1 A.C. 221.

[*Add at end of note 452*]
But see *Westland Helicopters Ltd v Sheikh Salah al-Hejailan (No.1)* [2004] EWHC 1625 (Comm); [2004] 2 Lloyd's Rep. 523 (challenge to arbitrator's award of interest under s.67 (lack of jurisdiction) and s.68 (serious irregularity)).

Form of award

32–115   [*Add to note 459: page* [152]]
cf. Tame Shipping Ltd v Easy Navigation Ltd [2004] EWHC 1862 (Comm); [2004] 2 Lloyd's Rep. 626 (reasons can be set out in separate "confidential" document); see below, para.32–145.

Correction of award or additional award

32–119   [*Add at end of paragraph: page* [153]]
The parties are nevertheless free to agree that the tribunal shall have further or different powers to correct an award or make an additional award outside the terms of s.57.[479a]

[479a] *Pirtek (UK) Ltd v Deanswood Ltd* [2005] EWHC 2301 (Comm); [2005] 2 Lloyd's Rep. 728 at [35].

[*Add to note 476: page* [153]]
Torch Offshore LLC v Cable Shipping Inc [2004] EWHC 787 (Comm); [2004] 2 Lloyd's Rep. 446; *Sinclair v Woods of Winchester Ltd* [2005] EWHC 1631 (QB); (2005) 102 Const. L.R. 127. But see *World Trade Corp v C Czarnikow Sugar Ltd* [2004] EWHC 2332 (Comm); [2005] 1 Lloyd's Rep. 422 at [8].

[*Add to note 477*]
Torch Offshore LLC v Cable Shipping Inc, above, at [27] ("claim" only applies to a claim which has been presented to the tribunal but has not been dealt with as opposed to an issue which remains undetermined as part of a claim); *World Trade Corp v C Czarnikow Sugar Ltd*, above, at [14] ("claim" does not mean a submission in support of a relevant question of fact as opposed to a claim for relief such as would have to be pleaded). See also *Pirtek (UK) Ltd v Deanswood Ltd* [2005] EWHC 2301 (Comm); [2005] 2 Lloyd's Rep. 728 (burden of proof).

[*Add to note 478*]
Torch Offshore LLC v Cable Shipping Inc, above; *Sinclair v Woods of Winchester Ltd*, above; para.32–148, below.

[Add to note 479]
Pirtek (UK) Ltd v Deanswood Ltd., above. The time-limits may be extended:
s.79, para.32–106, above.

Award as a defence

[Add to note 493: page [154]]   **32–123**
Contrast *Sun Life Assurance Co of Canada v Lincoln National Life Insurance
Co* [2004] EWCA Civ 1660; [2005] 1 Lloyd's Rep. 606 (no estoppel where
arbitration between one of the parties and a stranger).

10. Costs of the Arbitration

Costs

[Add at end of paragraph: page [155]]   **32–124**
An agreement in the parties' submission letter that they will share equally the
arbitrators' hourly charges does not imply that the costs of the arbitration
between the parties are to be similarly allocated.[499a]

[499a] *Carter v Harold Simpson Associates* [2004] UKPC 29; [2005] 1 W.L.R. 919.

[Add at end of note 502: page [155]]   **32–125**
Henchie (2004) 70 *Arbitration* 77.

[Add to note 515: page [156]]   **32–126**
See *Rotary Watches Ltd v Rotary Watches (USA) Inc*, unreported, noted (2005)
71 *Arbitration* 172.

[Add to note 521: page [157]]   **32–127**
But it might be argued, in certain circumstances, that costs could be awarded
on the basis of an estoppel or on the grounds that a party who initiates arbitration
impliedly consents to an order for costs being made against him if the tribunal
rules that it has no jurisdiction.

11. Powers of the Court in relation to the Award

Challenging the award: substantive jurisdiction

[Page [158]]   **32–132**
See generally Aeberli (2005) 21 *Arbitration International* 253.
Having regard to s.1(c) of the Act, the question arises whether the court still
retains in addition its inherent powers to rule on jurisdiction: see *ABB Lummus
Global Ltd v Keppel Fils Ltd* [1999] 2 Lloyds Rep. 24; *Vale do Rio Doce
Navegacao SA v Shanghai Bao Steel Ocean Shipping Co Ltd* [2000] 2 Lloyd's
Rep. 1; *J T Mackley & Co Ltd v Gosport Marina Ltd* [2002] EWHC 1315
(TCC); [2002] Build L.R. 367.

[*Add to note 529: page* [158]]

In *Republic of Ecuador v Occidental Exploration and Production Co* [2005] EWCA Civ 1116; [2006] 2 W.L.R. 70, the Court of Appeal rejected a claim that it was unable to adjudicate on a s.67 application on the ground of non-justiciability (bilateral investment treaty invoked).

[*Add to note 536*]

Zaporozhyve Production Society v Ashly Ltd [2002] EWHC 1410 (Comm); *Peoples Insurance Co of China v Vysanthi Shipping Co Ltd* [2003] EWHC 1655 (Comm); [2003] 2 Lloyd's Rep. 617; *Peterson Farms Inc v C&M Farming Ltd* [2004] EWHC 121 (Comm). [2004] 1 Lloyd's Rep. 603 at [18]; *Metal Distributors UK Ltd v ZCCM Investment Holdings plc* [2005] EWHC 156 (Comm); [2005] 2 Lloyd's Rep. 37 at [16]. But adducing new evidence is subject to control by the court: *Primetrade AG v Ythan Ltd* [2005] EWHC 2399 (Comm); [2006] 1 Lloyd's Rep. 457 at [62].

32–133   [*Add to note 540*]

Law Debenture Trust Corp v Elektrim Finance BV [2005] EWHC 1412 (Ch); [2005] 2 Lloyd's Rep. 755 (court rather than arbitrator to decide jurisdiction issue); Aeberli (2005) 21 *Arbitration International* 253, 254. It may also be appropriate in some cases for the court to grant an injunction under this subsection to prevent the arbitration from going ahead rather than leaving it to the tribunal to decide: *Zaporozhyve Production Society v Ashly Ltd* [2002] EWHC 1410 (Comm). See also *Arab National Bank v El-Abdali* [2004] EWHC 238 (Comm); [2005] 1 Lloyd's Rep. 541. *cf. Zaporozozhye Production etc. Society v Ashly Ltd* [2002] EWHC 1410 (injunction refused). An unsuccessful application under s.72 does not preclude a party from subsequently participating in the arbitration: *Hackwood Ltd v Areen Design Services Ltd* [2005] EWHC 2322 (TCC); (2006) 22 Const. L.J. 68.

32–134   [*Add to note 541 after Athletic Union of Constantinople v National Basketball Association: page* [159]].

; *JSC Zestafoni G Nikoladz Ferroalloy Plant v Ronly Holdings Ltd* [2004] EWHC 245 (Comm); [2004] 2 Lloyd's Rep. 335; *Westland Helicopters Ltd v Sheikh Salah al-Hejailan (No.1)* [2004] EWHC 1625 (Comm); [2004] 2 Lloyd's Rep. 523; *Vee Networks Ltd v Econet Wireless International Ltd* [2004] EWHC 2909 (Comm); [2005] 1 Lloyd's Rep. 192; *Primetrade AG v Ythan Ltd* [2005] EWHC 2399 (Comm); [2006] 1 Lloyd's Rep. 457 at [56].

Challenging the award: serious irregularity

32–137   [*Add to note 554: page* [160]]

Bulfracht (Cyprus) Ltd v Boneset Shipping Co Ltd [2002] EWHC 2292 (Comm); [2002] 2 Lloyd's Rep. 681; *Warborough Investment Ltd v S Robinson & Sons (Holdings) Ltd* [2003] EWCA 751; [2003] 2 E.G.L.R. 149; *Minermet SpA Milan v Luckyfield Shipping Corp SA* [2004] EWHC 729 (Comm); [2004] 2 Lloyd's Rep. 348, *Westland Helicopters Ltd v Sheikh Salah al-Hejailan (No.1)* [2004] EWHC 1625 (Comm); [2004] 2 Lloyd's Rep. 523; *Tame Shipping Ltd v Easy Navigation Ltd* [2004] EWHC 1862 (Comm), [2004] 2 Lloyd's Rep. 626; *Alphapoint Shipping Ltd v Rotem Amfert Negev* [2004] EWHC 2232 (Comm);

[2005] 1 Lloyd's Rep. 23; *Vee Networks Ltd v Econet Wireless International Ltd* [2004] EWHC 2909 (Comm); [2005] 1 Lloyd's Rep. 192; *Margulead Ltd v Exide Technologies* [2004] EWHC 1019 (Comm); [2005] 1 Lloyd's Rep. 324; *Home of Homes Ltd v Hammersmith & Fulham LBC* [2003] EWHC 807; (2003) 92 Const. L.R. 48; *Ronly Holdings Ltd v JSC Zestafoni G Nicoladze Ferroalloy Plant* [2004] EWHC 1354 (Comm); [2004] 1 C.L.C. 1168; *St George's Investment Co Ltd v Gemini Consulting Ltd* [2004] EWHC 2358 (Ch); *Bottiglieri di Navigazione SpA v Cosco Qingdao Ocean Shipping Co* [2005] EWHC 244 (Comm); [2005] 2 Lloyd's Rep. 1; *ASM Shipping Ltd of India v TTMI Ltd of England* [2005] EWHC 2238 (Comm); [2006] 1 Lloyd's Rep. 375; *Bernuth Lines Ltd v High Seas Shipping Ltd* [2005] EWHC 3020 (Comm); [2006] 1 Lloyd's Rep. 536 at [53]; *Claire & Co Ltd v Thames Water Utilities Ltd* [2005] EWHC 1022; [2005] Build. L.R. 366; *Cameroon Airlines v Transnet Ltd* [2004] EWHC 1829 (Comm); [2006] T.C.L.R. 1, *ABB AG v Hochtief Airport GmbH* [2006] EWHC 388 (Comm); [2006] 2 Lloyd's Rep. 1.

[*Add to note 555: page* [160]]
Westland Helicopters Ltd v Sheikh Salah al-Hejailan, above; *Republic of Ecuador v Occidental Exploration & Production Co (No.2)* [2006] EWHC 345 (Comm); [2006] 1 Lloyd's Rep. 773; *ABB AG v Hochtief Airport GmbH*, above. In *Lesotho Highlands Development Authority v Impregilo SpA* [2005] UKHL 43; [2006] 1 A.C. 221, the House of Lords held that a mere error of law by the arbitrators did not amount to an excess of power under s.68(2)(b).

[*At the end of sub-paragraph (c) in paragraph 32–137: page* [160], *insert new note 555a*]
555a *Westland Helicopters Ltd v Sheikh Salah al-Hejailan*, above.

[*Add to note 556*]
Torch Offshore LLS v Cable Shipping Inc [2004] EWHC 787 (Comm); [2004] 2 Lloyd's Rep. 446; *Tame Shipping Ltd v Easy Navigation Ltd*, above; *Alphapoint Shipping Ltd v Rolem Amfert Negev Ltd*, above; *Margulead Ltd v Exide Technologies*, above; *World Trade Corp v C Czarnikow Sugar Ltd* [2004] EWHC 2332 (Comm); [2005] 1 Lloyd's Rep. 422; *Marklands Ltd v Virgin Retail Ltd* [2003] EWHC 3428; [2004] 27 E.G. 130; *Fidelity Management SA v Myriad International Holdings BV* [2005] EWHC 1193 (Comm); [2005] 2 Lloyd's Rep. 508; *Protech Projects Constructions Pty Ltd v Al-Kharafi & Sons* [2005] EWHC 2165 (Comm); [2005] 2 Lloyd's Rep. 779; *Sinclair v Woods of Winchester Ltd* [2005] EWHC 1631; (2005) 102 Const. L.R. 127; *ABB AG v Hochtief Airport GmbH*, above.

[*Note 556a*]
Delete this note.

[*Add to note 557*]
Benaim (UK) Ltd v Davies Middleton & Davies Ltd [2005] EWHC 1370 (TCC); 102 Con. L.R. 1.

[*Add to note 558*]
Thyssen Canada Ltd v Mariana Maritime SA [2005] EWHC 219 (Comm); [2005] 1 Lloyd's Rep. 640; *Protech Projects Construction Pty Ltd v Al-Kharafi & Sons*, above.

[*Add to note 559: page* [160]]
Benaim (UK) Ltd v Davies Middleton & Davies Ltd, above.

[*Add to note 562: page* [161]]
See also *World Trade Corp v C Czarnikow Sugar Ltd*, above (weight of evidence); *Lesotho Highlands Development Authority v Impregilo SpA* [2005] UKHL 43; [2006] 1 A.C. 221 at [28].

32–138   [*Add to note 564: page* [161]]
Torch Offshore LLS v Cable Shipping Inc [2004] EWHC 787 (Comm); [2004] 2 Lloyd's Rep. 446; *Alphapoint Shipping Ltd v Rotem Amfert Negev Ltd* [2004] EWHC 2232 (Comm); [2005] 1 Lloyd's Rep. 23; *Newfield Construction Ltd v Tomlinson* [2004] EWHC 3051; (2004) 97 Const. L.R. 148; *Fidelity Management SA v Myriad International Holdings BV* [2005] EWHC 1193 (Comm); [2005] 2 Lloyd's Rep. 508; *ASM Shipping Ltd of India v TTMI Ltd of England* [2005] EWHC 2238 (Comm); [2006] 1 Lloyd's Rep. 375; *Bernuth Lines Ltd v High Seas Shipping Ltd* [2005] EWHC 3020 (Comm); [2006] 1 Lloyd's Rep. 537; *Cameroon Airlines v Transnet Ltd* [2004] EWHC 1829 (Comm); [2006] T.C.L.R. 1; *ABB AG v Hochtief Airport GmbH* [2006] EWHC 388 (Comm); [2006] 2 Lloyd's Rep. 1.

[*Add to note 565*]
But see *ASM Shipping Ltd of India v TTMI Ltd of England*, above, at [39] (tribunal not impartial in itself a substantial injustice).

[*Add at end of paragraph: page* [161]]
The element of serious injustice does not depend on the arbitrator having come to the wrong conclusion as a matter of law or fact but whether he was caused by adopting inappropriate means to reach one conclusion whereas had he adopted appropriate means he might well have reached another conclusion favourable to the applicant.[565a]

[565a] *Vee Networks Ltd v Econet Wireless International Ltd* [2004] EWHC 2909 (Comm); [2005] 1 Lloyd's Rep. 192 at [88]–[90]; *St George's Investment Co Ltd v Gemini Consulting Ltd* [2004] EWHC 2353 (Ch).

32–139   [*Add to note 570: page* [162]]
ASM Shipping Ltd of India v TTMI Ltd of England above, at [49].

Appeal on point of law

32–141   "There is no room for any appeal under section 69 against the findings of fact in the Award itself since these have to be accepted for the purpose of any application for permission to appeal": Cooke J. in *Demco Investments & Commercial SA v SE Banken Forsakring Holding Aktiebolag* [2005] EWHC 154 (Comm); [2005] 2 Lloyd's Rep. 650 at [35].

[*Add to note 572: page* [162]]
Dundas (2006) 72 *Arbitration* 111, 281.

[*Add to note 577: page* [162]]
JSC Zestafoni G Nikoladz Ferroalley Plant v Ronly Holdings Ltd [2004] EWHC 245 (Comm), [2004] 2 Lloyd's Rep. 335; *Vrinera Marine Co Ltd v*

Eastern Rich Operations Inc [2004] EWHC 1752 (Comm); [2004] 2 Lloyd's Rep. 465; *Alphapoint Shipping Ltd v Rotem Amfert Negev Ltd* [2004] EWHC 2232 (Comm); [2005] 1 Lloyd's Rep. 23; *Newfield Construction Ltd v Tomlinson* [2004] EWHC 3051 (Comm); (2004) 97 Const. L.R. 148; *Bottiglieri di Navigazione SpA v Cosco Quindao Ocean Shipping Co* [2005] EWHC 244 (Comm); [2005] 2 Lloyd's Rep. 1; *Surefire Systems Ltd v Guardian ECL Ltd* [2005] EWHC 1860 (TCC); [2006] Build. L.R. 534.

[After sub-paragraph (b) in paragraph 32–141: page [162] insert new note 577a]
577a *Marklands Ltd v Virgin Retail Ltd* [2003] EWHC 3428; (2004) 27 E.G. 130.

[Add to note 582: page [163]]   **32–142**
Alphapoint Shipping Ltd v Rotem Amfert Negev Ltd [2004] HC 2232 (Comm); [2005] 1 Lloyd's Rep 23 at [7] (conjoined applications under ss.68, 69). Refusal of an oral hearing is not contrary to Art.6 of the European Convention on Human Rights: *BLCT (13096) Ltd v J Sainsbury plc* [2003] EWCA Civ 884; [2004] 2 P.&C.R. 3.

[Add to note 586]
In *Demco Investments & Commercial SA v SE Banken Forsakring Holding Akhebolag* [2005] EWHC 1542 (Comm); [2005] 2 Lloyd's Rep. 650, Cooke J. reviewed the authorities and concluded that it is not now open to appeal under the 1996 Act on the basis that there is no evidence to support a finding of fact (at [35]–[48]). See also *Surefire Systems Ltd v Guardian ECL Ltd* [2005] EWHC 1860 (TCC); [2006] Build L.R. 534. *cf. Benaim (UK) Ltd v Davies Middleton & Davies Ltd* [2005] EWHC 1370 (TCC).

[Add at end of note 589: page [164]]   **32–143**
Vrinera Marine Co Ltd v Eastern Rich Operations Inc [2004] EWHC 1752 (Comm); [2004] 2 Lloyd's Rep. 465 at [15].

[Add new paragraph 32–143A: page [164]]
Combined applications. Applications under s.68 (challenge on the ground of   **32–143A** serious irregularity) and s.69 (for leave to appeal on a point of law) may be combined in one hearing[589a] but they involve two quite distinct processes of judicial analysis.[589b] In many cases determination of the s.69 application before that of the s.68 application may be logically preferable, but in each case it is a matter for the court whether the application for leave to appeal should be tried first.[589c]

589a *Bulfracht (Cyprus) Ltd v Boneset Shipping Co Ltd* [2002] EWHC 2292 (Comm); [2002] 2 Lloyd's Rep. 681; *Newfield Construction Ltd v Tomlinson* [2004] EWHC 3051; (2004) 97 Const. L.R. 148; *Alphapoint Shipping Ltd v Rotem Amfert Negev Ltd* [2004] EWHC 2232; [2005] 1 Lloyd's Rep. 23.
589b *Alphapoint Shipping Ltd v Rotem Amfert Negev Ltd*, above, at [5]–[7].
589c *ibid.*, at [7].

Right of appeal: exclusion agreements

[Add at end of paragraph: page [164]]   **32–144**
An exclusion agreement is not contrary to Art.6(1) of the European Convention on Human Rights.[593a]

[*Add to note 592: page* [164]]
Sukuman Ltd v Commonwealth Secretariat [2006] EWHC 304 (Comm);
[2006] 2 Lloyd's Rep. 53.

[*Add new note 593a after note 593*]
593a *Sukuman Ltd v Commonwealth Secretariat*, above.

Challenge or appeal: reasons for award

32–145 [*Page* [164]]
Where, by agreement of the parties, the arbitral tribunal makes an award
without stating its reasons for the award but sets out its reasons in a separate
"confidential" document, this does not preclude the court from looking at those
reasons for the purpose of an application under s.68 of the Act: *Tame Shipping
Ltd v Easy Navigation Ltd* [2004] EWHC 1862 (Comm); [2004] 2 Lloyd's Rep.
626; noted (2005) 71 *Arbitration* 98.

[*Add to note 595: page* [164]]
Alphapoint Shipping Ltd v Rotem Amfert Negev Ltd [2004] EWHC 2232
(Comm); [2005] 1 Lloyd's Rep. 23 at [5]; *Margulead Ltd v Exide Technologies*
[2004] EWHC 1019 (Comm); [2005] 1 Lloyd's Rep. 324 at [41]–[42].

Challenge or appeal: restrictions and time-limits

32–148 [*Add at end of note 602: page* [165]]
Torch Offshore LLS v Cable Shipping Inc [2004] EWHC 787 (Comm); [2004]
2 Lloyd's Rep. 446; *World Trade Corp v C Czarnikow Sugar Ltd* [2004] EWHC
2332 (Comm); [2005] 1 Lloyd's Rep. 422; *Sinclair v Woods of Winchester Ltd*
[2005] EWHC 1631 (QB); (2005) 102 Const. L.R. 127. (See para.32–119,
above).

[*Add to note 603*]
See also *Westland Helicopters Ltd v Sheikh Salah al-Hejailan (No.1)* [2004]
EWHC 1625 (Comm); [2004] 2 Lloyd's Rep. 523; *Thyssen Canada Ltd v
Mariana Maritime SA* [2005] EWHC 219 (Comm); [2005] 1 Lloyd's Rep. 640;
Sinclair v Woods of Winchester Ltd, above.

[*Add to note 604: page* [166]]
Thyssen Canada Ltd v Mariana Maritime SA, above; *Sinclair v Woods of
Winchester Ltd*, above.

32–149 [*Add to note 607: page* [166]]
Peterson Farms Inc v C&M Farming Ltd [2004] EWHC 121 (Comm); [2004]
1 Lloyd's Rep. 603; *JSC Zestafoni G Nikoladz Ferroalloy Plant v Ronly Holdings Ltd* [2004] EWHC 245 (Comm) 2004; [2004] 2 Lloyd's Rep. 335; *Westland
Helicopters Ltd v Sheikh Salah al-Hejailan (No.1)* [2004] EWHC 1625 (Comm);
[2004] 2 Lloyd's Rep. 523; *Vee Networks Ltd v Econet Wireless International Ltd*
[2004] EWHC 2909 (Comm); [2005] 1 Lloyd's Rep. 192; *Margulead Ltd v Exide
Technologies* [2004] EWHC 1019 (Comm); [2005] 1 Lloyd's Rep. 324; *Thyssen
Canada Ltd v Mariana Maritime SA* [2005] EWHC 219 (Comm); [2005] 1

Lloyd's Rep. 640; *ASM Shipping Ltd of India v TTMI Ltd of England* [2005] EWHC 2238 (Comm); [2006] 1 Lloyd's Rep. 375; *Primetrade AG v Ythan Ltd* [2005] EWHC 2399 (Comm); [2006] 1 Lloyd's Rep. 457; *Sinclair v Woods of Winchester Ltd* [2005] EWHC 1631 (QB); [2005] 102 Const. L.R. 127.

[*Add to note 608*]
JSC Zestafoni G Nikoladz Ferroalloy Plant v Ronly Holdings Ltd, above, at [63]–[64].

Challenge or appeal: supplementary orders

[*Add to note 609: page* [166]]   **32–150**
Republic of Kazakhstan v Istil Group Inc [2005] EWCA Civ 1468; [2006] 1 W.L.R. 596. *cf. Peterson Farms Inc v C&M Farming Ltd* [2003] EWHC 2298; [2004] 1 Lloyd's Rep. 614 (Tomlinson J.) (s.68 application).

Challenge or appeal: appeals to the Court of Appeal

[*Add to note 622: page* [167]]   **32–156**
See also (appeals to House of Lords) Sch.2(2) and *Henry Boot Construction Ltd v Alstom Combined Cycles Ltd* [2005] EWCA Civ 814.

Foreign awards

[*Add after the first reference to Dardana Ltd v Yukos Oil Co in note 658: page*   **32–160**
[170]]
; *Svenska Petroleum Exploration AB v Government of the Republic of Lithuania* [2005] EWHC 9 (Comm); [2005] 1 Lloyd's Rep. 515; *Ipco (Nigeria) Ltd v Nigerian National Petroleum Ltd* [2005] EWHC 726 (Comm); [2005] 2 Lloyd's Rep. 326; *Kanoria v Guinness* [2006] EWCA Civ 222; [2006] 1 Lloyd's Rep. 701. See also *Svenska Petroleum Exploration AB v Government of the Republic of Lithuania (No.2)* [2005] EWHC 2437 (Comm); [2006] 1 Lloyd's Rep. 181; *AIG Capital Partners Ltd v Republic of Kazakhstan* [2005] EWHC (Comm); [2006] 1 W.L.R. 1420 (sovereign immunity).

[*Add at the end of note 658*]
Ipco (Nigeria) Ltd v Nigerian National Petroleum Ltd, above.

Civil Jurisdiction and Judgments Act 1982

[*Add to note 660: page* [170]]   **32–162**
Shone (2005) 71 *Arbitration* 46.

Limitation

[*Add to end of note 664: page* [171]]   **32–164**
Good Challenger Navegante SA v Metalexportimport SA [2003] EWCA Civ 1668; [2004] 1 Lloyd's Rep. 67 (acknowledgement).

12. MISCELLANEOUS

Valuers, experts, etc.

32–166 [*Add to note 674: page* [172]]
Bernhard Schulte GmbH & Co KG v Nile Holdings Ltd [2004] EWHC 977 (Comm); [2004] 2 Lloyd's Rep. 352 at [68], [92]–[95] (apparent bias or unfairness not grounds for resisting determination by expert). *cf. Amec Civil Engineering Ltd v Secretary of State for Transport* [2005] EWCA Civ 291; [2005] 1 W.L.R. 2339 (adjudication).

[*Add to note 676*]
Thames Valley Power Ltd v Total Gas & Power Ltd [2005] EWHC 2208 (Comm); [2006] 1 Lloyd's Rep. 441.

Adjudication

32–169 See paras 37–255—37–262, below.

[*Add to note 683: page* [173]]
Pegram Shopfitters Ltd v Tally Weijl (UK) Ltd [2003] EWCA Civ 1750 at [8]

[*Add to note 684*]
But see *Amec Civil Engineering Ltd v Secretary of State for Transport*, above (duty to act independently, honestly and fairly).

[*Add to note 685*]
But see *Pegram Shopfitters Ltd v Tally Weijl (UK) Ltd*, above (challenge to the jurisdiction of the adjudicator).

CHAPTER 33

BAILMENT

			PARA.
■	1.	In general	33–001
□	2.	Possession and related matters	33–009
	3.	Gratuitous bailment	33–032
		(a) Deposit	33–032
		(b) Involuntary bailees	33–036
		(c) Mandate	33–040
		(f) Gratuitous loan for use	33–041
■	4.	Bailments for valuable consideration	33–044
		(a) The supply of services: statutory provisions	33–044
■		(b) Custody for reward	33–048
■		(i) In general	33–048
		(ii) Illustrations of custody for reward	33–057
		(c) Hire	33–063
		(i) Hire (unregulated by the Consumer Credit Act)	33–063
		(ii) Equipment leasing	33–081
		(iii) Statutory control of hiring	33–082
		(d) Work and labour	33–088
■		(e) Innkeepers	33–098
■		(f) Pledge	33–118
□		(i) Pledge at common law	33–118
□		(ii) Statutory control of pledges	33–134

1. In General

Definition of bailment

[*Note 7: page* [176]]   **33–001**
Marcq v Christie, Manson & Woods Ltd has been reported at [2004] Q.B.
286.

No one unifying theory

[*Note 37: page* [179]]   **33–006**
Marcq v Christie, Manson & Woods Ltd has been reported at [2004] Q.B.
286.

2. Possession and Related Matters

Conversion of the chattel by the bailee

33–014 *[Note 72: page* [183]]
Marcq v Christie, Manson & Woods Ltd has been reported at [2004] Q.B.
286.

Entitlement to sue

33–021 *[Add to note 99 after "below, para 33–026"): page* [186]]
HSBC Rail (UK) Ltd v Network Rail Infrastructure Ltd [2005] EWCA Civ
1437; [2006] 1 Lloyd's Rep. 358.

Insurable interest

33–025 *[Insert new footnote 113a after "full value" in line two of the text: page* [188]]
[113a] The extent of the bailee's insurance cover is a question of construction of the particular policy
and it is not the case that the bailee will in all cases be entitled to recover the full value of the goods
lost or damaged. In particular, the policy may be held to cover only the legal liabilities of the bailee
towards the bailor or a third party: see *Ramco (UK) Ltd v International Insurance Company of
Hanover* [2004] EWCA Civ 675; [2004] All E.R. (Comm.) 866. See further para.41–008.

Sub-bailment

33–026 *[Add to note 122: page* [189]]
It is, however, necessary to distinguish between consent to a sub-bailment and
consent to the creation of a direct contractual relationship between the bailor and
the sub-bailee. The two are "conceptually different": see *Targe Towing Ltd v
Marine Blast Ltd* [2004] EWCA Civ 346; [2004] 1 Lloyd's Rep. 721.

4. Bailments for Valuable Consideration

(b) *Custody for Reward*

(i) *In General*

Custody for reward

33–049 *[Add to note 255: page* [202]]
While it is not necessary as a matter of law for a bailee to show what the cause
of the damage was, the identification of the cause may be a "significant pointer
as to whether or not the bailee has exercised reasonable care": *Coopers Payne
Ltd v Southampton Container Terminal Ltd* [2003] EWCA Civ 1223; [2004] 1
Lloyd's Rep. 331 at [29].

[Add to note 258 after reference to Levison case: page [203]]
Euro Cellular (Distribution) plc v Danzas Ltd t/a Danzas AEI Intercontinental
[2003] EWHC 3161 (Comm); [2004] 1 Lloyd's Rep. 521 at [60]–[66].

Damages

[*Add to note 263: page* [203]]   **33–050**
The extent of the bailee's insurance cover is a question of construction of the particular policy and it is not the case that the bailee will in all cases be entitled to recover the full value of the goods lost or damaged. In particular, the policy may be held to cover only the legal liabilities of the bailee towards the bailor or a third party: see *Ramco (UK) Ltd v International Insurance Company of Hanover* [2004] EWCA Civ 675; [2004] All E.R. (Comm.) 866. See further para.41–008.

(e) *Innkeepers*

Defences: negligence of the guest

[*Note 654: page* [235]]   **33–109**
Update reference to *Cross and Tapper on Evidence* to (10th ed., 2005), p.140 n.49.

(f) *Pledge*

(i) *Pledge at Common Law*

Definition of pledge

[*Note 723: page* [240]]   **33–118**
Marcq v Christie, Manson & Woods Ltd has been reported at [2004] Q.B. 286.

Delivery essential for pledge

[*Note 739: page* [241]]   **33–121**
Update reference to *Benjamin's Sale of Goods* to (7th ed., 2006), paras 7–033, 18–235—18–239.

Pledges by mercantile agents or factors

[*Note 750: page* [243]]   **33–124**
Update reference to *Benjamin's Sale of Goods* to (7th ed., 2006), paras 7–034—7–054.

[*Note 751*]
Update reference to *Benjamin's Sale of Goods* to (7th ed., 2006), paras 7–055 *et seq.*, 7–069 *et seq.*

[*Note 752*]
Update reference to *Benjamin's Sale of Goods* to (7th ed., 2006), paras 7–049—7–052.

Pledge of bills of lading

33–125   [*Note 753: page* [243]]
Update reference to *Benjamin's Sale of Goods* to (7th ed., 2006), paras 5–140, 18–216, 18–234—18–239.

(ii) *Statutory Control of Pledges*

The Consumer Credit Act 1974

33–134   [*Note 813: page* [247]]
Update reference to *Benjamin's Sale of Goods* to (7th ed., 2006), paras 18–006—18–010.

CHAPTER 34

BILLS OF EXCHANGE AND BANKING

			PARA.
■	1.	Negotiable instruments	34–001
□		(a) The nature of negotiable instruments	34–001
□		(b) Bills of exchange	34–009
□		(i) Definitions and requirements	34–009
□		(ii) Capacity and authority of parties	34–040
□		(iii) The consideration for a bill	34–062
□		(iv) Transfer of bills	34–088
□		(v) General duties of holder	34–103
		(vi) Liabilities of parties	34–116
□		(vii) Discharge of bill	34–125
		(viii) Acceptance and payment for honour	34–144
		(ix) Lost instruments	34–147
		(x) Bills in a set	34–149
■		(c) Cheques	34–150
□		(i) General provisions	34–150
□		(ii) Crossed cheques	34–161
		(iii) Travellers' cheques	34–174
		(d) Promissory notes	34–186
□		(e) Negotiable instruments in the conflict of laws	34–198
		(i) General	34–198
		(ii) Form	34–205
□		(iii) Essential validity	34–208
		(iv) Performance	34–213
■	2.	Aspects of banking law	34–219
■		(a) Bank regulation	34–220
□		(i) Overview	34–220
□		(ii) The regulation of deposit-taking	34–226
□		(iii) EC harmonisation measures	34–240
■		(b) The relationship of banker and customer	34–242
□		(i) Definition of a bank	34–242
■		(ii) Definition of a customer	34–247
		(iii) Nature of the banker-customer relationship	34–250
□		(iv) Fiduciary relationship and duty of care	34–251
□		(v) Banks and undue influence	34–257
□		(vi) Banks as constructive trustees	34–275
□		(vii) Duty of secrecy	34–304
■		(viii) Termination of relationship	34–308
■		(c) The current account	34–309
□		(i) Rights and duties of the banker	34–309
□		(ii) Termination of duty to pay	34–318
□		(iii) Protection of paying banker in cases of unauthorised payment	34–330

			PARA.
☐		(iv) Special types of current accounts	34–345
☐	(d)	Discount and collection	34–352
☐	(e)	The giro system and electronic transfer of funds	34–367
☐	(f)	The deposit account	34–411
☐	(g)	Giving information on financial transactions	34–414
	(h)	The banker as bailee	34–418
☐	(i)	Bankers' commercial credits	34–422
☐		(i) The U.C.P.	34–422
☐		(ii) Types of documentary credits	34–457
☐		(iii) The contract between seller and buyer	34–470
		(iv) The relationship of issuing banker and buyer	34–478
☐		(v) The relationship of banker and seller	34–483
☐		(vi) The relationship of issuing and correspondent bankers	34–499
☐		(vii) The tender of documents	34–504
		(viii) The nature and effect of the trust receipt	34–522
	(j)	The banker's lien	34–525

1. Negotiable Instruments

(a) *The Nature of Negotiable Instruments*

Practical use of negotiable instruments

34–004   [*Note 11: page* [256]]
Update the reference to *Ellinger, Lomnicka and Hooley* to (4th ed., 2006), Ch.10, Sects. 8–11.

Promissory notes

34–005   [*Note 12: page* [256]]
Update the reference to *Benjamin* to (7th ed., 2006), Ch.24.

Effect of Consumer Credit Act 1974

34–008   [*Note 24: page* [258]]
Update the reference to *Ellinger, Lomnicka and Hooley* to (4th ed., 2006), pp.410–411.

(b) *Bills of Exchange*

[*Note 32: page* [259]]
Update reference to *Chalmers and Guest* to (16th ed., 2005) and to *Benjamin* to (7th ed., 2006), Ch.22.

(i) *Definitions and Requirements*

Unconditional order in writing

34–012   [*Note 48: page* [260]]
Update reference to *Benjamin* to (7th ed., 2006), para.22–042.

Bills addressed to drawee

[*Note 54: page* [261]]   **34-013**
Update reference to *Benjamin* to (7th ed., 2006), paras 22–018 *et seq.*

Authorised delivery

[*Add to note 140 at the end: page* [271]]   **34-035**
; *Abbey National plc v JSF Finance & Currency Exchange Co Ltd* [2006]
EWCA Civ 328.

(ii) *Capacity and Authority of Parties*

Sufficient signature

[*Note 164: page* [275]]   **34-043**
Update reference to *Chalmers and Guest* to (16th ed., 2005), para.3–023.

Personal liability of company's director

[*Delete ", if the bill is dishonoured," in second sentence of paragraph and add at*   **34-046**
end of that sentence: page [276]]
, unless it is duly paid by the company. Where a bill is presented for payment
and dishonoured, the bill is not "duly paid" for the purposes of s.349(4).[167a]

[167a] It may not even be necessary to present the bill for payment for s.349(4) to apply. A bill is
dishonoured by non-payment when presentment is excused and the bill is overdue and unpaid (Bills
of Exchange Act 1882, s.47(1)(b)). Presentment is excused where the drawee is not bound, as
between himself and the drawer, to pay the bill and the drawer had no reason to believe that it would
be paid if presented (Bills of Exchange Act 1882, s.46(2)(c), as applied in *Fiorentino Comm Giuseppe
Srl v Farnesi* [2005] EWHC 160 (Ch) (director held personally liable under s.349(4) despite fact
cheque not presented for payment)).

Forged indorsements: order bills

[*Note 188: page* [280]]   **34-056**
Update reference to *Chalmers and Guest* to (16th ed., 2005), para.3–066.

(iii) *The Consideration for a Bill*

Accommodation bill or party

[*Note 226: page* [288]]   **34-074**
Update reference to *Chalmers and Guest* to (16th ed., 2005), para.4–042.

Holder in due course

[*Note 232: page* [289]]   **34-075**
Update reference to *Chalmers and Guest* to (16th ed., 2005), para.4–057.

Position of original payee

34–083   [*Add to text at end of paragraph: page* [293]]
More recently, in *Dextra Bank & Trust Co Ltd v Bank of Jamaica*,[266a] Lord
Bingham and Goff, applying *Talbot v Von Boris* and *Hasan v Willson*, stated that
the payee of a cheque, obtained by a third party from the drawer in fraud of the
drawer, would acquire good title to the cheque provided that the payee had no
notice of that fraud.[266b]

[266a] [2002] 1 All E.R. (Comm.) 193, PC.
[266b] At [22]. And see *Abbey National plc v JSF Finance & Currency Exchange Co Ltd* [2006]
EWCA Civ 328, where, for the purposes of an interlocutory application, the Court of Appeal held that
the payee's knowledge should be assessed taking account of the wider circumstances in which the
transaction took place, including the fact that there had been a number of similar, previous transactions which the payee knew to be fraudulent.

(iv) *Transfer of Bills*

Overdue or dishonoured bills

34–093   [*Note 297: page* [297]]
Update reference to *Chalmers and Guest* to (16th ed., 2005), para.5–041.

Rights of holder: generally

34–095   [*Note 305: page* [298]]
Update reference to *Chalmers and Guest* to (16th ed., 2005), para.4–005.

Rights of holder in due course

34–096   [*Note 307: page* [299]]
Update reference to *Chalmers and Guest* to (16th ed., 2005), paras
4–062—4–069.

(v) *General Duties of Holder*

Presentment for payment

34–108   [*Note 341: page* [305]]
Update reference to *Chalmers and Guest* to (16th ed., 2005), para.6–022.

Notice of dishonour

34–112   [*Note 352: page* [307]]
Update reference to *Benjamin* to (7th ed., 2006), paras 22–121 *et seq.*

Noting or protest of bill

34–114   [*Note 360: page* [308]]
Update reference to *Benjamin* to (7th ed., 2006), paras 22–135 *et seq.*

(vi) *Liabilities of Parties*

Liability of drawer and indorser

[Note 377: page [310]]
Update reference to *Chalmers and Guest* to (16th ed., 2005), para.7–021.

34–117

Other signatures

[Note 380: page [310]]
Update reference to *Chalmers and Guest* to (16th ed., 2005), paras 7–031 *et seq.*

34–118

[Note 384]
Update reference to *Benjamin* to (7th ed., 2006), paras 22–052, 22–053.

Measure of damages for dishonour

[Delete from "The position is currently governed by a Practice Direction" in line 8 to the end of the paragraph and substitute: page [311]]
When calculating the appropriate rate of interest for a period from the date of the cause of action to the date of the judgment, the rate payable on judgment debts is a convenient starting point.[387a] However, the usual practice in the Commercial Court is to award interest at 1 per cent above base rate, unless such rate would be unfair to one or other of the parties.[387b] For small claims, it is easier to claim interest at the judgment rate.[387c]

34–120

[387a] See the notes to the CPR 1998 in the White Book, para.7.0.17. Contrast *Practice Note* [1983] 1 W.L.R. 377 (short-term investment account rate).
[387b] *Shearson Lehman Hutton Inc v Maclaine Watson & Co Ltd* [1990] 3 All E.R. 723.
[387c] CPR, Pt 12, r.6 (default judgments). On claims for interest generally, see *Chalmers and Guest on Bills of Exchange and Cheques* (16th ed., 2005), para.7–047.

(vii) *Discharge of Bill*

Discharge defined

[Note 403: page [314]]
Update reference to *Chalmers and Guest* to (16th ed., 2005), para.8–003.

34–125

Claims for repayment by drawee or acceptor

[Note 411: page [315]]
Update reference to *Ellinger, Lomnicka and Hooley* to (4th ed., 2006), Ch.12.

34–128

Present scope of doctrine

[Add new note 435a at the end of the first sentence: page [319]]
[435a] The defence of change of position is available against restitutionary claims based on unjust enrichment, but even then it is not open to a wrongdoer (*Lipkin Gorman (a firm) v Karpnale Ltd* [1991] 2 A.C. 548 at 580). There is some doubt as to whether it is available against a restitutionary claim based on the vindication of property rights, where the action is subject to the bona fide purchaser for value defence (*Foskett v McKeown* [2001] 1 A.C. 102 at 129; *Papamichael v National Westminster Bank* [2003] 1 Lloyd's Rep. 341 at 376).

34–136

[*Add to note 436 at the end*]
Commerzbank AG v Gareth Price-Jones [2003] EWCA Civ 1663 (noted by Birks, (2004) 120 L.Q.R. 373).

Assessment

34–137 [*Delete note 438: page* [320] *and substitute*]
Important recent cases on the availability of the change of position defence include: *Scottish Equitable plc v Derby* [2001] EWCA Civ 369; [2001] 2 All E.R. (Comm.) 274 and *Credit Suisse (Monaco) SA v Attar* [2004] EWHC 374 (Comm) (on the need for a causal link between the mistaken receipt and the change of position); *Dextra Bank & Trust Co Ltd v Bank of Jamaica* [2002] 1 All E.R. (Comm.) 193 and *Commerzbank AG v Gareth Price-Jones* [2003] EWCA Civ 1663 (on anticipatory change of position); *Niru Battery Manufacturing Co v Milestone Trading Ltd* [2002] EWHC 1425 (Comm); [2002] 2 All E.R. (Comm.) 705, 741, approved [2003] EWCA Civ 1446; [2004] 4 All E.R. (Comm.) 193 (on what constitutes "bad faith"); *Barros Mattos Junior v MacDaniels Ltd* [2004] EWHC 1188 (Ch); [2004] 3 All E.R. 299 (on a change of position which constitutes an illegal action); *Campden Hill Ltd v Chakrani* [2005] EWHC 911 (Ch) (on retention of benefit acquired as result of change of position). See, generally, Vol. I, paras 29–179 *et seq.*

Tracing order

34–138 [*Add to note 440 at the end: page* [320]]
See also *Bank of America v Arnell* [1999] Lloyd's Rep. Bank. 399.

[*Add to note 441 at the end*]
Bishopsgate Investment Management Ltd v Homan [1995] Ch. 211, CA; *Box v Barclays Bank plc* [1998] Lloyd's Rep. Bank. 185 at 203; *Shalson v Russo* [2003] EWHC 1637 (Ch); [2005] Ch. 281 at [140]–[141]. See also Smith, [1995] C.L.J. 290.

Acceptor holder at maturity

34–139 [*Note 445: page* [321]]
Update reference to *Chalmers and Guest* to (16th ed., 2005), para.8–058.

(c) *Cheques*

(i) *General Provisions*

Cheque truncation

34–154 [*Note 484: page* [326]]
Update reference to *Chalmers and Guest* to (16th ed., 2005), paras 13–021 *et seq.*

Post-dated cheques

34–157 [*Note 489: page* [327]]
Update reference to *Chalmers and Guest* to (16th ed., 2005), para.2–098.

(ii) Crossed Cheques

Protects true owner

[Add to note 503 at the end: page [330]]   **34–164**
; see also *Abbey National plc v JSF Finance & Currency Exchange Co Ltd*
[2006] EWCA Civ 328.

Effect of section 81A(1)

[Note 513: page [332]]   **34–169**
Update reference to *Chalmers and Guest* to (16th ed., 2005), para.14–039.

Negligence issue

[Amend note 515: page [332]]   **34–171**
Delete "*Linklaters v HKSB* [2003] 1 Lloyd's Rep. 545" and replace with
"*Linklaters (a firm) v HSBC Bank plc* [2003] EWHC 1113 (Comm); [2003] 1
Lloyd's Rep. 545 (noted by Ellinger, (2004) 120 L.Q.R. 226)."

(e) Negotiable Instruments in the Conflict of Laws

(iii) Essential Validity

Essential validity

[Note 592: page [345]]   **34–208**
Update reference to current edition of *Chalmers and Guest* to (16th ed., 2005),
para.12–015.

2. A<small>SPECTS OF</small> B<small>ANKING</small> L<small>AW</small>

(a) Bank Regulation

(i) Overview

Financial Services and Markets Act 2000

[Note 615: page [350]]   **34–220**
Update reference to *Ellinger, Lomnicka and Hooley* to (4th ed., 2006).

Other legislative controls

[Add to note 617 at the end: page [351]]   **34–222**
The Consumer Credit Act 1974 generally only regulates credit agreements of
up to £25,000 made with "individuals" (not companies), subject to exemptions.
But note that the Consumer Credit Act 2006, through amendment to the 1974

Act, abolishes the £25,000 financial limit so that all credit agreements are *prima facie* covered irrespective of the amount involved. The definition of an "individual" is narrowed in relation to partnerships so that only those of two or three persons are covered. Further exemptions have been introduced relating to agreements exceeding £25,000 which relate to the debtor's business and to "high net worth" debtors. See the Consumer Credit Act 2006, ss.1–4 (yet to come into force).

[*Add to note 618 at the end*]
But note that it was recently held by Judge Kershaw Q.C., sitting as a judge of the Queen's Bench Division, in *Governor & Company of the Bank of Scotland v Singh*, unreported, June 17, 2005, that the Regulations did not apply where a company director executed a guarantee to cover his company's indebtedness to the bank.

[*Add new note 621a after "by October 9, 2004", 22 lines from the start of this paragraph*]
621a EC Directive 2002/65 was implemented in the United Kingdom through the Financial Services (Distance Marketing) Regulations 2004 (SI 2004/2095), which came into force on October 31, 2004.

34–224 [*Delete first two sentences of note 624 and substitute: page* [352]]
The Money Laundering Regulations 2003 (SI 2003/3075) came into force, for the most part, on March 1, 2004. These Regulations repeal and replace the Money Laundering Regulations 1993 (SI 1993/1933) as amended and the Money Laundering Regulations 2001 (SI 2001/3641).

[*Amend note 624*]
Delete reference to the FSA's money laundering sourcebook.

Banking Codes

34–225 [*Page* [352]]
New editions of the *Banking Code* and the *Business Banking Code* came into effect on March 1, 2005.

(ii) *The Regulation of Deposit-taking*

Accepting deposits "by way of business"

34–231 [*Note 638: page* [355]]
Update reference to *Ellinger, Lomnicka and Hooley* to (4th ed., 2006), p.38.

Sanctions for unauthorised acceptance of deposits

34–236 [*Add to note 655 at end: page* [357]]
The court has jurisdiction under the Supreme Court Act 1981, s.37, to make an order freezing the bank accounts of third parties over which the person who has contravened the authorisation requirements of the 2000 Act has control. See *Financial Services Authority v Fitt* [2004] EWHC 1669 (Ch).

Statutory immunity of the F.S.A.

[*Add to note 662 at end: page* [377]]   **34–238**
The claim was eventually abandoned at the trial itself: see [2006] EWHC 816
(Comm).

(iii) *EC Harmonisation Measures*

EC single market in banking

[*Note 663: page* [358]]   **34–240**
Update reference to *Ellinger, Lomnicka and Hooley* to (4th ed., 2006),
pp.53–61.

(b) *The Relationship of Banker and Customer*

(i) *Definition of a Bank*

Who is a banker: scope of problem

[*Note 674: page* [359]]   **34–242**
Update reference to *Ellinger, Lomnicka and Hooley* to (4th ed., 2006), Ch.3.

Who is a banker: common law definition

[*Note 682: page* [360]]   **34–243**
Update reference to *Ellinger, Lomnicka and Hooley* to (4th ed., 2006), p.73.

(ii) *Definition of a Customer*

Account in nominee's name

[*Delete the first sentence of note 693 and substitute: page* [363]]   **34–249**
Money Laundering Regulations 2003 (SI 2003/3075), which came into force,
for the most part, on March 1, 2004, and which repeal and replace the Money
Laundering Regulations 1993 (SI 1993/1933) as amended and the Money Laundering Regulations 2001 (SI 2001/3641) (see para.34–224 above).

(iv) *Fiduciary Relationship and Duty of Care*

The General Rule

[*Note 697: page* [364]]   **34–251**
Update reference to *Ellinger, Lomnicka and Hooley* to (4th ed., 2006), Ch.5,
Sect. 4.

[*Add to note 698 at end of second sentence*]
; *Diamantides v JP Morgan Chase Bank* [2005] EWCA Civ 1612.

Every day transactions

34–255   [*Add to note 708 at the end: page* [367]]
(noted by Ellinger, (2004) 120 L.Q.R. 226).

[*Add to note 711 at the end*]
; *Abou-Rahmah v Abacha* [2005] EWHC 2662 (QB); [2006] 1 All E.R. (Comm.) 247 (receiving bank does not owe a duty of care to the payer of funds, who is not its customer and to whom it has undertaken no special responsibility, to pay money received only to the beneficiary identified in the payer's instructions or, in the case of discrepancies, to clarify the identity of the beneficiary with the payer); *Customs and Excise Commissioners v Barclays Bank plc* [2006] UKHL 28; [2006] 3 W.L.R. 1 (bank notified by a third party of freezing injunction granted to the third party against one of the bank's customers affecting an account held by the customer with the bank, owes no duty to the third party to take reasonable care to comply with the terms of the injunction); *Riyad Bank v Ahli United Bank (UK) plc* [2006] EWCA Civ 780 (where there is a contractual chain, the normal position is that the chain should not be by-passed by a claim in tort, but a duty of care may exist where discussions and representations are made directly to the party who suffers loss).

Information respecting new products

34–256   [*Amend note 713: page* [367]]
Delete "2003 editions" and replace with "2005 editions".

(v) *Banks and Undue Influence*

O'Brien guidelines in practice

34–262   [*Amend note 729: page* [370]]
Replace references to the 2003 editions of the *Banking Code* and *Business Banking Code* with references to the 2005 editions of both codes. Citation of paragraph numbers for each code remains unchanged.

Nature of the transaction

34–266   [*Add to note 743 at the end: page* [372]]
Mortgage Agency Services Number Two Ltd v Chater [2003] EWCA Civ 490; [2004] 1 P. & C.R. 4 (joint loan to mother and son).

Rescission

34–271   [*Add to note 762 at the end: page* [375]]
If the property subject to the security is jointly owned by a husband and wife then, even though the security may not be enforceable against the wife, it may be against the husband, and so the court may still order the property to be sold, under the Trusts of Land and Appointment of Trustees Act 1996, s.14, in order to realise the husband's share: see *First National Bank plc v Achampong* [2003] EWCA Civ 487; [2004] 1 F.C.R. 18, noted by Thompson, [2003] Conv. 314.

[*Amend note 767: page* [375]]   **34–272**
Delete "recission" at end of second sentence and replace with "rescission".

[*Add at end of note 767*]
See also J. Poole and A. Keyser, "Justifying Partial Rescission in English Law" (2005) 121 L.Q.R. 273.

[*Add to note 768 at the end: page* [376]]
Applied in *UCB Group Ltd v Hedworth* [2003] EWCA Civ 1717 (a case of sub-subrogation). By contrast, where an earlier charge is voidable for undue influence as against the husband and the bank, a replacement charge, taken out as a condition of discharging that earlier charge, will itself be voidable, even if undue influence was not operative at the time of such replacement: *Yorkshire Bank plc v Tinsley* [2004] EWCA Civ 816; [2004] 1 W.L.R. 2380 (see this Supplement, para.7–106A, above).

(vi) *Banks as Constructive Trustees*

Dishonest assistance

[*Add to note 795 at the end: page* [379]]   **34–279**
The nature of the accountability of the accessory or assister in equity, and the remedies available against him, are usefully examined by Elliott and Mitchell, (2004) 67 M.L.R. 16 (arguing that the assister is jointly and severally liable along with the trustee whom he has assisted).

Combined test of dishonesty

[*Delete "to Y without ensuring that the funds were utilised for the acquisition of the property." in fourth sentence of paragraph and substitute: page* [383]]   **34–288**
"to L. L, who knew of the undertaking given by S, did not take steps to ensure that it was utilised for the acquisition of property by Y. L simply paid out the money on Y's instructions."

[*Add to note 815 at the end*]
The Court of Appeal of New Zealand had also expressed (*obiter*) reservations about the subjective element of the combined test of dishonesty, see *US International Marketing Ltd v National Bank of New Zealand Ltd*, C.A. 144/02, October 28, 2003, at [62] and [78]–[79], noted by Yeo, (2004) 120 L.Q.R. 208.

Practical effect of *Twinsectra* on the position of banks

[*Delete entire paragraph 34–290 and replace with the following: pages* [383]–[384]]   **34–290**
Retreat from Twinsectra. The majority of their Lordships in *Twinsectra* held that for a defendant to be found to be dishonest "it must be established that the defendant's conduct was dishonest by the ordinary standards of reasonable and honest people *and* that he himself realised that by those standards his conduct was dishonest".[816a] The Privy Council has recently revisited the test of dishonesty in *Barlow Clowes International Ltd v Eurotrust International Ltd*[816b] and, although claiming merely to clarify an "ambiguity" in *Twinsectra*, has

altered the test by removing the requirement that the defendant must have subjectively appreciated that his conduct was dishonest. The change is a welcome one as it undoubtedly represents a more accurate interpretation of what Lord Nicholls said in *Tan*.[816c] Subjective elements remain relevant in that the court will consider such matters as the defendant's actual knowledge, or his actual level of experience and intelligence, before assessing whether an ordinary person would objectively consider the defendant's conduct dishonest.[816d] The decision does raises some thorny issues of precedent as *Twinsectra* is a decision of the House of Lords, but it is hoped that the English courts will be inclined to follow *Eurotrust* on this point. Treacy J. has already done so in *Abou-Rahmah v Abacha*.[816e]

[816a] [2002] 2 A.C. 164 at [27], *per* Lord Hutton (emphasis added).
[816b] [2005] UKPC 37; [2006] 1 W.L.R. 1476.
[816c] See n.815 above.
[816d] M. Conaglen and A. Goymour [2006] C.L.J. 18 at 20.
[816e] [2005] EWHC 2662 (QB); [2006] 1 All E.R. (Comm.) 247 at [40]–[52].

Unconscionability as the test of liability

34–301   *[Delete the ninth, tenth and eleventh sentences of paragraph and substitute: pages [387]–[388]]*

In *Criterion Properties plc v Stratford Properties LLC*,[838] the Court of Appeal held that an assessment of unconscionability based merely on whether the recipient had actual knowledge of the circumstances which gave rise to the breach of duty "was too narrow and one-sided a view of the matter".[839] The court was to have regard to the recipient's actions and knowledge in the context of the commercial relationship as a whole to determine whether the test of unconscionability was satisfied.

[838] [2002] EWCA Civ 1883; [2003] 1 W.L.R. 2108 at [38]; affd. on different grounds: [2004] UKHL 28; [2004] 1 W.L.R. 1846.
[839] In *Papamichael v National Westminister Bank plc* [2003] EWHC 164 (Comm); [2003] 1 Lloyd's Rep. 341 at [247], Judge Chambers Q.C. treated actual knowledge as a necessary condition for liability. More recently, in *Crown Dilmun v Sutton* [2004] EWHC 52 (Ch); [2004] 1 B.C.L.C. 468 at [200], Peter Smith J., reluctantly applying the Court of Appeal decision in *Criterion Properties*, held that "attribution of knowledge is not enough. It must be unconscionable for the . . . defendant to retain the benefit".

[Delete "however," from the twelfth sentence of paragraph 34–301]

(vii) *Duty of Secrecy*

Duty of Secrecy

34–304   *[Amend note 847: page [389]]*

Replace references to the 2003 editions of the *Banking Code* and *Business Banking Code* with references to the 2005 editions of both codes. Citation of paragraph numbers for each code remains unchanged.

[Amend note 851]

Delete "Process" in third sentence of n.851 and replace with "Proceeds".

[*Delete "2003 eds" in final sentence of paragraph 34–304 and substitute: page* [390]]
"2005 eds."

[*Add to note 851 at end*]
In general terms, a customer who opens an account at a bank in the UK must be taken to have accepted and be entitled to assume that the bank will act in accordance with applicable anti-money laundering and terrorism legislation (*Tayeb v HSBC Bank plc* [2004] EWHC 1529 (Comm); [2004] 4 All E.R. 1024 at [57], *per* Colman J.).

[*Add to note 852 at the end*]
See also *Rodaro v Royal Bank of Canada* (2002) 59 O.R. (3d) 74 (Ont. C.A.), noted by Ogilvie, (2004) 19 B.F.L.R. 103.

[*Amend note 853*]
Replace reference to the 2003 edition of the *Business Banking Code* with reference to the 2005 edition. Citation of paragraph numbers for the code remain unchanged.

Extraterritorial orders

[*Note 857: page* [391]]   **34–305**
Update reference to *Ellinger, Lomnicka and Hooley* to (4th ed., 2006), pp.188–195.

(viii) *Termination of Relationship*

Termination of relationship by consent

[*Amend note 864: page* [392]]   **34–308**
Replace references to the 2003 editions of the *Banking Code* and *Business Banking Code* with references to the 2005 editions of both codes. Citation of paragraph numbers for each code remains unchanged.

(c) *The Current Account*

(i) *Rights and Duties of the Banker*

Overdrafts

[*Add to note 878 at the end: page* [394]]   **34–312**
References to the bank's "usual rate of interest" or "usual terms" in standard form account opening agreements are not necessarily insufficiently certain to be enforceable as contract terms: whether such a provision fails for uncertainty depends on the evidence placed before the court: *Financial Institutions Services Ltd v Negril Negril Holdings Ltd* [2004] UKPC 40.

[*Add to note 880 at the end*]
affd. [2004] EWCA Civ 64 (but stating that the position would be otherwise where the bank had notice of the agreed limitation as between the account holders).

Combining accounts

34–313
[*Note 881: page* [394]]
Update reference to *Ellinger, Lomnicka and Hooley* to (4th ed., 2006), pp.229–248, 825–833.

[*Insert new paragraph at the end of note 884: page* [395]]
The new administration regime introduced into the Insolvency Act 1986 by the Enterprise Act 2002 includes a mandatory set-off rule in similar form to r.4.90: see r.2.85 of the Insolvency Rules 1986. Revised versions of r.2.85 and r.4.90 came into force on April 1, 2005 (see the Insolvency (Amendment) Rules 2005 (SI 2005/527)).

Effect of agreement

34–314
[*Add to note 891 at the end: page* [396]]
[2004] 2 Lloyd's Rep. 19; affd. [2004] EWCA Civ 1074; [2005] 1 Lloyd's Rep. 12.

Customer's remedies for dishonour

34–315
[*Note 893: page* [396]]
Update reference to *Ellinger, Lomnicka and Hooley* to (4th ed., 2006), pp.461–465.

Mandate and third parties

34–317
[*Add to note 907: page* [398]]
To similar effect, see *Tayeb v HSBC Bank plc* [2004] EWHC 1529 (Comm); [2004] 4 All E.R. 1024 at [75]–[77], *per* Colman J.

[*Add to note 908*]
In *Tayeb v HSBC Bank plc* [2004] EWHC 1529 (Comm); [2004] 4 All E.R. 1024, Colman J. held that mere suspicion as to the origin of funds transferred into a customer's bank account by a third party using the CHAPS electronic funds transfer system—as to which, see para.34–380 below—did not present the bank with a justifiable reason for returning those funds to the transferor without the customer's consent. A bank may have to freeze a customer's account where it knows or suspects that the account contains the proceeds of crime or risk committing a criminal offence under the Proceeds of Crime Act 2002, s 328 (see *Squirrell Ltd v National Westminster Bank plc* [2005] EWHC 664 (Ch); [2005] 1 All E.R. (Comm.) 749). A bank does not act in breach of contract by refusing to honour its customer's payment instructions where it knows or suspects that the money in the account is criminal property (see *K Ltd v National Westminster Bank plc* [2006] EWCA Civ 1039, where the Court of Appeal also held that the bank does not have to adduce evidence to support its suspicion or show that there were reasonable grounds for the suspicion).

(ii) *Termination of Duty to Pay*

When effective

[Main paragraph and note 913: page [399]]
Update references to the *Banking Code* and the *Business Banking Code* to
2005 editions.

Death of customer

[Note 916: page [399]]
Update reference to *Ellinger, Lomnicka and Hooley* to (4th ed., 2006),
pp.429–430.

Third party debt orders

[Note 930: page [401]]
Update reference to *Ellinger, Lomnicka and Hooley* to (4th ed., 2006),
pp.418–425.

[Add to note 933 at the end: page [402]]
Kuwait Oil Tanker Co SAK v Qabazard is now reported at [2004] 1 A.C. 300
and is noted by Rogerson, [2003] C.L.J. 576; Briggs, [2003] L.M.C.L.Q. 418;
Dickinson, (2004) 120 L.Q.R. 16.

[Insert new footnote 934a after "to the judgment debtor." in line 4]
934a In *Alawiye v Mahamood* [2005] EWHC 277 (Ch); [2006] 3 All E.R. 668, Lindsay J. held that,
in the absence of any contrary indication, the court could and should accept, as sufficient for the
purposes of an interim third-party debt order under CPR 72.4, evidence in which the judgment
creditor was able to say no more than that the judgment debtor had previously had an account with
the third-party bank and that it had previously been in credit. Lindsay J. also stated (*obiter*) that the
fact that the account had previously been overdrawn did not of itself preclude there being a debt to
the judgment debtor from the third party, at least where there was nothing to indicate that, overall,
the bank was not a debtor to the judgment debtor.

(iii) *Protection of Paying Banker in Cases of Unauthorised Payment*

Pass books and periodic statement

[Add to note 957 in line 5, after reference to Royal Bank of Scotland plc v Fielding: page [406]]
affd. [2004] EWCA Civ 64.

[Note 957]
Update reference to *Ellinger, Lomnicka and Hooley* to (4th ed., 2006), pp.215
et seq.

[Add to note 960: page [407]]
See also *Financial Institutions Services Ltd v Negril Negril Holdings Ltd*
[2004] UKPC 40 (conclusive evidence clause was not clear and unambiguous
and so was construed narrowly against the bank).

Tai Hing

34–338　　[*Note 970: page* [409]]
Update reference to *Ellinger, Lomnicka and Hooley* to (4th ed., 2006), pp.448–449.

Forged indorsement

34–339　　[*Note 974: page* [410]]
Update reference to *Ellinger, Lomnicka and Hooley* to (4th ed., 2006), pp.454–456.

Payment with negligence

34–340　　[*Note 981: page* [411]]
Update reference to *Chalmers and Guest* to (16th ed., 2005), para.14–028.

Irregularity in or absence of indorsement

34–341　　[*Note 983: page* [411]]
Update reference to *Chalmers and Guest* to (16th ed., 2005), para.17–003.

Where cheque avoided by forgery

34–342　　[*Note 984: page* [411]]
Update reference to *Chalmers and Guest* to (16th ed., 2005), paras 2–013, 3–062, 17–063.

(iv) *Special Types of Current Accounts*

Survivorship

34–348　　[*Add to note 1003 at the end: page* [414]]
; *Crill v Wood* (2003–04) 6 ITELR 590 (Royal Court, Jersey).

Partnership accounts

34–349　　[*Note 1008: page* [415]]
Update reference to *Ellinger, Lomnicka and Hooley* to (4th ed., 2006), pp.298–301.

Trust accounts

34–350　　[*Insert new note 1008a at the end of first sentence: page* [415]]
[1008a] For the nature of a trust account, see *Mann v Coutts & Co* [2003] EWHC 2138 (Comm); [2004] 1 All E.R. (Comm.) 1 at [154]–[165].

[*Amend note 1010: page* [415]]
Replace reference to *Hanbury and Martin's Modern Equity* (16th ed., 2001), p.582 with one to *Hanbury and Martin's Modern Equity* (17th ed., 2005), para.20–019.

(d) *Discount and Collection*

Non-transferable cheques

[*Add to note 1021 at the end: page* [417]]   **34–353**
noted by Ellinger, (2004) 120 L.Q.R. 226.

Causes of action

[*Note 1025: page* [418]]   **34–354**
Update reference to *Ellinger, Lomnicka and Hooley* to (4th ed., 2006),
pp.618–619.

[*Note 1028*]
Update reference to *Chalmers and Guest* to 16th ed., 2005), para.2–151.

[*Add to note 1031 at the end*]
noted by Ellinger, (2004) 120 L.Q.R. 226.

Protection of collecting banker

[*Note 1033: page* [419]]   **34–355**
Update reference to *Ellinger, Lomnicka and Hooley* to (4th ed., 2006),
Ch.15.

Instances of negligence

[*Amend text: page* [420]]   **34–356**
Delete sentence that begins "A relevant authorised person" in line 4, page
[420], of main paragraph, and update references in lines 22 and 23 to the *Banking
Code* and the *Business Banking Code* to 2005 editions.

[*Delete note 1042 and substitute*]
[1042] Money Laundering Regulations 2003 (SI 2003/3075) which came into force, for the most part,
on March 1, 2004. These new Regulations repeal and replace the Money Laundering Regulations
1993 (SI 1993/1933) as amended and the Money Laundering Regulations 2001 (SI 2001/3641) (see
para.34–224 above).

[*Note 1044*]
Update reference to *Ellinger, Lomnicka and Hooley* to (4th ed., 2006),
pp.630–633.

[*Add to note 1047 at the end: page* [421]]   **34–357**
noted by Ellinger, (2004) 120 L.Q.R. 226.

Other documents

[*Note 1052: page* [422]]   **34–359**
Update reference to *Benjamin* to (7th ed., 2006), paras 22–018—22–030.

Duty to customer

34–366 [*Insert new footnote 1073a after "with ordinary diligence." at the end of line 3 of main paragraph: page* [425]]

[1073a] By contrast, where a collecting bank collects an instrument for a remitting bank, it is a firmly established common law rule that the collecting bank has privity of contract with the remitting bank and not with the remitting bank's customer (*Grosvenor Casinos Ltd v National Bank of Abu Dhabi* [2006] EWHC 784 (Comm) at [34], Colman J.).

[*Note 1074*]

Update reference to *Ellinger, Lomnicka and Hooley* to (4th ed., 2006), pp.651 *et seq* and pp.355 *et seq*.

(e) *The Giro System and Electronic Transfer of Funds*

[*Note 1080: page* [426]]

Update reference to *Ellinger, Lomnicka and Hooley* to (4th ed., 2006), Ch.13.

Paper-based and electronic system

34–374 [*Insert in the tenth line of the text after "BACS Ltd" and before "("BACS")": page* [428]]

and, since December 1, 2003, BACS Payment Schemes Ltd,

Clearing house rules

34–379 [*Add to note 1096 at end: page [430]*]

See also *Tayeb v HSBC Bank plc* [2004] EWHC 1529 (Comm); [2004] 4 All E.R. 1024 at [57].

[*Amend note 1098*]

Update reference to New CHAPS Rules to Version 1.3, r.10.1.1.

UK clearing systems

34–380 [*Insert in the seventh line of the text after "BACS Ltd" and before "which provides": page* [431]]

and, since December 1, 2003, BACS Payment Schemes Ltd,

Position of paying banker

34–392 [*Add to note 1121 at the end: page* [436]]

And see also *Grosvenor Casinos Ltd v National Bank of Abu Dhabi* [2006] EWHC 784 (Comm) (held no privity of contract between drawee bank and holder of a bearer cheque who alleged that drawee bank had assured his own bank that it would be paid on presentation).

[*Add new paragraph 34–396A: page* [437]]

34–396A **Relationship between transferor and recipient (payee's) banker.** The recipient (payee's) bank does not owe a duty of care to a non-customer transferor of a giro transfer to pay money received only to the recipient identified in the transferor's instructions, or to clarify any discrepancies in those instructions as to the recipient's identity with the transferor.[1127a]

[1127a] *Abou-Rahman v Abacha* [2005] EWHC 2662 (QB); [2006] 1 All E.R. (Comm.) 247, where Treacy J. refused to follow *Royal Bank of Canada v Stangl* (1992) 32 A.C.W.S. (3d.) 17, Ontario Court, General Division.

Interposition of correspondent bank

[*Add to note 1129 at the end: page* [438]]   **34–397**
In *Grosvenor Casinos Ltd v National Bank of Abu Dhabi* [2006] EWHC 784 (Comm), Colman J. considered the Uniform Rules for Collections point to be of potentially wide application in international banking law and so was not prepared to decide it on a summary application.

Cases where payee claims payment is complete

[*Add to text at end of paragraph: page* [440]]   **34–402**
Similarly, in *Tayeb v HSBC Bank plc*,[1137a] where the payee's bank became suspicious of the origin of funds transferred into the payee's account using the CHAPS electronic transfer system and returned those funds to the payer's bank, Colman J. held that a CHAPS transfer was ordinarily irreversible once the payee's bank had authenticated the transfer, sent an acknowledgement message informing the payer's bank that the transfer had been received and credited the funds to the payee's account.[1137b]

[1137a] [2004] EWHC 1529 (Comm); [2004] 4 All E.R. 1024 (noted by Ellinger, (2005) 121 L.Q.R. 48).
[1137b] At [60] and [85]. However, the judge stated (at [60]) that there was an appropriate analogy with the practice in relation to documentary credits where, at the time of presentation of documents, a bank with cogent evidence of fraud can decline to make payment (*United Trading Corporation v Allied Arab Bank Ltd* [1985] 2 Lloyd's Rep. 554). He added (at [61]) that the same exception was likely to apply in respect of illegal transactions (see *Mahonia Ltd v JP Morgan Chase Bank* [2003] 2 Lloyd's Rep. 911).

Availability as if cash

[*Add to note 1142 at end: page* [442]]   **34–406**
See also *Tayeb v HSBC Bank plc* [2004] EWHC 1529 (Comm); [2004] 4 All E.R. 1024 at [88].

(f) *The Deposit Account*

Its nature

[*Note 1150: page* [444]]   **34–411**
Update reference to *Ellinger, Lomnicka and Hooley* to (4th ed., 2006), p.330.

(g) *Giving Information on Financial Transactions*

Banking references

34–417 [*Amend note 1165: page* [446]]
Replace references to the 2003 editions of the *Banking Code* and the *Business Banking Code* with reference to the 2005 editions. Citations of paragraph numbers for each code remain unchanged.

[*Note 1168: page* [447]]
Update reference to *Ellinger, Lomnicka and Hooley* to (4th ed., 2006), pp.673–675.

(i) *Bankers' Commercial Credits*

[*Note 1179: page* [448]]
Update reference to *Benjamin* to (7th ed., 2006), Ch.23.

(i) *The U.C.P.*

Purpose of credit

34–422 [*Note 1180: page* [449]]
Update reference to *Benjamin* to (7th ed., 2006), paras 23–217 *et seq.*

(ii) *Types of Documentary Credits*

Standby credits

34–464 [*Note 1227: page* [463]]
Update reference to *Benjamin* to (7th ed., 2006), paras 23–237 *et seq.*

Transfer and assignment of credits

34–465 [*Note 1228: page* [463]]
Update reference to *Benjamin* to (7th ed., 2006), paras 23–068 *et seq.*

[*Insert new footnote 1230a at the end of paragraph: page* [464]]
[1230a] The first beneficiary will usually want to keep information about his transaction with the second beneficiary away from the applicant for fear that the applicant will cut him out of the picture and deal directly with the second beneficiary. In *Jackson v Royal Bank of Scotland* [2005] UKHL 3; [2005] 1 W.L.R. 377 at [20]–[24], the House of Lords confirmed that an issuing bank owes the first beneficiary of a transferable letter of credit a duty of confidentiality with regard to this information (breach of duty of confidentiality when issuing bank reveals to applicant the extent of first beneficiary's "mark-up" on price charged).

Bank's duty to transfer

34–468 [*Note 1239: page* [466]]
Update reference to *Benjamin* to (7th ed., 2006), paras 23–079 *et seq.*

(iii) *The Contract between Seller and Buyer*

The documentary credit clause

[Add to note 1241 at the end: page [467]] **34–470**
Provision of a letter of credit is a condition precedent to any obligation on the part of the seller to perform any aspect of the loading operation which is the seller's responsibility (*Kronos Worldwide Ltd v Sempra Oil Trading Sarl* [2004] EWCA Civ 3; [2004] C.L.C. 136 at [19], *per* Mance L.J.).

Default after remittance of funds

[Note 1265: page [471]] **34–476**
Update reference to *Benjamin* to (7th ed., 2006), paras 23–056 *et seq.*

(v) *The Relationship of Banker and Seller*

The autonomy of an irrevocable credit

[Insert in line 10 of note 1305, after reference to Gold Coast Ltd v Caja de Ahorros **34–486**
del Mediterraneo: page [477]]
Banque Saudi Fransi v Lear Siegler Services Inc [2005] EWHC 2395 (Comm); [2006] 1 Lloyd's Rep. 273.

[Insert in line 6 of note 1307, after reference to Bank of Credit and Commerce v Somali Bank: page [478]]
Marconi Communications International Ltd v Pt Pan Indonesia Bank Ltd TBK [2004] EWHC 129 (Comm); affd. [2005] EWCA Civ 422.

[Amend note 1308]
Delete the second sentence of this note.

Illegality

[Add to the text at the end of paragraph: page [478]] **34–487**
The illegality exception to the autonomy doctrine is not confined to cases where payment of the credit infringes exchange control provisions. In *Group Josi Re v Walbrook Insurance Co Ltd*,[1310a] Staughton L.J. expressed the view that a court would restrain a bank from paying under a letter of credit being used as a means of payment of an illegal arms sale, at least where the illegality was clearly established and known to the bank. More recently, in *Mahonia Ltd v JP Morgan Chase Bank*,[1310b] Colman J. refused to strike out an illegality defence to enforcement of a letter of credit where the underlying contract was alleged to have been made for an illegal purpose, namely the contravention of US Securities law.

[1310a] [1996] 1 W.L.R. 1152.
[1310b] [2003] EWHC 1927 (Comm); [2003] 2 Lloyd's Rep. 911. It was later held at the trial of the action that there was no illegality which affected the transaction: *Mahonia Ltd v JP Morgan Chase Bank* [2004] EWHC 1938 (Comm).

The fraud rule

34–488   *[Note 1311: page* [478]]
Update reference to *Benjamin* to (7th ed., 2006), paras 23–141 *et seq.*

Ambit of rule

34–489   *[Insert in note 1315, at end of second sentence, line 5: page* [479]]
Balfour Beatty Civil Engineering v Technical & General Guarantee Co Ltd (1999) 68 Con. L.R. 180 at 190–191; *TTI Team Telecom International Ltd v Hutchison 3G UK Ltd* [2003] EWHC 762 (TCC.); [2003] 1 All E.R. (Comm.) 914.

[Note 1316]
Update reference to *Benjamin* to (7th ed., 2006), paras 23–152 *et seq.*

[Add to note 1320 at the end: page [480]]
For a critique, see Hooley, [2002] C.L.J. 279. The Singapore Court of Appeal has since recognised a separate "nullity" defence: *Beam Technology (Mfg) Pte Ltd v Standard Chartered Bank* [2003] 1 S.L.R. 597, noted by Chin and Wong, [2004] L.M.C.L.Q. 14.

Tender by third party

34–490   *[Add to note 1324 at the end: page* [480]]
In *Armlea plc v Gov & Co of the Bank of Scotland* (unreported, June 4, 2004), Lord Mackay (at [39]–[43]), sitting in the Outer House of the Court of Session, rejected a submission by a principal that it did not have to plead fraud when seeking an injunction against the bank to restrain payment under a demand guarantee (as opposed to where the bank wishes to avoid making payment, when fraud must be pleaded). Lord Mackay (at [44]–[46]) also rejected a submission that the fraud exception only applies to demand guarantees involved in international commerce but not to those involved in domestic commerce.

[Add new paragraphs 34–491A and 34–491B: page [481]]
34–491A   **Restrictions on beneficiary's right to call for payment.** In *Sirius International Insurance Corp (Publ) v FAI General Insurance Co Ltd*,[1326a] the Court of Appeal held that the principle of autonomy did not mean that a beneficiary could draw on a letter of credit when he had expressly agreed not to do so unless certain conditions were satisfied and those conditions had not been met. In this case, the restrictions were contained in a separate agreement made between the beneficiary (Sirius) and the applicant (FAI). May L.J. stated that "although those restrictions were not terms of the letter of credit, and although the bank would have been obliged and entitled to honour a request to pay which fulfilled its terms, that does not mean that, as between themselves and FAI, Sirius were entitled to draw on the letter of credit if the express conditions of this underlying agreement were not fulfilled. They were not so entitled".[1326b] The Court of Appeal was also of the opinion that if draw-down was attempted in these

circumstances, a court would be likely to grant an injunction restraining the beneficiary from drawing on the letter of credit in breach of express conditions contained in the underlying agreement. It should be noted that fraud was not alleged against Sirius and so the case does not fall within the fraud exception to the autonomy principle. The Court of Appeal held that an express condition of the separate agreement between the parties had not been met and that Sirius were not entitled to the proceeds of the credit. The House of Lords[1326c] reversed that decision on the ground that the condition had been satisfied. Their Lordships found it unnecessary to examine arguments about the autonomy principle.

[1326a] [2003] EWCA Civ 470; [2003] 1 All E.R. (Comm.) 865, noted by Hare, [2004] C.L.J. 288. For examples of Australian cases to similar effect, see *Selvas Pty Ltd v Hansen Yuncken (SA) Pty Ltd* (1987) 6 Australian Construction Law Rep 36; *Boral Formwork v Action Motors* [2002] N.S.W.S.C. 713.
[1326b] [2003] EWCA Civ 470 at [27].
[1326c] [2004] UKHL 54; [2004] 1 W.L.R. 3251.

The *Sirius* case raises important questions about the extent of the autonomy principle. There must be some concern as to how far it undermines the principle and its consequential benefits of commercial certainty. However, the English courts have not shown themselves willing to embrace the wider principle of "unconscionable demand" which has gained judicial support in Australia[1326d] and Singapore.[1326e] It is not entirely clear what constitutes unconscionablity, although it seems to be something more than unfairness and less than fraud, nor as to the standard of proof required to obtain injunctive relief on this ground.[1326f] The uncertainty that this creates is obvious. Nevertheless, there have been recent dicta which suggests that the current reluctance of the English courts to apply a concept of "unconsionability" may not last forever.[1326g]

34–491B

[1326d] See, *e.g. Olex Focas Pty Ltd v Skodaexport Co Ltd* [1998] 3 V.R. 380, where statute brought the concept into play.
[1326e] See, *e.g. Samwoh Asphalt Premix Pte Ltd v Sum Cheong Piling Pte Ltd* [2002] B.L.R. 459; *McConnell Dowell Construction (Aust) Pty Ltd v Semcorp Engineering and Constructions Pte Ltd* [2002] B.L.R. 450.
[1326f] See Ganotaki, [2004] L.M.C.L.Q. 148 at 152.
[1326g] See, especially, the dicta of Potter L.J. in *Montrod Ltd v Grundkotter Fleischvertriebs* [2001] EWCA Civ 1954; [2002] 1 All E.R. (Comm.) 257 at [59], and also that of Judge Thornton Q.C., sitting as a deputy High Court judge, in *TTI Team Telecom International Ltd v Hutchison 3G UK Ltd* [2003] EWHC 762 (TCC); [2003] 1 All E.R. (Comm.) 914 at [37].

(vi) *The Relationship of Issuing and Correspondent Bankers*

Compliance with instructions

[Note 1354: page [486]]
Update reference to *Benjamin* to (7th ed., 2006), paras 23–186 *et seq.*

34–501

(vii) *The Tender of Documents*

Technical defences

[Note 1372: page [489]]
Update reference to *Benjamin* to (7th ed., 2006), para.23–158.

34–507

CHAPTER 35

CARRIAGE BY AIR

			PARA.
☐	1.	Introduction	35–001
■	2.	International carriage	35–021
☐		(a) General	35–021
☐		(b) Passengers	35–027
■		(c) Baggage	35–052
☐		(d) Cargo	35–057
■		(e) Delay to passengers, baggage or cargo	35–072
■	3.	Non-international carriage	35–073

1. Introduction

The Warsaw Convention 1929

35–002   [*Replace from "When that Act" on line 7 of page* [500] *to end of para.35–002, and notes 5 and 6, with the following*]
The unamended Warsaw Convention continues to have effect as Sch.2 to the Carriage by Air Acts (Application of Provisions) Order 2004.[5] Schedule 3 to the same Order gives effect to Montreal Additional Protocol No. 1 of 1975. The two Schedules differ only in respect of the currency units by reference to which liability limits are prescribed.

[5] SI 2004/1899.

The Montreal Convention 1999

35–006   [*In note 17, delete "(not yet in force)" and substitute: page* [502]]
, which came into force on June 28, 2004

European Council Regulation No.2027/97

35–007—   [*Pages* [502]–[503]]
35–010   The Montreal Convention 1999 came into force for the European Community on June 28, 2004, and Council Regulation No.2027/97 was radically amended, and in effect replaced, by European Parliament and Council Regulation No.889/2002, as to which see paras 35–011 *et seq*. The Air Carrier Liability

Order 1998, giving effect to Council Regulation No.2027/98 was revoked with effect from the same date by the Air Carrier Liability Regulations 2004 (SI 2004/1418).

European Parliament and Council Regulation No.889/2002

[*For the second sentence of paragraph substitute: page* [503]]   **35–011**
The amending Regulation applied from June 28, 2004, the date on which the Montreal Convention entered into force for the European Community; the necessary changes to the law of the United Kingdom were made by the Air Carrier Liability Regulations 2004[34a] and the Air Carrier Liability (No.2) Regulations 2004.[34b]

[34a] SI 2004/1418.
[34b] SI 2004/1974.

Removal of financial limits

[*Add at end of paragraph: page* [504]]   **35–012**
European Parliament and Council Regulation No.785/2004 of April 21, 2004 on insurance requirements for air carriers and aircraft operators[37a] requires all air carriers and aircraft operators flying within, into, out of, or over the territory of a Member State to have specified levels of insurance cover in respect of their aviation-specific liability in respect of passengers (death and personal injury caused by accidents),[37b] for loss or destruction of or damage to baggage and cargo, and third parties (death, personal injury and damage to property caused by accidents). The insured risks must include acts of war, terrorism, hijacking, acts of sabotage, unlawful seizure of aircraft and civil commotion.[37c] In the United Kingdom, an air carrier or aircraft operator (other than a carrier or operator regulated by another Member State) who fails to comply with these requirements commits an offence.[37d] For the purposes of Regulation 785/04, the Civil Aviation Authority is the competent authority, except in cases where a permit under arts 113 or 115 of the Air Navigation Order 2000,[37e] which relate to certain aircraft registered outside the United Kingdom, where the Secretary of State is the competent authority.[37f]

[37a] O.J. No L138/1, 30.04.2004, which came into force on May 1, 2005. The Regulation does not affect the carriage of mail: Regulation, art.1(2).
[37b] The United Kingdom has set the minimum level at 100,000 SDRs per passenger: Civil Aviation (Insurance) Regulations 2005 (SI 2005/1089), reg.5.
[37c] Regulation 785/04, art.4(1).
[37d] Civil Aviation (Insurance) Regulations 2005 (SI 2005/1089), reg.4. For penalties, see reg.12.
[37e] SI 2000/1562.
[37f] Civil Aviation (Insurance) Regulations 2005 (SI 2005/1089), reg.3.

Conditions of carriage

[*Add at the end of paragraph: page* [504]]   **35–014**
Failure to comply with the requirements of Art.3a or Art.6 of the amended Regulation is made an offence by the Air Carrier Liability Regulations 2004.[39a]

[39a] SI 2004/1418.

Parties to the Conventions

35–015   *[For the first sentence of note 40 substitute: page* [505]]
s.2(1) as amended by SI 1999/213 and SI 2002/263 (and see the Carriage by
Air Acts (Application of Provisions) Order 2004 (SI 2004/1899), Arts 5(2) and
6(2)).

Scope of the Conventions

35–016   *[Note 42, for reference to 2000 Order, substitute: page* [505]]
Air Navigation Order 2005, SI 2005/1970, art.155(1).

[For note 43 substitute]
Carriage by Air Acts (Application of Provisions) Order 2004 (SI 2004/1899),
art.8 (excluding, in art.8(2), cases where members of the Armed Forces are
carried during a time of actual or imminent hostilities, severe international
tension, or great national emergency).

*[For the reference to the 1967 Order at the end of paragraph, and note 44,
substitute]*
Sch.1 to the Carriage by Air Acts (Application of Provisions) Order 2004,
under art.2(2) of which the carrier is liable only to the relevant postal administration and in accordance with the rules applicable to the relationship between
carriers and postal administrations.[44]

[44] Carriage by Air Acts (Application of Provisions) Order 2004 (SI 2004/1899), art.4.

Interpretation of the Convention

35–020   *[Note 48: page* [506]]
SI 2002/263 is now in force.

The starting-point for interpretation must always be the text of the Convention
and not the language used, even by a court of the highest authority, in formulating
a statement of its effect: *Re Deep Vein Thrombosis and Air Travel Group
Litigation* [2005] UKHL 72; [2006] 1 A.C. 495, commenting on over-reliance on
the formulation in *Air France v Saks*, 470 U.S. 392 (1985).

[For note 49 substitute:]
[49] Carriage by Air Acts (Application of Provisions) Order 2004 (SI 2004/1899), arts 5(1) and
6(1).

2. INTERNATIONAL CARRIAGE

(a) *General*

Definition

35–021   *[Note 57: page* [507]]
SI 2002/263 is now in force.

[*For notes 59 and 60 substitute: page* [508]]
[59] Carriage by Air Acts (Application of Provisions) Order 2004 (SI 2004/1899), Sch.2, art.1(2); Carriage by Air Act 1961, Sch.1, art.1(2), Sch.1A as inserted by SI 1999/1312, art.1(2), Sch.1B as inserted by SI 2002/263, art.1(2).
[60] Carriage by Air Acts (Application of Provisions) Order 2004 (SI 2004/1899), Sch.2, art.1(3); Carriage by Air Act 1961, Sch.1, art.1(3), Sch.1A as inserted by SI 1999/1312, art.1(3), Sch.1B as inserted by SI 2002/263, art.1(3).

Conventions provide exclusive cause of action

[*For note 62 substitute: page* [509]]   **35–022**
[62] Carriage by Air Acts (Application of Provisions) Order 2004 (SI 2004/1899), Sch.2, art.24(1); Carriage by Air Act 1961, Sch.1, art.24(1)(2), Sch.1A as inserted by SI 1999/1312, art.24(1)(2) (using different language), Sch.1B as inserted by SI 2002/263, art.29.

[*In note 63, insert before "Morris" in line 2*]
Deaville v Aeroflot Russian International Airlines [1997] 2 Lloyd's Rep. 67; *R. v Secretary of State for the Environment, Transport and the Regions Ex p. IATA* [2000] 1 Lloyd's Rep. 242.

[*In same note, add to citation of Re Deep Vein Thrombosis and Air Travel Group Litigation*]
and [2005] UKHL 72; [2006] 1 A.C. 495

Jurisdiction

[*For the first sentence of note 69 substitute: page* [510]]   **35–024**
Carriage by Air Acts (Application of Provisions) Order 2004 (SI 2004/1899), Sch.2, art.28(1); Carriage by Air Act 1961, Sch.1, art.28(1), Sch.1A as inserted by SI 1999/1312, art.28(1).

[*Note 70*]
SI 2002/263 is now in force.

[*For the citations in the first sentence of note 71 substitute:*]   **35–025**
Carriage by Air Acts (Application of Provisions) Order 2004 (SI 2004/1899), Sch.2, art.28(2); Carriage by Air Act 1961, Sch.1, art.28(2), Sch.1A as inserted by SI 1999/1312, art.28(2), Sch.1B as inserted by SI 2002/263, art.33(4).

Limitation of actions

[*For note 82 substitute: page* [511]]   **35–026**
[82] Carriage by Air Acts (Application of Provisions) Order 2004 (SI 2004/1899), Sch.2, art.29(1); Carriage by Air Act 1961, Sch.1, art.29(1), Sch.1A as inserted by SI 1999/1312, art.29(1), Sch.1B as inserted by SI 2002/263, art.35(1). English law will, as the *lex fori*, determine the method of calculating the period of limitation: Carriage by Air Acts (Application of Provisions) Order 2004 (SI 2004/1899), Sch.2, art.29(2); Carriage by Air Act 1961, Sch.1, art.29(2), Sch.1A as inserted by SI 1999/1312, art.29(2), Sch.1B as inserted by SI 2002/263, art.35(2).

[*In note 83, add: page* [512]]
Agtrack (NT) Pty Ltd v Hatfield [2005] HCA 38; *Air Link Pty Ltd v Paterson* [2005] HCA 39.

(b) *Passengers*

Passenger ticket

35–028   [*For note 93 substitute: page* [513]]
[93] Carriage by Air Acts (Application of Provisions) Order 2004 (SI 2004/1899), Sch.2, art.3(1).

[*In note 94, add*]
and see the cargo case of *Fujitsu Computer Products Corp v Bax Global Inc* [2005] EWHC 2289; [2006] 1 Lloyd's Rep. 231.

[*Note 95*]
SI 2002/263 is now in force.

Absence, irregularity or loss of passenger ticket

35–030   [*For the first line of note 103 substitute: page* [514]]
Carriage by Air Acts (Application of Provisions) Order 2004 (SI 2004/1899), Sch.2, art.3(2).

[*Note 106*]
SI 2002/263 is now in force.

[*For note 107 substitute:*]
[107] Carriage by Air Act 1961, Sch.1, art.34, Sch.1A as inserted by SI 1999/1312, art.34, Sch.1B as inserted by SI 2002/263, art.51. The Warsaw Convention 1929 is wholly excluded in such cases: Carriage by Air Acts (Application of Provisions) Order 2004 (SI 2004/1899), Sch.2, art.34.

Right of refusal

35–031   [*For the first sentence of note 108 substitute: page* [514]]
Carriage by Air Acts (Application of Provisions) Order 2004 (SI 2004/1899), Sch.2, art.33; Carriage by Air Act 1961, Sch.1, art.33, Sch.1A as inserted by SI 1999/1312, art.33, Sch.1B as inserted by SI 2002/263, art.27.

Liability for death and bodily injury

35–032   [*For note 111 substitute: page* 515]]
[111] Carriage by Air Acts (Application of Provisions) Order 2004 (SI 2004/1899), Sch.2, art.17.

[*Note 112*]
SI 2002/263 is now in force.

"Accident"

35–033   [*Page* [516]]
For a range of judicial views on the question whether an omission may amount to an accident (and whether a distinction can properly be drawn between act and omission in this context) see *Olympic Airways v Husain*, 124 S.Ct. 1221 (2004), pet. for rehearing denied, 124 S.Ct. 2065 (2004); *Povey v Qantas Airways Ltd*

[2005] HCA 33; (2005) 216 A.L.R. 427; *Deep Vein Thrombosis and Air Travel Group Litigation* [2003] EWCA Civ 1005; [2004] Q.B. 234, *per* Lord Phillips of Worth Matravers M.R. and the same case on appeal, [2005] UKHL 72; [2006] 1 A.C. 495, *per* Lord Mance. In *Olympic Airways v Husain*, the deceased passenger had been refused a change of seat to avoid the cigarette smoke to which he was allergic; this was an unusual event external to the passenger and so an "accident".

[*Note 121. For the first sentence substitute:*]
Re Deep Vein Thrombosis and Air Travel Group Litigation [2005] UKHL 72; [2006] 1 A.C. 495.

"Bodily injury"

[*Page* [516]]   **35–034**
There is no liability for mental injuries which are accompanied by, but not caused by physical injuries: *Ehrlich v American Airlines Inc* 360 F 3d 366 (2nd Cir, 2004).

Defences available to the carrier: "all necessary measures"

[*For the first line of note 124 substitute: page* [517]]   **35–035**
Carriage by Air Acts (Application of Provisions) Order 2004 (SI 2004/1899), Sch.2, art.20(1);

[*Delete second sentence and note 125*]
European Council Regulation No.2027/97 was radically amended, and in effect replaced, by European Parliament and Council Regulation No.889/2002, as to which see paras 35–011 *et seq*. The Air Carrier Liability Order 1998 was revoked with effect from the same date by the Air Carrier Liability Regulations 2004 (SI 2004/1418). Community air carriers now fall within the regime of the Montreal Convention 1999.

[*Note 126*]
SI 2002/263 is now in force.

Contributory negligence

[*Page* [518]]   **35–036**
European Council Regulation No.2027/97 was radically amended, and in effect replaced, by European Parliament and Council Regulation No.889/2002, as to which see paras 35–011 *et seq*. Community air carriers now fall within the regime of the Montreal Convention 1999.

[*For note 135 substitute:*]
[135] Carriage by Air Acts (Application of Provisions) Order 2004 (SI 2004/1899), Sch.2, art.21.

[*Note 138*]
SI 2002/263 is now in force.

Upper financial limit of liability

35–037   [*Page* [518]]
European Council Regulation No.2027/97 was radically amended, and in effect replaced, by European Parliament and Council Regulation No.889/2002, as to which see paras 35–011 *et seq.* Community air carriers now fall within the regime of the Montreal Convention 1999.

[*For note 141 substitute:*]
¹⁴¹ Carriage by Air Acts (Application of Provisions) Order 2004 (SI 2004/1899), Sch.2, art.22.

[*Note 145; page* [519]]
SI 2002/263 is now in force.

Misconduct

35–039   [*For the first sentence of note 149 substitute: page* [520]]
Carriage by Air Acts (Application of Provisions) Order 2004 (SI 2004/1899), Sch.2, art.25.

[*Note 152*]
SI 2002/263 is now in force.

Fatal accidents

35–045   [*Note 161: page* [522]]
SI 2002/263 is now in force.

Several actions by one passenger

35–046   [*Notes 164, 167, 168 and 169: pages* [522]–[523]]
SI 2002/263 is now in force.

[*In line 7: page* [522]]
The reference in the text to note 165 should now be to the Carriage by Air Acts (Application of Provisions) Order 2004.

[*For note 165 substitute:*]
¹⁶⁵ SI 2004/1899, art.7.

Overbooking

35–047   [*Last sentence, text to note 172: page* [523]]
Council Regulation 295/91 is with effect from February 17, 2005, repealed and replaced by European Parliament and Council Regulation No.261/2004 of February 11, 2004, for the text of which see OJ 2004 L46/1. In the United Kingdom, the Civil Aviation (Denied Boarding, Compensation and Assistance) Regulations 2005 (SI 2005/975) designate the Civil Aviation Authority as the body responsible for enforcement and the Air Transport Users Council as the body to receive complaints, and also make it an offence, subject to a defence of due diligence, for

an operating air carrier to fail to comply with its obligations under Regulation 261/2004.

Successive carriers

[For the first sentence of note 173 substitute: page [524]]   **35–048**
Carriage by Air Acts (Application of Provisions) Order 2004 (SI 2004/1899), Sch.2, art.1(3); Carriage by Air Act 1961, Sch.1, art.1(3), Sch.1A as inserted by SI 1999/1312, art.1(3), Sch.1B as inserted by SI 2002/263, art.1(3).

[For the first sentence of note 174 substitute:]
Carriage by Air Acts (Application of Provisions) Order 2004 (SI 2004/1899), Sch.2, art.30(1); Carriage by Air Act 1961, Sch.1, art.30(1), Sch.1A as inserted by SI 1999/1312, art.30(1), Sch.1B as inserted by SI 2002/263, art.36(1).

[For note 175 substitute:]
Carriage by Air Acts (Application of Provisions) Order 2004 (SI 2004/1899), Sch.2, art.30(2); Carriage by Air Act 1961, Sch.1, art.30(2), Sch.1A as inserted by SI 1999/1312, art.30(2), Sch.1B as inserted by SI 2002/263, art.36(2).

Contracting carriers and "actual" carriers

[Page [524]]   **35–049**
European Parliament and Council Regulation 2111/2005 of December 14, 2005 on the establishment of a Community list of air carriers subject to an operating ban within the Community and on informing air transport passengers of the identity of the operating air carrier and repealing Art.9 of Directive 2004/36, Arts 10–13, require the "air carriage contractor" to inform the passenger of the identity of the operating air carrier or carriers at the time of reservation, or on the identity of the relevant carrier becoming known, or at the latest at check-in (or on boarding if no check-in is required).

[Note 178: page [525]]
SI 2002/263 is now in force.

(c) *Baggage*

Forms of baggage

[For the first line of note 186 substitute: page [526]]   **35–052**
Carriage by Air Acts (Application of Provisions) Order 2004 (SI 2004/1899), Sch.2, art.22(3);

[Note 186, line 4]
SI 2002/263 is now in force.

Baggage check

[For note 189 substitute: page [526]]   **35–053**
[189] Carriage by Air Acts (Application of Provisions) Order 2004 (SI 2004/1899), Sch.2, art.4.

[*For note 191 substitute:*]
[191] Carriage by Air Acts (Application of Provisions) Order 2004 (SI 2004/1899), Sch.2, art.4(4).

[*Note 195: page [527]]*
SI 2002/263 is now in force.

Liability for damage, destruction or loss

35–054   [*Page [527]]*
Under European Parliament and Council Regulation No.889/2002, Community air carriers now fall within the regime of the Montreal Convention 1999.

[*For the first line of note 196 substitute:*]
Carriage by Air Acts (Application of Provisions) Order 2004 (SI 2004/1899), Sch.2, art.18(1);

[*For the first line of note 197 substitute:*]
Carriage by Air Acts (Application of Provisions) Order 2004 (SI 2004/1899), Sch.2, art.18(2);

[*Note 198: page [528]]*
SI 2002/263 is now in force.

35–055   [*Page [528]]*
[*For note 200 substitute:*]
[200] Carriage by Air Acts (Application of Provisions) Order 2004 (SI 2004/1899), Sch.2, art.22(2).

[*For note 202 substitute:*]
[202] Carriage by Air Acts (Application of Provisions) Order 2004 (SI 2004/1899), Sch.2, art.22(3).

[*In note 205, line 1, for the citation of the 1967 Order substitute:*]
Carriage by Air Acts (Application of Provisions) Order 2004 (SI 2004/1899), Sch.3, art.22(2)(3).

[*Note 206]*
SI 2002/263 is now in force.

[*For note 207 substitute: page [529]]*
[207] Carriage by Air Acts (Application of Provisions) Order 2004 (SI 2004/1899), Sch.2, art.22(2); Carriage by Air Act 1961, Sch.1, art.22(2)(a), Sch.1A as inserted by SI 1999/1312, art.22(2)(a), Sch.1B as inserted by SI 2002/263, art.22(2).

Time for making claims

35–056   [*For notes 208 to 210 substitute: page [529]]*
[208] Carriage by Air Acts (Application of Provisions) Order 2004 (SI 2004/1899), Sch.2, art.26(2); Carriage by Air Act 1961, Sch.1, art.26(2), Sch.1A as inserted by SI 1999/1312, art.26(2), Sch.1B as inserted by SI 2002/263, art.31(2).
[209] Carriage by Air Acts (Application of Provisions) Order 2004 (SI 2004/1899), Sch.2, art.35; Carriage by Air Act 1961, Sch.1, art.35, Sch.1A as inserted by SI 1999/1312, art.35, Sch.1B as inserted by SI 2002/263, art.52.

²¹⁰ Carriage by Air Acts (Application of Provisions) Order 2004 (SI 2004/1899), Sch.2, art.26(4); Carriage by Air Act 1961, Sch.1, art.26(4), Sch.1A as inserted by SI 1999/1312, art.26(4), Sch.1B as inserted by SI 2002/263, art.31(4).

(d) *Cargo*

Air waybill

[*For notes 211 to 215 substitute: page* [529]]   **35–057**
²¹¹ Carriage by Air Acts (Application of Provisions) Order 2004 (SI 2004/1899), Sch.2, art.5(1); Carriage by Air Act 1961, Sch.1, art.5(1).
²¹² Carriage by Air Acts (Application of Provisions) Order 2004 (SI 2004/1899), Sch.2, art.10(1); Carriage by Air Act 1961, Sch.1, art.10(1).
²¹³ Carriage by Air Acts (Application of Provisions) Order 2004 (SI 2004/1899), Sch.2, art.6(5); Carriage by Air Act 1961, Sch.1, art.6(5).
²¹⁴ Carriage by Air Acts (Application of Provisions) Order 2004 (SI 2004/1899), Sch.2, art.7; Carriage by Air Act 1961, Sch.1, art.7.
²¹⁵ Carriage by Air Acts (Application of Provisions) Order 2004 (SI 2004/1899), Sch.2, art.6(1)(2); Carriage by Air Act 1961, Sch.1, art.6(1)(2).

Statements in waybill

[*For note 217 substitute: page* [530]]   **35–058**
²¹⁷ Carriage by Air Acts (Application of Provisions) Order 2004 (SI 2004/1899), Sch.2, art.11(2); Carriage by Air Act 1961, Sch.1, art.11(2).

Absence of waybill, etc.

[*For the first line of note 219 substitute: page* [530]]   **35–059**
   Carriage by Air Acts (Application of Provisions) Order 2004 (SI 2004/1899), Sch.2, art.9;

[*Add to note 220*]
   There must be an identifiable notice; it is not sufficient that there are conditions from which the applicability of the Convention may be discovered: *Fujitsu Computer Products Corp v Bax Global Inc* [2005] EWHC 2289; [2006] 1 Lloyd's Rep. 231.

Cargo documentation under recent conventions

[*Notes 223 and 224: page* [530]]   **35–060**
SI 2002/263 is now in force.

Acceptability of goods for carriage

[*Note 226: page* [531]]   **35–061**
Amend the citation to CSC(24)1601.

[*Note 227*]
Amend the citation to art.3.1.1.2.

[*Note 229*]
   The Air Navigation (Dangerous Goods) Regulations 2002 are amended by SI 2004/3214, SI 2005/3356 and SI 2006/1092.

Liability for damage, destruction or loss

35–062   *[For the first line of note 231 substitute: page* [531]]
Carriage by Air Acts (Application of Provisions) Order 2004 (SI 2004/1899), Sch.2, art.18(1);

[For the first line of note 232 substitute:]
Carriage by Air Acts (Application of Provisions) Order 2004 (SI 2004/1899), Sch.2, art.18(2);

[Note 234: page [532]]
SI 2002/263 is now in force.

Upper financial limit of liability

35–063   *[For notes 239 and 240 substitute: page* [532]]
    [239] Carriage by Air Acts (Application of Provisions) Order 2004 (SI 2004/1899), Sch.2, art.22(2); Carriage by Air Act 1961, Sch.1, art.22(2)(3) (as amended by the Carriage by Air and Road Act 1979, s.4), Sch.1A as inserted by SI 1999/1312, art.22(2)(*a*), Sch.1B as inserted by SI 2002/263, art.22(2).
    [240] Carriage by Air Acts (Application of Provisions) Order 2004 (SI 2004/1899), Sch.2, art.22(2); Carriage by Air Act 1961, Sch.1, art.22(2)(*a*), Sch.1A as inserted by SI 1999/1312, art.22(2)(*a*), Sch.1B as inserted by SI 2002/263, art.22(2).

Stoppage in transit

35–064   *[For note 243 substitute: page* [533]]
    [243] Carriage by Air Acts (Application of Provisions) Order 2004 (SI 2004/1899), Sch.2, arts 12(4), 13(1); Carriage by Air Act 1961, Sch.1, arts 12(4), 13(1), Sch.1A as inserted by SI 1999/1312, arts 12(4), 13(1), Sch.1B as inserted by SI 2002/263, arts 12(4), 13(1).

[For the first sentence of note 244 substitute:]
Carriage by Air Acts (Application of Provisions) Order 2004 (SI 2004/1899), Sch.2, art.12(1); Carriage by Air Act 1961, Sch.1, art.12(1), Sch.1A as inserted by SI 1999/1312, art.12(1), Sch.1B as inserted by SI 2002/263, art.12(1).

[For the first sentence of note 245 substitute:]
Carriage by Air Acts (Application of Provisions) Order 2004 (SI 2004/1899), Sch.2, art.12(2); Carriage by Air Act 1961, Sch.1, art.12(2), Sch.1A as inserted by SI 1999/1312, art.12(2), Sch.1B as inserted by SI 2002/263, art.12(2).

[For note 246 substitute]
    [246] Carriage by Air Acts (Application of Provisions) Order 2004 (SI 2004/1899), Sch.2, arts 12(4), 13(1); Carriage by Air Act 1961, Sch.1, arts 12(4), 13(1), Sch.1A as inserted by SI 1999/1312, arts 12(4), 13(1), Sch.1B as inserted by SI 2002/263, arts 12(4), 13(1).

Delivery to the consignee

35–065   *[For notes 247 to 249 substitute: page* [533]]
    [247] Carriage by Air Acts (Application of Provisions) Order 2004 (SI 2004/1899), Sch.2, art.13(2); Carriage by Air Act 1961, Sch.1, art.13(2), Sch.1A as inserted by SI 1999/1312, art.13(2), Sch.1B as inserted by SI 2002/263, art.13(2). See the I.A.T.A. recommended Conditions of Carriage (CSC(24)1601), art.8.1.

²⁴⁸ Carriage by Air Acts (Application of Provisions) Order 2004 (SI 2004/1899), Sch.2, art.13(1); Carriage by Air Act 1961, Sch.1, art.13(1), Sch.1A as inserted by SI 1999/1312, art.13(1), Sch.1B as inserted by SI 2002/263, art.13(1).
²⁴⁹ CSC(24)1601, art.8.3.

Time for making claims: damage or delay

[*For the first sentence of note 254 substitute: page* [534]]   **35–067**
Carriage by Air Acts (Application of Provisions) Order 2004 (SI 2004/1899), Sch.2, art.26(2); Carriage by Air Act 1961, Sch.1, art.26(2), Sch.1A as inserted by SI 1999/1312, art.26(2), Sch.1B as inserted by SI 2002/263, art.31(2).

[*For notes 255 and 256 substitute:*]
²⁵⁵ Carriage by Air Acts (Application of Provisions) Order 2004 (SI 2004/1899), Sch.2, art.35; Carriage by Air Act 1961, Sch.1, art.35, Sch.1A as inserted by SI 1999/1312, art.35, Sch.1B as inserted by SI 2002/263, art.52.
²⁵⁶ Carriage by Air Acts (Application of Provisions) Order 2004 (SI 2004/1899), Sch.2, art.26(4); Carriage by Air Act 1961, Sch.1, art.26(4), Sch.1A as inserted by SI 1999/1312, art.26(4), Sch.1B as inserted by SI 2002/263, art.31(4).

Loss of cargo

[*For the first sentence of note 257 substitute: page* [535]]   **35–068**
Carriage by Air Acts (Application of Provisions) Order 2004 (SI 2004/1899), Sch.2, art.23; Carriage by Air Act 1961, Sch.1, art.23, Sch.1A as inserted by SI 1999/1312, art.23, Sch.1B as inserted by SI 2002/263, art.26.

[*Note 257, last line*]
SI 2002/263 is now in force.

[*For the first sentence of note 258 substitute:*]
Carriage by Air Acts (Application of Provisions) Order 2004 (SI 2004/1899), Sch.2, art.13(3); Carriage by Air Act 1961, Sch.1, art.13(3), Sch.1A as inserted by SI 1999/1312, art.13(3), Sch.1B as inserted by SI 2002/263, art.13(3).

Who can sue the carrier

[*For the first sentence of note 264 substitute: page* [535]]   **35–069**
Carriage by Air Acts (Application of Provisions) Order 2004 (SI 2004/1899), Sch.2, arts 13(3) and 24(1); Carriage by Air Act 1961, Sch.1, arts 13(3) and 24(1), Sch.1A as inserted by SI 1999/1312, arts 13(3) and 24(1), Sch.1B as inserted by SI 2002/263, arts 13(3) and 29.

[*For notes 266 and 267 substitute:*]   **35–070**
²⁶⁶ Carriage by Air Acts (Application of Provisions) Order 2004 (SI 2004/1899), Sch.2, art.24(1); Carriage by Air Act 1961, Sch.1, art.24(1), Sch.1A as inserted by SI 1999/1312, art.24(1), Sch.1B as inserted by SI 2002/263, art.29.
²⁶⁷ Carriage by Air Acts (Application of Provisions) Order 2004 (SI 2004/1899), Sch.2, art.24(2); Carriage by Air Act 1961, Sch.1, art.24(2), Sch.1A as inserted by SI 1999/1312, art.24(2), Sch.1B as inserted by SI 2002/263, art.29.

(e) *Delay to passengers, baggage or cargo*

Liability for delay

35–072   [*For notes 275 to 278 substitute: page* [537]]
[275] Carriage by Air Acts (Application of Provisions) Order 2004 (SI 2004/1899), Sch.2, art.19; Carriage by Air Act 1961, Sch.1, art.19, Sch.1A as inserted by SI 1999/1312, art.19, Sch.1B as inserted by SI 2002/263, art.19.
[276] Carriage by Air Acts (Application of Provisions) Order 2004 (SI 2004/1899), Sch.2, art.20; Carriage by Air Act 1961, Sch.1, art.20, Sch.1A as inserted by SI 1999/1312, art.20, Sch.1B as inserted by SI 2002/263, art.19.
[277] Carriage by Air Acts (Application of Provisions) Order 2004 (SI 2004/1899), Sch.2, art.20(2).
[278] Carriage by Air Acts (Application of Provisions) Order 2004 (SI 2004/1899), Sch.2, art.21; Carriage by Air Act 1961, Sch.1, art.21, Sch.1A as inserted by SI 1999/1312, art.21, Sch.1B as inserted by SI 2002/263, art.20.

[*For note 281 substitute:*]
[281] See I.A.T.A. recommended Conditions (PSC(24) 1724), Art.9.1.1.

3. Non-International carriage

Applicable rules

[*Substitute new paragraph: pages* [537]–[538]]
35–073   **Applicable rules.** The Conventions treated above regulate only international carriage. Carriage which is not international carriage as defined in any of the Conventions falls outside the Convention system. The applicable law is to be found in two sources. Community air carriers engaged in the carriage of persons or baggage are subject to European Parliament and Council Regulation No.889/2002,[282] which applies to national as well as international carriage. The liability of other air carriers, and Community air carriers engaged in the carriage of cargo, is governed by Schedule 1 to the Carriage by Air Acts (Application of Provisions) Order 2004,[283] which applies a modified version of the Montreal Convention 1999. Subject to the Regulation, the 2004 Order applies to all carriage by air other than carriage to which the Warsaw-Hague text, the MP4 Convention or the Montreal Convention 1999 applies, and Sch.1 applies to carriage which is not international carriage as defined in Schs 2 or 3 (applying the original Warsaw Convention and that Convention as amended by Montreal Additional protocol No.1 of 1975).[283a] To avoid giving too extensive a scope to the predecessor provisions, for it was arguable that the provisions of the United Kingdom Order applied to internal carriage in other countries, the House of Lords held that their application is limited to (a) carriage in which the places of departure and destination and any agreed stopping places are all within the United Kingdom or other British territory; and (b) non-convention carriage involving a place of departure or destination or an agreed stopping place in a foreign state and a place of departure or destination or an agreed stopping place in the United Kingdom or other British territory.[284]

[306]

²⁸² See paras 35–011 *et seq.*
²⁸³ SI 2004/1899. Note that art.2 is amended by SI 2004/1974.
²⁸³ᵃ Carriage by Air Acts (Application of Provisions) Order 2004 (SI 2004/1899), arts 3(1) and 4.
²⁸⁴ *Holmes v Bangladesh Biman Corp* [1989] A.C. 1112.

The modified convention regime under Schedule 1 to the 1967 Order

[Substitute new paragraph: page [538]]
The modified convention regime under Schedule 1 to the 2004 Order. Only **35–074** parts of the Montreal Convention 1999 are applied by the 2004 Order.²⁸⁵ Chapter II (Arts 3–16) dealing with documentation is omitted except for parts of Art.3 requiring the carrier to deliver a baggage identification tag for each piece of checked baggage. Liability for death or injury is unlimited but if the carrier proves an absence of fault there is no liability beyond 100,000 SDRs.²⁸⁶ There are no provisions regulating the carriage of mail and postal packages save for a provision that in these cases the carrier is liable only to the relevant postal administration and in accordance with the rules applicable to the relationship between carriers and postal administrations.²⁸⁷

²⁸⁵ Carriage by Air Acts (Application of Provisions) Order 2004 (SI 2004/1899).
²⁸⁶ *ibid.*, Sch.1, art.21.
²⁸⁷ *ibid.*, Sch.1, art.2(2). See the Postal Services Act 2000, s.90; *American Express Co v British Airways Board* [1983] 1 W.L.R. 701; *Post Office v British World Airlines Ltd* [2000] 1 All E.R. (Comm.) 532.

CHAPTER 36

CARRIAGE BY LAND

				PARA.
	1.	Introduction	36–001
		(a) General	36–001
		(b) Definition of carrier	36–005
■	2.	Internal carriage	36–007
■		(a) Goods	36–007
■		(i) Common and private carriers	36–007
		(ii) Introduction to carrier's duties and liabilities	36–013
		(iii) Carrier's liability imposed by law	36–014
■		(iv) Contractual liability	36–025
■		(v) Liability in tort	36–044
		(vi) Claims against the carrier	36–048
		(vii) Carrier's rights	36–049
■		(b) Passengers	36–054
		(c) Passengers' luggage	36–067
■	3.	International carriage	36–078
□		(a) Introduction	36–078
□		(b) Goods by rail	36–084
■		(c) Passengers, luggage and vehicles by rail	36–099
■		(i) Application and scope of the Convention	36–099
■		(ii) Passengers and hand luggage	36–103
■		(iii) Registered luggage and vehicles	36–111
■		(iv) Claims	36–114
□		(d) Goods by road	36–120
		(e) Passengers and luggage by road	36–150

2. INTERNAL CARRIAGE

(a) *Goods*

(i) *Common and Private Carriers*

The extinction of the common carrier

36–010 *[Delete "the Strategic Rail Authority" and the accompanying note from the second sentence: page* [545]]

[Add note 54a at the end of the fourth sentence: page [545]]
[54a] See McBain, "Time to abolish the common carrier" [2005] J.B.L. 545.

(iv) Contractual Liability

Construction of contracts

[Add to note 133 after second sentence: page [553]]   **36–028**
  In *Frans Maas (UK) Ltd v Samsung Electronics (UK) Ltd* [2004] EWHC 1502 (Comm); [2004] All E.R. (D) 362, the court held that the limitation provision under the BIFA Conditions was reasonable.

(v) Liability in Tort

Liability in tort

[Add to the end of note 258: page [565]]   **36–044**
  As to the employer's vicarious liability for the acts of his employees, see *Frans Maas (UK) Ltd v Samsung Electronics (UK) Ltd* [2004] EWHC 1502 (Comm); [2004] All E.R. (D) 362.

[Add to the end of note 264: page [566]]
  HSBC Rail (UK) Ltd v Network Rail Infrastructure Ltd [2005] EWHC 403 (Comm).

(b) Passengers

Common carriers

[Delete "the Strategic Rail Authority" from the third sentence: page [571]]   **36–054**

3. INTERNATIONAL CARRIAGE

(a) Introduction

Modification to COTIF: the Vilnius Protocol

[Delete the second and third sentences of the text, and add to text after the fourth   **36–080**
sentence: page [585]]
  By the Railways (Convention on International Carriage by Rail) Regulations 2005,[435a] the Vilnius Protocol was implemented as part of the law of the United Kingdom.

[435a] SI 2005/2092.

[Delete the final sentence of the text: page [586]]

[Add to the end of the paragraph: page [586]]
  The 2005 Regulations, and therefore the Protocol, entered into force on July 1, 2006.[436a] The United Kingdom has declared pursuant to Art.42 of the Protocol that it will not apply the CUI, APTU and ATMF (Apps E, F and G). In addition,

pursuant to an agreement between the United Kingdom and France, the CIV Uniform Rules and the CIM Uniform Rules will not apply to carriage by means of rail shuttle services carrying road vehicles and their passengers performed exclusively between the Channel Tunnel terminals at Cheriton in Kent and Coquelles in the Pas-de-Calais.

436a See London Gazette dated July 3, 2006; Railways (Convention on International Carriage by Rail) Regulations 2005, art.1 (SI 2005/2092).

Convention for Carriage of Passengers and Luggage by Road

36–082   *[Delete the fourth to eighth sentences and substitute: pages* [586]–[587]]
The possibility of signature and ratification grows remote, however, given that the United Kingdom's implementing legislation in respect of the CVR (the Carriage of Passengers by Road Act 1974) was repealed by the Statute Law (Repeals) Act 2004, s.1(1) and Sch.1, Pt 14.

(b) *Goods by Rail*

36–084—

36–119   *[Delete these paragraphs and the accompanying notes and substitute: pages* [587]–[602]]

36–084   **Scope of the Uniform Rules (CIM) under Appendix B to COTIF.**[452] CIM regulates the form and conditions of the contract of carriage of goods by rail, the performance of the contract, its modification, the disposal of the goods being carried, liability for loss, damage and delay, compensation and enforcement of claims by action.

452 See above para.36–078.

36–085   **Application of CIM.** CIM applies to every contract of carriage of goods by rail for reward when the place of taking over of the goods and the place designated for delivery are situated in two different Member States, irrespective of the place of business and the nationality of the parties to the contract of carriage.[453] It follows that CIM will apply even though the carriage is performed through the territory of a non-Member State[454] and that CIM will not apply if the place of taking over and the place of delivery are in the same State even though the carriage is performed through the territory of another State. CIM will also apply to contracts of carriage of goods by rail where only one of the place of taking over or place of delivery are in a Member State provided the parties to the contract agree that CIM will apply.[455] CIM will further apply where the international carriage is the subject of a single contract which contract includes carriage by road or internal inland waterway as a supplement to the trans-frontier carriage by rail or carriage by sea or trans-frontier inland waterway if the latter services are listed in accordance with Art.24 of COTIF.[456] However, CIM will not apply where the carriage is performed between stations situated on the territory of neighbouring States, when the infrastructure of the stations is managed by one or more infrastructure managers subject only to one of those

States.[457] Any stipulation in the contract of carriage which, directly or indirectly, derogates from CIM shall be null and void, but such nullity shall not operate to nullify the other provisions of the contract.[457a]

[453] Art.1(1).
[454] *Azienda Autonoma Ferrovie dello Stato v La Pace* 11 E.T.L. 137 (1976) (Corte di Cassazione Civile, Italy).
[455] Art.1(2).
[456] Art.1(3), 1(4). As to rail-road traffic, see also CMR, Art.2(1) and para.36–122 below.
[457] Art.1(6).
[457a] Art.5.

Interpretation of the Convention. Whilst there have been no English deci- 36–086
sions on the interpretation of CIM, some decisions of the courts in the Continental parties to the unmodified Convention have been reported. In view of the similarity of the provisions regarding the carrier's liability and the carrier's exemptions from liability between CIM and the Geneva Convention on the Contract for the International Carriage of Goods by Road (CMR),[458] the reported decisions on the interpretation of CMR are often of assistance in the interpretation of CIM.

[458] Some of these decisions have been reported in such periodicals as *European Transport Law* (E.T.L.) and *Lloyds Maritime and Commercial Law Quarterly* (L.M.C.L.Q.).

The carrier's role. Under the contract of carriage, the carrier undertakes to 36–087
carry the goods consigned for reward to the place of destination and to deliver them at the destination to the consignee.[459] For this service, the carrier is entitled to the payment by the consignor of the carriage charge, customs duties and other costs.[460]

[459] Art.6(1).
[460] Art.10(1).

Consignment note. CIM requires the contract of carriage to be confirmed by 36–088
a consignment note which accords with a uniform model.[461] The uniform model is to be established by international associations of carriers in agreement with customers' associations and relevant customs authorities.[462] The consignment note is *prima facie* evidence of the conclusion and conditions of the contract and the taking over of the goods being carried.[463] CIM specifies a number of formal requirements for the consignment note, stipulating the particulars which the consignment note must contain (*e.g.* places of issue, taking over and delivery, names of consignor, carrier and consignee, and details of the goods to be carried), the responsibility for which largely falls on the consignor.[464] However, the absence, irregularity or loss of the consignment note shall not affect the existence or validity of the contract which the Convention emphasises shall remain subject to CIM.[465] One consignment note shall be issued for each consignment and, unless the contracting parties agree otherwise, must not relate to more than one wagon load.[466] CIM contemplates that there will be two copies of the consignment note, the duplicate being given to the consignor.[467] CIM provides that the consignment note will not have effect as a bill of lading.[468]

[461] Art.6(2).
[462] Art.6(8).
[463] Art.12(1).
[464] Arts 7, 8.
[465] Art.6(2).
[466] Art.6(6).
[467] Art.6(4).
[468] Art.6(5).

36–089   **Loading, Carriage and Delivery.** CIM contemplates two types of consignments which may be carried by rail, namely packages and full wagon-loads. Unless the parties otherwise agree, the carrier is responsible for the loading and unloading of packages and the consignor is responsible for the loading of a wagon load and the consignee is responsible for the unloading of the wagon load.[469] The consignor is responsible for any defects in the packing of the goods unless the defects were apparent to the carrier on taking them over and the carrier made no reservations concerning the defects.[470] On arrival at the destination, the carrier must deliver the goods to the consignee and hand over the consignment note against the provision of a receipt and the payment of sums outstanding under the carriage contract.[471] Delivery also may be effected by the handing over of the goods to customs authorities, or the deposit of the goods for storage with the railway, with a forwarding agent or in a public warehouse, provided that such delivery is permitted by the provisions in force at the destination station.[472]

[469] Art.13(1).
[470] Art.14.
[471] Art.17(1). In Antwerp, it has been held that the consignee named in the consignment note who acts as agent for the final consignee will become a party to the contract by acceptance of the goods or the consignment note: *Sobelgra NV v Nationale Maatschappij der Belgische Spoorwegen (NMBS)* (1997) 33 E.T.L. 714.
[472] Art.17(2).

36–090   **Modification of the contract.** The consignor shall be entitled to dispose of the goods and to modify the contract of carriage by giving "subsequent orders". Such orders may require the carrier to delay delivery of the goods or to deliver the goods to a consignee or to a destination other than the one identified in the consignment note.[473] The modification of the contract appears to be limited to these matters and must be effected by the consignor producing to the carrier the duplicate consignment note on which the modifications must be entered.[474] Such modifications must be "possible, lawful and reasonable", must not interfere with the normal working of the carrier's undertaking nor prejudice the consignors or consignees of other consignments and must not have the effect of splitting the consignment.[475] The consignee will acquire the right to modify the contract of carriage once the consignment note is drawn up, unless the consignor reserves the right to himself or herself on the consignment note.[476] The consignor will lose the right to modify the contract when the consignee has acquired the right of modification or has accepted from the carrier the consignment note or the goods or has demanded both.[477] Similarly, the consignee will lose the right of modification when he or she has requested or accepted the consignment note or the goods. Additionally, the consignee will lose the right when he or she has instructed the carrier to deliver the goods to another person, who requests the carrier to hand over the consignment note and deliver the goods; that person will not be entitled to modify the contract.[478] The consignor may have a right of stoppage in transit *vis à vis* the consignee pursuant to the Sale of Goods Act 1979 if English law governs the contract between them.[479]

[473] Art.18(1).

[474] Art.19(1). If the carrier accepts the consignor's orders to deliver the goods to some person other than the consignee named in the consignment note without requiring the duplicate consignment note to be produced, it will be liable for any loss or damage arising from that omission: Art.19(7); *SA Nicolas Corman v SNCF* 11 E.T.L. 120 (1976) (Court of Appeal, Paris).

[475] Art.19(3), 19(4).

[476] Art.18(3).

[477] Art.18(2).

[478] Art.18(4), 18(5).

[479] See below paras 43–353—43–365.

Prevention of carriage or delivery. If the carriage of the goods has been prevented by circumstances,[480] the carrier must decide whether it is preferable (presumably in the interests of the person entitled to dispose of the goods) to modify the route or to ask the person entitled for instructions.[481] If it is impossible to continue the carriage or to effect delivery, the person entitled shall be asked for his or her instructions. If the carrier is unable to obtain instructions, he or she shall take such steps which he or she considers to be in the best interests of the person entitled.[482] If circumstances exist which prevent delivery, the carrier must ask the consignor or (if the consignee has modified the contract) the consignee for instructions.[483] If the consignee refuses delivery, the consignor may give instructions, even if he or she is unable to produce the duplicate consignment note.[484] If circumstances alter permitting delivery before the receipt of instructions, the carrier shall deliver the goods to the consignee.[485] If the goods are of a perishable nature or if the carrier does not receive instructions, the carrier may sell the goods and, after deducting relevant costs, place the proceeds of sale at the disposal of the person entitled.[486]   **36–091**

[480] The carrier will not be liable for any loss of or damage to the goods or delay caused by circumstances which are unavoidable by the carrier: Art.23(2).

[481] Art.20(1).

[482] Art.20(2).

[483] Arts 21(1), 21(4).

[484] Art.21(3).

[485] Art.21(2).

[486] Arts 22(3), 22(4).

Loss, damage and delay. The carrier is liable for loss (total or partial) of the goods, damage and delay (*i.e.* for exceeding the transit periods[487]) unless he or she can prove an applicable exception to that liability.[488] The carrier is liable for his or her own employees and for any other persons, including the managers of the railway infrastructure on which the carriage is performed, whose services he or she uses in the performance of the carriage.[489] There are two kinds of exceptions. The first type arises where the relevant loss, damage or delay was caused by (1) the fault of the person entitled; (2) an order given by the person   **36–092**

entitled other than as a result of the fault of the carrier; (3) inherent defect in the goods (decay, wastage, etc.)[490]; or (4) circumstances which the carrier could not avoid and the consequences of which he or she was not able to prevent.[491] The burden of proving any of these is on the carrier.[492] Thus far, the exceptions are very similar to those applicable to the common carrier at common law. But the second kind of exception comprises circumstances when loss or damage arises from the special risks inherent in one or more of the following circumstances: (a) carriage in open wagons when that has been agreed; (b) absence or inadequacy of packaging; (c) loading by the consignor or unloading by the consignee; (d) the nature of certain kinds of goods which particularly exposes them to loss or damage, especially through breakage, rust, interior and spontaneous decay, desiccation or wastage; (e) irregular, incorrect or incomplete description or numbering of packages; (f) the carriage of live animals; and (g) the carriage of consignments which, with the parties' agreement, must be accompanied by an attendant.[493] If the carrier establishes that loss or damage could be attributed to one or more of these exceptions, this is rebuttably presumed, unless in (a) above there is an abnormal shortage or a loss of a package.[494] If the goods are not delivered to the consignee or held at his or her disposal within 30 days after the expiry of the transit period, they are presumed to be lost.[495]

[487] The transit period is that which is agreed between the carrier and consignor or, in the absence of agreement, as specified in Art.16.

[488] A failure to comply with the instructions of the person entitled to dispose of the goods during carriage may also render the carrier liable for loss or damage caused thereby: Art.19(6). There is a facility by which the carrier may seek an exception to liability for losses arising by specified causes in respect of rail-sea traffic, provided that the relevant Member State made such provision in the listed services set out in Art.24(1) of COTIF.

[489] Art.40.

[490] Where there is wastage in transit of goods which, by reason of their nature, is caused by the sole fact of carriage, the carrier will be liable only to the extent that the wastage exceeds specified allowances: Art.31.

[491] Art.23(2).

[492] Art.25(1).

[493] Art.23(3). The unmodified Convention included an additional exception in respect of loss caused by a failure to comply with customs formalities. Such matters are now regulated by Art.15. The carrier is under a general duty to maintain its rolling stock put at a customer's disposal in good condition: *NMBS v NV Fonciere Carner* 11 E.T.L. 780 (1976) (Hof van Beroep, Brussels). See also Art.24 which concerns railway vehicles consigned as goods.

[494] Arts 25(2), 25(3).

[495] Art.29(1).

36–093   **Ascertainment of loss or damage.** Upon delivery, the person entitled may ask the carrier for an opportunity to examine the goods to determine the existence of any loss or damage. Any failure by the carrier to permit such an examination will entitle the person entitled to the goods to refuse to accept the goods, even when he or she has accepted the consignment note and/or paid the outstanding charges.[496] In the event of the discovery, presumption or allegation of partial loss of or damage to the goods, the carrier must, without delay prepare, if possible in the presence of the person entitled, a report concerning the condition of the goods and the nature, extent, cause and time of the loss or damage.[497] If the person entitled does not accept the report's findings, he or she can insist upon the circumstances surrounding the loss or damage to be investigated by an expert.[498]

[496] Art.17(4).
[497] Art.42(1).
[498] Art.42(3).

Upper financial limits of liability. The carrier's liability for loss of the goods, whether total or partial, is limited to 17 units of account[499] per kilogram of gross mass short,[500] unless the consignor and carrier agree that the consignor shall declare in the consignment note a value for the goods exceeding this limit or a special interest in delivery by entering an amount in figures on the consignment note, in which case compensation can be claimed up to the value or amount declared.[501] The compensation is calculated by reference to the commodity exchange quoted price or current market price or the usual value of the goods of the same kind and quality at the time and place at which the goods were taken over for the carriage.[502] The carrier must also refund the carriage charges, customs duties and other expenses paid in respect of the missing goods.[503] The carrier's liability for delay (*i.e.* for exceeding the transit periods) depends on whether actual loss or damage was thus caused. If actual loss or damage resulted from the delay, the compensation may not exceed four times the amount of the carriage charges, although the total compensation for the loss or damage caused by delay and otherwise may not exceed the compensation payable for a total loss.[504] The carrier's liability for damage is for the amount by which the goods have been diminished in value, but may not exceed the amount payable in respect of loss.[505] The maximum limits of compensation for loss, damage or delay are removed altogether if it was due to the carrier's wilful misconduct (namely, an act or omission which the carrier has committed either with intent to cause such loss or damage, or recklessly and with knowledge that such loss or damage would probably result).[506] The claimant may recover interest on the compensation payable at the rate of 5 per cent per annum from the time a claim, together with supporting documents, is submitted in accordance with the CIM Uniform Rules,[507] or failing such a claim, from the time of the commencement of legal proceedings in respect of the claim.[508]

36–094

[499] However, the carrier is free to assume a greater liability: Art.5. The unit of account is the Special Drawing Right (SDR) defined by the International Monetary Fund (IMF): COTIF, Art.9(1). Its value is expressed in the national currency of a State Member of the IMF in accordance with IMF methods of valuation: Art.9(2). States which are not Members of the IMF shall determine their own methods of calculating the value of the SDR: if their legislation does not permit this, the unit of account is deemed to be the equivalent of three gold francs, each gold franc weighing 1031 of a gramme and of millesimal fineness 900: Arts 9(3), 9(4). In any event the conversion of the gold franc must express in national currency a value approximating closely to the value calculated by reference to the IMF methods of valuation. In the case of judicial proceedings or arbitration in the United Kingdom, the SDR is converted into its sterling equivalent on the day of the judgment or award: Railways (Convention on International Carriage by Rail) Regulations 2005 (SI 2005/2092), reg.7.
[500] Art.30(2).
[501] Arts 34, 35.
[502] Art.30(1).
[503] Art.30(4). The charges do not include charges which would have been incurred in the event that the carriage was performed in accordance with the contract, would have contributed to the value of

the goods at the destination, and which were not incurred as a result of the incident giving rise to the claim (*Anon.*, Bundesgerichtshof, June 26, 2003, (2004) 39 E.T.L. 93). The claimant cannot recover any additional duty or VAT payable in respect of the goods which do not find themselves at their destination: *Anon.*, Cass. Paris, January 28, 1975; *cf. James Buchanan & Co Ltd v Babco Forwarding and Shipping (UK) Ltd* [1978] 1 Lloyd's Rep. 119; *contra Anon.*, Supreme Court of Denmark May 4, 1987 (1994) 29 E.T.L. 360 (CMR). See para.36–132, n.729 below.

[504] Arts 33(1), 33(2), 33(3).

[505] Arts 32(1), 32(2). Under the unmodified Convention, in the event of damage by deterioration, the carrier's liability is calculated under the provisions concerning damage not delay: *Anon.* 11 E.T.L. 787 (1976) (Bundesgerichtshof). Under Art.33(4), in the case of damage to goods, not resulting from the transit period being exceeded, the compensation payable under Art.33(1) shall, where appropriate, be payable in addition to that provided for in Art.32.

[506] Art.36.

[507] Art.43. If no supporting documents are provided within a reasonable time so that the amount of the claim can be finally settled, no interest shall accrue between the expiry of the time allotted and the actual submission of such documents: Art.37(3).

[508] Art.37(2).

36–095   **Successive and substitute carriers.** If carriage is governed by a single contract and is performed by several successive carriers, each carrier, by the very act of taking over the goods with the consignment note, shall become a party to the contract of carriage in accordance with the terms of the contract and shall assume the obligations arising therefrom. Each carrier shall be responsible in respect of carriage over the entire route up to delivery.[509] Where the carrier has entrusted all or part of the performance of the carriage to a substitute carrier, the carrier shall remain liable in respect of the entire carriage. The CIM provisions governing the liability of the carrier shall also apply to the liability of the substitute carrier for the carriage performed by him or her.[510] Actions based on the contract of carriage may be brought only against the first carrier, the last carrier or the carrier who performed that part of the carriage on which the event giving rise to the claim occurred.[511] A successive carrier may be sued if that carrier has been named, with his or her consent, in the consignment note as the carrier who must deliver the goods, even if that carrier has not received the goods or the consignment note.[512]

[509] Art.26.

[510] Arts 27(1), 27(2).

[511] Art.45(1).

[512] Art.45(2).

36–096   **Claims.** Claims against the carrier relating to the contract of carriage must be made in writing only by those persons who have the right to claim.[513] The consignor may bring an action against the carrier until such time as the consignee has taken possession of the consignment note or accepted the goods or demanded that the consignment note be handed over and that the goods be delivered or asserted his or her right to modify the contract.[514] From that time, the consignee may bring an action against the carrier unless and until the person to whom the consignee has ordered the carrier to deliver the goods has accepted the consignment note or the goods or has demanded both.[515] Actions based on CIM may be brought in the Member States designated by the parties' agreement or where the defendant is domiciled or resident or where the goods were taken over by the carrier or where the place designated for delivery is situated.[516]

[513] Arts 43(1), 43(2). The claim generally has to be supported by the consignment note: see Arts 43(3)–(6).
[514] Art.44(1)(a).
[515] Arts 44(1)(b), 44(2).
[516] Art.46(1).

Extinction of claims. Acceptance of the goods by the person entitled extinguishes all rights of action against the carrier arising from the contract of carriage in case of partial loss, damage or delay,[517] subject to four exceptions. First, claims for partial loss or damage can be made if the damage was ascertained by the preparation of a report (unless the report was not prepared solely by reason of the carrier's fault).[518] Secondly, claims for loss or damage which is not apparent and not discovered until after acceptance can still be made, provided the person entitled to claim asks the carrier for a report within seven days of acceptance and proves that the loss or damage occurred between the time of taking over the goods for carriage and the time of delivery.[519] Thirdly, claims for delay in delivery can be made within 60 days of acceptance.[520] Fourthly, the claim is not extinguished if wilful misconduct can be proved.[521]

36–097

[517] Art.47(1).
[518] Art.47(2)(a).
[519] Art.47(2)(b). See Clarke, "Non-apparent damage to goods in transit" [1982] L.M.C.L.Q 533.
[520] Art.47(2)(c).
[521] Art.47(2)(d).

Limitation of actions. All actions arising from the contract of carriage are time-barred after one year, or two years in the case of, *inter alia*, wilful misconduct.[522] The period of limitation runs, in the case of partial loss, damage or delay in delivery, from the date of delivery; in the case of total loss, from the 30th day after the expiry of the transit period.[523] A written claim suspends the running of the period of limitation until such date as the carrier rejects the claim in writing.[524]

36–098

[522] Art.48(1). The limitation provision applies to claims based on the contract of carriage, whether brought by or against the rail carrier: *Anon.*, Oberster Gerichtshof-Österreich, August 26, 2004 (2005) 40 E.T.L. 395.
[523] Art.48(2).
[524] Art.48(3).

(c) *Passengers, Luggage and Vehicles by Rail*

(i) *Application and Scope of the Convention*

Scope of the Uniform Rules (CIV) under Appendix A to COTIF. The CIV Uniform Rules regulate the making and performance of the contract of carriage of passengers, luggage and vehicles by rail, the liability of the rail carrier for death of, and personal injury to, passengers, for the failure to keep to the timetable, the liability of the passenger and the relations between carriers.

36–099

Application of CIV. CIV provides a unified set of rules to be applied to every contract of carriage of passengers by rail for reward or free of charge, when the

36–100

place of departure and the place of destination are situated in two different Member States, irrespective of the domicile or the place of business and the nationality of the parties to the contract.[525] CIV applies also to international carriage pursuant to a single contract which includes carriage by road or by internal inland waterway or, provided that the services are provided for in Art.24(1) of COTIF, by sea or trans-frontier inland waterway.[526] CIV also applies, as far as the liability of the carrier in the case of death or personal injury is concerned, to persons accompanying a consignment whose carriage is effected in accordance with the CIM Uniform Rules.[527] As with CIM, CIV will not apply where the carriage is performed between stations situated on the territory of neighbouring States, when the infrastructure of the stations is managed by one or more infrastructure managers subject only to one of those States.[528] Any stipulation in the contract of carriage which, directly or indirectly, derogates from CIV shall be null and void, but such nullity shall not operate to nullify the other provisions of the contract.[529]

[525] Art.1(1).
[526] Arts 1(2), 1(3).
[527] Art.1(4).
[528] Art.1(5).
[529] Art.5.

36–101   **Rail-sea carriage.** As mentioned above, CIV applies to a single contract of international carriage by rail and sea provided that the carriage is performed on services listed pursuant to Art.24(1) of COTIF.[530] It should be noted, however, that, whilst CIV may in certain circumstances cover aspects of rail-sea carriage, legislation in the United Kingdom has provided that as far as English law is concerned, the terms of the Athens Convention relating to the Carriage of Passengers and their Luggage by Sea 1974 are applied to any contract for international carriage by sea under which a place in the United Kingdom is the place of departure or destination.[531] The Athens Convention enables carriers by sea to limit their liability in respect of the death of, or personal injury to, a passenger. The terms of the Athens Convention have also been applied to carriage by sea within the United Kingdom.[532]

[530] Art.1(3).
[531] Merchant Shipping Act 1995, s.183. The Athens Convention came into force on April 30, 1987.
[532] Carriage of Passengers and their Luggage by Sea (Domestic Carriage) Order 1987 (SI 1987/670), which now takes effect as if made under the Merchant Shipping Act 1995, s.184. Under s.184(5), the term "contract of carriage" in the context of the Athens Convention excludes a contract which is not for reward.

36–102   **The carrier's role.** Under the contract of carriage, the carrier is obliged to carry the passenger and, where appropriate, the passenger's luggage and vehicle to the place of destination and to deliver the luggage and vehicle at the place of destination.[533] Subject to the terms of the contract, the carrier is entitled to advance payment of the carriage charge.[534]

[533] Art.6(1).
[534] Arts 8(1), 19, 25.

(ii) *Passengers and Hand Luggage*

The passenger's rights. The passenger in possession of a valid ticket is   **36–103**
entitled to be carried in accordance with the terms of the contract of carriage. The
passenger is also entitled to take with him or her articles which can be handled
easily (hand luggage), but it is the passenger's responsibility to supervise such
hand luggage.[535] If a passenger is unable to produce a valid ticket, the carrier may
require the passenger to pay a surcharge. If the passenger fails to pay the carriage
charge or the surcharge, the carrier may require the passenger to discontinue the
journey.[536] The carrier may also exclude a passenger from carriage or require a
passenger to discontinue his or her journey, without refunding the carriage
charge, if that passenger presents a danger for the safety and the good functioning
of the operations of the rail operations or for the safety of the other passengers
or if that passenger inconveniences other passengers in an intolerable man-
ner.[537]

[535] Arts 12(1), 15.
[536] Art.9(1).
[537] Art.9(2).

The ticket. The contract of carriage must be confirmed by one or more tickets   **36–104**
issued to the passenger. However, the absence, irregularity, or loss of the ticket
shall not affect the existence or validity of the contract, which remains subject to
the application of the CIV Uniform Rules.[538] The ticket is *prima facie* evidence
of the making and contents of the contract of carriage.[539] The terms and conditions of the contract are those which are legally in force in each Member State.
Such conditions will determine the form and content of tickets.[540] The ticket may
be established in the form of electronic data registration, which can be trans-
formed into legible written symbols.[541] However, the ticket must identify the
carrier and must state that the carriage is subject to the CIV Uniform Rules.[542] It
is incumbent on the passenger to ensure that on receipt of the ticket that it has
been made out in accordance with his or her instructions.[543] If the ticket is not
made out in the passenger's name, the ticket is transferable, provided that the
journey has not yet begun.[544]

[538] Art.6(2). This is subject to the carrier's right, as set out in Art.9, to demand a surcharge in the
event of the non-production of the ticket and to require the passenger to discontinue the journey if the
carriage charge or surcharge is not paid.
[539] Art.6(3).
[540] Arts 3(c), 7(1).
[541] Art.7(5).
[542] Art.7(2).
[543] Art.7(3).
[544] Art.7(4).

Liability for death and personal injury. In general under CIV the carrier is   **36–105**
liable for damage resulting from the death of, or personal injury or any other
physical or mental harm to, a passenger, when the damage is caused by an
accident arising out of the operation of the railway and happening while the
passenger is in, entering or alighting from, railway vehicles.[545] In the event of

death, the carrier is liable for damages comprising the necessary costs following the death (including transport and funeral expenses) and is liable to the passenger's dependents, whom the passenger was legally obliged to maintain, for the loss of support.[546] In the case of personal injury (whether or not it leads to death), or other physical or mental harm, the carrier is liable for damage comprising any necessary costs (including medical treatment and transport expenses) and compensation for financial loss due to incapacity to work or increased needs.[547]

[545] Art.26(1).
[546] Arts 27(1), 27(2). National law shall govern the rights of action of those whom the passenger was maintaining without a legal obligation so to do: Art.27(2).
[547] Art.28. National law shall govern the right to claim damages other than those set out in Arts 27 and 28: Art.29.

36–106   **Fatal accidents.** Regulation 5 of the Railways (Convention on International Carriage by Rail) Regulations 2005[548] provides that where under the Convention a person has a right of action in respect of the death of a passenger by virtue of his being a person whom the passenger was under a legally enforceable duty to maintain, no action in respect of the passenger's death may be brought for the benefit of that person under the Fatal Accidents Act 1976, although actions under that Act may be brought for the benefit of any other person. The Regulations further provide that in actions brought under CIV the same benefit shall be excluded in the assessment of damages as would be excluded under s.4 of the Fatal Accidents Act 1976. Where separate proceedings can be brought under CIV and under the Fatal Accidents Act 1976, a court may, in assessing damages under the 1976 Act, take account of any damages awarded in proceedings under the Convention.

[548] SI 2005/2092.

36–107   **Carrier's exemptions from liability for death and personal injury.** The carrier is relieved of liability for death or personal injury (a) if the accident was caused by circumstances not connected with the operation of the railway and which the carrier, despite the exercise of the care required in the circumstances, could not avoid and the consequences of which he or she could not prevent[549]; (b) to the extent that the accident was due to the passenger's fault[550]; and (c) if the accident was caused by the behaviour of a third party which the carrier, despite the exercise of the care required in the circumstances, could not avoid and the consequences of which it could not prevent.[551] If the accident is due to the behaviour of a third party and if the carrier is in any event not entirely relieved of liability, he or she shall be liable in full up to the limits imposed by CIV.[552]

[549] Art.26(2)(a).
[550] Art.26(2)(b).
[551] Art.26(2)(c). Another undertaking using the same railway infrastructure shall not be considered as a third party for the purposes of this provision.
[552] Art.26(3).

36–108   **Liability for delay.** The carrier is liable to the passenger for loss or damage resulting from the fact that the journey cannot, or could not reasonably, be continued on the same day because of a cancellation, the late running of a train or a missed connection. The damages for which the carrier is liable comprises the reasonable costs of accommodation and the reasonable costs of notifying persons expecting the passenger.[553] The carrier will be exempt from such liability in similar circumstances exempting the carrier from liability for death and personal injury.[554]

[553] Art.32(1). National law shall govern the passenger's right to claim other heads of damage: Art.32(3).
[554] Art.32(2). See para.36–107 above.

Liability for hand luggage. In the event that the passenger dies or sustains a personal injury, the carrier shall also be liable for loss or damage resulting from the total or partial loss of, or damage to, hand luggage.[555] In other cases, the carrier shall not be liable for hand luggage the supervision of which is the responsibility of the passenger, unless the loss or damage was caused by the fault of the carrier.[556]   **36–109**

[555] Art.33(1).
[556] Art.33(2).

Upper financial limits of liability. The amount of damages to be awarded in cases of death or personal injury under CIV are to be determined in accordance with national law. The limit of damages per passenger is fixed, for the purposes of the CIV Uniform Rules, at 175,000 units of account, where national law provides for an upper limit of less than that amount.[557] There is no specified financial limit of liability for delay. Where the carrier is liable for damage to, or loss of, hand luggage, the limit of compensation is 1,400 units of account per passenger.[558] The liability of the carrier is, however, not limited at all if the loss or damage results from an act or omission which the carrier has committed either with intent to cause such loss or damage or recklessly with the knowledge that such loss or damage probably will result.[559]   **36–110**

[557] Art.30(2). As to "units of account", see para.36–094, n.499 above.
[558] Art.34.
[559] Art.48.

(iii) *Registered Luggage and Vehicles*

Transport documents. A passenger may consign articles as registered luggage in accordance with the application general conditions of carriage.[560] The carrier's obligations concerning the forwarding of registered luggage must be established by a luggage registration voucher issued to the passenger. The absence, irregularity or loss of the voucher shall not affect the existence or validity of the contract of carriage, which remains subject to the application of the CIV Uniform Rules.[561] The voucher is *prima facie* evidence of the registration of the luggage and the contents of the contract of carriage.[562] The form and content of the voucher are determined in accordance with the general conditions of carriage.[563] The voucher must identify the carrier and must state that the   **36–111**

carriage is subject to the CIV Uniform Rules.[564] It is incumbent on the passenger to ensure that on receipt of the voucher that it has been made out in accordance with his or her instructions.[565] Similar provisions exist in respect of vehicles, for which a carriage voucher must establish the carrier's contractual obligations.[566]

[560] Art.12(2).
[561] Arts 16(1), 16(2). As to the responsibility of successive and substitute carriers, see Arts 38, 39.
[562] Art.16(3).
[563] Art.17(1).
[564] Art.17(2).
[565] Art.17(3).
[566] Arts 24, 25.

36–112   **Loss, damage and delay.** The carrier is liable for loss or damage resulting from the total or partial loss of, or damage to, registered luggage or the vehicle carried between the time of taking over by the carrier and the time of delivery as well as from delay in delivery.[567] The carrier will be relieved from this liability to the extent that the loss, damage or delay was caused by a fault of the passenger, an order given by the passenger other than as a result of the carrier's fault, an inherent defect or circumstances which the carrier could not avoid and the consequences of which he or she was unable to prevent.[568] Further, the carrier will be relieved of liability to the extent that the loss or damage arises from the special risks inherent in (a) the absence or inadequacy of packing, (b) the special nature of the luggage or vehicle, and/or (c) the consignment as luggage of articles not acceptable for carriage.[569] The person entitled to the luggage or vehicle may consider the luggage or vehicle lost, without adducing further proof, if has not been delivered within 14 days after a valid request for delivery has been made.[570]

[567] Arts 36(1), 47. It is rebuttably presumed that when the carrier took over the registered luggage that it was apparently in good condition and that the number and mass of the items of luggage corresponded to the entries on the voucher: Art.16(4). Delivery of the luggage or vehicle must be effected on surrender of the voucher: Art.22(1).
[568] Arts 36(2), 47. The carrier bears the relevant burden of proof: Art.37(1).
[569] Arts 36(3), 47. The carrier bears the initial burden of proof, which thereafter falls upon the claimant: Art.37(2).
[570] Art.40(1).

36–113   **Upper financial limits of liability.** The amount of the carrier's liability for loss of registered luggage, whether total or partial, depends on whether or not the passenger establishes the amount of loss or damage suffered. If the amount of loss is proved, the loss is limited to 80 units of account per kilogram of gross mass short or 1200 units of account per item of luggage; if not, the carrier must pay liquidated damages of 20 units of account per kilogram of gross mass short or 300 units of account per item of luggage.[571] The carrier must also refund the carriage charges.[572] Liability for damage is for the amount by which the luggage has been diminished in value, but may not exceed the amount payable in respect of loss.[573] As regards delay, if the passenger proves that he or she suffered loss or damage, the maximum amount payable as compensation is 0.80 units of account per kilogram of gross mass of the luggage or 14 units of account per item of luggage delivered late; but if loss or damage is not proved, the measure of damages is liquidated at 0.14 units of account per kilogram of gross mass of the luggage or 2.80 units of account per item of luggage delivered late.[574] The maximum limits of compensation for loss, damage or delay are removed altogether if it was due to the act or omission of the carrier which was done with the intent to cause loss or damage or recklessly with the knowledge that such loss or damage probably will result.[575] As regards vehicles, compensation for loss of or damage to the vehicle shall be calculated on the basis of the usual value of the vehicle subject to a limit of 8,000 units of account[576]; compensation for proven loss or damage resulting from delay is limited to the amount of the carriage charge.[577]

[571] Art.41(1).
[572] Art.41(2).
[573] Art.42.
[574] Art.43(1).
[575] Art.48.
[576] Art.45.
[577] Art.44.

(iv) *Claims*

Claims against carriers. A claim relating to liability for death or personal **36–114** injury must be addressed in writing to the carrier against whom an action may be brought. Where successive carriers performed the carriage under a single contract, the claim may also be made against the first or the last carrier as well as the carrier who has his or her principal place of business or whose agency concluded the contract in the State where the passenger is domiciled or resident.[578] An action in respect of death or personal injury may be brought only against the carrier (including substitute carriers) who was bound pursuant to the contract of carriage to provide the service of carriage in the course of which the accident happened.[579] Other claims based on the contract of carriage may be brought only against the first carrier, the last carrier or the carrier who performed that part of the carriage on which the event giving rise to the claim occurred.[580] A successive carrier may be sued if that carrier has been named, with his or her consent, in the voucher as the carrier who must deliver the luggage or vehicle, even if that carrier has not received them or the voucher.[581] Actions based on CIV may be brought before the courts or tribunals as agreed between the parties or in those Member States in which the defendant is domiciled or resident or has his or her principal place of business or agency which concluded the contract.[582]

[578] Art.55(1).
[579] Arts 26(5), 56(1).
[580] Arts 55(2), 56(2).
[581] Art.56(3).
[582] Art.57(1).

Extinction of claims. A claimant loses his right of action based on the **36–115** carrier's liability for death or personal injury if he or she does not give notice of the accident to one of the carriers to which a claim may be presented within 12 months of his or her becoming aware of the loss or damage.[583] Nonetheless, the right of action is not lost if (a) notice has been given to one of the carriers against a claim brought within the relevant period; (b) the carrier who is liable has learned of the accident within the relevant period in some other way; (c) notice of the accident has not been given, or has been given late, as a result of circumstances for which the claimant is not responsible; or (d) the claimant proves that the accident was caused by fault of the carrier.[584] As regards other claims, acceptance of the luggage by the person entitled extinguishes all rights of action against the carrier arising from the contract of carriage in case of partial loss, damage or delay,[585] subject to four exceptions. First, claims for partial loss or damage can be made if the damage was ascertained in accordance with CIV.[586] Secondly, claims for loss or damage which is not apparent and not discovered until after acceptance can still be made, provided the person entitled to claim asks the carrier for ascertainment within three days of acceptance and proves that the loss or damage occurred between the time of taking over and the time of delivery.[587] Thirdly, claims for delay in delivery can be made within 21 days of acceptance.[588] Fourthly, the claim is not extinguished if the person entitled proves that the loss or damage was caused by fault on the part of the carrier.[589]

[583] Art.58(1).
[584] Art.58(2).
[585] Art.59(1). It is assumed that this provision applies alike to vehicles.
[586] Arts 54, 59(2)(a).
[587] Art.59(2)(b).
[588] Art.59(2)(c).
[589] Art.59(2)(d). *cf.* CIM, Art.47(2)(d).

36–116   **Limitation of actions.** Actions for damages brought under CIV based on the carrier's liability for death or personal injury are time-barred in the case of a passenger who has sustained an accident, three years from the day after the accident. In the case of other claimants, actions are barred three years from the day after the death of the passenger or five years from the day after the accident, whichever is the earlier.[590] As regards all other claims, the period of limitation shall be one year (or two years in the case of wilful misconduct) (a) in the case of compensation for loss, from the 14th day after the person entitled calls for delivery, (b) in the case of compensation for partial loss, damage or delay in delivery, from the day when delivery took place, and (c) in all other cases involving the carriage of passengers, from the day of expiry of the validity of the ticket.[591] When a claim is made in writing to the carrier, the limitation period is suspended until the carrier against whom the claim has been made rejects it in writing.[592]

[590] Art.60(1).
[591] Arts 60(2), 60(3).
[592] Art.60(4).

(d) *Goods by Road*

The scope of CMR

[*Add to the end of note 624: page* [603]]
In *Anon.*, Hof van Cassatie van België, November 8, 2004 (2006) 41 E.T.L. 228, it was held that where the contract was silent on the mode of carriage and the circumstances were such that the parties did not contemplate road transport, CMR was inapplicable.

36–121

Delivery

[*Add at the end of note 686: page* [609]]
In *Anon.*, Oberster Gerichtshof-Österreich, May 16, 2002, (2003) 38 E.T.L. 512, it was held that delivery was not prevented if the carrier was able to carry the goods to the destination by alternative means.

36–127

The carrier's exemptions from liability: Article 17(2)

[*Add to the end of note 700: page* [611]]
In *Datec Electronic Holdings Ltd v United Parcels Service Ltd* [2005] EWHC 221 (Comm); [2005] 1 Lloyd's Rep. 470 at [127], reversed on other grounds [2005] EWCA Civ 1418; [2006] 1 Lloyd's Rep. 279 at [28], the court held that the consignment of a package worth more than U$50,000, pursuant to a contract which provided that the value of a package may not exceed US$50,000, did not constitute a wrongful act for the purposes of art.17(2).

36–129

[*Add to note 703 before "However, a 'wildcat' "*]
cf. *m/v Nord Cloud* (2006) 41 E.T.L. 79 (Hof van Beroep te Antwerpen).

[*Add at the end of note 708: page* [612]]
Anon., Oberster Gerichtshof-Österreich, February 13, 2003, (2004) 39 E.T.L. 244.

Upper financial limits of liability and measure of damages

[*Add to the end of note 724: page* [615]]
As to a claim for loss arising from a failure to place insurance cover, see *NV Valkeniersnatie* (2006) 41 E.T.L. 272 (Hof van Beroep te Antwerpen).

36–132

[*Add to note 729, line 11, after "para.98": page* [616]]
Anon., Bundesgerichtshof, June 26, 2003, (2004) 39 E.T.L. 93.

[*Add to end of note 737: page* [617]]
Such losses might be calculated in accordance with the applicable national law or Arts 17–28: *Anon.*, Bundesgerichtshof-Deutschland, March 3, 2005 (2005) 40 E.T.L. 729.

[*Add to note 738, line 1, after "Clarke op.cit. para.101"*]
Datec Electronic Holdings Ltd v United Parcels Service Ltd [2005] EWCA Civ 1418; [2006] 1 Lloyd's Rep. 279.

[*Add to note 738 at end of 4th last sentence, line 22: page* [617]]
Micro Anvika Ltd v TNT Express Worldwide (Euro Hub) NV [2006] EWHC 230 (Comm).

Interest

36–134   [*Add to the end of note 742: page* [618]]
Art.27 also applies to claims under Art.37: *Anon.*, Bundesgerichtshof, November 27, 2003, (2004) 39 E.T.L. 517.

The parties to the contract

36–135   [*Add to the end of note 746: page* [618]]
In *Royal & Sun Alliance Insurance Plc v MK Digital Fze (Cyprus) Ltd* [2006] EWCA Civ 629; [2006] 2 Lloyd's Rep. 110 at [3], the Court of Appeal held that the contract was not one to which the CMR Convention applied, because there was insufficient evidence that the claimant was a carrier, as opposed to a *commissionnaire de transport*.

Which carrier may be sued by those interested in the goods

36–139   [*Add to note 766 before "Clarke, op. cit. para.50": page* [622]]
Rosewood Trucking Ltd v Balaam [2005] EWCA Civ 1461; [2006] 1 Lloyd's Rep. 429.

Carrier's rights of recovery from other carriers

36–141   [*Add note to the end of the first sentence: page* [623]]
In *Rosewood Trucking Ltd v Balaam* [2005] EWCA Civ 1461; [2006] 1 Lloyd's Rep. 429, the Court of Appeal refused a carrier who compensated the first carrier but who was not the first, last or responsible carrier within the meaning of Art.36 to recover an indemnity from the responsible carrier.

Reservations at delivery and extinction of claims

36–144   [*Add note 786a at the end of the third sentence of the text: page* [625]]
Anon., Oberster Gerichtshof-Österreich, September 19, 2002, (2004) 39 E.T.L. 400.

Limitation of actions

36–145   [*Add to note 792 after the second sentence: page* [626]]
As to claims in delict or tort, see *Anon.*, Oberster Gerichtshof-Österreich, March 15, 2005, (2005) 40 E.T.L. 878.

[*Add to the end of note 793*]
See also *Frigo Express bvba v Frigo Traffic Company nv* (2004) 39 E.T.L. 521 (Hof van Cassatie van België) (claim by carrier against sub-carrier); *Transports Collomb Muret auto SA v Panini France SA* (2004) 39 E.T.L. 531 (Cour de Cassation de France) (claim by carrier against consignee).

[Add at the end of note 799: page [627]]]
See also *NV Optitrade ea v NV Cat Benelux* (2004) 39 E.T.L. 407 (Hof van Beroep te Antwerpen).

Jurisdiction

[Delete "the Brussels Convention on Jurisdiction . . . 1968" from the second sentence and substitute: page [628]]
Council Regulation (EC) No.44/2001

36–147

[Add to the end of note 809: page [629]]
Anon., Oberster Gerichtshof-Österreich, (2003) 38 E.T.L. 656, 658, 661; *DFDS Transport A/S v Dieter Mehrholz Internationale Transporte* (2004) 39 E.T.L. 74 (Supreme Court of Denmark); *Royal & Sun Alliance Insurance Plc v MK Digital Fze (Cyprus) Ltd* [2005] EWHC 1408 (Comm) at [55]–[69]; reversed on other grounds [2006] EWCA Civ 629; [2006] 2 Lloyd's Rep. 110.

[Add at the beginning of note 810]
Andrea Merzario Ltd v Internationale Spedition Leitner Gesellschaft mbH [2001] EWCA Civ 61; [2001] 1 Lloyd's Rep. 490.

[Add at the end of the second sentence of note 810]
Royal & Sun Alliance Insurance Plc v MK Digital Fze (Cyprus) Ltd [2005] EWHC 1408 (Comm) at [55]–[69]; reversed on other grounds [2006] EWCA Civ 629; [2006] 2 Lloyd's Rep. 110.

[Add before the final sentence of note 812]
In *Blue Water Shipping A/S v Melship Eesti OÜ* (2000) 35 E.T.L. 772, the Supreme Court of Denmark held that Art.39 referred to the residence of the defendant successive carrier and not the claimant successive carrier.

No contracting out

[Add to the end of the second sentence of note 817: page [629]]
Datec Electronic Holdings Ltd v United Parcels Service Ltd [2005] EWCA Civ 1418; [2006] 1 Lloyd's Rep. 279 at [24].

36–149

CHAPTER 37

CONSTRUCTION CONTRACTS

			PARA.
☐	1.	The nature of construction contracts	37–001
		(a) Definitions	37–001
		(b) Types of construction contract—payment	37–007
		(c) Types of construction contract—procurement	37–013
		(d) Standard forms of contract	37–016
☐		(e) Content of Standard Forms	37–020
		(f) Other contractual arrangements	37–034
■	2.	Formation of contract	37–039
■		(a) General principles	37–039
☐		(b) Contract/no contract	37–045
☐		(c) Tenders	37–051
		(d) Letters of intent	37–055
■	3.	Contract terms	37–058
		(a) General principles apply	37–059
■		(b) Contract documents	37–061
■		(c) Implied terms	37–067
■		(d) Statutes relevant to construction	37–076
■		(e) Tort in construction	37–087
■	4.	Particular features	37–091
		(a) Variations	37–091
■		(b) Instructions, certificates and approval	37–097
		(c) Completion, maintenance and performance	37–106
		(d) Extension of time and liquidated damages	37–110
		(e) Bonds and guarantees	37–116
		(f) Insurance	37–124
		(g) Retention	37–129
	5.	Payment	37–134
		(a) Measure and value	37–134
		(b) Interim payment and milestones	37–139
		(c) Obligation to pay	37–143
		(d) Cost-based payment	37–154
		(e) Price fluctuations	37–160
		(f) *Quantum meruit*	37–163
■	6.	Sub-contracts	37–166
■		(a) Sub-contractors	37–166
		(b) Nomination	37–171
☐	7.	The Contract Administrator	37–178
		(a) Engineers, architects and quantity surveyors	37–178
☐		(b) Role under contracts	37–183
		(c) Liability of Contract Administrator	37–190
		(d) Contract with employer	37–194

			PARA.
	8.	Breach and non-performance	37–198
		(a) General principles	37–198
		(b) Breach by employer	37–202
		(c) Breach by the contractor	37–206
		(d) Repudiation and discharge	37–212
		(e) Frustration and force majeure	37–216
		(f) The privity rule and its exceptions	37–219
		(g) Non-performance not amounting to substantial breach	37–224
	9.	Remedies by enforcement	37–227
		(a) Control by Contract Administrator	37–227
		(b) Claims	37–232
		(c) Determination	37–238
		(d) Final certificates	37–245
■	10.	Disputes	37–247
■		(a) Nature of disputes	37–247
		(b) Conditions precedent	37–248
		(c) Arbitration	37–250
□		(d) Litigation	37–252
□		(e) Adjudication	37–255
		(f) International disputes	37–263

1. THE NATURE OF CONSTRUCTION CONTRACTS

(e) *Content of Standard Forms*

Determination

[*Add new footnote 80A after the words "Clauses 7.9 to 7.12": page* [650]]   **37–032—**
80a It is to be noted that, in *Construction Partnership (UK) Limited v Leek Developments Limited*   **37–033**
[2006] C.I.L.L. 2357, TCC, the Court decided that the requirement that there be actual delivery of
notices under these provisions could be satisfied by faxed transmission.

2. FORMATION OF CONTRACT

(a) *General Principles*

General principles

[*Add to note 95: page* [653]]   **37–039**
See *Ove Arup & Partners International Ltd v Mirant Asia-Pacific Construction (Hong Kong) Ltd* [2003] EWCA Civ 1729; [2004] B.L.R. 49.

(b) *Contract/No Contract*

Decisions on contract/no contract

[*Add new paragraph 37–050A: page* [659]]   **37–050A**
In *ERDC Group Limited v Brunel University* [2006] EWHC 687 (TCC);
[2006] B.L.R. 255, the Court found that, for a period prior to September 1, 2002,

the series of letters of intent[135a] issued by Brunel, and worked to by ERDC, were sufficient to create a binding contract. However, on the unusual facts of the case, the court concluded that, in the period after September 1, 2002, there was no contract and, furthermore, the move to the non-contractual basis did not justify a departure from contract rates and prices in favour of remuneration based on ERDC's costs.

[135a] For a recent review of cases on letters of intent, see Whittaker "What are your intentions?" *New Law Journal* (July 28, 2006) p.1200.

(c) *Tenders*

Good faith

37–053   [*Add to note 143: page* [661]]
By way of comparison, see the Privy Council treatment of fairness and good faith in an appeal from the New Zealand Court of Appeal in *Pratt Contractors Ltd v Transit New Zealand* [2004] B.L.R. 143.

[*Add to note 143*]
For a recent case where the Court (in this case the Court of Appeal in the SAR of Hong Kong) decided that the terms of a settlement agreement were no more than an agreement to agree, applying *Walford v Miles*, see *Hyundai Engineering & Construction Company Limited v Vigour Limited* [2005] B.L.R. 416.

3. CONTRACT TERMS

(b) *Contract Documents*

Incorporated documents

37–064   [*Page* [666]]
See the approach of the Court of Appeal in *Aqua Design Ltd v Kier Regional Ltd* [2002] EWCA Civ 797; [2003] B.L.R. 111 to the question of whether certain provisions of the Standard DOM/1 Form of Sub-Contract were incorporated into a negotiated sub-contract.

(c) *Implied Terms*

General principles

37–067   [*Add to note 178: page* [667]]
See the decision of the Court of Appeal in *Ultraframe (UK) Ltd v Tailored Roofing Systems Ltd* [2004] EWCA Civ 585; [2004] B.L.R. 341.

(d) *Statutes Relevant to Construction*

Statutory implied terms

37–077   [*Add to end of note 221: page* [671]]
Contracts for the supply of materials are normally governed by the Sale of Goods Act 1979 (see Main Work, Vol. II, Chap.43); see *Jewsons Ltd v Boykan*

[2003] EWCA Civ 1030; [2004] B.L.R. 31 on fitness for purpose under s.14(3) in the building context.

4. PARTICULAR FEATURES

(b) *Instructions, Certificates and Approval*

Final certificate

[Add to note 337: page [684]]   **37–101**
See *Cantrell v Wright and Fuller Ltd* [2003] EWHC 1545 (TCC); [2003] B.L.R. 412.

6. SUB-CONTRACTS

(a) *Sub-Contractors*

No right to direct payment

[Add at end of paragraph: page [712]]   **37–169**
In each case, it is a question of construction of the contract as to what rights and obligations have been conferred, or imposed, on the parties.[543a]

[543a] *Actionstrength Ltd v International Glass Engineering IN.GL.EN SpA* [2003] UKHL 17; [2003] 2 A.C. 541 and *Brican Fabrications Ltd v Merchant City Developments Ltd* [2003] B.L.R. 512 (Court of Session).

7. THE CONTRACT ADMINISTRATOR

(b) *Role under Contracts*

Acting impartially

[Add new footnote 579a at the end of this paragraph: page [719]]   **37–186**
[579a] For a recent analysis of the duties of a "Construction Manager", where those duties involve the issue of certificates, see the judgment of Jackson J in *Scheldebouw BV v St James Homes (Grosvenor Dock) Limited* [2006] EWHC 89 (TCC); [2006] B.L.R. 113.

10. DISPUTES

(a) *Nature of Disputes*

Disputes under construction contracts

[Page [743]]
The question of whether a "dispute" or "difference" has in fact arisen may be   **37–247**
important in the context of dispute resolution procedures—such as arbitration or

adjudication—which require a "dispute" or "difference" to have arisen before those procedures can validly be operated. The most recent discussion of this topic, in the context of arbitration but equally applicable to adjudication, is in *Amec Civil Engineering Ltd v Secretary of State for Transport* [2005] EWCA Civ 291; [2005] B.L.R. 227. See also *Collins (Contractors) Ltd v Baltic Quay Management (1994) Ltd* [2004] EWCA Civ 1757; [2005] B.L.R. 63, where Clarke L.J. accepted as "broadly correct" the test set out in the form of seven propositions by Jackson J. in the first instance decision in *Amec* (above).

(d) *Litigation*

Presentation of claims

37–254   [*Add to note 772: page* [747]]

See the recent review of the decided cases on "global" claims by Lord Macfayden in *John Doyle Construction Ltd v Laing Management (Scotland) Ltd* [2002] B.L.R. 393 (Court of Session). Subsequent to the opinion of the Lord Ordinary, see the opinions of Lords MacLean, Johnston and Drummond Young in the Extra Division of the Inner House of the Court of Session (following a reclaiming motion by the management contractor) in *Laing Management (Scotland) Ltd v John Doyle Construction Ltd* [2004] B.L.R. 297.

[*Add new paragraph: page* [747]]

37–254A   **Alternative dispute resolution (ADR).** Where a commercial agreement between parties requires ADR to be undertaken, then the strong tendency of the courts, especially in the specialist divisions, is to refuse to permit a party to proceedings without having instituted ADR proceedings first.[778a] On the separate jurisdiction to stay proceedings in accordance with the principles set out in the CPR, see *Shirayama Shokusan Company Ltd v Danovo Ltd*,[778b] where Blackburne J. concluded that the court had jurisdiction to order the parties to mediate even where one party was opposed to any mediation (although presumably the prospects for success of such a process must be limited). A refusal by one party to mediate will often, though need not, have damaging costs consequences, and each case will depend on its own facts.[778c]

[778a] *Cable & Wireless plc v IBM UK Ltd* [2002] EWHC 2059 (Comm); [2003] B.L.R. 89.
[778b] [2003] EWHC 3306 (Ch); [2004] B.L.R. 207.
[778c] *The Wethered Estate Limited v Michael Davis & Others* [2005] EWHC (Ch); [2006] B.L.R. 86.

(e) *Adjudication*

The enforcement of adjudicator's awards

37–260   [*Sub-paragraph (2): page* [750]]

The adjudicator is permitted to take the initiative in ascertaining the facts and the law, but the proper ambit of the dispute will be determined by the notice of adjudication, properly construed, and the adjudicator will ordinarily have no jurisdiction to decide what is the real dispute between the parties: *McAlpine PPS*

Pipeline Systems Joint Venture v Transco Plc [2004] EWHC 2030 (TCC); [2004] B.L.R. 352.

[Sub-paragraph (4)]

However, in a contract where the obligation upon the employer was to pay certificates issues by the architect, then the contractor was entitled to summary judgment in respect of the sums certified but not paid, with any question of work not having been carried out correctly (or at all) being properly regarded as the subject for a separate claim, rather than a defence to the contractor's claim. The obligation to pay was triggered by the certificate, not by whether the work to which the certificate related had in fact been carried out properly (or at all): *Rupert Morgan Building Services (LLC) Ltd v Jervis* [2003] EWCA Civ 1563; [2004] B.L.R. 18.

[Sub-paragraph (5)]

The general law in relation to actual or apparent bias will apply to the conduct of adjudicators, but the courts have indicated that a robust approach will by taken, so that a telephone conversation with one side may not amount to apparent bias (*Amec Capital Projects Ltd v Whitefriars City Estates Ltd* [2004] EWCA Civ 1418; [2005] B.L.R. 1) and where the adjudicator receives privileged material, he may properly continue if he concludes that there can be no legitimate fear that he might not have been impartial (*Specialist Ceiling Services Ltd v ZVI Construction (UK) Ltd* [2004] B.L.R. 403). However, where an adjudicator is very critical of a party for not producing a witness who was never asked to attend, this may amount to bias (*A&S Enterprises Ltd v Kema Holdings Ltd* [2005] EWHC 3365; [2005] B.L.R. 76).

[Add new sub-paragraph (6)]

    (6) Although the possibility has been raised that some disputes may be so complex that it is impossible for them to be dealt with fairly within the timescales available in the adjudication process,[804a] such concerns have subsequently not found favour with the courts, particularly in cases where substantial extensions of time have been agreed between the parties.[804b]

[Add new sub-paragraphs (7) and (8)]

    (7) Where a contract has been entered into under duress, then that contract is voidable; and so, if it has in fact been avoided by the innocent party, then the agreement to adjudicate is unenforceable and the adjudicator will have no jurisdiction.[804c]

    (8) The adjudicator has the power to award costs in the event that an adjudication is discontinued.[804d]

[804a] *AWG v Rockingham Motorway Speedway Ltd* [2004] EWHC 888.
[804b] *CIB Properties Ltd v Birse Construction Ltd* [2005] 1 W.L.R. 2252.
[804c] *Capital Structures PLC v Time & Tide Construction Limited* [2006] B.L.R. 226.
[804d] *John Roberts Architects v Parkcare Homes (No.2)* [2006] EWCA Civ 64; [2006] 105 Con. L.R. 36.

CHAPTER 38

CREDIT AND SECURITY

				PARA.
□	1.		The Consumer Credit Act 1974	38–002
□		(a)	Terminology of the Act	38–013
□		(b)	Licensing of credit and hire businesses	38–056
□		(c)	Seeking business	38–061
		(d)	Antecedent negotiations	38–065
□		(e)	The agreement	38–070
□		(f)	Withdrawal and cancellation	38–085
□		(g)	Supply of information	38–117
□		(h)	Variation of agreements	38–127
□		(i)	Appropriation of payments and early settlement	38–137
□		(i–a)	Sums in arrears and default sums	38–143A
□		(j)	Restrictions on enforcement or termination of agreement	38–144
□		(k)	Security	38–160
□		(l)	Judicial control	38–180
□		(m)	Extortionate credit bargains	38–192
□		(n)	Ancillary credit businesses	38–208
■	2.		Loans and interest	38–223
□		(a)	Loans of money	38–223
□		(b)	Interest	38–248
□		(c)	Effect of the Consumer Credit Act 1974	38–262
■	3.		Hire-purchase agreements	38–270
		(a)	In general	38–270
□		(b)	At common law	38–275
□		(c)	Effect of the Consumer Credit Act 1974	38–320
■		(d)	Defective goods	38–344
■		(e)	Rights and liabilities of third parties	38–358
			(i) Assignment	38–358
□			(ii) Title of third parties	38–362
			(iii) Fixtures and accession	38–383
			(iv) Liens	38–386
■			(v) Execution and distress	38–390
			(vi) Insolvency	38–395
		(f)	Miscellaneous restrictions	38–402
□	4.		Conditional sale agreements	38–406
□	5.		Credit-sale agreements	38–431
□	6.		Credit and other payment cards, and checks	38–439
□	7.		Mortgages of personal property	38–481
□	8.		Mortgages of land	38–491

1. The Consumer Credit Act 1974

[Add new paragraph 38–001A: page [754]]
Regulation of financial activities. For the Financial Services and Markets Act
2000 and orders made thereunder, see Lomnicka and Powell, *Encyclopedia of
Financial Services Law*. Sections 59–61 of the Consumer Credit Act 2006 (see
para.38–012A, below) provides that the financial services ombudsman scheme is
to apply to consumer credit licensees. Schedule 2 to the 2006 Act inserts a new
Pt 3A in Sch.17 of the 2000 Act.

38–001A

Scope of the Act

For the removal of the general financial limit, see para.3–014, below.

38–002

Consumer hire agreement

For the removal of the general financial limit, see paras 38–014, 38–033,
below.

38–004

Extension of the Act

Sections 137–140 of the Act are repealed and replaced by ss.140A–140B by
the Consumer Credit Act 2006: see para.38–192, below.

38–005

Regulations, orders etc

[Add at end of note 18: page [755]]
SI 2004/1481, 1482, 1483, 1484, 2619, 3237, SI 2006/1273.

38–006

Contracting-out

[Add to note 25: page [755]]
See *Wilson v Robertsons (London) Ltd* [2005] EWHC 1425 (Ch); [2006] 1
W.L.R. 1248.

38–008

Banks and investment firms authorised in other EEA states

See now s.27A of the 1974 Act (consumer credit EEA firms) inserted by s.33
of the Consumer Credit Act 2006.
See also the Electronic Commerce Directive (Financial Services and Markets)
(Amendment) Regulations 2004 (SI 2004/3378) amending the Electronic Commerce Directive (Financial Services and Markets) Regulations 2002 (SI
2002/1775) and SI 2002/682, SI 2002/765.

38–011

Banking Code

[Page [757]]
See also the Business Banking Code, March 2005 (para.34–225 of the Main
Work).

38–012

[Add to note 39: page [757]]
The latest revision is March 2005.

Reform of consumer credit law

38–012A   *[Page [757]]*
The Consumer Credit Act 2006 received the Royal Assent on March 20, 2006. It comes into force on a day or days appointed by statutory instrument (s.71). One Commencement Order has been made (SI 2006/1508 (C.52) (operative June 10, 2006). For transitional provisions, see Sch.3.

The most important changes made by the Act are (1) the removal of the financial limits, (2) a requirement that debtors be given notice of sums in arrears and default sums, (3) the substitution of "unfair relationships between creditors and debtors" for extortionate credit bargains, (4) the tightening of controls over businesses requiring to be licensed, and (5) the application of the financial services ombudsman scheme (in the Financial Services and Markets Act 2000) to cover consumer credit businesses under the 1974 Act.

The following statutory instruments have also been made under the 1974 Act: Consumer Credit (Disclosure of Information) Regulations 2004 (SI 2004/1481) (operative May 31, 2005); Consumer Credit (Agreements) (Amendment) Regulations 2004 (SI 2004/1482) (operative May 31, 2005); Consumer Credit (Early Settlement) Regulations 2004 (SI 2004/1483) (operative May 31, 2005); Consumer Credit (Advertisements) Regulations 2004 (SI 2004/1484) (operative October 31, 2004); Consumer Credit (Miscellaneous Amendments) Regulations 2004 (SI 2004/2619) (operative in part October 31, 2004, and in part May 31, 2005); Consumer Credit Act 1974 (Electronic Communications) Order 2004 (SI 2004/3236) (operative December 31, 2004); Consumer Credit (Enforcement, Default and Termination Notices) (Amendment) Regulations 2004 (SI 2004/3237) (operative December 31, 2004).

EC Directives

38–012B   *[Page [758]]*
See the Financial Services (Distant Marketing) Regulations 2004 (SI 2004/2095) and the Electronic Commerce (EC Directive) Regulations 2002 (SI 2002/2013), as amended.

(a) *Terminology of the Act*

"Consumer credit agreement"

38–014   The general financial limit in the 1974 Act is removed by s.2 of the Consumer Credit Act 2006. The 2006 Act does away with the concept of "personal credit agreement" and substitutes therefor, in s. 8(1) of the 1974 Act, "consumer credit agreement". As a result, a consumer credit agreement is now defined as:

> "an agreement between an individual ('the debtor') and any other person ('the creditor') by which the creditor provides the debtor with credit of any amount".

"Individual" is re-defined (in s.189(1) of the 1974 Act) to include:

"(a) a partnership consisting of two or three persons not all of whom are bodies corporate; and

(b) an unincorporated body of persons which does not consist entirely of bodies corporate and is not a partnership".

But see the exemptions relating to high net worth debtors, and businesses, in the newly introduced ss.16A and 16B of the 1974 Act (paras 38–041A, 38–041B, below).

[Add to note 50: page [758]]
Section 185(5) is amended by s.5(8) of the Consumer Credit Act 2006.

[Add to note 52: page [759]]
SI 1989/1125 is revoked and replaced by SI 2004/1484 (amended by SI 2004/2619): see below, para.38–061.

"Regulated consumer credit agreement"

Section 8(3) of the 12074 Act is amended by s.5(1) of the Consumer Crerdit **38–015** Act 2006 so as to include ss.16A and 16B in addition to s.16: see paras 38–041A, 38–041B, below.

"Credit"

For the removal of the general financial limit, see para.38–014, above. **38–017**

[Add to note 62: page [759]]
Nejad v City Index Ltd [2000] C.C.L.R. 7 (C.A.) (allowing a client a "credit allocation" for future gambling did not constitute the provision of credit); *McMillan Williams v Range* [2004] EWCA Civ 294; [2004] 1 W.L.R. 1858 (payment of salary as an advance against commission did not constitute the provision of credit). It would seem that, at the time the agreement is made, it must be certain that credit will be provided: *ibid.*; *Tilby v Perfect Pizza Ltd* [2003] C.C.L.R. 9 (after-the-event insurance did not constitute the provision of credit).

"Credit not exceeding £25,000"

For the removal of the general financial limit, see para.38–014, above. But the **38–019** calculations in this paragraph are still relevant to the calculation of the financial limit in s.16B, para.38–041B, below

[Add in note 72, after Wilson v First County Trust Ltd: page [760]] **38–020**
Wilson v Robertsons (London) Ltd [2005] EWHC 1425 (Ch); [2006] 1 W.L.R. 1248.

[Add at end of note 72]
See *London North Securities Ltd v Meadows* [2005] EWCA Civ 956; [2005] C.C.L.R. 7.

"Running-account credit"

38–021   For "personal credit agreement" substitute "consumer credit agreement": see para.38–014 above.

[*Add to note 75: page* [761]]
See also *Goshawk Dedicated (No.2) Ltd. v Bank of Scotland* [2005] EWHC 2506 (Ch); [2006] C.C.L.R. 1.

"Credit limit"

38–022—   For the removal of the general financial limit, see para.38–014, above. But by
38–023   s.5(2) of the Consumer Credit Act 2006, the references to a £25,000 limit now refer to the limit in s.16B(1)(a) of the 1974 Act: see para.38–041B, below.

"Fixed-sum credit"

38–024   For "personal credit agreement" substitute "consumer credit agreement": see para.38–014 above.

"Restricted-use credit"

38–025   [*Add to note 90: page* [762]]
See *Office of Fair Trading v Lloyds TSB Bank plc* [2006] EWCA Civ 268; [2006] 2 All E.R. 821; see paras 38–029 and 38–454, below.

"Debtor–creditor–supplier" agreement

38–029   [*Add to note 103: page* [763]]
See above para.38–025, n.90.

[*Add to note 107: page* [764]]
See *Office of Fair Trading v Lloyds TSB Bank plc* [2006] EWCA Civ 268; [2006] 2 All E.R. 821, below, para.38–454 (existence of "arrangements" between credit card issuer and supplier abroad through network schemes such as Visa, Mastercard, etc.); *Bank of Scotland v Truman* [2005] EWHC 583; [2005] C.C.L.R. 3.

[*Add to note 109*]
cf., *Office of Fair Trading v Lloyds TSB Bank plc*, above.

"Credit-token agreement"

38–032   [*Add to note 120: page* [765]]
SI 1983/1553 is amended by SI 2004/1482 (amended by SI 2004/2619 and SI 2004/3236); see para.38–071, below. SI 1983/1564 is amended by SI 2004/3236.

"Consumer hire agreement"

The general financial limit provided for the in the 1974 Act is removed by s.2 of the Consumer Credit Act 2006. For the redefinition of "individual", see para.38–014, above.

[*Add to note 133: page* [766]]
Clark v Tull [2002] EWCA Civ 610; [2002] C.C.L.R. 4.

[*Text to note 134 and note 134*]
The £25,000 limit is removed by s.2(2) of the Consumer Credit Act 2006.

[*Add to note 136: page* [767]]
SI 1989/1125 is revoked and replaced by SI 2004/1484 (amended by SI 2004/2619); see para.38–061 below.

38–033

"Regulated" consumer hire agreement

[*Add to note 137: page* [767]]
See the new exemptions in ss.16A, 16B: paras 38–041A, 38–041B, below.

38–034

"Exempt agreement"

[*Page* [767]]
See the amendments of s.16 of the 1974 Act effected in relation to land mortgages by the Financial Services and Markets Act 2000 (Regulated Activities) Order 2001 (SI 2001/544), art.61.

38–036

[*Add after reference to Ketley v Gilbert in note 159: page* [768]]
O'Hagan v Wright [2001] NICA 26; [2003] C.C.L.R. 6; *Clarke v Tull* [2002] EWCA Civ 510; [2002] C.C.L.R. 4; *Thew v Cole* [2003] EWCA Civ 1828; [2004] R.T.R. 410; *Stevenson v Dudley Social Services* [2006] 3 C.L. 90 (Cty Ct).

[*Add to note 160*]
SI 1989/869 is amended by SI 2006/1273.

38–037

See also s.140A(5) of the 1974 Act inserted by s.19 of the Consumer Credit Act 2006, SI 2005/2967 and para.38–192, below.

[*Add to note 163: page* [768]]
October 31, 20045: see SI 2001/544.

38–039

[*Add at end of note 164: page* [769]]
and by Sch.17, para.47 of the Communications Act 2003.

38–040

[*Add to note 165: page* [769]]
Section 16(7) is repealed by s.70 and Sch.4 of the Consumer Credit Act 2006. But see s.16(7A), inserted by s.22(2) of the 2006 Act.

38–041

[*Add new paragraphs 38–041A and 38–041B: page* [769]]
"Exempt agreement": high net worth debtors. A new category of exempt agreements relating to high net worth debtors (and hirers) is introduced by s.3 of

38–041A

the Consumer Credit Act 2006 as s.16A of the 1974 Act (brought into force by SI 2006/1508 (C.52) on June 10, 2006). The implementation of this section is to be by order made by the Secretary of State.

38–041B   **"Exempt agreement": businesses.** A new exemption relating to business debtors is introduced by s.4 of the Consumer Credit Act 2006 (as s.16B of the 1974 Act). This is particularly important as a result of the removal of the general financial limit in the 1974 Act: see para.38–014, above. The exemption is for a consumer credit agreement by which the creditor provides the debtor with credit exceeding £25,000 if the agreement is entered into by the debtor wholly or predominantly for the purposes of a business carried on, or intended to be carried on, by him. A similar exemption is created in relation to consumer hire agreements. Agreements falling within s.16B are therefore not regulated, but exempt, agreements. See also, in relation to s.16B (4), SI 2006/1508 (C.52), operative June 10, 2006.

"Small agreement"

38–042   [*Add to note 173: page* [769]]
Section 17(2) is amended by s.5(3) of the Consumer Credit Act 2006 so as to refer to s.16B(1)(a) of the 1974 Act.

"Non-commercial agreement"

38–043   For the removal of the general financial limit in the 1974 Act, see para.38–014, above.

"Multiple agreement"

38–044   See (on the scope of s.18) *Wilson v First County Trust Ltd* [2001] Q.B. 407; *Burdis v Livsey* [2002] EWCA Civ 510; *London North Securities Ltd v Meadows* [2005] EWCA Civ 956; [2005] C.C.L.R. 7; *Ocwen v Coxall* [2004] C.C.L.R. 7 (Cty Ct); *Goshawk Dedicated (No.2) Ltd v Bank of Scotland* [2005] EWHC 2908 (Ch); [2006] C.C.L.R. 1.

"Part" of an agreement

38–046—   [*Page* [771]]
38–047   See the cases cited in para.38–044, above.

Consequences if part is a separate agreement

38–048   [*Add to note 212: page* [772]]
SI 1983/1553 is amended by SI 2004/1482 (amended by SI 2004/2619 and SI 2004/3236); see para.38–071, below.

"Total charge for credit"

[*Add to note 234: page* [774]]
SI 2004/1482 (amended by SI 2004/2619 and SI 2004/3236).

[*Add to note 239: page* [775]]
  Ocwen v Hughes [2004] C.C.L.R. 4 (Cty Ct) (optional credit insurance premiums); *London North Securities Ltd v Meadows* [2005] C.C.L.R. 7 (loan to pay off arrears under previous mortgage).

[*Insert new paragraph 38–055A: page* [775]]
Service of documents. Documents required or permitted to be served under   **38–055A**
the Act may be served as prescribed by ss.176, 176A (inserted by the Consumer Credit Act 1974 (Electronic Communications) Order 2004 (SI 2004/3236) (operative December 31, 2004)).

(b) *Licensing of Credit and Hire Businesses*

Businesses needing a licence

  New definitions of "consumer credit business" and "consumer hire business"   **38–056**
in s.189(1) of the Act are substituted by s.23 of the Consumer Credit Act 2006. Because of the removal of the general financial limit in the 1974 Act (see para.38–014, above) the result will be, when the relevant sections are brought into force, that licences will be required in respect of businesses that provide credit to individuals of any amount. However, s.189(1) (as amended) still refers to "regulated" consumer credit agreements. Licences will therefore not be required by businesses which provide credit only under exempt agreements, in particular those exempted under s.16B (see para.38–041B, above).

[*Add to note 252: page* [776]]
Section 185(5) is amended by s.5(8) of the Consumer Credit Act 2006. See also the new definition of "individual" in s.189(1), para.38–014, above.

Licensing and control

  See now the extensive changes made to the 1974 Act by ss.23–58 of the   **38–058**
Consumer Credit Act 2006.

[*Add at end of note 264: page* [777]]
SI 2000/291. Section 26 was amended by SI 2001/3649.

[*Add at end of note 271: page* [777]]
and by SI 2004/3236.

Unlicensed trading

  Section 40 of the 1974 Act is amended by s.26 of the Consumer Credit Act   **38–059**
2006. See also SI 2001/3649, art.170 (inserting new subs.(6)).

(c) *Seeking Business*

Advertising and quotations

38–061 Section 43(3) of the 1974 Act (financial and other limits relating to the regulation of advertisements) is amended by s.2(3) of the Consumer Credit Act 2006. As a result all credit advertisements regardless of the amount of credit or the nature of the security (other than an advertisement which indicates that the credit is available only to a body corporate) are potentially subject to control.

[Page [778]]
The Consumer Credit (Advertisement) Regulations 1989 are revoked and replaced by the Consumer Credit (Advertisement) Regulations 2004 (SI 2004/1484) (operative October 31, 2004) as amended by SI 2004/2619.

[Delete note 294 and substitute]
SI 1999/2725, as amended by SI 2000/1797. But these regulations are revoked in part by SI 2004/1484 (as amended by SI 2004/2619), above.

(e) *The Agreement*

Pre-contract disclosure

38–070 *[Page [781]]*
The Consumer Credit (Disclosure of Information) Regulations 2004 (SI 2004/1481), have now been made under s.55(1) of the Act (operative May 31, 2005). These regulations do not apply to agreements to which s.58 of the Act applies (see para.38–496 of the Main Work) nor in respect of distance contracts (as defined in reg.1(2)).

Form and content of agreement

38–071 *[Page [781]]*
The Consumer Credit (Agreements) Regulations 1983 are extensively amended by the Consumer Credit (Agreements) (Amendment) Regulations 2004 (SI 2004/1482) (operative May 31, 2005), as amended by SI 2004/2619 and SI 2004/3236.

Signing of agreement

38–072 *[Add to notes 339 and 341: page [782]]*
SI 1983/1553 is amended by SI 2004/1482 (as amended by SI 2004/2619 and SI 2004/3236); see para.38–071, above.

[Add to note 342]
Section 185(6) is amended by s.5(9) of the Consumer Credit Act 2006.

[Add at end of note 347]
as amended by SI 2004/1482 (as amended by SI 2004/2619 and SI 2004/3236).

Supply of copies

[*Text to note 362: page* [783]]
The copy may now be transmitted electronically: SI 2004/3236, art.2(3).

[*Page* [783]]
The Consumer Credit (Cancellation Notices and Copies of Documents) Regulations 1983 have been amended by the Consumer Credit (Miscellaneous Amendments) Regulations 2004 (SI 2004/2619) and by the Consumer Credit Act 1974 (Electronic Communications) Order 2004 (SI 2004/3236).

Notice of cancellation rights

[*Page* [784]]
The Consumer Credit (Cancellation Notices and Copies of Documents) Regulations 1983 have been amended by the Consumer Credit (Miscellaneous Amendments) Regulations 2004 (SI 2004/2619) (operative May 31, 2005) and by the Consumer Credit Act 1974 (Electronic Communications) Order 2004 (SI 2004/3236) (operative December 31, 2004).

[*Add to note 373*]
Goshawk Dedicated (No.2) Ltd v Bank of Scotland [2005] EWHC 2906 (Ch); [2006] C.C.L.R. 1.

[*Add to note 374*]
Section 185 is amended by s.7(3) of the Consumer Credit Act 2006.

[*Text to note 377: page* [784]]
The notice may now be transmitted electronically: SI 2004/3236, art.2(4).

Failure to comply

[*Add to note 383: page* [785]]
O'Hagan v Wright [2001] NICA 26; [2003] C.C.L.R. 6.

By s.15 of the Consumer Credit Act 2006, subss.(3)–(5) of s.127 of the 1974 Act cease to have effect. This means that the absolute bars to enforcement referred to in this paragraph will (when s.15 is brought into force) no longer apply and an enforcement order in cases of infringement will, in all cases, be dismissed only if the court considers it just to do so under s.127(1).

[*Add to note 391: page* [785]]
SI 1983/1553 is amended by SI 2004/1482 (as amended by SI 2004/2619 and SI 2004/3236): see para.38–071, above.

(f) *Withdrawal and Cancellation*

Agreement not to withdraw

[*Add to note 423: page* [788]]
See also *Lakin v Exe Haulage Ltd* [2006] 2 C.L. 105 (Cty Ct) (oral agreement to enter into future unregulated agreement upheld). *cf. Carson v Tazaki Foods Ltd* [2006] 2 C.L. 106 (Cty Ct).

Cancellable agreements

38–091 *[Page [788]]*
For a discussion of the various statutory provisions conferring rights of cancellation (and considered in paras 38–091—38–095) see Hellwege (2004) Camb. L.J. 712.

Exceptions

38–092 *[Add at end of note 441: page [789]]*
Coutts & Co v Sebestyen [2005] EWCA Civ 473; [2005] C.C.L.R. 4.

Consumer Protection (Cancellation of Contracts Concluded away from Business Premises) Regulations 1987

38–093 *[Add to note 450: page [789]]*
See also *Heininger v Bayerische Hypo-und Vereinsbank AG* (C481/99) [2004] All E.R. (EC) 1; *Schulte v Deutsche Bausparkasse Badenia AG* (C350/03) [2006] All E.R. (E.C.) 420 (mortgage transactions).

Consumer Protection (Distance Selling) Regulations 2000

38–094 *[Page [790]]*
These Regulations have been amended by the Consumer Protection (Distance Selling) (Amendment) Regulations 2005 (SI 2005/689). See also the amendments effected by SI 2004/2095, reg.25.
In *easyCar (UK) Ltd v Office of Fair Trading* (2005) (Case C–336/03), [2005] 2 C.M.L.R. 2, the European Court of Justice held that a car hire company which took bookings only via the internet did not come within Directive 97/7/EC as was exempted therefrom as providing "transport services" under Art.3(2).

[Insert new paragraph 38–094A: page [790]]

38–094A **Financial Services (Distance Marketing) Regulations 2004.** These Regulations (SI 2004/2095) give effect in the United Kingdom to Directive 2002/65/EC of the European Parliament and of the Council and give consumers a right to cancel most distance contracts for financial services during a set period after commencement of the contract.

Notice of cancellation

38–098 *[Note 482: page [792]]*
A new s.69(7) was substituted by SI 2004/3236, dealing with deemed service in the case of electronic communication.

Effect of notice

38–099 *[Add to note 483: page [792]]*
See *Goshawk Dedicated (No.2) Ltd v Bank of Scotland* [2005] EWHC 2906 (Ch); [2006] C.C.L.R. 1.

Cancellation: repayment of credit

[*Add to note 531: page* [795]]
amended by SI 2004/3236, art.7.

(g) *Supply of Information*

[*Insert new paragraph 38–117A: page* [800]]
Statements to debtor under fixed-sum credit agreement. Section 77A of the **38–117A**
1974 Act, inserted by s.6 of the Consumer Credit Act 2006, requires the creditor
to give to the debtor under a regulated agreement for fixed-sum credit an annual
statement in the form and with the content prescribed by regulation (see SI
2006/1508 (C.52)). Failure to comply renders the agreement unenforceable by
the creditor, and interest and default sums are irrecoverable, while the failure
lasts. The section does not apply to non-commercial or small agreements.

Information to debtor under running-account credit agreement

[*Notes 603 and 607: page* [800]] **38–118**
SI 1983/1577 has been amended by SI 2004/2619 and SI 2004/3236.

Periodic statements

Section 7 of the Consumer Credit Act 2006 enables regulations to be made **38–119**
(see SI 2006/1508 (C.52)) requiring a periodic statement under s.78(4) of the
1974 Act to contain information in the prescribed terms about the consequences
of the debtor: (a) failing to make payments as required by the agreement, or (b)
only making payments of a prescribed description in prescribed circumstances.

[*Add to note 613: page* [800]]
amended by SI 2004/3236, art.12.

[*Add to note 614*]
New subs.(2)(2A)–(2D) of s.185 are substituted by s.7(3) of the Consumer
Credit Act 2006.

Information to "surety"

[*Add at end of note 626: page* [801]] **38–120**
amended by SI 2004/2619 and SI 2004/3236.

Copy of security instrument

[*Add to note 634: page* [802]] **38–122**
SI 1983/1533 has been amended by SI 2004/1482 (as amended by SI
2004/2619).

Information as to settlement figure

38–124   [*Amend the text to note 642: page* [802]]
The period of 12 days prescribed by SI 1983/1564 is reduced to seven days by SI 2004/1483, reg.9, as from May 31, 2005.

[*Add to note 643*]
SI 1983/1564 is amended and SI 1983/1562 revoked and replaced by SI 2004/1483 (as amended by SI 2004/2619); see para.38–139, below.

(h) *Variation of Agreements*

Mutual variation by subsequent agreement

38–129—   For the removal of the general financial limit, see para.38–014, above. Section
38–132   82(2) does not apply if the modifying agreement is an exempt agreement as a result of 2.16(6C) (para.38–039, above): see SI 2005/2967.

38–131   [*Add to note 675: page* [805]]
Section 82(3) is amended by SI 2005/2967.

[*Add to note 676: page* [806]]
SI 1983/1553 is amended by SI 2004/1482 (as amended by SI 2004/2619 and SI 2004/3236); see para.38–071, above.

Cancellation of modifying agreement

38–133   [*Add to note 682: page* [806]]
Section 82(5) does not apply where the modifying agreement is an exempt agreement as a result of s.16(6C) (para.38–039, above).

Form, etc., of modifying agreement

38–135   [*Add to note 688: page* [807]]
SI 1983/1553 is amended by SI 2004/1482 (as amended by SI 2004/2619): see para.38–071, above.

(i) *Appropriation of Payments and Early Settlement*

Rebate on early settlement etc.

38–139—   [*Page* [808]]
38–140   The Consumer Credit (Rebate on Early Settlement) Regulations 1983 are revoked and replaced by the Consumer Credit (Rebate on Early Settlement) Regulations 2004 (SI 2004/1483) (amended by SI 2004/2619), but the 1983 Regulations continue to apply for a limited period to regulated consumer credit agreements entered into before the date on which the 2004 Regulations come into force (May 31, 2005). The 2004 Regulations incorporate an actuarial formula for

the calculation of the rebate in place of the various formulae provided for in the 1983 Regulations. Regulation 6 provides for the settlement date to be deferred by a month (or, at the option of the creditor, 30 days) in the case of agreements for a term of more than one year, and is thus less generous to the creditor than the 1983 Regulations.

(i–a) Sums in Arrears and Default Sums

[*Add new paragraphs 38–143A—38–143F*]

OFT to prepare information sheets on arrears and default. Section 86A of the 1974 Act (inserted by s.8 of the Consumer Credit Act 2006) requires the OFT to prepare, and give general notice of, an arrears information sheet and a default information sheet to help debtors who receive notices under s.86B or 86C (see paras 38–143B, 38–143C, below). The content of the information sheets may be prescribed by regulation. **38–143A**

Notice of sums in arrears under fixed-sum credit agreements etc. Section 86B of the 1974 Act (inserted by s.9 of the Consumer Credit Act 2006) requires a creditor or owner in certain circumstances to give to the debtor under a regulated agreement for fixed-sum credit, or a hirer under a regulated consumer hire agreement, who is in arrears under the agreement a notice of the sums in arrears. The notice must be given within 14 days. The form and content of the notice are to be prescribed by regulation (see SI 2006/1508 (C.52), operative June 10, 2006). A notice under s.86B must include a copy of the current arrears information sheet under s.86A (see para.38–143A, above). This section does not apply to non-commercial or small agreements. **38–143B**

Notice of sums in arrears under running-account credit agreements. Similar provision is made in s.86C of the 1974 Act (inserted by s.10 of the Consumer Credit Act 2006) requiring a creditor to give a notice of sums in arrears to a debtor under a regulated agreement for running-account credit. The notice must be given within the period specified for notices under s.78(4) (see para.38–119, above). The form and content of the notice are again to be prescribed by regulation (see SI 2006/1508 (C.52), operative June 10, 2006) and again must include a copy of the current information sheet under s.86A (see para.38–143A, above). The section does not apply to non-commercial or small agreements. **38–143C**

Failure to give notices of sums in arrears. By s.86D of the 1974 Act (inserted by s.11 of the Consumer Credit Act 2006) failure to give notice of sums in arrears under ss.86B or 86C above renders the agreement unenforceable during the period of non-compliance. **38–143D**

Notice of default sums. Section 86E of the 1974 Act (inserted by s.12 of the Consumer Credit Act 2006) requires a creditor or owner to give notice to the **38–143E**

debtor or hirer when a default sum becomes payable under a regulated agreement. By s.187A of the 1974 Act (inserted by s.18 of the 2006 Act) "default sum" is defined to mean a sum (other than a sum of interest) which is payable by the debtor or hirer under the agreement in connection with a breach of the agreement by him; but a sum is not a default sum simply because, as a consequence of his breach of the agreement, he is required to pay it earlier than he would otherwise have had to. The form and content of the notice, and the period within which the notice must be given, are to be prescribed by regulation (see SI 2006/1508 (C.52), operative June 10, 2006). This section does not apply to non-commercial or small agreements.

38–143F   **Interest on default sums.** Section 86F of the 1974 Act (inserted by s.13 of the Consumer Credit Act 2006) provides that, in respect of a regulated agreement, a debtor or hirer is only liable to pay interest in connection with a default sum (as defined in s.187A, see para.38–143E above) if the interest is simple interest.

(j) *Restrictions on Enforcement or Termination of Agreement*

Enforcement notice (non-default cases)

38–144   [*Add to note 722: page* [810]]
The notice must be in writing and given to the debtor in paper form: SI 2004/3237.

Default notice

38–147   [*Add to note 736: page* [811]]
Section 185(5) is amended by s.5(8) of the Consumer Credit Act 2006.

Form and content of default notice

38–148   [*Add to note 741: page* [811]]
The notice must be in writing and given to the debtor in paper form: SI 2004/3237.

[*Add to note 748: page* [812]]
Section 88(2) is amended by s.14(1) of the Consumer Credit Act 2006 and the period extended to 14 days (operative October 1, 2006: see SI 2006/1508 (C.52).

[*Add to note 749*]
By s.88(4A), inserted by s.14(3) of the Consumer Credit Act 2006, the notice must also include a copy of the current information sheet under s.86A (see para.38–143A). See also s.14(2) of the 2006 Act enlarging the scope of s.88(4) and SI 2006/1508 (C.52), art.3(2) and Sch.2.

Cumulative breaches

[*Add to note 754: page* [812]]
Section 88(3) is amended by s.14(1) of the Consumer Credit Act 2006 and the period extended to 14 days (operative October 1, 2006: see SI 2006/1508 (C.52)).

38–150

Notice of termination (non-default cases)

[*Add to note 759: page* [813]]
The notice must be in writing and given to the debtor in paper form: SI 2004/3237.

38–153

Copy of notices to "surety"

[*Add to note 771: page* [813]]
amended by SI 2004/2619 and SI 2004/3236.

38–154

(k) *Security*

"Security" defined

[*Add to note 795: page* [816]]
SI 1989/1125 is revoked and replaced by SI 2004/1484 (as amended by SI 2004/2619); see para.38–061, above.

38–161

Form and content of security instrument

[*Page* [817]]
The Consumer Credit (Guarantees and Indemnities) Regulations 1983 have been amended by the Consumer Credit Act (Electronic Communications) Order 2004 (SI 2004/3236), art.5.

38–164

Supply of copies to surety

[*Add to note 806: page* [817]]
SI 1983/1557 has been amended by SI 2004/2619 and SI 2004/3236.

38–166

Security provided by debtor or hirer

[*Add at end of note 814: page* [818]]
SI 2004/1482 (amended by SI 2004/2619 and SI 2004/3236).

38–168

Pledges

[*Add to note 843: page* [820]]
SI 2004/3236.

38–176

(l) *Judicial Control*

Time orders

38–183   Section 16(1) of the Consumer Credit Act 2006 adds a fourth situation (s.129 (1) (ba)) in which a time order can be made, on an application made by the debtor or hirer after he has been given a notice under s.86B or s.86C (see paras 38–143B, 38–143C, above). But see s.129A (para.38–183A, below).

[Add new paragraph 38–183A: page [824]]

38–183A   **Notice of intent.** A debtor or hirer can only make an application for a time order under s.129 (1) (ba) (see para.38–183, above) if he gives a "notice of intent" to the creditor or owner which indicates that he intends to make the application and that he wants to make a proposal to the creditor or owner in relation to his making payments under the agreement, and gives details of that proposal. This is provided for in s.129A of the 1974 Act (inserted by s.16(2) of the Consumer Credit Act 2006).

[Add new paragraph 38–186A: page [825]]

38–186A   **Interest payable on judgment debts.** By s.130A of the 1974 Act (inserted by s.17 of the Consumer Credit Act 2006) a creditor or owner who wants to be able to recover from a debtor or hirer under a regulated agreement post-judgment interest in respect of a judgment debt has to give the debtor a notice under this section (which notice may have to be repeated at intervals thereafter). The form and content of the notice are to be prescribed by regulation (see SI 2006/1508 (C.52)). This section does not apply to non-commercial or small agreements.

(m) *Extortionate Credit Bargains*

Unfair relationships

38–192—   Sections 137–140 of the 1974 Act, which deal with extortionate credit bar-
38–206   gains, are repealed by s.70 and Sch.4 of the Consumer Credit Act 2006. They are replaced by ss.140A–140D (inserted by ss.19–22 of the 2006 Act). The concept of an "extortionate credit bargain" is replaced by the much wider concept of an "unfair relationship" as between the creditor and the debtor, or an associate of the creditor and the debtor (s.140A). The court is given extensive powers to intervene if it determines that the relationship is unfair (s.140B). These powers can be exercised in relation to any credit agreement where the debtor is an individual (as defined in s.189(1), as amended: see para.38–014, above) or any related agreement (as defined in s.140C(4)). The fact that the agreement is an exempt, and not a regulated, agreement is immaterial, except that no order can be made in connection with a credit agreement which is an exempt agreement by virtue of s.16(6C) (see para.38–039, above). For transitional provisions, see Sch.3, paras 14–17, of the 2006 Act.

Rate of interest

[*Add to note 979: page* [830]]
Batooneh v Asombang [2003] EWHC 2111 (QB) (interest rate of 100 per cent on informal commercial loan reduced to 25 per cent).

38–198

[*Add to note 981*]
Paragon Finance plc v Pender [2005] EWCA Civ 760; [2005] C.C.L.R. 5.

(n) *Ancillary Credit Businesses*

Ancillary credit businesses

The Consumer Credit Act 2006, ss.24, 25, adds two further classes of ancillary credit business:

38–208

s.145(1) (da) debt administration
s.145 (1)(db) the provision of information services

See also SI 2006/1508 (C.52) and ss.24(2), (4), (6), 25(2), (5).

Credit brokerage

[*Add to notes 1028 and 1030: page* [835]]
Section 145(4) is amended by s.5(4) of the Consumer Credit Act 2006.

38–209

Exceptions

Further exceptions are created by subs.(5A) to (5D) of s.146 (added by the Financial Services and Markets Act 2000 (Regulated Activities) (Amendment) (No.1) Order 2003, SI 2003/1475). Section 146(5D) is amended by SI 2005/2967, art.3.

38–214

Credit reference agency

[*Add to note 1058: page* [837]]
Section 158(1) is amended by s.5(5) of the Consumer Credit Act 2006 and s.158(4) by s.5(6) of the 2006 Act.

38–215

Seeking business

Sections 151, 152, 154 and 156 of the 1974 Act are amended by s.25(3), (4) of the Consumer Credit Act 2006 (credit information services).

38–220

[*Add to note 1076: page* [839]]
SI 1989/1125 is entirely revoked, and SI 1999/2725 and SI 2000/1797 partially revoked, by SI 2004/1484 (operative October 31, 2004) (amended by SI 2004/2619): see para.38–061, above.

2. LOANS AND INTEREST

(a) *Loans of Money*

38–222A
[Insert new paragraph 38–222A: page [840]]
Regulatory provisions. For the Financial Services and Markets Act 2000 and orders made thereunder: see Lomnicka and Powell, *Encyclopedia of Financial Services Law*. For the extension of the financial services ombudsman scheme to consumer credit licensees, see para.38–001A, above.

Events of default

38–238
[Page [847]]
A notice of acceleration purporting to have been given under an "events of default" clause when no event of default has arisen will normally be merely ineffective and will not, in the absence of any contractual obligation (express or implied) between the person giving the notice and the borrower, give rise to any liability on the part of that person to the borrower: *Concord Trust v Law Debenture Trust Corp plc* [2005] UKHL 27; [2005] 1 W.L.R. 1591 at [30]–[45].

Student loans

38–247
[Add to notes 1202 and 1203: page [851]]
SIs 2003/1143; 2004/161; 2004/1030; 2004/1175; 2004/1602; 2004/2041; 2004/2752; 2005/5; 2005/52; 2005/1341; 2005/2084; 2005/2119; 2005/2598; 2005/2690; 2006/119; 2006/141; 2006/929; 2006/953; 2006/955.

(b) *Interest*

Compound interest

38–253
But see s.86F of the Consumer Credit Act 1974 inserted by s.13 of the Consumer Credit Act 2006, para.38–143F, above.

Rates of interest

38–256
But see the Credit Unions (Maximum Interest Rate on Loans) Order 2006, SI 2006/1276 (2 per cent per month) made under s.11(5) of the Credit Unions Act 1979.

Variation of interest rate

38–257
[Add to note 1243: page [855]]
But see *Sterling Credit Ltd v Rahman (No.2)* [2002] EWHC 3008 (Ch); [2003] C.C.L.R. 13 (no implied obligation to reduce interest rate); *Paragon Finance plc v Pender* [2005] EWCA Civ 760; [2005] C.R.L.R. 5 (lender forced to increase rates du to adverse financial circumstances).

Default interest

[*Add to note 1250: page* [856]]   **38–258**
Contrast *Jeancharm Ltd v Barnet Football Club Ltd* [2003] EWCA Civ 58;
[2003] 92 Const. L.R. 26 (default interest of 5 per cent per week held penal).

Contractual interest after judgment

But see s.130A of the Consumer Credit Act 1974 inserted by s.17 of the   **38–261**
Consumer Credit Act 2006.

(c) *Effect of the Consumer Credit Act 1974*

Consumer Credit Act

[*Add to note 1273: page* [858]]   **38–263**
But see para.38–014 above (removal of financial limit).

Extortionate credit bargains

Sections 137–140 are repealed by s.70 and Sch.4 of the Consumer Credit Act   **38–264**
2006 and replaced by ss.140A–140D inserted by ss.19–22 of the 2006 Act: see
para.38–192, above.

[*Add to note 1278: page* [858]]
Coutts & Co v Sebestyen [2005] EWCA Civ 473; [2005] C.C.L.R. 4.

3. Hire-Purchase Agreements

(b) *At Common Law*

Recovery by action

[*Add to note 1435: page* [872]]   **38–306**
See also *BMW Financial Services (GB) Ltd v Taylor* [2006] 1 C.L. 113 (Cty
Ct) (recovery of contractual indemnity costs).

Relief from forfeiture

[*Add after reference to Sport International Bussum BV v Inter-Footwear Ltd in note*   **38–308**
1448: page [873]]
The Jotunheim [2004] EWHC 671 (Comm); [2005] 1 Lloyd's Rep. 181.

(c) *Effect of the Consumer Credit Act 1974*

Scope of 1974 Act

[*Page* [880]]   **38–321**
But see para.38–014, above (removal of financial limit).

Extortionate credit bargains

38–323 Sections 137–140 repealed and replaced by new ss. 140A–140D: see para. 38–192, above.

Consent to repossession

38–328 [*Add to note 1535: page* [882]]
Hunter v Lex Vehicle Finance Ltd [2005] EWHC 223; [2005] B.P.I.R. 586.

(d) *Defective Goods*

Exclusion of implied terms: consumer agreements

38–354 [*Note 1644: page* [891]]
SI 1976/1813 was further amended by SI 2005/871.

(e) *Rights and Liabilities of Third Parties*

(ii) *Title of Third Parties*

Trade or finance purchasers

38–367 In *GE Capital Bank Ltd v Rushton* [2005] EWCA Civ 1556; [2006] 1 W.L.R. 899 at [39] Moore-Bick L.J. stated that the wording of s.29(2): "is intended to direct attention not merely to the business of the purchaser immediately prior to and at the time of the disposition but also the purpose for which the vehicle is bought."

[*Add to note 1691: page* [896]]
But see *GE Capital Bank Ltd v Rushton*, above, at [39].

Good faith and notice

38–372 [*Add to note 1697: page* [897]]
GE Capital Bank Ltd v Rushton, above.

Extent of protection

38–374 [*Add to note 1703: page* [898]]
cf. Freeman v Walker [2001] EWCA Civ 923; [2003] C.C.L.R. 4.

(v) *Execution and Distress*

Execution

38–390 [*Amend the text to note 1758: page* [903]]
Section 138B(1) of the Supreme Court Act 1981 has been repealed by s.109(3) and Sch.10 of the Courts Act 2003 and replaced by Sch.7, para.11, of that Act.

4. Conditional Sale Agreements

Scope of 1974 Act

[*Add to note 1827: page* [909]]
But see para.38–014, above (removal of financial limit). **38–410**

Extortionate credit bargains

Sections 137–140 are repealed and replaced by ss.140A–140D by the Con- **38–414**
sumer Credit Act 2006: see para.38–192, above.

Title to goods

[*Note 1861: page* [911]]
SI 1976/1813 was further amended by SI 2005/871. **38–423**

Defective goods

[*Note 1863: page* [912]]
SI 1976/1813 was further amended by SI 2005/871. **38–424**

5. Credit Sale Agreements

Scope of Consumer Credit Act

[*Add to note 1896: page* [914]]
But see para.38–014, above (removal of financial limit). **38–432**

[*Add to note 1903: page* [915]]
Sections 137–140 are repealed and replaced by ss.140A–140D by the Con- **38–433**
sumer Credit Act 2006: see para.38–192, above.

Implied terms

[*Note 1910: page* [915]]
SI 1976/1813 was further amended by SI 2005/871. **38–435**

6. Credit and Other Payment Cards and Checks

Consumer Credit Act 1974

[*Add to note 1958: page* [921]]
On the use of a credit card abroad, see *Office of Fair Trading v Lloyds TSB* **38–454**
Bank plc [2006] EWCA Civ 268; [2006] 2 All E.R. 821, where it was held that

s.75 liability attached in respect of transactions entered into abroad. See also *Bank of Scotland v Truman* [2005] EWHC 583; [2005] C.C.L.R. 3 and above paras 38–025, 38–029.

"Credit-token" and "credit-token agreements"

38–462 [*Add to note 2003: page* [924]]
SI 1983/1553 is amended by SI 2004/1482 (amended by SI 2004/2619 and SI 2004/3236): see para.38–071, above.

[*Add to note 2004*]
SI 1983/1557 is amended by SI 2004/2619 and SI 2004/3236.

Misuse of credit-token

[*Page* [927]]
38–475 The Consumer Protection (Distance Selling) Regulations 2000 have been amended by the Consumer Protection (Distance Selling) (Amendment) Regulations 2005 (SI 2005/689).

Regulation 14 of the Financial Services (Distance Marketing) Regulations 2004 (SI 2004/2095) makes similar provision with respect to the fraudulent use of a consumer's payment card in connection with a distance contract within the meaning of those Regulations. Again the protection is stated not to apply to an agreement to which s.83(1) of the Consumer Credit Act 1974 applies, but again the same result is achieved by removing the potential liability of the debtor for the first £50 of loss to the creditor in respect of any use of a card which is a credit-token and his liability for misuse of such a card by a person who acquired possession of it with his consent.

It is submitted that, in both the Regulations mentioned in this paragraph, the words "fraudulent use is made . . . of [that] card" will include fraudulent use of the details on the card which are supplied by the consumer to the supplier when entering into a transaction where the consumer is not physically present.

7. Mortgages of Personal Property

Mortgage or charge of choses in action

38–489 [*Page* [931]]
See para.38–014, above (removal of financial limit).

8. Mortgages of Land

Consumer credit

38–491 [*Text to note 2104a: page* [932]]
See now the Financial Services and Markets Act 2000 (Regulated Activities) Order 2001 (SI 2001/544), regs. 61, 90, 91 and the Financial Services Authority

(FSA) rules contained in the Mortgage Conduct of Business source book (operative October 31, 2004). See also Lomnicka and Powell, *Encyclopedia of Financial Services Law.*

Extension of Act

See para.38–014 above (removal of financial limit). But see s.140A of the **38–493** 1974 Act (inserted by s.19 of the Consumer Credit Act 21006): order under s.140B not to be made in connection with a credit agreement which is an exempt agreement by virtue of s.16(6C), paras 38–039, 38–192, 38–214, above, and SI 2003/1475; SI 2005/2967.

Form, etc.

[*Page* [932]] **38–494**
The Consumer Credit (Disclosure of Information) Regulations 2004 (SI 2004/1481) (see para.38–070, above) do not apply to agreements to which s.58 of the Act applies.

Special "pause" provisions

[*Add to note 2116: page* [933]] **38–496**
SI 1983/1557 has been amended by SI 2004/2619 and SI 2004/3236.

[*Add to note 2118*]
SI 1983/1557 has been amended by SI 2004/2619 and SI 2004/3236.

[*Text to note 2119*]
The unexecuted agreement may now be transmitted in electronic form: SI 2004/3236, art.2(2).

[*Add at end of note 2124*]
and by SI 2004/2619, SI 2004/3236.

Saving for registered charges

[*Add to note 2137: page* [934]] **38–499**
Section 177(3) is amended by s.24(5) of the Consumer Credit Act 2006.

CHAPTER 39

EMPLOYMENT

			PARA.
☐	1.	Introduction	39–001
☐	2.	The factors identifying a contract of employment	39–010
☐	3.	Formation of the contract	39–029
■	4.	Collective agreements and statutory awards of terms	39–043
		(a) Collective agreements as contracts	39–043
■		(b) Incorporation of collective agreements into individual contracts of employment	39–045
		(c) Statutory awards of terms	39–051
■	5.	Rights and duties under and associated with a contract of employment	39–054
■		(a) Duties of the employee	39–055
■		(b) Duties of the employer	39–074
☐		(i) Remuneration	39–074
☐		(ii) Other duties	39–096
■	6.	Termination of the contract	39–150
☐		(a) Termination by notice	39–150
■		(b) Termination by payment in lieu of notice	39–162
☐		(c) Termination by agreement or by expiry of fixed period	39–164
☐		(d) Termination under the doctrine of frustration	39–167
☐		(e) Assignment, winding up and changes in the employing enterprise	39–170
		(f) Summary dismissal	39–175
		(g) Wrongful dismissal or repudiation	39–186
☐		(h) Constructive dismissal	39–187
■	7.	Remedies, and rights incidental to the termination of employment	39–188
		(a) Statement of reasons for dismissal	39–188
		(b) Recovery of remuneration	39–189
		(c) Protection of the employee's accrued rights in the employer's insolvency	39–191
☐		(d) Damages for wrongful dismissal	39–193
■		(e) Equitable remedies and declarations	39–200
■		(f) Employment tribunal jurisdiction	39–205
		(g) Employer's damages	39–206
■	8.	Unfair and discriminatory dismissal	39–207
■		(a) Unfair dismissal	39–207
☐		(i) General considerations	39–207
■		(ii) Dismissal and effective date of termination	39–211
☐		(iii) Unfairness	39–215
☐		(iv) Remedies	39–228
		(b) Discriminatory and victimising dismissals	39–237

			PARA.
■	9.	Redundancy payments and procedure	39–243
□		(a) Redundancy payments	39–243
□		(b) Redundancy procedure	39–254
■	10.	Statutory dispute resolution procedures	39–258

1. INTRODUCTION

The Employment Act 2002

[Add to note 11: page [937]]   **39–002**
These provisions, which make significant changes to the costs regime for the Employment Appeal Tribunal and for employment tribunals, and which make various other changes designed to increase the efficiency of the management of applications to employment tribunals, were brought into effect from July 9, 2004.

The modern approach to definition of the contract of employment

[Add to text following note 29: page [939]]   **39–005**
It may also still be important for certain purposes to distinguish between the contract of employment and the contract of apprenticeship—compare Main Work, para.39–179, and para.39–196, n.1400; the way in which that distinction is to be drawn was considered by the Court of Appeal in *Flett v Matheson* [2006] EWCA Civ 53; [2006] I.R.L.R. 277.

The contract of service or personally to execute any work or labour: "workers" and "persons employed"

[Add to note 54: page [941]]   **39–009**
See *Wright v Redrow Homes (North West) Ltd* [2004] EWCA Civ 469; [2004] I.C.R. 1126 where the contracts of independent individual bricklaying contractors were construed as intended to require them to work "personally" so as to constitute them as "workers"; see also Main Work and Supplement, para.39–009, nn 60, 64; compare Main Work and Supplement para.39–022, nn 143–147.

[Add to notes 60, 64: pages [942] *and* [943]]
See also Main Work and Supplement, para.39–009, n.54; compare Main Work and Supplement para.39–022 nn 143–147. Compare now *Cotswold Developments Construction Ltd v Williams* [2006] I.R.L.R. 181, which confirms the role of mutuality of obligation in deciding whether the contractual relationship of "worker" and employer exists in a given case.

[Add to note 65: page [943]]
See *Mingeley v Pennock and Ivory* [2004] EWCA Civ 328; [2004] I.C.R. 727, where the relationship between a taxi-driver and the organisation co-ordinating his work was held not to amount to a contract personally to execute any work or labour; see also Supplement, para.39–023, n.150.

[*Add to note 66*]

See *South East Sheffield Citizens Advice Bureau v Grayson* [2004] I.R.L.R. 353, E.A.T., where an unpaid volunteer worker was held to fall outside this definition.

[*Amend text associated with note 67: page* [943]]

Instead of "the representatives of recognised trade unions", the text should now read "the representatives of workers".

2. THE FACTORS IDENTIFYING A CONTRACT OF EMPLOYMENT

Personal performance

39–022   [*Add to note 145: page* [950]]

The requirement of personal performance was strictly maintained and applied in *Staffordshire Sentinel Newspapers Ltd v Potter* [2004] I.R.L.R. 752, EAT, so that an express power for the worker to substitute another worker was treated as negating a contract of employment although the power was subject to the approval of the employer. Compare also Main Work and Supplement, para.39–009, nn 50, 60, 64.

The extent of the obligation to work or to employ

39–023   [*Add to note 150: page* [951]]

Compare now *Mingeley v Pennock and Ivory* [2004] EWCA Civ 328; [2004] I.C.R. 727, where the relationship between a taxi-driver and the organisation co-ordinating his work was held not to amount to a contract personally to execute any work or labour.

[*Add to note 152*]

Compare the decision in *Dacas v Brook Street Bureau (UK) Ltd* [2004] EWCA Civ 217; [2004] I.R.L.R. 358, regarding the relationship between the employment agency and the temporary agency worker—see further, Main Work and Supplement para.39–027, n.184. The approach in the *Dacas* case was applied to similar effect in *Bunce v Postworth Ltd (t/a Skyblue)* [2005] EWCA Civ 490; [2005] I.R.L.R. 557. See now also *Muscat v Cable & Wireless plc* [2006] EWCA Civ 220; [2006] I.R.L.R. 354, which refines the existing analysis of the circumstances in which, in a triangular employment relationship involving the intermediation of an employment agency, a contract of employment will be implied as between the worker and the end-user of his or her services; see also Supplement, para.39–027 n.185, p.[954].

[*Add to note 157*]

Compare, however, *Cornwall CC v Prater* [2006] EWCA Civ 102; [2006] I.C.R. 731, where the Court of Appeal displayed a greater willingness than had previously been shown to regard a sequence of casual work contracts as each consisting of a contract of employment, and as all being linked up into a period of "continuous employment", as to which see para.39–157, n.1089. But in the rather different context of unpaid voluntary workers, the approach in the *Carmichael* case received a stricter application in *Melhuish v Redbridge Citizens Advice Bureau* [2005] I.R.L.R. 419. Contrast, however, in the context of remunerated employment, *Wilson v Circular Distributors Ltd* [2006] I.R.L.R. 38, where the attempt to argue that the employer was under no clear obligation to provide work and that the claimant accordingly had no contract of employment was unsuccessful.

The intention of the parties

[*Page* [952]]   **39–025**
In *Smith v Reliance Water Controls Ltd* [2003] EWCA Civ 1153, Arden L.J. stressed the importance, in cases where there was an express change of status from employee to self-employed worker, of nevertheless weighing all the objective factors according to the test laid down in the *Market Investigations* case to assess whether the contract was a contract of employment.

[*Add to note 164: page* [952]]
Compare also *RNLI v Bushaway* [2005] I.R.L.R. 675, in which a contract of employment was held to arise between the end-user and the worker in a triangular employment situation despite an express agreement that the claimant was to be regarded as self-employed, which agreement contained an "entire contract" clause; see also Supplement, para.30–027, n.185.

Special cases: (2) agency workers

[*Add to note 184: page* [954]]   **39–027**
However, the Court of Appeal in *Dacas v Brook Street Bureau (UK) Ltd* [2004] EWCA Civ 217; [2004] I.R.L.R. 358, held that the temporary agency worker was not an "employee" of the agency, though she might be an employee of the end-user of her services. The approach in the *Dacas* case was applied to similar effect in *Bunce v Postworth Ltd (t/a Skyblue)* [2005] EWCA Civ 490; [2005] I.R.L.R. 557.

[*Add to note 185: page* [955]]
See now also *Muscat v Cable & Wireless plc* [2006] EWCA Civ 220; [2006] I.R.L.R. 354, which refines the existing analysis of the circumstances in which, in a triangular employment relationship involving the intermediation of an employment agency, a contract of employment will be implied as between the worker and the end-user of his or her services. Compare also *RNLI v Bushaway* [2005] I.R.L.R. 675, in which such a contract was implied despite an express agreement that the claimant was to be regarded as self-employed, which agreement contained an "entire contract" clause.

[*Add to notes 186, 187*]
With effect from various dates in 2004, amendments were made to the Employment Agencies Act 1973 by s.31 and Sch.7 of the Employment Relations Act 1999, and the Regulations cited in n.187 were revised and replaced by the Conduct of Employment Agencies and Employment Businesses Regulations 2003 (SI 2003/3319).

3. FORMATION OF THE CONTRACT

Public policy, restraint of trade, and illegality

39–032   *[Page [957]]*
The Gangmasters Licensing Act 2004, the essential provisions of which were brought into effect from April 1, 2005, requires individuals to be licensed as gangmasters if they are to engage in the supplying of workers for the use of their services in agricultural work and various kinds of gathering, harvesting, processing or packaging of foodstuffs. Sections 12–14 of that Act create a series of criminal offences involving the disregarding of these licensing requirements, including an offence of acting as a gangmaster without a licence, and an offence of entering into arrangements with gangmasters who are not licensed. The principles discussed in this paragraph of the Main Work will apply to determine whether and when contracts of employment will be rendered unenforceable because their formation or performance involves the commission of one or more of those offences.

[Add to note 221: page [958]]
The decision of the EAT was upheld by the Court of Appeal in *Vakante v Addey & Stanhope School* [2004] EWCA Civ 1065; [2004] 4 All E.R. 1056.

[Add to note 228]
The approach in the *Woolston Hall Leisure* case was reiterated and applied in *Colen v Cebrian (UK) Ltd* [2003] EWCA Civ 1676; [2004] I.C.R. 568, and in *Wheeler v Qualitydeep Ltd (t/a Thai Royale Restaurant)* [2004] EWCA Civ 1085; [2005] I.C.R. 265, where the requirement of active participation by the employee in the illegality as to performance was insisted upon.

Unlawful advertisements for employment

39–034   *[Add at end of paragraph: page [962]]*
(9) *Age.* Provisions generally comparable to those relating to discrimination, harassment and victimisation relating to sex, race, disability, religion or belief and sexual orientation have now been made, with effect from 1 October 2006, with regard to age by the Employment Equality (Age) Regulations 2006 (SI 2006/1031). See also paras 39–166A, 39–208, 39–216A of the Supplement for an account of the way in which these Regulations alter the law concerning retirement from employment.

4. COLLECTIVE AGREEMENTS AND STATUTORY AWARDS OF TERMS

(b) *Incorporation of Collective Agreements into Individual Contracts of Employment*

Express incorporation

39–046   *[Add to note 333: page [969]]*
Compare, however, *Ackinclose v Gateshead MBC* [2005] I.R.L.R. 79, EAT, where it was held that when a contract of employment only made reference to a

national agreement as the relevant collective agreement without any further reference or incorporation, a successor agreement would not thereby be incorporated so as to take effect following transfer of the employment in question from a local authority employer party to the national bargaining structure to a private employer not party to that structure. Contrast, however, *Griffiths v Salisbury DC* [2004] EWCA Civ 162, where an agreement implementing the national agreement was held to be incorporated in the individual contract and where therefore a backdated pay freeze imposed under that agreement was effective.

Incorporation by implication

[*Add to note 346: page* [970]]   **39–048**
    Compare *Kaur v MG Rover Group Ltd* [2004] EWCA Civ 1507; [2005] I.R.L.R. 40, where a set of provisions concerning job security in a collective agreement were held to be inappropriate for incorporation into individual contracts of employment, as to certain of them because they were aspirational in character, and as to certain others because they were essentially collective undertakings rather than undertakings to individuals.

5. Rights and Duties Under and Associated with a Contract of Employment

(a) *Duties of the Employee*

Duties to disclose information

[*Add to notes 408–411: page* [976]]   **39–060**
    The decision in *Tesco Stores Ltd v Pook* [2003] EWHC 823; [2004] I.R.L.R. 618, Ch D, suggests that a sufficiently senior employee may in certain circumstances come under a generally implied duty to disclose his own breaches of trust as well as those of other employees.

(b) *Duties of the Employer*

(i) *Remuneration*

Remuneration

[*Add to note 502: page* [984]]   **39–074**
    Compare *Judge v Crown Leisure Ltd* [2005] EWCA Civ 571; [2005] I.R.L.R. 823, where the Court of Appeal upheld a decision of an employment tribunal that a verbal promise at a Christmas party eventually to place the claimant on the same salary scale as another employee was too indefinite to have contractual force, rejecting, however, the argument that this was a question of intention to create legal relations.

[*Add to note 511: page* [985]]
    Compare also now *Horkulak v Cantor Fitzgerald International* [2004] EWCA Civ 1287; [2005] I.C.R. 402.

The national minimum wage

39–076 [*Page* [986]]

Sections 44–46 of the Employment Relations Act 2004 make extensive additions and amendments to the regime for the enforcement of the national minimum wage, with effect from April 6, 2005.

General restrictions on deductions made, or payments received, by employers

39–093 [*Add to note 716: page* [1001]]

It was held in *Farrell Matthews & Weir v Hansen* [2005] I.C.R. 509 (EAT) that there was no reason to construe s.27(3) as meaning that non-contractual bonuses could not come within the definition of wages unless they were actually paid.

[*Add to note 725: page* [1002]]

It was re-confirmed in *Elizabeth Claire Care Management Ltd v Francis* [2005] I.R.L.R. 858 that non-payment of remuneration may qualify as "deduction from wages".

(ii) *Other Duties*

Action in tort

39–100 [*Add to note 767: page* [1006]]

Update reference to *Clerk & Lindsell* to 18th ed., 2004.

[*Add to note 769*]

In *Barber v Somerset County Council* [2004] UKHL 13; [2004] 1 W.L.R. 1089, the House of Lords broadly endorsed the guidelines laid down in *Sutherland v Hatton*, though applying them to somewhat different outcomes in the particular cases which were under appeal.

The Working Time Regulations

39–108 [*Add to note 812: page* [1010]]

See also now the Working Time (Amendment) Regulations 2006 (SI 2006/99).

[*Add to note 823: page* [1011]]

Compare, as to collective agreements, *Prison Service v Bewley* [2004] I.C.R. 422, EAT. The provisions of the 1999 Regulations which permitted exemption in respect of "partly measured working time" were revoked by the Working Time (Amendment) Regulations 2006 (SI 2006/99).

[*Add to note 824*]

The issue of whether this entitlement can be discharged by the payment of "rolled-up" holiday pay has been referred to the ECJ by the Court of Appeal in *Caulfield v Marshalls Clay Products Ltd* [2004] EWCA Civ 422; [2004] 2 C.M.L.R. 45. In the joined cases of *Robinson-Steele v RD Retail Services Ltd,*

Caulfield v Hanson Clay Products Cases C-131 and C-257/04 [2006] I.C.R. 932, the ECJ held the practice of payment of "rolled-up holiday pay" to be unlawful, as failing to comply with the paid holiday obligations imposed by the Working Time Directive.

The rights of the employee [or worker] in relation to trade union membership and activities

[*Pages* [1012]—[1013]]

39–111—
39–112

The material in these paragraphs is extensively affected by, and should now be read subject to, the provisions of ss.29–32 of the Employment Relations Act 2004, which came into force on October 1, 2004. The Act established new or enhanced rights for workers not to be offered inducements relating to trade union membership and collective bargaining, and extended their rights not to suffer detrimental action in circumstances relating to trade union membership.

Sections 29–32 of the 2004 Act make a series of additions and amendments to ss.146–151 of the Trade Union and Labour Relations (Consolidation) Act 1992; s.29 of the 2004 Act inserts new ss.145A–F into the 1992 Act. In particular it should be noted that s.31 of the 2004 Act amends ss.146–151 of the 1992 Act to extend the existing protections of employees against detrimental action by their employer for being, or not being, a member of a trade union or for taking part in the activities of their union to workers who are not employees. The heading to these two paragraphs is accordingly amended, as shown above, to refer to the larger category of "workers" rather than the more limited category of "employees" (see para.39–009 of the Main Work).

Statutory rights of employees to time off

[*Page* [1013]]

39–113

A new kind of statutory right to time off has been conferred on employees by s.40 of the Employment Relations Act 2004, which by inserting a new s.43M into the Employment Rights Act 1996 protects employees from being subjected to detriment by the employee by reason of being summoned for or being absent from work on jury service, with effect from April 6, 2005.

Equality clauses in contracts of employment

[*Add to note 887: page* [1017]]

39–122

Compare *Allonby v Accrington & Rossendale College* Case C-256/01 [2004] I.R.L.R. 224, ECJ, as to the construction of the "same employment" concept in accordance with art.141(1) of the EC Treaty. Compare also now *DEFRA v Robertson* [2005] EWCA Civ 138; [2005] I.C.R. 750, expounding the notion of attributability of differences between terms and conditions of employment to a "single source" which had been articulated by the ECJ in *Lawrence v Regent Office Care Ltd* Case C-320/00 [2002] E.C.R. 1–7325.

Disability discrimination during the period of employment

[*Page* [1022]]

39–131

The Disability Discrimination Act 2005 amends and extends in various respects the provisions of the Disability Discrimination Act 1995 concerning disability discrimination in employment. Specific amendments of the existing law will be mentioned in this Supplement as and when they are brought into force.

[*Add to note 935: page* [1022]]
See now *Archibald v Fife Council* [2004] UKHL 32; [2004] I.R.L.R. 651 on the meaning of the concept of reasonable adjustment.

Rights in connection with parenthood and family responsibility

39–140 [*Add to note 951: page* [1025]]
Section 12 of the Work and Families Act 2006, amending new s.80F of the ERA 1996, extends the category of employees who are entitled to request flexible working by including "carers" (to be defined in regulations) within the scheme.

References and testimonials

39–142 [*Add to note 968: page* [1027]]
Compare now also, to comparably restrictive effect, *Aspin v Metric Group Ltd* [2004] EWHC 1265.

Trust and confidence and other implied duties

39–145 [*Add to note 993: page* [1029]]
Compare the application of the implied obligation in favour of a senior manager in *Horkulak v Cantor Fitzgerald International* [2003] EWHC 1918 (QB) [2004] I.C.R. 697. In *Waltham Forest LBC v Omilaju (No.2)* [2004] EWCA Civ 1493; [2005] I.R.L.R. 35 it was re-asserted that the test of whether an act was capable of breaching the implied obligation was an objective one, so that the employee's subjective loss of trust and confidence was not sufficient in itself. In *Nottinghamshire CC v Meikle* [2004] EWCA Civ 859; [2004] 4 All E.R. 97, the objectivity of the test had been likewise asserted, but to the contrary effect that it was not necessary for the employee subjectively to have lost confidence in her employer in an overall sense. The decision in *Horkulak v Cantor Fitzgerald International* was upheld in the Court of Appeal with regard to the application of the implied obligation to the exercise of a contractual discretion as to the level of bonus payment to be awarded: [2004] EWCA Civ 1287; [2005] I.C.R. 402.

[*Add to note 1001*]
Compare now *Crossley v Faithful & Gould Holdings Ltd* [2004] EWCA Civ 293; [2004] I.R.L.R. 377, in which it was held that there is no general obligation upon the employer to take reasonable care for the employee's economic well-being, and that the application of the criteria articulated in the *Scally* case did not require disclosure on the present facts. To similar effect has been *Lennon v Commissioner of Police of the Metropolis* [2004] EWCA Civ 130.

The extensions and limits of the implied obligation of trust and confidence

39–146

[Add to note 1005 : page [1030]]
Compare also now *Bunning v GT Bunning & Sons Ltd* [2005] EWCA Civ 104 where it was held to be arguable that a failure to conduct a proper risk assessment of the continued employment of the employee as a welder, as required by Regulations when she became pregnant, might constitute a serious breach of the implied obligation as to trust and confidence. Compare now also *Greenhof v Barnsley MBC* [2006] I.R.L.R. 98, where it was held that a serious failure to make reasonable adjustments in favour of a disabled person as required by the Disability Discrimination Act 1995 amounted to a breach of the implied obligation as to trust and confidence, and a constructive dismissal.

[Add to note 1006]
In *Holladay v East Kent Hospitals NHS Trust* [2003] EWCA Civ 1696 it was held that the breach of the implied obligation must be a material cause of the event (arrest on suspicion of theft) which had caused the employee harm, but that it was not necessary to conclude that the event would not have occurred but for the breach.

[Add to notes 1008 and 1009: page [1031]]
See now *Eastwood v Magnox Electric plc, McCabe v Cornwall County Council* [2004] UKHL 35; [2005] 1 A.C. 503, in which the House of Lords seeks authoritatively to draw the boundary between the area of exclusion of liability for breach of the implied term of trust and confidence envisaged in the *Johnson* case, and the area of pre-dismissal conduct on the part of the employer, apparently including conduct capable of being treated as constructive dismissal, within which liability for breach of the implied term may arise.

Duties to avoid less favourable treatment of part-time work and fixed-term work

39–148

[Add to note 1023 : page [1032]]
See for the judicial construction of this Regulation, and the clarification of the notion of comparable workers which it articulates, *Mathews v Kent and Medway Towns Fire Authority* [2006] UKHL 8; [2006] I.C.R. 365.

39–149

[Page [1032]]
In *Department for Work and Pensions v Webley* [2004] EWCA Civ 1745; [2005] I.C.R. 577 it was confirmed that the employer's allowing a fixed-term contract to expire by effluxion of time without renewal does not in itself constitute a detriment, or less favourable treatment of a fixed-term employee than of a permanent employee, within reg.3 of the 2002 Regulations.

6. TERMINATION OF THE CONTRACT

(a) *Termination by Notice*

Form of notice

39–152

[Add to note 1043: page [1034]]
See, as to contingent or equivocal notice, *Rai v Somerfield Stores Ltd* [2004] I.C.R. 656, EAT.

"Continuous employment"

39–157   [*Add to note 1089: page* [1038]]
Compare *Cornwall CC v Prater* [2006] EWCA Civ 102; [2006] I.C.R. 731, where the Court of Appeal displayed a greater willingness than had previously been shown to regard a sequence of casual work contracts as being linked up, by periods of "temporary cessation of work" into a period of "continuous employment". See also Supplement, para.39–023 n.157.

(b) *Termination by Payment in Lieu of Notice*

The statutory and contractual effects of payment in lieu of notice

39–163   [*Page* [1042]]
See now *Hardy v Polk Ltd* [2004] I.R.L.R. 420 (EAT), where Burton J. held, in effect, that s.86 did not create an entitlement to payment in lieu of notice, or a claim in debt for failure to give the statutory minimum period of notice or payment in lieu thereof.

(c) *Termination by Agreement or by Expiry of Fixed Period*

Termination by subsequent agreement

39–166   [*Add to note 1152: page* [1045]]
Compare *Solectron Scotland Ltd v Roper* [2004] I.R.L.R. 4, EAT as to the validity of a compromise agreement which could be regarded as limiting the application of the TUPE Regulations.

[*Add new paragraph 39–166A: page* [1046]]

39–166A   **Retirement.** The notion of "retirement" from employment is one which is far from precise either in practical or in legal terms. In practical terms its normal or approximate meaning is the ending of the employment of a worker by reason of his or her having reached the end of his or her normal working life or career. In legal terms this may take various forms, such as termination of the contract of employment by the employing enterprise, perhaps by notice to terminate, or termination by expiry of a fixed-term contract of employment, or it might be regarded as termination by agreement, whether prior or ad hoc, or it might consist of termination by the worker (the latter especially in the case of so-called "early retirement", itself a notion with further imprecisions). (Compare Freedland, *The Personal Employment Contract* (2003), pp.400–401, 429–431.) Without defining the notion of "retirement", the Employment Equality (Age) Regulations 2006 (SI 2006/1031) have attached very significant new legal incidents to it; see also paras 39–034, 39–208 and 39–216A of the Supplement. At this point, attention is drawn in particular to the way in which reg.47 and Sch.6 create, first, a duty upon an employer who intends to retire an employee to give the employee notice in writing of "the date on which he intends to retire the employee" and of the employee's right to make a request not to retire on that date (Sch.6, paras 2–4), and secondly, a duty upon the employer to consider such a request not to retire (Sch.6, paras 5–7). (Refusal of such a request is not required to be justified; but an internal appeal against refusal must be provided: Sch.6, para.8.) An employee may complain to an employment tribunal of failure to fulfill these duties of notification, and may be awarded amounts of compensation which are defined and limited in various ways up to the amount of eight "weeks' pay": Sch.6, para.11.

(d) *Termination under the Doctrine of Frustration*

Frustration

[*Add to notes 1164, 1165: page* [1046]]   **39–167**
   Compare now the restricted approach to frustration of the contract of employment which was taken in *Four Seasons Healthcare Ltd v Maughan* [2005] I.R.L.R. 324.

(e) *Assignment, Winding-up and Changes in the Employing Enterprise*

Transfer of employment: (2) the effect of the Transfer Regulations

[*Add to text after note 1193: page* [1049]]   **39–171**
   With effect from April 6, 2006, the existing Transfer of Undertakings (Protection of Employment) Regulations were revised and replaced by the Transfer of Undertakings (Protection of Employment) Regulations 2006 (SI 2006/246). This paragraph will be revised accordingly in the next edition of the Main Work; in this Supplement, attention is drawn to the most important relevant changes. The changes affecting this paragraph consist of a widening of the scope of the Regulations to cover cases where services are outsourced, insourced or assigned by a client to a new contractor ("service provision changes"): see reg.3(1)(b), (3); and the making of provisions which clarify the ability of employers and employees to agree to vary contracts of employment in circumstances where a relevant transfer occurs: see regs 4(4)–(5), 9.

[*Add to notes 1193 and 1198*]
   Compare *Martin v South Bank University*, Case C-4/01 [2004] I.R.L.R. 74, ECJ, as to the application of the Acquired Rights Directive and the Transfer Regulations to early retirement benefits.

Dissolution of partnership

[*Add to note 1206: page* [1050]]   **39–172**
   See now, however, *Stevens v Bower* [2004] EWCA Civ 496; [2004] I.C.R. 1582 where the approach taken in *Harold Fielding Ltd v Mansi* was rejected and it was held that the employees in question had continuity of service despite the change in the status of their employer from that of a partnership of solicitors to that of a sole practitioner.

(h) *Constructive Dismissal*

Termination as the result of constructive dismissal

39–187   [*Add to note 1308: page* [1060]]
In *Waltham Forest LBC v Omilaju (No.2)* [2004] EWCA Civ 1493; [2005] I.R.L.R. 35 it was held that the final act or "last straw" in a series of actions which cumulatively amounted to constructive dismissal need not itself be a breach of contract or unreasonable; but it had to be more than very trivial and had to be capable of contributing, however slightly, to a breach of the implied obligation as to mutual trust and confidence. Compare also now *Bunning v GT Bunning & Sons Ltd* [2005] EWCA Civ 104, in which the judgment of Wall L.J. adds further support to the notion of the "last straw" as articulated in the *Omilaju* case.

[*Add to note 1311*]
In *Kerry Foods Ltd v Lynch* [2005] I.R.L.R. 681, the doctrine in *Johnson v Unisys Ltd* received an important application or extension, in that it was held that where an employing enterprise sought to impose a six-day week on an employee working a five-day week, its conduct amounted not to a repudiatory breach of the obligation as to mutual trust and confidence, but rather to a giving of lawful notice to terminate the contract of employment coupled with an offer of re-engagement on different terms.

7. REMEDIES, AND RIGHTS, INCIDENTAL TO THE TERMINATION OF EMPLOYMENT

(d) *Damages for Wrongful Dismissal*

Damages for loss of earnings following wrongful dismissal

39–193   [*Add to note 1384: page* [1066]]
See also now *Wise Group v Mitchell* [2005] I.C.R. 896.

[*Add to note 1385*]
See now *Harper v Virgin Net Ltd* [2004] EWCA Civ 271, in which it was held that damages for wrongful dismissal should not include compensation for the chance that, if the employee had not been dismissed with insufficient notice, she would have become time-qualified to make a claim for unfair dismissal. The decision in *Harper v Virgin Net Ltd* was followed and applied in *Wise Group v Mitchell* [2005] I.C.R. 896.

Damages for other lost benefits

39–195   [*Add to note 1394: page* [1066]]
Note the way in which the decision in the *Lavarack* case was distinguished by the Court of Appeal in *Horkulak v Cantor Fitzgerald International* [2004] EWCA Civ 1287; [2005] I.C.R. 402.

Damages for injury to feelings or reputation

[Add to note 1404: page [1068]]
An appeal to the House of Lords was allowed in *Eastwood v Magnox Electric plc* [2004] UKHL 35; [2005] 1 A.C. 503: see this Supplement, para.39–146, nn.1008 and 1009, above.

39–196

Deductions for Social Security contributions and benefits

[Note 1412: page [1068] Punctuation misplaced; the first three lines should read:-]
Claims for damages for wrongful dismissal would seem not to be affected by the recoupment provisions either of the Social Security (Recovery of Benefits) Act 1997, which applies to "payments in consequence of any accident, injury or disease" [etc.].

39–198

(e) *Equitable Remedies and Declarations*

Declaration and other remedies

[Add to note 1441: page [1072]]
Compare *Kaur v MG Rover Group Ltd* [2004] I.R.L.R. 279, Q.B.D., where a declaration was granted of contractual entitlement not to be made redundant. The decision was reversed on appeal on other, substantive, grounds ([2004] EWCA Civ 1507; [2005] I.R.L.R. 40), but remains of interest as to this remedial point.

39–203

(f) *Employment Tribunal Jurisdiction*

Jurisdiction of employment tribunals in relation to contracts of employment

[Add to note 1460: page [1073]]
Compare *Peninsula Business Services Ltd v Sweeney* [2004] I.R.L.R. 49, E.A.T., denying entitlement to commission payments which would normally have accrued due at a date later than that of termination of employment, and where the rules of the commission scheme excluded post-termination accrual.

39–205

8. UNFAIR AND DISCRIMINATORY DISMISSAL

(a) *Unfair Dismissal*

(i) *General Considerations*

Employments covered and employments specifically excluded

[Add to note 1478 : page [1075]]
As to the implicit exclusion of employees working abroad, see *Lawson v Serco Ltd* [2004] EWCA Civ 12. See now *Lawrence v Serco Ltd* [2006] UKHL 3;

39–208

[2006] I.C.R. 250, in which the House of Lords allowed the appeals of certain claimants in a group of joined appeals, remitting their cases to the employment tribunal for re-hearing, and further explicated the territorial scope of the right not be unfairly dismissed.

[Add to note 1484: page [1076]]
The upper age limit, specified in the text to which this footnote is attached, was abolished with effect from October 1, 2006 by the Employment Equality (Age) Regulations 2006 (SI 2006/1031), Sch.8, para.25. See also paras 39–166A, 39–216A of the Supplement.

(ii) *Dismissal and Effective Date of Termination*

The effective date of termination

39–213   *[Add to note 1538: page [1080]]*
Compare *Fitzgerald v University of Kent at Canterbury* [2004] EWCA Civ 143; [2004] I.C.R. 737, in which it was held that a retrospective agreement did not validly alter the effective date of termination. But compare also now *Palfrey v Transco plc* [2004] I.R.L.R. 916 (EAT) where a later agreement for payment in lieu of notice was held to have advanced the effective date of termination.

39–214   *[Add to note 1540: page [1081]]*
In *Harper v Virgin Net Ltd* [2004] EWCA Civ 271; [2004] I.R.L.R. 390 it was held that the legislation did not bring about a further postponement of the effective date of termination to the later date at which a contractual notice period, longer than the statutory minimum notice period, would have expired.

(iii) *Unfairness*

Introduction

39–215   *[Page [1081]]*
A new specially designated ground of unfair dismissal has been created by s.40 of the Employment Relations Act 2004, which, by inserting a new s.98B into the Employment Rights Act 1996, renders it unfair to dismiss an employee by reason of his or her being summoned for or being absent from work on jury service, unless the employer shows the likelihood of substantial injury to the undertaking being caused by the absence on jury service. This provision was effective from April 6, 2005.

[Add to note 1547]
As to the impact of the Human Rights Act 1998 on the adjudication of unfairness, see *X v Y (Employment: Sex Offender)* [2004] EWCA Civ 662; [2004] I.R.L.R. 625.

Substantial reasons for dismissal

39–216   *[Add to text at end of paragraph: page [1083]]*
With effect from April 6, 2006, the existing Transfer of Undertakings (Protection of Employment) Regulations were revised and replaced by the Transfer of

Undertakings (Protection of Employment) Regulations 2006 (SI 2006/246). This paragraph will be revised accordingly in the next edition of the Main Work; in this Supplement, attention is drawn to the most important relevant changes. The changes affecting this paragraph consist of provisions which clarify the circumstances under which it is unfair for employers to dismiss employees for reasons connected with a relevant transfer: see reg.7.

[*Add new paragraph 39–216A*]

Retirement. Among the very significant new legal incidents which the **39–216A** Employment Equality (Age) Regulations 2006 (SI 2006/1031) have attached to the notion of "retirement" (as to which see also paras 39–034, 39–208, 39–216A of this Supplement) has been a special regime for "retirement" within the law of unfair dismissal. This special regime has been created by Sch.8, paras 21–23, introducing new ss.98ZA to 98ZH into the Employment Rights Act 1996 and making consequential amendments. Those new sections between them (i) identify "retirement" as a ground or reason for dismissal; (ii) prescribe the circumstances in which "retirement" cannot be, may be or will be deemed to be the reason or principal reason for a dismissal; (iii) lay down the rules according to which dismissal by reason of retirement will be treated as fair or unfair; and (iv) lay down certain special rules as to the remedies for unfair dismissal in the case of dismissals by reason of retirement.

Reasonableness of dismissal

[*Add to note 1578: page* [1084]]

This should now be considered in conjunction with the provisions about **39–217** statutory dispute resolution procedures, detailed in paras 39–258—39–262 of the Main Work. The provisions came into force on October 1, 2004.

Dismissal by reason of trade union membership, non-membership or activity

[*Page* [1085]]

The reference in the text to s.46 of the Trade Union and Labour Relations **39–219** (Consolidation) Act 1992 should be to ss.146–151 of that Act.

Section 152 of the 1992 Act has been amended by s.32 of the Employment Relations Act 2004 so as to make the dismissal of an employee unfair where it is for making use of the services of his union or refusing to accept certain specified inducements in respect of trade union membership or collective bargaining. This provision was brought into effect on October 1, 2004.

Dismissal during lock-out, strike or other industrial action

[*Add to note 1621: page* [1087]]

The provisions of s.238A of the 1992 Act concerning "protected industrial **39–220** action" have been amended by the Employment Relations Act 2004. Sections 27–28 of the 2004 Act, which, by amending s.238A and adding a new s.238B to the 1992 Act, increase the protections against the dismissal of employees taking official lawfully organised industrial action by extending the "protected period" from 8 to 12 weeks, by exempting days of lock-out from the 12-week protected period, and also defining more closely the actions which employers and unions should undertake by way of recourse to conciliation and mediation with regard to "protected industrial action". These provisions were brought into effect on April 6, 2005.

(iv) *Remedies*

Compensation for unfair dismissal: the basic award

39–232   [*Add to note 1690: page* [1093]]
The lower age limit, which was specified in the text to which this footnote is attached, was, so far as it had continued to be applicable, abolished with effect from October 1, 2006 by the Employment Equality (Age) Regulations 2006 (SI 2006/1031), Sch.8, para.35. See also paras 39–166A, 39–248 of this Supplement.

Compensation for unfair dismissal: the compensatory award

39–233   [*Add to note 1706: page* [1094]]
The principle in the *Norton Tool* case was upheld on the appeal to the House of Lords in *Dunnachie v Kingston-upon-Hull City Council* [2004] UKHL 36.

9. REDUNDANCY PAYMENTS AND PROCEDURE

(a) *Redundancy Payments*

Redundancy Payments

39–248   [*Add to notes 1830, 1832: page* [1105]]
The lower age limit of 18 and the upper age limit of 65 and the tapering provisions after the age of 64, which were specified in the text to which these footnotes are attached, were, so far as they had continued to be applicable, abolished with effect from October 1, 2006 by the Employment Equality (Age) Regulations 2006 (SI 2006/1031), Sch.8, paras 30, 32, 35. See also paras 39–166A, 39–252 of the Supplement.

Exclusions from the Act

39–252   [*Add to note 1857: page* [1107]]
The upper age limits which were specified in the text to which this footnote is attached, were, so far as they had continued to be applicable, abolished with effect from October 1, 2006 by the Employment Equality (Age) Regulations 2006 (SI 2006/1031), Sch.8, para.30. See also paras 39–166A, 39–248 of the Supplement.

(b) *Redundancy Procedure*

Consultation with the representatives of recognised trade unions or of employees

[Add to text at end of paragraph: page [1109]]   **39–255**
With effect from April 6, 2006, the existing Transfer of Undertakings (Protection of Employment) Regulations were revised and replaced by the Transfer of Undertakings (Protection of Employment) Regulations 2006 (SI 2006/246). This paragraph will be revised accordingly in the next edition of the Main Work; in this Supplement, attention is drawn to the most important relevant changes. There are no major changes directly affecting this paragraph, but attention is drawn to a new duty on the old transferor employer to supply information about the transferring employees to the new transferee employer (by providing what is described as "employee liability information"): see reg.11.

[Add to note 1879: page [1109]]   **39–256**
See, as to the making of the award, *Susie Radin Ltd v GMB* [2004] EWCA Civ 180; [2004] 2 All E.R. 279.

[Text at note 1886: page [1110]]
With effect from April 6, 2006, the existing Transfer of Undertakings (Protection of Employment) Regulations were revised and replaced by the Transfer of Undertakings (Protection of Employment) Regulations 2006 (SI 2006/246). This paragraph will be revised accordingly in the next edition of the Main Work; in this Supplement, attention is drawn to the most important relevant changes. There are no major changes directly affecting this paragraph, but compare Supplement, above, para.39–255.

10. STATUTORY DISPUTE RESOLUTION PROCEDURES

Introduction

[Page [1111]]   **39–258**
In connection with the statutory dispute resolution procedures, reference should now be made to the right for workers to be accompanied by certain trade union officials or fellow workers at non-trivial disciplinary and grievance hearings. That right was originally conferred by ss.10–12 of the Employment Relations Act 1999. Section 37 of the Employment Relations Act 2004 amended s.10 of the 1999 Act, with effect from October 1, 2004, in order further to clarify the role of the companion at such disciplinary and grievance hearings.

The statutory dispute resolution procedures

[Note 1902: page [1111]]   **39–259**
The Employment Act 2002 (Dispute Resolution) Regulations 2004 were duly enacted on March 12, 2004 with the SI number SI 2004/752, to come into force on October 1, 2004.

CHAPTER 40

GAMING AND WAGERING

			PARA.
☐	1A.	Gambling Act 2005	40–A001
■	1.	Definitions	40–001
■		(a) Wagering contracts	40–001
■		(b) Gaming contracts	40–013
■	2.	Effects of gaming and wagering contracts	40–017
■		(a) Enforcement	40–017
■		(b) Recovering back money paid	40–028
■		(c) Recovering back money or property deposited	40–031
■		(d) Principal and agent	40–033
■		(e) Partnership	40–042
■		(f) Stakeholders	40–043
■		(g) Prizes for lawful games	40–047
■		(h) Securities	40–048
■		(i) Loans in general	40–059
		(i) Loans to pay lost bets	40–060
		(ii) Loans for future betting	40–065
■		(j) Loans for gaming on licensed premises	40–077
■		(k) Gambling with stolen money	40–081
■		(i) Illegal wagers	40–082
☐		(ii) Lawful wagers	40–083
		(iii) Change of position	40–087
■		(l) Gaming chips	40–088

1A. GAMBLING ACT 2005

40–A001   **Contracts which relate to gambling generally enforceable.** Part 17 of the Gambling Act 2005 will, when that Part is brought into force,[a1] fundamentally change the law with regard to gaming and wagering contracts as discussed in Ch.40 of the Main Work. So far as the effects of gaming and wagering contracts are concerned, that discussion is mainly concerned with the restrictions on the validity of such contracts and of certain associated transactions which had been imposed by the Gaming Acts 1710, 1835, 1845 and 1892, as interpreted in the cases discussed in Pt 2 of that Chapter (paras 40–018—40–088). Section 334 of the 2005 Act will repeal all those provisions,[a2] though not with retrospective effect,[a3] thus rendering most of that discussion obsolete; s.356 will also repeal the remaining provisions of those Acts, as well as the Gaming Act 1968, s.16 which is discussed in paras 40–057, 40–058 and 40–077—40–080 of the Main Work. Section 335(1) of the 2005 Act marks a fundamental shift in the approach of the law to the legal effects of gambling contracts by laying down the general rule that contracts which relate to gambling are to be legally enforceable. This general rule is, under the Act, subject to two principal exceptions; the general rule and the exceptions to it are discussed in paras 40–A004—40–A007 of this Supplement. By way of introduction, a (necessarily brief) account must be given of the principal elements of the structure of this complex legislation and of its terminology, so far as these matters relate to the legal effect of gambling contracts under the Act.

[a1] By order made under s.358(1); at the time of writing, no order has been made bringing Pt 17 of the Act (ss.334–338), with which the following discussion is mainly concerned, into force.
[a2] s.334(1).
[a3] s.334(2).

General scheme of the Act. The main purpose of the Act is to create a new **40–A002** scheme for the regulation of gambling in Great Britain, to be supervised by a body (the Gambling Commission) created by the Act.[a4] The scheme does not extend to "spread bets" (such as contracts for differences) which are regulated under the Financial Services and Markets Act 2000,[a5] or to the National Lottery.[a6] The general principle underlying the Act is that commercial gambling which does not fall within either of these exceptions is unlawful, so that the provision of facilities, or the use of premises, for gambling is an offence unless a licence has been obtained from the appropriate local authority[a7] and the conditions of the licence have been complied with.[a8] It is also an offence under the Act to invite or permit a child or young person to take part in commercial gambling[a9] and for a young person to engage in such gambling[a10] or to provide facilities for such gambling.[a11] The licencing requirements described above,[a12] and the offences resulting from failure to comply with them do not extend to "private" gaming or betting or to certain other non-commercial gaming or betting.[a13]

[a4] s.20.
[a5] s.10.
[a6] s.15, except for the purposes of ss.42 and 335 (below, paras 40–A004 and 40–A005).
[a7] s.2.
[a8] ss.33(2), 37(1).
[a9] s.46.
[a10] s.48.
[a11] s.50.
[a12] At nn 7 and 8.
[a13] ss.296, 297–302.

Terminology of the Act. "Gambling" in the Act means gaming, betting and **40–A003** participating in a lottery.[a14] "Gaming" means playing (*i.e.* participating in) a game of chance (not including a sport) for a prize.[a15] "Betting" means "making or accepting a bet on (a) the outcome of a race, competition or other event or process, (b) the likelihood of anything occurring or not occurring, or (c) whether anything is or is not true."[a16] The events on which the outcome of the bet depends in some important respects resemble those which could be the subject of a wager (an expression which forms no part of the definition of "gambling", "gaming" or "betting" in the 2005 Act) within the definition which had been formulated at common law for the purposes of the earlier Gaming Acts[a17] which are to be repealed. The phrase "making a bet" is not defined, but it can be inferred that the person making the bet must pay or deposit a stake or make some other payment in order to participate in the bet.[a18] "Betting" in the 2005 Act does not include activities regulated under s.22 of the Financial Services & Markets Act[a19]; contracts for differences (Main Work para.40–010) fall into this category,[a20] as do so-called "spread bets". On the other hand, the concept of "gambling" under the 2005 Act is wider than that of a wager under the common law definition in that it includes participating in a lottery[a21] and in that the concept of betting includes pool betting.[a22]

The concept of "gambling" under the 2005 Act is also not in terms restricted to cases in which the party to whom money is to be paid on the outcome of the bet has no other "interest" in the contract than the sum or stake that he will win or lose.[a23] The existence of such an "interest" was thought to be one reason why contracts of insurance were not wagers where the requirement of the insured's having an "insurable interest" was satisfied. But, as is pointed out in para.40–005 of the Main Work, a contract of insurance was not necessarily a wager merely because the requirement of insurable interest was not satisfied; and in such cases the contract of insurance was nevertheless void under s.4 of the Marine Insurance Act 1906 and might be illegal under the Marine Insurance (Gambling Policies) Act 1909. Neither of these enactments is repealed or amended by the 2005 Act, in spite of the fact that by s.4 of the 1906 Act a contract of marine insurance is "deemed to be a gaming or wagering contract"[a24] where "the assured has not an insurable interest as defined by this Act"[a25] and that "every contract of marine by way of gaming or wagering is void."[a26] The absence of any reference to these provisions in the 2005 Act seems to indicate a legislative intention not to change the law with regard to insurance without interest, at any rate with regard to marine insurance, and probably with regard to insurance generally since the provisions of the 1906 Act are, where appropriate, regarded as applicable to contracts of insurance generally.[a27] It follows that insurance, even without interest, is not subject to the regulatory provisions which form the bulk of the 2005 Act, and that Pt 17 of that Act, which relates to the legality and enforceability of gambling contracts, does not apply to contracts of insurance which are void for want of insurable interest.

[a14] s.3.

[a15] s.6.

[a16] s.9.

[a17] See Main Work, paras 40–001—40–012.

[a18] See Gambling Act 2005, s.11(1) ("despite the fact that he does not deposit a stake in the normal way of betting"), 11(1)(b) ("required to pay").

[a19] Gambling Act 2005, s.10.

[a20] Financial Services and Markets Act 2000 (Regulated Activities) Order 2001 (SI 2001/544), art.85.

[a21] Gambling Act 2005, s.3(1).

[a22] Gambling Act 2005, s.12(1); contrast Main Work para.40–003 for the view that pool betting was not "wagering" under the previous law.

[a23] See Main Work, para.40–005 for this requirement under the previous law.

[a24] Marine Insurance Act 1906, s.4(2).

[a25] *ibid.*, s.4(2)(a); see also s.4(2)(b) ("interest or no interest policy").

[a26] *ibid.*, s.4(1).

[a27] *cf. Locker & Woolf Ltd v W Australian Insurance Co Ltd* [1936] 1 K.B. 408 at 414.

Enforceability of contracts relating to gambling: s.335(1). At common law, **40–A004** the general rule was that wagering contracts were legally enforceable, though this rule was subject to qualifications stated in para.40–017 of the Main Work. The restrictions on the enforceability of such contracts imposed by the legislative provisions referred to in para.40–A001 of this Supplement are to be removed by the repeal of those provisions by the 2005 Act,[a28] but this repeal will not, of itself, restore the common law rule by which wagering contracts were, in general, legally enforceable.[a29] It was therefore necessary for that Act to contain a specific provision to this effect. This is made by s.335(1), which provides that "the fact that a contract relates to gambling shall not prevent its enforcement". Four points must here be made about this provision.

The first arises from what is in substance the double negative contained in the phrase "shall not prevent". The subsection does not in terms say that contracts relating to gaming shall be enforceable; it merely says that the fact of a contract's being so related shall not prevent its enforcement. It therefore does not rule out the possibility that enforcement may be refused on some ground other than the fact that the contract relates to gambling. The significance of this point is further considered in the discussion in paras 40–A005 and 40–A006 below of one of the exceptions to the general principle of enforceability laid down by the 2005 Act.[a30]

Secondly, s.335(1) refers to "the fact that a contract relates to gambling". This phrase is wide enough to cover, not only the gambling contract itself, but also associated transactions. Problems that have in the past arisen (and may continue to arise) out of associated transactions such as agency arrangements related to gambling, partnerships, stakeholders, securities and loans for gambling,[a31] would all seem to be covered by the phrase and such related transactions will, as a general rule, be enforceable by virtue of s.335(1).

Thirdly, the only direct effect of s.335(1) is to make the contracts covered by it enforceable; but the enforceability of such contracts will also have repercussions on a number of further legal effects of such contracts which had given rise to problems under the previous law. Thus if money is paid or property deposited under a gambling (or related) contract[a32] there will no longer be any question of its being recoverable by the payee or depositor merely because that contract is a gambling contract. The payment or deposit will simply have been made under a valid contract and any right to its return will depend on the terms of the contract, or on other rules of law governing the recoverability of payments or deposits made under a contract. The fact that a payment is made under a gambling contract which will, under s.335(1), be enforceable will also have repercussions on the law relating to gambling with stolen money.[a33]

Fourthly, the general principle of the enforceability of contracts relating to gambling is, under the 2005 Act, subject to two significant exceptions. Enforcement may be refused on the ground of "unlawfulness"; and the Gambling Commission is given power to "void" certain bets. These exceptions are discussed in paras 40–A00—40–A007 below.

[a28] Above, para.40–A001.
[a29] See Interpretation Act 1978, s.16.
[a30] *cf.* Gambling Act 2005, s.337(1).
[a31] See Main Work, paras 40–033—40–080.
[a32] See *ibid.*, paras 40–028—40–032.
[a33] See *ibid.*, paras 40–081—40–087; below, paras 40–082—40–083 of this Supplement.

40–A005 **Unlawfulness: s.335(2).** Section 335(2) of the 2005 Act provides that "subsection (1) is without prejudice to any rule of law preventing the enforcement of a contract on the ground of unlawfulness (*other than a rule relating specifically to gambling*)." The first question that arises from this provision is its effect on cases in which the unlawfulness is due to failure to comply with the provisions of the Act, outlined above, such as its licensing requirements. In one sense, those requirements might be said to consist of rules of law "relating specifically to gambling" and so not to fall within the restriction on the enforceability of contracts contained in s.335(2). But it is submitted that this reasoning would be contrary to the policy of the Act in that it would allow a party to a gambling contract who had failed to comply with the Act nevertheless to enforce the contract. Such a conclusion can, and should, be avoided by arguing that, in cases of this kind, the "unlawfulness" arises, not "specifically" because the transaction is a bet, but because the making of the contract constitutes a form of activity which is prohibited, with penal sanctions, by law (in this case, by other provisions of the Act itself). The purpose of the words italicised above appears to be to exclude the argument that gambling contracts are "unlawful" *as such* because their enforcement would be contrary to public policy; for if this argument were accepted, s.335(2) would (but for those italicised words) wholly negate the validating effect on gambling contracts of s.335(1). The purpose of subs.(2) is, in the terms of the Explanatory Notes[a34] to the Act, to ensure that subs.(1) "does not . . . override any other rule that prevents enforcement on the ground of unlawfulness. Therefore gambling contracts may be void on the same basis as any other contract (for example, on the basis of lack of intention, mistake or illegality)." The rule that a contract may be void or for illegality because it is one to engage in a form of activity that is prohibited by legislation with penal consequences is of general application in that it applies to all contracts, of whatever nature; and the rule is not excluded, by the words italicised above, from the restriction on enforceability in s.335(2) merely because the activity happens to be gambling.

It follows from the above reasoning that, if a person who provided facilities for gambling did so without the requisite licence, or failed to comply with conditions of the licence, and so committed an offence under the Act,[a35] then that person would, under the law relating to illegal contracts, not be entitled to enforce the contract; the other party's ability to enforce it would depend on the degree of his knowledge of or complicity in the failure. Conversely, if that other party committed the offence of cheating contrary to s.42 of the Act, then that other party would not be entitled to enforce the contract, though the victim of the offence might be able to do so. Where the gambling amounts to an offence because it is between the holder of a licence and a child or young person, any money paid (*e.g.* by way of stake) by the child or young person must be returned to the child or young person,[a36] even (it seems) to a young person who is himself guilty of an offence by gambling[a37]; and the provider of the facilities for gambling "may not give a prize to the child or young person."[a38] It follows from this last provision that the contract under which the prize is to be given is not enforceable by the child or young person. A further possible ground of unlawfulness under the 2005 Act lies in the provision of credit for gambling. In this respect, the Act maintains the policy of some of the earlier gaming legislation,[a39] which it will repeal,[a40] to restrict the giving of such credit. For example, it provides that an operating licence may restrict the giving of credit "in connection with the licensed activities"[a41]; and that certain premises licences shall be subject to the condition that the licensee does not "give credit in connection with gambling authorised by the licence."[a42] Failure to comply with such a condition would be an offence under the Act.[a43] It is also an offence under the Act to supply, install or make available for use a gaming machine which is designed or adapted to permit money to be paid by means of a credit card.[a44] In the first two cases, it follows that the licensee could not enforce the terms of the credit against the person to whom it had been granted; and it is arguable that the illegality of the loan would also infect the gambling transaction itself. The latter argument could also be available in the third case, though it would not affect the legal relations between the cardholder and the issuer of the card (assuming the issuer to be a person other than the licensee). A premises licence must also be subject to the condition that the premises shall not be used for gambling on Christmas Day.[a45] Such gambling would therefore be unlawful and contracts relating to it unenforceable.

Unlawfulness of a contract relating to gambling can also result from rules of law other than those contained in the 2005 Act: *e.g.* where the gambling was prohibited by other rules of law, or where the event on which the outcome of a bet depended involved the commission of an illegal act, whether by one or more of the parties to the bet or by one of the participants in the gaming on which the bet was placed. In such cases, the contract would be invalid, not because it related to gambling, but because it could be said to encourage breaches of the law. It is submitted that the same reasoning could apply where the unlawfulness arose because the conduct in question, though not contrary to law, was contrary to public policy on grounds other than the mere fact that it related to gambling. This was the position at common law before the Gaming Acts of 1710, 1835, 1845 and 1892. As explained in para.40–017 of the Main Work, at common law wagers were generally valid but a wager could not be enforced if enforcement was "against sound policy"[a46]: *e.g.* because it tended to cause public disorder.[a47] While the repeal by the Gambling Act 2005 of earlier legislation invalidating wagering contracts will not of itself restore the earlier common law rules,[a48] the wording of s.335(2) will, it is submitted, leave it open to the courts to develop grounds of public policy on which they could refuse to enforce contracts relating to gambling; again, the reason for such refusals would be, not that the contract related to gambling, but that its enforcement would be contrary to public policy on some other ground. In relation to the example given above,[a49] of a wager causing public disorder, it should be emphasised that the first of the "licensing objectives" stated in s.1(a) of the 2005 Act is "preventing gambling from being a source of crime or disorder, being associated with crime or disorder or being used to support crime." It is submitted that a contract which tended to subvert any part of this objective should not be enforceable by virtue of s.335(1) but should be denied enforceability by virtue of s.335(2). In the case of most commercial gambling, a contract which had such a tendency would in all probability involve the breach of a condition of the relevant licence and so amount to an offence under the Act. But the scope of s.335 is quite general: it applies not only to commercial gambling, but also to gambling which is not subject to any licensing requirements, such as private and non-commercial gambling.[a50] The court may thus not only enforce contracts relating to such gambling, but also refuse to enforce them on the ground of "unlawfulness" (not relating specifically to gambling).

[a34] See para.829 of the Explanatory Notes; for further discussion of this Note, see below, para.40–A006 of this Supplement.
[a35] Gambling Act 2005, ss.33(2), 37(2).
[a36] *ibid.*, ss.58, 83(1)(a).
[a37] *ibid.*, s.48.
[a38] *ibid.*, s.83(1)(b).
[a39] Especially Gaming Act 1710, s.1 and Gaming Act 1968, s.16.
[a40] Above, para.40–A001 of this Supplement.
[a41] Gambling Act 2005, s.81(2)(a); see also s.81(2)(b).
[a42] *ibid.*, s.177(2)(a).
[a43] *ibid.*, ss.33(1) and (2), 37(1) and (2).
[a44] *ibid.*, s.245.
[a45] *ibid.*, s.183.
[a46] *Good v Elliott* (1790) 3 T.R. 693 at 695.
[a47] *Eltham v Kingsman* (1818) 1 B. & Ald. 683.
[a48] See Interpretation Act 1979, s.16.
[a49] At n.47.
[a50] See Gambling Act 2005, ss.33(1)(b)(v) and (vi), 37(7).

40–A006   **Scope of s.335(2).** The grounds on which the courts may refuse to enforce a contract relating to gambling are by no means exhaustively stated in s.335(2). That subsection states only *one* such ground, *i.e.* unlawfulness (other than a rule relating specifically to gambling). Enforcement may also be refused on other grounds, such as the failure of the parties to reach agreement, lack of contractual intention, invalidating causes such as mistake, misrepresentation or duress, and any other ground on which a contract may be void, voidable or unenforceable irrespective of its being a contract relating to gambling. The Explanatory Note to s.335, indeed, includes among its illustrative list of rules that prevent "enforcement on the grounds of unlawfulness" not only "illegality" but also "lack of intention" and "mistake".[a51] It is, however, respectfully submitted that to regard "lack of intention" or "mistake" as illustrations of "unlawfulness" is, to say the least, unusual; and that it may be misleading when the exact legal effects of such factors fall to be considered. The possibility that enforcement may be refused on account of these factors, and of other factors such as those listed above in this paragraph, follows, not from the exception to enforceability contained in s.335(2), but from the negative language of s.335(1).[a52] The subsection does not say that contracts relating to gambling are enforceable; it says only that the fact of a contract's being so related does not prevent its enforcement. Where the contract is affected by some invalidating cause such as those listed above, it simply does not fall within the scope of s.335(1). The same is, *a fortiori*, true where the alleged contract is impugned for lack of intention, *e.g.* because it contains an "honour" or similar clause, as appears to be common in the case of agreements between football pool promoters and participants in such betting.[a53] In such cases there is simply no "contract" which could be made enforceable by virtue of s.335(1).

[a51] Explanatory Note, para.829.
[a52] See above, para.40–A004 of this Supplement.
[a53] See Main Work paras 40–003 and Vol.I, para.2–157.

Voiding a bet. Section 336 of the 2005 Act will confer on the Gambling **40–A007** Commission[a54] power, in certain cases,[a55] to make an order that any contract or other arrangement in relation to a bet is to be void, if the Commission is "satisfied that the bet was substantially unfair".[a56] The power is exercisable in relation to a bet accepted by or through the holder of (a) a general operating licence, (b) a pool betting licence, or (c) a betting intermediary licence.[a57] It is thus restricted to commercial gambling and so does not, for example, extend to private and non-commercial gaming or betting.[a58] The effects of an order under s.336 are that (a) any contract or other arrangement in relation to the bet is void, and (b) that any money paid in relation to the bet (whether by way of stake, winnings, commission or otherwise) must be repaid to the payor.[a59] In deciding whether a bet is "unfair" the Commission is required to take account of any of a list of factors (set out in s.336(4)) that applies to the case in question. The list is not intended to be exhaustive[a60]; it includes "the fact that either party to the bet supplied insufficient, false or misleading information in connection with it".[a61] An order under s.336 can be made only within six months of the beginning of the day on which the bet is determined[a62]; but where the circumstance which makes the bet unfair would also amount to a factor vitiating the contract under general principles of law, a party to the contract could rely on that circumstance even after the expiry of the six month period by way of defence to an action on the bet under s.335. This follows from the discussion in paras 40–A005 and 40–A006 of "unlawfulness" and other grounds on which the court may refuse to enforce a contract relating to gambling. This reasoning would also apply where the contract was one in respect of which no order under s.336 could be made: *e.g.* because the contract related to private gaming or betting. An order under s.336 may relate to the whole or any part of a betting transaction[a63] and may make incidental provisions about other parts of a transaction one part of which is made void by the order,[a64] and about related bets.[a65] Any order made by the Commission under s.336 is subject to appeal to the Gambling Appeals Tribunal[a66] from which a further appeal lies on a point of law to the High Court with leave of the Tribunal or the court.[a67]

An order under s.336 will no doubt normally be sought by the party to the contract who is prejudiced by the unfairness of the bet. But nothing in the section limits the power of the Commission to cases in which the order is sought by that person. On the contrary, s.338 suggests that the Commission may act on its own initiative in this respect. That section applies "where the Commission has reason to suspect that it may wish to make an order under section 336(1) in respect of a bet"[a68] and empowers the Commission in such a case to make an "interim moratorium" order by which an obligation to pay money in relation to the bet ceases to have effect for 14 days.[a69] It seems also to be possible for an order under s.336 to be made on the application of a third party who might be prejudiced by the enforcement of, or the retention of money paid under, the bet.[a70]

[a54] Created by Gambling Act 2005, s.20.
[a55] See below, after n.56.
[a56] *ibid.*, s.336(3).
[a57] *ibid.*, s.336(1).
[a58] Within Pt 14 of the 2005 Act (ss.295–302).
[a59] *ibid.*, s.336(2).
[a60] See the words "in particular" in the opening phrase of s.336(4).
[a61] s.336(4)(a).
[a62] s.336(5).
[a63] s.337(2).
[a64] s.337(3)(a).
[a65] s.337(3)(b).
[a66] Established by s.140.
[a67] s.143.
[a68] s.338(1).
[a69] ss.338(2), (3); the time can be extended: s.338(4).
[a70] *e.g.* by the victim of a theft of money used by the thief for gambling: see below, para.40–083 of this Supplement.

1. DEFINITIONS

(a) *Wagering Contracts*

Wagering contract defined

40–001   [*Add to note 1: page* [1115]]
The definition of "wagering contract" quoted in para.40–001 of the Main Work was formulated for the purposes of s.18 of the Gaming Act 1845. This definition will be made obsolete by the repeal of s.18 by the Gambling Act 2005: see above, para.40–A001 of this Supplement. The 2005 Act does not use the expressions "wagering contract" or wager. For the meaning of "gambling" in the 2005 Act, see above, para.40–A003.

Future uncertain event

[Add to note 3: page [1116]]

Some of the elements of the common law definition of a wagering contract are reflected in the definition of "betting" in s.9 of the Gambling Act 2005.

40–002

No other interest

[Add to note 18: page [1117]]

The rules stated in s.4(2) of the Marine Insurance Act 1906 and in the Marine Insurance (Gambling Policies) Act 1909 appear not to be affected by the Gambling Act 2005: see above, para.40–A003.

40–005

(b) *Gaming Contracts*

Statutory definitions

[Add to note 56: page [1121]]

The Gaming Act 1968 will be repealed by the Gambling Act 2005: above, para.40–A001. Elements of the definition quoted in the Main Work at n.56 are reflected in the definitions of "gaming" and "game of chance" in s.6 of the 2005 Act. The basic concept of "gaming" remains "playing a game of chance for a prize" (s.6(1)). The other legislation cited in para.40–014 of the Main Work is also (except for the National Lottery Act 1993) repealed by the 2005 Act.

40–014

Lawful and unlawful gaming

[Add at end of paragraph: page [1121]]

For the repeal of the Gaming Act 1968, see above, para.40–A001 of this Supplement; for the principal categories of cases in which gambling will be unlawful under the Gambling Act 2005, see *ibid.*, para.40–A002.

40–015

2. Effects of Gaming and Wagering Contracts

(a) *Enforcement*

Under the Gaming Act 1845, s.18

[Add new text after note 76: page [1123]]

The repeal of s.18 of the Gaming Act 1845 by the Gambling Act 2005 will make the discussion in paras 40–018—40–024 of the Main Work obsolete: see above, para.40–A001.

40–018

Excepted transactions

[Add to note 96: page [1125]]

The reference in s.412 of the Financial Services and Markets Act 2000 to s.18 of the Gaming Act 1845 is to be deleted by ss.334(1)(e) and 356 and Sch.17 of

40–025

the Gambling Act 2005 but without change of substance since under s.335(1) contracts which relate to gambling will, in general, be enforceable: see above, para.40–A004 of this Supplement.

Distance contracts

40–026   [*Add to note 97: page* [1125]]
For amendments of the Consumer Protection (Distance Selling) Regulations 2000, see above, Vol.I, para.2–026.

(b) *Recovery Back Money Paid*

Gaming Act 1845 s.18

40–029   [*Add to note 107: page* [1126]]
The repeal of s.18 of the Gaming Act 1845 by the Gambling Act 2005 (see above, para.40–A001) will make the reasoning of para.4–029 of the Main Work obsolete. Money paid under a contract relating to gambling will continue to be irrecoverable, but on the different ground that the payment was made under a valid contract. Where the gambling contract is illegal or defective in some other way, the right (if any) to recover money paid under it will be governed by the general rules of law relating to the recovery of money under illegal or otherwise defective contracts.

Overpayment

40–030   [*Add to note 113: page* [1127]]
The reasoning of *Morgan v Ashcroft* [1938] 1 K.B. 49 (Main Work, Vol.I, para.29–038) will be undermined by the repeal of s.18 of the Gambling Act 1845 by the Gambling Act 2005 (see above para.40–A001) and by the enforceability (in general) of contracts relating to gambling by virtue of s.335(1) of the 2005 Act (see above, para.40–A004). After these developments, there seems to be no reason why the normal rules relating to the recovery of overpayments made under valid contracts (*e.g.* under a mistake) should not apply to overpayments made under gambling contracts.

(c) *Recovering Back Money or Property Deposited*

Lawful wagers

40–032   [*Add to note 122: page* [1127]]
The reasoning of *Universal Stock Exchange v Strachan* [1896] A.C. 166, in so far as it is based on the voidness of the debt, will become obsolete when contracts relating to gaming become generally enforceable by virtue of s.335(1) of the Gambling Act 2005 (above, para.40–A004). The same is true of other parts of the reasoning of para.40–032 of the Main Work so far as they are based on the assumption that the wagering contract is void.

(d) *Principal and Agent*

[Add new paragraph 40–032A before paragraph 40–033: page [1128]]

Gambling Act 2005. The agency situations discussed in Main Work paras 40–033—40–039 will generally give rise to enforceable contracts as contracts related to gambling by virtue of the Gambling Act 2005, s.335(1), above para.40–A004 of this Supplement. The provisions of the Gaming Acts 1845 and 1892 discussed in the above paragraphs of the Main Work are to be repealed by the Gambling Act 2005: see above, para.40–A001.

40–032A

Excepted transactions

[Add to note 143: page [1130]]

Section 412 of the Financial Services and Markets Act 2000 is to be amended, but without change of substance, by the Gambling Act 2005, ss.334(1)(e) and 356 and Sch.17: see above, para.40–025 of this Supplement.

40–041

(e) *Partnership*

Partnership for betting

[Add to note 147: page [1130]]

A partnership for betting will generally be an enforceable contract as a contract related to gambling by virtue of the Gambling Act, 2005, s.335(1), above para.40–A004 of this Supplement. Section 1 of the Gaming Act 1892 is to be repealed by the 2005 Act (see above, para.40–A001).

40–042

(f) *Stakeholders*

Gaming Act 1845, s.18

[Page [1131]]

A contract with a stakeholder for the purposes of gambling will generally be enforceable as a contract related to gambling by virtue of the Gambling Act 2005, s.335(1), above, para.40–A004 of this Supplement. Section 18 of the Gaming Act 1845 is to be repealed by the 2005 Act, above, para.40–A001 of this Supplement.

40–044

Gaming Act 1892, s.1

[Page [1131]]

Section 1 of the Gaming Act 1892 is to be repealed by the Gambling Act 2005, above para.40–001A of this Supplement.

40–045

(g) *Prizes for Lawful Games*

Gaming Act 1845, s.18

40–047   *[Page* [1132]]
Section 18 of the Gaming Act 1845 is to be repealed by Gambling Act 2005, see above, para.40–A001 of this Supplement; but the policy of the third limb of s.18 of the 1845 Act is maintained by s.339 of the 2005 Act. This section provides that "participating in a competition or other arrangement under which a person may win a prize is not gambling for the purposes of this Act unless it is" gaming, participating in a lottery, or betting within specified other provisions of the Act. Such prize *competitions* are to be distinguished from prize *gaming*, which is regulated by Pt 13 (ss.288–294) of the 2005 Act.

(h) *Securities*

In general

40–048   *[Add to note 161: page* [1132]]
By virtue of s.335(1) of the Gambling Act 2005 contracts relating to gambling will, as a general rule, be enforceable (see above, para.40–A004 of this Supplement). It follows that if the loser gives the winner a cheque in payment, an action can be brought on the cheque no less than on the bet. If, however, a debt is incurred in relation to gambling in violation of the restrictions on the giving of credit imposed by the terms of a licence (see s.81 of the 2005 Act) or by virtue of the Act itself (see *ibid.*, s.177), then the contract by which credit was given would not be enforceable on the ground of unlawfulness (see s.335(2), above para.40–A005 of this Supplement) and the creditor would not be able to enforce the security any more than the contract under or in respect of which it was given.

Excepted transactions

40–050   *[Add to note 166: page* [1133]]
For amendment of the legislation referred to in n.166, see above, paras 40–025 and 40–041 of this Supplement. In line 3 of the text of para.40–050, substitute "1845" for "1945"; for the repeal of s.18 of the Gaming Act 1845, see above, para.40–A001 of this Supplement.

Gaming wagers and wagers on games

40–051   *[Page* [1133]]
For the repeal of the Gaming Acts 1710, 1835 and 1968, see above, para.40–A001 of this Supplement.

Gaming Acts 1710 and 1835

40–052   *[Page* [1133]]
For the repeal of the Gaming Acts 1710 and 1835, see above, para.40–A001 of this Supplement. It should be noted that the Act of 1710 referred not only to

securities given for money won by gaming, etc., but also to securities for repaying money lent in connection with gaming. Where the loan contravenes the restrictions on the giving of credit imposed by or under the Gambling Act 2005 (see ss.81, 177) the reasoning in para.40–048 of this Supplement will apply, so that neither the loan nor the security will be enforceable: see s.335(2) of the 2005 Act (above, para.40–A005 of this Supplement). This reasoning would not apply to the gambling contract itself or to a security given in respect of losses incurred under it, so that these would be enforceable by virtue of s.335(1) of the 2005 Act (above, para.40–A004 of this Supplement).

Securities for loans to pay debts already lost

[*Page* [1134]]   **40–053**
For "debts" in the heading to this paragraph, substitute "bets". For the repeal of the Gaming Acts 1710, 1835 and 1892, see above para.40–A001 of this Supplement. These repeals will make the reasoning of para.40–053 of the Main Work obsolete; but neither the contract of loan nor the security could be enforced if the loan contravened the restrictions on the giving of credit imposed by the Gambling Act 2005: see above, para.40–052 of this Supplement.

Securities for loans of gaming chips

[*Page* [1134]]   **40–054**
For the repeal of the Gaming Acts 1710, 1835, 1845 and 1968, see above para.40–A001 of this Supplement, making the reasoning of para.40–054 of the Main Work obsolete; the reasoning of para.40–053 of this Supplement will, *mutatis mutandis*, apply.

New promise to pay

[*Page* [1135]]   **40–056**
The repeal of the Gaming Acts 1710, 1835 and 1845 (see above, para. 40–A001 of this Supplement) will make the reasoning of para.40–056 of the Main Work obsolete.

Gaming Act 1968, s.16

[*Add new text after note 192: page* [1135]]   **40–057**
For the repeal of the Gaming Act 1968, see above, para.40–A001 of this Supplement.

(i) *Loans in General*

Introductory

[*Page* [1136]]   **40–059**
The discussion of loans related to gaming in paras 40–059—40–076 is largely based on cases concerned with the effects on such loans of the Gaming Acts

1710, 1835, 1845 and 1892. The repeal of those Acts (above, para.40–A001 of this Supplement) will make most of that discussion obsolete. Under s.335(1) of the Gambling Act 2005, contracts relating to gambling are, in general, enforceable (see above, para.40–A004 of this Supplement); but under s.335(2) enforcement of such contracts may be refused on the ground of "unlawfulness" (see above, para.40–A005 of this Supplement). Thus if the gambling itself is carried on in contravention of the Act and amounts to an offence under it, the common law principle, that a loan made to enable a person to play an illegal game is irrecoverable, will continue to apply (see Main Work, para.40–059 at n.201). Where the loan itself amounts to the giving of credit in contravention of the 2005 Act (see ss.81, 177), the unlawfulness of the loan will be a ground for refusing its enforcement. Where the loan is not affected by such (or any other) unlawfulness, the giving of a security in respect of it will no longer affect the enforceability of the loan.

[*Add to note 202: page* [1136]]
For amendment of this legislation (Financial Services and Markets Act 2000, s.412), but without change of substance, see above paras 40–025 and 40–041 of this Supplement.

(j) *Loans for Gaming on Licensed Premises*

Gaming Act 1968, s.16

40–077   [*Add new text: page* [1142]]
For the repeal of the Gaming Act 1968, s.16 by the Gambling Act 2005, see above, para.40–A001 of this Supplement; this repeal will make the discussion in Main Work, paras 40–077—40–080 obsolete. For restrictions on credit for gambling under the Gambling Act 2005, see above, paras 40–048 and 40–052 of this Supplement.

(k) *Gambling with Stolen Money*

(i) *Illegal Wagers*

Stolen money used to pay losses under illegal wagers

40–082   [*Add to note 248: page* [1144]]
In so far as the outcome of *Clarke v Shee and Johnson* (1774) 1 Cowp. 197 was based on the ground that the recipient of the stolen money had provided no consideration for the payment of it to him because his promise to the thief was void on the ground of illegality, that reasoning is not affected by the Gambling Act 2005; see further below, para.40–083 of this Supplement.

(ii) *Lawful Wagers*

Stolen money used to pay losses under lawful wagers

40–083   [*Add at end: page* [1144]]
The reasoning of *Lipkin Gorman v Karpnale Ltd*[250a] will be undermined by the repeal of s.18 of the Gaming Act 1845 by the Gambling Act 2005[250b] and by the

provision of s.335(1) of the latter Act that "the fact that a contract relates to gambling shall not prevent its enforcement".[250c] Since on such facts the club will be bound by its promise to pay his winnings to Cass (the thief of the money), that promise would, unless defective for some reason other than that it was contained in a contract relating to gambling, bind the club; it would therefore constitute consideration for the payment of the money to the club. The assumption on which this view is based is that the gambling was lawful. If it was unlawful, *e.g.* because the club lacked a requisite licence or had failed to comply with a condition of its licence, then its promise would be illegal and void,[250d] so that in such a case the reasoning of the *Lipkin Gorman* case would still apply.

The further question arises whether that reasoning would also still apply where it was arguable that the bet was "unfair" so that the Gambling Commission could make an order under s.336 of the 2005 Act, that any contract or other arrangement in relation to the bet was to be void and that any money paid in relation to the bet was to be repaid.[250e] It is submitted that the possibility that such an order might be made would not deprive the club's promise of its potential of constituting consideration for the payment. The power to make the order is discretionary[250f] so that there can be no certainty of its being exercised. The club's promise may then be of doubtful value but this is not sufficient to negative the possibility of its amounting to consideration.[250g] Moreover, the power to make an order under s.336 is exercisable only for six months after the determination of the bet[250h]; and, if no attempt were made during that time to obtain such an order, there would be no doubt that the club's promise (unless it were otherwise defective) would then constitute consideration for the payment to it of the stolen money. Where the bet is indeed unfair, there may, however, be a mechanism under the Act by which the victim of the theft can indirectly secure the return of the stolen money, or at least of part of it. It has been suggested in para.40–A007 of this Supplement that there is nothing in s.336 which expressly restricts the power to apply for an order under the section to the parties of the bet. If this is right, an application for such an order could be made by the victim of the theft. The effect of the order (in cases of the present kind) would be that any money paid in relation to the bet "shall be repaid to the person who paid it and repayment may be enforced as a debt by that person".[250i] The person entitled to repayment would indeed be the thief, but the victim of the theft would then have a civil claim against the thief for the restitution of the stolen money. It is an open question whether such a claim would be a proprietary claim or a personal one (under which the victim of the theft would rank equally with the thief's other creditors). In this respect, the claim against the thief could be less advantageous to the victim than the claim against the club was in the *Lipkin Gorman* case.[250j] On the other hand, in a restitution claim against the thief the partial defence of change of position *by the club*, that prevailed in the *Lipkin Gorman* case[250k] would not be available to the thief since that defence is not available to a defendant who has changed his position in bad faith.[250l] Nor would change of position by the club afford it a partial defence to an order to make repayment (if the bet is unfair) under s.336. Such repayment "may be enforced as a debt due to that person"[250m] (*i.e.* the payer of the money). In actions for the recovery of a debt there is no defence of change of position; and even if there were such a defence it would not be available to the recipient of a payment who was responsible for the unfairness of the bet.[250n] In this respect the rights of the victim of the theft against the thief might actually be more favourable to him, if he could invoke s.336, than his rights against the club were in the *Lipkin Gorman* case.

250a [1991] 2 A.C. 548.
250b See above, para.40–A001 of this Supplement.
250c See above, paras 40–A004 and 40–A006 of this Supplement.
250d See above, para.40–A005 of this Supplement.
250e See above, para.40–A007 of this Supplement.
250f s.336(1) begins with the words "The Commission *may* make an order . . . ".
250g *cf.* above, Vol.I, para.3–051.
250h Gambling Act 2005, s.336(5).
250i *ibid.*, s.336(2)(b).
250j Above, n.250a.
250k Main Work, para.40–087.
260l *ibid.*, Vol.I, para.29–183.
260m Gambling Act 2005, s.336(2)(b).
250n The reasoning at n.above would apply by way of analogy.

(l) *Gaming Chips*

Gaming chips treated as money

40–088   *[Page [1147]]*

The discussion in Main Work, para.40–088 will be rendered obsolete by the repeal by the Gambling Act 2005 of the Gaming Acts 1710, 1892 and 1968 (above para.40–A001 of this Supplement) and of other legislation indirectly referred to in that discussion; and by the general principle stated in s.335(1) of the 2005 Act making contracts related to gambling enforceable (above, para. 40–A004 of this Supplement).

CHAPTER 41

INSURANCE

			PARA.
	1.	The nature of insurance	41–001
☐	2.	Insurable interest	41–003
■	3.	The event insured against	41–016
		(a) The nature of the event	41–017
☐		(b) The time of the event	41–022
		(c) The place of the event	41–024
■		(d) The nature of the loss or damage	41–025
☐	4.	*Uberrima fides*	41–028
☐	5.	The parties	41–039
☐	6.	The contract of insurance	41–044
■	7.	Conditions and warranties	41–052
	8.	Assignment	41–060
☐	9.	Claims	41–063
■	10.	The rights of the insurer upon payment	41–081
■	11.	Specific types of insurance contract	41–087
☐		(a) Liability insurance	41–088
☐		(b) Motor insurance	41–091
☐		(c) Reinsurance	41–094
■		(d) Insurance against financial loss	41–096
		(e) Fire insurance	41–098
		(f) Life insurance	41–099
		(g) Marine insurance	41–100

2. INSURABLE INTEREST

Definition of insurable interest

[*Update note 24: page* [1152]]   **41–004**
O'Kane v Jones is now reported at [2004] 1 Lloyd's Rep. 389.

The relevance of the risk of financial loss

[*Update note 31: page* [1153]]   **41–005**
O'Kane v Jones is now reported at [2004] 1 Lloyd's Rep. 389.

Types of insurable interest

[*Delete "but only in the event insured against" from note 46 and substitute: page*   **41–006**
[*1154*]]
but only in the profits or the subject matter lost

Insurance of another's interest

41–008 [*Add to note 77 after the first sentence: page* [1156]]
Indeed, the assured may insure another as an undisclosed principal, provided that the insurer is willing to contract with an undisclosed principal: *Talbot Underwriting Ltd v Nausch Hogan & Murray (The Jascon 5)* [2006] EWCA Civ 889; [2006] 2 Lloyd's Rep. 195.

[*Add to the end of note 81*]
cf. *Talbot Underwriting Ltd v Nausch Hogan & Murray (The Jascon 5)* [2006] EWCA Civ 889; [2006] 2 Lloyd's Rep. 195.

[*Add to the end of note 88: page* [1157]]
Ramco (UK) Ltd v International Insurance Co of Hannover Ltd [2004] EWCA Civ 675; [2004] 2 Lloyd's Rep. 595 at [8].

[*Add to the end of note 89*]
Ramco (UK) Ltd v International Insurance Co of Hannover Ltd [2004] EWCA Civ 675; [2004] 2 Lloyd's Rep. 595.

[*Add to the end of note 90*]
Ramco (UK) Ltd v International Insurance Co of Hannover Ltd [2004] EWCA Civ 675; [2004] 2 Lloyd's Rep. 595.

[*Add to the end of note 91*]
BP Exploration Operating Co Ltd v Kvaerner Oilfield Products Ltd [2004] EWHC 999 (Comm); [2005] 1 Lloyd's Rep. 307.

Life Assurance Act 1774

41–012 [*Update note 107: page* [1159]]
O'Kane v Jones is now reported at [2004] 1 Lloyd's Rep. 389.

The Marine Insurance Act 1906

41–014 [*Update note 123: page* [1160]]
O'Kane v Jones is now reported at [2004] 1 Lloyd's Rep. 389.

3. THE EVENT INSURED AGAINST

(b) *The Time of the Event*

Event and loss during period of cover

41–023 [*Add to the end of note 180: page* [1166]]
In *Bolton Metropolitan Borough Council v Municipal Mutual Insurance Ltd* [2006] EWCA Civ 50; [2006] 1 W.L.R. 1492, the Court of Appeal held that in respect of a claim relating to mesothelioma under a public liability policy

insuring against "injury" which took place during the policy period, the "injury" took place when the disease first occurred or manifested itself, not when the body was first exposed to asbestos.

(d) *The Nature of the Loss or Damage*

Nature of loss

[Add at the end of note 188: page [1167]]   **41–025**
Horbury Building Systems Ltd v Hampden Insurance NV [2004] EWCA Civ 418; [2004] 2 C.L.C. 453 at [13]–[27].

[Add at end of note 194: page [1168]]
affd. [2004] EWCA Civ 277; [2004] Lloyd's Rep. I.R. 481.

4. *UBERRIMA FIDES*

Utmost good faith

[Note 206: page [*1169*]]   **41–028**
Update reference to *Good Faith and Insurance Contracts* to (2nd ed., 2004).

The duty to disclose material facts

[Add at the end of the first sentence of note 220: page [*1171*]]   **41–029**
Whitlam v Hazel [2004] EWCA Civ 1600; [2005] Lloyd's Rep. I.R. 168.

[Update note 222]
O'Kane v Jones is now reported at [2004] 1 Lloyd's Rep. 389.

[Add at the end of note 223]
Doheny v New India Assurance Co Ltd [2004] EWCA Civ 1705; [2005] Lloyd's Rep. I.R. 251 at [16]–[20].

[Update note 225]
O'Kane v Jones is now reported at [2004] 1 Lloyd's Rep. 389.

[Add at the end of the second sentence of note 226: page [*1172*]]
North Star Shipping Ltd v Sphere Drake Insurance plc [2005] EWHC 665 (Comm); [2005] 2 Lloyd's Rep. 76; [2006] EWCA Civ 378; [2006] 2 Lloyd's Rep. 183; *ERC Frankona Reinsurance v American National Insurance Co* [2005] EWHC 1381 (Comm).

Scope of duty of disclosure

[Add at end of note 231: page [*1172*]]   **41–030**
In order to determine whether a particular person is the assured's agent to know, it is necessary to analyse both the nature of the relationship between that

person and the assured and the nature of the information in question: *ERC Frankona Reinsurance v American National Insurance Co* [2005] EWHC 1381 (Comm) at [132].

[*Add to note 238 at end of first sentence: page* [1173]]
WISE (Underwriting Agency) Ltd v Grupo Nacional Provincial SA [2004] EWCA Civ 962; [2004] 2 Lloyd's Rep. 483; *Doheny v New India Assurance Co Ltd* [2004] EWCA Civ 1705; [2005] Lloyd's Rep. I.R. 251 at [16]–[20].

[*Update note 240: page* [1174]]
O'Kane v Jones is now reported at [2004] 1 Lloyd's Rep. 389.

Time of disclosure

41–031 [*Add at end of the first sentence of note 253: page* [*1175*]]
Swiss Reinsurance Co v United India Insurance Co Ltd [2005] EWHC 237 (Comm); [2005] Lloyd's Rep. I.R. 341 at [35]–[36].

Misrepresentation

41–032 [*Add to note 259, after reference to the Economides case: page* [*1176*]]
Rendall v Combined Insurance Co of America [2005] EWHC 678 (Comm); [2005] 1 C.L.C. 565.

Honesty

41–034 [*Add to note 265, after reference to Merchants' and Manufacturers' Insurance case: page* [*1176*]]
Whitlam v Hazel [2004] EWCA Civ 1600; [2005] Lloyd's Rep. I.R. 168 at [28].

Effect of non-disclosure or misrepresentation

41–035 [*Update note 272: page* [1177]]
Drake Insurance plc v Provident Insurance plc [2003] EWCA Civ 1834 is now reported at [2004] Q.B. 601.

Affirmation

41–036 [*Add to the end of note 287: page* [1179]]
As to the affirmatory effect of a contractual notice of cancellation, see *Mint Security Ltd v Blair* [1982] 1 Lloyd's Rep. 188 at 198; *WISE (Underwriting Agency) Ltd v Grupo Nacional Provincial SA* [2004] EWCA Civ 962; [2004] 2 Lloyd's Rep. 483.

Statements of Insurance Practice

41–038 [*Delete note 301 and substitute: page* [1180]]
For the texts of the latest versions of the Statements of Insurance Practice, see *www.abi.org.uk.*

[*Delete final sentence of paragraph and substitute: page* [1181]]

Although mere statements of practice, the statements provide that they shall be taken into account in arbitration and any other referral procedures.

5. THE PARTIES

The insurer

[*Add note 310a at end of the first sentence: page* [*1182*]]   **41–040**
[310a] See McMeel, "The FSA's insurance conduct of business regime: a revolution in (consumer) insurance law?" [2005] L.M.C.L.Q. 186.

Broker

[*Add to end of note 321: page* [*1183*]]   **41–042**
As to the broker's entitlement to claim commission from either the insurer or the assured, see *Carvill America Inc v Camperdown UK Ltd* [2005] EWCA Civ 645; [2005] 1 C.L.C. 845.

[*Add to note 325 after the reference to Jackson & Powell: page* [1183]]
As to the assumption of a duty of care, see *European International Reinsurance Co Ltd v Curzon Insurance Ltd* [2003] EWCA Civ 1074; [2003] 1 Lloyd's Rep. 793.

Lloyd's

[*Add to note 329 before the final sentence: page* [1184]]   **41–043**
Heath Lambert Ltd v Sociedad de Corretaje de Seguros [2004] EWCA Civ 792; [2004] 1 W.L.R. 2820.

[*Add to the end of note 329*]
Heath Lambert Ltd v Sociedad de Corretaje de Seguros [2006] EWHC 1345 (Comm).

[*Add to the end of note 340: page* [*1186*]]
In *Goshawk Dedicated Ltd v Tyser & Co Ltd* [2006] EWCA Civ 54; [2006] 1 Lloyd's Rep. 566, the Court of Appeal held that there is an implied term in a contract of insurance between an assured and a Lloyd's underwriter that the Lloyd's broker will make available to the underwriter documents previously shown to the underwriter during the placement of the risk or the presentation of a claim; in addition, certain premium accounting documents would be disclosable to the underwriter.

6. THE CONTRACT OF INSURANCE

Open covers and declarations

[*Add at end of note 351: page* [*1187*]]   **41–045**
As regards the insurer's obligations towards his reinsurer in deciding whether or not to accept a risk which would be ceded to the reinsurer, see *Bonner v Cox*

Dedicated Corporate Member Ltd [2004] EWHC 2963 (Comm) at [255]; [2005] EWCA Civ 1512; [2006] 2 Lloyd's Rep. 152 at [85]–[111].

Payment of premium

41–050   [*Add before the final sentence of note 373: page* [*1189*]]
Heath Lambert Ltd v Sociedad de Corretaje de Seguros [2004] EWCA Civ 792; [2004] 1 W.L.R. 2820.

[*Add to the end of note 378: page* [1190]]
As regards the position in respect of marine insurance, see *Heath Lambert Ltd v Sociedad de Corretaje de Seguros* [2004] EWCA Civ 792; [2004] 1 W.L.R. 2820; see above, para.41–043, n.329.

Repayment

41–051   [*Add at the end of note 402: page* [*1192*]]
cf. Swiss Reinsurance Co v United India Insurance Co Ltd [2005] EWHC 237 (Comm); [2005] Lloyd's Rep. I.R. 341.

[*Add at the end of the first sentence of note 403*]
Swiss Reinsurance Co v United India Insurance Co Ltd [2005] EWHC 237 (Comm); [2005] Lloyd's Rep. I.R. 341.

[*Add new paragraph*]

41–051A   **Construction of insurance contracts**. Insurance contracts are subject to the same approach to contractual construction as other commercial contracts, namely that the words of the contract will be interpreted to divine their contextual meaning consistently with the commercial sense and purpose of the policy, even if that is at odds with the literal meaning of the contract.[404a] Therefore, where a word is used in an insurance policy which has a technical, legal connotation, the court will not necessarily infer that the parties intended that meaning and will inquire into the ordinary, commercial meaning to be ascribed to the word.[404b] There is one rule of construction applicable to ordinary contracts which applies with particular force in the context of insurance contracts, namely that *verba chartarum fortius accipiuntur contra proferentem*: *i.e.* where the contractual provision is ambiguous, the provision will be construed against the person who drafts or puts forward the provision, which in many cases will be the insurer.[404c] The construction of contractual terms "against the insurer" is not limited to cases where the insurer has produced the wording. If the insurer seeks to rely on a provision, such as a condition precedent, warranty or an exclusion, so as to extinguish or reduce his or her basic obligations, the court will resist such a construction unless the contractual terms are especially clear.[404d]

[404a] *Sirius International Insurance Co (Publ) v FAI General Insurance Ltd* [2004] UKHL 54; [2004] 1 W.L.R. 3251, at [18]–[19]; *Blackburn Rovers Football & Athletic Club Plc v Avon Insurance Plc* [2005] EWCA Civ 423; [2005] Lloyd's Rep. I.R. 447 at [9].

[404b] *Wooldridge v Canelhas Comercio Importacao e Exportacao Ltda* [2004] EWCA Civ 984; [2005] 1 All E.R. (Comm.) 43 ("robbery"); *cf. Dobson v General Accident Fire & Life Assurance Corp plc* [1990] 1 Q.B. 274 ("theft").

[404c] *Tektrol Ltd v International Insurance Co of Hanover Ltd* [2005] EWCA Civ 845; [2005] 1 All E.R. (Comm.) 132.

[404d] *Tektrol Ltd v International Insurance Co of Hanover Ltd* [2005] EWCA Civ 845; [2005] 1 All E.R. (Comm.) 132; *Royal & Sun Alliance Insurance Plc v Dornoch Ltd* [2005] EWCA Civ 238; [2005] 1 All E.R. (Comm.) 590; *Blackburn Rovers Football & Athletic Club Plc v Avon Insurance Plc* [2005] EWCA Civ 423; [2005] Lloyd's Rep. I.R. 447 at [9].

7. CONDITIONS AND WARRANTIES

Construction of terms

[Add at the end of note 407: page [1193]]
affd. [2004] EWCA Civ 622; [2004] Lloyd's Rep. I.R. 354 at [40]–[46].

41–053

Conditions precedent

[Add to the end of note 412: page [1193]]
As to a claims control clause in a reinsurance policy, see *Eagle Star Insurance Co Ltd v Cresswell* [2004] EWCA Civ 602; [2004] 2 All E.R. (Comm.) 244.

41–054

[Add to the end of note 415: page [1194]]
Whether or not there is a class of insurance term as an innominate term, the breach of which will entitle the insurer to decline the claim as opposed to terminate the contract, is now in doubt, given the Court of Appeal's decision in *Sirius International Insurance Corp v Friends Provident Life & Pensions Ltd* [2005] EWCA Civ 601; [2005] 1 C.L.C. 794, although (putting aside the sense of that decision) it must be questioned whether the Court of Appeal was free to overrule the court's decisions in *Alfred McAlpine v BAI* and *K/S Merc-Scandia v Lloyd's Underwriters*.

[Add to the end of the first sentence of note 416: page [1194]]
Tektrol Ltd v International Insurance Co of Hanover Ltd [2005] EWCA Civ 845; [2005] 1 All E.R. (Comm.) 132; *Royal & Sun Alliance Insurance Plc v Dornoch Ltd* [2005] EWCA Civ 238; [2005] 1 All E.R. (Comm.) 590.

Waiver

[Add to the end of note 435: page [1196]]
Fortisbank SA v Trenwick International Ltd [2005] EWHC 399 (Comm); [2005] Lloyd's Rep. I.R. 464.

41–057

[Delete "there is prejudice to the assured thereby, or" from the penultimate sentence: page [1196]]

9. CLAIMS

Notice of loss

[Add to the end of note 483: page [1201]]
In *Tioxide Europe Ltd v Commercial Union Assurance Co Plc* [2005] EWCA Civ 928; [2005] All ER (D) 281 (Jul.), the relevant notice was given to the wrong

41–064

addressee. For an example of a clause which exercised the court's powers of interpretation, see *Royal & Sun Alliance Insurance Plc v Dornoch Ltd* [2005] EWCA Civ 238.

[*Add to the end of note 486: page* [*1201*]]
See also *Sirius International Insurance Corp v Friends Provident Life & Pensions Ltd* [2005] EWCA Civ 601; [2005] 1 C.L.C. 794, where the Court of Appeal disapproved *Alfred McAlpine v BAI* in so far as it recognised that there might be an innominate term of an insurance contract, the breach of which would entitle the insurer to decline the insurance claim, rather than terminate the contract.

[*Add to the end of note 487*]
As to the impact of prejudice in determining what is a reasonable time, see *Shinedean Ltd v Alldown Demolition (London) Ltd* [2006] EWCA Civ 939.

[*Add to the end of the paragraph*]
There is no rule of law which relieved an assured of the obligation to comply with policy provisions concerning the notification of a claim or loss where the insurer had earlier repudiated liability under the policy on other grounds.[490a]

[490a] *Nasser Diab v Regent Insurance Co Ltd* [2006] UKPC 29.

Details of loss

41–065
[*Add to the end of note 491: page* [1202]]
As to the adequacy of particulars provided by the assured, see *Super Chem Products Ltd v American Life and General Insurance Co Ltd* [2004] UKPC 2; [2004] Lloyd's Rep. I.R. 446 at [28]–[30].

Choice of law

41–068
[*Add to the end of the penultimate sentence of note 511: page* [*1204*]]
Travelers Casualty & Surety Co of Europe Ltd v Sun Life Assurance Co of Canada (UK) Ltd [2004] EWHC 1704 (Comm); [2004] Lloyd's Rep. I.R. 846.

Fraudulent claims

41–069
[*Add to text after the first sentence: page* [*1204*]]
Beyond that simple axiom, the law is currently in an uncertain state.[512a]

[512a] *Interpart Comerciao e Gestao SA v Lexington Insurance Co* [2004] Lloyd's Rep. I.R. 690; *Marc Rich Agriculture Trading SA v Fortis Corporate Insurance NV* [2004] EWHC 2632 (Comm).

[*Add to the end of note 515*]
Axa General Insurance Ltd v Gottlieb [2005] EWCA Civ 112; [2005] Lloyd's Rep. I.R. 369.

[*Add after the second sentence of note 516*]
cf. *Axa General Insurance Ltd v Gottlieb* [2005] EWCA Civ 112; [2005] Lloyd's Rep. I.R. 369.

The burden of proof

[Line 5 of note 528: page [1206]]
The *Kastor Navigation* case was affd., [2004] EWCA Civ 277; [2004] Lloyd's
Rep I.R. 481.

41–070

Multiple Causes

[Add to note 557 before reference to Kuwait Airways case: page [1208]]
Midland Mainline Ltd v Eagle Star Insurance Co Ltd [2004] EWCA Civ 1042;
[2004] 2 Lloyd's Rep. 604.

41–073

The amount recoverable

[Add to the end of note 569: page [1210]]
Thor Navigation Inc v Ingosstrakh Insurance Co Ltd [2005] EWHC 19
(Comm); [2005] 1 Lloyd's Rep. 547.

41–074

Rateable proportion clauses

[Update note 584: page [1211]]
Drake Insurance plc v Provident Insurance plc [2003] EWCA Civ 1834 is now
reported at [2004] Q.B. 601.

41–077

[Update note 585]
Phillips v Syndicate 992 Gunner is now reported at [2004] Lloyd's Rep. I.R.
426.

10. THE RIGHTS OF THE INSURER UPON PAYMENT

Contribution

[Update note 645: page [1217]]
O'Kane v Jones is now reported at [2004] 1 Lloyd's Rep. 389.

41–086

[Update note 647]
O'Kane v Jones is now reported at [2004] 1 Lloyd's Rep. 389.

11. SPECIFIC TYPES OF INSURANCE CONTRACT

(a) *Liability Insurance*

General characteristics

[Delete "s.310 and Companies Act 1989, s.137(1)" from note 661 and substitute:
page [1219]]
ss.309A, 309B and 309C, introduced by the Companies (Audit, Investigations
and Community Enterprise) Act 2004, s.19.

41–088

[Add after the first sentence in note 662: page [1219]]
In *Lumbermens Mutual Casualty Co v Bovis Lend Lease Ltd* [2004] EWHC
2197 (Comm); [2005] Lloyd's Rep. 74, the court held that a liability will not be
established by a settlement agreement where that settlement agreement does not
identify the specific cost of discharging the liability in question. Accordingly,
where under a global settlement agreement, the assured agreed to receive, not
pay, a single sum in settlement of all claims and counterclaims, the assured's
liability for the counterclaims was held not to have been established and extrinsic
evidence could not be adduced for that purpose. This proposition is questionable.
The decision in *Lumbermens* was subjected to a disapproving critique in *Enterprise Oil Ltd v Strand Insurance Co Ltd* [2006] EWHC 58 (Comm); [2006] 1
Lloyd's Rep. 500 at [150]–[175].

[Add to the end of note 663]
cf. *Sun Life Assurance Co of Canada v Lincoln National Life Insurance Co*
[2004] EWCA Civ 1660; [2005] 1 Lloyd's Rep. 606.

Employers' liability

41–089 *[Delete note 666 and substitute: page [1219]]*
Employers' Liability (Compulsory Insurance) Regulations 1998 (SI
1998/2573). As to reg.3, see *R (on the application of Geologistics Ltd) v
Financial Services Compensation Scheme* [2003] EWCA Civ 1877; [2004]
Lloyd's Rep. I.R. 336, at [20]–[22].

Statutory assignment

41–090 *[Delete the reference to Tarbuck case from note 669 and substitute: page [1220]]*
In the matter of *OT Computers Ltd (in administration)* [2004] EWCA Civ 653;
[2004] 2 All E.R. (Comm.) 331; *Freakley v Centre Reinsurance International Co*
[2005] EWCA Civ 115; [2005] Lloyd's Rep. I.R. 303.

[Add to note 672 before 2nd sentence]
See *Centre Reinsurance International Co v Curzon Insurance Ltd* [2004]
EWHC 200 (Ch); [2004] 2 All E.R. (Comm.) 28.

(b) *Motor Insurance*

Road Traffic Act 1988

41–091 *[Add to note 681 after first sentence: page [1221]]*
cf. *Slater v Buckinghamshire County Council* [2004] Lloyd's Rep. I.R. 432.

[Add to the end of note 690: page [1222]]
The defendant to a claim for damages for personal injury is not entitled to
counterclaim for a breach of this statutory duty for purely economic losses in
connection with the defendant's liability to the claimant, as opposed to the
defendant's own injuries: *Bretton v Hancock* [2005] EWCA Civ 404; [2005]
Lloyd's Rep. I.R. 454 at [42]–[50].

Third parties and uninsured drivers

[Delete note 703 and substitute: page [1223]] **41-093**
The current agreement dated August 13, 1999 (and called "Compensation of Victims of Uninsured Drivers"), is between the M.I.B. and the Secretary of State for the Environment, Transport and the Regions, and applies to claims arising on or after October 1, 1999. It is effectively based upon the original 1945 agreement, with subsequent agreements in 1946, 1971, 1972 and 1988. A more complex scheme (first introduced in 1969) covers the position of untraced drivers. This is now governed by the Untraced Drivers Agreement dated February 14, 2003, the immediate predecessor to which was the 1996 Agreement. The M.I.B.'s liability under the 2003 Agreement is dependent on establishing that the untraced driver would have been liable to the victim and that that liability is of a kind required to be covered by compulsory insurance under the Road Traffic Act 1988. Applicants for compensation under these agreements, however, cannot rely on the doctrine of direct effect in the event that there is any shortfall in the cover provided by them and the cover required to be legislated by the United Kingdom by EC Directives 72/166, 84/5 and 90/232: *Evans v Motor Insurers' Bureau* [1999] Lloyd's Rep. I.R. 30. However, in *Evans v Secretary of State for the Environment, Transport and the Regions* [2001] EWCA Civ 32; [2002] Lloyd's Rep. I.R. 1 at [4], the Court of Appeal indicated that the victim might have the right to enforce the Agreement pursuant to the Contracts (Rights of Third Parties) Act 1999. Clause 31(5) of the Untraced Drivers Agreement dated February 14, 2003, confirms that the Agreement is intended to benefit the victim. As to the level of compensation obtainable under the agreements, see *Evans v Secretary of State for the Environment, Transport and the Regions* (Case C-63/01) [2004] Lloyd's Rep. I.R. 391 (ECJ). As to the relationship between the M.I.B. and the Secretary of State, see *Sharp v Pereira* [1999] Lloyd's Rep. I.R. 242.

[Add to the end of note 704: page [1224]]
Phillips v Rafiq [2006] EWHC 1461 at [12], QB.

[Add at end of note 705]
In *Pickett v Motor Insurers Bureau* [2004] EWCA Civ 6; [2004] Lloyd's Rep. I.R. 513, the Court of Appeal considered whether the M.I.B. was liable under the 1988 Agreement where the claimant, who was also the owner of, but a passenger in, the vehicle, knew that the vehicle was uninsured. The court held that the claimant had not withdrawn her consent to be carried in the vehicle because she had not unambiguously required the vehicle to be stopped so that she could get out, thus permitting the M.I.B. to rely on an exception to liability. The 1999 Agreement provides that the relevant knowledge is that of the claimant as opposed to the person suffering the relevant injury, whereas the 1988 Agreement applied the relevant exception to the knowledge of the person who suffered the injury. This distinction proved to be critical in *Phillips v Rafiq* [2006] EWHC 1461 (QB), where the deceased's wife brought the proceedings and was entitled to maintain the claim against the M.I.B. even though her husband was aware that the driver was uninsured.

(c) *Reinsurance*

General characteristics

41–094   [N*ote 709: page* [1224]]
Update reference to *The Law of Reinsurance in England and Bermuda* to (2nd ed., 2004).

[*Add at the end of the second sentence of note 713: page* [1225]]
American International Marine Agency of New York Inc v Dandridge [2005] EWHC 829 (Comm); [2005] All ER (D) 48 (May) ("follow the leader" clause).

[*Add to the end of note 713*]
For a case where the terms of the underlying insurance are summarised in the reinsurance contract itself, see *Toomey v Banco Vitalcio De Espana SA de Seguros y Reaseguros* [2004] EWCA Civ 622; [2005] Lloyd's Rep. I.R. 423.

Liability of the reinsurer

41–095   [*Add to the beginning of note 718: page* [1225]]
CGU International Insurance plc v Astrazeneca Insurance Co Ltd [2005] EWHC 2755 (Comm); [2006] Lloyd's Rep. I.R. 409.

[*Line 4 of note 722: page* [1226]]
Assicurazioni Generali SpA v CGU International Insurance plc was affirmed, [2004] EWCA Civ 429; [2004] 2 Lloyd's Rep. I.R. 457.

(d) *Insurance against Financial Loss*

Types of financial loss insurance

41–096   [*Add to the end of note 733: page* [1227]]
Pilkington United Kingdom Ltd v CGU Insurance plc [2004] EWCA Civ 23; [2004] Lloyd's Rep. I.R. 891.

CHAPTER 42

RESTRICTIVE AGREEMENTS AND COMPETITION

			PARA.
	1.	Introduction	42–001
■	2.	Competition rules under the EC Treaty	42–004
□		(a) In general	42–004
□		(b) Article 81(1)	42–011
□		(c) Article 81(3): Individual and block exemption	42–031
□		(d) Application of Article 81 to specific agreements	42–035
■		(e) Article 82	42–061
□		(f) Enforcement in the national courts	42–065
□		(g) Enforcement at the Community level	42–073
■	3.	United Kingdom competition law	42–077
■		(a) Introduction	42–077
■		(b) The Chapter I Prohibition: agreements	42–084
■		(c) The Chapter II Prohibition: abuse of a dominant position	42–123
■		(d) Market investigations	42–133
■		(e) Investigation and enforcement	42–136
		(f) The Competition Commission	42–144
■		(g) The Competition Appeal Tribunal	42–145
		(h) Miscellaneous	42–146

2. COMPETITION RULES UNDER THE EC TREATY

(a) *In General*

Purpose of this section

[Note 10: page [1233]]
See now Kerse and Khan, *EC Antitrust Procedure* (5th ed., 2005).

42–004

Principal sources of law

[Note 22: page [1234]]
See now *Butterworths Competition Law Handbook* (12th ed., 2006).

42–008

European Economic Area

[Page [1235]]
For the position on the EEA Enlargement Agreement, see *http://secretariat .efta.int/Web/EuropeanEconomicArea/EEAAgreement/eeaenlargementagree ment.*

42–010

(b) *Article 81(1)*

Undertaking

42–013   *[Note 42: page* [1237]]
The CFI's judgment in *FENIN* was upheld on appeal by the ECJ: Case C-205/03, judgment of July 11, 2006.

Effect on trade between Member States

42–027   *[Page* [1242]]
The Commission has published *Guidelines on the effect on trade concept in Articles 81 and 82 of the Treaty*, [2004] O.J. C 101/81.

(c) *Article 81(3)*

Agreements likely to satisfy Article 81(3)

42–032   *[Page* [1243]]
The Commission has published *Guidelines on the application of Article 81(3) of the Treaty*, [2004] O.J. C 101/97.

Block exemptions currently in force

42–034   *[Note 104: page* [1245]]
See now *Butterworths Competition Law Handbook* (12th ed., 2006).

[Note 106]
Regulation 240/96 was replaced, with effect from May 1, 2004, by Regulation 772/2004, [2004] O.J. L 123/11.

(d) *Application of Article 81 to Specific Agreements*

Mergers

42–037   *[Page* [1247]]
Regulation 4064/89 was replaced, with effect from May 1, 2004, by Regulation 139/2004, [2004] O.J. L 24/1.

[Note 136: page [1248]]
See now Cook and Kerse, *EC Merger Control* (4th ed., 2005).

Intellectual property licences

42–054   *[Note 164: page* [1253]]
See now Cornish, *Intellectual Property: Patents, Copyright, Trade Marks and Allied Rights* (5th ed., 2003).

Technology transfer agreements

[*Page* [1254]]
Regulation 240/96 was replaced, with effect from May 1, 2004, by Regulation 772/2004, [2004] O.J. L 123/11. The European Commission has also published *Guidelines on the application of Article 81 of the EC Treaty to technology transfer agreements*: [2004] O.J. C 101/2.

Agency agreements

[*Page* [1255]]
In Case T-325/01 *DaimlerChrysler v Commission*, judgment of September 15, 2005, the CFI annulled a finding of an infringement of Art.81(1) by the Commission because the Commission had incorrectly concluded that DaimlerChrysler's dealers were not agents.

(e) *Article 82*

Examples of abusive contractual provisions

[*Page* [1258]]
One of the abusive practices for which the European Commission fined Microsoft €497 million in March 2004 was that it had made the availability of its *Windows Client PC Operating System* conditional upon the simultaneous acquisition of *Windows Media Player*: *Microsoft* Commission Decision of March 24, 2004; the case is on appeal to the Court of First Instance, Case T-201/04, judgment pending.

Refusal to contract as abusive conduct

[*Page* [1258]]
One of the abusive practices for which the European Commission fined Microsoft €497 million in March 2004 was that it had refused to supply *Interoperability Information* and allow its use for the purpose of developing and distributing work group server operating system products: *Microsoft* Commission Decision of March 24, 2004; the case is on appeal to the Court of First Instance, Case T-201/04, judgment pending.

(f) *Enforcement at the National Level*

Role of the national courts

[*Page* [1258]]
In Cases C-295/04 to C-298/04 *Manfredi*, judgment of July 13, 2006, the ECJ dealt with several questions concerning the rights of third parties to claim damages for harm caused by a prohibited agreement under Art.81.

Effect of the Modernisation Regulation

42–067 [*Add at the end of the paragraph: page* [1259]]
The Commission has published a *Notice on the co-operation between the Commission and the courts of the EU Member States in the application of Articles 81 and 82 EC.*[191a]

[191a] OJ 2004 C 101/54

Causes of action in English law

42–071 [*Add to note 199, at the end: page* [1260]]
The Court of Appeal reversed the judgment of the High Court, and Crehan was awarded damages for the harm he had suffered: [2004] EWCA Civ 637; [2004] E.C.C. 28. Subsequently the House of Lords reversed the judgment of the Court of Appeal, with the result that Crehan's claim for damages was unsuccessful: judgment of July 19, 2006, [2006] UKHL 38; [2006] 3 W.L.R. 148.

Role of national competition authorities

42–072 [*Page* [1260]]
The Commission has published a *Notice on Co-operation within the Network of Competition Authorities*, [2004] O.J. C 101/43.

(g) *Enforcement at the Community Level*

Commission investigations and adverse decisions

42–074 [*Line 12, after "... written and oral rights of defence": page* [1261]]
The Commission has adopted this implementing regulation, Regulation 773/2004, [2004] O.J. L 123/18.

Fines and other remedies

42–076 [*Note 207: page* [1261]]
The Commission has revised the guidelines for the setting of fines in antitrust cases: the new guidelines are available at *http://ec.europa.eu/comm/competition/antitrust/legislation/fines_en.pdf.*

3. UNITED KINGDOM COMPETITION LAW

(a) *Introduction*

Reform of the law

42–077 [*Add, at the end of the paragraph: page* [1262]]
A number of statutory instruments have been adopted to amend the Competition Act in order to make it compatible with the principles of the EC modernisation package. See in particular the Competition Act 1998 and Other Enactments

(Amendment) Regulations 2004[213a]; The Competition Act 1998 (Land Agreements Exclusion and Revocation) Order 2004[213b]; the Competition Act 1998 (Determination of Turnover for Penalties)(Amendment) Order 2004[213c]; and the Competition Act 1998 (Appealable Decisions and Revocation of Notification of Excluded Agreements) Regulations 2004.[213d] A further statutory instrument has been adopted containing the rules of the Office of Fair Trading: see the Competition Act 1998 (Office of Fair Trading's Rules) Order 2004.[213e]

[213a] SI 2004/1261.
[213b] SI 2004/1260.
[213c] SI 2004/1259.
[213d] SI 2004/1078.
[213e] SI 2004/2751.

Guidelines

[Page [1264]]   **42–082**
The Guidelines referred to in the text have been replaced by a fresh set, written in the light of the EC Modernisation Regulation and the consequent changes to the Competition Act 1998: they are available on the website of the OFT, *http://www.oft.gov.uk.*

(b) *The Chapter I Prohibitions: Agreements*

Effect on trade within the United Kingdom

[Add, at the end of sub-paragraph (ii): page [1266]]   **42–087**
The Commission has published *Guidelines on the effect on trade concept in Articles 81 and 82 of the Treaty.*[225a] It has also published a *Notice on cooperation within the network of competition authorities.*[225b]

[225a] [2004] O.J. C 101/81.
[225b] [2004] O.J. C 101/3.

[Add at the end of sub-paragraph (iv)]
The system of notifying agreements for individual exemption has been abolished by the Competition Act 1998 and Other Enactments (Amendment) Regulations 2004.[227a]

[227a] SI 2004/1261.

Agreements, decisions and concerted practices

[Page [1266]]   **42–089**
The OFT's decision in *Hasbro UK Ltd* was upheld on appeal to the Competition Appeal Tribunal, Case Nos. 1014/1/1/03 and 1015/1/1/03 *Argos Ltd and Littlewoods Ltd v OFT* [2004] CAT 24; [2005] Comp.A.R. 588; see similarly Case Nos. 1021/1/1/03 and 1022/1/1/03 *JJB Sports plc v Office of Fair Trading* [2004] CAT 17; [2005] Comp.A.R. 29.

Relevant differences between the Chapter I prohibition and EC law

42–091 [*Page* 1267]]
The exclusion of vertical agreements from the Chap. I prohibition will be repealed with effect from May 1, 2005 as a result of the Competition Act 1998 (Land Agreements Exclusion and Revocation) Order 2004 (SI 2004/1260).

[*Add at the end of sub-paragraph (ii)*]
This is no longer the case since the adoption of the OFT's new Guideline *Agreements and concerted practices* OFT 401, December 2004.

Appreciability

42–092 [*Page* [1268]]
Since the adoption of the OFT's new Guideline *Agreements and concerted practices* OFT 401, December 2004, the OFT now applies the same standards on appreciability as the European Commission: see in particular paras 2.15–2.21 of the Guideline.

Schedule 2: competition scrutiny under other enactments

42–101 [*Add at the end of the paragraph: page* [1272]]
Some amendments to Sch.2 are effected by para.49 of the Competition Act 1998 and Other Enactments (Amendment) Regulations 2004.[262a]

[262a] SI 2004/1261.

Schedule 3: "general exclusions"

42–102 [*Add, at the end of the paragraph: page* [1272]]
Some amendments to Sch.3 are effected by para.49 of the Competition Act 1998 and Other Enactments (Amendment) Regulations 2004.[262b]

[262b] SI 2004/1261.

Schedule 3, para.2: s.21(2) agreements

42–104 [*Page* [1272]]
Schedule 3, para.2 is repealed with effect from May 1, 2007 by the Competition Act 1998 and Other Enactments (Amendment) Regulations 2004.[264a]

[264a] SI 2004/1261.

Schedule 3, para.4: services of general economic interest

42–106 [*Note 268: page* [1273]]
See now OFT Guideline 421 *Services of general economic interest* OFT 421, December 2004.

Repeal of the exclusion order for vertical agreements

[*Page* [1275]]
The exclusion of vertical agreements from the Chap. I prohibition will be repealed with effect from May 1, 2005 as a result of the Competition Act 1998 (Land Agreements Exclusion and Revocation) Order 2004 (SI 2004/1260). The OFT has adopted a new Guideline *Vertical agreements* OFT 419, December 2004 explaining the application of the Competition Act 1998 to vertical agreements.

42–115

Sections 4 and 5: individual exemption

[*Page* [1277]]
The system of notifying agreements for individual exemption has been abolished by the Competition Act 1998 and Other Enactments (Amendment) Regulations 2004 (SI 2004/1261).

42–118

Sections 12–16: notification

[*Page* [1278]]
The system of notifying agreements for individual exemption has been abolished by the Competition Act 1998 and Other Enactments (Amendment) Regulations 2004 (SI 2004/1261).

42–122

(c) *The Chapter II Prohibition: Abuse of a Dominant Position*

Abuse of a dominant position

[*Page* [1280]]
Note the new Guidelines issued by the OFT in December 2004, in particular *Abuse of dominant position* OFT 402; *Market definition* OFT 403; and *Assessment of market power* OFT 415.

42–128

Section 20–24: notification

[*Page* [1281]]
The system of notifying conduct to the OFT has been abolished by the Competition Act 1998 and Other Enactments (Amendment) Regulations 2004.[310a]

42–132

[310a] SI 2004/1261.

(e) *Investigation and Enforcement*

Power to investigate

[*Note 327: page* [1283]]
See now *Powers of investigation* OFT 404, December 2004.

42–137

Penalties

42–139   *[Add to text after note 338: page* [1284]]
The maximum penalty is now calculated by reference to worldwide turnover rather than UK turnover as a result of the Competition Act 1998 (Determination of Turnover for Penalties) (Amendment) Order 2004.[338a]

[338a] SI 2004/1259.

[Note 340: page [1283]]
See now *OFT's Guidance as the appropriate amount of a penalty* OFT 423, December 2004.

Cartel offence

42–141   *[Note 349, page* [1284]]
See now *Powers for investigating criminal cartels* OFT 515, January 2004.

(g) *The Competition Appeal Tribunal*

The Competition Appeal Tribunal

42–145   *[Add to line 9, after "... apply from June 20, 2003": page* [1286]]
The Competition Appeal Tribunal (Amendment and Communications Act Appeal) Rules 2004[358a] amend the Competition Appeal Tribunal Rules 2003.

[358a] SI 2004/2068.

CHAPTER 43

SALE OF GOODS

			PARA.
☐	1.	In general	43–001
☐		(a) Introduction	43–001
☐		(b) Definitions	43–005
■	2.	Formation of the contract	43–008
☐		(a) Contract of sale	43–008
☐		(b) Capacity of parties	43–021
		(c) Formalities	43–022
☐		(d) Subject-matter	43–023
		(e) The price	43–039
■	3.	Terms of the contract	43–042
☐		(a) Conditions, warranties, misrepresentations and puffs	43–042
■		(b) Implied terms	43–061
☐		(i) Implied terms about title	43–062
☐		(ii) Implied term as to correspondence with description	43–073
☐		(iii) Implied terms about quality and fitness for purpose	43–081
☐		(iv) Sale by sample	43–101
☐		(v) Exclusion of terms implied by sections 13, 14 and 15	43–104
☐		(c) Stipulations as to time	43–113
■	4.	Consumer protection	43–114
☐		(a) Additional remedies of the buyer in consumer cases	43–114
☐		(b) Cancellation rights	43–135
☐		(c) Consumer Protection Act 1987	43–138
☐		(d) Consumer guarantees	43–155
☐		(e) Other enactments	43–156
■	5.	Effects of the contract	43–160
☐		(a) Transfer of property as between seller and buyer	43–160
☐		(b) When the risk passes	43–216
■		(c) Transfer of title	43–221
☐		(i) Sale by person not the owner	43–221
■		(ii) Effect on title of writs of execution	43–260
■		(iii) Effect of limitation	43–261
■	6.	Performance of the contract	43–262
☐		(a) Duties of seller and buyer	43–262
☐		(b) Rules governing delivery	43–267
☐		(i) Place of delivery	43–269
☐		(ii) Time for delivery	43–271
☐		(iii) Goods in possession of third person	43–277
☐		(iv) Expenses in connection with delivery	43–279
☐		(v) Delivery of the wrong quantity	43–280
☐		(vi) Instalment deliveries	43–287
☐		(vii) Delivery to a carrier	43–294

				PARA.
☐		(c)	Examination and acceptance	43–301
☐		(d)	Payment	43–319
■	7.	Remedies of the seller		43–331
☐		(a)	Rights of unpaid seller against the goods	43–331
☐			(i) Unpaid seller's lien	43–342
☐			(ii) Stoppage in transit	43–353
☐			(iii) Sub-sales and other subsequent transactions	43–366
☐			(iv) Resale by the seller	43–371
☐		(b)	Action for the price	43–386
☐		(c)	Action for damages	43–395
☐		(d)	Other remedies of the seller	43–412
■	8.	Remedies of the buyer		43–415
☐		(a)	Damages for non-delivery	43–415
☐		(b)	Damages for delay in delivery	43–433
■		(c)	Damages for defective quality	43–438
☐			(i) Diminution in value	43–438
☐			(ii) Losses other than diminution in value	43–443
☐		(d)	Other remedies of the buyer	43–464
	9.	Supplementary		43–475

1. In General

(a) Introduction

Sale of Goods Act 1979

43–002   [*Note 3: page* [1291]]
Update reference to *Benjamin's Sale of Goods* to (7th ed.), paras 1–008, 10–009.

(b) Definitions

Definitions

43–005   [*Note 19: page* [1292]]
Update reference to *Benjamin's Sale of Goods* to (7th ed.), para.18–006.

[*After the definition of "Plaintiff" on page* [1293] *insert*]
"Producer" means the manufacturer of goods, the importer of goods into the European Economic Area or any person purporting to be a producer by placing his name, trade mark or other distinctive sign on the goods"[23a];

[23a] Inserted by reg.6(1) of the Sale and Supply of Goods to Consumers' Regulations 2002 (SI 2002/3045).

[*After the definition of "Property" on page* [1293] *insert*]
"Repair" means, in cases where there is a lack of conformity in goods for the purposes of s.48F of this Act, to bring the goods into conformity with the contract;[24a]

[24a] Inserted by reg.6(2) of the Sale and Supply of Goods to Consumers' Regulations 2002 (SI 2002/3045).

[Add to note 28: page [1294]] **43–006**
; *GE Capital Bank Ltd v Rushton* [2005] EWCA Civ 1556; [2006] 1 W.L.R.
899.

2. FORMATION OF THE CONTRACT

(a) *Contract of Sale*

Transactions outside the Act

[Add to note 59: page [1297]] **43–013**
The Trading Stamps Act 1964 has been repealed by the Regulatory Reform
(Trading Stamps) Order 2005 (SI 2005/871).

[Note 66: page [1298]] **43–014**
Update reference to *Benjamin's Sale of Goods* to (7th ed.), para.1–047.

[Add to note 73: page [1299]] **43–015**
The Consumer Credit Act 2006 removes the financial limit: see above,
para.38–014.

Conditional sale agreements

[Add to note 77: page [1299]] **43–016**
The Consumer Credit Act 2006 removes the financial limit: see above,
para.38–014.

Credit-sale agreements

[Add to note 82: page [1299]] **43–017**
The Consumer Credit Act 2006 removes the financial limit: see above,
para.38–014.

[Note 89: page [1300]] **43–018**
Update reference to *Benjamin's Sale of Goods* to (7th ed.), para.1–066.

[Note 94: page [1301]] **43–020**
Update reference to *Benjamin's Sale of Goods* to (7th ed.), paras
1–048—1–049.

(b) *Capacity of Parties*

Capacity of parties

Section 3 of the 1979 Act has been amended by the Mental Capacity Act 2005, **43–021**
Sch. 6, para.24. The effect of mental incapacity is now dealt with in s.7 of the
2005 Act.

[*Note 96: page* [1301]]
Update reference to *Benjamin's Sale of Goods* to (7th ed.), para.2–028.

(d) *Subject-matter*

Problem cases

43–031   [*Note 116: page* [1304]]
Update reference to *Benjamin's Sale of Goods* to (7th ed.), paras 1–114, 1–115.

Sale of goods already perished

43–033   [*Note 128: page* [1305]]
Update reference to *Benjamin's Sale of Goods* to (7th ed.), paras 1–121—1–134.

[*Note 129*]
Update reference to *Benjamin's Sale of Goods* to (7th ed.), para.19–113.

43–034   [*Note 131: page* [1306]]
Update reference to *Benjamin's Sale of Goods* to (7th ed.), para.1–126.

Operation of section 7

43–038   [*Notes 146 and 147: page* [1307]]
Update reference to *Benjamin's Sale of Goods* to (7th ed.), paras 6–058, 6–033 respectively.

3. TERMS OF THE CONTRACT

(a) *Conditions, Warranties, Misrepresentations and Puffs*

Contractual promises: conditions and warranties

43–044   [*Note 164: page* [1309]]
Update reference to *Benjamin's Sale of Goods* to same paras of the 7th ed. (2006).

Misrepresentations external to the contract

43–046   [*Note 174: page* [1310]]
Update references to *Benjamin's Sale of Goods* to same paras of the 7th ed. (2006).

[*Add to note 176: page* [1311]]
For a recent example see *Thompson v Christie Manson & Woods Ltd* [2004] EWHC 1101 (QB) (attribution of vase by auctioneer without warning of non-

finality of attributions). The decision was reversed [2005] EWCA Civ 555; [2005] P.N.L.R. 38.

[*Add to note 180*]
For an example see *Lucas Laureys v Graham Earl*, QBD (David Foskett Q.C.), November 3, 2005, where the statement was by an agent to sell a classic car: but it was held that he had simply passed on information given him by his principal.

Effect of breach of condition

[*Add to note 210: page* [1313]]   **43–053**
See discussion of the view that the Act confers no right of second tender in two Scottish cases, *JH Ritchie Ltd v Lloyd Ltd* 2005 S.L.T. 64 and *Lamarra v Capital Bank plc*, 2005 S.L.T. (Sh. Ct.) 21. However, it should be borne in mind that in Scots law the right to reject is not based on the concept of condition.
Update reference to *Benjamin's Sale of Goods* to same para. of the 7th ed. (2006).

Limitation of right to reject in non-consumer cases

[*Note 227: page* [1315]]   **43–057**
Update reference to *Benjamin's Sale of Goods* to (7th ed., 2006), paras 12–025 and 18–284.

Rescission for misrepresentation

[*Note 230: page* [1316]]   **43–059**
Update reference to *Benjamin's Sale of Goods* to (7th ed., 2006), para.12–120.

[*Add to note 231*]
For an example of rejection of goods not in their former state which had been fraudulently misrepresented as new but were "worthless from the beginning", see *Kellogg Brown & Root Services Inc v Aerotech Herman Nelson Inc* (2004) 238 D.L.R. (4th) 595.

Remedies in tort

[*Note 237: page* [1316]]   **43–060**
Update reference to *Clerk and Lindsell* to (19th ed., 2006), paras 8–83 *et seq.*

[*Note 239: page* [1317]]
Update reference to *Benjamin's Sale of Goods* to (7th ed., 2006), paras 12–121 *et seq.*, and that to *Clerk and Lindsell* to (19th ed., 2006), paras 8–111 *et seq.*

(b) *Implied Terms*

(i) *Implied terms about title*

Implied terms about title

43–062 [*Note 243: page* [1317]]
The Trading Stamps Act 1964 is repealed by the Regulatory Reform (Trading Stamps) Order 2005 (SI 2005/871).

Effect of breach of section 12

43–067 [*Note 267: page* [1319]]
Update reference to *Benjamin's Sale of Goods* to same para of the 7th ed. (2006).

Total failure of consideration despite use of goods

43–068 [*Note 274: page* [1320]]
Update reference to *Benjamin's Sale of Goods* to same paras of the 7th ed. (2006).

[*Note 276*]
Update reference to *Benjamin's Sale of Goods* to same para of the 7th ed. (2006).

Change of position no defence

43–070 [*Note 282: page* [1321]]
Update reference to *Benjamin's Sale of Goods* to same para of the 7th ed. (2006).

Exclusion of section 12

43–072 [*Note 290: page* [1322]]
Update reference to *Benjamin's Sale of Goods* to same para of the 7th ed. (2006).

(ii) *Implied term as to correspondence with description*

Identification

43–078 [*Note 319: page* [1325]]
Update reference to *Benjamin's Sale of Goods* to same paras of the 7th ed. (2006).

(iii) *Implied Terms about Quality and Fitness for Purpose*

Implied term as to satisfactory quality

43–082 [*Note 328: page* [1326]]
The Trading Stamps Act 1964 is repealed by the Regulatory Reform (Trading Stamps) Order 2005 (SI 2005/871).

Satisfactory quality

[*Add to note 344: page* [1329]]   **43–086**
For consideration of the role of expert evidence see *Friarwood Ltd v Champagne Cattier SA* [2006] EWCA Civ 1105.

[*Add to note 346: page* [1330]]
Bramhill v Edwards [2004] EWCA Civ 403; [2004] 2 Lloyd's Rep. 653 (American mobile home slightly wider than UK regulations permitted; not of unsatisfactory quality, objective test considered). See a note by Twigg-Flesner (2005) 121 L.Q.R. 205.

Reliance may be rebutted

[*Add to note 382: page* [1334]]   **43–096**
The *Britvic* case is discussed by Sealy [2003] C.L.J. 260.

Reasonably fit for purpose

[*Add to note 392: page* [1335]]   **43–097**
It has been held that the seller of a software package may be liable if he does not make clear, at least in general terms, that not all packages are compatible: *Brocket v DGS Retail Ltd* [2004] C.L. Jan. 322.

(iv) *Sale by sample*

Bulk to correspond with sample

[*Note 412: page* [1337]]   **43–102**
Update reference to *Benjamin's Sale of Goods* to (7th ed., 2006), para. 11–078.

(v) *Exclusion of Terms Implied by Sections 13, 14 and 15*

Dealing as consumer

[*Add to note 431: page* [1339]]   **43–106**
The *R & B* case was followed in *Feldaroll Foundry plc v Hermes Leasing (London) Ltd* [2004] EWCA Civ 747 (Lamborghini for managing director of finance company: company dealt as consumer). But see Twigg-Flesner (2005) 121 L.Q.R. 41.

Reasonableness

[*Add to note 448: page* [1341]]   **43–108**
In *Balmoral Group Ltd v Borealis (UK) Ltd* [2005] EWHC 1900 (Comm) a clause in the sale of borecene (a polymer) limiting liability to replacement or refund of the price was held unreasonable. Some reliance was placed on the fact that earlier claims had been settled (*cf.* text to n.446, above); and on the insurance position, see at [398]–[426].

International sales

43–110   [*Add to note 457: page* [1342]]
Balmoral Group Ltd v Borealis (UK) Ltd [2005] EWHC 1900 (Comm).

Common law

43–112   [*Note 468: page* [1343]]
Update reference to *Benjamin's Sale of Goods* to (7th ed., 2006), para.
13–012.

<h3 align="center">4. Consumer Protection</h3>

<h3 align="center">(a) Additional Remedies of the Buyer in Consumer Cases</h3>

Introduction

43–114   [*Note 500: page* [1345]]
A full discussion of the changes effected by the Regulations now appears in
the 7th ed. of *Benjamin's Sale of Goods* (2006) at paras 12–071 *et seq.*

Enforcement

43–124   [*Add to note 516: page* [1349]]
See Harris (2003) 119 L.Q.R. 541.

Rescission

43–127   [*Add to note 521: page* [1350]]
See a note on rescission under the Regulations by Hogg in [2003] S.L.T.
277.

Exclusion by contract

43–134
[*Note 533: page* [1353]]
Update reference to *Benjamin's Sale of Goods* to (7th ed., 2006), para.
25–104.

<h3 align="center">(b) Cancellation Rights</h3>

43–135—   [*Pages* [1353]–[1355]]
43–137   The cancellation rights referred to in paras 43–135—43–137 are discussed by
Hellwege [2004] Camb. L.J. 712. See also the cancellation rights conferred by
the Supply of Extended Warranties on Domestic Electrical Goods Order 2005 (SI
2005/37).

Consumer credit transactions

[Delete note 535: page [1353] and substitute]
As amended by the Consumer Credit Act 2006, *i.e.* a credit agreement where the buyer is an individual (as defined in s.189(1) of the 1974 Act as amended) other than an exempt agreement under ss.16, 16A, 16B. See above, paras 38–014, 38–015.

43–135

Consumer Protection (Cancellation of Contracts concluded away from Business Premises) Regulations 1987

[Add to end of note 540: page [1353]]
SI 2003/1400.

43–136

Consumer Protection (Distance Selling) Regulations 2000

[Page [1354]]
These regulations have been amended by the Consumer Protection (Distance Selling) (Amendment) Regulations 2005 (SI 2005/689). See also the amendments effected by SI 2004/2095, reg.25, SI 2005/55.

The Consumer Credit (Disclosure of Information) Regulations 2004 (SI 2004/1481) (see para.38–070, above) do not apply to distance contracts (as defined in reg.1(2) of those Regulations).

The information requirements of the Regulations have been supplemented by the Electronic Commerce (EC Directive) Regulations 2002 (SI 2002/2013, as amended by SI 2003/115, SI 2003/2500, SI 2004/1178).

43–137

(c) *Consumer Protection Act 1987*

Defences

[Add to note 587: page [1358]]
See *O'Byrne v Sanofi Pasteur MSD Ltd* [2006] 1 W.L.R. 1606 (ECJ).

43–148

Consumer safety

[Note 595: page [1359]]
Update reference to Miller, *Product Liability and Safety Encyclopedia* to (1979–2006).

43–151

The General Product Safety Regulations 1994

These Regulations have been repealed and replaced by the General Product Safety Regulations 2005 (SI 2005/1803).

43–153

Misleading price indications

The Consumer Protection (Code of Practice for Traders on Price Indications) Approval Order 1988 has been revoked and replaced by the Consumer Protection

43–154

(Code of Practice for Traders on Price Indications) Approval Order 2005 (SI 2005/2705).

(d) *Consumer Guarantees*

Consumer guarantees

43–155   [*Page* [1360]]
See also the Supply of Extended Warranties on Domestic Electrical Goods Order 2005 (SI 2005/37).

[*Add to note 617*]
; and *Benjamin's Sale of Goods* (7th ed.), para.14–070.

(e) *Other Enactments*

Enterprise Act 2002

43–157   [*Add to note 621: page* [1361]]
See SI 2003/1368, SI 2003/1374, SI 2003/1375, SI 2003/1399, SI 2003/1593, SI 2004/935, SI 2004/1517, SI 2004/2095, SI 2005/917, SI 2005/2340, SI 2005/2418, SI 2005/2468, SI 2005/2759.

Advertisements etc

43–159   [*Add to note 627: page* [1361]]
and amended by SI 2005/871.

[*Add to note 630*]
See SI 2003/3183.

[*Amend the text to note 633*]
The Price Marking Order 1999 has been revoked and replaced by the Price Marking Order 2004 (SI 2004/102).

5. Effects of the Contract

(a) *Transfer of Property as between Seller and Buyer*

Specific goods in a deliverable state

43–168   [*Note 654: page* [1364]]
Update reference to *Benjamin's Sale of Goods* to (7th ed.), paras 5–019—5–020.

Sale or return

43–176   [*Note 671: page* [1367]]
Update reference to *Benjamin's Sale of Goods* to (7th ed.), paras 5–055, 5–056.

Appropriation of unascertained or future goods

[*Note 681: page* [1368]]
Update reference to *Benjamin's Sale of Goods* to (7th ed.), para.19–100.

43–179

Appropriation unconditional

[*Note 694: page* [1370]]
Update reference to *Benjamin's Sale of Goods* to (7th ed.), para.19–100.

43–182

Shipbuilding contracts

[*Note 703: page* [1371]]
Update reference to *Benjamin's Sale of Goods* to (7th ed.), paras 5–090—5–092.

43–186

Materials not yet incorporated

[*Add to note 706: page* [1371]]
But see *Petromec Inc v Petroleo Brasileiro SA Petrobras* [2004] EWHC 1180 (Comm); [2005] 1 Lloyd's Rep. 219 at [36].

43–187

Requirements for passing of property in undivided share

[*Notes 720, 722, 723: pages* [1373]–[1374]]
Update references to *Benjamin's Sale of Goods* to (7th ed.), paras 5–111, 5–113, 5–113 respectively.

43–191—
43–192

[*Note 726: page* [1374]]
Update reference to *Benjamin's Sale of Goods* to (7th ed.), paras 5–114, 18–293.

43–193

[*Note 728*]
Update reference to *Benjamin's Sale of Goods* to (7th ed.), paras 5–116, 18–293.

43–195

Extent of undivided share

[*Note 733: page* [1375]]
Update reference to *Benjamin's Sale of Goods* to (7th ed.), paras 5–121—5–123.

43–196

[*Note 734*]
Update reference to *Benjamin's Sale of Goods* to (7th ed.), paras 5–121, 5–123, 7–067.

Deemed consent by owner to dealings in bulk goods

[*Note 737: page* [1376]]
Update reference to *Benjamin's Sale of Goods* to (7th ed.), para.5–125.

43–197

Situations outside s.20A

43–198 [*Note 741: page* [1376]]
Update reference to *Benjamin's Sale of Goods* to (7th ed.), para.5–129.

Seller's right of disposal

43–200 [*Note 747: page* [1377]]
Update reference to *Benjamin's Sale of Goods* to (7th ed.), paras 5–132, 18–211.

[*Note 748*]
Update reference to *Benjamin's Sale of Goods* to (7th ed.), para.19–098.

43–201 [*Note 749: page* [1377]]
Update reference to *Benjamin's Sale of Goods* to (7th ed.), paras 18–214, 20–077.

[*Note 750*]
Update reference to *Benjamin's Sale of Goods* to (7th ed.), paras 5–138, 18–221.

"Romalpa" clauses: retention of title

43–203 [*Page* [1378]]
In *Benford Ltd v Lopecan SL* [2004] EWHC 1897 (Comm); [2004] 2 Lloyd's Rep. 618 the question was raised (but not answered) as to whether a retention of title clause would be effective if there was a defence to a claim for the price of the goods (at [18]).

[*Note 754*]
Update references to *Benjamin's Sale of Goods* to (7th ed.), paras 5–141, 25–141, 25–150.

[*Add to note 757*]
On proposals by the Law Commission for reform: see Law Com Consultation Paper No. 164 (2002); Law Com. Consultation Paper No. 176 (2004); Law Com. Report No. 296 (2005).

43–204 [*Note 774: page* [1380]]
Update reference to *Benjamin's Sale of Goods* to (7th ed.), para.5–146.

Products

43–205 [*Note 781: page* [1381]]
Update reference to *Benjamin's Sale of Goods* to (7th ed.), paras 1–058—1–059, 5–148—5–149.

Proceeds of sale

43–207 [*Note 800: page* [1383]]
Update reference to *Benjamin's Sale of Goods* to (7th ed.), para.5–154.

Voluntary agreements

[*Page* [1386]]
Correct the title of this paragraph to read **Voluntary arrangements**

43–214

(b) *When the Risk Passes*

Goods to which risk relates

[*Note 846: page* [1386]]
Update reference to *Benjamin's Sale of Goods* to (7th ed.), paras 18–300,
19–110, 20–087, 21–003, 21–011, 21–013, 21–020, 21–043, 21–100.

43–217

[*Note 848: page* [1387]]
Update reference to *Benjamin's Sale of Goods* to (7th ed.), paras 6–004,
18–300.

[*Notes 850 and 851*]
Update references to *Benjamin's Sale of Goods* to (7th ed.), paras 6–006—
6–008.

Qualifications

[*Note 857: page* [1388]
Update reference to *Benjamin's Sale of Goods* to (7th ed.), paras 6–026—
6–032.

43–219

Consumer sales

[*Add to note 861: page* [1388]
See now *Benjamin's Sale of Goods* (7th ed.), Ch.6.

43–220

(c) *Transfer of Title*

(i) *Sale by Person not the Owner*

(1) *Estoppel*

Estoppel

[*Note 873: page* [1389]]
Update reference to *Benjamin's Sale of Goods* to (7th ed.), para.7–008.

43–224

[*Add new paragraph after paragraph 229: page* [1392]]
Estoppel by judgment. Where, in an action between two parties brought to
determine the ownership of goods, title to the goods is established by judgment,
the unsuccessful party will be estopped *per rem judicatam* from claiming the
goods and that estoppel will bind also his privies, *i.e.* those claiming title from
or through him, but only if the title claimed was acquired after (and not before)
the date of the judgment.[900a]

43–229A

[900a] *Powell v Wiltshire* [2004] EWCA Civ 534; [2005] Q.B. 117.

(3) *Sales under Special Powers or Court Orders*

Sales under special powers or court orders

43–233   [*Note 903: page* [1393]]
Update reference to *Benjamin's Sale of Goods* to (7th ed.), paras 7–109, 7–114.

[*Add to note 908*]
S.138B of the Supreme Court Act 1981 has been repealed by s.109(3) and Sch.10 of the Courts Act 2003 and replaced by Sch.7, para.10 of that Act.

[*Add to note 911*]
Police Reform Act 2002, Sch.4, para.10.

[*Add to note 912: page* [1394]]
Police Reform Act 2002, Sch.4, para.10.

[*Add at the end of para.(ii) of this paragraph: page* [1394]]
to the trustee for civil recovery[914a]; and to administrators of companies.[914b]

[914a] Proceeds of Crime Act 2002, s.267 and Sch.7.
[914b] Insolvency Act 1986, Sch. B1, paras 59, 70–72, inserted by s.248 and Sch.16 of the Enterprise Act 2002.

(6) *Disposition by Seller in Possession*

Seller in possession

43–241   [*Note 931: page* [1396]]
Update reference to *Benjamin's Sale of Goods* to (7th ed.), para.7–055.

Delivery or transfer

43–244   [*Note 944: page* [1397]]
Update reference to *Benjamin's Sale of Goods* to (7th ed.), para.7–062.

(7) *Disposition by Buyer in Possession*

Buyer in possession

43–247   [*Note 955: page* [1398]]
Update reference to *Benjamin's Sale of Goods* to (7th ed.), para.7–069.

"Having ... agreed to buy"

43–249   [*Note 969: page* [1399]]
For the removal of the general financial limit in the Consumer Credit Act 1974: see para.38–014 above.

Mercantile agents

43–254   [*Note 978: page* [1401]]
Update reference to *Benjamin's Sale of Goods* to (7th ed.), para.7–081.

Delivery or transfer

43–256   [*Note 982: page* [1401]]
Update reference to *Benjamin's Sale of Goods* to (7th ed.), para.7–077.

(ii) *Effect on Title of Writs of Execution*

Effect on title of writs of execution

[*Page* [1403]]
S.138 of the Supreme Court Act 1981 has been repealed by s.109(3) and Sch.10 of the Courts Act 2003 and replaced by the provisions contained in Sch.7 to that Act.

43–260

(iii) *Effect of Limitation*

[*Insert new paragraph 43–261A: page* [1404]]
Actions for recovery of property obtained through unlawful conduct etc. By s.27A of the Limitation Act 1980 (inserted by s.288 of the Proceeds of Crime Act 2002) none of the time limits given in the preceding provisions of the 1980 Act apply to any proceedings under Ch.2 of Pt 5 of the 2002 Act (civil recovery by the Director of the Asset Recovery Agency of proceeds of unlawful conduct). The Director has 12 years in which to bring proceedings for a recovery order from the date on which his cause of action accrued. Moreover, if proceedings are started by the Director for a recovery order in respect of a chattel, s.3(2) of the 1980 Act does not prevent a claimant from asserting on an application under s.281 of the 2002 Act (victims of theft, etc.) that the property belongs to him, or the court making a declaration in his favour under that section. If the court makes such a declaration, his title to the chattel is to be treated as not having been extinguished by s.3(2) of the 1980 Act.

43–261A

6. Performance of the Contract

(a) *Duties of Seller and Buyer*

Export and import licences

[*Note 1028: page* [1405]]
Update reference to *Benjamin's Sale of Goods* to (7th ed.), para.18–308.

43–265

Letters of credit

[*Note 1032: page* [1406]]
Update reference to *Benjamin's Sale of Goods* to (7th ed.), Ch.23.

43–266

(b) *Rules Governing Delivery*

Delivery

[*Note 1040: page* [1407]]
Update reference to *Benjamin's Sale of Goods* to (7th ed.), para.8–002.

43–267

(i) *Place of Delivery*

Place of delivery

43–269 *[Note 1048: page* [1408]*]*
Update reference to *Benjamin's Sale of Goods* to (7th ed.), paras 8–018—8–024.

Delivery at buyer's premises to unauthorised person

43–270 *[Add to note 1049 after Galbraith & Grant Ltd v Block: page* [1408]*]*
Computer 2000 Distribution Ltd v ICM Computer Solutions plc [2004] EWCA Civ 1634; [2005] Info. T.L.R. 147.

(ii) *Time for Delivery*

No time fixed

43–272 *[Add to note 1054: page* [1409]*]*
Hick v Raymond [1893] A.C. 22 at 29; *SHV Gas Supply & Trading SAS v Naftomar Shipping & Trading Co Ltd Inc* [2005] EWHC 2528 (Comm); [2006] 1 Lloyd's Rep. 163.

[Add new paragraph 43–274A: page [1409]*]*
43–274A **Variation of delivery time**. The buyer may agree to an extension of the time fixed for delivery and such an agreement will constitute an effective variation of the contract of sale provided that sufficient consideration to support the variation moves from the promisee.[1058a]

[1058a] *South Caribbean Trading Ltd v Trafigura Beheer BV* [2004] EWHC 2676 (Comm); [2005] 1 Lloyd's Rep. 128; see para.3–079, above.

Waiver of delivery time

43–275 *[Add to note 1059: page* [1409]*]*
See also *Fleming & Wendeln GmbH & Co v Sanofi SA/AG* [2003] EWHC 561 (QB); [2003] 2 Lloyd's Rep. 473. Contrast *South Caribbean Trading Ltd v Trafigura Beheer BV*, above, at [112] (estoppel cannot be invoked where unconscionable to do so); see para.3–095, above.

Force majeure

43–276 *[Note 1060: page* [1409]*]*
Update reference to *Benjamin's Sale of Goods* to (7th ed.), para.8–088.

(iii) *Goods in Possession of Third Person*

Goods in possession of third person

43–277 *[Note 1068: page* [1410]*]*
Update reference to *Benjamin's Sale of Goods* to (7th ed.), paras 8–013, 18–193, 18–196.

(iv) *Expenses in Connection with Delivery*

Expenses of delivery

[*Note 1073: page* [1411]]   **43–279**
Update reference to *Benjamin's Sale of Goods* to (7th ed.), paras 19–009,
19–011, 20–008, 20–012, 21–002, 21–010, 21–012, 21–014.

(v) *Delivery of Wrong Quantity*

Defective delivery

[*Note 1076: page* [1411]]   **43–280**
Update reference to *Benjamin's Sale of Goods* to (7th ed.), paras 8–052,
12–031.

(vi) *Instalment Deliveries*

Stated instalments

[*Notes 1095 and 1097: pages* [1413]–[1414]]   **43–288**
Update references to *Benjamin's Sale of Goods* to (7th ed.), para.8–077.

Anticipatory breach: repudiation accepted

[*Note 1110: page* [1415]]   **43–292**
Update reference to *Benjamin's Sale of Goods to* (7th ed.), paras
9–010—9–017.

[*Note 1113*]
Update reference to *Benjamin's Sale of Goods* to (7th ed.), para.9–020.

(vii) *Delivery to a Carrier*

Delivery to a carrier

[*Note 1126: page* [1417]]   **43–294**
Update reference to *Benjamin's Sale of Goods* to (7th ed.), paras 8–014,
19–011, 20–012, 21–072.

Reasonable contract with carrier

[*Note 1131: page* [1417]]   **43–295**
Update reference to *Benjamin's Sale of Goods* to (7th ed.), paras 8–015,
18–245.

Notice to enable insurance

[*Note 1132: page* [1418]]   **43–296**
Update reference to *Benjamin's Sale of Goods* to (7th ed.), paras 18–246,
19–117, 20–039, 20–089.

[*Note 1133: page* [1418]]
Update reference to *Benjamin's Sale of Goods* to (7th ed.), paras 18–248, 20–039, 20–091.

Deterioration

43–298   [*Note 1140: page* [1419]]
Update reference to *Benjamin's Sale of Goods* to (7th ed.), paras 6–022, 18–249, 19–118, 20–091.

Seller's responsibilities at point of delivery

43–299   [*Note 1142: page* [1419]]
Update reference to *Benjamin's Sale of Goods* to (7th ed.), paras 6–019, 11–067, 18–255.

(c) *Examination and Acceptance*

Place for examination

43–302   [*Note 1152: page* [1420]]
Update references to *Benjamin* to (7th ed., 2006), paras 12–043, 19–156, 20–108, 20–109 and 21–102.

Intimation of acceptance

43–305   [*Note 1159: page* [1421]]
Jones v Gallagher is now reported at [2005] 1 Lloyd's Rep. 377.

Lapse of reasonable time

43–310   [*Add to note 1182: page* [1424]]
The emphasis of *Jones v Gallagher* (now reported at [2005] 1 Lloyd's Rep. 377) seems to be that the question is one of fact. See also *Hawkins v C.D. Bramall plc*, HH Judge Dowse, [2004] C.L. June 94 (car rejected after six days but buyer continued to drive it for nine months and 14,000 miles, during which car damaged in collision: held nothing to prevent reliance on original rejection); *A.C. Daniels & Co Ltd v Jungwoo Logic*, Q.B.D. (HH Judge Hicks Q.C., April 14, 2000 (injection mould: valid rejection after 13 months); *Lamorra v Capital Bank plc*, below, n.1187a (Range Rover returned after two months and 6000 miles, but had been rejected soon after delivery). On *Jones v Gallagher* see Bradgate (2004) 120 L.Q.R. 558; and on *Clegg v Olle Andersson* see Reynolds (2003) 119 L.Q.R. 544.

Attempts at repair

43–311   [*Insert new note 1187a at end of paragraph: page* [1424]]
Two Scottish cases consider the problem of attempts to repair defective goods. In the first, *JH Ritchie Ltd v Lloyd Ltd* 2005 S.L.T. 64, the defect was rectified

but the vendor refused to say what the defect had been. The buyer, who purported to reject, was held by a majority of an Extra Division of the Court of Session to have no right to do so as the goods were compliant on final delivery. The dissenting opinion of Lord Marnoch, pointing out that the Act does not envisage the possibility that the defect is not adequately remedied, and that there is nothing in it permitting a second tender, is persuasive. In the second, *Lamarra v Capital Bank plc* 2005 S.L.T. (Sh. Ct.) 21, a new and very expensive Range Rover acquired suffered from many defects and despite attempts at rectification it was held that it had not at the time of delivery come within the basic definition of satisfactory quality, and that the Act (actually the Supply of Goods (Implied Terms) Act 1973, as the case was one of hire-purchase) conferred no right of second tender.

Return to seller

[*Note 1198: page* [1426]]   **43–316**
Update reference to *Benjamin's Sale of Goods* to same paras of the 7th ed. (2006).

Refusal to take delivery

[*Note 1207: page* [1426]]   **43–318**
Update references to *Benjamin's Sale of Goods* to (7th ed., 2006), paras 19–219, 20–139.

(d) *Payment*

Credit

The Consumer Credit Act 2006 removes the financial limit: see above, para.   **43–329**
38–014.

7. Remedies of the Seller

(a) *Rights of Unpaid Seller against the Goods*

Remedies of seller who retains the property in the goods

[*Note 1260: page* [1431]]   **43–333**
Update reference to *Benjamin's Sale of Goods* (7th ed., 2006), para.15–011.

(i) *Unpaid Seller's Lien*

Effect of grant of credit

[*Note 1329: page* [1437]]   **43–343**
Update reference to *Benjamin's Sale of Goods* to (7th ed., 2006), para. 15–034.

The seller's possession

43–345   *[Note 1346: page* [1438]]
Update references to *Benjamin's Sale of Goods* to (7th ed.), paras 15–038—15–039.

[Note 1350]
Update references to *Benjamin's Sale of Goods* to (7th ed.), paras 15–038—15–039, 18–235.

Termination of the lien

43–348   *[Note 1367: page* [1439]]
Update references to *Benjamin's Sale of Goods* to (7th ed.), paras 5–131, 18–211, 20–075.

Delivery to buyer ends lien

43–350   *[Note 1379: page* [1440]]
Update references to *Benjamin's Sale of Goods* to (7th ed.), para.15–050.

[Note 1380: page [1441]]
Update references to *Benjamin's Sale of Goods* to (7th ed.), para.15–050.

Waiver of lien

43–351   *[Note 1387: page* [1441]]
Update references to *Benjamin's Sale of Goods* to (7th ed.), para.15–057.

[Add to note 1388 at end]
cf. Clifford Harris & Co v Solland International Ltd [2005] EWHC 141 (Ch); [2005] 2 All E.R. 334.

[Note 1390]
Update references to *Benjamin's Sale of Goods* to (7th ed.), para.15–059.

Effect of sub-sales and other dispositions

43–352   *[Note 1396: page* [1442]]
Update references to *Benjamin's Sale of Goods* to (7th ed.), paras 15–092—15–099.

(ii) *Stoppage in Transitu*

Right of stoppage in transit

43–353   *[Note 1403: page* [1442]]
Update references to *Benjamin's Sale of Goods* to (7th ed.), para.15–064.

Shipment on buyer's ship: transfer of bill of lading

[*Note 1442: page* [1445]]   **43–358**
Update references to *Benjamin's Sale of Goods* to (7th ed.), para.18–211.

[*Note 1443*]
Update references to *Benjamin's Sale of Goods* to (7th ed.), paras
18–166—18–167.

Buyer obtains delivery before arrival

[*Note 1448: page* [1446]]   **43–359**
Update references to *Benjamin's Sale of Goods* to (7th ed.), paras 21–072 *et
seq.*, 15–074.

Other provisions as to transit

[*Note 1461: page* [1447]]   **43–361**
Update references to *Benjamin's Sale of Goods* to (7th ed.), paras 15–082,
18–214, 20–077.

(iii) *Sub-sales and Other Subsequent Transactions*

Stoppage in respect of price payable under sub-sale

[*Note 1521: page* [1452]]   **43–370**
Update references to *Benjamin's Sale of Goods* to (7th ed.), para.15–100.

[*Note 1522*]
Update references to *Benjamin's Sale of Goods* to (7th ed.), para.15–100.

(iv) *Resale by Seller*

Power of the seller to pass a good title to a second buyer

[*Note 1530: page* [1453]]   **43–372**
Update references to *Benjamin's Sale of Goods* to (7th ed.), para.15–102.

[*Note 1532*]
Update references to *Benjamin's Sale of Goods* to (7th ed.), para.15–103.

[*Note 1533: page* [1454]]
Update references to *Benjamin's Sale of Goods* to (7th ed.), para.15–102.

[*Note 1535*]
Update references to *Benjamin's Sale of Goods* to (7th ed.), para.15–104.

Right to resell

43–373 *[Note 1540: page [1454]]*
Update references to *Benjamin's Sale of Goods* to (7th ed.), para.15–106.

Repudiation or fundamental breach by the buyer

43–374 *[Note 1548: page [1455]]*
Update references to *Benjamin's Sale of Goods* to (7th ed.), para.15–109.

Seller's remedies after termination

43–375 *[Note 1561: page [1456]]*
Update references to *Benjamin's Sale of Goods* to (7th ed.), para.15–113.

Where the seller retains property in the goods

43–376 *[Note 1566: page [1456]]*
Update references to *Benjamin's Sale of Goods* to (7th ed.), para.15–115.

[Note 1570: page [1457]]
Update references to *Benjamin's Sale of Goods* to (7th ed.), para.15–116.

Where the buyer has property in the goods

43–377 *[Note 1571: page [1457]]*
Update references to *Benjamin's Sale of Goods* to (7th ed.), para.15–117.

[Note 1577]
Update references to *Benjamin's Sale of Goods* to (7th ed.), para.15–118.

Statutory right of resale

43–378 *[Note 1591: page [1458]]*
Update references to *Benjamin's Sale of Goods* to (7th ed.), para.15–121.

The seller's power of resale when he is out of possession

43–380 *[Note 1602: page [1459]]*
Update references to *Benjamin's Sale of Goods* to (7th ed.), para.15–125.

Express reservation of the right of resale

43–382 *[Note 1609: page [1460]]*
Update references to *Benjamin's Sale of Goods* to (7th ed.), para.15–129.

Forfeiture of deposits

43–385 *[Note 1618: page [1461]]*
Update references to *Benjamin's Sale of Goods* to (7th ed.), paras 15–132—15–133.

(b) *Action for the Price*

Action for price when property has passed

[*Note 1621: page* [1462]]   **43–386**
Update references to *Benjamin's Sale of Goods* to (7th ed.), para.16–003.

[*Note 1627*]
Update references to *Benjamin's Sale of Goods* to (7th ed.), para.20–071.

[*Note 1628*]
Update references to *Benjamin's Sale of Goods* to (7th ed.), para.20–128.

[*Note 1630: page* [1462]]   **43–387**
Update references to *Benjamin's Sale of Goods* to (7th ed.), paras
16–021—16–022, 16–059, 20–126—20–128.

Claim for price due on "a day certain"

[*Note 1650: page* [1464]]   **43–391**
Update references to *Benjamin's Sale of Goods* to (7th ed.), paras
19–212—19–214.

[*Note 1651*]
Update references to *Benjamin's Sale of Goods* to (7th ed.), paras
16–025—16–026, 19–212—19–215.

[*Note 1652: page* [1465]]
Update references to *Benjamin's Sale of Goods* to (7th ed.), paras 16–026,
19–212—19–213, 19–215.

Action for the price outside section 49

[*Note 1655: page* [1465]]   **43–392**
Update references to *Benjamin's Sale of Goods* to (7th ed.), paras
16–027—16–028.

Conditional sale agreements

[*Note 1664: page* [1466]]   **43–393**
Update references to *Benjamin's Sale of Goods* to (7th ed.), para.16–028.

(c) *Action for Damages*

The relevant "market"

[*Note 1723: page* [1472]]   **43–401**
Update references to *Benjamin's Sale of Goods* to (7th ed.), paras
20–133—20–136 (*cf. ibid.* para.19–216).

Proof of the market price

43–406   *[Note 1742: page* [1474]]
Update references to *Benjamin's Sale of Goods* to (7th ed.), paras 16–075—16–076.

(d) *Other Remedies of the Seller*

Miscellaneous remedies of the seller

43–413   *[Note 1800: page* [1478]]
Update references to *Benjamin's Sale of Goods* to (7th ed.), Ch.24.

8. REMEDIES OF THE BUYER

(a) *Damages for Non-Delivery*

Damages where there is an available market

43–416   *[Add to notes 1821 and 1823: page* [1480]]
On the possible relevance of the buyer's lack of financial resources, see above paras 26–095A—26–095D, 26–097.

[Note 1823: page [1480]]
Update references to *Benjamin's Sale of Goods* to (7th ed.), para.17–009.

The relevant time for taking the market price

43–418   *[Note 1838: page* [1482]]
Update references to *Benjamin's Sale of Goods* to (7th ed.), paras 19–176—19–186, 20–114—20–116, 21–031.

[Note 1841]
Update references to *Benjamin's Sale of Goods* to (7th ed.), para.17–008.

Repudiation not accepted

43–422   *[Note 1873: page* [1485]]
Update references to *Benjamin's Sale of Goods* to (7th ed.), paras 19–179—19–181.

Purchase of near equivalent

43–426   *[Note 1892: page* [1487]]
Update references to *Benjamin's Sale of Goods* to (7th ed.), para.17–025.

[Note 1898: page [1488]]
Update references to *Benjamin's Sale of Goods* to (7th ed.), para.17–024.

Loss of profits under sub-sale

[Note 1914: page [1490]] **43–428**
Update references to *Benjamin's Sale of Goods* to (7th ed.), paras
17–030—17–033.

[Note 1920: page [1490]] **43–429**
Update references to *Benjamin's Sale of Goods* to (7th ed.), paras
17–032—17–033.

[Note 1922]
Update references to *Benjamin's Sale of Goods* to (7th ed.), paras
17–032—17–033.

Loss of future business

[Add to note 1926: page [1491]] **43–430**
cf. *Jackson v Royal Bank of Scotland* [2005] UKHL 3; [2005] 1 W.L.R. 377
(loss of repeat orders caused by breach of obligation to maintain confidence; see
Vol.I, para.26–055.)

(b) *Damages for Delay in Delivery*

Resale prices are irrelevant

[Note 1950: page [1493]] **43–434**
Update references to *Benjamin's Sale of Goods* to (7th ed.), para.17–039.

(c) *Damages for Defective Quality*

(i) *Diminution in Value*

Breach of warranty

[Note 1965: page [1496]] **43–438**
Update references to *Benjamin's Sale of Goods* to (7th ed.), paras
19–190—19–199, 20–114.

Prima facie rule only

[Add to note 1988; page [1498]] **43–440**
See also *Louis Dreyfus Trading Ltd v Reliance Trading Ltd* [2004] EWHC 525
(Comm); [2004] 2 Lloyd's Rep. 243.

Damages for the cost of adaptations, or of substitute goods

[Note 1993: page [1499]] **43–441**
Update references to *Benjamin's Sale of Goods* to (7th ed.), para.17–056.

Buyer performing sub-contract despite seller's breach

43-442   [*Note 1998: page* [1499]]
Update references to *Benjamin's Sale of Goods* to (7th ed.), paras 17–039, 17–057—17–058.

[*Add to note 1999*]
See the *Louis Dreyfus* case, above (parties contemplated sale of the same goods to the sub-buyer under a specific contract).

(ii) Losses other than Diminution in Value

The buyer's failure to discover the defect

43-444   [*Note 2008: page* [1501]]
Update references to *Benjamin's Sale of Goods* to (7th ed.), para.17–060.

Additional or wasted expenses

43-446   [*Note 2015: page* [1501]]
Update references to *Benjamin's Sale of Goods* to (7th ed.), para.17–062.

The buyer's loss of profit

43-449   [*Note 2027: page* [1503]]
Update references to *Benjamin's Sale of Goods* to (7th ed.), para.17–066, 43–459.

Loss of future business

43-452   [*Add to note 2045: page* [1505]]
cf. also *Jackson v Bank of Scotland* [2005] UKHL 3; [2005] 1 W.L.R. 377 (see Vol.I, paras 26–055, 26–062A).

Compensation paid by the buyer to a sub-buyer

43-459   [*Note 2070: page* [1508]]
Update references to *Benjamin's Sale of Goods* to (7th ed.), para.17–076.

[*Note 2075*]
Update references to *Benjamin's Sale of Goods* to (7th ed.), para.17–077.

Compensation paid to sub-buyers in a series of "string contracts"

43-460   This paragraph was cited in the *Louis Dreyfus* case, above, at [24].

43-461   [*Add to note 2095 at end: page* [1510]]
See also the *Louis Dreyfus* case, above.

(d) *Other Remedies of the Buyer*

Restitution: recovery of money paid to the seller

[*Note 2110: page* [1512]] **43–465**
Update references to *Benjamin's Sale of Goods* to (7th ed.), paras 4–002 *et seq.*

Specific performance

[*Add to note 2124: page* [1513]] **43–466**
See Harris, (2003) 119 L.Q.R. 541.

Injunction

[*Note 2156: page* [1516]] **43–471**
Update references to *Benjamin's Sale of Goods* to (7th ed.), paras 1–007—1–011.

CHAPTER 44

SURETYSHIP

			PARA.
□	1.	In general	44–001
□	2.	Formation of the contract	44–016
		(a) Agreement	44–016
		(b) Consideration	44–019
□		(c) Grounds of vitiation of the contract	44–024
		(d) Effect on surety of vitiation of the transaction guaranteed .	44–036
□	3.	Formalities	44–038
■	4.	Construction of the contract	44–055
	5.	Discharge of debtor	44–068
■	6.	Discharge of surety	44–070
		(a) Discharge of surety by payment or set-off	44–070
■		(b) Discharge of surety through discharge of principal debtor .	44–071
□		(c) Discharge of surety through variation of contract between debtor and creditor	44–089
□		(d) Discharge of surety on other grounds	44–099
	7.	Surety's right to indemnity and contribution	44–108
	8.	Legislative protection of sureties	44–128
		(a) Unfair Contract Terms Act 1977	44–129
		(b) Unfair Terms in Consumer Contracts Regulations 1999	44–132

1. In General

New tenancies: breaking privity of contract

44–008   [*Add to note 37: page* [1526]]
cf. Legends Surf Shops plc v Sun Life Assurance Soc. plc [2005] EWHC 1438 (Ch); [2006] 1 P. & C.R. D. G1.

Guarantees and indemnities: the significance of the distinction

44–012   [*Add new text at end of paragraph: page* [1528]]
Thirdly, certain other rules of law apply to guarantees (where only a secondary liability is undertaken) but not to indemnities (where a primary liability is undertaken), for example, the rule that any material variation of the contract between the debtor and the creditor will in principle discharge a guarantor but not a person undertaking a primary liability.[48a]

[48a] *Holme v Brunskill* (1877) 3 Q.B.D. 495 (on which see Main Work, paras 44–089 *et seq.*); *Marubeni Hong Kong and South China Ltd v The Mongolian Government* [2005] EWCA Civ 395; [2005] 1 W.L.R. 2497.

Guarantees and indemnities: the distinction itself

[*Page* [1528]]   **44–013**
The first sentence of this paragraph was quoted by the Court of Appeal with apparent approval in *Marubeni Hong Kong and South China Ltd v The Mongolian Government* [2005] EWCA Civ 395; [2005] 1 W.L.R. 2497 at [20].

[*Add new text after note 49*: page [1528]]
In this respect, while the presence or absence of the language of "guarantee" in the document is not conclusive, outside the context of documents issued by banks (on which see Main Work, para.44–014 performance bonds), the absence of language appropriate to provide for the creditor "the additional security of a demand bond" creates a strong presumption in favour of a merely secondary liability.[49a]

[49a] *Marubeni Hong Kong and South China Ltd v The Mongolian Government* [2005] EWCA Civ 395; [2005] 1 W.L.R. 2497 at [30].

Performance guarantees

[*Add to note 54, at end*: page [1529]]   **44–014**
Banque Saudi Fransi v Lear Siegler Services Inc [2005] EWHC 2395; [2006] 1 Lloyd's Rep. 273.

[*Add new text after note 58*]
However, it has been held that cases where documents are issued by banks which are "described as, or assumed to be, performance bonds ... provide no useful analogy for interpreting a document which was not issued by a bank and which contains no overt indication of an intention to create a performance bond or anything analogous to it."[58a]

[58a] *Marubeni Hong Kong and South China Ltd v The Mongolian Government* [2005] EWCA Civ 395; [2005] 1 W.L.R. 2497 at [28], *per* Carnwath L.J.

[*Add to note 65*: page [1530]]
; applied in *Tradigrain SA v State Trading Corp of India* [2005] EWHC 2206 (Comm); [2006] 1 Lloyd's Rep. 216.

2. FORMATION OF THE CONTRACT

(c) *Grounds of Vitiation of the Contract*

Creditor on constructive notice: *Barclays Bank plc v O'Brien*

[*Add to note 131 on page*: [1538]]   **44–030**
cf. Moody v Condor Insurance Ltd [2006] EWHC 100 (Ch); [2006] 1 All E.R. 934, where it was held that fraud in the principal debtor practised on a commercial guarantee corporation and unknown to the creditor did not affect the validity of the guarantee.

3. Formalities

Written agreement; or note or memorandum

44-049 *[Add to text at end of paragraph: page* [1550]*]*
On the other hand, it has held that "[t]he purpose of the Statute of Frauds 1677 is to protect people from being held liable on informal communications because they may be made without sufficient consideration or expressed ambiguously or because such a communication might be fraudulently alleged against the party to be charged. That being so, the logic underlying the authorities[240a] would appear to be that where . . . there is an offer in writing made by the party to be bound which contains the essential terms of what is offered *and* the party to be bound accepts that his offer has been accepted unconditionally, albeit orally, there is a sufficient note or memorandum to satisfy section 4."[240b]

[240a] *Lever v Koffler* [1901] 1 Ch. 543, though the learned judge also referred to other cases cited in Vol.1, para.4–027, n.126, of the Main Work. (Footnote not in original.)
[240b] *J Pereira Fernandes SA v Mehta* [2006] EWHC 813 (Ch) at [16]; [2006] 2 All E.R. 881, *per* Judge Pelling Q.C.

[Add new paragraph 44–049A]
44-049A **Rectification and the Statute.** Where as a result of a shared mistake a guarantee instrument does not record the common intention of the parties, and the creditor is entitled to invoke the court's equitable jurisdiction to rectify the instrument so as to accord with their common intention, the creditor's claim under the instrument as so rectified does not offend s.4 of the Statute of Frauds.[240c]

[240c] *GMAC Commercial Credit Development Ltd v Sandhu* [2004] EWHC 716 (Comm); [2006] 1 All E.R. (Comm.) 268, esp. at [58]; following *USA v Motor Trucks Ltd* [1924] A.C. 196, PC (land contract) and see Main Work, Vol.1, para.5–094.

Signature to memorandum

44-051 *[Add to text at end of paragraph: page* [1551]*]*
On the other hand, it has been held that where an alleged guarantee was contained in an email sent with the would-be guarantor's authority, the automatic insertion of an email address in the message by an internet service provider did not constitute a signature by its writer within the meaning of s.4 as it did not represent any intention to authenticate the message by the writer.[249a] However, Judge Pelling Q.C. accepted that: "if a party or a party's agent sending an e-mail types his or her or his or her principal's name to the extent required or permitted by existing case law in the body of an e-mail, then . . . that would be sufficient signature of the purposes of section 4 [of the Statute of Frauds]."[249b]

[249a] *J Pereira Fernandes SA v Mehta* [2006] EWHC 813 (Ch); [2006] 2 All E.R. 881 at [25]–[30].
[249b] *ibid.*, at [31].

4. Construction Of The Contract

Impact of modern approach to construction

[Add to text at end of paragraph: page [1555]]

44–057

On the other hand, in *Vodafone Ltd v GNT Holdings (UK) Ltd*[277a] the High Court applied the "new approach" to construction found in *Investors Compensation Scheme Ltd v West Bromwich Building Society*[277b] to the construction of a guarantee. There a director of a company, company A, had signed on its notepaper a guarantee of the obligations of its subsidiary, company B. The guarantee was expressed to be for the benefit of company C. However, company B had entered an agreement not with C but with company D, which was in the same group of companies as company C. Company C was merely a holding company and no company in the group other than company D had entered such an agreement. In these circumstances, it was held that the guarantee was given by company A in respect of company C's liabilities to *company D*; the circumstances led the judge "to the conclusion that something went wrong with the drafting of the [guarantee] letter. . . . To construe it literally would be a commercial nonsense."[277c] In *Static Control Components (Europe) Ltd v Egan*[277d] the Court of Appeal agreed that the ordinary principles of contractual construction as set out in *Prenn v Simmonds*[277e] and the *Investors Compensation Scheme* case applied equally to contracts of guarantee, even where there was no ambiguity in the words used by the document.[277f] Moreover, if the court's purpose is the "ascertainment of the meaning of the document by the objective approach described by the House of Lords" in these cases, then "it may be that the concept that a guarantee should be 'strictly construed' now adds nothing."[277g] The Court of Appeal therefore construed a guarantee in respect of "the price of all Trade Goods that you may supply to the trader" as in the context applying to past debts in respect of goods supplied as well as future ones: any other construction would make "no commercial sense" where the guarantee had been preceded by a guarantee for a lesser amount in respect of existing debts and where the purpose of the later guarantee was clearly known by the guarantor to cover existing indebtedness beyond this lesser amount.[277h] By contrast, in *Dumford Trading AG v OAO Atlantrybflot*[277i] a differently constituted Court of Appeal considered that (apart from the doctrines of rectification or misnomer[277j]), where an existing person is named as guarantor in the guarantee document, there is a danger that extrinsic evidence from the surrounding matrix of facts could create an ambiguity otherwise not present.[277k] Where, therefore, company A in a group of companies was identified as guarantor by the document of guarantee, the court should not look at extrinsic evidence (such as the postal address given for this company) so as to construe this unambiguous reference as being to company B, a very similarly-named company in the same group.[277l]

[277a] [2004] All E.R. (D) 194 (Mar.).

[277b] [1998] 1 W.L.R. 896.

[277c] [2004] All E.R. (D) 194 (Mar.) at [74] *per* Christopher Moger Q.C. sitting as a deputy judge of the High Court. *cf. Amalgamated Investment & Property Co Ltd (In Liquidation) v Texas Commerce International Bank Ltd* [1982] Q.B. 84 (guarantee expressed on its terms to cover loan by bank held in the "factual matrix" of the contract also to cover loan by bank's subsidiary).

[277d] [2004] EWCA Civ 392; [2004] 2 Lloyd's Rep. 429.

²⁷⁷ᵉ [1971] 1 W.L.R. 1381 at 1385.

²⁷⁷ᶠ [2004] EWCA Civ 392 at [13], [28].

²⁷⁷ᵍ *ibid.*, at [19] *per* Holman J.

²⁷⁷ʰ *ibid.*, at [15]–[16], [31]–[32]. This construction could also be supported by the reference in the later guarantee document to a guarantee of the "whole debt": *ibid.*, at [17], [36].

²⁷⁷ⁱ [2005] EWCA Civ 25; [2005] 1 Lloyd's Rep. 289. It is to be noted that these observations were made in the context of an application for summary judgment under Pt 24 CPR.

²⁷⁷ʲ On which see Main Work, paras 5–092—5–113 and 12–075 respectively.

²⁷⁷ᵏ [2005] EWCA Civ 25 at [36]; [2005] 1 Lloyd's Rep. 289.

²⁷⁷ˡ *ibid.*

Conditional guarantees

44–060   *[Add new note 285a at the end of the first sentence: page [1556]]*

²⁸⁵ᵃ It has been held that English law does not recognise any wider relief in equity based on the mere expectation of a guarantor than is afforded by the determination whether or not the guarantee is conditional on some circumstance, for example, the execution of a guarantee by a third person: *Capital Bank Cashflow Finance Ltd v Southall* [2004] EWCA Civ 817; [2004] 2 All E.R. (Comm.) 675 at [16], discussing *Bleyer v NevilleJefferson Advertising Pty Ltd* (NSW, 1987) (unreported).

[Add new text after note 289]

While a guarantee may also be held to be conditional on the execution of a second guarantee on identical terms contained in a different document, in this situation the first guarantee document does not on its face point to a conclusion that execution of the second is necessary for the first guarantee's validity and the fact that all the documents formed part of some larger transaction is not by itself sufficient.²⁸⁹ᵃ

²⁸⁹ᵃ *Capital Bank Cashflow Finance Ltd v Southall* [2004] EWCA Civ 817; [2004] 2 All E.R. (Comm.) 675 at [17].

6. DISCHARGE OF SURETY

(b) *Discharge of Surety through Discharge of Principal Debtor*

Discharge of debtor through debtor's breach of contract

44–085   *[Add text at end of paragraph: page [1570]]*

For example, in *Manx Electricity Authority v J P Morgan Chase Bank*⁴⁰⁴ᵃ the Court of Appeal held that where the main contract is breached by the principal debtor, a guarantor under a performance guarantee remained liable under it to the creditor even where the contract guaranteed had subsequently ceased to exist. "A repudiatory breach [by the debtor] will in the normal course of events lead to the termination of the repudiated contract (although of course it may not do so). It would be extraordinary if a performance guarantee was intended to case to operate in exactly the situation in which its beneficiary most needs it—when the contract has failed because the principal has repudiated it."⁴⁰⁴ᵇ

⁴⁰⁴ᵃ [2003] EWCA Civ 1324; 2003 WL 22187638.

⁴⁰⁴ᵇ *ibid.*, at [37] *per* Rix L.J. See similarly at [47] *per* Chadwick L.J.

Discharge of debtor by operation of law

[*Note 415: page* [1572]]
Hindcastle Ltd v Barbara Attenborough Associates Ltd [1997] A.C. 10 was applied in *Scottish Widows plc v Tripipatkal* [2003] EWHC 1874 (Ch); [2003] B.P.I.R. 1413.

(c) *Discharge of Surety through Variation of Contract between Debtor and Creditor*

Variation of contract between creditor and debtor

[*Add to text of note 418 after reference to Howard de Walden Estates Ltd v Pasta Place Ltd: page* [1572]]
Marubeni Hong Kong and South China Ltd v Government of Mongolia [2004] EWHC 471 (Comm); [2004] 2 Lloyd's Rep. 198 at [58]–[60]; affd. [2005] EWCA Civ 395; [2005] 1 W.L.R. 2497.

[*Add new text to note 421: page* [1573]]
; *Barclays Bank plc v Kingston* [2006] EWHC 533; [2006] 1 All E.R. (Comm.) 519.

Agreement to allow variation or giving of time

[*Add new text at end of paragraph: page* [1575]]
So, notably, where a contract of guarantee provided that the guarantor's liability "under or pursuant" to the loan agreement was not to be affected by an arrangement which the creditor may make with the principal debtor and that the creditor could "agree to any amendment, variation, waiver or release . . . in respect of an obligation of the [principal debtor] under the Loan Agreement", the question remained whether subsequent contracts of loan between the principal debtor and the creditor which "replaced" the loans guaranteed were indeed "amendments" or "variations" of the guarantor's liability "under or pursuant to" the loans guaranteed or whether they were "substantially different", whether in purpose, amount or terms, so as to fall outside the permitted variation provision in the guarantee contract.[448a] In so holding, the Court of Appeal approved the statement of the law found in *Rowlatt on the Law of Principal and Surety* (1898), according to which "assent, whether previous or subsequent to a variation, only renders the surety liable for the contract as varied, where it remains a contract within the general purview of the original guarantee . . . If a new contract is to be secured there must be a new guarantee".[448b] On the other hand, where a clause in a contract of guarantee allows the creditor to vary the loan with the principal debtor but the creditor later agrees in writing with the guarantor not to renegotiate the loan without the latter's consent, then this subsequent agreement in effect reinstates the rule in *Holme v Brunskill*,[448c] with the result that any variation of the loan to the potential detriment or disadvantage of the guarantor discharges him.[448d]

[448a] *Triodosbank NV v Dobbs* [2005] EWCA Civ 630; [2005] 2 Lloyd's Rep. 588 at [11]–[13], [19], *per* Longmore L.J., with whom Neuberger and Chadwick L.JJ. at [27] and [29] respectively agreed.
[448b] *ibid.,* at [14].
[448c] (1877) 3 Q.B.D. 495 on which see Main Work, Vol.2, para.44–089.
[448d] *Lloyds TSB Bank plc v Hayward* [2005] EWCA Civ 466.

(d) Discharge of Surety on Other Grounds

Altering the terms of guarantee

44–099   [*Add to second sentence after "held to be whether" in line 5: page* [1576]]
"there is an alteration which affects the very nature and character of the instrument" or

[*Note 457*]
Amend reference to *Raiffeisen Zentralbank Osterreich AG v Crosseas Shipping Ltd* to: [2000] 1 W.L.R. 1135 at 1146–1148, *per* Potter L.J.

[*Add at end of text of note 457*]
cf. *Bank of Scotland v Henry Butcher & Co* [2003] EWCA Civ 67; [2003] 2 All E.R. (Comm.) 557 at [72]–[74] where an alteration by some co-guarantors was held to be plainly beneficial to the others who were not as a result discharged.

Neglect of creditor in relation to securities

44–104   [*Add new text at end of paragraph: page* [1579]]
This effect on the liability of a guarantor of neglect of a creditor in relation to securities may be excluded by the terms of the guarantee, though it has been said that the proper approach to such an alleged exclusion "should seek to interpret the guarantee as a whole as a commercial document and to give it a sensible meaning", rather than treat it "with the traditional hostility shown to exemption clauses".[485a] Nevertheless, where such an alleged exclusion was contained in the creditor's standard document in circumstances where the guarantor had been encouraged to give the guarantee on the basis that the principal debtor had given valuable security and that, if need be, the creditor would realise the market value of that security properly, then it was held that neglect would reduce the guarantor's liability "unless the terms of the guarantor clearly indicate otherwise".[485b] With respect, this approach to the construction of such an exclusion is to be approved: a contract term excluding the *reduction* of a guarantor's liability is not an exclusion clause properly so-called as it seeks to preserve the guarantor's liability where equity would reduce or extinguish it; and the approach also reflects both the modern approach to construction of commercial contracts which sets them in their factual matrix and preserves a certain force to the traditional maxim of interpretation *contra proferentem* appropriate in the context of the exclusion of this equitable protection for guarantors.[485c]

[485a] *Barclays Bank plc v Kingston* [2006] EWHC 533; [2006] 1 All E.R. (Comm.) 519 at [29], *per* Stanley Burton J. cf. *American Express v Hurley* [1985] 3 All E.R. 564 at 571, where Mann J. treated such an exclusion as "exclusion of liability for negligence" and *Continental Illinois National Bank*

& Trust Company of Chicago v Papanicolaou ("The Fedora") [1986] 2 Lloyd's Rep. 441 at 444, where a clause which ruled out any "deductions or withholdings" by the guarantor was not treated as an exclusion of liability by the creditor as it did not prevent the guarantor later claiming independently against the creditor.

485b *Barclays Bank plc v Kingston, ibid.*, at [29].

485c *cf.* Main Work, Vol.2, para.44–057 and accompanying text in this Supplement, above, and esp. *Liberty Mutual Insurance Co (UK) Ltd v HSBC Bank plc* [2002] EWCA Civ 691 at [56].